TEX UNBOUND

WE ARE INDEBTED FOR TeX, WHICH DESERVES SIMULTANEOUS RECOGNITION AS THE TEXT FORMATTER OF CHOICE AND THE MOST IDIOSYNCRATIC PROGRAMMING LANGUAGE KNOWN TO US. · STEPHEN WARD and ROBERT HALSTEAD Jr (1990) ·

TeX UNBOUND

LaTeX & TeX Strategies for
Fonts, Graphics, & More

ALAN HOENIG

Oxford   New York

OXFORD UNIVERSITY PRESS

1998

Oxford University Press

Oxford   New York

Athens   Auckland   Bangkok   Bogota   Bombay   Buenos Aires
Calcutta   Cape Town   Dar es Salaam   Delhi   Florence   Hong Kong
Istanbul   Karachi   Kuala Lumpur   Madras   Madrid   Melbourne
Mexico City   Nairobi   Paris   Singapore   Taipei   Tokyo   Toronto   Warsaw

and associated companies in
Berlin   Ibadan

Copyright © 1998 by Oxford University Press, Inc.

Published by Oxford University Press, Inc.
198 Madison Avenue, New York, New York 10016

Oxford is a registered trademark of Oxford University Press

Library of Congress Cataloging-in-Publication Data
Hoenig, Alan.
TeX unbound: LaTeX & TeX strategies for fonts, graphics, & more
/ Alan Hoenig.
p.   cm.
Includes index.
ISBN 0-19-509685-1; 0-19-509686-X (pbk.)
1. LaTeX (Computer file) 2. TeX (Computer file) 3. Computer
fonts. 4. METAFONT 5. Computer graphics. 6. Computerized
typesetting. 7. Mathematics printing—Computer programs.
8. Technical publishing—Computer programs. I. Title.
Z253.4.L38H64 1998
686.2'2544536—dc21   97-5918

3 5 7 9 8 6 4 2

Printed in the United States of America
on acid-free paper

For my home team,
Jozefa, Hannah, Sam

INTRODUCTION

The reader contemplating this book has a right to know what the author's goals are—or are not—for this volume. The nongoals are easy—this book will *not* discuss the various typesetting commands supported by LaTeX and TeX (except casually or in passing). It's much better to consult the canonical works by Knuth (1986a) or by Lamport (1994), or any of the several excellent books this canon has inspired, for that kind of information.

Anyone who knows the slightest bit about typesetting with LaTeX or TeX knows there is more to fine typesetting than the commands of the TeX language. It's important to know this material well, but there are other issues concerning document production that the canon barely touches upon. For instance:

- How can I make full use of the many commercial digital fonts? And how may I use them to typeset technical texts in a fully professional manner? And if I use these fonts, can I also typeset mathematics in a visually compatible way? (See chapters 7 through 10 in this book.)

- What about graphics—How may I prepare and include images and graphic material for my TeX document? (Chapters 11 through 15.)

- Do the Internet, multimedia, and hypertext have any relevance to TeX (and vice versa)? (Chapter 2.)

- Can TeX be made to fit into the suite of general office and educational software that is so ubiquitous, or is TeX *sui generis*? (Chapter 5.)

- Low-level query: What is TeX and why should I care? What is LaTeX, and how does it differ from TeX? Where did TeX come from? How do I best bring myself up to speed as a TeX user? (Chapters 1 through 4.)

It is my intention to provide discussions of these and similar queries in the pages that follow.

These are disparate issues, linked only by their absence in a standard "TeXtbook." Some of this material is elementary, while other bits are quite advanced. As a result, it's hard to fix a single label on this book as to level—it is neither elementary, nor intermediate, nor advanced, but all three at once.

Three informal parts of the book attempt to deal with these issues. In the first part—the first five chapters—we present surveys of useful areas—what computer typesetting and TEX involve exactly; what Internet resources there are for the TEX-aware author; introductions to METAFONT and Meta-Post, TEX's graphic siblings; logical document structure (including SGML) and LATEX; and some tips and suggestions for using TEX alongside standard office and academic software (but a discussion of HyperTEXt also appears here).

Chapters 6 through 10 comprise the lengthy second part and form an extended discussion of virtual fonts and related issues, including a discussion of font installation and selection for both plain TEX and LATEX, so authors will know how to use non-Computer Modern fonts in their TEX documents. After an extensive examination of the virtual font concept, several chapters present instructions for carrying out many virtual font projects:

- simple EC font creation;

- installing outline fonts for use by LATEX and TEX;

- creating real small caps fonts;

- oblique (slanted) and unslanted italic fonts;

- old style figures in fonts;

- better footnote numbers with expert fonts;

- introduction to foreign language typesetting;

- underlining and striking-out of extensive passages of text;

- bold fonts when no bold font exists;

- f-words (that is, words that end in f);

- alternate fonts containing special characters and exotic ligatures;

- kern tracking and letterspacing;

- previewing output using that contains PostScript fonts;

- hints and suggestions for properly scaling fonts at different sizes; and

- creating and installing new math packages, so authors can properly typeset mathematics using MathTime, Lucida, Euler, or Mathematica math fonts, plus sans serif, typewriter, Fraktur, calligraphic, and blackboard bold fonts.

The "new math" section contains an extensive "rogues' gallery" showing how combining various roman faces with math fonts leads to different visual effects.

The last five chapters—the final portion of the book—addresses a fun question. How do you create and place graphic images in a document? There are many excellent tools to accomplish this, but even with the limited discussion we're restricted to, there's lots to say. After some general discussion, we focus on four very special approaches:

- the LaTeX picture environment and extensions thereto;

- METAFONT and MetaPost (siblings to TeX); and

- two packages powered by TeX front-ends, PSTricks (a TeX front-end to the PostScript language) and MFPIC (a TeX front-end to META-FONT).

Appendices 1 and 2 present whirlwind introductions to TeX and LaTeX, whereas appendix 3 reveals how I and Oxford University Press produced this book (which was *entirely* by means of TeX and its siblings and friends).

What's the best way to use this book? I hope that everyone will find the time to sit back, relax, and read everything from cover to cover, but this is not practical for most readers. Please do, though, take time to riffle through this volume. Note that several chapters conclude with compendia or lists of commands that just may prove useful. Note too that the entries in the bibliography have back references, so it's possible to find out where in the book a citation was discussed. Finally, you will ignore the index at your peril! Every effort has been made to make the index complete and consistent. Who would guess that discussion of underlining appears in a virtual font chapter—but the index points you to the proper page.

One principle silently informs much of the book's discussion. I call this "Hayes's Principle of Software."

> No matter how many palettes of buttons and how many menu options are offered, users of a program will always want to do something the author has not foreseen. Adding still more buttons and menus is not the answer. [Hayes (1995)]

This is why TeX (or a comparable descendent program) will endure in the face of huge advertising efforts by software giants. But there's another result of Hayes's Principle—authors of TeX documents tend to be on their own private cutting edge in their inadvertent journey to the unforeseen. One final purpose of this book is to enhance the insight of a TeX user, who, while now conscious of ever more things to do within TeX, will now know ever more ways to carry them out.

ACKNOWLEDGMENTS

I am grateful indeed for HarperCollins' permission to quote from Patrick O'Brian's novel *Master and Commander* (© 1970 by Patrick O'Brian) in chapter 9. Likewise, I am pleased that Vikram Seth allowed me to quote his *Hymn* from his novel *A Suitable Boy* (© 1993 by Vikram Seth) in chapter 14. John Wiley & Sons has given permission to use the extract from Steven Weinberg's *Gravitation and Cosmology* (© 1972 John Wiley & Sons, Inc.), which appears prominently in chapter 10. Many thanks.

Several companies, including Adobe Systems, Altsys, Bitstream, Carter & Cone, Corel Corporation, Monotype Corporation, SoftQuad, TCI Software Research, Waterloo Maple Software, Wolfram Research, and Y and Y were very generous with their advice and support, and I am pleased to be able to acknowledge this here. The support of several special colleagues at John Jay College was important to me.

No author is an island, and many people, wittingly or not, contributed to the project that became this book. Like every other TEX user, I extend my warmest gratitude to Don Knuth, not only for TEX and METAFONT themselves, but also for his leadership in the sharing of ideas and information. I know that his attitude has rubbed off on many members of the TEX community, for otherwise, what could account for the extraordinary cooperation, friendliness, and tutelage afforded me over the years by many clever (and busy!) people? Among them, the insights of Nelson Beebe, Barbara Beeton, John Hobby, Jozefa Hoenig, Alan Jeffrey, David Ness, Mitch Pfeffer, Tomas Rokicki, and Michael Spivak considerably aided this book's quality. Some may be surprised to find themselves in this short list, but I hope no one is surprised to find themselves off it! If I have inadvertently left someone out (mea culpa!—and my sincerest apologies), it's an accident of my increasingly undependable memory. Among the many helpful people at Oxford, I am especially indebted to Don Jackson and to my editor, Bill Zobrist, and to the exemplary production staff.

There is one other asset without which I know this book would have languished in some scriptatorial limbo, and that is the support, encouragement, and love from my family, Jozefa, Hannah, Sam, and Mabel. Thanks, guys!

Huntington, New York   Alan Hoenig
July, 1997

CONTENTS

1 About TEX and LATEX   3

2 TEX, the Internet, and Multimedia   42

3 Mostly Metafont   58

4 Logical Documents via LATEX   98

5 TEX in the Workplace   117

6 Installing and Selecting Fonts   130

7 Virtual Fonts, Virtuous Fonts   166

8 Virtual-Font Projects   201

9 More Virtual Fonts   257

10 New Math Fonts   287

11 Graphic Discussions   345

12 Graphics via TEX and LATEX   368

13 Using Metafont and MetaPost   390

14 PSTricks   441

15 Mfpic Pictures   494

Appendix 1: Basic TEX Commands   511

Appendix 2: More About LATEX   530

Appendix 3: Producing this Book   541

Sources and Resources   547

Index   555

TEX UNBOUND

CHAPTER I

· ·

ABOUT TEX AND LATEX

1.1 An overview

It is surprising how difficult it is to automate the process of typesetting. The TEX (ideally pronounced to rhyme with *blec-c-c-ch*) typesetting system is (arguably) the best way to do this by computer. TEX was designed to cope with the intricacies of mathematical and technical typesetting *and* especially to deliver beautifully typeset documents. The source of the "TEX" logo is the Greek root τεχ (tau epsilon chi), which forms part of words like "technology."

What is LATEX, and how does it differ from TEX? In ways we will discuss, TEX typesetting commands have been used to create many new commands that are easier and more convenient to use; these new commands comprise the LATEX system. But behind the scenes, all LATEX commands need to be resolved in terms of primitive TEX commands, which is why it is proper to say that LATEX is TEX. In the remainder of this chapter, "TEX" is usually a synonym for "TEX and LATEX" because most of this material applies equally well to LATEX or to plain TEX. Sometimes, for emphasis, we will say "LATEX and TEX" explicitly. An extended discussion of LATEX appears later (in chapter 4 and appendix 2).

For the best possible printed appearance of your document, TEX is the tool of choice. Because of this, and because it's free (that is, the original program code is free and many implementations of it are free), it's become a preferred alternative (and often the standard) for electronically distributing documentation, preprints and reprints, and technical reports. If an author prepares a file containing the text of a message sprinkled with the formatting instructions that LATEX or TEX obeys, then anyone else anywhere in the world can print this message *precisely* as intended using their local version of TEX. The files we feed to the TEX program contain only printable ASCII characters, so these files are easy to transfer from one computer to another.

In addition to this portability, TEX documents are stable. Work on the basic TEX "engine" has now been frozen (except for bug fixes) so a decade-old TEX document can be rerendered today.

Type:	-	--	---	\$ - \$	``	''	?`	!'	ff	fi	fl	ffi	ffl
To get:	-	–	—	–	"	"	¿	¡	ff	fi	fl	ffi	ffl

Figure 1: TEX's ligature mechanism helps typeset several different characters.

1.1.1 Typographic niceties

LATEX and TEX are hardly the only systems purporting to paint digital characters on a laser-printed page. But even at this late date, few other systems do it as well as TEX does. Let's see what lies behind this extravagant claim.

Over the centuries, printers (doubtless attempting to mirror the flowing appearance of fine handwriting) became accustomed to replacing certain pairs of adjacent letters by single characters termed *ligatures*. Early printers used far more ligatures than do current typesetters, but some ligatures have survived until now (or at least until the advent of computer typesetting!). Today, knowledgeable typesetters would replace letter groups "fl" and "fi" by the typographic equivalents fl and fi (look closely at the differences). Other ligatures that should be used include ff, ffi, and ffl, and TEX can actually accommodate other exotic ligatures if the need arises. Human authors could, of course, be taught to somehow select them as they key in their texts, but this is a bad idea—computers that never err should do it instead. The task of creating ligatures automatically is apparently beyond the capabilities of most computer typesetting systems, and it's becoming increasingly common to read books in which some (or all!) of the f-ligatures are missing.

TEX uses its ligature mechanism to improve the appearance of often misused characters like dashes and quotes. Depending on how an author enters a dash and on the context (math mode or not), LATEX or TEX typesets four different dash-like quantities. Quotes are handled in similar ways, so a TEX document will contain proper left and right double "quotes." Figure 1 summarizes these (and a few other) results.

TEX can also *kern* adjacent letters. A kern is a dollop of horizontal spacing that is added or subtracted between character pairs to improve the appearance of the letters. Probably the best example of kerning appears in the logo **TOYOTA** (compare with **TOYOTA**)—each letter is kerned to its neighbor. Most of the time, kerning is negative—letters are moved together. (But every so often, as with adjacent o's, TEX has to impose positive kerning to further separate adjacent letters.) Figure 2 on the next page compares and contrasts kerned text with its unkerned counterpart.

It's not always possible to end words on lines without splitting them in two parts. The rules concerning this hyphenation are nontrivial and vary from language to language. (Sometimes the rules vary from region to region within a single language; British and American rules are completely differ-

Kerned	TOYOTA
Unkerned	TOYOTA
Kerned	**IRRAWADDY**
Unkerned	**IRRAWADDY**
Kerned	JAVA WAVE
Unkerned	JAVA WAVE

Figure 2: Kerning

ent.) Although TEX works hard to set type without the necessity of hyphenating, TEX does contain algorithms that ensure proper hyphenation about 95% of the time. (Corrections to a word's hyphenation are easy to specify.) In general, TEX works hard to compute proper line breaks in a paragraph. In extreme cases, the last word of a paragraph influences the line break of the first line, so neither TEX nor LATEX will compute line breaks until the entire paragraph is known to it.

The particular strengths of LATEX and TEX lie in the areas of setting complex tables and mathematics and other technical material. (See figure 3 on the following page for mathematics, and figure 4 on page 7 and especially the front endpaper for examples of tables.) For mathematical typesetting, TEX is even able to distinguish between math in the context of display or text—compare the displayed formula

$$\sum_{i=0}^{\frac{m}{2}} \frac{k}{x_i}$$

to the same expression $\sum_{i=0}^{\frac{m}{2}} \frac{k}{x_i}$ set within text.

1.1.2 Scholarly detritus

Papers written for a scholarly or technical audience require many supporting aids, such as indexes, footnotes, tables of contents, lists of figures, glossaries, bibliographies, and so on. Most of these can be handled automatically by TEX; some, like indexes, will always need some manual intervention.

TEX can write material to an external file and later retrieve information from that file. That's how it is possible to prepare this material. Certain commands will cause TEX to write phrases with page numbers to files, which TEX can read back in on a subsequent run. This is why LATEX runs, for example, sometimes conclude with an injunction to rerun the file through LATEX, even though no additional changes have been made.

$$\mathcal{K} \ll \begin{pmatrix} 1 & 1 & \cdots & 1 \\ \xi_1 & \xi_1^2 & \cdots & \xi_1^n \\ \xi_2 & \xi_2^2 & \cdots & \xi_2^n \\ \vdots & \vdots & \ddots & \vdots \\ \xi_m & \xi_m^2 & \cdots & \xi_m^n \end{pmatrix} \sqrt{1 + \sqrt{1 + \sqrt{1 + \sqrt{1 + \sqrt{1 + \sqrt{1 + \theta}}}}}}$$

$$\int_0^{\frac{\pi}{2}} e^{e^{-x^2}}\, dx \qquad \overbrace{\{\underbrace{\alpha, \ldots, \alpha}_{k\ \alpha\text{'s}}, \underbrace{\beta, \ldots, \beta}_{l\ \beta\text{'s}}\}}^{} \\ \underbrace{\phantom{\{\alpha, \ldots, \alpha, \beta, \ldots, \beta\}}}_{k + l\ \text{elements}}$$

Figure 3: TEX does mathematics.

In the case of footnotes and floating objects (like figures and tables), TEX is adept at figuring out how much space to leave to accommodate the item and at moving a figure or table to the next page if the current page is already too full (that's why they're called "floats"). Automatic numbering of footnotes, tables, and so on, is also possible.

Sometimes, external programs work in concert with TEX. In the case of index preparation, an author inserts various commands in the manuscript, and LATEX or TEX obligingly spits the material to a separate index file. Another program, such as *MakeIndex*, is needed to sort the entries properly and merge identical entries together. In the case of bibliography preparation, an author may well like to prepare a collection of entries pertaining to her field of specialty, say, and have only a small number of entries selected for a particular report. The bibliographic information will need special formatting to accommodate itself to the needs of the journal. This is done by a program, usually BIBTEX.

No matter what flavor of TEX an author uses, these abilities are always present. However, in plain TEX an author has to work harder, because relatively few high level commands exist. The more complete a macro package is, such as LATEX (see page 33), the easier these capabilities become.

Although the major advantage of using a program like TEX (plus perhaps helpers like BIBTEX or *MakeIndex*) is convenience, the major payoff occurring whenever the original manuscript undergoes revision. Changes to pagination, page layout, and so on, which occur as a result of the document's revision, automatically propagate to these ancillary materials.

1.1.3 Why is TEX hard?

Any reader with even a smattering of LATEX or TEX experience knows that this versatility and perfectionism comes at a cost—TEX is widely perceived to be a hard tool to use and master. Why should this be so?

For one reason, there is rarely immediate feedback with a TEX document, and this may contribute to this perception. Like any computer sys-

AT&T Common Stock		
Year	*Price*	*Dividend*
1971	41–54	$2.60
2	41–54	2.70
3	46–55	2.87
4	40–53	3.24
5	45–52	3.40
6	51–59	.95*

* (first quarter only)

Figure 4: TEX sets a handsome table. This famous example is from chapter 22 of *The TEXbook*.

tem, TEX does what you tell it to do, rather than what you mean to tell it to do, and this leads to some frustration. But even factoring out these effects, LATEX or TEX can be hard. In an effort to apply to virtually all typesetting scenarios, some of TEX's rules seem arcane, counterintuitive, and just plain weird. The conscientious author is saved by three trends:

1. LATEX and TEX are like fine musical instruments. While it may take years to achieve virtuosity (as with the cello), it's easy to do simple things right away.

2. A large body of users of TEX is struggling hard to make LATEX and TEX easier to use, and they are generous in making their work available to others.

3. There is invariably more than one way to accomplish something in LATEX or TEX. If one approach fails, there's hope that a second way will work.

Tenner (1996) discusses (among many other fascinating topics) the "revenge effects" of complicated computer systems; his discussion of TEX appears on pages 192–193 of his book. TEX makes short work of complicated tables and equations that are difficult and costly to typeset using traditional methods. But there are times an author wants to make an adjustment—closing up some vertical space, adding a hair rule—that is trivial with traditional systems but embarrassingly time-consuming with TEX. Authors should forego the general power that TEX provides in favor of doing things simply and easily, perhaps by sticking to macro packages like LATEX and only using straightforward math and text markup. Time-consuming changes, no matter how trivial they may appear, are not appropriate for short reports and letters, and may only pay off for large-scale projects (books), where even a multiday effort at TEX programming is still only a small percentage of the total time spent writing and keying in the manuscript.

1.2   A brief history of TEX

The origin of the TEX system lies in the dissatisfaction of one author with the galley proofs of his work in the middle and late 1970s. The author was computer scientist and Stanford University professor Donald Knuth, and the proofs were for his typographically challenging and still ongoing work, *The Art of Computer Programming*. He found that not only did the typesetters make many mistakes in the first pass, but they introduced new ones in the process of correction! By 1977, though, Knuth had seen a book printed via high-resolution rasterization and was impressed that the technology now existed to generate digital output that could (at least in theory) surpass the then-traditional hot metal technology. The words of Knuth (1986f) himself describe his reaction:

> Digital typesetting means patterns of 0s and 1s, and computer science can be thought of as the study of 0s and 1s. Therefore, it dawned on me for the first time that I, as a computer scientist, would be able to help solve the printing problem that was worrying me so much. I didn't need to know about metallurgy or optics or chemistry or anything scary like that; all I had to do was construct the right pattern of 0s and 1s and send it to a high-resolution digital typesetter …; then I'd have my books the way I wanted them. In other words, the problem of quality printing has been reduced to a problem about 0s and 1s. Therefore it was almost an obligation for a computer scientist like myself to study the problem carefully.

Work on TEX began officially on May 5, 1977; the first version of TEX was available at Stanford in 1979 and was written in *SAIL*, the Stanford Artificial Intelligence Language. This version was completely rewritten by 1982, this time using Pascal. (Actually, it was written using WEB; see subsection 1.9.2 on page 35.)

Relatively recent changes   In the summer of 1989, Knuth decided to make a few more changes to TEX, largely to make typesetting in languages other than American English easier. TEX3.0, released on the Ides of March, 1990, makes it easier to incorporate multiple hyphenation patterns and fonts with more than 128 characters, features demanded by non-English typesetting. (Fonts may now contain up to 256 characters.) TEX also supports the use of *virtual* or *composite fonts*. A virtual font is one we build up from characters and accents appearing in one or more fonts. Knuth urges everyone to switch to this new TEX as quickly as possible. Fortunately, all files compiled in TEX82 will compile perfectly with TEX3.0. No conversion for source files is needed.

Relatively recent changes to LATEX   At about the same time the new TEX was coming into being, it was felt that a new version of the LATEX macro system was also needed. The effort at upgrading this package is not yet complete, but the international team doing this work has already released several

modules that will presumably be part of the proposed LATEX3, and has released a stable interim LATEX, the so-called LATEX2$_\varepsilon$, that *everyone* should
switch to.

Logo   The origin of the strange name and logo "TEX" is the Greek root
"$\tau\epsilon\chi$." Because of this background, its pronunciation involves a soft, guttural, sound. Nowadays, mostly people speaking languages containing a
throat-clearing guttural retain this original pattern. Most Americans pro-
nounce it either as "a Texan would"[Knuth (1979)] or as "tek"; the computer
doesn't seem to mind.

The author of TEX   TEX groupies can't help wanting to know more about
Don Knuth. His non-TEXnical writings, such as Knuth (1986f), Knuth
(1991), and Thiele (1996), provide useful and entertaining insight, as does
Knuth's home page at

```
http://www-cs-faculty.stanford.edu/~knuth
```

on the World Wide Web.

1.2.1   How does one "TEX" differ from any other?

TEX has been placed in the public domain by its author. Anyone can use
the ideas in the source code of the program TEX (and of its siblings), can
use sections of the code outright, and can compile TEX on any computer.
But control of the name "TEX" remains in Knuth's hands, and only those
programs that truly conform to the TEX standard may use the name "TEX."
   The standard is the "Trip TEX" test, a tripartite (triptych) suite of procedures specifically designed to trip up TEX lookalikes and implementations
not fully conforming to TEX as its author envisioned it. Output from this
run must be identical to the official run, modulo certain allowable devia-
tions like date and time. Anybody using any program called "TEX" on any
computer will be assured that that program will render a document in the
same way as any other similarly named program on any other computer.
   Because it takes work to port TEX to any particular computer, some people have taken to selling their "versions" of TEX. Such TEX's are functionally
identical to any other TEX by virtue of Trip TEX. Of course, additional value
may exist in the form of front ends, printer drivers and previewers (which
are not part of TEX), and support.

1.3   The TEX life cycle

In principal, TEX is easy to use. We prepare a *source file* containing the text
of our document together with various instructions to TEX. Next, we run
this file through the TEX program and finally feed the output of this step
into a separate program that is responsible for the actual generation of ink

Life Cycles

LATEX/TEX Life Cycle: Word Processing Life Cycle:

- Prepare source file.   • Prepare document file.

- Feed source through TEX.   • Print this file.

  ○ Make necessary corrections.   ○ Revise as necessary.

- Use device driver to print document.

  ○ Preview the document if desired.

on paper. This is the *TEX life cycle.* The process during which TEX ingests the document file is called *compilation;* we speak of TEX having *compiled* a document.

It's helpful to understand this life cycle by comparing it to that of a traditional office word processor. The word processing life cycle consists of only two steps: keying in the text together with the word processing formatting commands and printing it.

Word processors and desktop publishing packages provide a large choice of formats, but because of their organization around menus and such, they can provide a large but ultimately finite choice of format choices; even a moderately experienced LATEX or TEX user can coax an infinite number of typesetting formats from TEX. This is yet another advantage of LATEX and TEX.

1.3.1 Another perspective

With a slight shift of focus, another difference between TEX and word processing becomes clear. Authors who follow the TEX way use distinct tools for different purposes—a text editor has as its only job the preparation of a source file, the typesetting engine (TEX) only does typesetting, and only the device driver or previewer is responsible for rendering images.

In contrast, a WYSIWYG word processor is responsible for all those tasks, together with the added overhead of the WYSIWYG display itself and conformance to a slick graphics operating system like *Windows95* or the Macintosh *System 7.* Is it a wonder that even the fanciest of word processors has trouble approaching TEX's typesetting standard?

These comments may make choices on the part of beginning writers easier. Clever user interfaces may be of prime importance to a beginner wholly intimidated by computers, but an experienced hand may feel that such displays add little value to a document and that a TEX system is well worth grappling with.

1.4   A working TEX system

A complete TEX system is actually a concert between several different component pieces of hardware and software. There are at least three different but necessary pieces of software.

First is a version of TEX for a particular computer and operating system. At this time, there are versions of TEX available for every reasonable computer. In the unlikely event that there isn't, it's possible to customize TEX by doing a reasonable amount of spade work yourself. The TEX program is in the public domain (and in electronic form), and all you need to do is make whatever changes (if any) are called for and recompile the TEX source code in a robust Pascal compiler that works on your system. (Most likely, you will translate the original Pascal WEB source to a C source program using the freely available web2c utility, and then use a robust C compiler to compile TEX.) TEX was originally written in Pascal, and depending on how you "pretty print" the listing, it amounts to between 20,000 and 30,000 lines of code. TEX exercises all the dark corners of any compiler, so you need a compiler that has itself been thoroughly debugged. In case you need help with this project, there are plenty of individuals who have been through this exercise and can probably help you out. (There is a white lie of omission in this account. All this source code is written in WEB, so some mastery of this WEB system must be acquired.)

Do we need a special version of LATEX to match our hardware? The core LATEX files, which "sit" on top of TEX, are ASCII files, and we can easily transfer ASCII files from one computer to another. However, proper behavior of LATEX will require us to install LATEX and in that process to create a special binary format file for use by our computer. (Additional discussion of format files appears on page 19.) In general, binary files may not be transferred from one type of hardware to another (but format files are easy to construct).

Next is a *text editor*. This was discussed earlier and is necessary for preparing the document source file.

Finally there are the *device driver* and *screen previewer*. TEX's output is a file containing commands to typeset all the letters, rules, and special symbols in the document. Unfortunately, different printers obey distinctly different sets of such commands. Therefore, TEX employs a generic, no-frills, *device-independent* language in which to express these commands. That's why the output file from TEX has the extension .dvi, to suggest *device-independence*. In this way, the TEX program is relevant to virtually any hardware setup, but it does mean that we need yet another program, a so-called device driver. The purpose of this program is simply to translate TEX's generic, device independent typesetting commands into commands that our particular printer understands.

Everybody will want to arm themselves with a *screen previewer*, a special-purpose device driver. Remember, TEX is not WYSIWYG, and we frequently want to see what the TEX document will look like without going to the bother of printing it out. (This may be because we share printing facilities in some computer center, or because your printer takes a long time to deliver a single page. Anyone who has tried generating TEX output on a dot matrix printer knows that feeling.) A video monitor is just a special purpose printing device, and it is usually a straightforward matter to write a device driver to paint the image of the page on a monitor screen.

It makes sense to choose hardware on the basis of TEX software. For example, you'll want to make *really* sure that the printer is one for which a device driver exists. (Or else make sure that the printer is one that will *emulate*—imitate—a supported printer. For example, there are many laser printers for sale, each with its own protocol for generating printed images. There are relatively few laser printer device drivers available. Among these few with support are the Hewlett-Packard laser printers, which many other laser printers emulate well. Since there are several Hewlett-Packard laser printer drivers available, an HP-like laser printer may be a safe bet.)

TEX also runs well on printers that understand the PostScript page description language. This PostScript language is another means for creating device-independent files, because the mechanism for rendering the PostScript document resides in the printer itself. Consequently, we need a special PostScript printer in order to take advantage of the PostScript technology. (That there are hundreds of beautiful digital PostScript fonts is another inducement to use PostScript.) Special dvi-to-PostScript postprocessors translate a .dvi file to a PostScript equivalent. Many such programs are available from any number of vendors. Fortunately, one of the best, *dvips* by Tomas Rokicki, is freely available.

Other commercially available digital fonts follow the True Type font protocol. A True Type-to-pk package written by Konstantin Vasil'ev is available from the support/ttftogf area of any CTAN archive.

1.4.1 Miscellaneous TEX software tools

Other software tools not necessarily TEX-specific are often helpful. *Spell check* programs work well with TEX source documents. Some can be configured to recognize misspellings in TEX commands as well as in "regular" words, so many TEX errors due to misspelled LATEX or TEX commands can be eliminated before the TEX compilation process gets under way. Grammar checkers are less successful. Streams of LATEX or TEX commands seem to be cases of bad grammar and lower the perceived reading level of the document. However, it should be possible to run a document through a "detex" utility and to run the resulting ASCII document, stripped of all TEX markup commands, through the grammar checker. One such program, detex by Daniel Trinkle (in the support section of any of the vast CTAN Internet TEX archives; see chapter 2), is also used for spell checking; the detex'ed

> ### Software Components of a Complete System
>
> - An ASCII text editor.
>
> - A version of TeX appropriate for your computer and its operating system.
>
> - A printer device driver for your printer.
>
> - A previewer to preview your TeX output on your screen. (Optional, but highly recommended.)
>
> In addition to these mandatory components, you may want to investigate other software tools (spell checkers and so on) and macro packages (LaTeX, $\mathcal{A}_{\mathcal{M}}\mathcal{S}$TeX, Seminar, etc.)

file is run through the spell checker in this raw form. Some editors, notably Emacs, are sufficiently TeX-aware to allow spell-checking from within the program.

Macro packages are different from programs in that the macros are software written in terms of TeX's commands with the great advantage that (1) these files are printable ASCII and so are easily exchanged from computer to computer and (2) these macros will work anywhere that TeX will. In addition to the packages already mentioned, you may also come across references to SliTeX and Seminar, style and macro packages for making slides (for company presentations and so on). It's important to emphasize—when we use a macro package like LaTeX or $\mathcal{A}_{\mathcal{M}}\mathcal{S}$TeX, we are still using TeX.

Many of these macro packages require special fonts, which are usually distributed with their macros. It is *your* responsibility to make sure you get the font pixel files appropriate for your printer. (See section 1.7 on page 21 for a discussion of pixel files.) Although the Computer Modern fonts that come with a canonical TeX installation are free, and although many other fonts are available at no cost, many more are proprietary and require some form of purchase or lease before use.

1.5   Getting TeX

Although the TeX software is "free"—within the public domain—it often takes work to port it to a particular computer. This is true of implementations for the original IBM PC and for the Apple Macintosh, for example. In any case, device drivers and screen previewers were never part of the original TeX package. Consequently, some firms sell their implementations for TeX.

An interesting recent phenomenon is the availability of several public domain TEX implementations for microcomputers. One or more such implementations exist for all kinds of personal computer, including IBM-type computers, Apple Macintosh, Amiga, Atari, and Acorn. Some of them may even be as good or better than commercial products. Of course, when we use a public domain version, we are on our own. Companies have "helplines" for users who find themselves in trouble. With rare exceptions, no such lifelines exist for users of public domain TEXs. Public domain implementations are available from user groups (TUG, Dante, GUT, and so on), from Internet archives, and from special TEX CD-ROMs.

When acquiring a TEX "package," make sure it's complete. In addition to the TEX executable, the associated ancillary files TEX needs, various important input files, and the latest version of important macro packages, we must make sure additional utilities are part of the suite even if your current plans don't include using them. I have in mind here the METAFONT program (and the MetaPost program if possible), various TEXware utilities (of which `tftopl`, `vftovp` and their inverses `pltotf` and `vptovf` are probably the most important), and the METAFONTware utilities. The TEX program should be version 3.1415 or higher, and the METAFONT program should be version 2.71 or higher.

1.5.1   Unique TEXs

Although each implementation of TEX is typographically equivalent to any other, a few are worthy of special notice by virtue of some distinguishing feature. A few of these special TEXs are worthy of mention here.

The em-TEX software collection is especially interesting—it's a complete implementation of TEX, METAFONT, all TEXware and MFware programs, printer drivers, previewers, and documentation (in English and German) for PC-DOS and OS/2 operating systems, and it's all free. Several executables of TEX and METAFONT are provided, from "small" to "huge" versions. (These designations refer to the speed and/or the amount of material these TEXs and METAFONTs can process.) Eberhard Mattes is the man behind this prodigious effort, but there are those who wonder if "Eberhard Mattes" doesn't refer, like the fictional "Nicolas Bourbaki," to a dedicated group of workers. In any case, this material is all available free for downloading from any CTAN site (see chapter 2), and some user groups like UK TUG make it available to their members for a nominal fee. Furthermore, there is a special em-TEX Internet list, so this is one important instance where public domain software does have some support. Over the last several years, Mattes has proven to be a conscientious developer, providing bug fixes in a timely way and keeping up with the latest master source files of TEX, METAFONT, and their friends.

Tom Rokicki is well-known in TEX circles for his *dvips* post-processor (it converts `.dvi` output to a form suitable for rendering on a PostScript printer). Less well known but just as impressive is TEXView, his version of

TEX for the NextStep operating system. NextStep, which runs on the Intel-486 architecture among others, is a flavor of Unix (BSD 4.2) onto which has been grafted a very convenient windowing system. NextStep contains a version of Display PostScript, which means that TEX documents that incorporate PostScript graphics and PostScript fonts may be previewed effortlessly (including color). Because Unix is a multitasking system, an author can run a document through TEX, begin the previewing process, and continue editing. One odd feature has proven invaluable—the ability to measure actual distances on a page with clicks of a mouse. It's surprising how often it is possible to fix a bug in a LATEX or TEX file by simply knowing how much extra or missing space there is. See Hoenig (1994) for further details on this system. The manuscript for this book was prepared using TEXView. Most of the TEXView enhancements can be found incorporated into the web2c TEX kits for Unix platforms. (As a result of various corporate acquisitions, NextStep is now called OpenStep.)

Lightning Textures, by Blue Sky Research, is a version of TEX for the Macintosh. Its distinguishing feature is its ability to show TEX output produced simultaneously as text is keyed in. The freely available InstantTEX for NextStep (originally by Dmitri Linde and now maintained by Gregor Hoffleit) provides the same functionality—it's great for debugging macros. InstantTEX is freely available from several ftp sites, including

    peanuts.leo.org/pub/comp/platforms/next/Text/tex/apps

and its mirrors. The file will have a name like InstantTeX.3.11d.NIHS.b.tar and there is an accompanying "readme" file as well.

AucTEX is not an implementation, but an editing enhancement available to Unix users of the Emacs editor. With it, Emacs becomes highly TEX-aware, making available a large number of shortcuts, command completion, automatic indentation, special outlining, online documentation, the ability to customize (provided you can program in Lisp, the language in which it is programmed), and a good bit more. Kresten Krab Thorup is its author, and it is available from any CTAN site.

1.5.2 Updating TEX; extending TEX

How often will your TEX executables have to be updated? TEX and META-FONT have been declared frozen by their author, so new "versions" will never exist. To be sure, the fixing of bugs will require new program modules, but at this point in TEX's life, all the serious bugs have (likely) been caught, and any remaining problems are not apt to show up in ordinary work. Each time the TEX source is revised, its version gains another digit in the expansion of $\pi = 3.14159\ldots$, so its version number slowly converges to π. (In the same way, METAFONT's version number converges to $e = 2.71828\ldots$.) Any versions of TEX or METAFONT that are current as of the mid-1990s are stable and likely won't need upgrading, even for bug fixes.

However, the TEX code is available to all, and its algorithms may be used by others to design new typesetting systems. Some such systems are beginning to appear.

NTS, the "new typesetting system," is taking shape under the direction of an international team of programmers. Their goal is to design a system that will process all existing LATEX and TEX documents and will possess several other important strengths [Taylor (1994)].

Yannis Haralambous and John Plaice are designing the Omega project [Plaice (1994), Haralambous (1996), Plaice and Haralambous (1996)], essentially an extension of TEX to 16-bit characters. This extension will make it possible to implement new ways to handle clusters of characters so that the typesetting of foreign languages, ones far more exotic than English, will be straightforward. Preliminary versions of Omega are already available for downloading.

Michael Vulis pioneered a commercial extension to TEX, called VTEX. It allowed for several nonstandard treatments of fonts and for the use of scalable fonts. The extension to scalable fonts, for example, meant that it was easy to use only a few main fonts and scale them as needed. In this way, it was possible to fit TEX on the "small" laptop computers of that era (early 1990s). VisualTEX, the successor to this program, provides many enhanced features to help authors compose documents and refine their use of fonts.

I know of no comparable plans underway to extend METAFONT, the graphics companion program to TEX. MetaPost, a descendent of META-FONT, is discussed in chapters 3 and 13.

1.6   Installing and running TEX

Installing TEX involves three things:

1. placing the TEX executable (and all other executables) in a place your system knows about (usually with other executable files);

2. placing other files in directories the executables know about; and

3. preparing a *format file* for use by TEX.

Installation may also involve deciding what kind of executable to install.

It's very likely a guide of some sort will accompany any implementation. It may be printed or may be some file with a name like README, INSTALL, or something similar. This guide should be the resource of choice during any installation.

1.6.1   The executable

The *executable file* is what most people refer to as TEX, the actual program. On Unix (and some other) systems, TEX may come in source form so that you or someone at your site will need to compile it first. This is a straight-forward process, even for those ignorant of programming. (Carefully follow the detailed instructions in the local guide.)

It may be necessary to choose the type of executable. On computers running with an Intel chip (286, 386, 486, Pentium, and so on), users often have a choice of TEX's for the type of chip. Programs optimized for the chip type generally operate faster. Thus, if you have a 386-computer or better, you should probably choose to install a `tex386.exe` module over one named simply `tex.exe` or `tex186.exe`.

When TEX runs, it appropriates the computer's memory and uses it to store and manage quantities that are important to it. The more computer memory the program can handle, the more you can do with TEX—you can run larger macro packages, more complicated macros, and typeset larger pages. Varieties called "big TEX" or "huge TEX" refer to the quantity of computer memory that the module can handle, and refer also to some min-imum quantities of memory necessary for these memory-hungry programs. (Check the local guide for details.) Sometimes (as on DOS systems), the larger the capacity of the program, the more sluggish will TEX run, but if your computer is reasonably fast (say a 486 or better) and possesses ample quantities of memory, you should choose the "biggest" module optimized for the chip (e.g., `btex386` or even `htex386`; h=huge) because the penalty in performance will generally not be objectionable (particularly in comparison with the peace of mind from knowing that any macro package will work fine with your TEX).

The TEX executable belongs in a directory or folder in the system's path.

1.6.2 Other files

Without a host of related files containing important information, TEX will be incapable of any action. These files need to be placed in a directory or folder that TEX knows about. For example, the `.tfm` files (see the next sec-tion) often need to be in a place named something like

```
\tex\fonts\tfm
```

(DOS) or

```
/usr/local/lib/tex/fonts/tfm
```

(Unix). If, for some reason, it is necessary to put these auxiliary files in some non-standard locations, you will have to let TEX know by setting some environment variable, which is an operating system's way of allowing you to name a special place for storing information it will use. Environment variables are set within the operating system, so at your system prompt, type something like

```
set TEXFONTS=\myplace\tfm
```

but check the local guide for particular details. If at all possible, you should strenuously try to adhere to the default directory structure. Many setup problems have to do with TEX's (alleged) inability to find files that aren't in places it expects.

Font and string pool information   Most beginners are surprised to learn that TEX itself doesn't care at all about the shapes of the letters and symbols it places on the page. TEX is only interested in the *space* that these letters occupy. TEX's typesetting universe assumes all characters sit in boxes. TEX composes a page by butting these boxes together to form rows, and builds the page by stacking rows on top of each other. (The process is not quite this simple, but the process can be elaborated to encompass all of TEX's typesetting.) Therefore, all that TEX needs are files that contain the measurements of these boxes. These files are called *TEX font metric* files, or *font metric files* or simply .tfm files, and TEX needs access to one .tfm file for each font in any document.

Many of TEX's error messages are stored as character strings in a file as a special *string pool* file. Although normally called tex.pool on sophisticated systems, MS-DOS and PC-DOS truncate the name charmingly to tex.poo.

Input files   Lots of files store information about the text of a document and its formatting. There are several types of these *input files*. Usually LATEX or TEX can find these files if they're in the current working directory, perhaps the parent to this work directory, and (at least) one other dedicated location, probably with a name like

```
/usr/local/lib/tex/inputs
```

on Unix systems or

```
\tex\inputs
```

on DOS systems.

One other important input file is the document file you're working on. This will typically be in the current working directory, which is where TEX will expect to find it.

1.6.3   Initializing TEX with format files

The author of TEX wrote TEX so that its built-in commands are at as low a level as possible, so low that they are inefficient for the typical user of TEX. These are TEX's *primitive commands*. He anticipated that individuals would create their own *macro packages* to put many useful macros at a user's fingertips, and he set the example by creating the file plain.tex to contain a wide variety of useful macros. Everybody's TEX files contain commands that are not primitive to TEX, but which occur in plain or are based on definitions

in plain. Therefore, you always need to be sure that the contents of this file
(or a file comparable to this one) become known to TEX each time you use
TEX.

Moreover, the file plain.tex is long, so to save time, TEX has been given
the ability to transform it to an equivalent file in which all the macros are
expressed in a special binary format that the TEX program can read at high
speed. This transformed file is a *format file*; for example, the format file
corresponding to plain.tex is plain.fmt. The creation of this format file
is regarded as an initialization procedure for TEX, since TEX *always* looks
for a format file whenever it starts up, and without one, ceases operation.
As with TEX's other files, all format files need to be in a special place on the
hard disk, in a place named something like /usr/local/lib/tex/formats.

We need to run a special version of TEX called initex to create a format file. Some implementations provide separate initex program modules,
while others combine the two, and allow us to run initex by executing TEX
with a special software switch.

At initialization time, we include information about hyphenation and
non-American authors should take care that they don't reduce the portability of their documents. For example, all of an author's efforts at the fine tuning of line breaks when, say, British hyphenation is in effect, can be nullified
if the document is later processed by a TEX that only understands American
hyphenation.

Any time we plan to use a macro package extensively, it's a good idea to
use initex to create a corresponding format file containing those macros.
This is certainly the case with LATEX or $\mathcal{A}_{\mathcal{M}}\mathcal{S}$TEX. Detailed information
on preparing the format file is usually part of a system installation guide.
The format file will also incorporate hyphenation information, which is a
set of rules and patterns to guide TEX when it has to hyphenate words at
the ends of lines. Hyphenation patterns exist for many languages other than
American English.

However, if we use smaller macro files, or don't plan on using a large
macro package all that often, TEX is perfectly happy to work with this file
"as is"; we need not convert every macro file to its format equivalent.

Many (most?) readers use LATEX, which requires its own format file. The
old version of LATEX (now frozen at version 2.09) required using the file
lplain.tex as the base to create the format file. The new LATEX2$_\varepsilon$, which
is LATEX now, is a much larger package, and it's an especially good idea to
create the corresponding format file.

1.6.4 Running TEX

Suppose you have the file mychapter.tex composed plain TEX, and you
want run it through the TEX program. (The document file has the extension

Creating Format Files

Consult the local guide first. Proceed with the instructions here only if there is no information.

A typical format file needs to know something about macros. The special version of TeX called `initex` is usually invoked by typing something like

```
initex      or      tex /i
```

Try each of these commands. When they work, you will see a double asterisk prompt on the monitor:

```
**
```

In response, type

```
\input plain \dump
```

In addition, format files need to contain hyphenation information. Macro designers who think their files will be made into format files are usually careful to input a hyphenation file named `hyphen.tex` automatically. If you want to substitute non-American patterns, do not fail to put a copy of the nonstandard hyphenation file into a TeX input directory. Save the original `hyphen.tex` under a new name, and rename the non-American hyphenation file `hyphen.tex`. (But beware of portability problems this procedure may introduce!)

At the ** prompt, type

```
\input plain \dump
```

to create the format file `plain.fmt`. After the run has finished, move `plain.fmt` to the formats directory.

To create a LaTeX(that is, LaTeX2$_\varepsilon$) format, follow the complete directions in the LaTeX2$_\varepsilon$ installation guide called `install.txt`. This will tell you to run `initex` on the file `latex.ltx`.

`.tex`.) Unless there is a graphic user interface that sits over your version of TeX, you execute TeX at the command line with the statement

```
tex mychapter
```

But what if the document is a LATEX file? You need to tell TEX to read the appropriate format file; in this case you type

```
tex &latex mychapter
```

or

```
tex '&latex mychapter'
```

if you're running under Unix. Often, there may be a system script, alias, batch file, or whatever so that typing latex is equivalent to tex &latex.

If you omit the file name (typing simply tex or tex &latex, TEX will enter interactive mode and expect further input in response to its prompts of * or **.

1.7   Inking the page

Neither TEX nor LATEX (nor any other macro package) actually paints the page. TEX simply creates a file, the .dvi file, which precisely records the position of each character, rule, and other graphic element in the document. Other programs take responsibility for using this information to place ink on the page. Remember, the TEX program needs only to know how much space is required for each character, rule, and typographic element on the page.

1.7.1   The characters of a font

It's the province of the device driver (or previewer, just another type of device driver) to deal with the characters of a digital font. Information in the .dvi file tells it where to position each character, and then the driver paints each character where it is supposed to be.

Bitmap fonts   How does the driver know these shapes? One way to store shape information is within a collection of *pixel files*. Computer printers generate their shapes by putting lots of tiny dots next to each other in such a way that they form patterns which our eyes resolve into letters and graphs. Office laser printers, for example, are capable of placing as many as 600 dots per inch to the left or right and up or down. Only the dots needed to create a character are printed, and the human eye smoothes out any jaggedness as it perceives the image. Pixel files, or *bitmap fonts*, provide instructions as to which dots to blacken and which to leave blank.

There are lots of pixel files because TEX needs a different file for each font of "type" at each size and at each magnification. What's the difference between the *size* of a font and the *magnification* of a font? Type designers of old took care to slightly redesign each font of type at different sizes. Subtle issues of spacing require that the proportions between thick and thin strokes, the size of the white areas within some letters, and so on be readjusted at each size. *The TEXbook* makes this point early on, on page 16, which shows the difference between 10-point type and 5-point type magnified two hundred percent. That and the following demonstrations have members from the Computer Modern Roman families. Computer Modern Roman type at a 10-pt design size (type size or just *size*) is referred to as cmr10.

If you look closely, you can also see these effects of *optical scaling* in fonts that are more closely sized. Look closely at the difference between 12-point type and 10-point type magnified by 20%.

12-point: The lazy brown fox jumped quickly.
10-point magnified by 20%:   The lazy brown fox jumped quickly.

and at the differences between cmr17 and cmr10 magnified 70% (actually 72.8%).

17-point: The lazy brown fox jumped quickly.

10-point magnified by 70%:
The lazy brown fox jumped quickly.

Although TEX has been designed to appreciate this subtle difference in type sizing, many computer typesetting systems do *not*. Therefore, prevailing electronic fonts of type construct different type sizes by taking a single font and magnifying it by whatever amount necessary to get the size you want. That is, there is generally no difference between *type size* and *magnification* unless you work with Computer Modern types. (Recently, there are some indications that the non-TEX world may be beginning to perceive the importance of this distinction. Adobe's Multiple Master technology is one sign of this trend.)

The many different font files that normally come with TEX often confuse users, but now we know why they are necessary. TEX *does* distinguish between size and magnification, and TEX's ability to make this distinction calls this diversity into being.

On DOS systems (and any others that impose rigid lengths on possible file names), the necessity for having many different fonts at different sizes and magnifications calls an intricate directory structure into being. All cmr10 fonts at any magnification have the name cmr10.pk. The magnification is distinguished by creating different directories to hold pixel files with like magnifications. For fonts rendered to print on a 300 dpi printer, fonts at magnification 1000 (normal size) appear in directories named something like

    \tex\fonts\dpi300

while for 120% magnification, since $360 = 1.2 \times 300$, the directory will be

    \tex\fonts\dpi360

Bitmap Technology: Pros and Cons

- **Pros:**

  - Compact font files.

  - Easy to preview

  - Relatively compact .dvi files.

  - Computer Modern fonts, which respect the distinction between a font's size and its magnification, are freely available; this super-family of fonts contains individual fonts for most typesetting purposes, including mathematics.

  - Documents containing only bitmap fonts print relatively rapidly.

- **Cons:**

  - Device-dependent font descriptions.

  - Relatively sparse selection of fonts.

  - May be difficult to find a service bureau to render typeset-quality documents (but see the discussion of PostScript below to see how this technology copes with this limitation).

1.7.2 Scalable fonts and a PostScript postscript

PostScript technology has come to dominate the world of computer type-setting and desktop publishing. Files fully (and carefully) prepared in Post-Script are device-independent and are generally ASCII (so they can be freely transferred across computer platforms). "Device independence" means any PostScript device. (With the Level 2 enhancement, PostScript supports some binary encoding, so such files may no longer be pure ASCII. Such files may still be moved across platforms as Adobe took great care to ensure this.)

Since PostScript files are independent of the printer resolution, fonts for PostScript cannot rely on bitmap descriptions, which are inherently tied to a printer's resolution. (See chapter 3 for a further discussion of this important topic.) Each character in a PostScript font is given by a mathematical description of the outline of that character (hence, the appellation 'outline font'); this description is not dependent on any printer resolution. Nevertheless, any raster printing device is, in the final analysis, a set of bitmap

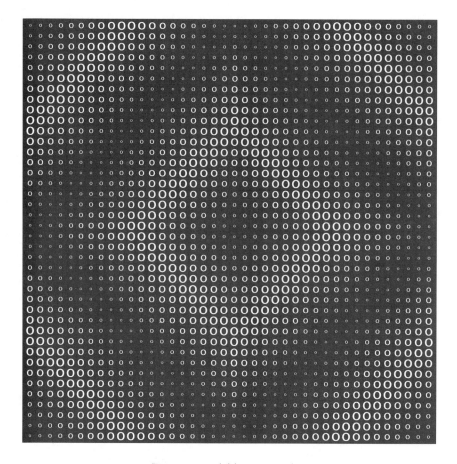

Figure 5: Scalable typography.

images, but it's the job of the special PostScript printer to resolve the outline descriptions to their bitmap equivalents.

PostScript fonts are called *scalable fonts* because the technology scales these outline descriptions up or down to get different sizes. Old-time typographers may (rightly) deplore the loss of design detail in such font scaling, but outline fonts do make the composition of figure 5 rather straightforward. (The plain TEX code for this figure appears in the appendix to this chapter.)

TEX and PostScript technology coexist quite companionably. To render a .dvi file on a PostScript printer, the .dvi file must be translated to the PostScript language. A variety of dvi-to-PostScript converters exist for this purpose; one such, and one of the most highly regarded, is the freely available *dvips* by Tomas Rokicki. (It has been compiled for virtually every computer platform.) The end product of the translation is a series of statements in the PostScript language, which are either transmitted immediately to the printer or saved to a special file with a .ps extension.

Beware—these .dvi postprocessors are savvy enough to embed bitmap descriptions into the output .ps file in the proper format for printing on a PostScript printer. Only now the file has become device-dependent—it will print properly only on the printer for which the bitmaps were created. Post-Script does try to scale the bitmap image, but an inevitable loss of quality accompanies this operation. Thus, if you plan to print the document later via phototypesetter, you'll have to regenerate the .dvi and .ps files with the proper bitmaps.

Outline fonts   All the Computer Modern bitmap fonts are free. Very few outline fonts are free. A few font families, like Utopia, have been donated by their copyright owners to the public domain, and they can be found on the CTAN archives; see chapter 2. In particular, outline equivalents of the Computer Modern fonts (the BaKoMa fonts by Basil Malyshev and the Blue Sky fonts) are also there.

Any of the hundreds of outline fonts that are commercially available can be used with LaTeX or TeX. They will require some special installation procedures; see chapters 6 and 7 for full details. It is possible to typeset mathematics with compatible fonts; see chapter 10 for advice and procedures.

Any .ps files containing references to proprietary scalable fonts may **not** be freely distributable because the PostScript converter may embed these fonts into the .ps file. In contrast, since the Computer Modern fonts *are* freely distributable, any author relying solely on these fonts can freely distribute .dvi files.

1.7.3 *Phototypesetters and service bureaus*

Most of us rarely produce TeX documents on devices more sensitive than a laser printer. Nevertheless, we should in principle be prepared to view laser output as proof output in preparation for high-quality phototypeset output. When a document is rendered on a high-resolution phototypesetter, typically on special paper of some kind, it can be used as a master by a printer to do the actual printing of books or manuscripts. Studies have shown that the range of 500–600 dpi is a watershed in the appearance of output. Above that range, printed output looks "real"; below it, the printing appears unprofessional.

When documents are prepared using bitmap fonts exclusively, it is the responsibility of the phototypesetter's device driver to use fonts at the proper resolution. It may be difficult to find commercial phototypesetters with TeX-savvy device-driver software. (It is possible to use PostScript technology to print bitmap phototypeset output; see the box on page 27.)

If a document is prepared using PostScript outline fonts, and only outline fonts, one needs to locate a PostScript phototypesetter. Such service bureaus may be listed under the "desktop publishing" category in local yellow page directories. *Linotronic* brand output devices are particularly common. The service bureau needs the .ps file that the dvi-to-PostScript post-

Outline (PostScript) Technology: Pros and Cons

- **Pros:**

  - PostScript has become a de facto standard.
  - Pure PostScript output files are device-independent.
  - PostScript output files are (mostly) printable ASCII and thus easy to exchange between computers.
  - A huge selection of fonts is available.

- **Cons:**

  - Special PostScript printer hardware may be costly.
  - PostScript files may be huge.
  - It may be problematic to typeset mathematics properly (but see chapter 10 for extensive discussion of this issue).
  - PostScript output is difficult to preview.
  - Very few outline fonts are available for free; others are proprietary and must be bought.
  - Printing may proceed relatively slowly (compared to bitmap output).
  - Output files containing proprietary font information are not freely distributable.
  - PostScript fonts require some special installation procedures for use with LATEX or TEX.

processor. It is usually not enough to blindly run a `.dvi` file through the postprocessor. *Header files* define PostScript macros that the postprocessor uses or contain information defining the fonts and will be needed by the phototypesetter. Conscientious programs like *dvips* are careful to include the header files into the `.ps` file. In this context, font files are themselves treated as header files and may be incorporated into the resulting `.ps` file.

Programs like *dvips* know how to include bitmap font information into their output so that the bitmap fonts will print properly on the PostScript printer. If you can generate your own bitmap fonts at the proper high resolution (using METAFONT; see chapters 3 and 13 to learn how), and if you instruct the postprocessor to include these bitmaps in the `.ps` file, the PostScript service bureau will properly render the bitmap document.

Preparing Files for a Service Bureau

Bitmap fonts. If your file contains bitmap fonts and bitmap inclusions, you need to bring the .dvi file only to an appropriate service bureau (which can be located via commercial announcements in TEX-related journals like *TUGBoat*). The service bureau is responsible for using Computer Modern fonts at the proper resolution for its phototypesetter.

Alternatively, the procedure for outline fonts (below) works for bitmap fonts, but there is greater responsibility on the author for preparing bitmap font files for inclusion in the output .ps file.

PostScript outline fonts. Documents may reference outline fonts, or outline fonts plus bitmap fonts, together with scalable graphics. In that case, an author will need to prepare a postprocessed .ps file from the .dvi file. The *dvips* command to do this is

```
dvips -o mychapter.ps mychapter
```

assuming that mychapter.dvi contains the compiled document. Other postprocessors will employ similar syntax.

The resulting .ps file may be quite large, and may not fit on a single floppy disk! If you possess a Syquest removable disk cartridge, it should be possible to bring the cartridge directly to the bureau; this medium seems to have become the de facto standard for the service bureau industry (at least in the United States).

In the absence of such media, authors may need to compress the file with a utility like gzip, pkzip, or zip. Sometimes the compressed file is itself too large, and (since subsequent compressions will do no good) it will be necessary to split the file into disk-sized chunks which can be reconstituted on the service bureau's hard disk. Such splitting and joining utilities will be available on computer bulletin boards and archives. File transmission by modem is also possible, but only if robust transfer protocols such as kermit are used.

If your document refers to bitmap fonts, these will be included in the output .ps file in such a way as to appear properly when the .ps file is rendered, *provided the resolution and characteristics of the bitmap fonts match those of the phototypesetter.* Consequently, it is the responsibility of the author to have generated and used high-resolution bitmaps. (Use METAFONT to generate Computer Modern fonts at high resolution. This simple procedure appears in chapter 3.)

1.7.4 Just for fun

We normally use TEX to place type on a page, but neat effects are possible if one extends the meaning of "type." Early on, for example, Knuth (1987)

1.250000

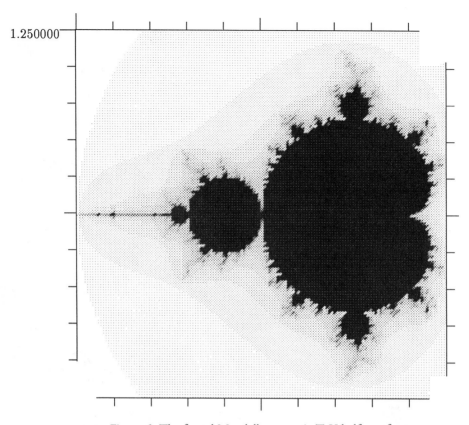

Figure 6: The fractal Mandelbrot set via TEX halftone fonts.

showed that if we define a font, each of whose glyphs is a small rectangle in a different shade of halftone gray, then it is possible to typeset halftone pictures. [Hoenig (1989) applied this technique to the generation of fractal images; see figure 6.] This appeared to be a good way to display large quantities of data, such as a digital representation of a painting.

We shouldn't take this process too seriously—meaningful halftones seriously strain TEX's memory resources and make it difficult to generate images at resolutions greater than 300 dpi. Knuth (1993, pp. 88–89) himself has suggested another way of making the translation from numerical database to visual representation, this time via encapsulated PostScript.

TEX can also help make beautiful music, as figure 7 on page 30 shows. This sample, produced by Don Simons, uses the MusixTeX package, developed by Daniel Taupin, Ross Mitchell, and Andreas Egler, together with the pmx Fortran preprocessor (by Don Simons), which makes it easier to write an input file. All of this material is available from any CTAN archive (see chapter 2), or from the ftp site

ftp.gmd.de/music

or from

    http://ftp.gmd.de/music/README.html

on the World Wide Web.

1.8   Document files

1.8.1   Preparation

In the first stage of the TEX cycle, we prepare the *source file*, which contains all of our text, equations, charts, tables, and so on, together with the TEX formatting commands. We can't use TEX to prepare this file—TEX contains no built-in text editor. A *text editor* or *word processor* is the first of the several additional programs we need to work with TEX.

Virtually any text editor will serve, but be careful how it is used. TEX will accept files that contain *only* printable ASCII characters; anything that's not ASCII in a file will confuse TEX. Most commercial word processors embed formatting commands into a document file by means of various non-ASCII characters, but it is equally true that most such programs may be instructed to output just ASCII text. (Remember, we won't need the word processor formatting commands, because TEX will take care of all that for us.) Various word processors use different buzz words to refer to pure ASCII files. Some such terms are *nondocument files, unformatted file*, and *program files*.

Many public-domain word processors and text editors are perfect vehicles for preparing TEX source files. Often, they only output ASCII files, and, being in the public domain, they are cheap. A common choice for a TEX editor is Emacs, most common on Unix workstations, and now ported to every computer platform. Emacs has many commands specially tailored for use with LATEX or TEX.

1.8.2   What do TEX commands look like?

LATEX and TEX reserve ten characters for their own use; see figure 8 on page 31. Otherwise, when TEX encounters a letter or symbol such as an "A" or "9" it interprets the symbol as a command to typeset that symbol (to typeset an uppercase A or the numeral 9). We call the character that alerts TEX to an immediately following command the *escape character*, but this character bears no relation to the key marked "escape" or "esc" on many keyboards.

We issue explicit commands to TEX by means of one of several hundred commands beginning with the backslash, the usual escape character for TEX. Immediately following the backslash are one or more characters, which may be followed by additional information that the command needs. For example, the command

    \noindent

Figure 7: Music typeset completely by TEX. This piece is from *Ayres for the Violin, Part 4* by Nicola Matteis (late 17th century).

\	Escape symbol	%	Comment symbol
{ }	Grouping symbols	#	Parameter symbol
^	Superscript indicator	&	Tabbing symbol
_	Subscript indicator	~	Non-break space
$, $$	Math mode toggles		

Figure 8: TEX's reserved symbols.

suppresses indentation at the beginning of a paragraph while

```
\vspace{1in}
```

instructs LATEX to skip one inch of vertical space.

It's important that special reserved characters begin or introduce special formatting instructions, because you never know when you might want to include the word "noindent" or "vspace" within the document. By the way, there are special commands to typeset any of the reserved symbols, so it is possible (and easy) to typeset a backslash or a dollar sign within the document.

1.8.3 More about TEX's commands

TEX contains a rich set of several hundred or so commands. Although by themselves they do just about anything we might wish, their real strength flows from the ability to string commands together to form new commands for special typesetting purposes.

We might create our own personal \newchapter command to begin a new page, skip down a third of the page, center the chapter title, skip a quarter of an inch, suppress indentation on the first paragraph, and set the first two words of the chapter in a small caps font. These new commands are called *macros*.

Creating a macro is a lot like writing a computer program. TEX possesses several commands to test conditions and perform action on the basis of the test, to perform looping, and to handle input/output operations. Tricky macros can take a long time to write and test, but more often than not, it's possible to write simple macros on the fly that make typesetting much easier.

TEX lets us place all our personal macro definitions into a separate *style file*. The document would contain special instructions for TEX to read and assimilate those macros before typesetting. Publishers, for example, could exploit this by making generic style files available to their authors while commissioning a designer to prepare a style file to implement a specialized book layout. The typeset document file remains the same, and only the macro definitions change. LATEX exploits this philosophy to the hilt. This concept is so important that it is worth an illustrative example.

In a math article, I might typeset the theorem

■   THEOREM There is no royal road to typesetting. Fine typesetting
             is inherently difficult.

via

```
\theorem There is no ... difficult.
```

But all I have to do to get

THEOREM. *There is no royal road to typesetting. Fine typesetting is inherently difficult.*

is alter the definition of \theorem in my style file and rerun the document through TEX. The document file itself remains untouched.

This method of command structure has another important result. We are free to revise the text of our document, secure in the knowledge that TEX will incorporate the revised text into the layout. For example, the TEX source for this paragraph begins with

```
\droppedcap This method of command ...
```

and it is the responsibility of the \droppedcap macro to perform the machinations necessary for the proper positioning of the dropped cap and the subsequent wrapping of the text around it. But if we wanted to revise this paragraph so that it begins differently, all we need do is perform the revision (leaving the \droppedcap instruction in place) and rerun the revised source file through TEX, which attends to the positioning of a new dropped cap and the wrapping of the new text around it automatically.

1.8.4   *L*A*TEX and TEX are not WYSIWYG*

WYSIWYG—"what you see is what you get"—refers to the ability of a software package to show at the monitor what a document will look like as the document is being created. Large numbers of users feel that this is the way computer composition systems should work. TEX is not a WYSIWYG system, and experienced computer typographers as well as TEX users agree that this is the best way for a computer typesetting system to be.

What you see in WYSIWYG software is *all* you get. Computing machinery excels at making decisions, and there are many decisions to be made in any typesetting process. But in a WYSIWYG system, we are responsible for many of the details that should otherwise be left for the computer—otherwise, how would the computer know what to display? In the expression

$$e^{-x^2}$$

whose responsibility is it for the spacing in the exponents (superscripts) in this expression? In a WYSIWYG system, it is often ours. As a practical matter, anybody quickly tires of making these tedious decisions over and over.

But there are other things that a typesetting system should do automatically. Suppose, for example, we typeset a set of numbered exercises in a math text. With TEX, it's easy to design an \exercise macro to automatically number the exercises. In case we decide to insert new exercises at the *beginning* of the exercise set, all we do is revise the source file by placing the new problems wherever they belong and rerun the revised source file through TEX. In a WYSIWYG system, we might actually have to renumber the problems by hand—a ghastly (and highly error-prone) prospect.

Typesetting decisions can be more subtle. Typesetting systems should pay careful attention to deciding the best way to break lines in a paragraph. How can a WYSIWYG program do that, since (in admittedly extreme cases) the last word of a paragraph can influence the line break at the first line?

1.8.5 Some popular macro packages

Over the years, an increasing number of people have brought a variety of macro packages into being. LATEX and $A_{\mathcal{M}}S$TEX are the two most widely used packages, with LATEX leading $A_{\mathcal{M}}S$TEX in popularity. But even when not using any of these, TEX invokes the plain set of macros. The most primitive TEX commands are at far too low a level to be of much use to most users, so the macro collection plain.tex serves as a common base on which many macro packages build. Therefore, all TEX users use some macro package.

LATEX was originally written by Leslie Lamport (but its recent revision is courtesy of an international team of which he is a member). He defined hundreds of new macros in clever ways so that the LATEX syntax is sometimes quite a bit different from plain TEX syntax. Many LATEX users feel that LATEX commands are easier to master than those of raw TEX, and there are many more LATEX users than there are plain TEX users. However, that power has a price, and it can be difficult to make LATEX do things that aren't part of the LATEX model. (Sometimes, though, it's possible to resort to the use of plain TEX within the LATEX document. After all, when you use LATEX, you are still using TEX.)

Michael Spivak wrote $A_{\mathcal{M}}S$TEX to make it easy to typeset mathematical papers, especially for journals. Current versions of $A_{\mathcal{M}}S$TEX include additional math fonts containing special characters that aren't in TEX's native fonts. Spivak has created a second-generation macro package, $L_{A\mathcal{M}}S$-TEX, whose name suggests its function. It is a synthesis of the capabilities of both LATEX and $A_{\mathcal{M}}S$TEX, although its syntax is its own. $L_{A\mathcal{M}}S$-TEX is the first of the second-generation macro packages to appear. Another on the horizon is the LATEX3 project, modules of which have already been distributed.

Both LATEX and $A_{\mathcal{M}}S$TEX are in the *public domain*, as are $L_{A\mathcal{M}}S$-TEX and the new LATEX modules. This means that anyone is free to obtain and pass along this software.

In the summer of 1990, the American Mathematical Society announced a new macro package, the amsmath package, which combines the features of both of its parents, $\mathcal{A}_{\mathcal{M}}\mathcal{S}$TEX and LATEX. The Society maintains a public-domain archive at the Internet node e-math.ams.org. Anyone is welcome to access a variety of TEX macro packages and fonts using anonymous file transfer protocol (ftp) or World Wide Web browsers. (METAFONT enthusiasts should be aware that this software includes the METAFONT sources for the Society's special TEX fonts, including their *Euler math fonts*.

1.9 Friends of TEX

In the process of developing the TEX program, Knuth relied on utility programs to facilitate program development, test integrity of output, and make life easier. Some of these friends of TEX, like WEB and METAFONT, are useful tools in their own right.

1.9.1 *Metafont and MetaPost*

TEX is often subject to the criticism that it cannot efficiently handle graphics within documents. That's an unfair criticism, since TEX has a sibling program that excels at the creation of figures that can easily become part of a TEX document. This sibling is METAFONT, the design tool Knuth used to create each character in each of the fonts that are part of the standard TEX distribution package. All of those fonts are members of the so-called Computer Modern family of typefaces. METAFONT has the ability, like TEX, to form new macro commands and to such an extent that it too can be considered a programming language.

MetaPost, by John Hobby, is a descendant of METAFONT, and its language is remarkably similar to its ancestor. It produces PostScript graphics instead of fonts and so directly serves as a graphic tool for TEX documents intended for PostScript output. In 1995, MetaPost was placed in the public domain.

METAFONT will not complain if you use it to generate forms other than font characters, and a small but enthusiastic group of METAFONT users have shown that METAFONT can be quite effective in preparing graphic images and dingbats. It is trivial to incorporate such graphics into a TEX document. As a special bonus, METAFONT can serve as a neat on-line calculator and equation solver (see chapter 13 for further details).

The Computer Modern family is created from a small set of METAFONT program files. All that needs to be done to generate a **bold faced font** versus *italic* versus unslanted italic versus *slanted (oblique)* versus ... is to appropriately change the values of the 60 or so numerical parameters that are part of each of these METAFONT programs. This book has not been typeset using the Computer Modern types. All the volumes of *Computers and Typesetting* are set in Computer Modern. Figure 9 on the facing page compares the Roman and italic forms of Computer Modern with Adobe Garamond, the text

Mathematical books and journals do not look as beautiful as they used to. It is not that their mathematical content is unsatisfactory, rather that the old and well-developed traditions of typesetting have become too expensive. Fortunately, it now appears that mathematics itself can be used to solve this problem.	Mathematical books and journals do not look as beautiful as they used to. It is not that their mathematical content is unsatisfactory, rather that the old and well-developed traditions of typesetting have become too expensive. Fortunately, it now appears that mathematics itself can be used to solve this problem.
Mathematical books and journals do not look as beautiful as they used to. It is not that their mathematical content is unsatisfactory, rather that the old and well-developed traditions of typesetting have become too expensive. Fortunately, it now appears that mathematics itself can be used to solve this problem.	*Mathematical books and journals do not look as beautiful as they used to. It is not that their mathematical content is unsatisfactory, rather that the old and well-developed traditions of typesetting have become too expensive. Fortunately, it now appears that mathematics itself can be used to solve this problem.*

Figure 9: Computer Modern is on the left in this display, and the corresponding variant of Garamond is on the right.

face used in this book. The text in this figure is from Knuth (1979). Few people have followed Knuth's lead in generating versatile METAFONT font programs.

The number of METAFONT users is a tiny fraction of the number of LaTeX and TEX users. One reason is the absence (so far) of macro packages like LaTeX to make METAFONT more accessible; METAFONT is widely if unfairly viewed as being more difficult to use than TEX. The small group of dedicated METAFONTers testify that METAFONT can be quietly addictive.

1.9.2 The WEB system of structured documentation

The source of the TEX and METAFONT programs are Pascal programs of between 20,000 and 30,000 lines. How can any one person reasonably expect to write, test, and *debug* such mammoth programs? Knuth's answer was the WEB system of structured documentation.

WEB provides an environment for combining TEX commands together with Pascal programming commands in a single source from which typeset documentation and program source files can be quickly generated. In the process of creating a web, it's possible to make more visible the structure of each program module and the interrelationships between modules. At its highest and best use, a web is a literate document that can be read with as much pleasure and profit as a classic novel. The printed programs [Knuth (1986b), Knuth (1986d)] for TEX and METAFONT are actually webs (as is the source for MetaPost), and large parts of these are fun to read; see Knuth (1992). Other valuable information on WEB can be found in Knuth (1983), Sewell (1989), and Knuth (1992).

WEB is not a system for beginners—since you're dealing with three systems, you have to watch out for three kinds of errors (TEX, the computer language, and WEB). Nevertheless, reliable software can be rapidly created using WEB.

Associated with WEB are two programs, TANGLE and WEAVE. If a .web file is fed into WEAVE, the output is a TEX document file from which TEX can generate high-quality documentation. If TANGLE acts on the web file, the output is an ugly language source file which is then fed to the appropriate compiler. Programmers are encouraged to only make changes on the original .web file. The source has been "tangled" to make tampering with the source file much less attractive than modifying the WEB file.

Much effort has gone into adapting the WEB environment toward languages other than Pascal. Silvio Levy in conjunction with Knuth has created a CWEB environment for the C and C++ languages. In addition, WEB systems now exist for Modula-2, C and C++, Fortran, and several other high-level languages. The bibliography in Knuth (1992) is particularly rich in pointers to these other efforts.

At a party celebrating the publication of the five-volume *Computers and Typesetting* series [Knuth (1986f)], Knuth expressed the opinion that WEB may be the most important piece of research to emerge from his ten-year involvement with typography, more important even than TEX or META-FONT.

1.9.3 Other utilities

Figure 10 on the next page lists the full panoply of additional tools available to users of TEX and METAFONT. Over the years, virtually all of them have been useful to me at one time or another. The first group in this table form the original group of "TEXware," described by Knuth and Fuchs (1986). Discussion for two additional virtual font utilities appears in Knuth (1990). Finally, for completeness, we list a group of utilities that will be of use to users of METAFONT and MetaPost; complete documentation for them can be found in Knuth, Rokicki, and Samuel (1989).

If you will be installing PostScript fonts or anticipate any work with virtual fonts, you will need the tools tftopl, vftovp, and their opposites pltotf and vptovf. Work with METAFONT will require the tools gftopk to render the fonts usable and gftodvi to monitor and preview METAFONT work in progress. If you plan to print METAFONT or MetaPost programs, you will need the mft prettyprinter. The program listings in chapter 13 have all been formatted with mft.

pooltype	Converts string pool files output by TANGLE into a slightly more symbolic format that may be useful when TANGLEd programs are being debugged.
tftopl	Converts a binary TEX font metric .tfm file into an ASCII property list .pl file, and checks the .tfm file for correctness.
pltotf	Converts an ASCII property list .pl file into its equivalent .tfm file.
dvitype	Reads a .dvi file, converts it into a symbolic form, and tests the correctness of the file.
vftovp	Analogous to tftopl; verifies virtual font .vf files and converts them to symbolic ASCII virtual property list files.
vptovf	Analogous to pltotf; converts a virtual property .pl into its binary equivalent.
gftype	Reads the generic font output produced by METAFONT and converts it to symbolic form.
gftopk	This program reads a .gf file and packs it into a .pk file, which is significantly smaller than a .gf file.
gftodvi	Converts the generic font output produced by METAFONT into a .dvi format that can be printed or previewed.
mft	Converts a METAFONT source file to a TEX file for "prettyprinting."

Figure 10: Here are additional friends of TEX and METAFONT.

1.10 Learning and joining

Although the numbers of users of LATEX and TEX are (as of yet) dwarfed in magnitude by users of famous commercial products, the growth in use of TEX is astonishing. For consider this: an idiosyncratic product, passed along by word of mouth, has no public-relations dollars behind it. The reaction of users learning it was "free" was often the same—if it is so good, why isn't anyone selling it?

But as these words are written, it has become clear that there will always be a prominent place for TEX. Although there is widespread perception that LATEX and TEX may be difficult to use well, no desktop publishing package is particularly easy. Furthermore, TEX has been able to perform certain nice things from the beginning that some famous commercial programs are still struggling over, and this has won the hearts of several mainstream publishers. Scientists the world over will never relinquish LATEX or TEX— how else will they *unambiguously* capture on the page their technical expressions? Furthermore, the many millions of pages of LATEX and TEX electronic manuscript already in existence require TEX's continued presence.

It can be difficult, though, to bring oneself up to speed in the conventions of LATEX or TEX. Except for the odd university course here and there, there tends not to be formal instruction in these programs. Moreover, many practicing scientists won't realize that they need these tools until the opportunity to avail themselves of these courses is long past. This section makes some broad suggestions for learning how to use LATEX and TEX.

There are many varied resources on computer networks, and we will explore these in chapter 2. Some suggestions for useful books follow.

The TEX bible is of course *The TEXbook*, by Donald E. Knuth [Knuth (1986a)], the author of both TEX and METAFONT. Everything to be known about the TEX language appears in this volume, which is also volume A of Knuth's series *Computers and Typesetting*. Everything about METAFONT appears in *The METAFONTbook* [Knuth (1986c)], which is volume C of *Computers and Typesetting*. The remaining volumes present the WEB listings of the computer programs for TEX and METAFONT [Knuth (1986b), Knuth (1986d)] (volumes B and C). Volume E [Knuth (1986e)] presents the METAFONT programs for each of the characters in the Computer Modern family of typefaces. All of these books are casebound but less-expensive paperbound versions of *The TEXbook* and *The METAFONTbook* are available.

The comprehensive guides to LATEX and to $A_{\mathcal{M}}S$TEX appear in *LATEX: A Document Preparation System* [Lamport (1994)], now in its second edition, and *The Joy of TEX* [Spivak (1990)], written by the authors of these systems. The *LATEX Companion* [Goossens, Mittelbach, and Samarin (1994)], in the short time it has appeared, has proven to be an essential resource for users of LATEX.

A plethora of books is appearing to fill the need for introductory TEX materials. As always, the quality varies. Of great interest is Michael Doob's *Gentle Introduction to TEX* [Doob (1990)], because it is being distributed in electronic form and has graciously been placed in the public domain by its author. Michael Spivak has also written the *PC TEX Manual* [Spivak (1987)]. Spivak's explanation of $L_{\mathcal{A}\mathcal{M}}S$-TEX appears in Spivak (1989).

Some advanced books are by Eijkhout (1992), Salomon (1995), and von Bechtolsheim (1994). The sources and resources section lists several other books on TEX, but this is by no means an exhaustive survey of all books about TEX.

1.10.1   The public domain

The five-volume *Computers and Typesetting* series contain everything there is to know about TEX and METAFONT, including the WEB documents from which the programs can be derived. All of the methods and ideas in these books are in the public domain; feel free to use any of them. Control only of the names TEX and METAFONT has been retained. Programs may only use these names if they conform to published standards.

User Groups

TUG: TEX Users Group (Int'l; American & English)
P. O. Box 1239, Three Rivers, CA 93271-1239 USA   Tel: 1 209 561-0112
Email: TUG@mail.tug.org   Web: http://www.tug.org/

CsTUG (Czech and Slovak)
  % FI MU
  Botanicá 68a
  CZ-602 00 Brno, Czech Republic
  Tel: 420 5 41212352
  email: cstug@cstug.cz
  ftp: ftp.cstug.cz/pub/tex
CyrTUG (Russian)
  Mir Publishers
  2 Pervyi Rizhskii Pereulok
  Moscow 129820, Russia
  Tel: 095 286-0622, 286-1777
  email: cyrtug@cemi.rssi.ru
DANTE e.V. (German speaking)
  Postfach 101840
  D-69008 Heidelberg
  Germany
  Tel: +49 06221/29766
  email: dante@dante.de
  ftp: ftp.dante.de
  Web: www.dante.de
Estonian User Group (Estonian)
  Astrophysical Observatory, Toravere
  EE 2444 Estonia
  email: saar.aai.ee
EFT (Greek)
  366, 28th October St.
  GR-671 00 Xanthi
  Greece
  Tel: 30 541 28704
  email: apostolo@platon.ee.duth.gr
GUST (Polish)
  Inst. Matematyki Uniwersytetu Gdanskiego
  ul. Wita Stwosza 57
  80-952 Gdansk, Poland
  Web: www.gust.org.pl/GUST/ GUThp.html
GUTH (group being formed) (Spanish)
  GMV SA, Isaac Newton 11
  PTM Tres Cantos
  E-28760 Madrid, Spain
  email: jsanchez@gmv.es
  Web: gordo.us.es/Actividades/GUTH
GUTenberg (French speaking)
  c/o IRISA
  BP 10
  F-93220 Gagny principal, France
  email: gut@irisa.fr
  ftp: ftp.univ-rennes1.fr
  Web: www.ens.fr/gut

ITALIC (Irish; not a formal group)
  Mailing list: ITALIC-L@irlearn.ucd.ie
  subscription requests to:
    listserv@irlearn.ucd.ie
  email: pflynn@www.ucc.ie
ITEXnici (group being formed) (Ital.)
  Giovanni MenoZero Pensa
  email: pensa@dsi.unimi.it
  Web: www.dsi.unimi.it/Users/
    Students/pensa/tex/ uitug.htmol
JTUG (Japanese)
  Environmental Information, Keio Univ.
  5322 Endo, Fujisawa-shi
  JP-252 Japan
  Tel: 81 466 47 5111
  email: ns@keio.ac.jp
Lithuanian TEX Users Group (Lithuanian)
  Akademijos 4
  LT-2600 Vilnius, Lithuania
  Tel: +370 2 279 609
  email: vytass@ktl.mii.lt
  Web: vtex.mii.lt/tex/
NTG (Dutch)
  Postbus 394
  NL-1740 AJ Schagen
  The Netherlands
  email: ntg@nic.surfnet.nl
  Web: www.ntg.nl/ntg/
Nordic TEX Group (Scandinavian langs.)
  Dept. of Informatics, Univ. of Oslo
  P.O. Box 1080 Blindern
  N-0316 Oslo, Norway
  email: nordictex@kth.se
  Web: www.ifi.uio.no/~dag/ntug/
TEXCeH (Slovenian)
  University of Ljubljana
  Jadranska 19
  SI-1111 Ljubljana, Slovenia
  email: texceh@uni-lj.si
  Web: vlado.mat.uni-lj.si/texceh
UK TUG (United Kingdom)
  c/o Peter Abbott
  1 Eymore Close, Selly Oak
  Birmingham B29 4LB,UK
  email: uktug-enquiries@tex.ac.uk
  Web: www.tex.ac.uk/UKTUG

1.10.2 Joining the TEX community

TEX, METAFONT, and their friends form a rich set of tools. Many workers have spent many happy hours adapting TEX to various specialized tasks or to creating special front ends that might be just what you were looking for. Although the many computer networks form a platform for the communication of this news, the various user groups provide a more formal forum for the exchange of important news. Not only do the larger of these groups publish their own newsletters, but they often sponsor annual meetings.

The TEX Users Group—TUG—is the original user group organization. Originally an offshoot of the American Mathematical Society, it is now an independent organization. TUG serves as a clearinghouse for all information on TEX, and members receive the journal *TUGboat*, the transactions of the TEX User Group. See TUG (1979).

Other user group organizations have since arisen, and the addresses of most of them appear in the box on the preceding page. New user groups, particularly behind the former Iron Curtain, are constantly being formed. (The attention of English-speaking readers must certainly be drawn to UK TUG, whose journal *Baskerville* is well worthwhile.)

1.11 Appendix: Scalable typography

It's well worth your while to try and generate figure 5 on page 24 before glancing at the solution presented below. I found that the versions I generated on the way to this figure were just as entertaining as the original. Figure 5 used Lucida Sans demibold type.

```
\input colordvi
\newdimen\myfontsize \myfontsize=10.2pt
\newdimen\fontinc     % font increment for linear scaling
\fontinc=-.8pt        % default
\def\fontid{lsd at\myfontsize}%% or choose your own font...
\def\DefineFonts{% these fonts are linearly scaled
  \font\0=\fontid\relax \advance\myfontsize by\fontinc
  \font\1=\fontid\relax \advance\myfontsize by\fontinc
  \font\2=\fontid\relax \advance\myfontsize by\fontinc
  \font\3=\fontid\relax \advance\myfontsize by\fontinc
  \font\4=\fontid\relax \advance\myfontsize by\fontinc
  \font\5=\fontid\relax \advance\myfontsize by\fontinc
  \font\6=\fontid\relax \advance\myfontsize by\fontinc
  \font\7=\fontid\relax \advance\myfontsize by\fontinc
  \font\8=\fontid\relax \advance\myfontsize by\fontinc
  \font\9=\fontid\relax \let\bigfont=\0
}
\DefineFonts
\newdimen\letterwidth \newdimen\charht
\setbox0=\hbox{\bigfont T}%
  \letterwidth=\wd0 \charht=\ht0
  \ifdim\wd0<\ht0 \letterwidth=\ht0 \advance\letterwidth by2truept
  \baselineskip=\letterwidth
```

```
  \fi
\newdimen\voff % amount of vertical opffset for each character
\setbox0=\hbox{\9 N}\charht=\ht0
\def\getvoffset{% compute offset to center each char vertically
  \voff=\charht \advance\voff by-\ht\charbox \divide\voff by2
}

%% Any 10-letter word will do...
%% \def\word{\\U\\N\\D\\U\\L\\A\\T\\I\\O\\N}
\def\word{\\O\\O\\O\\O\\O\\O\\O\\O\\O\\O}

\def\row{\noindent\hskip2pt\word\word
 \delta=-\delta
 \word\word\hskip2pt\par}

\newif\ifdec \newif\ifinc % decreasing size or increasing
 \dectrue % start with big letters and decrease in size
\newcount\startfont \newcount\nextfont
\newcount\maxfonts \maxfonts=9
\newcount\delta \delta=-1
\startfont=\maxfonts \advance\startfont by1
\newcount\rowdelta \rowdelta=-1
\everypar={%
 \advance\startfont by \rowdelta
 \ifnum \startfont>\maxfonts \rowdelta=-1 \startfont=\maxfonts \fi
 \ifnum \startfont<0 \rowdelta=1 \startfont=0 \fi
 \ifnum\rowcount>\halfway \delta=\rowdelta \else\delta=-\rowdelta
 \fi \nextfont=\startfont }

\newbox\charbox
\def\\#1{\setbox\charbox=\hbox{%
  \expandafter\csname\the\nextfont\endcsname #1}%
  \getvoffset\hbox to\letterwidth{%
  \hss\raise\voff\box\charbox\hss}%
  \advance\nextfont by \delta
  \ifnum\nextfont>\maxfonts \delta=-\delta \nextfont=\maxfonts \fi
  \ifnum\nextfont<0 \delta=-\delta \nextfont=0 \fi }
\newcount\rowcount \rowcount=\maxfonts \multiply\rowcount by4
  \advance\rowcount by 4
\newcount\halfway \halfway=\rowcount \divide\halfway by 2

\let\MyBlack=\Black % default
\def\MyBlack{\Color{0 0 0 .8}}

\setbox0=\vbox{\vskip2pt%
\loop \row \advance\rowcount by-1 \ifnum\rowcount>0 \repeat
\vskip2pt}
\dimen0=40\letterwidth \advance\dimen0 by4pt

%% Uncomment this line for white chars on black background
\noindent\rlap{\MyBlack{\vrule width\dimen0 height\ht0}}%
  \White{\box0}

%% Uncomment this line for black chars on a white background
%% \noindent\box0
```

CHAPTER 2

· ·

TEX, THE INTERNET, AND MULTIMEDIA

Freedom is not free.

This slogan of the American Legion might well be rephrased by a struggling TEX author:

Free software is not free.

How can anyone call TEX "free" when it may take many valuable hours to run a TEX problem to earth? While users of commercial versions of TEX can (and should!) avail themselves of the company helpline, people using free implementations have no such resource—or do they? It is the goal of this chapter to show how the Internet and related topics might be useful in this regard. The Internet provides a mechanism for answering puzzling questions, just like an expensive vendor helpline, although the turnaround may be longer.

Multimedia and Internet are such trendy topics (as of summer 1996 when this was written) that we can be sure of an impending backlash. Nevertheless, serious users of LATEX and TEX will find themselves constantly relying on these resources, and this chapter hopes to demonstrate why this should be so. There are any number of decent books exploring the Internet; Krol (1994) is as good as any.

2.1 Internet resources

2.1.1 Archives

As you become more at ease with LATEX and TEX, you will learn of style files, miscellaneous utilities, intriguing documents and reports, and other oddments of the TEX world that you might care to own. The overwhelming

Comprehensive TEX Archive Network

`tug2.cs.umb.edu`	Boston, Massachusetts, USA
`ftp.tex.ac.uk`	Cambridge, England
`ftp.dante.de`	Stuttgart, Germany

majority of this material is freely available and will have been deposited in *archives* for your convenience. A computer archive is a host on the network with room to store massive amounts of information. Such hosts become repositories for large collections of files available to everyone.

Some years ago, the TEX community came together (under the leadership of a small team) to establish a *comprehensive TEX archive network*, which quickly become known by its initials CTAN. Material submitted to any single CTAN archive is mirrored to its CTAN mates, and so the CTAN resource quickly became an indispensable source of material relating to LATEX and TEX. You will need to learn to access it (or to gain access to a CD-ROM snapshot of its contents; see on page 52), because it is such a vital resource.

There is well over one gigabyte of information in which to browse, "information" in the form of documentation, macros, source code, binary executables, important tools and utilities, fonts, and much, much more. The box on the next page contains the description of the top-level directories. (Some CTAN archives store other, non-TEX material too.)

At the moment (summer, 1997), three hosts comprise the CTAN network. They are

`tug2.cs.umb.edu`

in the United States (at University of Massachusetts, Boston),

`ftp.tex.ac.uk`

in the United Kingdom (originally at Aston University, and now at Cambridge University) and

`ftp.dante.de`

sponsored by Dante, the user group organization for German-speaking users of LATEX and TEX, housed at the University of Stuttgart. (Dante graciously donated the computer for use at the American CTAN site.)

Other archives Several other archives are also worthy of mention.

Top-Level Directories of a CTAN Site

- **tools** contains the various archiving tools that users may find useful.

- **biblio** contains bibliography-related files, such as BibTEX.

- **digests** contains back issues of TEX-related electronic newsletters.

- **info** contains files and tutorials that document various aspect of TEX.

- **dviware** contains the various dvi-to-whatever filters and drivers.

- **fonts** contains a large collection of fonts, both sources and precompiled.

- **graphics** contains utilities and macros related to graphics use in TEX.

- **help** contains files that provide an overview of the archive and the TEX system.

- **indexing** contains utilities and related files for indexing documents.

- **language** contains language- or alphabet-specific files (fonts, hyphenation patterns, support macros) for TEX.

- **macros** contains macros for TEX and its derivatives in unique subdirectories.

- **support** contains files and programs that can be used in support of TEX (editors, file-conversion, etc.).

- **systems** contains complete system setups, organized by operating system.

- **web** contains WEB-related files and utilities.

- The site `ftp.cs.ruu.nl`, which is physically located in the Netherlands.

- Nelson Beebe's `tuglib` archive at `math.utah.edu` and at `ftp.math.utah.edu/pub/tex/bib` contains many relevant bibliography files for the user of TEX.

- The master site for the TEX programs is at `labrea.stanford.edu`; it's where Knuth deposits files when bugs have been fixed.

- The American Mathematical Society maintains `e-math.ams.org` as a distribution site and help center for the LATEX and TEX material whose development they have sponsored.

Important ftp Sites

ftp.dante.de ⎫	
ftp.tex.ac.uk ⎬	CTAN
labrea.stanford.edu	The Source
ftp.math.utah.edu	tuglib
e-math.ams.org	AMS archives
ftp.gust.org.pl/pub/TeX	GUST archives

- The Polish TEX User Group, GUST, maintains an archive at ftp.gust.org.pl/pub/TeX that contains much interesting material not available elsewhere, including work by Bogusław Jackowski and his colleagues.

- Figure 1 on the following page lists known sites that mirror the main CTAN sites.

Finally, note that many other large sites have "tex" areas for browsing, but may not be formally maintained.

No software system is an island, and you will find yourself needing additional software utilities in the course of your TEX (or computer) career. Most of these can be found at ftp archives; some important ones appear in the box on page 47. (CD-ROM collections of many of these archives are also available from CD-ROM vendors like Walnut Creek CDROM and Prime Time Freeware; see page 52.)

Finding files   The box on page 48 summarizes some important and useful commands for negotiating an ftp session, but these procedures work well providing you know the location of the file, a dubious assumption. Suppose first that you are in the middle of an ftp session, you know the name of a file, but you don't know where it is. To determine its location, type

    quote site index ⟨file-name⟩

and wait for the computer's response.

But what if you don't know the file's name? Most archives maintain a complete index of the archive, stored in a file that might be named ls-lr in the root directory. It may sometimes be necessary to download this file and peruse it for the exact file name you are after.

But what if you don't know which archive contains the file you need? The Archie system was designed to answer these questions. The next few paragraphs contain a very brief introduction to using this system via email.

Nodes and Locations	Top Directory
ftp.cdrom.com (California)	/pub/tex/ctan
dongpo.math.ncu.edu.tw (Taiwan)	/tex-archive
gw.pacbell.com (California)	/mirror/ftp.shsu.edu/
	tex-archive
ftp.center.osaka-u.ac.jp (Japan)	/CTAN
ftp.ccu.edu.tw (Taiwan)	/pub/tex
ftp.cs.rmit.edu.au (Australia)	/tex-archive
ftp.duke.edu (North Carolina)	/tex-archive
ftp.gwdg.de (Germany)	/pub/dante
ftp.jussieu.fr (France)	/pub4/TeX/CTAN
ftp.loria.fr (France)	/pub/unix/tex/ctan
ftp.mpi-sb.mpg.de (Germany)	/pub4/tex/mirror/ftp.dante.de
ftp.muni.cz (The Czech Republic)	/pub/tex/CTAN
ftp.riken.go.jp (Japan)	/pub/tex-archive
ftp.uni-bielefeld.de (Germany)	/pub/tex
ftp.uni-stuttgart.de (Germany)	/tex-archive (/pub/tex)
ftp.u-aizu.ac.jp (Japan)	/pub/CTAN
ftpserver.nus.sg (Singapore)	/pub/zi/TeX
kadri.ut.ee (Estonia)	/pub/tex
src.doc.ic.ac.uk (England)	/packages/tex/uk-tex
sunsite.unc.edu (North Carolina)	/pub/packages/TeX
wuarchive.wustl.edu (Missouri)	/packages/TeX

Figure 1: Known CTAN mirrors.

Archie   There are a dozen or so Archie servers throughout the world. In the United States, these are

```
archie.unl.edu
archie.internic.net
archie.rutger.edu
archie.sura.net
```

To locate a file, send mail to archie at any of these locations (for example, archie@archie.unl.edu). The message needs no subject or other identifiers, and the text of the message should consist of one or more commands recognized by the Archie system. The most important such command is prog followed by the file name you are seeking. If the message were

```
prog texbook.tex
```

Archie would report on the locations of this file, provided it is one of the 2.5 million files located at any of 1200 servers it monitors. Actually, prog

Other Important ftp Sites

When no path is given, begin exploring at the root.

`emsworth.andrew.cmu.edu`	Applications for X Window System
`gatekeeper.dec.com`	DEC programs, and much more
`ftp.jcu.edu.au`	Freeware for DEC Alpha/OSF systems
`ftp.ncsa.uiuc.edu`	Useful material for the Macintosh and PC
`sunsite.unc.edu`	Software for Sun Microsystems computers
`archive.umich.edu`	A huge pot-pourri of useful material
`wsmr-simtel20.army.mil`	DOS archive (often too busy to access)
`wuarchive.wustl.edu/systems`	Mirror for the Simtel DOS archive
`ftp-os2.nmsu.edu/os2`	OS/2 software
`ftp.cica.indiana.edu`	MS-Windows software
`nic.funet.fi`	Macintosh software
`oak.oakland.edu/pub2/macintosh`	Macintosh software
`oak.oakland.edu/pub/misc/os2`	OS/2 software
`sumex-aim.stanford.edu`	Macintosh software
`garbo.uwasa.fi`	Immense quantities of software for many systems

It's often difficult to log on to the Simtel site. The location `systems/ibmpc` at `wuarchive.wust.edu` mirrors Simtel and is much easier to access. At this same site, branches `amiga/`, `atari/`, and `unix/` below `systems` contains much software for these platforms. Note that `oak.oakland.edu` is another mirror for Simtel.

The huge Garbo archive contains software for PCs, Windows3, Windows3.1, Macintosh, NextStep, and Unix in named branches below the root.

supports the common wildcard specifications of many operating systems, so

```
prog tex*.tex
```

is also a valid message.

2.1.2 *Lists and newsgroups*

So many people use the Internet that it's likely that some of them share your interests, whatever they are. Many lists and newsgroups have been set up to facilitate communication between like-minded people. Several such groups apply to people who are interested in LATEX and TEX.

Some Useful Commands Within ftp

`pwd`	print working directory
`ls`	list directory contents (terse form)
`dir`	list directory contents (verbose)
`cd` ⟨*dir-name*⟩	change to new directory
`ascii`	prepare to load ASCII data files
`binary`	prepare to load binary files
`quote site index` ⟨*string*⟩	locate file(s) `string`
`quit`	close connection and end session

When you subscribe to a list, you add your name to a list of people who receive copies of all messages sent to the list. Thus, a list is like a clearinghouse for communications from people with similar interests. This works as long as you maintain interest in the field. It may happen that either your interest wanes, or the volume of activity is such that list messages clog your computer's reader (much like junk surface mail), at which time you will want to unsubscribe from the list. Using a list properly involves four steps:

1. subscribing to the list;

2. posting to the list;

3. reading the postings of the list; and

4. unsubscribing from the list.

Of course, there's nothing special about reading contributions—they appear as regular mail. Once you have joined a list, you mail to the list by posting mail to the addresses listed on the next page and on page 50.

Subscribing to and unsubscribing from a list require posting special messages, but *not* to the list, for that will broadcast these administrative directives to the whole list rather than to the list maintainer. List members who receive such messages often erupt in angry *flames* at these trivial postings that contribute to the junk-mail ambiance of a list.

The subscription and termination procedures depend on the type of the list. TEX-related lists are generally either Listserv lists or Internet lists, each of which use slightly different procedures. It's not apparent which list is of which type, so you should try each of the following procedures; one of which is sure to work.

Note first that each list has a ⟨*list*⟩-name appended to a ⟨*host*⟩-name. For the `latex-l` list, `latex-l` is the ⟨*list*⟩-name, and `dhdurz1.bitnet` is the ⟨*host*⟩. Figure 2 on page 51 summarizes the procedures. Sending mail with the single word `help` to any listserver will get you a special help document

Some TeX-Related Internet Lists

List Name	Purpose
4TeX@nic.surfnet.nl	Users of 4AllTeX system
atmtug-l@tamvm1	Texas A&M Univ. TeX Users Group discussion
ctan-ann@urz.Uni-Heidelberg.de	Announcements of submission to the CTAN archives; highly recommended
ctt-Digest@shsu.edu	Digests of the postings to the newsgroup comp.text.tex
ellhnika@dhdurz1	Greek-TeX discussion list
emtex-user@ methan.chemie.fu-berlin.de	For users of emTeX
fontinst@cogs.susx.ac.uk	Technical discussion of fontinst and virtual font matters
gust-l@pltumk11.BITNET	Polish TeX users
gut@frulm11.bitnet	French TeX discussion group
info-tex@shsu.edu	summary of comp.text.tex
italic-l@irlearn.ucd.ie	Irish users of TeX
ivritex@taunivm.bitnet	For Hebrew users
latex-help@ sumex-aim.stanford.edu	Help with LaTeX queries
latex-l@dhdurz1.bitnet	Issues of LaTeX development
litprog@shsu.edu	Literate programming (WEB and friends) discussion list
majordomo@vvv.vsu.ru	List cyrtug-t2 to discuss Russian T2 encoding
metafont@ens.fr	users of METAFONT
pstricks-request@mail.tug.org	PSTricks users
tex-fonts@math.utah.edu	About fonts for use with TeX and LaTeX

detailing these and other procedures. Listserver addresses are either of the form

> listserv@⟨*host*⟩

or

> ⟨*list*⟩-request@⟨*host*⟩

More Internet Lists

List Name	Purpose
mutex@stolaf.edu	Masaryk University discussion list
nordictex@kth.se	LaTeX and TeX in use in Scandinavia
nts-l@dhdurz1.bitnet	NTS is the New Typesetting System, a proposed successor to TeX which will be 100% backward compatible with TeX
rustex-l@ubvm.bitnet	Russian TeX discussion group (lately the concentration has been on Russian rather than TeX)
spanish-tex@eunet.es	Spanish users
tex-d-l@vm.gmd.de	German users
tex-d-pc@dhdurz1.bitnet	German TeX-on-a-PC discussion
tex-euro@dhdurz1.bitnet	Issues for European users
tex-ibm@dhdurz1	TeX-IBM Distribution list
tex-l@ubvm.bitnet	General TeX issues
tex-nl@nic.surfnet.nl	Dutch users
texceh@uni-lj.si	Users in Slovenia
TeXhax@tex.ac.uk	Useful summaries of TeX queries
texrox-l@tamvm1	The TeXrox information list
typo-l@irlearn.ucd.ie	Typography and TeX (the discussion emphasizes typography rather than TeX these days)
uktex-l@dhdurz1.bitnet	Issues for LaTeX and TeX in the United Kingdom
vmstex-l@uicvm.uic.edu	VMS TeX discussion group
yunus@trmetu.bitnet	Turkish-TeX discussion list

If latex-l were a listserv list, you would subscribe to it by sending mail like

```
Subscribe latex-l John Doe
```

List Type	Admin Address	Subscribing	Terminating
Listserv	`listserv@`⟨*host*⟩	Subscribe ⟨*list*⟩ Your Name	Signoff ⟨*list*⟩
Internet	⟨*list*⟩`-request@`⟨*host*⟩	Anything	Anything

Figure 2: List administrative details.

to `listserv@dhdurz1.bitnet`; the name of the list is necessary since the host might administer several different lists. You unsubscribe by posting

```
Signoff latex-l
```

to the same address. Sometimes `unsubscribe` is a synonym for `signoff`.

If the `fontinst` list were an Internet list, you could subscribe and unsubscribe by sending empty mail to

```
fontinst-request@cogs.susx.ac.uk
```

since the empty mail simply toggles your subscription on and off.

Upon first subscribing to a list, the first thing you receive from it should be a manifesto of the administrative details (subscribing, unsubscribing, etiquette, and so forth) that have just been sketched here. It is a good idea to file this mail away for future reference. Do not be surprised if some lists appear to be moribund—activity levels vary greatly by list and by time.

2.1.3 Newsgroups

Operationally, *newsgroups* act like restricted lists. You can post material to the group, but you have to make an active effort to read material on the group—it's not automatically distributed as list material would be. There are several news readers available, and you should talk to a guru at your site to determine the procedures available to you.

Information so basic that nobody wants to waste time with its discussion tends to migrate to documents called FAQ, frequently asked questions. A FAQ may be posted within your newsgroup, or it may be archived separately in the special group *news.answers*. Users of LATEX and TEX will be most interested in the group `comp.text.tex` that generates an immense amount of traffic.

2.2 The World Wide Web and hypertext

As you gain experience with `ftp` archives, you'll note a tendency to prowl up and down the directory structure. The `cd` command is the only navigation tool available, and you'll surely wonder why there isn't a better way. The World Wide Web—WWW or W3—provides that better way.

First of all, it provides a graphic interface to Internet resources (although a line-oriented text browser to WWW is also available). Navigating from one site to another, or from one directory to another, is as simple as pointing and clicking with a mouse.

But second and most important, it allows for *hypertext links* in a Web document by which you can effortlessly follow thoughts and related ideas to related bits of information.

2.2.1 Web locations

Once on the Web, where do you go? The host machine's name, the path on the machine, and the nature of the site come together to form any document's URL, its uniform record locator. For example,

```
ftp://ftp.tex.ac.uk/tex-archive/fonts/utilities/fontinst
```

is the URL for the *fontinst* package for virtual fonts on one of the CTAN servers and indicates it is an `ftp` site at `ftp.tex.ac.uk`, and the package resides in the `/tex-archive/fonts/utilities/fontinst` directory. The URL

```
http://www.yahoo.com/
```

is the Web location ("`http://`" part stands for *hypertext transfer protocol*) on the host `www.yahoo.com`.

There are a number of URLs of special LATEX and TEX interest. These are summarized in the boxes on the facing page, on page 54, and on page 55. (The information in this box is found at the TUG home page

```
http://www.tug.org/
```

in a file maintained by Sebastian Rahtz.)

2.3 CD-ROMs

CD-ROMs frequently contain collections of archive material and provide the same convenience that `ftp` archives do. The rainbow-silvery platters add sex appeal to an otherwise putty-colored computer room. For the aficionado of LATEX and TEX, there are several CD-ROMs that will be of special interest. These CD-ROMs are inexpensive by any standard; none of them costs more than forty dollars.

Two provide slightly different snapshots of the CTAN archive. The oldest of the pair is *Prime Time TEXcetera*, a single disk containing the CTAN archive as of approximately late spring, 1994 (although the company promises to release periodic updates)[Prime Time Freeware (1994)]. The more recent entry is a two disk set entitled "TEX CD-ROM," produced as of July 1995 [Walnut Creek (1995)].

Some Interesting WWW Sites, Part 1

TEX User Groups

http://www.tug.org/   The TEX Users Group
http://www.cl.cam.ac.uk/UKTUG/   The UK TEX Users Group
http://www.dante.de/   DANTE (German-speaking TEX Users)
http://www.ens.fr/gut/   L'association GUTenberg
http://www.ifi.uio.no/~dag/ntug/ntug.html   Nordic TEX Users
   Group
http://ei0.ei.ele.tue.nl/ntg   Dutch TEX users group
http://www.dsi.unimi.it/Users/Students/pensa/tex/   Italian TEX
   Users
http://noa.huji.ac.il/tex/www/top.html   TEX in Israel

Online help from O'Reilly and Associates, Inc.

http://jasper.ora.com//texhelp/Plain.html   Plain TeX
http://jasper.ora.com//texhelp/LaTeX.html   LaTeX
http://jasper.ora.com//texhelp/BibTeX.html   BibTeX
http://jasper.ora.com//texhelp/MakeIndex.html   Make Index
http://jasper.ora.com//texhelp/SliTeX.html   SliTeX

FAQ, documentation

http://nsi.net.kiae.su/latex/latex2e.html   Complete TEX and
   WEB site
http://www.cogs.susx.ac.uk/cgi-
   bin/texfaq2html?introduction=yes   Frequently Asked Questions
   (prepared by the UK TeX Users Group)
http://www.loria.fr/tex   The LaTeX Navigator
http://www.tex.ac.uk/TeXdoc/TeXdocs.html   TeX-related
   documentation
http://curia.ucc.ie/info/TeX/menu.html   Information about TeX at
   University College, Cork
http://theory.lcs.mit.edu/~dmjones/texindex.html   David Jones's
   index of TEX macros
http://molscat.giss.nasa.gov/LaTeX/   Hypertext Help with LaTeX
http://www.stsci.edu/ftp/software/tex/ltxcrib/   LaTeX
   Command Summary by Chris Biemesderfer
http://www.chem.emory.edu/latex.faq   TeX and LaTeX FAQ from
   Emory Univ.
http://riceinfo.rice.edu/Computer/Documents/Classes/Unix/
   class/class.html   Intro to LaTeX is from a short course at Rice Univ.
http://www.cs.stir.ac.uk/guides/latex/guide.html   Document
   preparation with LaTeX comes from the Univ. of Sterling, UK

Both of these packages mirror the CTAN directory structure exactly. The convenient single-disk format of the Prime Time disk has to be weighed against the access techniques. For technical reasons, all files are stored in gigantic .zip archives. (This is a means of compressing and bundling many

Some Interesting WWW Sites, Part 2

CTAN interfaces

`http://www.ucc.ie/cgi-bin/ctan` CTAN Search by Peter Flynn
`http://www.shsu.edu/cgi-bin/ctan-index` ftp.SHSU.edu CTAN
Index
`http://jasper.ora.com/ctan.html` CTAN-Web Home Page
`http://www.tex.ac.uk/tex-archive/` Index of /tex-archive/ on
ftp.tex.ac.uk

TEX Journals

`http://www.cl.cam.ac.uk/TeXdoc/TTN/ttn.html` TeX and TUG News
`http://www.univ-`
`rennes1.fr/pub/GUTenberg/publications/publis.html` Cahiers
Gutenberg
`http://www.dsi.unimi.it/Users/Students/pensa/tex/Tipo/`
`Tipo.html` Italian TeX Journal

Packages and programs

`http://www.aip.org/aip/pubserv.html` The REVTeX package
`http://www.ferberts.com/AAS/EMSsubm.html/AASTeX` or
`ftp://aas.org/pubs/aastex-misc/FAQ` AASTeX FAQ
`http://www.idris.fr/~girou/english/PSTricks` PSTricks site
prepared by Denis Girou
`http://www.diku.dk/users/kris/Xy-pic.html` XYpic by Kristoffer
Rose
`http://e-math.ams.org/web/tex/tex-resources.html` AMS-TeX
and AMS-LaTeX resources
`http://www.arch.su.edu.au/~peterw/latex/harvard` Harvard
package for bibliographies in LaTeX by Peter Williams
`http://www.wfu.edu/Academic-`
`departments/Economics/ftp/emtexgi.html` Windows interface for
emTeX (EMTEXGI)

Projects

`http://www.cl.cam.ac.uk/CTAN/latex/` LaTeX 2e
`http://xxx.lanl.gov/hypertex/` HyperTeX
`http://www.iesd.auc.dk/~amanda/auctex/` AUC-TeX
`http://www.ens.fr/omega/` Omega Home Page
`http://www.cs.ruu.nl/people/otfried/html/hyperlatex.html` The
Hyperlatex package
`http://www.cs.cornell.edu/Info/People/raman/aster/demo.html`
ASTER demo (spoken mathematics)
`http://cbl.leeds.ac.uk/nikos/tex2html/doc/latex2html/`
`latex2html.html` LaTeX to HTML

files together. The disk contains the utility pkunzip and unzip necessary
to unzip—uncompress and unbundle—these archives.) However, because
a .zip file is apt to be large, it takes time and disk space to unzip a col-

Some Interesting WWW Sites, Part 3

TEX Vendors

http://www.tcisoft.com/tcisoft.html   TCI Research
http://www.crl.com/~pti/   Personal TeX Inc.
http://www.YandY.com/   Y&Y Inc. Home Page
http://www.bluesky.com/   Blue Sky Research
http://e-math.ams.org/web/tex/commercial-tex-vendors.html   list
  of vendors (including some without Web connections)

Miscellaneous

http://www.math.utah.edu/~beebe   Nelson Beebe's home page
http://meyer.fys.ku.dk/~tex/TeXcrazy.html   TeX crazy page
http://www.uwa.edu.au/HGrk/GreekGIF/   Metafont to GIF
http://www.mat.uc.pt/~pedro/ntcientificos/TeXportugues.html
  LaTeX in Portuguese
http://www.mat.uc.pt/~pedro/ntcientificos/dcpic.html   block
  diagrams
http://mixing.qc.dfo.ca/pub/emacs-add-ons/hilit-LaTeX.el
  LaTeX highlighting in emacs

lection, although the unzip process is extremely easy to perform. Along with each .zip archive comes a list of the files in the .zip archive and some minimal explanation of the nature of this archive. Prime Time Freeware distributed a 100-page manual containing some background material about LATEX and TEX and some terse description of the material on the disk.

All of the contents of the Walnut Creek archive are unbundled, but until you get used to it, it's hard to be sure which of the two disks in the set contains which files. However, the first volume contains the binaries and sources for the TEX programs compiled for several architectures, while the second contains the remainder of the archive. None of the files are archived together—all occur singly in the same directory as on the actual archive. This makes it easy to access the files on these disks. Once your TEX system is completely installed, you will most likely need only the second disk. Another advantage of the Walnut Creek set is its timeliness—it is (at the moment, anyway) the most recent offering. No printed documentation accompanies this package, but none is needed.

(Incidentally, both of these companies offer additional software collections on CD-ROM at low prices. You should consider some of these alternative offerings, which contain many software tools you may need sooner or later.)

The third edition of *4AllTEX* [Dol and Frambach (1995)] is an exciting event for users of TEX, particularly for DOS users. This edition is the first of the CD-ROM packages to have been prepared by dedicated and knowledgeable users of TₑX, Wietse Dol and Erik Frambach, supported by the Nederlandstalige TₑX Gebruikersgroep (NTG), the TₑX organization for Dutch-speaking people. Each disk contains about 640 megabytes of TₑX tools. The set includes a 160-page manual, containing valuable background information about TₑX and about the tools on the CD-ROMs. Although the set is targeted for DOS users, there is so much information nonspecific to any operating system that all TₑX authors might find it useful.

The disks make no attempt to mirror the CTAN directory structure. The second disk contains many tools and packages organized logically. But it's the first disk that makes this set unique, for it allows an author to run a fully operational and robust TₑX system "right out of the box." Once the TₑX system has been installed, a simple but powerful system of menus allows an author to access and use the various parts of the LATₑX or TₑX production cycle.

Installation of *4AllTₑX* is simple. One mounts the first CD-ROM of the set and executes a batch file in its root directory. (Note though that this system, although it calls itself "DOS-based," really uses a replacement for command.com. The replacement, 4dos, works better than the original, has a lot of Unix-like power built into it, and seems to have no adverse effects on any programs that expect the usual command.com to be present. It too is highly recommended.)

An aspiring user has three choices for installation of the *4AllTₑX* system: either to run TₑX exclusively from the CD-ROM (slow); to install a few files on the hard disk, but leave the bulk of the system on the CD-ROM (respectable performance speeds on many recent multimedia and office computers); or to install the entire system on a hard disk. This third option requires in excess of 300 megabytes of disk space, and although much (most) of this material may be deleted later, the deletion must be done by hand. Furthermore, unless a large amount of disk space is available at the outset, the installation may fail. (The documentation does not note that the utility acd, which is on the disks, can delete whole directory subtrees at once, so the process of pruning and cleaning up after a full installation is easy.)

The most recent TₑX-related CD-ROM is TₑX Live (1997), which was first issued in May 1996. Its team of compilers, led by Sebastian Rahtz, intends to release updates every six months or so. (A second edition has appeared in the summer of 1997, as this manuscript was being readied for publication.) *TₑX Live* contains ready-to-run implementations of TₑX for the most popular of Unix platforms, including Linux, Digital Equipment, Hewlett-Packard, Silicon Graphics, Sun Microsystems, and NeXT systems. In addition to executables of TₑX, many other programs, such as META-FONT, *MakeIndex, dvips,* xdvi, and BⁱⱯTₑX are also provided. Non-Unix users may well be attracted by the very complete collection of macros, fonts, and documentation conforming to the TₑX Directory Structure (see chapter 6), and all users will be attracted by the low price, twenty dollars (or its rough equivalent) to members of recognized user groups. *TₑX Live* is available from GUTenberg, TₑX Users Group, or UK TₑX Users Group.

Although you can transfer the material from the CD-ROM to your own hard disk, *TEX Live* has been specially designed so that it's possible to run these programs directly off the CD-ROM. The adjustments to the system's search path are described in the accompanying documentation. The version of TEX chosen for *TEX Live* is teTEX, by Thomas Esser, which supports the TEX Directory Structure (TDS), with which it is easy to add fonts, macro packages, and so on, to a computer system, easy for TEX to then find this material, and easy for a systems administrator to remove this material. (See chapter 6 for further discussion of TDS.)

. . . .

CHAPTER 3

MOSTLY METAFONT

METAFONT is the sibling of TEX responsible for all the letterforms in the Computer Modern family of fonts. METAFONT is a true programming language, one specifically created for designing digital type. As with TEX, METAFONT generates enthusiasm in a dedicated band of users.

The glyphs or individual characters in each Computer Modern font are graphic objects, and so it is also proper to regard METAFONT as a graphics generator; we will explore that aspect of METAFONT in chapter 13. In this chapter, we will focus on other aspects of METAFONT usage, and we will see how useful METAFONT can be even with no knowledge of the META-FONT language. Mostly, METAFONT will be useful to anyone who needs to generate LATEX or TEX fonts at odd sizes or to anyone who doesn't yet have an on-line calculator on their computer.

Because they have the same author, we expect parallels between META-FONT and TEX even though each of the two programs does very different things. First, both programs are written using WEB, Knuth's literate programming tool. Woven printouts of TEX and METAFONT are easy to follow. Second, both programs are in the public domain (although implementations of METAFONT for a particular computer may not be free). Third, both programs actually provide new computer languages for typesetting professionals and allow us to create powerful and sophisticated macros.

Finally, both programs follow similar paradigms. METAFONT is an *image compiler* in the same way that TEX is a *document compiler*. The TEX typesetting process is a three-step process: (1) prepare the document file separately, including formatting commands; (2) run the document through TEX to generate the .dvi file; and (3) print (or view) the .dvi file on the printer. We have an analogous METAFONT life cycle.

1. Prepare a file containing commands to generate the images.

2. Run this file through METAFONT, making corrections as necessary, until a *generic font file*, a .gf file, is produced.

Installing METAFONT

Here's how to install METAFONT:

1. Follow the instructions in the local guide. If possible, adhere closely to the directory structure of the default installation process. (Otherwise, it will be your responsibility to set environment variables to point to your own directories.)

2. Move all executable files, like `mf.exe` or `virmf.exe`, possibly `inimf.exe` (unless the first two are combined into one), `gftodvi` and `gftopk`, and others into a directory on your path.

3. There will be an input directory with a name like `/usr/local/lib/mf/inputs` or `\mf\inputs`. Explore it, looking for a file named something like `local.mf`. It contains information about common printer modes and about your own system that will be useful to METAFONT. We will need this file name in order to create the base file.

4. Create the base file; see the box on page 61.

3. Do some other trivial bookkeeping, and so prepare to use the new fonts in a TEX document.

As in TEX, but unlike most computer graphic systems, there is a distinction between the source file and the compiled image.

MetaPost is a language similar to METAFONT. Its main difference lies in its output—it generates PostScript output directly and so is well suited to create graphics for a LATEX or TEX document, provided you have access to a PostScript printer. MetaPost gets much greater treatment later on in chapter 13, but the two systems are so similar that it makes sense to discuss some details of MetaPost in this chapter; see page 89.

3.1   Installing Metafont

As with TEX, METAFONT comes with a large collection of files that have to be in their proper places. On Unix systems, it will also be necessary to compile the program itself, but implementations for personal computers will have been compiled already.

3.1.1   Types of files

A working METAFONT needs three kinds of files:

1. input files, which contain information used to create letterforms or graphic objects (as in TEX, METAFONT only reads ASCII files);

2. a *pool file*, which contains the text of all error messages; and

3. the *base file*, explained in subsection 3.1.2.

METAFONT looks for these types of files in different directories and folders, and you should follow the local installation instructions in this matter. If you decide to place them in nonstandard locations, you'll need to set *environment variables*, which are pointers to these new locations. If at all possible, use the default locations for your implementation.

Unix users should follow the directions that come with their METAFONT kit. In any case, the executable files should be placed in a directory on your system's search path. There may be an executable called inimf, but the main one will be mf or perhaps virmf. In addition, other utilities such as gftodvi (which converts METAFONT output to .dvi form for convenient inspection), gftopk (which compresses METAFONT output into a useful form that device drivers can read), and mft (a METAFONT prettyprinting program) belong in a path directory as well.

3.1.2   Base files

As with TEX, METAFONT primitives are at such a low level as to be practically useless. Serious users will depend on a *base file* to contain useful constructs defined in terms of the primitives. Knuth provided two widely used bases, the plain base, suitable for most generic work, and cmbase, for creating Computer Modern fonts. A base file is exactly analogous to a TEX format file. The base files plain.base and cmbase.base (or plain.bas and cmbase.bas on DOS systems) are ASCII files, and they take too long to load in ASCII format. One of the first steps in any installation is to create binary equivalents that METAFONT can read at high speed.

A special executable file has the responsibility for creating the binary base file. For some implementations, this is a separate file called inimf, but on others, it is invoked with a special switch. See the box on the facing page to see how to create the binary base file.

3.2   Running Metafont

Now that we have successfully installed METAFONT, let's run it. Before playing with a new program, it's a good idea to learn how to start it *and* how to stop it.

3.2.1   Starting and stopping

We'll see shortly that we can run METAFONT with a command line that tells METAFONT what we expect it to do. But it can also be invoked for interactive use by typing something like mf at the system prompt. In interactive

---

Creating a Base File for METAFONT

To create a version of `plain.base` (`plain.bas` on DOS systems), the ASCII file `plain.mf` must be in the METAFONT `...\inputs` directory.

1. First, determine the name of file containing local additions or changes. Common names are `local.mf` or `waits.mf`. You'll find this file in a place named `../mf/inputs` or `.../texmf/metafont/local`.

2. Type `inimf` (or perhaps `mf-i` or `mf /i`) at the system prompt.

3. The initial prompt is a double asterisk **. Enter

   ```
   plain; input local; dump; bye.
   ```

   in response to this prompt. (If necessary, replace the word `local` with another name for a file with local additions.) METAFONT will shortly report the creation of the base file `plain.base` or `plain.bas`.

4. Move the base file to the bases directory (one with a name like `.../mf/bases`).

You may need a different base for your METAFONT work. Here's how to create `cm.base` (or `cm.bas`), and it's easy to generalize this procedure for any other base.

1. Create a short file `cm.mf` containing the lines

   ```
   input plain;
   input local; input cmbase; dump;
   bye.
   ```

   and type `inimf cm`.

2. Move the base file `cm.base` to the `...\bases` subdirectory.

3. When you need this base, issue the command

   ```
   mf &cm ...
   ```

---

mode, METAFONT prompts you with one or two asterisks (* or **) for instructions.

The double asterisk prompt occurs only at the beginning of a session, and means that the next thing you type will be interpreted as a file name for METAFONT to read. So if you type `myfont` (followed by the "enter" key) in response to the **, METAFONT will attempt to read a file `myfont.mf`.

At this point, it's easy to forget or mistype the name of the file. If this happens, METAFONT complains that it can't find myfomt.mf (say) and that you should type in another file name. This is an opportunity to correct a typing error, but you may truly have forgotten the file name and will wish to exit METAFONT to investigate the proper name of the file (or perhaps to move it to a directory that METAFONT is aware of). The undocumented solution is to simply type control-z (^Z) or perhaps control-d, the conventional end-of-file symbols in DOS and Unix. (This trick also works for TEX and for MetaPost.)

Normally, the proper response to the single asterisk prompt is any valid sequence of METAFONT commands. Two important commands are "bye" and "end," either of which will gracefully end the session.

When METAFONT doesn't like something you've said, it treats it as an error. Its error format is similar to that of TEX. The error prompt is an exclamation point !, the context of the error, and a message. If you respond with an x, METAFONT will exit.

3.2.2 *"Fonts" and fonts*

It's easy to place anything in a TEX document as long as TEX thinks it is a well-formed font. Consequently, one easy way to place an image into a report is by means of a "font" consisting of one or a few characters, each of which is not any usual letterform, but is rather some arbitrary image. After all, TEX does not check to see that an "A" of a font actually resembles an "A." When requested to print an A, it checks the .tfm file to determine how much space to leave, and leaves it to the device driver to pull in the bitmap image at printing time. Of course, if the image is a graph or a smiley instead of an actual A, who's to complain? The crests of figure 1 on the next page were produced this way.

Another example makes this clear. It's much too hard to create a real letterform font, so our example will contain only a single graphic character.

In general, the preparation of source files may require detailed knowledge of the METAFONT language. A METAFONT travelog appears later on in this volume. As we'll shortly see, it is possible to make slight changes to existing source files for slightly new fonts without knowing much about METAFONT commands.

3.2.3 *An example font*

Copy the following lines *exactly* to a file grampa.mf.

```
mode_setup;
u#:=8pt#;
define_pixels(u);
beginchar("A", u#, u#, 0);
  pickup pencircle scaled .04u;
```

Figure 1: Medieval Japanese heraldic crests (80-pt size), rendered by Alan Jeffrey.

```
z.center=(.5w,  .5h);
z.eye.left=(.3w,  .5h); z.eye.right=(.7w,  .5h);
z.nose=(.5h,  .25h);
draw fullcircle scaled u shifted z.center;       % the face
draw fullcircle scaled .13u shifted z.eye.left; % left eye
draw fullcircle scaled .13u shifted z.eye.right;% right
filldraw fullcircle scaled .175u shifted z.nose;% nose
mouthlength=.3w;
draw (.5w-.5 mouthlength ,.14h)--
  (.5w+.5 mouthlength ,.14h);                    % mouth
z0=(0,.5h); z1=(w,.5h);
filldraw fullcircle scaled .175u shifted z0;   % left tuft
filldraw fullcircle scaled .175u shifted z1;   % right
endchar;
bye.
```

Now, if you type

```
mf grampa
```

METAFONT will begin. It begins by reading the file grampa.mf and following the instructions contained therein. The command

```
mf grampa.mf
```

is also acceptable, but the default extension .mf is automatically supplied by METAFONT if you don't include it. METAFONT spits something out to the screen that should look something like

```
This is METAFONT, C Version 2.71
(grampa.mf [65] )
Output written on grampa.2602gf (1 character, 2236 bytes).
```

provided there were no typing errors in grampa.mf. Character A has the ASCII value of 65, so we learn that a generic font file grampa.2602gf now exists. On DOS systems, the file extension is truncated; on such a system, the file would be grampa.260. As usual, a .log file records this and other information as well.

In case METAFONT did report an error, the best strategy for beginners is simply to take note of the line number, type x in response to METAFONT's complaint, use an editor to fix the offending line in grampa.mf, and commence the experiment again.

Some implementations may automatically display the image for you on-screen as part of the run. If not, or if you want to see more detailed information about your image, invoke the program gftodvi by typing

```
gftodvi grampa.2602gf
```

to create file grampa.dvi, which is as previewable as any other .dvi file. (If gftodvi complains, it may be because a special gray font does not exist on your system. In that case, you will need to run METAFONT on this halftone font gray.mf. Follow directions in Appendix H of *The METAFONTbook* [Knuth (1986c)], or consult local documentation.) Figure 2 on the facing page should look very similar to what you see in your own experiment.

3.2.4 *Customizing the mode*

Although you have created your first font, it is unusable for two reasons: there is no .tfm file and METAFONT assumed that the resolution of the output device is 2602 dots per inch. (See page 72 for the origin of the mysterious number 2602.) Almost certainly this does not match your printer's resolution.

Figure 2: Grampa. METAFONT's "smoke" mode looks like this.

METAFONT takes care to match the image it creates with the resolution and other characteristics of the device on which the image will ultimately appear. The font's *mode* refers to a collection of parameters that should match the printer. The most important such parameter is the number of pixels per inch or the dots per inch (often 600 for a typical laser printer). Modes have names, and you'll have to check either the local documentation or the local.mf file. (Check the METAFONT ...\inputs area for this file.)

Therefore, now type something like

```
mf \mode=imagen; input grampa
```

to customize the mode. On Unix systems, since some of these symbols have meanings to the shell, it will be necessary to type

```
mf '\mode=imagen; input grampa'
```

Soon there will be a file called grampa.300gf and a new file called grampa.tfm. If you like, you can run grampa.300gf through gftodvi, but the image will be much coarser. (Do you see why? The resolution is only 300 dpi rather than 2602 dpi as it was before.)

Here's an explanation of the command line

```
mf '\mode=imagen; input grampa'
```

(possibly without the apostrophes). Normally, METAFONT expects the material following the 'mf' to represent the name of a file. That is, it's what we would type in response to the ** prompt in an interactive session. We "escape" this convention with the escape character '\'. (Without the backslash, METAFONT seeks the oddly named file mode=imagen.mf.) Now, we can add whatever commands we like to the command line, and we separate one from the next with a semicolon ';', the standard statement separator in METAFONT. Once we've escaped the command line convention, we can't go back. To input a file, we now need the explicit input command. This is the only time the backslash is needed in METAFONT use. This backslash convention applies in an interactive session as well. We type

```
\mode=imagen; input grampa
```

in response to the **.

Proof and smoke modes   What if we don't specify any mode to META-FONT? The default is proof mode in which METAFONT creates large scale images surrounded by a bounding box. In proof mode, METAFONT will also indicate and label key points in the design process. If the design is still not good enough, these key point labels are useful for making revisions. Figure 3 on the next page shows the 'Œ' ligature from cmb10. It was part of the output of a run invoked by the command

```
mf &cm cmr10
```

The designations 12r, 12, 121 (on the left of the figure) and the many other labels refer to points given those names in the METAFONT program for that character. That is, 12r corresponds to a point named z_{12r} (or z12r using METAFONT input conventions).

smoke mode is similar to proof. Traditionally, typefounders cast each trial letter in metal. When held close to the flame of a lit candle, it becomes covered with sooty lampblack. Were they to then press this type hard against a sheet of paper, the lampblack would make a smoky impression on paper, and that's how typefounders of old monitored their progress. In META-FONT's smoke mode, a large image is bracketed by right angle markers at the corners of what would be the bounding box. If you print smoke images, you can align them at the brackets and see not only how your design is coming, but how effective the relative spacing between characters is. Figure 2 on the preceding page is an example of a smoke mode display. That figure was the product of this command:

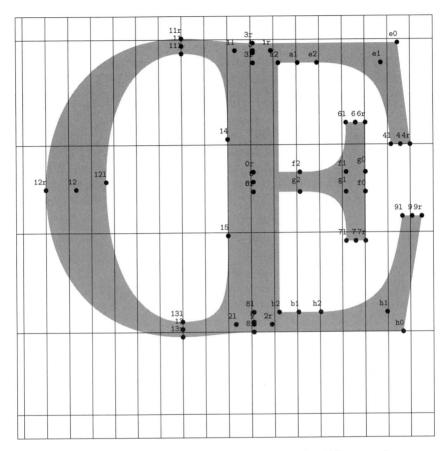

Figure 3: One page of output from `gftodvi`. We see the Œ ligature of `cmr10` in proof mode superimposed on a grid with the key points labeled.

```
mf '\mode=smoke; input grampa'
```

In both modes, the METAFONT pixel file has the extension 2602gf or perhaps just 260 (as in DOS systems). Many implementations of META-FONT will display the smoke or proof mode images onscreen and will not generate tfm files. (You're not supposed to do actual typesetting with proof or smoke characters.)

3.2.5 Packing pixels

We call the two files grampa.300gf and grampa.2602gf *generic font files*, and generic font files tend to be large. Contemporary device drivers expect fonts to be in packed pixel, or pk, format, which saves room on disks. The gftopk utility performs this conversion for us if we type

```
gftopk grampa.300gf grampa.300pk
```

You will need to move `grampa.tfm` with all the other `.tfm` files and to move `grampa.300pk` with all the other `.pk` files, but be careful, especially if you are a DOS user.

Caveat for DOS users   Since DOS filenames can have only three characters in the extension, files like `grampa.300gf` and `grampa.2602gf` would be truncated to `grampa.300` and `grampa.260`. In DOS systems only, we agree to call these pixel file `grampa.pk`, and to distinguish one `.pk` file from the other by moving each with all other pk files with the same magnification and resolution. This is the origin of the ramified network structure on DOS systems for containing all of TEX's pixel files. In this hierarchy of subdirectories that separates a given magnification from the others, `grampa.pk` belongs in a place likely named something like `...pixels\300`. (Check the local documentation for specifics.)

3.2.6   From Metafont into TEX

The font `grampa` is just like any other font in TEX, except that only one character is available for typesetting. In plain TEX, if we type

```
\font\silly=grampa
\def\grampa{{\silly A}}
```

near the beginning of our document, and `\grampa` anyplace thereafter, we get ☻. Since TEX will complain about missing characters if we attempt to typeset any character in the `grampa` font other than A (for this is the only character in the font), it makes sense to embed the logo in a macro. The LATEX way to create that command is similar:

```
\newfont{\silly}{grampa}
\newcommand{\grampa}{{\silly A}}
```

(Although LATEX\newfont is no longer documented in official documentation, it still works. It takes two arguments; the first is the command sequence by which the font will be used, and the second is the name of the font.)

3.3   Some Metafont conventions

In this section, we present a short discussion of METAFONT conventions so that program listings like the one on page 62 are meaningful. Except for comments, everything in a `.mf` file supports the creation of an image. As in TEX, comments are preceded by percent signs. The METAFONT interpreter ignores everything from a % to the end of that line.

METAFONT programs have the look and feel of "real" programs. As in the C language, the semicolon separates one statement from the next. Variables may have names, and the parameters in a macro (like a subroutine)

From METAFONT **to** TEX

These steps summarize the steps for generating printable fonts from a source file.

1. Prepare the source file.

2. Run this file through METAFONT, via a command like

   `mf \mode=⟨mymode⟩; input ⟨myfile⟩`

   (On Unix systems, it will be necessary to surround the command arguments with single quotes.) As in any TEX run, it may be necessary to correct the input file and run it through METAFONT again.

3. In proof or smoke mode, many METAFONT implementations will display each image onscreen as it is created. If not, or you need additional insight into the image, run the resulting `.gf` file through `gftodvi` to create a previewable `.dvi` file of your images.

4. Use `gftopk` to generate packed pixel files from the `.gf` file. Move this resulting `.pk` file to the proper place on your system.

5. To use the new font, declare it in the TEX document.

may have descriptive titles (in stark contrast with TEX, where macro parameters are identified by numbers only). METAFONT contains all the capabilities (but one) that anyone expects of a mature programming language—loops, decision making, macros, input facilities, variable assignments, and so on; but alas, the output facility is severely restricted (but see section 3.8 on page 89 for a discussion of MetaPost).

METAFONT provides for several types of variables. In addition to purely numeric variables, we can have pairs of numbers (which represent the location of points on a plane), paths (the connections between several points), pictures, and others. Usual arithmetic conventions prevail, so a statement like

```
mouthlength=.3w;
```

makes the variable `mouthlength` to be 30% of w, a variable representing the width of the completed image. METAFONT allows subscripts to be part of names, so

```
z.center=(.5w, .5h);
```

is equivalent to a mathematician's $z_{center} = (.5w, .5h)$; this places the point z_{center} at the geometric center of the part of the image's bounding box above the baseline. The variables w and h refer to the width and height above the baseline of the type. We use verbs and adjectives like fill, scaled, shifted, draw, and so on, so METAFONT knows what to do with the image components.

3.3.1 Sharped units

METAFONT allows us two ways to interpret distances within a program. Actual distances—dimensions of characters, the width of a space, and so on—must be independent of mode. The basic unit is a printer's point, and all other allowable units (picas, centimeters, Didot points, and so on) are interpreted as multiples of points.

Directions for creating an image strongly depend on our printer. At the time it prepares to create the bitmap description of the image, METAFONT needs to know which pixels to blacken. Pixels (from *picture elements*) are the basic building blocks of any bitmap image, the individual dots out of which raster devices, including monitors, ink jet printers, laser printers, phototypesetters, and dot matrix printers, compose their images. (Typewriters and daisy wheel printers are not raster devices.)

The *sharp convention* supports this dual interpretation. When the suffix # follows a variable, METAFONT interprets it as an actual distance, invariant from mode to mode. In grampa.mf the statement

```
u#:=8pt#;
```

sets u# to be eight actual points. These sharped units must appear as arguments in the beginchar command, which generates the values that belong in the device-independent .tfm file.

The instructions between beginchar and endchar are pixel blackening instructions, so variable values should record numbers of pixels rather than actual dimensions. All variables should appear without the # suffix, which means they refer to pixel quantities rather than dimensions. The connection between a variable and its sharped equivalent is not automatic. There are commands (like define_pixels and its relatives, which we don't discuss here) to make the connection explicit. The variable u, then, will be equal to the number of pixels in 8 true points; this value will vary with the mode (that is, from printer to printer).

Let's look at another example to make this clear. Suppose T#=1in# (one true inch). Associated with T# is the unsharped variable T. In the event that we are creating fonts for a 300 dpi laser printer, then T=300. If we are creat-

Figure 4: Here's how METAFONT creates a rectangle. The left rectangle is the goal. Suppose two imaginary printers have resolutions of 4 dpi and 8 dpi. The middle and right figures show how METAFONT approximates the rectangles for these printers.

ing fonts for a phototypesetter with a resolution of 1200 dpi, then T=1200, but in both cases T#=1in#.

In the same way, there are always 72.27 pt#s in an inch. On the other hand, if we are creating a font for a 300 dpi device, one pt (without the #) is the whole number of pixels that best satisfies the equation 72.27 pt = 300.

Figure 4 illustrates this concept. On the left is a rectangle which META-FONT aspires to create for two very coarse printers, with hypothetical resolutions of four and eight dots per inch. We want the rectangle to be one inch wide (1in#, in METAFONT terms). The METAFONT draw instruction will make a line 1in long. For the 4 dpi printer, METAFONT will blacken four pixels in the horizontal direction. For the 8 dpi printer, our command will blacken eight pixels. In the first case, 1in=4 (pixels always being understood), while 1in=8 in the second case.

3.3.2 Coordinate systems

Implicit always is the underlying coordinate system METAFONT uses to determine the positions of its points and paths. This coordinate system is only slightly more general than the street grid that urbanites in Manhattan, Seattle, Brooklyn, and many other cities and towns take for granted. Any position in an image or piece of type can be uniquely determined by specifying two quantities—its distance to the right or left of some fixed vertical line, and its distance above or below a fixed horizontal line. In a METAFONT image, the fixed horizontal line is the baseline while the left edge of the type plays the role of the vertical line. The *origin* is the intersection of these two lines. The grid in figure 5 on the following page shows a portion of the coordinate plane. One dot is at the origin. Other dots mark the locations of points $(-1, 0)$, $(4, 8)$, and $(8, 1)$. The designation $(4, 8)$ means that the point can be found at the location four units to the right of the origin and eight units above it. Negative signs imply distances to the left or below the coordinate axes. Normally, the grid lines do not appear.

METAFONT also supports the *coordinate* or *ordered pair notation* with which we fix points. Two quantities are separated by a comma and surrounded by parentheses. A time-honored tradition calls these horizontal and vertical distances the x and y coordinates, and a pair is *ordered* because

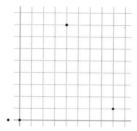

Figure 5: The typical coordinate system.

the *x*-value must come first. A point written

   $(-3, 4\text{pt}\#)$

is three pixels to the left of the origin and four sharped (true) points above it. The point

   $(1\text{pt}, h)$

is as many pixels to the right of the origin as there in one point and at the height of the type; *h* is one of the several variables that will have been defined by the immediately preceding beginchar.

   METAFONT's author did his type design using graph paper in which there were 36 squares for each true point. Proof and smoke modes assume a proofing device in which each of these tiny squares represents the width of a single pixel. Consequently, there will be $36 \times 72.27 \approx 2602$ dots per inch in this hypothetical device, and that is the origin of the 2602 in the .gf file extension for proof and smoke output.

   For points, METAFONT knows about the convenient notation in use by generations of mathematicians. If *x* and *y* refer to horizontal and vertical distances, then let *z* refer to the point itself. METAFONT artists are free to assign names to points, but may also choose to number points. Thus, we might choose to let z_1, z_2, z_4, z'_5 represent four distinct points. After having defined these points, the artist may also refer individually to the components of these points: x_1, y_1, x_4, y'_5, and so on. A subscript may also take the form of descriptive names, such as z_{center} on page 70. METAFONT's input rules allow us to type z1, z2, z4, z5', x1, y1, x4, y5', and z.center for these quantities.

3.3.3 Prescription versus description

Most programming languages are *prescriptive*; it's up to the programmer to prescribe the operations to get a result. Suppose we need the solutions to

$$
\begin{aligned}
2x + y &= 0 \\
4x + 3y &= 3.
\end{aligned}
$$

Using the computer requires actually coding the solutions in terms of the coefficients. Such a program would request the coefficients and constants for this system, and, after checking some special cases, would spit out the solution ($x = -1.5$, $y = 3$).

Contrast this with the *descriptive* METAFONT way. Simply enter the two equations

```
2x+y=0;
4x+3y=3;
```

and type show x, y;. After all, the information necessary to extract values for x and y is contained within these two equations. METAFONT allows us to *describe* the problem in this way. Typing the two equations constitutes a description of the relationship that governs x and y. Having read the description, METAFONT can deduce the solutions (at least for linear equations, but even for some nonlinear equations).

We can take advantage of METAFONT's readiness to solve equations and use METAFONT as a calculator. This procedure is described and displayed on the following page. *The METAFONTbook* [Knuth (1986c), p. 61] suggests a more formal method for using METAFONT interactively.

Type designers can spend time describing the relationships between the components of each letter, knowing METAFONT will take care of the solution details. (Refer to volume E of *Computers and Typesetting* for a virtuoso display of the use of these techniques.) Technical illustrators have been slow to avail themselves of these advantages. Although a technical illustration is not a piece of type, its components frequently have to adhere to rigid relationships, and METAFONT users have demonstrated over and over that many types of figures are easily produced by METAFONT.

It is possible to program in METAFONT using the ـusual" prescriptive method if need be.

3.3.4 Modes

Somewhere in the . . . \inputs directory (or folder) that was set up by the installation process there should be a file with a name like local.mf. It's a good idea to peruse it and get familiar with its contents. Most of the file contains definitions of modes that METAFONT will recognize. A typical excerpt follows:

```
mode_def imagen = % imagen mode (Canon engine)
proofing:=0;       % no, we're not making proofs
fontmaking:=1;     % yes, we are making a font
tracingtitles:=0;  % no, don't show titles in the log
pixels_per_inch:=300;
blacker:=0;        % Canon engine is black enough
fillin:=.2;        % and it tends to fill in diagonals
```

A METAFONT and METAPOST Calculator

At the prompt, enter mf. You will see a double asterisk prompt. In response, enter \relax; forgetting neither the backslash nor the semicolon. Now, you see a single asterisk, in response to which you should enter statements describing your problem. Remember:

• Always terminate statements with semicolons.

• Terminate the entire session with bye.

• To begin a new problem, type something like numeric x; or numeric x, y; to initialize variables that may have values already.

• Use the show command to display results.

• Refer to Knuth (1986c, chapter 8) for a complete discussion of available operators.

Here is a snapshot of a short calculator session.

```
localhost:113# mf
This is METAFONT, C Version 2.71
**relax;
*show 123+456-789;
>> -210
*3x+2=11; show x;
>> 3
*numeric x, y;
*2x+y=0; 4x+3y=3;
*show x, y;
>> -1.5
>> 3
*show cosd 45;
>> 0.7071
*show sqrt 8.5;
>> 2.91548
*bye
Transcript written on mfput.log.
```

```
o_correction:=.6;
enddef;
```

Frequently, the initialization process inimf pulls in local.mf so that its contents are part of your METAFONT binary base file. You especially need to go through this file to learn the METAFONT name for your printer. When you've found it, look backward to the preceding mode_def statement for the name of the mode. It's this name that should appear in the command line for this run. In the above excerpt, the name of the mode is imagen.

In case your printer does not appear in this list, all is not lost. Search local.mf for another printer with a similar description; there will surely be one with your printer's resolution. Karl Berry maintains the file modes.mf that can be downloaded from CTAN and other archives. This file is surely the definitive collection of METAFONT mode definitions. If the mode_def for your printer is not here, you should be able to adapt the most appropriate one for your use.

3.4 Metafont as graphics engine

Why don't more people use METAFONT for their graphics? Perhaps it is because relatively few artists have the quantitative background necessary for METAFONT. The reverse is also true—relatively few technical authors have enough interest in the looks of their illustrations to pursue METAFONT aggressively.

A thoughtful criticism relates to the device dependence of METAFONT's output and the reliance on TEX device drivers to use METAFONT output. It is difficult to find a service bureau with a TEX device driver for its photo-typesetters. Fortunately, strategies exist for incorporating METAFONT output into printable PostScript files; see page 87. The most important such strategy is to replace METAFONT by MetaPost, John Hobby's adaptation of METAFONT to produce PostScript output rather than generic font output. (See chapter 13 for an extensive discussion of MetaPost.) Although PostScript files require printers that understand this language, these printers have become so ubiquitous that it is proper to regard a PostScript file as being *de facto* printable anywhere, and so it is no longer true that lack of device drivers prevents TEX or METAFONT output from printing.

No doubt the biggest drawback to METAFONT acceptance is the failure of a front end to appear and make METAFONT more accessible to casual users, a front end that identifies and defines some simple, useful commands in the same way that LATEX does for TEX. METAFONT's macro language is easily as sophisticated as TEX's and would surely make such an effort feasible. Hardware front ends could also make METAFONT easier to use. I have found that it is tedious to enter coordinates of points into a file. After taping tracing graph paper over an original, I squint to interpolate key points for a particular drawing. Some scheme whereby I slide a mouse and click to enter coordinates would be very welcome. Let these remarks be a call to action!

The concept of a "pleasing curve" is crucial to METAFONT's success in drawing handsome figures. After all, there are an infinite number of smooth curves that might pass through the points z_1, z_2, and z_3. Which one should METAFONT choose?

The basis of METAFONT's pleasing curves are Bézier curves. The process begins with two points z_1 and z_2. Next, METAFONT determines two intermediate points, call them z_{1p} and z_{p2}, which lie off the curve. These *control points* are carefully chosen. It then erects a scaffolding of "girders" hung from these points, the lowest elements of which define the outline of the curve. Although this process sounds complicated, the mathematics behind it is simple, and it's easy for METAFONT to draw virtually any curve by piecing enough small Bézier curves together. Figure 6 on the next page

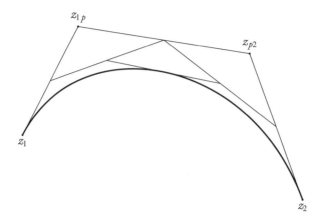

Figure 6: A path with some of its Bézier scaffolding.

shows a path together with its Bézier control points and some of the Bézier scaffolding. The process by which METAFONT chooses the control points is more complicated, for it depends on the other points in the path.

Normally we can't exactly reproduce a given curve *exactly* with Bézier curves, but we can get close. For example, it's possible to draw a pseudo-quarter-circle with Bézier curves differing from the real thing by less than 0.06%. Bézier curves seem so natural that relatively few points are needed to determine the outline of a letterform, and some of the interesting comments by Haralambous (1991b) address that issue. Its nice curves have other applications. I used MetaPost to draw a smooth curve for an arched opening between living and dining rooms in my house. The results were much nicer than the quarter circles the contractor would have chosen.

3.5   Meta-ness

What does the "meta" in the name "METAFONT" mean? METAFONT allows us to create our drawing instructions in terms of parameters whose value we can specify right *before* METAFONT does the actual drawing. If we are clever in the ways we execute this strategy, we can generate different families of fonts, each of which might be strikingly different from other siblings in this family by simply adjusting the values of these parameters.

It's possible to follow a crude example with nothing but a passing famil-iarity with METAFONT. In addition to demonstrating the way to create a simple character in a meta-way, it will also demonstrate a few more aspects of the METAFONT language.

First, here's a naïve way to draw an uppercase, sans serif 'I'. (The *serifs* are the extensions that finish off the ends of a stroke in a letter form in a Roman type, the kind of type used in most book and magazine typesetting. An "I" has four serifs, two each at the top and bottom. Some letters, like "e," have no serifs. Some fonts (like this one), called sans serif, lack serifs altogether; *sans* is French for "without.")

```
mode_setup; % a naive sans serif I
beginchar("I", 1pt#, 7pt#, 0);
   z1l=origin; z1r=(7pt,0);              % points on bottom
   y2l=y2r=3.85pt; x2l=.1pt; x2r=6.9pt;% points in middle
   z3l=(0, 7pt); z3r=(1pt, 7pt);        % points on top
   fill z1l--z1r..z2r{up}..z3r--z3l..z2l{down}..z1l..cycle;
   % draw outline and fill it in to create the letterform
endchar;
bye.
```

Explaining this code   The initial mode_setup command instructs META-FONT to prepare the character for the appropriate mode; the values of several variables are adjusted accordingly. The command beginchar is a macro that takes four arguments—the name of the letter, its width, its height above the baseline, and its depth below the baseline. We use sharped units here, because these are to be the actual dimensions of the letter and should be the same regardless of the device they are intended for. (Aspiring META-FONTers: a common error is to forget to use sharped units in beginchar. The use of unsharped units is syntactically okay, but it often makes META-FONT throw up its hands in despair at working with large numbers.)

Six key points determine this character; see figure 7 on the following page. Points z_{1l}, z_{2l}, and z_{3l} run up the left side of the letter while z_{1r}, z_{2r}, and z_{3r} run up the right. META FONT provides flexible ways of making these coordinates known. We can use coordinate pair notation, or we may specify the x- and y-coordinates separately. (Here, w and h refer to the width and height of the character; beginchar automatically sets up these values.) Note that the middle points are actually located slightly above the geometric midpoint of the character and specify that this part of the letter should be slightly narrower than the top and bottom. Finally, we draw the outline and fill it in before ending the character. In this drawing process, z1l--z1r means to connect the points with a straight line, while the path connector .. (as in z1r..z2r{up}) instructs META FONT to draw a curved line, as pleasing as possible, between points. The direction specifiers {up} and {down} tell META FONT to draw its curve such that the nib is traveling in these directions when it is at those points. The outline of the letter comes out crisp and razor sharp.

META FONT designers, like all designers, have to be alert for pesky optical illusions that can cause a well-thought-out design to look clumsy. It happens that a thin, vertical, perfect rectangle will look thicker along the middle than it is. Architects call this illusion *entasis* and the narrowing of the middle

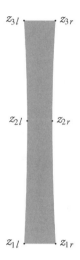

Figure 7: A simple and naïve 'I', courtesy of METAFONT.

helps counteract this illusion. (The ancient Greek engineers who narrowed the columns of the Parthenon surely knew this.) Another visual illusion dictates that something placed at the geometric center of a rectangle actually *appears* to be slightly below center, which is why we applied the narrowing at 3.85 pt rather than at 3.5 pt, the halfway point.

Criticizing this example   One drawback with this example is that any alterations we want to make would require substantive changes to the program. For example, if the letter were to be 8-pt tall, we would need to change the argument to beginchar, the values of y2l and y2r (that is, y_{2l} and y_{2r}), and the locations of the points z3l and z3r (z_{3l} and z_{3r}).

A better way   Let's redo this example, embedding some meta-instruction into the program. In addition to our own parameters, we can also take advantage of the parameters like w and h (the width and height of the type) that beginchar automatically creates. The boxed portions draw attention to the added meta-ness.

```
mode_setup; % a less naive sans serif I
stem# =1pt#;  cap# =7pt#;  nib# =.4pt#;  tightness =0.1;
define_pixels(nib);
beginchar("I", stem#, cap#, 0);
pickup pencircle scaled nib;
z1l=origin; z1r=( w ,0);
y2l=y2r= .55h ; x2l= tightness*w ; x2r= w -x2l;
z3l=(0, h ); z3r= (w, h) ;
```

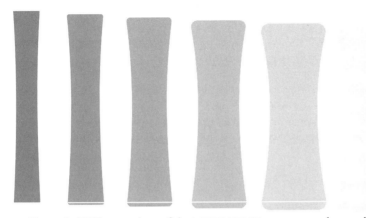

Figure 8: Different values of the METAFONT parameters change the appearance of the letters. The white horizontal line indicates their position on the baseline.

```
filldraw
  z1l--z1r..z2r{up}..z3r--z3l..z2l{down}..z1l..cycle;
endchar;
bye.
```

There are four parameters in this version in addition to the w and h (and d, the depth of the type below the baseline) that are always available—the stem width (stem#), the height (cap#), the diameter of the pen nib (nib#) with which we draw and fill in the outline of the letter, and a tightness parameter, which gives a measure of the amount by which we narrow the middle of the letter to combat entasis. The only other new feature is the use of define_pixels to create a variable nib that is unsharped; nib measures the number of pixels in the distance nib#, and we use the unsharped variables in the letter program so the drawing corresponds to the resolution of the printing device. This is a meta-version of an 'I'. See Knuth (1986c, p. 32) for another sans serif 'I'.

The advantage of this version is that we need not alter the program to make changes in the appearance of the letter—we simply change the values of the parameters. Because of the careful way we wrote the program, these changes propagate automatically to the letterform. Figure 8 shows how changes to these parameters affect the appearance of the letter. Because the characters are drawn with thick pens, parts of some variants descend below the baseline.

3.6 Computer Modern fonts

Donald Knuth's METAFONT programs for Computer Modern typefaces are the prime example of meta-design. Volume E of *Computers and Typesetting* [Knuth (1986e)] contains all the programs and some explanation of the METAFONT code. All of the programs are written in terms of about

Computer Modern at 10 point, magnified.
Computer Modern at seventeen points.

Figure 9: Both types here are at 17.28-pt. The strange number '17.28' arises
from the fact that 10-pt at magstep 3 is in fact 17.28. The difference between
the geometrically magnified type and the font designed specifically for this size
is clear.

60 parameters, and twiddling values for these give rise to all the 75 fonts
or so in this family; see figure 9 and figure 10 on page 82. The programs
demonstrate a virtuoso use of METAFONT, and you should not expect to
understand all of the programs without some effort.

All Computer Modern font names conform to a single naming convention. They begin with the letters 'cm', followed by one to four letters identifying the font type, followed by one or two digits for its size. Thus, cmr10
is the Computer Modern Roman at a 10-pt size, cmbx12 is a 12-pt, bold
extended font, while cmss9 is a sans serif font at 9-pt. Beginners often confuse cmti10 with cmmi10. The first is a text italic font, and offers *an italic
font* for use in text-only work. The second is a math italic font, and generates the italic letters (and some other symbols) specifically used in mathematics. In Computer Modern, text *italic* (we type \textit{italic} using LaTeX syntax or {\it italic\/} in plain TeX) is different from math
italic ($italic$). In the same way, text italic is *different* from math italic
different (typed $different$).

The Computer Modern fonts have deliberately been designed so that,
say, cmr5 is not cmr10 at half-size. Subtle details of spacing and thicknesses
of the strokes need careful adjustment from one size to the next; this *optical
scaling* of type has been largely ignored by digital type founders outside of
the world of TeX until now (although the development of Adobe Multiple
Master technology for scalable fonts may signal a change). Old-style metal-
type designers took this carefully into account in designing their fonts, but
this detail has largely been lost in the collection of commercial software fonts
for computers. While the meta-font cmr5 is *not* cmr10 at half size, a Post-
Script 5-pt font *is* identical to a 10-pt size at half mast. You can remind
yourself of the difference optical scaling makes by referring to the demonstration on page 16 of *The TeXbook* [Knuth (1986a)] and to figure 9.

In the best case, a font we create with METAFONT exhibits a high degree of meta-ness. The font is described in terms of a variety of parameters,
and all it takes to generate a Roman font versus a **bold-faced** font versus a
typewriter font versus … is to twiddle the values of these parameters. Several layers of files are used to generate the 75 or so fonts. Even if you embark
on your own font design project, you may care to follow this structure. It's

well suited for organizing all the software tasks involved in generating any
fonts. Besides the special base file, we use three other types of files to create
any Computer Modern font, and we need to know about them in case we
want to create a custom font of our own. Refer to the box on page 84 for a
summary of the steps in this procedure.

Computer Modern fonts need their own base cm.base; see the box on
page 61 to see how to create it. This file defines many commands appropriate only for the Computer Modern family. Once created, invoke it using the
notation similar to selecting format files by TEX. Type mf &cm ... instead
of just mf .. (or mf '&cm ...' under Unix).

3.6.1   Parameter files

All parameter files are named after the font whose parameter values are in the
file. We create cmr10 with the parameter file cmr10.mf, and run METAFONT
by typing

```
mf &cm cmr10
```

or perhaps

```
mf &cm \mode=. . . ; input cmr10
```

when we need actual fonts for a particular printer. Under Unix, these command lines might be entered mf '&cm cmr10', etc.

In the Computer Modern family, there are about 60 such parameters,
and it is the job of *parameter files* to set specific values for these. (Although
most of these are numeric, a handful are logical variables, and may only be
'true' or 'false'.) These files all end with statements of the form

```
generate roman
```

where generate here is a synonym for input, and the file name following
(roman in this case) is the name of the *driver file*, the second type of font file.

3.6.2   Driver files

Once the values of the important parameters are known to METAFONT, control is handed over to any of several *driver files* that make sure that the final
stage—the actual creation of the letterforms—is handled properly.

Driver files are short and contain three small sections. In the first few
lines, METAFONT takes care of some bookkeeping. It decides on a

```
font_coding_scheme
```

and executes some additional important commands, such as mode_setup,
which tells METAFONT how to adapt its drawing instructions to any of the

Computer Modern Sans Serif	*CM Sans Serif Italic*
Computer Modern Typewriter	*Computer Modern Slanted*
Computer Modern Dunhill	**Computer Modern Fibonacci**
Computer Modern Funny Font	*Matching Funny Italic Font*

Figure 10: This chart shows several additional members of the Computer Modern family of fonts. All fonts are at 10-pt, except the Fibonacci font, which only comes in 8-pt

numerous printing or viewing devices you might be using. If you don't execute this statement, METAFONT assumes a default raster resolution of 2602 pixels (dots) per inch.

The second part of a driver file contains a series of statements such as

```
input romanu;
```

which tells METAFONT to read in the contents of a *program file.* METAFONT will read `romanu.mf` containing instructions for constructing the uppercase letters.

The final section of a driver file specifies information METAFONT needs for creating constants for the font, such as the size of a quad or the interword space. Here appear all the `ligtable` entries, the information about the kerning between adjacent letters. A ligtable program like

ligtable "g": "j" kern .5u#

instructs TEX to add an extra *.5u#* of space whenever a *g* is followed by a *j* in the same font (so 'logjam' looks fine). The complete set of rules describing ligtables can be found in Knuth (1986c, pp. 316–317).

Any font's font metric file contains this measurement information for use by TEX and is the origin of the magic used by TEX to insure that letters are spaced properly with respect to their neighbors.

3.6.3 *Program files*

The program files contain the actual METAFONT descriptions of each character. Each description is given in terms of parameters whose values have been made known (by this point) in a parameter file. It makes no sense to examine any such file in detail, since detailed knowledge of what goes on requires a detailed knowledge of the METAFONT language. (But see chapter 13 for some elementary discussion of METAFONT and MetaPost.) Each file such as `romanu.mf` or `punct.mf` (which creates the punctuation) contains groups of statements bounded by `beginchar` and `endchar` pairs.

People approach type design under the assumption that all Roman types look alike. Nothing could be more mistaken. Figure 11 on the next page

GARAMOND ROMAN TYPE	12345 abcde fghij klmno
COMPUTER MODERN ROMAN TYPE	12345 abcde fghij klmno
GARAMOND BOLD TYPE	**12345 abcde fghij klmno**
CM BOLD EXTENDED	**12345 abcde fghij klmno**
GARAMOND ITALIC TYPE	*12345 abcde fghij klmno*
COMPUTER MODERN TEXT ITALIC	*12345 abcde fghij klmno*

Figure 11: Comparison of Garamond with Computer Modern.

compares Computer Modern type with Adobe Garamond (the text face you are reading).

Figure 10 on the facing page displays a samples from several Computer Modern fonts. All of these different fonts are the product of judicious twiddling of the font parameters; see Knuth (1986e).

3.6.4 Custom Computer Modern fonts

TEX distributions contain a large selection of Computer Modern fonts at several sizes and magnifications. Nevertheless, it's common to want a Computer Modern font at other than one of these canonical sizes or magnifications. It's easy to generate new fonts at new sizes, but the use of these renegade fonts will limit the portability of your document, for it is unlikely that an independent site will have the same custom fonts.

Changing the magnification simply requires a slight modification of the METAFONT command line. For example, I can generate cmr10 at a 30% enlargement by changing the value of the variable mag. Note that increasing the size of a 10-pt font by 30% yields a 13-pt font.

The command

```
mf &cm \mode=imagen; mag=1.3; input cmr10
```

does this. (Don't forget the backslash, and change the mode name, and other parameters as necessary.) The "&cm" refers to a special cm base that we use to generate Computer Modern fonts.

The successful result of this run will be a .log file and two other files: cmr10.tfm and cmr10.390gf (which DOS truncates to cmr10.390). The metric .tfm file may be discarded; there surely is another copy elsewhere with the rest of the .tfm files. These .tfm files depend on the design size of the font but not on magnification, so successive runs of METAFONT for different magnifications of the same font size generate duplicate .tfm files.

Now use gftopk to convert the .gf file to packed pixel format, and place this new pixel file in the proper directory. For DOS systems, this means creating a new pixel directory like ...\pixel\390 and placing the packed pixel file cmr10.pk here. Unix users will place the pixel file cmr10.390pk with other pixel files.

Custom Computer Modern Fonts

There are three types of changes that will make a unique Computer Modern font—changes of magnification, of size, or of some more complicated combination of parameters.

Magnification   To generate a font at a different magnification, we will generate the font using METAFONT in the usual way with a minor change to the command line. For example,

```
mf &cm \mode=hplaser; mag=1.0833; input cmr12
```

generates a "mock 13-pt" font by magnifying the 12-pt font by slightly more than 8%.

New sizes   There are two methods.

1. *Naïve Method.* Find the parameter file of an existing font closest in size to the font you need, and make a copy of it, giving the copy the new name. At the beginning of this new parameter file, redefine pt# as shown in the text to magnify the font by the appropriate amount.

2. *Conscientious Method.* Use the Sauter files to set up a new parameter file with carefully adjusted values of the font parameters.

To use this file in a document, plain TEX users should remember that TEX's magnification conventions are slightly different than those of META-FONT. A METAFONT magnification mag=1.3 corresponds to a TEX magnification of 1300. Thus, either a statement like \magnification 1300 at the start of the document, or a declaration like

```
\font\xiii=cmr10 scaled 1300
```

will make the font visible to TEX. LATEX users would most likely regard the magnified font as a new 13-pt font and make it available via an NFSS declaration of the form

```
\DeclareFontShape{OT1}{cmr}{m}{n}{ <13> cmr10 }{}
```

Then \fontsize{13}{15}\selectfont will switch to this font. The second number in the command—here, 15—sets the baselineskip.

3.6.5 Poor person's font sizing

What we just did was to create a copy of a 10-pt font we could use at 13-pt. Another modification will generate an actual 13-pt font, subject to certain caveats (see below). The creator of Computer Modern was careful to express all units in terms of pt#'s, so all we need to do is to make METAFONT think that one pt# is 30% larger than normal! Make a copy of cmr10.mf called cmr13.mf. At the head of file cmr13.mf insert the statement

```
pt#:=1.3;
```

right after the font_size command (which should also be changed); don't overlook the colon right before the = sign. Now compile cmr13 in the usual way and move the packed pixel file to the right directory. If we declare the font in plain TEX by typing

```
\font\XIII=cmr13
```

then \XIII will select this font. If, in LATEX, we add the NFSS declaration

```
\DeclareFontShape{OT1}{cmr}{m}{n}{ <13> cmr13 }{}
```

to a package file or to the preamble of a document, then a command like

```
\fontsize{13}{16}\selectfont
```

selects the new font size.

Because a real 13-pt font is closer in appearance to a 12-pt font (which exists in the Computer Modern suite), it would be better to use a 12-pt font as the base font. In this alternative approach, we edit a copy of cmr12.mf into cmr13.mf by placing the statement pt#:=1.08333; after font_size 12pt#. The constant 1.08333 arises as the decimal equivalent of the fraction 13/12.

3.6.6 Better fonts at new sizes

Conscientious LATEX and TEX users are well aware of the difference between a font that is magnified to a particular size and one that is properly scaled for that size. While figure 9 on page 80 and the display on page 16 of *The TEXbook* focus on one end of the problem, figure 12 on the following page indicates the scope of the problem in a different way. In this figure, two out of the dozens of parameters that control a font have been selected and are plotted against design size. If the values were linear—that is, if we could scale up or down in the simplest manner—then the plots would exactly overlap the dashed lines. Close observers will see that the deviation from linearity is at most some few thirty-sixths of a point, but the human eye is

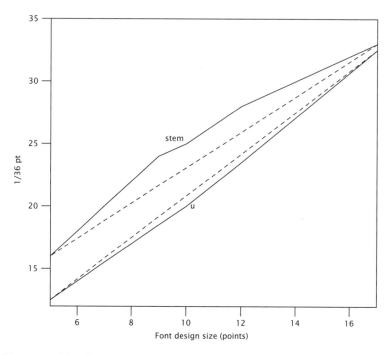

Figure 12: Two font parameters (called "u" and "stem") plotted against font size. If the scaling were linear, the solid lines and the dashed lines would coincide.

easily sensitive to small amounts in types, and so it is important to use actual values of the parameters.

How in general can we construct a new size CM font in which all the METAFONT parameters are set to give the best scaled font possible? John Sauter provided one solution several years ago. He looked at these parameters and watched them change as the font size varied. From the resulting functions, he was able to interpolate values for these parameters for fonts at other than the standard sizes. His files can be found in any CTAN archive (in the area /tex-archive/fonts/cm/sauter). To create, say, a cmr13 font (Computer Modern Roman at 13 pt), create a file cmr13.mf with the lines

```
design_size := 13;
input b-cmr;
```

and create the font in the usual way (run METAFONT, run gftopk, place pixel and font metric files in the appropriate places). Unix users will find scripts to do all this automatically for them. The documentation accompanying the package explains the significance of b-cmr.

3.7   PostScript and Metafont

Everyone knows that PostScript is a page description language, that it needs special printers, and that its fonts are given in terms of outline descriptions. The advantage of PostScript is its device independence. Font outlines are rasterized at almost the last stage of the printing process, within the printer. (In contrast, TEX's bitmap fonts are rasterized by METAFONT in the computer.) PostScript files can be freely exchanged from one PostScript printer to the next since it is the printer's job—not the computer's—to prepare the material for printing (subject, that is, to various font licensing agreements). A file containing pure PostScript is as device-independent as a `.dvi` file. (You do need a PostScript printing device, but programs for rendering Post-Script on non-PostScript platforms do exist; see chapter 9 for further discussion.) For better or worse, PostScript has become a thoroughly entrenched technology, and it seems safe to conclude that the PostScript printing technology will remain dominant over time.

3.7.1   PostScript as a device driver

It was always a problem to find service bureaus with phototypesetters *and* TEX device drivers. PostScript technology helps resolve this difficulty. Most good dvi-to-ps converters can incorporate bitmaps into the `.ps` files they create in ways that are compatible with PostScript printing, so we can print the resulting file on any PostScript printer or phototypesetter. PostScript phototypesetters are plentiful, and so we can generate high quality output anywhere—but beware! If the `.ps` file contains 300 dpi bitmaps, they won't look as good as they ought to, even though the purely PostScript fonts will appear properly.

Therefore, it is up to us to update the bitmaps in a `.ps` file whenever we are moving the file from one printer to another. METAFONT output for different printers should be generated and stored separately. Before moving to another printer, regenerate the `.ps` file using bitmaps of the proper resolution.

3.7.2   Bitmaps into PostScript

We create PostScript files from LATEX or TEX output by running the usual `.dvi` file through any good dvi-to-ps converter. For *dvips*, one would type something like

```
dvips -o foo.ps foo
```

to generate `foo.ps` from `foo.dvi`. Any pixel fonts that the document requests will have their bitmaps included in `foo.ps`.

For information on how to use virtual fonts to select between bitmap fonts specific to different devices, refer to chapter 9.

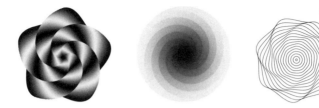

Figure 13: METAFONT writes Encapsulated PostScript.

3.7.3   Interfacing Metafont to Encapsulated PostScript

Bogusław Jackowski has proven to be one of the most innovative and creative of METAFONT programmers; his work is well worth seeking out. He recently wrote a METAFONT-EPS interface to allow an artist to use META-FONT commands to create files containing encapsulated PostScript for inclusion in TEX documents by *dvips*, or for inclusion in *Adobe Illustrator*, *Fontographer*, and *CorelDRAW* files. Here's how it works.

There are a dozen or so METAFONT commands in this package that supersede their native METAFONT equivalents. These commands write encapsulated PostScript commands to the METAFONT .log file. Of course, METAFONT writes lots of other stuff in the .log file, and therefore this file feeds into a filter program in the second step of this process. Either of two filters (provided with the package) strips away the non-PostScript material, leaving pure encapsulated PostScript.

Two filters are provided—in the awk language and in the TEX language. The awk utility is a batch text-editing tool that appears on most computer platforms, and the awk filter runs quickly and efficiently. Some flavor of awk is usually freely available from the Internet for any computer. The second filter is written in the TEX language, and works relatively slowly but has one great advantage—wherever METAFONT goes, TEX is usually not far behind. METAFONT artists are almost sure to have access to TEX, but how many of them have awk at hand?

The MFToEPS package provides a relatively small subset of commands with which to generate PostScript images, but because all of the underlying power of METAFONT remains available, fascinating special effects are possible, as in figure 13. To use this package, the prototypical METAFONT file looks something as follows.

```
input mftoeps;
eps_mode_setup;
⟨some METAFONT code⟩
find_BB ⟨list of paths⟩;
write_preamble jobname;
⟨more METAFONT code using MFToEPS commands⟩
write_postamble;
```

⟨*more METAFONT commands, possibly*⟩
```
end.
```

Next, run METAFONT on this file using a command very much like this
example.

```
mf '\mode=imagen; yeseps:=1; input ⟨myfile⟩'
```

(The MFTOEPS package works only when yeseps has a known value.) The
result of this incantation will be an inflated `.log` file ready for further processing. In the presence of the file `spliteps.tex` (which is part of the package), type

```
tex '\def\inputname{⟨myfile⟩.log}\input spliteps'
```

to generate the `.eps` files, which are ready for other programs, or for reuse
in a TEX document via *dvips* or other postprocessor.

The MFTOEPS package is at CTAN/graphics/MFPS and at

```
ftp.pg.gda.pl or its synonym ftp.gust.org.pl
```

in the directory

```
TeX/GUST/contrib/BachoTeX95/B_Jackowski
```

3.8   MetaPost

While a graduate student at Stanford University, John Hobby was closely
involved in the development of METAFONT. Since then, he has created a di-
alect of METAFONT called MetaPost whose output is PostScript code rather
than generic fonts. The commands of MetaPost and METAFONT are the
same, with very few exceptions. Any METAFONT commands that specifically refer to pixels don't appear in outline-oriented MetaPost. For example, there is no need for the sharp convention; all numeric quantities measure things in PostScript points. (A PostScript point is what *The TEXbook*
calls a "big point." There are exactly 72 big points in an inch.) Conversely,
outline fonts call for commands that would have made no sense for pure
METAFONT. MetaPost, for example, has commands for dealing with color
and shades of gray which would make no sense to METAFONT.

One other important difference between METAFONT and MetaPost lies
in the handling of text. Unlike METAFONT, MetaPost has the extensive ability to incorporate TEX fragments into its output. Now, graphics can contain
perfectly typeset, perfectly positioned labels that match the text of the document. Many of the diagrams in this book were prepared with MetaPost.

This program has now been placed in the public domain, and the source
and executables for selected platforms (OS/2, DOS as of this writing; and it

is part of the web2c distribution) may be obtained from CTAN. The manuals [Hobby (1993)] and [Hobby (1992)] for MetaPost may be freely downloaded from the AT&T server. More comments appear in chapter 13.

3.8.1   The MetaPost cycle

A MetaPost program consists of drawing commands sandwiched between pairs of

    beginfig(⟨number⟩);

and

    endfig;

commands. The file is run through MetaPost by means of a command like

    mp ⟨myfile⟩

where ⟨myfile⟩.mp is the ASCII file containing the MetaPost descriptions of the graphic. If MetaPost discovers any errors, it reports them in the same way as does METAFONT, and the MetaPost artist has to make corrections and revisions to ⟨myfile⟩.mp until it comes out right.

In addition to a .log file, the output of a successful run is a series of files with names like myfile.1, myfile.2, and so on. (That is, the file name is the same as the input file, and the numeric extensions match the number in each beginfig statement.) These output files are like encapsulated Post-Script files.

3.8.2   From MetaPost to TeX

It should be possible to include MetaPost output in a LaTeX or TeX document with any good .dvi-to-PostScript postprocessor. Recent versions of *dvips* work for sure. LaTeX users must include

    \usepackage{epsf}

in the preamble of the document. Then, a statement like

    \epsfbox{myfile.1}

will include the MetaPost output file myfile.1. Several caveats: within certain environments such as center, flushleft, and so on, it may be necessary to include the command \leavevmode or \noindent before the call to \epsfbox.

Plain TeX users should place the line

    \input epsf

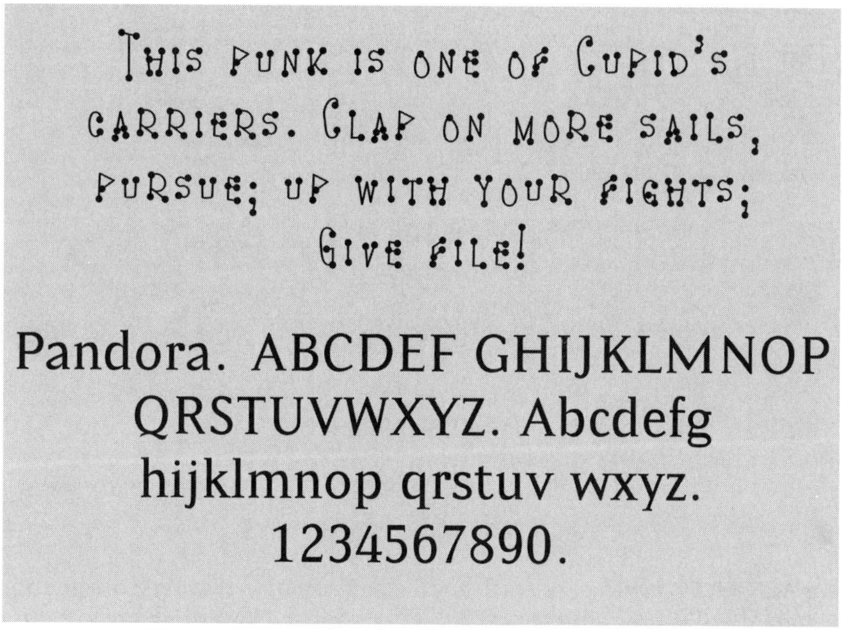

This PUNK IS ONE OF CUPID'S
CARRIERS. CLAP ON MORE SAILS,
PURSUE; UP WITH YOUR FIGHTS;
GIVE FILE!

Pandora. ABCDEF GHIJKLMNOP
QRSTUVWXYZ. Abcdefg
hijklmnop qrstuv wxyz.
1234567890.

Figure 14: Examples of Punk and Pandora meta-fonts.

somewhere near the beginning of the file. Then, place the graphic in the document with the \epsfbox command.

All users should check the epsf documentation for interesting other capabilities of the \epsfbox or \epsffile command (its synonym). Note that because the MetaPost is PostScript output, it may not be possible to preview the document any longer.

3.8.3 Installing MetaPost

The installation procedure for MetaPost is slightly different than for META-FONT; carefully check the installation guide accompanying the program.

As with both TEX and METAFONT, MetaPost needs special binary files present before it can run. This binary file is equivalent to some ASCII file of macro definitions. For TEX, the binary file is a format .fmt file. For METAFONT, it is a base .base or .bas file, and for MetaPost, it is a memory mem file. Special mem files need to be created in ways analogous to a META-FONT base file, and these files belong in the mp subdirectory (which will be at the same level as your tex subdirectory). In addition to plain.mp, the precursor of plain.mem, the standard distribution contains mfplain.mp from which mfplain.mem is the product. Invoking this base file allows MetaPost to mimic METAFONT in such a way that many METAFONT files—including the files for creating Computer Modern fonts—can run through MetaPost properly.

QUI NESCIT DISSIMULARE
NESCIT VIVERE

FELICITAS HABET
MULTOS AMICOS

Figure 15: A Dürer Roman font.

3.9   Other Metafont work

The METAFONTbook begins with a warning (page viii) that type design can be hazardous to other interests. And it's true, as the loyal (but small) cadre of METAFONT and MetaPost users will cheerfully attest. Yet despite this, very little other meta-METAFONT design work has appeared (although many people have used METAFONT as a computer drafting tool with great suc-

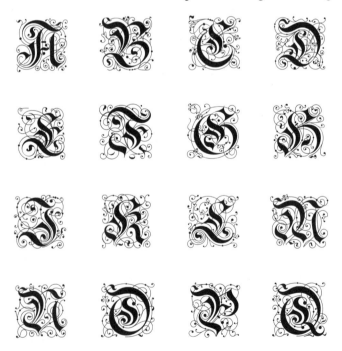

Figure 16: Illuminated initials by Yannis Haralambous.

cess). There are some important and interesting meta-fonts in existence, all downloadable from the appropriate subdirectory in the fonts area of CTAN.

Another of Knuth's font designs, although it dates from the mid-1980s, still maintains an up-to-the-minute appearance. The Punk types (see figure 14 on page 91) are important because they represent what is probably the shortest set of METAFONT programs for a complete 128 character font. For details, see Knuth (1988).

Neenie Billawala designed a meta-font family, Pandora, and although her generating programs differ substantially from Knuth's, she maintained the same file structure—parameter files, driver files, and program files—as in the Computer Modern fonts, and has created a special base file for Pandora. Reading her METAFONT programs deepens one's knowledge of the METAFONT language, but there is no matching math family, and advice about generating the fonts at sizes other than 10-pt is sketchy. The definitive report on Pandora appears in Billawala (1989).

One other meta design project, discussed by Hoenig (1990), was motivated by the observation that Albrecht Dürer had designed an uppercase font several hundred years ago using ruler and compass constructions only. Could METAFONT render these letters today? And while we're at it, can we embed sufficient meta-ness in each program to generate corresponding Dürer fonts, such as a sans serif, a typewriter-like font, a boldface font, an oblique font, and an informal font (inspired by Adobe Systems' Stone Informal font)? The answer is a qualified yes. The Roman uppercase is handsome, designed as it was by a major artist, but the further the variant fonts deviate from the pure Roman, the less successful they appear. There are no characters but the uppercase letters, and they look best at large sizes (figure 15 on the preceding page).

Yannis Haralambous has been involved in major font creation projects and has created a variety of fonts for foreign languages and dialects. He uses METAFONT to create these, frequently employing a program like *Fontographer* as a front end to METAFONT. Anyone interested in font design (with or without the aid of METAFONT) would do well to seek out his work; Haralambous (1991b) and Haralambous (1991a) include important discussions of these fonts. Here (figure 16 on the facing page) we show some illuminated initials he crafted.

A particularly interesting font design project involves the sans serif face Malvern (figure 17 on the next page) by Damian Cugley. He has some novel ideas about type design; for example, his fonts contain intermediate caps as well as small caps. The manual accompanying his font package is worth reading for comments about font design. This material appears in the fonts/malvern area of any CTAN archive.

The medieval Japanese heraldic crests rendered by Alan Jeffrey (shown earlier in figure 1 on page 63) present another example of METAFONT usage.

A leisurely stroll through the fonts area of the CTAN archives reveals many other strange and wonderful fonts. There are several dingbat fonts, fonts for non-European alphabets, non-terrestrial alphabets (Elvish), and

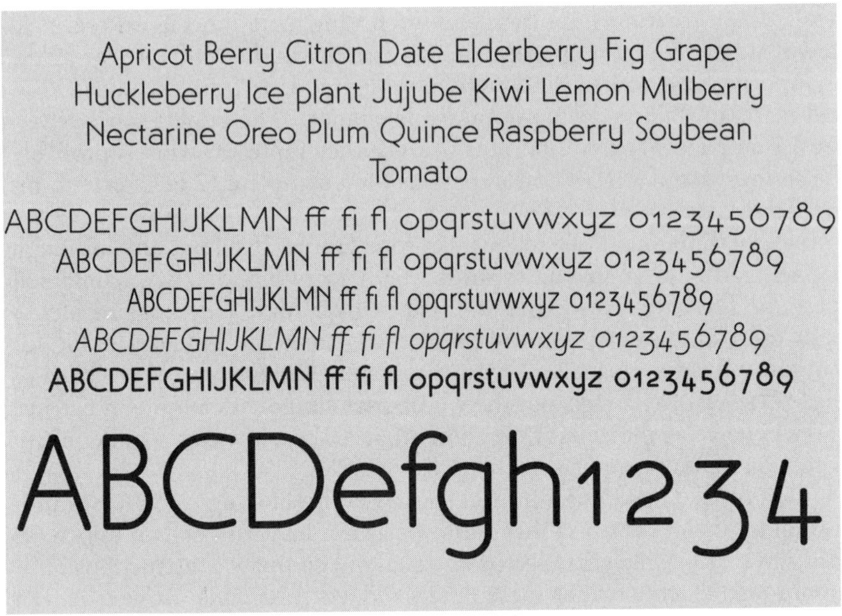

Apricot Berry Citron Date Elderberry Fig Grape
Huckleberry Ice plant Jujube Kiwi Lemon Mulberry
Nectarine Oreo Plum Quince Raspberry Soybean
Tomato

ABCDEFGHIJKLMN ff fi fl opqrstuvwxyz 0123456789
ABCDEFGHIJKLMN ff fi fl opqrstuvwxyz 0123456789
ABCDEFGHIJKLMN ff fi fl opqrstuvwxyz 0123456789
ABCDEFGHIJKLMN ff fi fl opqrstuvwxyz 0123456789
ABCDEFGHIJKLMN ff fi fl opqrstuvwxyz 0123456789

ABCDefgh1234

Figure 17: A sampling of Malvern types.

others. Figure 18 on the next page displays one of the dingbat fonts, and figure 19 on page 96 shows a miscellaneous few other fonts.

In 1988, D. Wujastyk, in [Wujastyk (1988b)] and [Wujastyk (1988a)], compiled a comprehensive list of fonts usable with TEX. Some of these are fonts designed using METAFONT. (Surely it's time for an update?) Most can be downloaded from any of the CTAN archives, although these articles predate the CTAN structure. Appendix B in Walsh (1994) displays samples of many fonts in the archive.

3.10 Learning more about Metafont

Much less has been written about METAFONT than about TEX. The major reference remains *The METAFONTbook*, by Donald E. Knuth, METAFONT's author [Knuth (1986c)]. Additional information can be extracted from *METAFONT: The Program,* [Knuth (1986d)], volume D of the series *Computers and Typesetting.* Volume E of this series [Knuth (1986e)]contains all there is to know about using METAFONT to generate the Computer Modern fonts and provides large renditions of all the characters in these fonts; this volume is the "coffee table" member of the series. The bibliographies within these books provide references to other articles relevant to computer font design and Knuth's ideas on these subjects.

Even though MetaPost is not quite the same as METAFONT, the manuals for MetaPost[Hobby (1992), Hobby (1993)] are also helpful. Much of these

Figure 18: An anonymous dingbat font (bbding) from CTAN.

Apple Berry Cherry Date
Eggplant 123456790

A B C D E F G H I

J K L M

N O P Q R S T U V

W X Y Z

abcdefghijklmnopqrstuvwxyz

Fig Gooseberrry Kiwi Lemon
Nourishment Orange 0123456789

ABCDEFGHIJKLMNOPQRSTU

VWXYZ abcde

fghijklmnopqrstuvwxyz

Peach Pear Plum Persimmon 0123456789

ABCDEFGHIJKLMNOPQRST

UVWXYZ abcde

fghijklmnopqrstuvwxyz

Figure 19: Miscellaneous meta-fonts. The calligraphic Calligra font appears to be an anonymous contribution. The Blackboard Bold font (bbold10) is by Alan Jeffrey and the Fraktur font is by Yannis Haralambous.

files contains core METAFONT material discussed from a viewpoint slightly different from that of Knuth.

Of recent interest is the electronic pamphlet on METAFONT by Geoffrey Tobin [Tobin (1994)]. It can be downloaded from the /documentation area of any of the CTAN archives. Finally, do not neglect the METAFONT source files for fonts on CTAN. Many authors have been conscientious about documenting their modifications within their code; these tips are invaluable.

CHAPTER 4

. . . .

LOGICAL DOCUMENTS
VIA LaTeX

4.1 What is logical document structure?

Imagine yourself as a computer user, but blind. The situation isn't as dreadful as you might think—certain gadgets let the computer read ASCII files out loud, and TEX input files, which are pure ASCII, work well in this arrangement. (For a discussion of an actual such system, see both Raman (1995) and Gibbs (1996).)

Now imagine the computer reading a TEX input file to you. Certain situations arise.

- The computer reads the following fragment out loud.

```
...the frammis contains the {\it octothorpe\/} which ...
```

  What's the purpose of the \it italic command? Did the author intend to emphasize that word, or did it connote the first appearance of a key term? The visual context available to a sighted reader may be enough to resolve this issue, but an unsighted auditor cannot be sure.

- A paragraph concludes, and a sequence of TEX commands follows, commands for some extra vertical space, formatting a phrase in italic, adding additional vertical space, and (finally!) resumption of the text.

  The blind listener—you—is confused by this markup. Did the author on a whim attempt some typographic filigree, or was it an attempt to make it easier for a sighted reader to determine the organization of the document? If the former, then presumably the original discussion will continue. If the latter, we need to prepare ourselves for a new discussion.

These examples show there are really two structures to a document—its *visual structure* and its *logical structure*. For the sighted majority of us, it requires a subtle adjustment in perspective to perceive this distinction, because we're unused to thinking about a document except when we are reading it.

A better way to create the document would be to organize it so it made sense to a blind auditor as well as to a sighted reader by somehow making the formatting instructions reflect the purpose they serve. For example, the first source fragment above might be better keyed in as

```
...the frammis contains the {\em octothorpe\/} which ...
```

in which case the \em suggests that the expression in the group will be emphasized when typeset, or as

```
...the frammis contains the \keyterm{octothorpe} whi...
```

which clearly identifies the octothorpe as an important term. (An octothorpe is the true name for the symbol #. Frammis is wholly imaginary.)

In the same way, if the string of formatting instructions referred to above in the second list item were encapsulated in a definition like

```
\def\newsection{...}
```

then it would be clear not only to the reader of the printed document but also to the peruser of the input, be they blind or sighted, what the author intended by the string of formatting commands—namely, that they were intended to mark the beginning of a new section.

In this logical approach, we use commands not only to control the final typeset appearance but also the structure of our paper. This is the basis of *logical document structure.*

Advantages accrue to logical markup. TEX allows definitions of macros to be isolated in a separate file. It's easy to bury the details of formatting in these files, so the final look of the typeset document changes merely by using one or the other of these style files. For example, after

```
\get{hismacs}
   ...
...the {\em octothorpe\/} which..
```

might typeset "the *octothorpe* which" whereas after

```
\get{hermacs}
   ...
...the {\em octothorpe\/} which..
```

we might see "the <u>octothorpe</u> which" or "the OCTOTHORPE which." The author need not worry about these onerous details, but only on using the

\em command to express the relation of emphasis. (The macro \get is imaginary, but its name expresses its function. Of course, we could easily define a \get macro to fetch macro files.)

Once a document file is freed from explicit formatting commands, it is easy to use computer tools to organize groups of documents, and make indexing, searching for topics, and so on, feasible.

4.1.1 General markup

Using a system of general markup, not only should it be possible to identify all parts of a document by their function, but also possible to process documents by any "well-formed" formatting system. The most renowned such system is SGML (Standardized General Markup Language) which generally uses angle brackets < and > to delimit SGML instructions. It is possible to configure TEX so that < serves as the escape character, a function usually allocated to the backslash. Once that change is achieved, it should be possible to define TEX commands identical to the SGML markup, so that SGML documents can be typeset by TEX. Individuals on the Internet have reported great success with this approach, but at present there is no freely available package to do that. Useful references to SGML include the canonic work by Goldfarb (1990) and an introduction by Turner, Douglas, and Turner (1996).

4.1.2 Logical markup in TEX

There are several extensive macro packages available for achieving logical markup with TEX. The most well-known is LᴬTEX.

TEX watchers report that most TEX users are in fact LᴬTEX users. Undoubtedly, the reason for its popularity is not due to the logical structure it provides but because it makes TEX easier to use. There is a price: strict adherence to LᴬTEX standards may make it difficult to do lots of things that are possible under plain TEX. The structure plus restrictiveness of LᴬTEX are precisely the reasons why LᴬTEX has become so popular with many publishers. Authors, normally prone to exotic flights of typographic fancy, find themselves sharply reined in when asked to submit manuscripts in LᴬTEX. (Since LᴬTEX *is* TEX, it's possible much of the time to use plain TEX commands within a LᴬTEX document. Therefore, it is possible to subvert the advantages of LᴬTEX, but few authors seem aware of this.)

One hundred percent logical markup is a target to which we should all aim, but on which we never land. At the very least, some awkward page or line breaks have to be fixed manually (by adding an explicit \hfill\break or \vfill\eject or \newpage). These are among the least logical examples of markup, but there are times when TEX itself needs a helping hand. [Donald Knuth expects TEX to do 95% of any typesetting task. The final five percent requires the judgment of a human and would be difficult to automate. See the helpful discussion of this issue in Goossens, Mittelbach, and Samarin (1994, p. 529).]

4.2 LATEX

Leslie Lamport is the original author of LATEX, which dates from the early 1980s. It has been frozen at version 2.09.

In the late 1980s, Frank Mittelbach and Rainer Schöpf began work on a significantly revamped version of LATEX. That work continues, but an interim version dubbed LATEX2$_\varepsilon$ has since become *the* official LATEX—the version that is supported by Leslie Lamport and by these workers and an international team. Since it is backwardly compatible with LATEX2.09, older documents are not obsolete. Among the many advantages of the new LATEX is the New Font Selection Scheme, which makes font selection logical but simple.

The current LATEX is LATEX2$_\varepsilon$; from now on "LATEX" means LATEX2$_\varepsilon$. It is continuously undergoing debugging and evolutionary improvements. New versions with the official imprimatur of the LATEX development team are made available twice a year, generally mid-December and July, and can be downloaded from the CTAN archives thereafter. This new LATEX is of necessity a large and unwieldy package; it's a good idea to peruse the article by Carlisle (1996b) for an overview of the files in the LATEX system. LATEX has become quite stable, and the LATEX team has reverted to their work on LATEX3.

LATEX is a very large package, and typically, it is used as a format file. That is, at initex time, the original ASCII files containing the LATEX macros are translated to a binary file that TEX can read at high speeds. If we call the resulting format latex.fmt, then we invoke LATEX by typing something like

```
tex &latex myfile
```

or perhaps tex '&latex myfile' on Unix. (Many systems will provide for meaningful aliases, so perhaps latex will stand for tex &latex on such a system.)

4.3 LATEX conventions

Although LATEX responds to many of the original plain TEX commands, a conscientious author will use the logical document commands of LATEX wherever possible. For example, authors should almost never use a naked font-changing command. What would be the reason for italicizing a phrase with the \it command? If we want emphasis, we should use LATEX's \em command. If we want the title of a subsection to be italicized, then we should use the \subsection command, and so on.

> **Conventions**
>
> LaTeX documents obey the same input conventions as any other TeX document files.
>
> The basic unit of LaTeX documents is the environment.
>
> In the usual way, LaTeX commands may accept arguments. LaTeX commands may have a variant star form (e.g., \verb and \verb*). Commands may also accept optional arguments that are delimited by square brackets.

It's important for LaTeX authors to understand how LaTeX lets us organize a document in a logical way, and that's what we discuss here. An intensive, whirlwind LaTeX short course appears in Appendix 2. All of the conventions for preparing plain TeX documents apply to LaTeX too.

An author new to LaTeX learns a lot about LaTeX structure by looking at one of the shortest possible LaTeX document files.

```
\documentclass{article} %%      The PREAMBLE
\begin{document} %%              The DOCUMENT begins.
   Hello, world!
\end{document} %%               The DOCUMENT ends.
```

The typeset page consists of a short greeting plus page number. The actual typesetting is done within a 'document' environment, while administrative details pertaining to the document are segregated in an initial preamble.

4.3.1   Environments

The basic "unit" of a LaTeX document is the *environment*, a portion of a document in which the text is formatted in a distinctive way. Environments all have simple descriptive names: center centers all lines, tabular typesets a table or chart, quotation sets off a long quotation, itemize and enumerate format lists, and so on. Environments may often be nested within each other—in case, for example, one item of a list is itself a list. As we see above, the entirety of a document fits into a document environment.

One enters and exits any environment using a pair of matching \begin and \end commands. These commands take as argument the name of the environment (although some environments demand additional parameters) and an ironclad rule demands that \begin and \end commands be properly matched when nested.

4.3.2 *Commands and conventions*

Some commands need additional information in order to take effect. A LATEX \begin needs to know the name of an environment, for example. Recall that arguments (parameters) to commands need to be surrounded by a pair of curly braces. LATEX extends the syntax for certain commands.

Many commands can be followed by an asterisk (*). The star form is similar but distinctly different from the original command. For example, \vspace is the LATEX way of adding vertical white space. All such white space is subject to TEX's insistence on discarding this space whenever it appears at the beginning of a page. (This rule is what makes it so hard for beginners to vertically center a title on a separate title page.) But LATEX provides \vspace*, the command to add vertical space that is *never* discarded. Not all commands have a star form, and when the star alternative exists, you can't predict just how it will differ from the native command. In practice, though, it proves easy to keep track of commands and their star forms.

Many LATEX commands accept *optional arguments*, that generally follow the command name but precede the required arguments. For example, LATEX provides \\ as a new-line indicator in environments like center or tabular but with an optional length that adds additional space between the lines. You might type \\[1pc] instead of simply \\ to get an additional pica separation between consecutive lines. It's the responsibility of the \caption command to add the caption to a figure and also to add an entry to the list of figures that might appear. In case a caption is long, \caption permits an author to specify an abbreviated caption in an optional argument, and it is this abbreviation that will appear in the list of figures. Thus, although

```
\caption{Four score and seven years ago, ....
... shall not perish from the earth.}
```

is legal,

```
\caption[Gettysburg Address]{Four score and seven years...
... shall not perish from the earth.}
```

is preferable.

LATEX provides an extensive palette of typesetting commands. From the standpoint of logical structure, the most important of these are \em (for emphasis) and sectioning commands like \part, \chapter, \section, and the like.

With the current version of LATEX comes the *New Font Selection Scheme*; familiarly *NFSS*. An extensive discussion of this appears in chapter 6.

Nothing has been said so far of technical typesetting in LATEX. Most of the capability of plain TEX survives intact, but some revised commands are also available.

4.3.3   The preamble

There is more to a document than its printed image—states must be declared, flags and switches must be set, and new commands made known. Although this information has great bearing on the printed appearance of the document, it generates no type itself. These declarations belong in the preamble. (Although new commands may appear anywhere, it's a good idea to collect them all together in the preamble.)

The preamble for an early draft of this chapter looked like the following.

```
\documentclass[twoside]{article}
  \usepackage{resource,epsf}
  \makeindex                  %  generates index entries
  \newcommand{\foo}{...}      %  a personal command
  \title{Logical Documents}
\begin{document}              %  document begins
  ...
```

Of these declarations, only the \documentclass is required. The .cls *class file* contains the instructions needed to resolve the appearance of segmenting commands \section and so on. Here, option twoside adds further restrictions on the appearance. Additional .sty *package files* provide further information or restrictions and are brought in by the command \usepackage. Here, epsf.sty contains the macros so LATEX can import certain graphic files, and the macros of resource.sty particularize the action of article.cls to make sure the manuscript conformed to the publisher's requirements.

A declaration like \title{...} frequently confuses beginners. Doesn't this command typeset the title of the piece, and so why is it in the preamble? In fact, \title (and its siblings \author and \date) serve merely to store information but do no typesetting themselves. That's the responsibility of a \maketitle command, which may only appear *after* \begin{document}.

4.3.4   LATEX209

Many readers may possess a huge collection of "old" LATEX documents, so a few words on the differences between the two flavors of LATEX may be in order.

LATEX209 used style files where the current LATEX uses class files. Consequently, a 209 document began with a \documentstyle command. LATEX now examines this first command, and if it is a ...style command, it processes the file in a 209 compatibility mode. Some users have reported that this processing is very slow, but as desktop computers get increasingly fast, this objection should rapidly recede in importance. It is advantageous to switch to the new LATEX as rapidly as possible. Only this version will be supported, and it has many improved features that are worth exploiting.

4.3.5 Floats

A frustrating component of many LATEX documents (and plain TEX documents, too) are the *floats*, which refer to things like figures, tables, and so on whose position can neither be predicted nor precisely controlled. An author may want a figure to appear after a certain paragraph, say, but what should TEX do at typesetting time if there is only an inch of available space on that page while the figure itself is three inches high? TEX holds components like this in a special place and inserts them when there is room, such as at the top of the next page. An item like this—which can float back and forth in the document as revisions are made—is called a float.

The situation was particularly troublesome whenever there were several floats in a document. It was even possible (in the original LATEX) for floats to appear out of order—figure 4 might actually precede figure 3 in the final text! Other complaints centered about floats migrating to the end of the document.

Within LATEX, floats are placed by the figure and table environments (and by their star variants). The underlying macros have been substantially improved so floats never appear out of order. It is still possible for floats to appear at the end of the document, but that is often a signal that at least one float is too tall for the page.

The current LATEX provides a number of parameters to fine tune float placement; see Goossens, Mittelbach, and Samarin (1994) for all of the details. For the current book, these parameters and their values (together with the commands to set them)

```
\setcounter{topnumber}{2}
\setcounter{bottomnumber}{2}
\setcounter{totalnumber}{4} %            value of 2 also OK
\setcounter{dbltopnumber}{2}
\renewcommand{\topfraction}{0.9}
\renewcommand{\bottomfraction}{0.5}
\renewcommand{\textfraction}{0.1}
\renewcommand{\floatpagefraction}{0.8}
\renewcommand{\dbltopfraction}{0.9}
\renewcommand{\dblfloatpagefraction}{0.8}
```

have worked well. [These suggestions are due to Granger (1994).]

4.3.6 Other parts of a document

LATEX supports the automatic generation of the front and back matter that surround a document, further advantages of using LATEX.

As part of their job, the segmenting commands (\part, \section, etc.) write page information to an auxiliary .toc file that LATEX later uses to create tables of contents when the \tableofcontents command appears in

the file. In the same way, the \caption command in the figure and tabular environments generates information that you can instruct LATEX to
use to create lists of tables or figures in the presence of \listoffigures or
\listoftables.

The back matter to a book consists of bibliography, index, and perhaps
a glossary or other similar sections. Although LATEX commands will throw
off index entries and references to other scholarly works, you'll need separate
programs to process this material.

4.3.7 Index preparation

For index preparation, the tool of choice is *MakeIndex* by Pehong Chen and
Michael Harrison. To typeset comprehensive indexes, authors need to know

1. how to mark their documents; and

2. how to generate and process the index data.

Marking the document   The command \index is the basic tool for generating an index entry. It takes a single argument, the term for the index. Of
course, one can't know the page number of this entry until the document
has been run through LATEX, and \index is responsible for making sure that
TEX throws this information off at typesetting time.

Index entries can appear in several variations, and some characters have
special meanings that tell the *MakeIndex* processor how to handle these variations. One character controls the sublevels of the entry, another the formatting of the entry, and a third the treatment of the page number in the
typeset index.

These conventions are summarized in the box on the facing page, which
also suggests one or two convenient index techniques. We can force an entry
to the end of all entries for that letter by insisting that it be alphabetized as if
it ended with numerous additional z's; the @ ensures it typesets properly. For
example, we might place α at the end of the a's by indexing it under 'azzzz'.
We could force it to the beginning of the a's by indexing under 'aaaa'.

We may use any of these conventions in conjunction with any other. For
example,

```
\index{Greek letter!aaaa@$\alpha$|textit}
```

generates an entry like

> Greek letter
> α, *92*

where *MakeIndex* will place this first among all subentries (after all, few
things can precede 'aaaa').

Index Conventions

- Use the ! to control entry sublevels. For example,

```
\index{index entries!long}
```

   generates entries something like

   index entries
      long, 14

- Since the markup for an entry may be different from its alphabetiza-
   tion, \index uses the symbol @ to control formatting. For example,

```
\index{azzzz@$\alpha$}
\index{alpha@$\alpha$}
\index{alpha@\texttt{\symbol{'134}alpha}}
```

   add three entries to the index. The first two will print as α, but will
   appear in different places. The third entry prints '\alpha' as if it were
   alphabetized as alpha (\symbol{'134} is one way to print the backslash).

- The vertical bar | uses any following declarations that follow it to *en-
   capsulate* the page number. Thus,

```
\index{entry|see{exit}}
\index{exit|textit}
\index{index|(}
 ...
\index{index|)}
```

   leads to entries like

   entry, *see* exit
   exit, *29*
   index, 29–33

   in the final index.

Remember, the \index command does not typeset anything, but only
generates a line of information (pagination plus information about sublevels, typesetting the index entry, and so on) in an external index file. Fortunately, all of these conventions can be combined inside macros. For the
class file for this book, a command \fil typesets a file name in tt and generates an index entry for it which also be in tt. Roughly speaking, its (LATEX)

The Index Cycle

1. Prepare the LaTeX document to contain the index.

   - Place the command \makeindex in the preamble of the document.
   - Use the package makeidx via a \usepackage command.
   - Insert the command \printindex at the position in the document where you want the index to appear.

2. Run the file through LaTeX once. This generates a file with extension .idx. If the file is myfile.tex, then the raw index file will be myfile.idx.

3. Run *MakeIndex* on this file. Typically, the command line will be something like

   ```
   makeindex myfile.idx
   ```

   and the result will be an .ind file (in this case, myfile.ind).

4. In the presence of the new .ind file, run your file one more time through LaTeX.

definition is

```
\newcommand{\fil}[1]{\index{#1@\texttt{#1} file}{\tt #1}}
```

which ensures that file names receive identical treatment (provided that we use this new command to refer to names of files).

The LaTeX \index command is responsible for spitting entries plus page numbers to a separate .idx file. Certain options control subentries, format instructions for the entry, and so on. Then, *MakeIndex* processes the .idx file and works it into a form for typesetting by LaTeX. The precise details appear in the box on this page. During the preparation of this manuscript, I found it useful to also use the package showidx (by Leslie Lamport) which typesets the index entries in the margin of a draft.

Many other details, and descriptions of useful packages to supplement or replace the makeindex package, can be found in Goossens, Mittelbach, and Samarin (1994, chapter 12).

4.3.8 Bibliographies

The program BIBTEX by Oren Patashnik lets LATEX *or* TEX users maintain bibliography references in master files separate from document files. Entries in the `.bib` file are categorized as any of numerous reference types (book, tech report, article, misc, etc.) which gets a unique key. Inside the entry, BIBTEX expects the information to be associated with certain keywords (`publisher="Oxford University Press"` and so on). Authors use the `\bibliography` command to fix the name of the `.bib` file and specify the style of bibliography formatting using the `\bibliographystyle` command. (BIBTEX style files possess a `.bst` extension. A large collection of `.bst` files resides in the `biblio/bibtex` area of CTAN.) A summary of the BIBTEX production cycle appears in the box on the following page.

Nelson Beebe maintains extensive bibliographies of TEX- and LATEX-related material at `ftp.math.utah.edu`. He has written `bibclean`, a syntax checker and `.bib`-file pretty-printer, freely available from the same archive, plus a few other worthwhile bibliographic utilities [Beebe (1993a), Beebe (1993b)].

Additional information, including additional packages for indexing and bibliography preparation, appears both in Lamport (1994) and Goossens, Mittelbach, and Samarin (1994).

4.4 Modifying LATEX commands

It is sometimes necessary to modify LATEX commands for special purposes. Much of the time it's straightforward for anyone with a few weeks (or less) of LATEX experience. As a case study, let's examine a small change needed for this book involving the `\caption` command. It's a good idea to create a private style or class file to hold these modifications.

4.4.1 The problem

The raw `\caption` command supplied the proper caption, but displayed the text of the caption in the prevailing size of the text typeface. The author wanted a caption at a smaller size. While this could "easily" have been achieved by adding

```
\fontsize{9}{10}\selectfont
```

at the beginning of each occurrence of caption texts, this is a bad idea. The manuscript source files would become riddled with nonstructural markup labels. Furthermore, in case the publisher's production staff disliked this idea or imposed additional changes, a whole new bunch of explicit changes would be necessary.

A better approach might be to redefine `\caption`:

```
\renewcommand{\caption}[1]{ ... }
```

Bibliographies with BibTeX

Assume that file `resource.bib` contains the collection of citations, that `plain.bst` is the desired bibliography style, and that your document file is `mybook.tex`. Make sure `resource.bib` is in a directory visible to TeX.

1. Use commands like `\cite{⟨key⟩}%%`   `<<cite          index`
   to point to references. For example,

```
\cite{texbook}%% <<cite index
```

refers to *The TeXbook* provided `resource.bib` contains an entry like

```
\@BOOK{texbook,
 title      = "The \TeX\ Book",
 author     = "Donald E. Knuth",
 ...
}
```

See Lamport (1994)and Goossens, Mittelbach, and Samarin (1994) for the extended syntax rules for these bibliographic entries.

2. Include commands like

```
%% \bibliography{resource} \bibliographystyle{plain}
```

in your source file to point BibTeX toward your references and toward the style file (here, `plain.bst`).

3. Run your file through LaTeX, thereby creating `mybook.aux`, which contains your citations (among other information).

4. Run the BibTeX program by typing something like `bibtex mybook`. BibTeX reads the `.aux` file and creates `mybook.bbl`, which contains the bibliographic information in a form suitable for typesetting by LaTeX. (You'll also see a BibTeX `.blg` log file.)

5. Type `latex` `mybook` *twice* more to resolve citations properly. The bibliography will be part of the finished document.

Since this command has an optional argument, this brute-force redefinition is a bad idea.

4.4.2 Examine the source

A better first step is to examine the definition \caption in a LaTeX macro file. Upon loading a fresh copy of latex.ltx (the source for LaTeX2$_\varepsilon$) into a text editor, and using the editor's search facility, we find the line

```
\def\caption{\refstepcounter\@captype
  \@dblarg{\@caption\@captype}}
```

as its definition. There are many mystifying aspects to this definition, but most can be ignored. Only two are of any interest to an author.

First of all, the defining mechanism is the plain TeX \def command. This line states that any reference to \caption in a document will be replaced by

```
\refstepcounter\@captype \@dblarg{\@caption\@captype}
```

If an author knows anything about LaTeX or TeX command sequences, it's that they may contain sequences of letters only. How therefore can all these @ signs be legal?

4.4.3 Private command names

TeX identifies a character in a document file by means of two numbers—its ASCII equivalence (by which an 'A' is equivalent to the number 65) and its category code. The ASCII convention is universal, but the category codes are a special TeX construct. TeX will think a character is a letter, regardless of its ASCII code, if it possesses the category code for a letter. Moreover, category codes can be assigned and changed by those who know what they're doing.

Before the definition of \caption, the at-sign "@" has been made a letter by virtue of a category-code change. For the duration of that assignment, command names like \@captype are legal, because @ is a letter. Some time later, following all of these definitions, the category code of @ is restored to its usual value, making @ a non-letter again.

The value of private command names like \@captype is that it will be impossible for any author to inadvertently redefine them, since any name containing @ is not legal in the normal document context.

LaTeX provides two commands to make private command names accessible. The first, \makeatletter makes @ behave like a letter. The second, \makeatother, undoes this behavior; normally, @ possesses the numerical category code assigning it a category called "other." For more on category codes, see *The TeXbook*, page 37 ff.

4.4.4 *Identifying the component*

We cannot proceed further without a leap of faith—faith that the framers of LaTeX were careful how they named their commands. Therefore, we may ignore things like "\refstepcounter" and "\@captype" and proceed to explore \@caption. In latex.ltx, we find that the definition of this command immediately follows \caption.

```
\long\def\@caption#1[#2]#3{\par\addcontentsline{\csname
  ext@#1\endcsname}{#1}{\protect\numberline{\csname
  the#1\endcsname}{\ignorespaces #2}}\begingroup
    \@parboxrestore
    \normalsize
    \@makecaption{\csname fnum@#1\endcsname}{\ignorespaces #3}\par
  \endgroup}
```

Since we are not interested in making any changes that will affect the table of contents, we make another leap of faith and ignore everything except \@makecaption, which should control the formatting of the caption, which is our goal.

A moment of slight panic sets in when a careful search of latex.ltx fails to locate other occurrences of \@makecaption. But this is hardly surprising. If this command is truly in charge of formatting the caption, then it will be the job of the class files to specify the formatting, not the main collection of LaTeX macros. And sure enough, a search of article.cls reveals this definition.

```
\long\def\@makecaption#1#2{%
  \vskip\abovecaptionskip
  \sbox\@tempboxa{#1: #2}%
  \ifdim \wd\@tempboxa >\hsize
    #1: #2\par
  \else
    \hbox to\hsize{\hfil\box\@tempboxa\hfil}%
  \fi
  \vskip\belowcaptionskip}
```

Making sense of this definition is the most difficult part of the exercise. Here's the basic idea. If the caption is short enough to fit on a single line, it is centered on the page. Otherwise, it is set as a paragraph. (The caption is first typeset in a box, and the box's width is measured. Typesetting decisions are based on comparing this width to \hsize, the width of the text.) With this interpretation in hand, the needed revisions are trivial. The following material should appear in an author's personal package file.

```
\long\def\@makecaption#1#2{%
  \vskip\abovecaptionskip
  \sbox\@tempboxa{ \fontsize{9}{10}\selectfont #1: #2}%
```

Revising a Command

- Do not make any revisions in the original macro files! Revised definitions should be part of a personal package file.

- Look for the definition of the command in `latex.ltx` (for LaTeX2ε) or the relevant class or style file.

- Regard the odd @ symbol as a letter.

- Ignore embedded definitions that appear not to be relevant to the modification that is needed. Track the important sub-definitions to their lowest level. Make the appropriate revisions to this command.

- Since the defining operation will involve the use of @ as a letter, surround the revised definition with a pair of commands `\makeatletter` and `\makeatother` if you're making these changes outside of a package or class file.

```
\ifdim \wd\@tempboxa >\hsize
   \fontsize{9}{10}\selectfont  #1: #2\par
\else
   \hbox to\hsize{\hfil\box\@tempboxa\hfil}%
\fi
\vskip\belowcaptionskip}
```

When this package is subsequently used via the `\usepackage` command, the additional command `\makeatletter` is silently supplied and so is not needed explicitly. If you plan to include this definition explicitly in your document, then this code *must* be surrounded by the

`\makeatletter`

and

`\makeatother`

commands.

4.5   Other structured macro packages

4.5.1   The synthesis

Michael Spivak used know-how gained from the original LATEX, together
with experience gained through the development of $\mathcal{A}_{\mathcal{M}}\mathcal{S}$TEX (the mathematical TEX macro package he also wrote) to develop a package that synthe-
sizes the functionality of both LATEX and $\mathcal{A}_{\mathcal{M}}\mathcal{S}$TEX in one. It is upwardly
compatible with existing $\mathcal{A}_{\mathcal{M}}\mathcal{S}$TEX files, but uses different syntax to achieve
its document structuring. LAMS-TEX offers some significant features.

First, it offers freedom to adjust the numbering of lists, document segments, equation tags, and so on with its unique quote mechanism. Normally, an equation number is supplied via the \tag command; we type

```
$$2\times3=3\times2\tag$$
```

to typeset something like

$$(18) \qquad\qquad 2 \times 3 = 3 \times 2$$

To get

$$(*) \qquad\qquad 2 \times 3 = 3 \times 2$$

simply replace \tag by \tag"$(*)$". The next time \tag is called, the
proper tag number appears. To get the tag (18′), replace \tag by \tagp after
the LAMS-TEX definition

```
\define\tagp{\Offset\tag0 \newpost\tag{$'$} \tag}
```

has been given. (In LAMS-TEX terms, this definition instructs LAMS-TEX
not to bump up the tag counter this time, and to affix the prime post—
after—the tag number.) In the same way, a wide variety of tags and other
formats can be easily controlled by an author.

LAMS-TEX also provides cross-referencing facilities, lists and sublists up
to five levels, an extensive indexing facility equivalent or subsuming that of
MakeIndex, a powerful verbatim construction, superior capabilities for typesetting commutative diagrams and complex matrices, and powerful table
writing commands. BIBTEX is compatible with it. LAMS-TEX lacks anything comparable to the NFSS of LATEX.

Although the LAMS-TEX software is freely available (on CTAN, among
other sources), you will need to consult its detailed manual [Spivak (1989)]
for instruction.

4.5.2   Extended `plain` macros

It might be appropriate to regard Karl Berry's `eplain` package—available
from CTAN—as a kit for manufacturing your own structured macro package. Much criticism of LATEX has centered about its incompatibility with

the original `plain` macros written by Knuth for TEX. The `eplain` macros remedy this by adding to `plain` those macros that Knuth "missed" and by adding macro tools useful for constructing personal structured macros. ($L\!A\!M\!S$-TEX too is upwardly compatible with `plain`.)

From a structured point of view, perhaps `plain`'s biggest lack is omission of macros for any front-matter support, cross-referencing, bibliography preparation, and all but rudimentary indexing. `eplain`'s remedy is to provide interfaces to BIBTEX and *MakeIndex* and to provide a repertoire of cross-referencing commands that reproduce the functionality of the `\label`, `\ref`, and `\pageref` commands of LATEX. Several macros allow an author to generate tables of contents, lists of figures and whatnot, and other front matter easily.

Another big complaint about LATEX alleges that it is difficult to alter the formatting of the LATEX segmenting commands. While this is not as difficult as is thought, it is true that `eplain` building blocks make it easy to create these commands yourself. For example, a home-brewed `\chapter` command might have the definition

```
\def\chapter#1{%
    \advance\chapno by 1 \secno=0  % initialize counters
    \writenumberedtocentry{chapter}{#1}{\the\chapno}% TOC
    \formatchapter{#1}}
```

where `\formatchapter` contains the details of the formatting.

`eplain` lacks any special font-selection scheme. Nothing comparable to NFSS is supported.

The `eplain` package comes with a comprehensive set of documentation files in general ASCII form and in Emacs `texinfo` form.

4.5.3 The `texinfo` system

Few authors seem aware of the `texinfo` system for documentation preparation. `texinfo` documentation files are suitable for on-line presentation or printing, and it is sensible to have a only a single file for both purposes.

The printing part is courtesy of TEX, while the on-line part is done either by the GNU Emacs editor or by a special viewing utility. When created properly, these files are of great use. Emacs advocates know how easy it is to go to a "next" or "previous" screen and how to follow related topics and sub-topics back and forth in a `texinfo` file in a manner reminiscent of hypertext.

Even without viewing, a `texinfo` file can be prepared and printed normally by TEX (in the presence of the `texinfo.tex` macro file). The escape character has been redefined to be the @ sign, and (except for boiler plate details at the beginning of any document) formatting markup is limited but powerful. Preparation of tables of contents, indexes, and bibliographies is enabled. To get a taste for this system, here follow excerpts from a simple texinfo file. (The commands that control only the online display have been suppressed.)

```
\input texinfo    @c -*-texinfo-*-
@setfilename testing 1-2-3
@settitle Short and Sweet
@setchapternewpage odd
@titlepage
@sp 10
@center @titlefont{Short and Sweet}
@page
@vskip 0pt pus 1filll
Copyright @copyright{} 1996 A. U. Thor
@end titlepage
@chapter First Chapter
@cindex first chapter

This is the contents of the first chapter.

Here is a numbered list.

@enumerate
  @item
  This is the first item.
  @item
  This is the second item.
@end enumerate

@TeX{} typesets this file for a printed manual.

@unnumbered Concept Index
@printindex cp

@contents
@bye
```

Given that @ has become the escape character, this sequence of commands should be easy to interpret. After printing a title page, this file generates a single page, which looks as follows.

> This is the contents of the first chapter.
> Here is a numbered list.
>
> 1. This is the first item.
> 2. This is the second item.
>
> TEX typesets this file for a printed manual.

Thereafter, the file arranges for a concept index (texinfo allows for several different varieties), a table of contents, and concludes.

The texinfo system is another example of ways in which document files can be given structure. Documentation and the material itself is available from the ftp archive prep.ai.mit.edu/pub/gnu

. . . .

TEX IN THE WORKPLACE

There are several ways TEX can be used together with conventional software products. Some suggestions for doing so form the basis of this chapter.

5.1 Word processors

Astonishingly, the query "how can I convert TEX output to WordPerfect form?" is common on computer text forums. Such a task is doomed for a simple reason—TEX can format text in ways that are impossible for an office word processor, so what would the conversion process do when confronted with a commutative diagram or fancy table? Since TEX can do everything a word processor can do, the reverse—transformations from word processor format to TEX—has a better chance of succeeding.

Rich text format   Something called *rich text format* forms the basis of this transformation. Word processors provide authors with numerous options when it comes time to save a file. Among the options frequently available is rich text format, which saves the document using an `.rtf` extension. Both Microsoft Word and WordPerfect word processors provide this option. Rich text involves creation of a purely ASCII text, using format markup that is astonishingly similar to TEX. The trouble is that official documentation of the rich text standard remains elusive. Several workers in the TEX community have created useful tools for translating `.rtf` format to a LATEX or TEX file. Not only can these programs create `.rtf` output, but are able to read `.rtf` documents for further word processing.

The `.rtf`-tools in figure 1 on page 119 require you to save your document in `.rtf` format. The paragraphs

> This is a paragraph of text which has been created for demonstration purposes. It contains some words that are in *italics* and others that are in **bold**. Due to the nature of WORD, it is also possible <u>to underline</u> things, although this is typically frowned on in typesetting circles.
> Here is another paragraph.
> And still one more...

lead to the following TEX-like gibberish when rendered into rich text format by Microsoft Word.

```
{\rtf1\ansi \deff4\deflang1033{\fonttbl{\f4\froman\fcharset0
\fprq2 Times New Roman;}}
{\stylesheet{\f4\fs20
\snext0 Normal;}
{\*\cs10 \additive Default Paragraph Font;}}
{{\creatim\yr1996\mo5\dy30\hr10\min53}
{\version1}{\edmins4}{\nofpages0}{\nofwords0}{\nofchars0}%
  {\vern49213}}
\widowctrl\ftnbj\aenddoc\formshade \fet0\sectd
\linex0\endnhere {\*\pnseclvl1\pnucrm\pnstart1\pnindent720
\pnhang{\pntxta .}}{\*\pnseclvl2\pnucltr\pnstart1\pnindent720
\pnhang{\pntxta .}}{\*\pnseclvl3\pndec\pnstart1\pnindent720
\pnhang{\pntxta .}}{\*\pnseclvl4\pnlcltr\pnstart1\pnindent720\pnhang
{\pntxta )}}{\*\pnseclvl5\pndec\pnstart1\pnindent720\pnhang
{\pntxtb (}{\pntxta )}}{\*\pnseclvl6\pnlcltr\pnstart1
\pnindent720\pnhang{\pntxtb (}{\pntxta )}}
{\*\pnseclvl7\pnlcrm\pnstart1\pnindent720
\pnhang{\pntxtb (}{\pntxta )}}{\*\pnseclvl8
\pnlcltr\pnstart1\pnindent720\pnhang
{\pntxtb (}{\pntxta )}}
{\*\pnseclvl9\pnlcrm\pnstart1
\pnindent720\pnhang{\pntxtb (}{\pntxta )}}\pard\plain \f4\fs20
This is a paragraph of text which has been
created for demonstration purposes.
It contains some words that are in {\i italics} and
others that are in {\b bold}.
Due to the nature of WORD, it is also possible
{\ul to underline things}, although this is typically
frowned on in typesetting circles.
\par Here is another paragraph.
\par And still one more...
\par }
```

A few of the header lines at the beginning of the file have been eliminated from this display, and some lines have been folded to fit on this page, but otherwise this is a verbatim display.

Several freely available tools appear on CTAN and other archives. The accompanying documentation for most of these programs freely admits that complicated layouts—tables and equations, to no one's surprise—can cause problems. The table in figure 1 on the next page summarizes the available public software. Commercial products are also available from

K-Talk Communications, Inc.
1287 King Avenue, Suite 203, Columbus, OH 43212;
(614) 488-8818; email lisa@ktalk.com

and from

Design Science
4028 Broadway, Long Beach, CA 90803
(310) 433-0685; email mtinfo@mathtype.com.

TEX or LATEX to RTF

Tex2RTF (June 1995)
ftp://ftp.aiai.ed.ac.uk
/pub/packages/tex2rtf
http://www.aiai.ed.ac.uk
/~jacs/tex2rtf./html
ftp://CTAN/support/tex2rtf

For SPARC Open Look, SPARC Motif, and Windows 3.1 platforms.

latex2rtf
CTAN/support/latex2rtf

Source and makefiles available.

RTF to LATEX or TEX

RTFLATEX (July 1995)
ftp://hprib.lps.u-psud.fr/pub/rtflatex
ftp://CTAN/support/rtflatex

Aggressively supported and maintained by its author, Daniel Taupin, this tool comes with Turbopascal source, C source, and DOS executable.

rtf2TeX (May 1992)   ftp://CTAN/support/rtf2tex
rtf2LaTeX (August 1993)   ftp://CTAN/support/rtf2latex

These last two may have particular problems with .rtf output stemming from Win-Word6.

w2latex
ftp://CTAN/support/w2latex

This is C source and must be compiled. It does not yet handle WinWord6 .rtf.

WINW2LTX
ftp://CTAN/support/winw2ltx

Unlike the others in this list, this is a set of macros in two versions for WinWord2 and WinWord6.

Figure 1: LATEX and TEX to .rtf, and back. The dates given are those of the last known revision.

Other techniques   When you have no choice and must work with a word processor, it may be still necessary from time to time to include bits of TEX output in the word processor. This may be the only way to include an equation or table into an office report. One way to do this when working with PostScript is to create mini-TEX documents, one for each bit of text. It is easy to process each of them as usual and use *dvips* to create encapsulated PostScript files that may then be included in the word processing file, perhaps as a graphic or other special case (the details will vary from word processor to word processor). Be warned, though—this may dramatically increase the size of the resultant word-processor document file.

And don't neglect the low-tech solution. It's always possible to retype a WordPerfect document in TEX or even vice versa.

5.2   Spreadsheets

The cellular, repetitive calculations of a spreadsheet are a natural for the computer, but workers err in spending any time at all trying to coerce the spreadsheet program to properly format this material—this is a natural task for LATEX or TEX.

We note two things. First, every spreadsheet can save a workspace as an ASCII file, and every robust program provides several options for doing so. At the very least, it should be possible to save the file as a comma-separated variable format, in which each of the values of a cell is separated from its neighbors with a comma. (If a data field already contains a comma, it is surrounded with double quotes.) Really lucky users will find that they can specify the character for separating neighboring values.

The second observation—that we can use any character as a tab character in tables, not just the ampersand &—renders this previous fact important, because we can make the comma perform tabbing in a document, and then set a spreadsheet as an elaborate table in TEX.

Here's a small and illustrative example. The following

```
Tokyo,27540,1.1,30058.91,
Mexico City,21615,3.4,28243.57,
Sao Paulo,19373,3.5,25510.54,
Seoul,17334,3.2,22301.62,
"New York, NY",14628,0,14628,
```

was produced by the Excel spreadsheet program. What we see here was saved as comma-separated variable format. The original spreadsheet contained four cells per row, corresponding to a city, its 1992 population in thousands, its rate of growth (percent), and its estimated population for the year 2000, again in thousands. (The information is from the 1996 *Information Please* almanac, which regards a city as that contiguous region containing population densities greater than 5000 persons per square mile. Political boundaries are irrelevant in this analysis.) Because the name of New York City was entered with a comma, Excel has prudently quoted the string.

At this point, some readers will use an editor, Perl, or awk for rudimentary data processing. I used my editor to replace the final commas with \cr or \\ (depending on whether I am using plain TEX or LATEX) and then add a simple prelude template to typeset the table. The statements

```
\let\savedcomma=,
\catcode'\,=4
\catcode'\"=\active \def"#1,#2"{#1\savedcomma #2}
```

belong in either type of document. The first \catcode change makes a comma act like a tab character. Then, the next \catcode makes the quotes active (that is, it is a single-character command) and we define it, under the limiting assumption that no cell has more than one comma, so that a quoted string typesets the way we expect.

Thereafter, we simply tack the material fore and aft to make a recognizable table out of it. In LATEX, I type

```
\begin{tabular}{lrrr}
Tokyo,27540,1.1,30058.91\\
Mexico City,21615,3.4,28243.57\\
Sao Paulo,19373,3.5,25510.54\\
Seoul,17334,3.2,22301.62\\
"New York, NY",14628,0,14628\\
\end{tabular}
```

to get a simple table. With the conventions of plain TEX (which work even in a LATEX document), I can type

```
\newskip\ssskip \ssskip=1.5pc plus 1pc minus.5pc
  % spreadsheet skip
$$\vbox{\tabskip=\ssskip
\halign to\textwidth{
  \bf #\hfil&    % col 1
  \hfil#\hfil&   % col 2
  \hfil\it#\thinspace\%\hfil& % col 3
  #\hfil\cr      % col 4 and end of template
  \sc\quad city\hfil&
   \omit\hfil\sc1996 pop.&\omit\hfil\sc growth\hfil&
   \omit\hidewidth\hfil\sc 2000 pop. (est.)\hidewidth\cr
  &\omit\hfil\sc(1000s)\hfil&\omit\hfil\sc rate\hfil&
   \omit\hfil\hidewidth\sc(1000s)\hfil\hidewidth\cr
\noalign{\smallskip}
  Tokyo,27540,1.1,30058.91\cr
  Mexico City,21615,3.4,28243.57\cr
  Sao Paulo,19373,3.5,25510.54\cr
  Seoul,17334,3.2,22301.62\cr
  "New York, NY",14628,0,14628\cr
}}$$
```

to typeset the table

CITY	1996 POP. (1000S)	GROWTH RATE	2000 POP. (EST.) (1000S)
Tokyo	27540	1.1 %	30058.91
Mexico City	21615	3.4 %	28243.57
Sao Paulo	19373	3.5 %	25510.54
Seoul	17334	3.2 %	22301.62
New York, NY	14628	0 %	14628

quite attractively (and far nicer than any spreadsheet could have done by itself).

Spreadsheets are often wide—too wide to fit on a sheet. Adjustments to the alignment template can help select and typeset portions of the data. For example, if we include with other definitions

```
\def\zgobble#1{\tabskip0pt}
```

to zero out the tabskip glue (the rubber length found between columns of a table) and then gobble its argument, then we can typeset the first and third columns only of the foregoing table as follows. After typing

```
$$\vbox{\tabskip=\ssskip
\halign{
  \tabskip\ssskip\bf #\hfil&    % col 1
  \zgobble{#}&                  % col 2
  \tabskip\ssskip\hfil\it#\thinspace\%\hfil& % col 3
  \zgobble{#}\cr                % col 4; end of template
  \sc\quad city\hfil&&\omit\hfil\sc growth\hfil&\cr
\noalign{\smallskip}
⟨the spreadsheet data as above⟩
}}$$
```

the table collapses into the following form.

CITY	GROWTH
Tokyo	*1.1%*
Mexico City	*3.4%*
Sao Paulo	*3.5%*
Seoul	*3.2%*
New York, NY	*0%*

5.3   Hypertext

It's common for a statement in a document to refer either to another part of the same document or to another document entirely. Here are some common examples.

- An entry in an index tells us that mention of the composer Mozart appears on page 409. (Entries in tables of contents, lists of figures, and their ilk are similar references.)

- An author reminds us that equation 12 follows from equations 10 and 11 above.

- The same author reminds us that the results in the current report build upon those presented in an earlier paper. The proper bibliographic reference to the early paper is provided.

It's a nuisance to thumb one's way to distant spots in one document or to another document entirely. *Hypertext* presents a better way—let computers do the work. For documents properly organized, it's a matter of simply clicking on an entry or citation and having the image scroll to the referred location, or even to another document. And the remote document need not be a document at all—it can be a graphic image, a recording, or even a fragment of film.

There are currently three main contexts for hypertext.

- Users of the World Wide Web experience this firsthand all the time. Web documents are deliberately formatted to allow effortless wandering down strands of related topics in a, well, web-like manner.

- The family of programs denoted by the umbrella name *Acrobat* (by Adobe) produces documents with hypertext links.

- Special TEX archives directly provide hypertext facilities for their documents, including special software tools.

Even though hypertext is best viewed onscreen, and LATEX and TEX exist for the production of printed output, the usual advantages accompany the LATEX source for hypertext documents. The source files are freely interchangeable with distant colleagues, and it's easy to make changes to this source. With LATEX or TEX as the markup, it's easy to generate a printed approximation to the hypertext original.

Everything about hypertext is in a state of flux since everything about it is still so new. Standards are being upgraded, and tools are still in the process of development. The discussion that follows attempts to survey the hypertext as of mid-1996. Special TEX publications exploring this area include the *TUGboat* (vol. 16(2)), June, 1995, *Baskerville* (vol. 5(2)), March 1995, and *Cahiers Gutenberg* (no. 19), January 1995.

5.3.1 Hypertext on the Web

The *lingua franca* of the World Wide Web is *hypertext markup language,* commonly known as HTML, a special instance of SGML. Documents created with HTML are rendered onscreen with a Web browser, one of the few readily available examples of a document compiler for an SGML system. See Flynn (1995) for more about HTML. Nelson Beebe maintains a complete list of titles of books on HTML and on the Perl language in the BIBTEX database files sgml.bib and unix.bib at

    ftp://ftp.math.utah.edu/pub/tex/bib

Perl is quite useful for these conversion activities and other data processing activities.

When preparing LATEX documents for conversion to HTML, it is currently necessary to restrict oneself to a subset of LATEX. In particular, tables and equations cannot be easily translated into HTML. It is a common strategy to embed bitmap images of a compiled equation or table into the HTML document, but this swells the size of the document, sometimes unmanageably so, and makes for poor viewing unless the bitmap resolution exactly matches that of the viewing device.

12x	Written in C, it is restricted to a subset of LATEX.
Hyperlatex	A package in GNU Emacs lisp; see Schwarzkopf (1995).
tex2RTF	Converts to other formats than .rtf, one of which is HTML.
texihtml	This Perl script translates texinfo source into HTML format. The texinfo system is a structured macro package, analogous to LATEX but more restricted, that is used for all documentation on the GNU project.
texi2html	Derives HTML versions of documentation from Texinfo documents.
LaTeX2HTML	A Perl-based system; see the text for further information.
LATEX-to-HTML	A conversion procedure by Xavier Leroy based on the Caml language.

Figure 2: Tools for converting from LATEX into HTML.

Figure 2 on the following page summarizes the tools for conversion from LATEX or TEX into HTML; figure 3 on page 125 provides their Internet locations. Of these tools, the most robust appears to be LaTeX2HTML, which supports its own mailing list (to subscribe, send a message to

    latex2html-request@mcs.anl.gov

with the message subscribe). A gigantic Perl script, it makes it feasible to use familiar text-editing concepts, used to create a standard LATEX document, to create a complex hypermedia document. Some care is needed when using this tool.

Currently, LaTeX2HTML exhibits a strong Unix bias, in the sense that directory separators are '/' and file names are long. It should be straightforward to adapt this material to other operating systems. In addition to the on-line material cited in figure 2, the interested reader is well advised to seek out the detailed tutorial by Goossens and Saarela (1995). Both Flynn (1995) and Goossens and Saarela (1995) provide information on the reverse commute, converting an HTML document to TEX or LATEX.

5.3.2 Acrobat

Adobe's *Acrobat* programs aim at a TEX-like goal: to render all documents in a common format so that they can be previewed or rendered by any computer. It achieves this by ingesting a document and distilling it to a common denominator, the so-called *portable document format* (sort of a slimmed-down PostScript); files in this format have the extension .pdf. One impor-

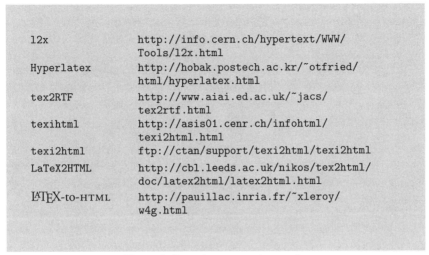

l2x	http://info.cern.ch/hypertext/WWW/Tools/l2x.html
Hyperlatex	http://hobak.postech.ac.kr/~otfried/html/hyperlatex.html
tex2RTF	http://www.aiai.ed.ac.uk/~jacs/tex2rtf.html
texihtml	http://asis01.cenr.ch/infohtml/texi2html.html
texi2html	ftp://ctan/support/texi2html/texi2html
LaTeX2HTML	http://cbl.leeds.ac.uk/nikos/tex2html/doc/latex2html/latex2html.html
LATEX-to-HTML	http://pauillac.inria.fr/~xleroy/w4g.html

Figure 3: Locating conversion tools.

tant by-product is the ability to preview PostScript files onscreen (see also chapter 9). A second is added value, in that Acrobat allows the addition of hypertext links plus other aspects that the Acrobat reader is able to respond to.

To anyone steeped in the TEX gestalt (freely available software of the highest caliber for every computer platform), Acrobat is frustrating. Not only is the program proprietary and costly, but it is not available for every platform. The distiller is slow; it can take close to a minute to distill a single page on a fast desktop computer (admittedly a complex page, but still!). Fortunately, the entire .pdf standard is public [Bientz and Cohn (1993)] and Acrobat readers are free. Acrobat and .pdf seem to be emerging as a standard (and distilled documents can contain valid URLs that can be passed to a Web browser). Recent versions (3.51 or greater) of GhostScript, the GNU PostScript clone, read .pdf files and several other free non-Adobe .pdf readers have become available. As of this writing, there seems not to be any public distiller-like utility, but such a facility will soon be available from within GhostScript (version 4.x). Moreover, the accompanying *Ghostview* utility will support the previewing of .pdf files thereafter.

It's easy to use Acrobat with TEX. We would simply create a .ps file for our document (with a program like *dvips*), and then run this file through the Distiller, one of the component programs of Acrobat or through recent versions of GhostScript. Interested readers will want to keep their eyes focused on two additional projects. Lesenko (1996) and colleagues are creating a special tool dvipdf to directly convert TEX output into the .pdf format. Sojka, Thanh, and Zlatuška (1996) are writing a new program, called tex2pdf, which will read standard TEX (or LATEX) input files and directly render .pdf output.

`hyperbasics.tex`	Some basic set of macros.
`lanlmac.tex`	A plain TEX package.
`hyperlatex.tex`	A variety of styles, but only for the old LATEX2.09.
`hyperref.dtx`	The package by Rahtz and Haralambous for LATEX2_ε.
`hyper.dtx`	Similar to `hyperlatex` but for LATEX2_ε.

Figure 4: All these hypertext packages are available either from `ftp://xxx.lanl.gov/pub/hypertex/` via `ftp` or from the Web at the site `http://xxx.lanl.gov/hypertex/`.

LATEX authors are already accustomed to linking two points in a document by means of the `\label` and `\ref` or `\pageref` commands. Paper doesn't support hyperlinking, but if we revise our macros to recognize these links, and enhance some of the TEX postprocessing tools, it may be possible to create a hyperTEXt document by simply recompiling the document. If a hypertext version of *dvips* is used, `dvihps`, then the resultant `.ps` file may be passed to the Acrobat Distiller for final processing and subsequent hyperviewing via the Acrobat Reader. Haralambous and Rahtz (1995) present a very useful discussion of their `hyperref` package for LATEX2_ε. Although there are other hypertext macro packages, `hyperref` is particularly useful because of the special processing it supports, so the final `.pdf` file exploits the Acrobat Reader to the hilt. For example, running a new auxiliary `.rep` file through a special utility lets Acrobat place a thumbnail table of contents onscreen, each of whose entries is "hot," so it's easy to jump back and forth from section to section. However, it's worth emphasizing that if you include `hyperref` among the LATEX packages in a document (making sure it is the *last* such package listed in the `\usepackage` command), then you otherwise prepare the document in the usual way—`hyperref` silently adds the hypertext links in the background. This observation holds true for all other hypertext packages as well.

The `hyperref` package and all supporting tools are at CTAN. Macros are stored in `macros/latex/contrib/supported/hyperref`, while `dvihps` appears in `dviware/dvihps`. Figure 4 lists other hypertext macro packages.

Additional advice and help on converting existing TEX documents (that may have been compiled using device-dependent bitmap fonts) to `.pdf` files is on hand in several places on the World Wide Web. The documents "TEX and PDF: Solving Font Problems" (at `http://emrg.com/texpdf.html`) and "Creating Quality Adobe PDF Files form TEX with *dvips*" by Kendall Whitehouse, at

```
http://www.adobe.com/supportservice/SOLUTIONS/2d7a.htm
```

address special font issues, while Berthold Horn's "Acrobat PDF from TEX," at `http://www.YandY.com/pdf_from.pdf` is more global in scope.

5.3.3 Hypertext archives

The story of the Los Alamos e-print archives [Doyle (1995)] is fascinating. Created in 1991 by Paul Ginsparg, they were intended to act as a convenient repository for papers in high-energy physics. They now form a collection of 25 archives in narrow specializations in physics, mathematics, economics, computation, and linguistics, containing more than 25,000 papers. Over 90% are submitted as TEX source, with the remainder comprising Post-Script files; and the majority of these were created by passing the results of TEX through *dvips*.

An auto-TEXing script now processes all submissions automatically. Curiously, the TEX-ability of a submission seems to correlate well with the scientific quality of the work.

In 1993, provisions were made to provide hypertext functionality to the archives. This was done by developing hypertext versions of macro packages (`lanlmac` was the first) and then encouraging the use of software tools capable of supporting hypertext. Let us note once again that once the hypertext macro package is chosen by an author, nothing special in the way of TEX markup need be done—all hypertext linkages are prepared silently when the document is processed by TEX and `dvihps`. Of course, the hyper-aware author may well choose to structure a document to take advantage of hypertext opportunities, but that is a matter of personal choice and experience.

One early tool was `dvihps`, modified by Mark Doyle, which could produce hyper-PostScript, itself suitable for input into Acrobat. Members of the team soon realized that hyper-PostScript is an end in itself, and several tools to work with hyper-PostScript and hyper-`.dvi` have appeared. These are summarized in figure 5 on the following page and are all available via `ftp` access from

```
xxx.lanl.gov/pub/hypertex/
```

Anyone can download any item from the archive and either distill it and hyperview it via Acrobat or with the hyperpreviewers given in figure 5 on the next page. Acrobat implementations exist for DOS, Windows, the Macintosh operating system, and a few flavors of Unix. These platforms, together with those for the hyperpreviewers, are sufficiently rich so that workers on virtually any computer platform will have access to hyperTEXt.

5.4 TEX in science

TEX input files are created according to rules that are easy for an author to follow but whose creation follows strict rules. It should be possible for

	Hyper Previewers
xhdvi	Extension of xdvi for X-Windows (Unix)
HyperTEXview	Extension of Rokicki's TEXview for NeXTStep (the NeXtStep operating system)
DirectTEX	Full Macintosh implementation.
	Conversion to Hyper-PostScript
dvihps	Extension of *dvips*; output is distillable by Acrobat
ghostview	Hacked version of Ghostview to support hyper-PostScript

Figure 5: Tools for working with hyper-dvi and hyper-PostScript.

other applications to generate or read TEX source files, and we are seeing this increasingly often.

One program where this is handled in a useful way is the *Mathematica* system for doing mathematics [Wolfram (1996)]. This program consists of a kernel that can be compiled on different computers, coupled to a front-end interface, which makes the most of a particular operating system. The *Mathematica* language provides a wide variety of commands and syntax rules for evaluating mathematical expressions. Furthermore, commands can be blocked together to form new commands, functions, and procedures.

One of *Mathematica*'s commands is TeXForm, to convert an expression to TEX syntax. For example, part of a *Mathematica* session could consist of the following exchange.

In[23] := **(x + y)^2 / Sqrt[x y]**

Out[23] := $\dfrac{(x+y)^2}{\sqrt{xy}}$

The expression on the top is the 23rd input expression or instruction that was typed in the current *Mathematica* session. The output line rewrites this in an on-screen approximation to standard notation. *Mathematica* recognizes the % character as a shorthand representation for the immediately preceding output expression, so if we type

In[24] := **TeXForm[%]**

we observe

Out[24]//TeXForm={{{{\left(x + y \right)}^2}}\over
{{\sqrt{x\,y}}}}

which typesets properly as

$$\frac{\left(x + y \right)^2}{\sqrt{x\,y}}$$

Mathematica front ends frequently provide the means for translating sessions integrating both text and mathematics into a single entity. Several workers, such as Smith (1993), have shown how to do this using Unix-shell conventions; fortunately, his technique can be easily extended to non-Unix systems. The `bilo` system by Barnett and Perry (1994) describes a different system of conventions for accomplishing similar goals. In this system, a *Mathematica* script containing some special markup, in addition to standard *Mathematica* expressions, automatically generates a document that can be run through TEX. Their software is available from

```
mondrian.princeton.edu/pub/bilo
```

for anonymous `ftp` downloading.

CHAPTER 6

INSTALLING AND SELECTING FONTS

6.1 Preliminaries

We can use any digital fonts with LaTeX or TeX. Most of these fonts were not designed with TeX in mind, so they need some preparation.

- *Font installation* refers to the process by which we reorganize the characters in the font and perform additional bookkeeping to make it usable by TeX.

- *Font selection* refers to the instructions we apply in a TeX document to select a certain font for typesetting.

Font installation leads to considerations of *virtual fonts*, the subject of the next few chapters. This chapter concerns itself with font selection—that is, making a new font family known to TeX in such a way that \it or \bf or \large will do the right thing with respect to the new fonts.

6.1.1 How should font selection work?

The TeXbook pioneered the use of *nicknames* like \it and \bf to select fonts. The original LaTeX adapted these, and set up a few more, such as \sf and \sc.

The contemporary LaTeX or TeX author has a right to expect font nicknames to observe context sensitivity. That is, if we typed

```
ham {\it and\/} eggs
```

we get

ham *and* eggs

in the body of the document, but we might see

> ham *and* eggs

in a footnote,

> ham *and* eggs

in a computer program, and even

> ham *and* eggs

in a heading or subheading. The font selection schemes of this chapter respect context sensitivity.

6.1.2 Caveat: Why switch fonts explicitly?

There should always be a logical reason for switching fonts—the structure of the document should require the new font to help make that structure apparent. If so, then a macro call should perform the font switching for us. For example, LaTeX's \section macro automatically switches to a larger and bolder typeface to emphasize the beginning of the section; there is no need for us to refer to this new font separately. Font switching is useful mainly to people writing books like this one, or to people writing macros.

6.1.3 Plan of this chapter

It's impossible to study font selection without some reference to the digital fonts themselves. Before getting started with font selection, we need to consider ways to conveniently name the files containing a font's digital description. We also need to consider basic font installation techniques, otherwise it won't be possible to exercise the font selection.

6.2 Naming digital fonts

Commercial fonts typically come as a set of several files. The .pfb file (less frequently, a .pfa file or a file with no extension whatever) contains the actual outline descriptions for the glyphs in each font, and these files should be collected in a special area on the computer. The metric information for the font resides in an associated .afm file. Other files, with extensions .inf (information) and .pfm, are irrelevent to LaTeX and TeX.

Fonts already have names given them by their designers. The problem lies in associating this name with the font files. In a perfect world, the file names would be identical to the font name, and this is possible on certain operating systems. The ubiquitous PC-DOS, though, restricts the initial part of file names to eight characters, and for that reason, we must know how to name font files in ways that are acceptable to restrictive systems.

Adobe Fonts

pac	Adobe Caslon	pad	Adobe Garamond
phv	Helvetica	plc	Lucida
pmn	Minion	ppl	Palatino
ptm	Times	psy	Symbol

Monotype Fonts

mbv	Baskerville	mur	Centaur
mdn	Dante	mgs	Gill Sans
mjn	Janson	mmo	Modern
mnt	Times New Roman	mtw	Twentieth Century

Fonts from Miscellaneous Foundries

bb7	Bernhard Modern (Bitstream)
bch	Chianti (Bitstream)
zgl	Galliard (Carter & Cone)
hlb	Lucida Bright (Bigelow & Holmes)

Figure 1: Some font families and their abbreviations.

6.2.1 One naming scheme

The PC-DOS file-naming convention allows only eight characters in a file's base name. Karl Berry has suggested a system—admittedly imperfect, but perhaps the best one can do—for mapping a lengthy font name into a file name that's eight or fewer characters long. If the font files are renamed accordingly, then we can deduce the nature of the font by examining its file name. A full description of this naming scheme can be found at the archive site ftp.cs.umb.edu or in the documentation for *dvips*. This scheme does *not* apply to the original Computer Modern TEX fonts, which retain their original names.

This scheme assumes that only eight characters or fewer are available for naming the font file, and it allocates individual characters in the new name to various aspects of the name. Schematically, these eight characters look like

FNNW[S][V]7V

where F designates a digital type foundry, NN is an abbreviation for the font's name, W is the font's weight, S is its shape, one or more V's will indicate the variant nature of this font (if any), and 7 is a digit to indicate the encoding of the font. Bracketed items are optional. We refer to the initial three characters (FNN in the above notation) as the *font family*.

Some additional comments on this shorthand notation is in order. The most common foundry abbreviations are p for Adobe (think PostScript), b for BitStream, and m Monotype. A font flouting this scheme will begin with a z.

r   regular
s   semibold
b   bold
x   extra bold

Figure 2: Some common font weights.

The next two letters are reserved for the typeface name. The hundreds and hundreds of available faces guarantees that many of these designations will be cryptic, even for common typefaces—Adobe Garamond is ad. Figure 1 on the facing page lists some font families and their abbreviations.

The *weight of a font* refers to characteristics like "bold" or "light," aspects which naturally seem to be a visual counterpart of heaviness. Figure 2 lists some common weight attributes.

The *shape of a font* refers not to individual idiosyncrasies, but rather to shape attributes that are perceptible across font families, such as being upright or italic. Figure 3 lists some common font shapes. Note that we omit the shape character in case the font is upright.

When a font is dedicated to some special purpose, we call it a *font variant*. Fonts containing special swash forms of an uppercase alphabet, or special ligatures, or a display form of the font are examples of font variants; perhaps the font is dedicated to swash forms of uppercase ($\mathcal{A}$ $\mathcal{B}$ $\mathcal{C}$). Variant fonts that contain additional double-f ligatures and small caps fonts are called *expert fonts*. Recently, the Bitstream foundry has begun offering the selection of characters found in an expert font in two separate fonts—a distinct small caps font and an extensible math symbols font. Figure 4 on the next page lists some font variants.

Up to two variant indicators can be present in a file name, but it is convenient to combine one variant indicator with the encoding digit. The original TeX fonts contained 128 characters, and are called 7-bit encodings, because 128 is the largest number that 7 bits can access. If we allow ourselves one additional bit, then an 8-bit encoding can contain 256 characters. Consequently, we use 7 and 8 to identify fonts containing 128 or 256 characters. The *encoding* of a font refers to the order and selection of the glyphs in the font.

c   small caps   i   italic   o   oblique (slanted)

Figure 3: Some common shapes of fonts.

9	oldstyle digits	x	expert
w	swash	l	alternate
e	extension	i	titling
d	display	s	small caps only
p	ornament		

Figure 4: Some common font variants.

The following table lists several encoding-variant pairs.

7t	original TEX encoding
8t	Cork 256-char encoding
8a	Adobe standard encoding
8x	expert font encoding
8l	Adobe encoded alternate font
8e	Adobe encoded extension font

The Cork encoding is a scheme (decided upon at the city of Cork in 1990) for assigning all allowable 256 positions in a TEX font to additional characters used in European languages.

As an example, consider the Adobe Garamond fonts, the body fonts for this book. The file names on the distribution disks were gdrg____.afm, gdrg____.pfb and so on, and we need to rename them (they follow the Adobe standard encoding) as follows:

padr8a	AGaramond-Regular
padri8a	AGaramond-Italic
pads8a	AGaramond-Semibold
padsi8a	AGaramond-SemiboldItalic
padb8a	AGaramond-Bold
padbi8a	AGaramond-BoldItalic

so we have files padr8a.pfb and padr8a.afm, and so on. The Adobe Garamond family is particularly rich in special fonts. Here are just a few of them with appropriate new names.

padr8x	AGaramondExp-Regular (regular expert)
padri8x	AGaramondExp-Italic (italic expert)
padr8l	AGaramondAlt-Regular (alternate font)
padr8i	AGaramond-Titling (titling capitals)

6.2.2 Naming scalable math fonts

TEX will need the *font* names for each of the four math families. As we will see in later chapters, we'll typically be creating viable math fonts by marrying third-party math fonts to a variety of text fonts using the soon-to-be-discussed mechanism of virtual fonts. It's convenient to adhere to some new naming conventions to keep all the fonts straight.

1. All new math fonts have names beginning with 'z' since they don't follow a canonical naming scheme.

2. All math font names begin with a root, consisting of a leading z, followed by two characters indicating the math font software, followed finally by the three character family name identifying the text fonts used. If mt stands for MathTime fonts and pad suggests the Adobe Garamond fonts, then the root for math fonts created out of these component fonts would be zmtpad.

3. All math font names consist of the root followed by zero or one math variant identifiers:

    (a) No identifier indicates the *math Roman font.*

    (b) A trailing m is for the *math italic font.*

    (c) A trailing y indicates a *math symbol font.*

    (d) A final v is a *math extension font.*

   For example, a collection of MathTime-Garamond fonts, family zmt-pad, will have names zmtpad, zmtpadm, zmtpady, and zmtpadv according to this convention.

Sizing math fonts   Although a single dimension is enough to fix the size of text fonts, math fonts need to come in three sizes—for normal work, for script size (subscript x_i or superscript $g^{\alpha\beta}$), and for second-order script size (when scripts themselves have scripts, as in e^{-2x^2}). Given the optically scaled fonts of Computer Modern, at the normal 10-pt size, these three dimensions are 10 pt, 7 pt, and 5 pt; in case the first- and second-order scripts are geometrically scaled from the main font, values of 10 pt, 7.4 pt, and 6 pt seem to work better. The term *optical scaling* refers to types that are subtly redesigned at different sizes and are therefore not geometrically similar to each other at these different sizes.

6.2.3 Aliases and alias files

Scalable outline fonts may have long, descriptive names:

```
MTwentiethCentury-UltraBoldCondensed.
```

Although most operating systems will allow the font files to bear the same names as the font, at least one (MS-DOS and its siblings) does not. Even on systems that allow lengthy file names, it may be a good idea to use short names for the font files so that system commands for moving, copying, and so on are easy to type. In order to use the font description to render a page, the PostScript printer needs to be fed the contents of this file. Sometimes the document file will incorporate the font file, sometimes programs like *dvips download* it to the printer automatically, and sometimes an author performs the downloading separately. In any event, once the font description reaches the printer, the printer has no way of knowing the name of the computer file containing this description. It knows only the font name that has been embedded inside the font file. LaTeX and TeX font-selection schemes refer only to the font files themselves. Therefore, we are going to need some way to make a correspondence between, say, the font file padr8a and the font AGaramond-Regular. It is the purpose of a *map file* or *alias file* to make these correspondences explicit.

The alias file for *dvips* is called psfonts.map. Including a line like

```
padr8a    AGaramond-Regular </psfonts/padr8a.pfb
```

in this file not only makes explicit the equivalence between a font and its file, but will cause *dvips* to download the font file padr8a.pfb from the directory /psfonts. (Unix syntax is shown here.) One part of any installation process must ensure that the proper alias information becomes part of psfonts.map.

Downloading   PostScript printers need the description of all characters in a font before it can draw characters from this font on a page. The .pfa and .pfb font files on your computer contain this information. The act of transferring this information from the computer to the printer is *downloading*.

Some postprocessors will do the downloading providing certain information appears in the map file indicating the location of the font file; *dvips* is one such. The fonts are downloaded over and over again as they are reused in document after document. Printing slows down this way; downloading is a time-consuming process.

Some authors prefer to download all special fonts when they turn the printer on. Many utilities exist to do this, such as pcsend and pcdown on DOS. Such a strategy requires careful planning to make sure no fonts are omitted, but printing goes much faster.

Finally, some fonts need no downloading. Most PostScript printers have font information *resident* in the printer for about three dozen fonts, such as Times Roman, Helvetica, and others. It's quickest to print with these fonts, but they are used so often as to have become typographic clichés.

6.3   Font installation

We install a new font so LaTeX or TeX can easily use it. Bitmap fonts created by METAFONT are the easiest fonts to install (see subsection 6.3.2 on page 139), and no one will be surprised to learn that fonts created for the non-TeX world need some massaging to make them TeX-acceptable.

6.3.1 Where do font files live on your computer?

Early implementations of TEX made a simple assumption about files they needed—all like files were located in a single place (or at most a small number of places). In such *traditional systems*, all .tfm files could be found in a single directory named something like /usr/local/lib/tex/fonts/tfm or \tex\fonts\tfm. Format files and virtual fonts had their own place, and when authors began demanding outline fonts, the .afm and .pfb files were stored in their own locations. Provision was often made for several areas for input files, but this fixed number was generally agreed on at the time of installation and not changed thereafter.

TEX directory structure   On multiuser and networked systems, it was becoming painfully clear to the maintainers of these systems that this simple system fell far short of perfection. On occasion, people were submitting macro files (for example) that had the same name as a pre-existing file, but a completely different function. Moreover, when packages of related files (say a virtual font and the associated font metrics for it and its component raw fonts or a macro package comprising several files) needed updating or deletion, it is difficult to know which files to revise or remove.

For that reason, the TEX community has begun promulgating a scheme whereby each grouping of files occupies its own directory within the directory tree in which all TEX files reside. It is up to the implementation of TEX to incorporate the ability to search this highly ramified directory tree. The *TEX Directory Structure* (TDS) standard supports this initiative. All the executables on the *TEX Live* CD-ROM support TDS (see chapter 2).

A TDS tree has a root that is generically known as texmf. On a particular system, this root may actually be the root of the file system, the directory /usr/local, \tex, or something similar. Below the texmf root, TDS reserves a series of names for top level names identifying the components of a complete TEX system. For example, tex includes all TEX files, including macros and fonts contains all font-related files. Further directory branches below the top level makes it possible to unambiguously store and retrieve TEX files of any stripe. An excellent source for further information is the *TEX Live* CD-ROM that contains documentation (in the texmf/doc/help area). More important, most of the material on this CD-ROM is organized according to the TDS conventions. The CD-ROM thus becomes a very exemplar of TDS.

It's important to understand how font files appear in this order. Font files need the additional structure

    texmf/fonts/⟨type⟩/⟨supplier⟩/⟨typeface⟩/

where ⟨type⟩ may be any of

- afm for Adobe font-metric files;

- gf for generic font bitmaps;

- pk for packed bitmap files;

- source for METAFONT source files, property list files, and so on;

- tfm for TEX font metrics;

- type1 for Type 1 fonts in any format; and

- vf for virtual fonts.

The level ⟨*supplier*⟩ refers to the digital foundry (adobe, monotype, etc.) or to public (freely redistributable fonts) or ams. Finally, ⟨*typeface*⟩ refers to cm (for Computer Modern), to latex (for those fonts part of the standard LATEX distribution), or to a familiar name for a typeface family (times, agaramon, euler, and so on). The font files for Adobe Garamond might be stored in directories with names like these:

```
texmf/fonts/tfm/adobe/agaramon/
texmf/fonts/vf/adobe/agaramon/
texmf/fonts/afm/adobe/agaramon/
texmf/fonts/type1/adobe/agaramon/
```

and, incidentally, the LATEX style files and font descriptor files would be stored in

```
texmf/tex/latex/vfinst/
```

assuming that the VFINST utility (see subsection 63.5 on page 143) had been used to create this material.

Bitmap fonts produced by METAFONT require a slight expansion of this scheme since bitmaps are specific not only to the type of device (usually specified by the mode used in the METAFONT process) but also to the resolution (given in dots per inch) of the font. This requires two additional directory levels under pk and gf.

```
texmf/fonts/pk/⟨mode⟩/⟨supplier⟩/⟨typeface⟩/dpi⟨nnn⟩/
texmf/fonts/gf/⟨mode⟩/⟨supplier⟩/⟨typeface⟩/dpi⟨nnn⟩/
```

Some of the font files for cmr10 for the Hewlett-Packard LaserJet 4 would therefore appear in the following places on a TDS system.

```
texmf/fonts/pk/ljfour/public/cm/dpi300/
texmf/fonts/tfm/public/cm/
```

Installing Bitmap Fonts

- **The metric file.** Place the .tfm file with the other metric files, probably in a directory like /tex/fonts/tfm or \tex\tfm for traditional systems or a more specific place like /texmf/fonts/ tfm/public/cm/ on a TDS system.

- **The pixel file.**

  ○ In DOS systems, place the pixel file, which has an extension .pk, in a subdirectory whose name reflects that magnification and resolution of the printing device for which the fonts were created. For example, the directory might have a traditional name like \tex\fonts\pk\dpi300 or a TDS name like /texmf/fonts/pk/epson/public/cm/ dpi300.

  ○ In non-DOS systems, the bitmap extension might reflect the resolution and be something like .300pk. Place this file with the other pixel files as appropriate.

6.3.2   Bitmap fonts

New bitmap fonts must come to you in the form of .pk files and associated .tfm files. Installation simply requires placing the .tfm files and the associated .pk packed pixel files in the proper locations. For a TDS system, see page 137.

In a traditional system, place the .tfm file with your other .tfm files. The pixel file may have any of several file extensions. In MS-DOS, it will be .pk, and it must be placed in an appropriate directory whose name provides information about the resolution of the printer and magnification of the font. Such a directory may have a name like \tex\fonts\pk\300; consult the system documentation.

On other operating systems, the font's extension will contain information about the resolution and may be something like .300pk or .400pk.

In case the font is distributed as a METAFONT program file, you will have to run it through METAFONT and perform the associated bookkeeping. Consult the procedure given in chapter 3.

6.3.3   Scalable outline fonts

Figure 5 on page 141 (after a similar figure by Alan Jeffrey) reminds us of the types of files that enter the document process whenever outline fonts are present. The grey rectangle in this figure covers the part under control of the installation process.

The `.pfb` or `.pfa` files are the easy part—postprocessors like *dvips* know how to handle them properly. The interesting part involves the `.afm` file, for from it we must somehow generate a metric file—the `.tfm`—that TEX understands.

Although most scalable fonts are proprietary and require some purchase agreement for their use, many free fonts do exist for downloading. The outline version of Computer Modern fonts on CTAN are in the `fonts/cm` area, and intrigued readers should also check the Web site

```
http://cuiwww.unige.ch/search-form.html
```

for pointers to over 600 available fonts.

The installation process requires several steps. In addition to creating the `.vf` and `.tfm` files themselves, the fonts should be renamed according to the font naming conventions described above, `psfonts.map` must be updated, a font description file needs to describe the new fonts for use by the New Font Selection Scheme (NFSS) of LATEX, and all of these files need to be stored in their appropriate places on the system. There are two ways to carry out this procedure. One way is via the PostScript-specific extension to NFSS called PSNFSS (courtesy of Sebastian Rahtz) which consists of premade metric and style files that are available for retrieval from any CTAN site. The other way is via the VFINST installation utility, written by me. It consists of a shell script or batch file plus two Perl scripts. VFINST automatically performs all of the installation tasks for a font enthusiast and is available from any CTAN archive, the `fonts/utilities/vfinst` area.

6.3.4   An overview of PSNFSS

The designation 'PSNFSS' refers to a set of files—styles, fonts, metrics—by which an author can use NFSS to select common PostScript font families for typesetting. The entire suite of files is due to Sebastian Rahtz, an apparently tireless worker for the TEX community.

Setup is simple. First off, though, an author must make a commitment to the Berry font-naming convention, as PSNFSS follows this convention religiously and rigorously. You will need to rename commercial fonts in accordance with this scheme.

Next, you'll need the metrics for the PostScript fonts. These can be found in the `fonts/metrics` area of CTAN (and on the *TEX Live* CD-ROM also). Other PSNFSS files, including the manual `psfnss2e.tex`, appears in the `macros/latex/packages/psnfss` area. Note that metric files are segregated by digital foundry—adobe, `monotype`, and so on—and if you have expert fonts, you should retrieve the metric font files from the `xadobe` and `xmonotype` areas.

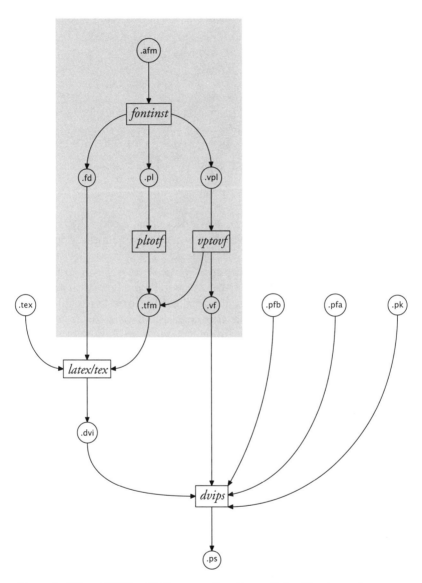

Figure 5: When LATEX or TEX uses outline fonts, all the files shown here may enter the TEX production cycle. The shaded portion of this figure shows the portion of the cycle influenced by the installation process. MetaPost has drawn this figure, which is a slightly modified form of a similar figure by Alan Jeffrey that appears as part of the documentation for his *fontinst* package.

Using PSNFSS

All font files and metric files must be named according to Karl Berry's font-naming scheme.

1. Retrieve all metric files and place in the appropriate places on your system.

2. Make the mapping additions known to the device driver.

3. Use the package file that relates the new fonts to the NFSS.

In the usual way, you'll need to place these files where LaTeX knows to find them. TeX needs the .tfm files, LaTeX need the .fd files, and the driver needs the .vf files. (The driver will also need the outline files, usually with extension .pfb, but with rare exceptions, these will not be in CTAN.)

The driver needs to know that the fonts you'll be referring to correspond to outline files, and so you'll need to make additions to the alias file, or map file, that drivers use to make this correspondence; for *dvips*, this file is psfonts.map. You will find the additions you'll need in files with names like

⟨*font-family*⟩.map

So, for example, pad.map contains the alias information for Adobe Garamond, whose font family is called pad. Add these additions to the map file (or consult the driver documentation to see how to load the supplementary information on the fly). Note also that you might have to make slight alterations to these additions to accord with your system.

A package file describes these fonts so LaTeX's NFSS can make sense of them. Retrieve this file and place in an appropriate area of your own system. Then, after typing

\usepackage{times}

(here times.sty is the package for Adobe Times Roman fonts) usual font commands like \bf, \textit, and so on now refer to the Times fonts.

The overwhelming advantage of PSNFSS is that all font files have been created for you. In many cases, though, PSNFSS will not be appropriate.

• PSNFSS files may not have been provided for your font family.

• You may require font variants that are not part of the PSNFSS collection, such as an italic small caps font. (How does one set the *LaTeX* logo in italics otherwise?)

- Some of the other font variants may not satisfy purists. All oblique fonts in the PSNFSS suite have the same slant as the Computer Modern Roman Slanted font. In fact, an oblique font should match the slant of the italic, and italic fonts have a wide variety of slants.

For any of these reasons, therefore, authors may prefer to "roll their own" fonts, or perhaps use the VFINST installation tools described below.

6.3.5 An overview of **VFINST**

VFINST automatically renames your font files according to the conventions we've discussed previously. For each upright raw font it installs, you get several virtual fonts:

- the upright font;

- a small caps font (mock or real, depending on the presence of true small caps fonts);

- a slanted (oblique) font; and

- an underline font.

For each raw italic font you install, you get:

- the italic font;

- an oblique small caps font (mock or real);

- an unslanted italic font; and

- an underline font.

These fonts are named properly and placed in the proper places. If an italic font is present, the unslanted italic and oblique (slanted) fonts use the proper italic angle of the font.

You also get two test files, one for plain TEX (`testpln.tex`) and one for LATEX (`testltx.tex`), showing how to use the new fonts. You can find VFINST in CTAN/fonts/utilities/vfinst.

Prerequisites for VFINST   This utility relies on other publicly available tools to do its work. Foremost among these is Alan Jeffrey's *fontinst* software, a special TEX file for creating virtual fonts. You can retrieve the latest version of *fontinst* from CTAN in the `fonts/utilities/fontinst/inputs` area.

The other important tool is Perl, a language specially designed to manipulate text and files that has been ported to every computer platform and is freely available. Perl scripts are likely (like TEX source files) to be system-independent. It is not necessary to know anything about the Perl language to use it with VFINST; simply place the Perl executable somewhere on your computer's search path.

Where to get Perl? The major `ftp` archives for your computer platform should contain it. For example, the Simtel archive and its many mirrors hold DOS versions. I got my NextStep version from the archive at `ftp.cs.orst.edu`. Walnut Creek CD-ROM offers an inexpensive CD-ROM that contains source or binary versions of Perl for everything from Amiga to Xenix by way of Macintosh and MS-DOS. (Walnut Creek, 4041 Pike Lane, Suite D, Concord, CA 94520-9909, USA; 1 (800) 786-9907; or-der@cdrom.com; `http://www.cdrom.com`.)

Installation and set up: A detailed look   Please refer to `vfinst.tex`, which is part of the package, for additional explanation.

To install VFINST, create a new directory, possibly something like

```
/usr/local/vfinst
```

or

```
\tex\vfinst
```

Copy all VFINST files into that directory. Also create a working directory below this, with a name like

```
/usr/local/vfinst/work
```

or

```
\tex\vfinst\work
```

There are some things that need setting at the beginning of the shell script (batch file). These *must* be set up properly—VFINST won't work properly otherwise, and there are no default settings for these parameters. VFINST works on both traditional and TDS systems.

A variety of variables needs proper definition; see the documentation `vfinst.tex` for further details. Some of these will contain path names; it is imperative that *none* of these path names end with the path separator symbol (slash or backslash). Another group of parameters—labeled "wizards only"—should already have been set for you.

On certain systems, like Unix, you'll need to make VFINST executable (`chmod +x vfinst`, followed by `rehash`). If your TEX is a multitasking application, such as the excellent TEXView on NextStep, you'll need to make the application quit and restart it to make your new fonts visible to it.

***Running* VFINST**   Once everything has been set up, make sure you are in the `work` directory and just enter

```
../vfinst
```

> ### Using VFINST
>
> The VFINST package is for the simple installation of families of scalable fonts.
>
> 1. Create a special directory for the package and a working directory directly below this.
>
> 2. Place the files in the package (one shell script or batch file plus additional Perl files) into this directory. Adjust the parameters in the script.
>
> 3. Copy all of your fonts—outline files plus .afm files—into the working directory.
>
> 4. Execute VFINST from the working directory.
>
> 5. Follow the further instructions that VFINST issues.

(or maybe ..\vfinst on DOS) to begin the font installation process. As it processes the fonts, it pauses each time a new font family is encountered and prompts you for a *three-character* family name. If you like the suggestion it makes, just press the enter key. But if you want to adhere to Karl Berry's font-naming scheme, you may enter that abbreviation then. But keep this family designation in mind, especially if you're a LATEX user—it's this abbreviation that you'll use in LATEX to switch between families of fonts. Even though you may enter a single three-letter designation, VFINST may create more than one family of fonts, and those designations will consist of four characters. For example, in the presence of all the expert fonts for the Adobe Garamond fonts, with Berry family name pad, VFINST creates two font families, padx, with proper small caps members but mono-height numerals, and pad9, with old style digits. On TDS installations, VFINST may also request a typeface name and a typeface supplier from you.

Occasionally, VFINST queries you more than once for a font-family designation, an artifact reflecting inconsistency on the part of the font provider. For example, the font family may be AGaramond on regular fonts but may be AGar for the expert fonts. In such instances, you must simply enter the identical family designation for each query.

Upon completion, VFINST lets you know what it expects you to do next. It will have created several additional scripts or batch files for you to execute.

6.4   Plain TEX font selection

Plain TEX's "font selection" appears in Knuth (1986a, pp. 350–351) and these pages in *The TEXbook* display the forbidding nature of these declarations, the point of which is to establish nicknames for fonts. Damian Cugley's PDCFSEL font-selection scheme for plain TEX makes it easy to adjust font nicknames according to context. These macros are not as flexible as the NFSS of LATEX, but the entire macro file is less than 3500 bytes in length, which means that it's easy to incorporate the entire file as part of the document. This should work with any extensive macro package in addition to plain TEX, but not LATEX.

The value of PDCFSEL lies in being able to identify *contexts* in which font nicknames take on particular meanings. Thus, \it might select the usual *italics* in the body of a paper, but might select *sans serif italics* in a section heading. The collection of fonts defined for any such context is a *fontset*; we've described two fontsets in the beginning of this paragraph. We define a fontset by setting up templates for PDCFSEL to apply when it creates font nicknames. Each template explains to PDCFSEL how to load the font at various sizes.

6.4.1   Getting PDCFSEL

You'll need to get two files from the macros/plain/contrib/pdcmac area of CTAN; these are pdccode.tex and pdcfsel.dtx. (The extension .dtx refers to Cugley's own system of structured TEX documentation, which is distinct from docstrip despite the use of the same file extension.) Place these two files in a work directory, and issue the command

```
tex '&plain pdcfsel.dtx'
```

The output will be the macro file pdcfsel.tex you need, as well as pdcfsel.dvi, which should be printed and retained as the full documentation for this system.

6.4.2   Using PDCFSEL

First, we need to make a correspondence between various nicknames and the fonts themselves. In pure text (no mathematics), we might define an elaborate text template by

```
\def\bodytemplate{%
  \f{tt}{cmtt}%
  \@\f{rm}{padr7t}\@\f{sc}{padrc7t}\@\f{ob}{padro7t}%
  \@\f{it}{padri7t}\@\f{si}{padric7t}\@\f{ui}{padriu7t}%
  \@\f{bf}{padb7t}\@\f{bc}{padbc7t}\@\f{bo}{padbo7t}%
  \@\f{bi}{padbi7t}\@\f{bsi}{padbic7t}\@\f{bui}{padbiu7t}%
}%
```

which contains a collection of rules for associating fonts with nicknames. Here, the strings rm, sc, ob, and so on will become the nicknames \rm, \sc, and \ob. Note that the nickname references in any template must appear *without* the leading backslash.

Special commands associate a font nickname with the font file. The prefixes to the nicknames, here \@ and \f, tell PDCFSEL how to load fonts to go with these nicknames. The \@ command explains that the associated font can be scaled, so we form a small caps font by scaling padrc7t to whatever size we specify in another part of the font selection.

The typewriter font (that will become \tt) is not scaled—we form the font by appending the size to the given font name, and so no \@ is present at this part of the template. At 10-pt, the \tt font will be cmtt10, and so on. (It will be up to us to make sure we use this template only at sizes *nn* for which cmtt*nn* exists.)

The prefix \f indicates fonts that won't be used in a mathematics setting.

This template defines several new and unfamiliar nicknames. Here, \ob and \bo will be regular and bold oblique (slanted); \si, \bc, and \bsi are italic small caps, bold small caps, and bold italic small caps; and \bi and \bui are bold italic and bold unslanted italic fonts.

We can define as many templates as we wish. In this same document, we might define a simpler template

```
\def\headingtemplate{%
  \f{rm}{cmss}\f{it}{cmssi}%
}
```

to establish a correspondence between \rm and \it and various sans serif fonts, presumably for use in a section heading.

Templates can also set fonts up for use in mathematics. In this next example, we presume the existence of these fonts:

- padr7t, padri7t, padb7t, and padbi7t, the four Adobe Garamond fonts for regular and bold series, in upright and italic shapes (moreover, we assume the presence of the Greek capitals in these fonts as befits true math Roman fonts);

- mtex, the MathTime extension font;

- zmtpadm, a math-italic font comprising some characters from the Adobe Garamond fonts and many from the MathTime math-italic fonts; and

- zmtpady, a math-symbols font employing glyphs from the MathTime symbol font and from the Garamond fonts.

(We'll see later how to construct these fonts.) The MathTime fonts are a set of proprietary math fonts that were designed to be compatible with Times

Roman, but also work well with other text fonts. The template for these fonts should look like this.

```
\def\mathtemplate{%
  \@\m{rm}{padr7t}\@\m{it}{padri7t}%
  \@\f{bf}{padb7t}\@\f{bi}{padbi7t}%
  \@\M{mi}{zmtpadm}\@\M{sy}{zmtpady}%
}
```

All the fonts are scalable, which explains the \@ prefix. The new prefixes \m and \M instruct PDCFSEL to prepare the fonts for mathematics. \M is for fonts that will be used in text, script (sub- or super-), and scriptscript (scripts of scripts) modes; \m is only in text and script modes.

The \fontset command establishes the correspondence between an actual context and the fonts. For example,

```
\fontset{body}\bodytemplate{10}{12pt}{}{}
```

causes PDCFSEL to define a command \bodyfonts to invoke this fontset. That is, \bodyfonts defines an environment in which 10-pt type is set on a 12-pt baseline such that the nicknames suggested in the body template invoke those fonts. (We'll see the point of the two empty arguments shortly.) Similarly, after

```
\fontset{heading}\headingtemplate{10}{12pt}{}{}
```

a command \headingfonts makes it possible to use \rm and \it to typeset 12-pt sans serif fonts on a 14-pt baseline. We use these commands with grouping in the usual way. That is, after typing

```
\input pdcfsel
\def\bodytemplate{...}
\def\headingtemplate{...}
\fontset{body}\bodytemplate{10}{12pt}{}{}
\fontset{heading}\headingtemplate{12}{14pt}{}{}
\bodyfonts

\centerline{\headingfonts Short {\it and\/} Sweet}

{\it This\/}  is a test...
```

we get

Short *and* Sweet

This is a test …

Mathematics requires only a bit more setup. One of \fontset's jobs is to establish nicknames set up by a template. In math, there are many fonts used that don't require any nicknames whatever—they are selected and chosen by the typesetting engine. PDCFSEL provides an \xfontset command for these instances. In the process of setting up math fonts that will use the math template given above, we write

```
\xfontset{scriptscript}\mathtemplate{6}
\xfontset{script}\mathtemplate{7.4}
```

which use the template to set up script and scriptscript fonts at sizes of 7.4 and 6 points. We follow these with

```
\fontset{body}\mathtemplate{10}{12pt}%
  {script}{scriptscript}
```

to complete the font setup and to provide the \bodyfonts command, which invokes the math template nicknames and the proper math fonts. Here, the final two arguments of \fontset refer to the script and scriptscript contexts that should already have been set up. Incidentally, it's not necessary to stick to these names. It would have been quite all right to type

```
\xfontset{tiny}\mathtemplate{6}
\xfontset{small}\mathtemplate{7.4}
\fontset{body}\mathtemplate{10}{12pt}{small}{tiny}
```

instead.

In summary, then, we prepare for mathematics in a document by beginning a document like this. Note the explicit declarations necessary to invoke the MathTime extension font.

```
\input pdcfsel

\font\tenex = mtex at 10pt % extension font
\textfont3=\tenex \scriptfont3=\tenex
  \scriptscriptfont3=\tenex

\def\mathtemplate{%
  \@\m{rm}{padr7t}\@\m{it}{padri7t}%
  \@\f{bf}{pads7t}\@\f{bi}{padsi7t}%
  \@\M{mi}{zmtpadm}\@\M{sy}{zmtpady}%
}

\xfontset{scriptscript}\mathtemplate{6}
\xfontset{script}\mathtemplate{7.4}
\fontset{body}%
  \mathtemplate{10}{12pt}{script}{scriptscript}

\bodyfonts
```

PDCFSEL, a Font Selection Scheme for Plain TEX

We can use this macro file to organize font usage around different contexts or fontsets. For use with scalable fonts, we need to define a template to make a correspondence between font nicknames and the font files themselves.

To use PDCFSEL for fonts in a nonmathematical setting, follow the example on page 148.

For math fonts, use the examples on the preceding page as a guide.

⟨ *Text of the paper* ⟩

The MathInst and *MathKit* software described in chapter 10 automatically incorporates this material in a style file for users of plain TEX.

6.5 The New Font Selection Scheme

Font selection in the older version of LATEX was like that of plain TEX. The current LATEX incorporates the New Font Selection Scheme (NFSS) of Frank Mittelbach and Rainer Schöpf, and the convenience this scheme provides is worth the effort to switch to the new LATEX. NFSS offers font selection based on logical design and context. Within NFSS, fonts are categorized by five attributes:

- *encoding,*
- *family,*
- *series,*
- *shape,* and
- *size.*

We select fonts by specifying their attributes. Of course, at some point someone has to tell LATEX which particular font belongs to a given 5-tuple of encoding, font family, series, shape, and size. That's an easy job, made even easier since software like *fontinst* produces this information automatically. The following discussion is intended to summarize the more relevant aspects of NFSS. For greater detail, see Goossens, Mittelbach, and Samarin (1994).

6.5.1 Font attributes

Some remarks about the font attributes are in order.

Encoding   The different glyphs (characters) of a font appear in a certain order. The letter 'A' comes before 'B', which precedes 'C', and so on, but there is order between other characters as well. This ordering is the *encoding*, or sometimes the *code page*, of the font. For LaTeX and TeX, encodings are denoted by short, cryptic sequences. T1 and OT1 denote the new Cork encoding and the original TeX font encoding. The encodings for the original math italic (letters), symbols and extension fonts are OML, OMS, and OMX.

Family   A group of fonts belongs to the same family if they possess common visual characteristics; fonts in a family "go" well with each other. Within the standard suite of TeX fonts there are several families, of which cmr, containing the standard serif text fonts; cmss, containing the text fonts without serifs; and cmtt, containing typewriter type are the most prominent. The Garamond family, in which this book is set, is yet another family. Font families may contain one font or many fonts.

Series   Individual fonts may also be characterized by weight (bold versus medium or normal, for example) and width (extended versus narrow), but NFSS groups these two characteristics together under the term *series*. The cmr family contains three series, medium (m), bold extended (bx), and bold (b). While many fonts belong to the medium series, the bold series contains only one font (cmb10). For the Garamond fonts you are reading, there are three series: bold (b), semibold (s), and medium (m).

Shape   We use font *shape* to group together fonts whose members possess similar geometrical attributes. The cmr family contains more shapes than any other TeX family, encompassing fonts with the normal upright shape, italic, slanted, small caps, and upright italic shapes. Among the shapes in the Garamond family are normal, *italic*, and SMALL CAPS. We use the same designations for the bold fonts—**normal**, *italic*, and SMALL CAPS—but the type is set in a different series.

Size   It's common to speak of a font "at 10-pt" as if that were a received standard. Font size is a relative measure—Garamond at 14 pt is sure to be 40% larger than the same cutting at 10 pt, but we may *not* conclude anything about the relative size of 10 pt Garamond with 10 pt Times Roman, or with any other font from another family. Here are two fonts at the same size (10-pt):

Adobe Garamond Lucida Bright Regular

For improved visual compatibility, we'll have to scale up the Garamond size, scale down the Lucida, or adopt some middle ground.

One often sees books and documents typeset willy nilly with Times Roman and Helvetica at the same size, but 10-pt Helvetica is far too big for

10-pt Times Roman. Trial and error is the proper tool for determining the proper font size of Helvetica to best match a given size of Times Roman.

6.5.2   Using NFSS

There are a variety of commands as part of NFSS, falling naturally into three categories.

1. *High-level commands* are used most commonly and make it easy to perform the most frequent and most important font-switching tasks.

2. *Mid-level commands* assume less about the typesetting process and so require more savvy on the part of an author. However, they provide more control over font selection.

3. *Low-level commands* provide the information LATEX needs to match its commands to the various fonts you want to use. Although many of these commands are simple to use, many authors will cheerfully go through life never using even one of them.

The high- and mid-level commands will normally be the only font commands in a LATEX document, and our discussion summarizes them. Low-level commands typically belong in auxiliary files—font descriptor .fd files or package .sty files—that LATEX reads separately.

6.6   NFSS: High-level commands

6.6.1   Commands versus declarations

The important NFSS elements occur in two forms:

- *active command form*, and

- *declaration form*.

Active commands take an argument and do something to that argument; declarations change the state of the the typesetting world and must be enclosed in curly brackets. High-level commands appear on this page. Thus, the active command \texttt is equivalent to the declaration \ttfamily, but their syntax differs; we get typewriter by typing either

```
\texttt{typewriter}   or   {\ttfamily typewriter}
```

(or by typing {\tt typewriter}; the original command syntax remains in force).

6.6.2   "Old" LATEX font commands

For the sake of completeness and/or compatibility with LATEX209 documents that predate the current version of LATEX, the old font-changing commands are still available. Commands like \bf and \tt work as before.

NFSS: High-Level Commands

These high-level font-changing commands are new to the New Font Selection Scheme.

Active Command Form	Declaration Form	Sample
`\textnormal{...}`	`{\normalfont...}`	class default
`\emph{...}`	`{\em...}`	*emphasis*
Family Commands		
`\textrm{...}`	`{\rmfamily...}`	roman family
`\textsf{...}`	`{\sffamily...}`	sans serif family
`\texttt{...}`	`{\ttfamily...}`	`typewriter`
Series Commands		
`\textmd{...}`	`{\mdseries...}`	upright, medium series
`\textbf{...}`	`{\bfseries...}`	**bold-face series series**
Shape Commands		
`\textup{...}`	`{\upshape...}`	normal, upright shape
`\textit{...}`	`{\itshape...}`	*italic shape*
`\textsl{...}`	`{\slshape...}`	*slanted shape*
`\textsc{...}`	`{\scshape...}`	Small Caps Shape

Special Math Commands

`\mathcal{...}`, `\mathrm{...}`, `\mathbf{...}`,
`\mathsf{...}`, `\mathtt{...}`, `\mathnormal{...}`,
`\mathit{...}`

Size-Changing Declarations

`\tiny, \scriptsize, \footnotesize, \small, \normalsize,`
`\large, \Large, \LARGE, \huge, \Huge`

6.6.3 NFSS commands in context

The high-level commands on the facing page work in *context*. Thus, the same command can select a different font depending on preceding font commands. For example, the appearance of

```
{⟨context-command⟩ now to \itshape test}
```

depends on the context. Our document might contain any of the following

```
now to test
```

now to *test*
now to *test*

depending on whether the context was set by \ttfamily, \rmfamily, or
\bfseries (equivalently, \texttt, \textrm, or \textbf).

Changing font size should be done by the usual LaTeX sizing commands,
\tiny, \scriptsize, and so on on up through \Huge. These commands in
the current LaTeX have been made context sensitive so that issuing \large
in the midst of bold text will lead to \large-sized bold type. That is, type
something like

```
\bfseries really \large big
```

to get

really big

6.6.4 *Typesetting mathematics*

When NFSS is set up properly, an author will not need to know much about
it. All the math toggle switches (\[, \(, etc.), commands like \alpha or
\int, and so on work as they should, and all the usual math commands
behave as we expect.

There are seven new active commands that work only in mathematics,
and here they are (with examples):

Declaration	*Example*	
\mathcal	$\mathcal{K}$	$\mathcal{K}$
\mathrm	child_i	child$_i$
\mathbf	$\mathbf{x\times y}$	$\mathbf{x \times y}$
\mathsf	Quill	Quill
\mathtt	$\mathtt{hbox}$	hbox
\mathnormal	$\mathnormal{z}$	z
\mathit	Son_k	*Son*$_k$

What about text font-switching commands? Will they work in math mode?
Declarations will not work in math mode, but active commands will. To get

$$FV = \text{future value} = p\frac{(1+i)^n - 1}{i}$$

we can type

```
\[
  \mathit{FV}=\mathrm{future value}=..
\].
```

6.6.5 Examples

Here is an example of these commands in use. One way to get the ugly display

> Mathematics books and journals do not look as **beautiful as they used to.** It is not that their mathematical content *is unsatisfactory,* **rather that the old and** well-developed traditions of typesetting HAVE BECOME TOO EXPENSIVE.

is by typing

```
\textsf{Mathematics books and journals do not look as}
\textbf{beautiful as they used to.}
\textnormal{It is not that their mathematical content}
\textit{is unsatisfactory,}
\textbf{rather that the old and}
\textmd{well-developed traditions of typesetting}
\textsc{have become too expensive.}
```

Using declarations, we could type

```
{\sffamily Mathematics books and journals do not look as }
{\bfseries beautiful as they used to.  }
{\normalfont It is not that their mathematical content }
{\itshape is unsatisfactory, }
{\bfseries rather that the old and }
{\mdseries well-developed traditions of typesetting }
{\scshape have become too expensive.}
```

instead. This next example of (equally atrocious) typesetting

> Fortunately, **it now *appears that* mathematics** *itself can be used to* solve this problem.

shows how size and font commands interact. One way to get it is to type the following.

```
{\sffamily \large Fortunately, \bfseries it
\Large now \itshape appears that
\normalsize mathematics \mdseries itself
\small can be \itshape used to
\footnotesize \upshape solve this problem.}
```

NFSS: Mid-Level Commands

Command	Example
\fontencoding	\fontendcoding{OT1}
\fontfamily	\fontfamily{cmr}
\fontseries	\fontseries{b}
\fontshape	\fontshape{it}
\fontsize	\fontsize{12}{14}
\usefont	\usefont{OT1}{pgd}{b}{sc}
\selectfont	\selectfont

6.7   NFSS: Mid-level commands

With the commands listed on this page we can change individual attributes of the current font. These characters are *declarations*, so they must be enclosed within a group, but they are declarations of a particularly primitive form. At this level, NFSS has separated the choice of the font from the act of switching to that font. (High-level commands like \large or \bfseries both select new fonts *and* switch to the new font.) NFSS provides two new commands, \selectfont and \usefont, to activate a selection. Mid-level commands like \fontseries or \fontshape will *not* take effect until you type \selectfont. For example,

```
\fontseries{b}This is a {\selectfont pretty} tale
```

generates

This is a **pretty** tale

even though the new font series was declared at the start of the sentence. The \selectfont began the bold type, not the \fontseries command.

The \usefont command combines the preceding four commands together with an automatic \selectfont. To get

Four score and *seven years ago...*

we can type

```
\normalfont\fontfamily{hls}\selectfont Four score and
 \fontsize{9}{10}\fontfamily{pad}\fontseries{b}
 \fontshape{it}\selectfont seven years ago...
```

or

```
\normalfont\fontfamily{hls}\selectfont Four score and
\fontsize{9}{10}
\usefont{OT1}{pad}{b}{it}seven years ago...
```

among other things. Here, hls and pad denote the Lucida Bright sans serif and Adobe Garamond font families.

We use the \fontsize command to change the size of the current font. Two arguments are required—font size and baseline skip. Thus

```
\fontsize{11pt}{13pt}
```

specifies an 11-pt size and a 13-pt skip between consecutive baselines; it's equivalent to \fontsize{11}{13}. While \fontsize makes a new specification, the actual change will not happen unless an active command, declaration, or the command \selectfont appears. Typing

```
{big things \fontsize{8}{9}\selectfont come in
\fontsize{6}{7}\selectfont small packages}.
```

results in

big things come in small packages.

Obviously, the new baseline skip values are irrelevant for this example, but \fontsize always requires that second argument. (Reminder: it also requires \selectfont to take effect.)

If you're confused about the current font, \normalfont or \textnormal will switch to the basic font.

Too many fonts and sizes makes a document ugly and reader-unfriendly.

6.8   NFSS: Low-level font interface

Whose responsibility is it to ensure that font attributes are tied to real fonts? The lowest level font commands perform that task. These commands are easy to use, but some software generates them automatically.

Two commands

```
\DeclareFontFamily and \DeclareFontShape
```

anchor attributes to actual fonts. \DeclareFontFamily needs three arguments [the third is for special purposes not discussed here; see Goossens, Mittelbach, and Samarin (1994)]. The first two are the encoding and the family identifiers.

The important work is done by \DeclareFontShape, which takes six arguments (the final argument is generally empty and we will not discuss it here). The first four arguments are the font encoding, font family, series, and shape, followed by a single expression combining information about the font sizes with the system name of the font. We will discuss some of the more important aspects of the font sizing shortly, but if <-> represents the entire available size range, and if we choose the identifier padx to represent the Adobe Garamond family (the 'x' suggests that expert fonts were present to create genuine small-caps fonts), then inclusion of the lines

```
\DeclareFontFamily{OT1}{padx}{}
  \DeclareFontShape{OT1}{padx}{m}{n} { <-> padr7t  }{}
  \DeclareFontShape{OT1}{padx}{m}{sc}{ <-> padrc7t }{}
  \DeclareFontShape{OT1}{padx}{m}{it}{ <-> padri7t }{}
  \DeclareFontShape{OT1}{padx}{b}{n} { <-> pads7t  }{}
  \DeclareFontShape{OT1}{padx}{b}{sc}{ <-> padsc7t }{}
  \DeclareFontShape{OT1}{padx}{b}{it}{ <-> padsi7t }{}

  \renewcommand{\rmdefault}{padx}
```

in a style file will ensure that subsequent (nonmath) text will be printed in Garamond. For this to work, we need fonts padr7t, padrc7t, and so on, on our system, which stand for the regular, regular small caps, regular italic, semibold regular, semibold small caps, and semibold italic variants. The redefinition of \rmdefault ensures that the upright Garamond variant is the default typeface.

We (or a package like *fontinst*) can place the \Declare... commands in a separate *font-descriptor* .fd file. The font descriptor base name should be named by the encoding and font family, so TEX expects to find the above commands in OT1pad.fd; leave the \renewcommand in the package or class file. The .fd file itself belongs in a directory from which LATEX can read.

6.8.1 Sizing fonts

The fifth argument to \DeclareFontShape must consist of a series of sizes enclosed by angle brackets followed by font names. The macro associates a particular font with the associated size. For example

```
\DeclareFontShape{OT1}{cmr}{m}{n}{
  <5> cmr5 <7> cmr7 <9> cmr9 <10> cmr10 }{}
```

contains instructions to NFSS about fonts with OT1 encoding in the cmr family, the medium series, and normal shape and at sizes of 5 pt, 7 pt, 9 pt, and 10 pt. When these attributes and sizes are chosen, NFSS must use fonts cmr5, cmr7, cmr9, and cmr10.

Bitmap fonts   Generally, bitmap fonts are used at the size at which they have been created. Bitmap fonts cannot be scaled up or down in size without a severe loss in quality.

NFSS: Low-Level Text Font Commands

Low-level commands anchor a 5-tuple of attributes (encoding, family, series, shape, and size) to a font at a certain size. Every font used in a document must be matched to a \DeclareFontShape command.

- Three arguments characterize a family:

\DeclareFontFamily{⟨*encoding*⟩}{⟨*family*⟩}{⟨*options*⟩}

(in this text, we do not discuss the ⟨*options*⟩ argument at all).

- Six arguments match a font to its attributes with the \DeclareFontShape command:

\DeclareFontShape{⟨*encoding*⟩}{⟨*family*⟩}{⟨*series*⟩}%
 {⟨*shape*⟩}{⟨*size/font name*⟩}{⟨*options*⟩}

(in this text, we will not discuss the ⟨*options*⟩ argument at all).

- There will be one \DeclareFontFamily per family, but as many \DeclareFontShape's as necessary to match actual fonts to sets of NFSS attributes.

Outline fonts and font scaling In contrast with bitmap fonts, outline fonts are infinitely scalable up or down, so "one size fits all"—that is, we use a single master font file to generate individual fonts at different sizes. (These fonts actually correspond to different magnifications of the master font.) The size information for this important special case is <->, which we have already seen above in specifications for a Garamond font family.

Other considerations We have already seen on page 151 that some families of fonts don't look good next to each other because their natural sizes are incongruous. The use of a scaling factor to make one font closer in size to the other may be appropriate. For example, a sans serif font may need to be adjusted a bit to make it visually compatible with the Roman font. We will need either to scale the Garamond font up or scale the Lucida Bright text down.

In chapter 10, we will see that it is convenient to match the size of text fonts to a family of math fonts. Then, the fonts will be scaled at the time they are made ready for use by TEX (that is, the scaling will be incorporated into the virtual font, but virtual fonts have not yet been discussed). However, the scaling can also be done by a LATEX \DeclareFontShape command. For example, Garamond fonts have to be scaled up by as much as 34% to match the x-height of Lucida Bright, so we need a statement like

```
\DeclareFontShape{OT1}{pad}{m}{n}{<-> [1.337] padr7t }{}
```

to make this juxtaposition.

scaled Garamond vs. Lucida Bright regular

The use of the optional [...] argument scales all font sizes by the given amount. In this example, the size of padr7t is multiplied by 1.337, and thus increased about 34%. (Of course, with such large scaling factors, there are bound to be new problems. Now, the x-heights of the fonts are compatible, but the Garamond ascenders look too big compared to Lucida, among other things. Not every font family is visually compatible with every other.)

6.8.2　New math fonts

Typically, mathematics requires four special fonts:

1. math roman;
2. math italic;
3. math symbols; and
4. math extensions font.

These fonts, moreover, have to be grouped in special math families (functional groups, having nothing in common with the font families of NFSS). In the Computer Modern font family, the math roman font is cmr10, which does double duty as both text and math Roman. This font contains many characters, such as the uppercase Greek letters and some math operator symbols, that are largely irrelevant in text, but are vital to many technical expressions. In the following chapters, you will see how to create a text roman font containing enough of the requisite math symbols to make a font usable both in text and math modes.

Literal expression in mathematics like x or y are formed from italic letters, but these expressions obey different spacing and other conventions. For example, ligatures are not used in math so though {\itshape ff} yields *ff*, ff yields ff. Although there is substantial overlap between a text and a math italic font, it is better that they be separate. The symbols and extension fonts are altogether special, containing dozens of special-purpose characters.

As we have seen, the behind-the-scenes machinations by which plain TEX sets up math fonts is daunting. NFSS improves this situation—that is, the same machinations are well hidden by easy-to-use macros.

NFSS: Low-Level Math-Font Commands

- To set up sizes for math fonts, use \DeclareMathSizes.

- To set up fonts for math, use \DeclareSymbolFont.

- To set up fonts for an alternate version, use
  \DeclareMathVersion and \SetSymbolFont.

- As with all fonts, all fonts must be made visible to LaTeX with
  appropriate \DeclareFontFamily and \DeclareFontShape
  commands; these may be placed in an .fd file. All other low-
  level math commands belong in the style or package file.

The template package in subsection 6.8.6 on page 163 suggests the
commands and declarations, and the portions needing customization, to install and use a family of text and math fonts.

Here are the tasks to be done by us when selecting a suite of math fonts
for use by LaTeX.

1. We need to specify math-font sizes to NFSS.

2. We need to make new fonts visible to NFSS.

3. NFSS needs to know how the various math fonts will be used.

4. We can group different styles of mathematical typesetting using distinct *versions*.

6.8.3 Math-font sizes

LaTeX needs to know how to set subscripts (H_2O) and superscripts ($E = mc^2$), and sub- or superscripts themselves attached to sub- or superscripts
(e^{-x^2}). At the default size of 10-pt, we find that TeX uses a 7-pt type for
scripts, and 5-pt for second-order scripts; 10-pt is to be used for text math.
We code this for NFSS with the line

```
\DeclareMathSizes{10}{10}{7}{5}
```

but this assumes that the smaller fonts are optically scaled, as is the case for
Computer Modern fonts. When using geometrically scaled outline fonts, a
line like

```
\DeclareMathSizes{10}{10}{7.4}{6}
```

is appropriate. Indeed for a variety of the most popular sizes and magnifications, reasonable values for scalable fonts are laid out by means of these
declarations.

```
\DeclareMathSizes{5}{5}{5}{5}
\DeclareMathSizes{6}{6}{5}{5}
\DeclareMathSizes{7}{7}{5}{5}
\DeclareMathSizes{8}{8}{6}{5}
\DeclareMathSizes{9}{9}{7}{5}
\DeclareMathSizes{10}{10}{7.4}{6}
\DeclareMathSizes{10.95}{10.95}{8}{6}
\DeclareMathSizes{12}{12}{9}{7}
\DeclareMathSizes{14.4}{14.4}{10.95}{8}
\DeclareMathSizes{17.28}{17.28}{12}{10}
\DeclareMathSizes{20.74}{20.74}{14.4}{12}
\DeclareMathSizes{24.88}{24.88}{17.28}{14.4}
```

A line like \DeclareMathSizes{30}{}{}{} tells LATEX to suppress mathematical typesetting at 30-pt.

6.8.4 Making fonts visible to NFSS

We make fonts visible using \DeclareFontShape together with the encompassing \DeclareFontFamily; see subsection 6.8 on page 159.

6.8.5 Purposes for individual math fonts

Each individual math font has a special purpose. Roughly speaking, LATEX
takes the operators from the roman font, the letters for variable names from
the math italic font, lots of symbols from the symbol font, and all the large
symbols from the extension font. \DeclareSymbolFont incorporates these
facts. The first of its five arguments specify the functionality, and the final
four record the encoding, family, series, and shape. In addition to usual encodings, like T1 (Cork encoding) or OT1 (original TEX encoding), there are
three additional encodings that show up: OML, OMS, and OMX (which
stand for "original math letter encoding," "original math symbol encoding,"
and "original math extension encoding"). Suppose all math fonts belong to
the zmtpad family (we will be using an initial z to represent a math family;
mt represent the MathTime math fonts, and the pad the Adobe Garamond
text fonts that are used—at least here—with the math fonts). With the usual
conventions of NFSS in place, the font declarations take this form.

```
\DeclareSymbolFont{operators}    {OT1}{zmtpad}{m}{n}
\DeclareSymbolFont{letters}      {OML}{zmtpad}{m}{it}
\DeclareSymbolFont{symbols}      {OMS}{zmtpad}{m}{n}
\DeclareSymbolFont{largesymbols}{OMX}{zmtpad}{m}{n}
```

6.8.6 A style or package template

If you make use of *fontinst* to install fonts (as you certainly should), you will almost never need to adjust \DeclareFont... commands yourself. (But you will need to remember to move the .fd files to the proper place on your hard disk.) You will need to provide a link between the new fonts and NFSS. If you are using *only* text fonts, a single line like

```
\renewcommand{\rmdefault}{ pad }
```

is all you need (of course, change the boxed material as appropriate). If you plan to use new math fonts, you'll need a package file modeled after the following short template. (See chapter 10 for its explanation and for discussion of tools that do this work for you.)

```
\NeedsTeXFormat{LaTeX2e}% NFSS package template
\ProvidesPackage{ zmtpad }%
   [1994/04/29 MathTime math+ AGaramond ]
\renewcommand{\rmdefault}{ pad }      % default text face
\newcommand{\mathdefault}{ zmtpad } % default math family
\newcommand{\mathextension}{ mtex } % math large symbol font
\newcommand{\sfdefault}{ hls } % Lucida sans serif
\newcommand{\caldefault}{ pzc }
%   pzc = Zapf Chancery math calligraphic
\renewcommand{\bfdefault}{b}
%
\DeclareSymbolFont{operators}    {OT1}{\mathdefault}{m}{n}
\DeclareSymbolFont{letters}      {OML}{\mathdefault}{m}{it}
\DeclareSymbolFont{symbols}      {OMS}{\mathdefault}{m}{n}
\DeclareSymbolFont{largesymbols}{OMX}{\mathextension}{m}{n}
\DeclareSymbolFont{italic}       {OT1}{\rmdefault}{m}{it}
\DeclareSymbolFont{bold}{OT1}{\rmdefault}{\bfdefault}{n}
%
\SetMathAlphabet{\mathbf}{normal}%
   {\encodingdefault}{\rmdefault}{b}{n}%
\SetMathAlphabet{\mathsf}{normal}%
   {\encodingdefault}{\sfdefault}{m}{n}%
\SetMathAlphabet{\mathrm}{normal}%
   {\encodingdefault}{\rmdefault}{m}{n}%
\SetMathAlphabet{\mathit}{normal}%
   {OT1}{\rmdefault}{m}{it}%
\SetMathAlphabet{\mathtt}{normal}%
   {\encodingdefault}{cmtt}{m}{n}%
```

NFSS: Creating New Math Versions

1. Declare a new version.

2. Make sure the font family and shape for each of the four new math fonts appears, either in the package or style file or in separate font descriptor .fd files.

3. Use a series of \SetSymbolFont commands (rather than \DeclareSymbolFont) to relate the functionality of each font with the font.

4. Use the command \mathversion whenever this new version is to be invoked. As with all font declarations, the scope of the new version needs to be restricted using grouping symbols.

```
\SetMathAlphabet{\mathcal}{normal}%
  {OT1}{\caldefault}{m}{n}
%
\DeclareMathSizes{10}{10}{7.4}{6}% plus other sizes
                              % as appropriate
\endinput                     % END of template
```

(The boxed material is what needs to be changed.) Math fonts and their installation, and the details for customization of this template, will be covered in great detail in chapter 10.

6.8.7 New versions

Typesetting mathematics requires four fonts—operators, letters, symbols, and large symbols—acting in concert. Normally, one such *suite* of math fonts will be sufficient for a document, but sometimes we will need to juxtapose different such suites. NFSS refers to each such collection of math fonts as a *version* and creates two versions by default, a normal version and a bold version.

Normal version is in vogue by default, and preparing for a new version requires the steps in the box on this page.

Creating a new version   In this book, we use MathTime fonts, which match Garamond fonts far better than Computer Modern math fonts. The needs of this book are such that I may need to compare and contrast Math-Time and Computer Modern typesetting. A special cmr math version allows for that. Creating this version involved four steps.

First, I declared a new cmr math version. Second, I made sure that the following font-shape commands appeared either in four separate .fd files or in my package file. Third, four \SetSymbolFont commands told LATEX how to use these fonts. \SetSymbolFont used an extra argument to indicate the version.

```
\DeclareMathVersion{cmr}              %% Step 1
\DeclareFontFamily{OT1}{cmr}{}        %% Step 2
  \DeclareFontShape{OT1}{cmr}{m}{n}%
    {<5> cmr5 <7> cmr7 <10> cmr10}{}
\DeclareFontFamily{OML}{cmr}{}
  \DeclareFontShape{OML}{cmr}{m}{it}%
    {<5> cmmi5 <7> cmmi7 <10> cmmi10}{}
\DeclareFontFamily{OMS}{cmr}{}
  \DeclareFontShape{OMS}{cmr}{m}{n}%
    {<5> cmsy5 <7> cmsy7 <10> cmsy10}{}
\DeclareFontFamily{OMX}{cmr}{}
  \DeclareFontShape{OMX}{cmr}{m}{n}{<-> cmex10}{}
\SetSymbolFont{operators}{cmr}    {OT1}{cmr}{m}{n} %% Step 3
\SetSymbolFont{letters}  {cmr}    {OML}{cmr}{m}{it}
\SetSymbolFont{symbols}  {cmr}    {OMS}{cmr}{m}{n}
\SetSymbolFont{largesymbols}{cmr}{OMX}{cmr}{m}{n}
```

With these declarations in a package file, or the preamble of a document, everything is properly set up now. Finally, I can typeset

$$E = \int_0^\infty \left\{ \frac{e^{-x^2}}{\frac{1}{2}} \right\} dx \qquad E = \int_0^\infty \left\{ \frac{e^{-x^2}}{\frac{1}{2}} \right\} dx$$

by using \mathversion, which must be issued *outside* of the math switch. I typed

```
\newcommand{\mathsample}{
  \[ E=\int_0^\infty
    \left\{\frac{e^{-x^2}}{\frac{1}{2}}\right\}dx \]}
\setbox8=\vbox{\hsize=10pc \mathsample }
\setbox6=\vbox{\hsize=10pc\mathversion{cmr} \mathsample }
\[ \box8 \box6 \]
```

to put MathTime and Computer Modern math adjacent to each other.

CHAPTER 7

. . . .

VIRTUAL FONTS,
VIRTUOUS FONTS

When talking about computers, we use the adjective "virtual" to describe a thing that behaves like something else. Virtual disks are really memory blocks that simulate hard disks, while virtual memory uses a disk to mimic a computer's memory. A virtual font looks to LATEX or TEX like any other font, but it really is pieced together from other fonts or collections of typographic elements. It may be

- a composite of several different fonts somehow mixed together (in a special way, according to precise rules);

- a single font whose characters are (for very good reasons) scrambled in some new order;

- a collection of constructed characters, each built from several components (like accented letters are), which behaves like a font;

- individual horizontal or vertical rules each treated as a character in a font;

- a collection of text, graphics, or PostScript files, each treated as a single character within the virtual font;

- a conglomerate of all (or some) of the above.

This and the next few chapters explore virtual fonts, consider situations that need them, and provide procedures for constructing them. It's messy constructing virtual fonts by hand, but a few freely available resources make it easy.

The box on the facing page lists some virtual-font projects. For most people, the only application of virtual fonts may be to perform the proper installation of outline fonts (that is, PostScript fonts) for use by TEX. (We

166

Virtual-Font Projects

Here is a partial list of virtual-font applications.

- installing PostScript fonts (or any non-TeX fonts) for use by LaTeX and TeX;

- creating a true SMALL CAPS font for use with PostScript fonts;

- adding additional ligatures to a font so TeX and LaTeX can select them automatically;

- changing the metrics of individual characters to add more or less space around punctuation, dashes, or small caps;

- transforming existing scalable fonts to create simple variant fonts like *slanted (oblique)* or *unslanted italic fonts*;

- creating "poor person's bold" fonts for fonts that do not exist in a bold version;

- creating special <u>underlining fonts to underline extended portions of text while not messing up</u> TeX's <u>line breaking or hyphenation algorithms</u> (and similarly for special ~~overstrike~~ overstrike fonts);

- creating special fonts containing quaint alternate characters;

- creating fonts with oldstyle digits;

- creating better footnote numbers;

- making the input easy when typesetting in languages using many accented letters;

- enable math typesetting in font families other than Computer Modern;

- previewing PostScript fonts on a monitor.

will use the term *installation* to describe the entire process of making fonts usable by TeX.) Many tasks difficult or impossible to accomplish with macros become trivial when implemented via virtual fonts.

The next few sections explain in detail the concept of virtual fonts. This and the next few chapters then show how to implement most of these virtual font applications.

Discussion of virtual fonts appeared originally in Knuth (1990) and Knuth (1989a). For other treatments, consult Goossens, Mittelbach, and Samarin (1994), Jeffrey (1995), and Doob and Platt (1993).

7.1 The virtual-font concept

Let's begin by journeying to a different planet, one on which a system like TEX has been developed, but on which all languages contain only two distinct characters, which we can call 'e' and 'f', together with the double-f ligature 'ff'. A close examination of a font on this hypothetical planet makes it easier to understand the kinds of problems arising in real, terrestrial fonts, and how virtual fonts can solve them.

A table listing the characters of any TEX font would contain only three characters.

0	1	2
e	f	ff

These three characters have been numbered using the usual computer science convention that starts with 0. These numeric labels serve to identify the position in the font of each character.

These numeric positions also play an important role for TEX, for .dvi files contain typesetting commands based *not* on the glyph name ('A', 'B', "comma," or whatever) but on each numeric label. For any 'e' in the input file, the .dvi file contains the instruction to typeset character 0 in the current font. The lowercase 'e' had better be in that position! This correspondence between character and character number is built into the TEX program, and that's true for both the distant planet and for ours.

Difficulties arise when we try to use a commercial font instead of Computer Modern. We will suppose that the commercial font we want contains three characters, but they are 'e', 'f', and '&'. To get the ligature, we need to purchase a separate font, which contains the 'ff' plus two other characters. A further difficulty surfaces when we examine the layout of the fonts:

0	1	2		0	1	2
f	e	&		ff	%	$

The characters in the main font are in the wrong order, and this leads to disaster. To see why, let's select the commercial font, and now suppose we type f. TEX expects an 'f' to occupy position 1 of the font table, and so puts an instruction (in the .dvi file) to typeset character 1. But character 1 in the non-TEX font is the glyph 'e', and that's what gets typeset—not the 'f' that we requested. Moreover, it does not appear that we can typeset the ff without an explicit call to the auxiliary font. Apparently, the input file will look different whether we typeset with the usual TEX fonts or with some other fonts, and this is unacceptable.

Virtual fonts have been created to deal with this (and other) exigencies. As far as an author is concerned, a virtual font is just another font. But it

0 Γ 0	1 Δ 1	2 Θ 2	3 Λ 3	4 Ξ 4	5 Π 5	6 Σ 6	7 Υ 7
8 Φ 10	9 Ψ 11	10 Ω 12	11 ff 13	12 fi 14	13 fl 15	14 ffi 16	15 ffl 17
16 ı 20	17 J 21	18 ` 22	19 ´ 23	20 ˜ 24	21 ˇ 25	22 ˘ 26	23 ° 27
24 ¸ 30	25 ß 31	26 æ 32	27 œ 33	28 ø 34	29 Æ 35	30 Œ 36	31 Ø 37
32 ´ 40	33 ! 41	34 " 42	35 # 43	36 $ 44	37 % 45	38 & 46	39 ' 47
40 (50	41) 51	42 * 52	43 + 53	44 , 54	45 - 55	46 . 56	47 / 57
48 0 60	49 1 61	50 2 62	51 3 63	52 4 64	53 5 65	54 6 66	55 7 67
56 8 70	57 9 71	58 : 72	59 ; 73	60 ¡ 74	61 = 75	62 ¿ 76	63 ? 77
64 @ 100	65 A 101	66 B 102	67 C 103	68 D 104	69 E 105	70 F 106	71 G 107
72 H 110	73 I 111	74 J 112	75 K 113	76 L 114	77 M 115	78 N 116	79 O 117
80 P 120	81 Q 121	82 R 122	83 S 123	84 T 124	85 U 125	86 V 126	87 W 127
88 X 130	89 Y 131	90 Z 132	91 [133	92 " 134	93] 135	94 ^ 136	95 · 137
96 ` 140	97 a 141	98 b 142	99 c 143	100 d 144	101 e 145	102 f 146	103 g 147
104 h 150	105 i 151	106 j 152	107 k 153	108 l 154	109 m 155	110 n 156	111 o 157
112 p 160	113 q 161	114 r 162	115 s 163	116 t 164	117 u 165	118 v 166	119 w 167
120 x 170	121 y 171	122 z 172	123 – 173	124 — 174	125 ˝ 175	126 ~ 176	127 ¨ 177

Figure 1: A font table for Computer Modern Roman fonts (here, cmb10). The upright numbers in the upper left of each box give the character number using the usual decimal representation. The italic numbers in the lower right are the octal equivalents.

provides a mechanism whereby (behind the scenes), real fonts (*raw fonts*) can be combined so that the resulting *virtual font* conforms to the usual TEX conventions to eliminate any need for marking up the input file differently. In our example, a virtual font would

1. select the 'e' and 'f' from the main font, and reorder them in a TEX-acceptable way; and

2. include the ligature from the expert font in the last position in the table for the virtual font.

We call an auxiliary font containing ligatures and other special symbols an *expert font*, and we'll follow the terrestrial convention of labeling raw fonts by appending '8a' or '8x' (expert) to them. So raw font foo8a and expert font foo8x come together in the virtual font foo7t. (Chapter 6 ex-

32 40	33 ! 41	34 " 42	35 # 43	36 $ 44	37 % 45	38 & 46	39 ' 47
40 (50	41) 51	42 * 52	43 + 53	44 , 54	45 - 55	46 . 56	47 / 57
48 0 60	49 1 61	50 2 62	51 3 63	52 4 64	53 5 65	54 6 66	55 7 67
56 8 70	57 9 71	58 : 72	59 ; 73	60 < 74	61 = 75	62 > 76	63 ? 77
64 @ 100	65 A 101	66 B 102	67 C 103	68 D 104	69 E 105	70 F 106	71 G 107
72 H 110	73 I 111	74 J 112	75 K 113	76 L 114	77 M 115	78 N 116	79 O 117
80 P 120	81 Q 121	82 R 122	83 S 123	84 T 124	85 U 125	86 V 126	87 W 127
88 X 130	89 Y 131	90 Z 132	91 [133	92 \ 134	93] 135	94 ^ 136	95 _ 137
96 ' 140	97 a 141	98 b 142	99 c 143	100 d 144	101 e 145	102 f 146	103 g 147
104 h 150	105 i 151	106 j 152	107 k 153	108 l 154	109 m 155	110 n 156	111 o 157
112 p 160	113 q 161	114 r 162	115 s 163	116 t 164	117 u 165	118 v 166	119 w 167
120 x 170	121 y 171	122 z 172	123 { 173	124	174	125 } 175	126 ~ 176	

Figure 2: A font table for a PostScript font (Adobe Garamond). Boxes are empty wherever there is no character in that position for this font.

plains the conventions surrounding the notations 8a, 8x, and 7t.)

$$
\begin{array}{ccc}
0\ 1\ 2 & 0\ 1\ 2 & 0\ 1\ 2
\end{array}
$$

$$
\boxed{\text{f} \mid \text{e} \mid \text{\&}} + \boxed{\text{ff} \mid \text{\%} \mid \$} \Rightarrow \boxed{\text{e} \mid \text{f} \mid \text{ff}}
$$

$$
\text{foo8a} \qquad\quad \text{foo8x} \qquad\quad \text{foo7t}
$$

Font foo7t uses selected characters from the two raw fonts, and orders this selection in a way meaningful to TEX. Not all the characters from raw fonts need be part of the final virtual font.

To be sure, this unrealistic, alien font provides a contrived example. But with real commercial fonts, these same problems—writ large because real fonts have so many more characters—need the practical solutions that virtual fonts provide.

7.2   Digital fonts and font tables

Font tables for the Computer Modern TEX fonts and for PostScript outline fonts contain a maximum of 256 positions; 256 is one of the magic numbers of computer science. See figures 1–3 for examples of real font tables.

	161 ¡ 241	162 ¢ 242	163 £ 243	164 / 244	165 ¥ 245	166 ƒ 246	167 § 247
168 ¤ 250	169 ' 251	170 " 252	171 « 253	172 ‹ 254	173 › 255	174 fi 256	175 fl 257
	177 – 261	178 † 262	179 ‡ 263	180 · 264		182 ¶ 266	183 • 267
184 ‚ 270	185 „ 271	186 " 272	187 » 273	188 … 274	189 ‰ 275		191 ¿ 277
	193 ` 301	194 ´ 302	195 ^ 303	196 ˜ 304	197 ¯ 305	198 ˘ 306	199 ˙ 307
200 ¨ 310		202 ° 312	203 ¸ 313		205 ˝ 315	206 ˛ 316	207 ˇ 317
208 — 320							
	225 Æ 341		227 ª 343				
232 Ł 350	233 Ø 351	234 Œ 352	235 º 353				
	241 æ 361				245 ı 365		
248 ł 370	249 ø 371	250 œ 372	251 ß 373				

Figure 3: The upper half of a PostScript font for Adobe Garamond Regular.

(For a slightly different representation, refer to the font tables beginning on page 427 of *The TEXbook*.) Although there are a maximum of 256 positions in any digital font, there may be more characters that are present. Only 256 of them will be accessible.

A casual glance reveals significant differences between the layouts for the two fonts. Each slot of the Computer Modern font is filled (up till character 127), whereas there are many unfilled slots in the PostScript fonts. Some characters, like the uppercase Greek letters or the ff, ffi, and ffl ligatures, do not appear anywhere in the PostScript font, while certain PostScript characters appear nowhere in the Computer Modern layout. Other characters are in disparate positions. All the Scandinavian ligatures (æ, and so on) appear in the fourth row of the Computer Modern font table, but cluster together near the very end of the PostScript font table.

Positions in any font table are numbered starting from zero up to 255. We know that terrestrial TEX selects characters *not* by the character name but according to its position in the font table, so a command to typeset an 'A' is relayed as an instruction to

> typeset the character from the currently selected font that occu-
> pies position 65 in that font

since that's the numeric label of the 'A' slot. (All character positions are given
here in decimal notation. Computer scientists may be more comfortable
with a character's octal position, which is why that information also appears
in the tables.)

When using PostScript outline fonts, it's useful to be able to typeset in
a "fake font"—our virtual font—which looks real to TEX but is in fact an
amalgam of one or more raw, component fonts. We arrange this virtual
font so the characters in the virtual font are in the same order as in any
other Computer Modern font. That way, macros will seldom have to be
redefined for different fonts, a particularly important issue for mathematics
typesetting.

Associated with a font table is the *font-encoding vector* or just the *encoding
vector* or *code page*. The encoding vector is the list of the character names in
the order in which they occur in the font table. For a TEX font (figure 1 on
page 169), the encoding vector is the list beginning

> Gamma, Delta, Theta, Lambda, Epsilon, Pi, Sigma, Upsilon,
> Phi, Psi, Omega, ff, fi, fl, ffi, ffl, dotlessi, ...

and so on. If we let '.notdef' designate a font position for which no character is defined, then for a PostScript font (such as in figure 2 on page 170),
the encoding vector is a list that begins

> .notdef, ..., .notdef (32 times in total),
> space, exclam, quotedbl, numbersign, dollar, ...

7.3   What comprises a virtual font?

TEX does not deal with any character information beyond the metrics associated with a font. It expects to find this information in a `.tfm` file, and
so each virtual font must be accompanied by a font metric file in the usual
way. This file should be placed in a suitable location.

The details behind the construction of the virtual characters appear in
the actual virtual font file, a file with the extension `.vf`. There needs to
be a location on a hard disk to store virtual fonts, in the same way that
there are places for `.tfm` files, format files, input files, and so on. The places
have different names depending on whether your system is traditional or
complies with the TDS standard (see chapter 6).

The actual virtual font `.vf` file contains fragments of dvi language that
specify the way that a virtual character should be created. That means that
a character in a virtual font can be anything that occurs in a `.dvi` file. In
theory, one virtual character can typeset an entire page or document! Typically, virtual characters are not so complex. In the alien-planet example,
the virtual font simply remapped characters (placed them in a different and
more suitable order) and merged characters together from raw fonts.

7.4 What we will need: Preparation

We've seen in the previous chapter that VFINST or PSNFSS takes care of the most common virtual font task—the installation of scalable fonts to make them usable by TEX. However, there are many reasons to use virtual fonts, so we now begin a lengthy, conscientious look at virtual fonts. We need to understand, too, the sequence of steps that VFINST performs.

First, virtual fonts are a feature of TEX3. In order to proceed, that version must be installed.

Many authors will be preparing documents for output on PostScript printing devices. Since TEX only knows how to write .dvi files, we will always need a dvi-to-PostScript converter. Frequently these programs require an auxiliary map file to "map" the long font names to the short file names that are all that some operating systems, notably MS-DOS and its relatives, can handle. Because it is freely available, and available for all computer platforms, we will usually refer to *dvips* and its map file psfonts.map. Each of its entries pairs a short, DOS-acceptable name for a *raw* font with its long, given font name. These short aliases are the names that we should use in the process of virtual-font creation. For each short alias in the map file, there must be a .tfm file under that name.

The map file may serve other functions. It may aid in the process of downloading, and it may be where we specify certain types of transformations on a font (see the discussion on page 186).

At print time, how does the printer get the information about the shapes of the characters in the document? For bitmap fonts, it's the responsibility of the printer driver to include the bitmap information in the instructions it transmits to the printer. For scalable fonts, the situation is different. The outline information on all fonts must be transmitted to the printer, for it is the printer that ultimately converts the outline to raster form for printing. In most PostScript-compatible printers, descriptions of 35 or so common fonts, including Times Roman and Helvetica, are resident—built-in—to the printer. If you use other, nonresident fonts, you will need to *download*—transmit—this font information to the printer, and this downloading can be accomplished in different ways. It is also possible to include the font information in the PostScript version of the document.

7.5 The purpose of a simple installation

If we examine the three font tables in this chapter (figures 1–3), we see that the problem of constructing a virtual font from a PostScript font is not hopeless. Most characters are in the same positions, including all upper- and lowercase letters, digits, and much of the punctuation. We may divide the remaining characters in an outline font into two groups:

- special characters like fi, —, ¿, and the English quotation marks " ", which are selected by TEX's ligature mechanism; and

---

Software for Creating/Using Virtual Fonts

We will need:

- TEX3;

- device drivers—both a printer driver and screen previewer—
  that understand the language of virtual fonts;

- (optional) at least one PostScript font or other raw font;

By "PostScript font" we mean the outline file *plus* font metric file
for that font. The font metric file will have the file extension .afm,
while the outline file will have an extension like .pfb or .pfa (or
occasionally no extension at all).

- the matching "expert font" for the outline text font above (optional);

- the software tools afm2tfm (part of the *dvips* package) and *fontinst*; and

- the TEXware programs vptovf and pltotf along with their inverses tftopl and vftovp (these should be part of any complete TEX suite anyway).

- characters like æ, Œ, or ç, which are invoked by control sequences or
  control words (here, \ae, \OE, and \c{c}).

(Actually, there's a third group—those characters present in cmr10 but ab-
sent entirely from a standard Type1 font, such as the ligatures ff, ffi, and
ffl. We'll see later how to deal with these.) We would like to make sure we
have access to *these* members of a font *without* having to change the rules
by which we create our source documents. Actually, just in case an author
has been silly and has used a non-standard convention to typeset a symbol
(such as getting ¿ by typing \char62 or \symbol{62} rather than ?'), we
would like the layout of the virtual font to adhere as closely as possible to
the original TEX font layout.

The ligatures of the first group can be handled in a nonvirtual way by
adjusting the font metric files so TEX plucks the ligature from the proper
font position; no remapping is necessary. This requires a modification of
the .tfm only.

Characters accessed by TEX commands present more of a challenge. The definition for each such command relies on being able to locate special characters by their position in the font table. TEX therefore expects œ to be character 27 in a font, since that's where it is in the Computer Modern family. When constructing ç, it expects the cedilla to be in position 24 for the same reason. Typically, though, these characters do not appear in those positions in the raw PostScript font (œ and cedilla occupy positions 250 and 203). Macros could be redefined, but it's a bad idea to have macro definitions depend on the current font. We require our virtual-font utility to reorder—to remap—these characters in the font. For example, virtual character 27 consists of the raw character 250. That way, when the virtual font is the current font, \oe will correctly typeset the œ glyph.

The afm2tfm utility (part of *dvips*) is an excellent tool for creating this elementary kind of virtual font—a font consisting of the remapping of the characters in a single raw font. Because the source for this program has been made available, afm2tfm has been ported to every significant computer architecture, and executable binaries are freely available from friends or software archives (the same applies to *dvips* itself). But afm2tfm suffers from several disabilities: it can't create a virtual font out of more than one raw file, it can't create the .fd font descriptors that LATEX now uses, and it doesn't mimic the original TEX font layout as closely as it might. Nevertheless, simple installations are so common that it is important to detail this process precisely.

The box on the following page summarizes the steps for creating virtual fonts using afm2tfm. We use this procedure whenever this simple manipulation is sufficient. (More complicated finagling is best carried out with *fontinst*; see below.) This process involves using or creating several file types. If an outline font is foo, that means the distribution diskette should include foo.afm and foo.pfb. It is necessary to rename the files foo8a.afm and foo8a.pfb, and from these we will generate foo7t.vpl, foo7t.tfm, and foo7t.vf, the virtual font files. Finally, we create a font metric file foo8a.tfm.

The program afm2tfm can also create pseudo-small caps fonts and other fonts that have undergone simple geometric transformations, like slanting or extension. Check the documentation to learn how.

Once we've created the virtual font and placed all the files where they belong, we access any virtual file just as if it were a normal TEX font (which it is). For example, we could declare

```
\font\psfont=foo7t at 10.5pt
```

in a plain TEX document and use it via the command \psfont which has become a font changing command like \it or \tt. Although we never again refer to the raw font file explicitly, TEX does. Behind the scenes, whenever a TEX device driver resolves the meaning of a virtual font, it refers to the component raw fonts; the raw fonts must be present on our system.

Simple Font Installation with afm2tfm

We use `afm2tfm` to install a font whenever a single raw font is the sole component of a virtual font. Here are the steps in the procedure, assuming we begin with font files `foo8a.afm` and one of `foo8a.pfb`, `foo8a.pfa`, or `foo8a` (depending on the computer system and the way the fonts are distributed). From these, we follow these steps to create a virtual font `foo7t`. (See the previous chapter for the significance of the final 8a and 7t suffixes.)

1. Issue the command

```
afm2tfm foo8a.afm -v foo7t.vpl foo8a.tfm >tmp
```

   at the prompt.

2. Issue the command

```
vptovf foo7t.vpl foo7t.vf foo7t.tfm
```

   at the prompt.

3. The file `tmp` contains a single line like

```
foo8a FullNameOfTheFont
```

   Add this line to the end of the file `psfonts.map`. If you want `dvips` to download the file automatically, revise the line to look like

```
foo8a FullNameOfTheFont </psfonts/foo8a.pfb
```

4. Move the two `.tfm` files, a single `.vf` file, and the original font files to their proper directories. Make sure also that the revised version of `psfonts.map` is where it belongs.

7.6   Introduction to *fontinst*

The *fontinst* package by Alan Jeffrey does everything `afm2tfm` does and more. It can create a virtual font from several raw fonts, for example, and it automatically produces an auxiliary `.fd` file used by LaTeX's NFSS to select the font. The *fontinst* package is written entirely in TeX, and TeXegetes will enjoy perusing `fontinst.sty` to watch TEX do things it was never intended for. Writing it in the TEX language ensures that *fontinst* runs on every platform that TEX does. You can retrieve *fontinst* from any CTAN archive, under `fonts/utilities/fontinst`. The discussion in this chapter supplements `fontinst.tex`, the documentation of the package.

We use *fontinst* by preparing a simple plain TEX file. Typically, this file will be short and will consist of a command to `\input fontinst.sty`, followed by a variety of commands that tell *fontinst* how to create the virtual font. Normally, `.vf` and `.tfm` files are binary files, file types that TEX cannot write. Therefore, *fontinst* reads and writes property list files and special metric and encoding files instead. These are all in ASCII, and the property files in particular are ASCII equivalents to `.vf` and `.tfm` files with extensions `.vpl` and `.pl`. Part of your TEX installation should include the utilities vptovf and pltotf (together with their inverses vftovp and tftopl), and we would then use these utilities to create the font files we need.

After each successful run of *fontinst* there will be three new kinds of files in your working directory:

- `.pl` files—one for each raw font—which feed into pltotf to create a `.tfm` file;

- `.vpl` files—one for each virtual font—which feed into vptovf to create one `.vf` and one `.tfm` file; and

- an `.fd` *font descriptor file*—one for each font family—which NFSS will use to relate the font attributes to individual fonts.

(There are also some new `.mtx` files and the usual `.log` file that you can delete.) It is necessary to run all `.vpl` files through vptovf and all `.pl` files through pltotf to generate the binary metric files that TEX needs. A map file like `psfonts.map` for *dvips*, must be updated; see chapter 6.

All `.tfm` files belong with your other `.tfm` files. The `.vf` files belong in a special place as well, where *dvips* expects to find virtual files. The `.fd` files belong in a TEX inputs directory.

7.6.1 Installing fontinst

The *fontinst* package consists of the core file `fontinst.sty` together with some documentation, some samples, and many examples. In addition to `fontinst.sty` itself, there is group of files with extensions .mtx and .etx. Move these files to one of your TEX input directories to complete the installation; on a TDS installation, this would be a place like ⟨*texmf*⟩/tex/generic/fontinst.

Goals The *fontinst* package provides a new language for the creation of virtual fonts of all types. Our goal in this and subsequent chapters shall be to develop familiarity with these procedures so that we can install any font with (relatively) little work.

Although *fontinst* works *much* slower than afm2tfm, it is much faster than creating .vpl files by hand.

7.7   Simple font installation with *fontinst*

The box on page 196 lists many of the problems—and solutions—I ran into while preparing the many virtual fonts used in this book. The reader should refer to it frequently in the course of an actual *fontinst* installation.

7.7.1   New commands

Figure 4 on page 180 displays one way to use *fontinst* to install the Times Roman fonts that are resident in every PostScript printer. Most *fontinst* installation files resemble this display.

Much of this file is standard boilerplate. The first line

```
\input fontinst.sty
```

makes *fontinst* known to TEX.

The pair of commands \installfonts and \endinstallfonts (with no arguments) surrounds the sequence of commands that do the bulk of the work. One or more \installfamily commands now follow. The first argument specifies the encoding, the second the family designation, and the third a set of commands that will be executed each time the family is loaded. See the *fontinst* documentation for further details on this third argument; it will be empty in nearly all our work.

```
\installfamily{⟨encoding⟩}{⟨family⟩}{⟨fd-commands⟩}
```

The workhorse command in any installation file is the \installfont command, which takes eight parameters. The last parameter allows us to specify size information for the font. For scalable fonts, it is nearly always empty because scalable fonts are, well, scalable to any size. (Bitmap fonts, created specifically for different sizes, require nonempty entries.) Parameters 4–7 provide space for the encoding, family, series, and shape values that *fontinst* uses to create the NFSS .fd file. Consult the previous chapter and examples in this and subsequent chapters to see how these parameters fill out. The very first parameter stores the file name of the virtual font you want to create.

That leaves the second and third parameters. In order to understand their significance, we need a small digression to consider the process of font creation.

7.7.2   Creating fonts

There are two aspects to font creation:

1. *Metric:* We need procedures for constructing each glyph or character in the virtual font. I use the term 'metric' to encompass these structural aspects, which ultimately involve measuring the glyphs for use by TEX.

2. *Encoding:* We need to decide on the order of the glyphs in the font and specify any additional rules that the characters need to live by. For example, rules might concern ligatures (any time an i follows a single f, replace it by fi; any time an *A* appears at the beginning of a word, replace it by $\mathcal{A}$) or math symbols (any time interior material gets too tall, replace a delimiter by the next larger size).

For *fontinst*, these instructions should be in *metric files*, with an .mtx extension, and *encoding files*, with extension .etx. In the second position of the \installfont command, we place a list of metric files to be inserted. *fontinst* reads them to find out how to construct the characters. The third position records the name of an encoding file, which *fontinst* reads to learn which characters to include, how to order them, and what ligature and other special rules to follow.

Schematically, a \installfont instruction looks like this:

\installfont{⟨*font-name*⟩}{⟨*metric-files*⟩}{⟨*encoding-file*⟩}
    {⟨*encoding*⟩}{⟨*family-name*⟩}{⟨*series*⟩}{⟨*shape*⟩}{⟨*size*⟩}

7.7.3 Metric files

The task of preparing metric files is lightened because *fontinst* reads three types of metric files:

1. .mtx files, using a format specific to *fontinst*;

2. .afm files, the ASCII metric files that come with each scalable outline font; and

3. .pl files, the ASCII equivalents to a TEX .tfm file.

fontinst reads the first two types automatically, but you will need to use the program tftopl (which should accompany your version of TEX) to create the third file. For example, type

```
tftopl cmr10.tfm cmr10.pl
```

to do the obvious thing.

In fontinst, earlier definitions take precedence over later definitions. That is, if any construct appears more than once in a series of files that *fontinst* reads, only the first one counts; later definitions are silently ignored. Therefore, *the order in which fontinst reads files is critical!* This philosophy is central to the way *fontinst* works, as we'll see.

```
\input fontinst.sty

\installfonts
   \installfamily{OT1}{ptm}{}
   \installfont{ptmr7t}{ptmr8a,latin}{OT1}{OT1}{ptm}{m}{n}{}
   \installfont{ptmrc7t}{ptmr8a,latin}{OT1c}{OT1}{ptm}{m}{sc}{}
   \installfont{ptmri7t}{ptmri8a,latin}{OT1}{OT1}{ptm}{m}{it}{}
   \installfont{ptmb7t}{ptmb8a,latin}{OT1}{OT1}{ptm}{bx}{n}{}
   \installfont{ptmbc7t}{ptmb8a,latin}{OT1c}{OT1}{ptm}{bx}{sc}{}
   \installfont{ptmbi7t}{ptmbi8a,latin}{OT1}{OT1}{ptm}{bx}{it}{}
\endinstallfonts
\bye
```

Figure 4: One way to install Times Roman. This example uses the original TEX encoding but does not include any expert fonts. Two series are installed—regular and bold. Within each series, three shapes are installed—upright, small caps (which use encoding file OT1c.etx), and italic.

The file latin.mtx is the "metric file of last resort." It provides instructions for creating 401 glyphs found in Latin alphabets. Of those 401, some can't be faked (they're unfakable)—there's no way to print characters like 'A' unless the A is in the font, but many other glyphs can be faked. Accented letters can be built from letters and accents, and small caps can be taken from an uppercase font set at 80% of the current design size. Of course, there isn't room for all 401 of these characters in a single font anyway. (The limit is 256.) But because many of these characters have been previously defined in metric files, *fontinst* will ignore many of the definitions in latin.mtx— remember, glyph constructs have no effect if defined previously. But if you have neglected to define a glyph that you later call for, the definitions in latin.mtx serve as safety net. That is why all the \installfont commands in figure 4 and in many *fontinst* examples contain lists of metric files that terminate with a call to latin.mtx.

7.7.4 Encoding files

Once the metric files have done their job (of constructing the glyphs), a single encoding file chooses the group of characters that belong in the font and their proper order (encoding). This file also specifies certain ligature and other rules for the font to abide by.

Encoding files tend have names to reflect their encoding. Thus, the encoding file for the OT1 encoding is simply OT1.etx. Similar files, OT1c.etx and OT19.etx, would set up a small caps and an old-style figures font using OT1 encoding. There are several more variants in the *fontinst* distribution.

7.8 Progressive examples

It's time to consider examples using *fontinst* to create virtual fonts.

7.8.1 *Simple font installation*

The simplest way to use *fontinst* is to run TEX on the file fontinst.sty and to then type

```
\latinfamily{ptm}{}
\bye
```

in response to TEX's star prompt *. This works presuming that all the fonts in the ptm family (Times Roman) have been named in accordance with Karl Berry's font-naming scheme and that all font metric files are in places that TEX can read from.

This method is best for authors who plan never to need any fonts more exotic than these. Subsequent examples are designed to show of the power of *fontinst* and to teach its intricacies in a tutorial manner.

7.8.2 *Easy EC fonts*

The Cork encoding, denoted by T1, refers to the standard agreed on at a TEX meeting held in Cork, Ireland in September 1990. At that time, agreement was reached for sets of 256-character fonts for use by LATEX and TEX. (The TEX standard had at that time only been extended to 256 character fonts for a short time.) The ecr fonts look like the usual Computer Modern fonts, but these fonts have been extended according to the Cork standard. Virtual fonts provide an easy way to generate ecr fonts from raw, Computer Modern fonts.

For each virtual ecr font, a corresponding cmr font acts as the single raw font. We will need the property list .pl file as well.

Here are the steps to create a virtual ecr10 from a raw cmr10 font. The installation file makeecr.tex should resemble

```
% This is makeecr.tex, for use with fontinst.
\input fontinst.sty
  \installfonts
    \installfamily{T1}{ecr}{}
    \installfont{ecr10}{cmr10,latin}{T1}{T1}{ecr}{m}{n}{}
  \endinstallfonts
\bye
```

although you'll need additional \installfont statements for members of this family that are italic, boldface, and so on.

Now enter these statements at the system prompt:

```
tftopl cmr10.tfm cmr10.pl
tex makeecr
vptovf ecr10.vpl ecr10.vf ecr10.tfm
rm *.log *.pl *.vpl *.mtx
```

Accessing New Virtual Fonts

To access new virtual fonts in a document, use the standard TEX conventions. Let's suppose a new virtual font vfont belongs to font family fam.

In **plain TEX**, type something like

```
\font\myfont=vfont at 12pt
```

and from then on, use the control sequence \myfont to switch to that font.

When using **NFSS and LATEX**, *fontinst* will have produced a file like OT1fam.fd or T1fam.fd. *Carefully* move this file to an input directory, where "care" is appropriate because if an existing file with this name is there already, the contents of the new .fd file needs to be merged with the existing .fd file. Then, type

```
\renewcommand{\rmdefault}{fam}
```

to enable the font family.

after which you'll need to move the .tfm and .vf files to their proper places. In other words, we first need the ASCII property list file, after which we can invoke TEX and *fontinst*. Thereafter, we create binary font files using the virtual property .vpl file produced by *fontinst*. Finally, we clean up. (Unix syntax is shown.) This example does not require an addendum to psfonts.map unless you are using scalable versions of the Computer Modern fonts.

Drawbacks of easy ecr10   During the creation of ecr10.vpl, *fontinst* reports that 34 glyphs are missing—that is, of the full complement of characters that belong in a T1-encoded font, *fontinst* complained 34 times that it couldn't make the glyph. Most of these are various diacritics (ring, ASCII tilde, and so on) and accented letters that use these missing diacritics, but a few are more problematic, including the sterling symbol and French quotations. If you use these characters, the mock ecr10 font will not be suitable.

Moreover, there is no premium on disk space from using these fonts. The .vf and .tfm files require roughly 4 k and 5.7 k apiece, comparable with an actual .pk file at laser-printer resolution.

7.8.3   Installing outline fonts

Although VFINST or PSNFSS takes care of scalable font installation, we are now in a position to understand a simple installation ourselves. We may begin by renaming the font files to conform to a TEX-font naming standard. Suppose we have Adobe Garamond Roman fonts to install. We rename the regular font files to padr8a.pfb and padr8a.afm, for example.

   As an example, we can create the OT1-encoded font padr7t from these. This new font will belong to font family pad and have NFSS designations of m and n (medium series, normal shape). With this information, we prepare an installation file that looks like

```
% This is file makepad.tex
\input fontinst.sty
\installfonts
  \installfamily{OT1}{pad}{}
  \installfont{padr7t}{padr8a,latin}{OT1}{OT1}{pad}{m}{n}{}
\endinstallfonts
```

although a real installation will likely contain several \installfont commands. The \installfont command is quite straightforward. It:

- constructs a font for family pad;

- uses glyph information from padr8a.afm, and supplements it (if necessary) with instructions from latin.mtx;

- applies the OT1 encoding to it; and

- uses the four parameters OT1, pad, m, and n for the NFSS .fd file.

Incorporating expert fonts   For the vast majority of outline fonts, the only way to get the ff, ffi, and ffl ligatures is from an expert font, because these characters are rarely present in the base font. However, latin.mtx does create mock characters with these names because slots are provided for these ligatures by the encoding files. Therefore, the way to get the honest double-f ligatures is simply to include the expert font name in the list of metric files in an \installfont command. That is, the above skeletal installation file would become

```
% This is file makepad.tex
\input fontinst.sty
\installfonts
  \installfamily{OT1}{pad}{}
  \installfont{padr7t}{padr8a, padr8x, latin}{OT1}%
    {OT1}{pad}{m}{n}{}
\endinstallfonts
```

Installing Outline Fonts with FONTINST

- Initial preparation: make sure .afm files are in a TEX input directory. For any raw bitmap fonts, use tftopl create the ASCII .pl file for that font.

- Prepare an installation file similar to makepad.tex on the previous page, and run plain TEX on it.

- For each .pl and .vpl file, use pltotf and vptovf to create the .vf and .tfm files. Move these files to their proper places.

- Add an entry like

```
padr8a AGaramond-Regular </psfonts/padr8a.pfb
```

and maybe

```
padr8x AGaramondExp-Regular </psfonts/padr8x.pfb
```

(if expert fonts are present) to the map file psfonts.map.

The box on this page summarizes the bookkeeping involved in completing the installation. This discussion is for pedagogical completeness only, for in this case it's better to use \latinfamily (see page 181) or PSNFSS or VFINST (chapter 6).

7.8.4 Small caps

EVERYONE KNOWS WHAT SMALL CAPS LOOK LIKE. There are two ways to create small caps fonts.

We do it the wrong way if we fake a small caps font by piecing together regular caps together with caps at 80% (say) of the design size. This unfortunate compromise implies that the thickness of the lowercase small caps are only 80% the thickness of the uppercase strokes. In true small caps, the thickness of the strokes should be the same even as the font switches from upper to lowercase. Figure 5 on the facing page shows the difference. Using expert fonts in a virtual font makes true small caps fonts possible (see next section). Aspiring authors should insist on real small caps, but the jury-rigged variety is increasingly common.

Note that VFINST automatically creates small caps virtual fonts. It uses

Making Small Caps Fonts

Fake: Add a line like

```
\installfont{padrc7t}{padr8a,latin}%
  {OT1c}{OT1}{pad}{m}{sc}{}
```

to the installation file. Proceed as usual to construct the virtual fonts.

Real: In the presence of expert or small caps fonts named like padr8x, add a line like

```
\installfont{padrc7t}{padr8a,padr8x,latin}%
  {OT1c}{OT1}{pad}{m}{sc}{}
```

to the installation file. Proceed as usual to construct the virtual fonts.

In the actual file, the family name (here pad), the encoding (here OT1), and other aspects of the font files may be different. The installation file looks similar to that on page 183.

the auxiliary small caps or expert fonts if they are present at the time of installation and otherwise sets up the jury-rigged, mock versions.

The true SMALL CAPS characters are found in special *expert fonts* furnished separately by a digital foundry. Not all text fonts have matching expert fonts, but they are being made available increasingly often. On occasion, as with Bitstream fonts, the separate fonts containing the small caps characters are called small caps fonts. Typically, an expert font contains the characters you see in figure 6 on the following page.

To create real small caps, it is sufficient to include the small caps .afm file in the list of metric files for *fontinst* to read. Small caps characters have different names than the corresponding characters in a regular font—for example 'Asmall' instead of 'a'—so there is no danger of *fontinst* not realizing what

THE QUICK BROWN FOX TYPESETS THE LAZY BROWN DOG (REAL).
THE QUICK BROWN FOX TYPESETS THE LAZY BROWN DOG (FAKE).

Figure 5: Caps/small caps typesetting—real and fake.

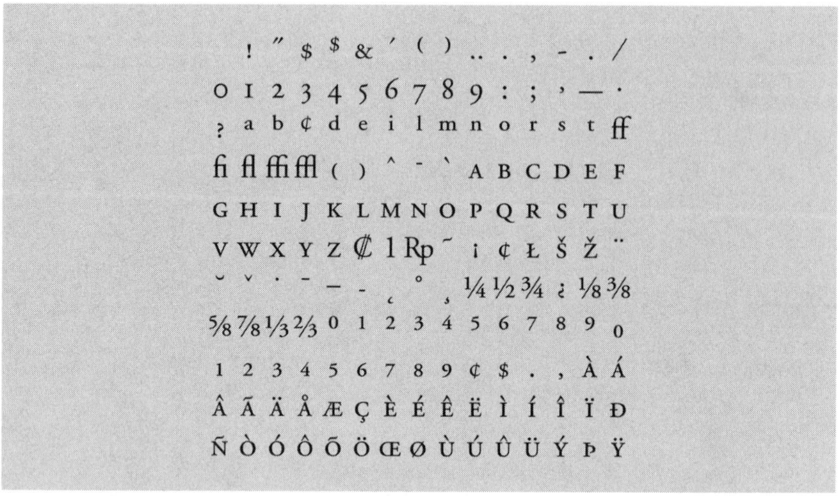

Figure 6: Characters in a typical expert font (Adobe Garamond expert).

character it is dealing with. Of course, `latin.mtx` makes sure all characters in the Latin character set are defined, so we make sure we choose the small caps character set by choosing the small caps encoding file `OT1c.etx` (or `T1c.etx` for those following the T1 encoding). The installation file needs to install another font. For Adobe Garamond, this line would look like this.

```
\installfont{padrc7t}{padr8a,padr8x,latin}%
  {OT1c}{OT1}{pad}{m}{sc}{}
```

Although `latin.mtx` would attempt to create mock small caps glyphs, those definitions are superseded by the real definitions in the small caps `.afm` file.

If the expert (or small caps) auxiliary font is not present, the mock definitions in `latin.mtx` take effect. They will be present in the font provided we choose a small caps encoding. The command to install this font is slightly simpler.

```
\installfont{padrc7t}{padr8a,latin}%
  {OT1c}{OT1}{pad}{m}{sc}{}
```

(The `\installfont`'s belong in an install file like the one on page 183, and you must follow the procedure sketched in the box on page 184.)

7.8.5 Oblique and unslanted italic

Often, simple changes to font geometry are all that's needed to create a new font. *The METAFONTbook* discusses methods whereby shearing yields oblique and unslanted italic from text Roman and regular italic fonts. Other simple transformations that are useful are a geometric scaling of the font (which can also be done at the time the font is defined in a document), scaling the font only in the horizontal or vertical directions, and re-encoding the font. For bitmap fonts, these transformations must be done at the time the font is created (except for re-encoding), but we can easily perform these transformations for outline fonts by means of an appropriate virtual font *provided* our dvi-to-PS converter is able to perform font transformations itself. The *fontinst* documentation sketches the process for simple virtual fonts, and we outline the procedure in the case that we want to create an oblique or unslanted italic font from a virtual font constructed out of several raw font components. Normally, though, VFINST will automatically create these fonts at the time of installation.

How much slant?   To get an approximation for the amount of slant, use a text editor to examine the `.pfb` or `.afm` file for the *italic* version of the font. Somewhere near the beginning of the file will be a line of the form

```
ItalicAngle -18.5
```

which indicates that the italic lists to the right by 18.5° (degrees); the minus sign means that Adobe Systems employs a coordinate system with slightly different conventions. The figure given here (18.5°) is right for Adobe Garamond, but varies from font family to font family. The *fontinst* commands need the *tangent* (to three decimal places) of this angle. *Finding the tangent* means using mathematics to associate a special number with the angle. Old-time readers may have dusty volumes of numerical tables that yield this information, but up-to-the-minute readers need simply locate a scientific calculator, check that the calculator expects input in degrees, punch in the angle, and then tap the key marked `tan`. The display will give the results. For 18.5°, the tangent is 0.335.

The *fontinst* commands use this value without the decimal point; that is, it uses this number multiplied by 1000. Before creating virtual fonts, we need to shear the raw fonts by an amount specified by the tangent. The installation commands to create oblique and unslanted italic virtual fonts for Adobe Garamond pad fonts begin by creating oblique and unslanted raw fonts.

```
%% Regular fonts
\transformfont{padro8a}{\slantfont{335}{\fromafm{padr0}}}
\transformfont{padru8a}{\slantfont{-335}%
   {\fromafm{padri8a}}}
%% Expert fonts (if present)
\transformfont{padro8x}{\slantfont{335}{\fromafm{padr8x}}}
\transformfont{padriu8x}{\slantfont{-335}%
   {\fromafm{padri8x}}}
```

Include the lines for the expert fonts only if they are present. In an installation file, the

```
\transformfont
```

commands can precede the \installfonts command. After the

> \installfamily

statement, we will include two new \installfont commands.

```
\installfont{padro7t}{padro8a,[padro8x,]latin}%
    {OT1}{OT1}{pad}{m}{sl}{}
\installfont{padriu7t}{padriu8a,[padriu8x,]latin}%
    {OT1}{OT1}{pad}{m}{ui}{}
```

Here, the bracketed material should be included only if the expert files are present.

The *dvips* driver needs to know about these transforms, so lines like

```
%% Regular fonts
   padro8a    AGaramond-Regular      ".335 SlantFont "
   padriu8a   AGaramond-Italic       "-.335 SlantFont"
%% Expert fonts
   padro8x    AGaramondExp-Regular   ".335 SlantFont"
   padriu8x   AGaramondExp-Italic    "-.335 SlantFont"
```

belong in psfonts.map. The parameter is negative for an unslanted italic because we need to rotate each character in a counterclockwise (negative) direction. The \transformfont commands makes oblique/unslanted italic versions of the raw fonts, which are stitched together in the proper ways by the all of the \installfont commands. *The resulting oblique font provides another way to emphasize material,* as does the unslanted italic font. (The unslanted italic really is unslanted; an optical illusion makes it appear to lean to the left.)

7.9   More virtual-font projects

These projects all use the *fontinst* package, but are *not* performed by VFINST.

7.9.1   Adjustments to individual characters

At times, it will be necessary to adjust the spacing for individual characters. Some house styles demand a bit of space surrounding an em-dash — like this. European publishers may adjust punctuation to provide some space separating a semicolon from the preceding text. These are simple adjustments to make.

As an illustration, let's make the change to the dash in the OT1-encoded Adobe Garamond font. If we create a short file newdash.mtx like

```
\relax
   This is file newdash.mtx, a fontinst file.
\metrics
```

```
\resetglyph{emdash}
   \movert{167}
   \glyph{emdash}{1000}
   \movert{167}
\endresetglyph
\endmetrics
```

then any \installfont command for this family should be revised

```
\installfont{padr7t}{padr8a,[padr8x,] newdash, latin}{OT1}
   {OT1}{pad}{m}{n}{}
```

—that is, the newdash file should follow all font files but should precede the call to latin.mtx. After the resulting virtual fonts are created and installed, typing --- in this font will automatically place additional space around the em-dash. The funny constant 167 arises as the amount of space—167/1000 units (one-sixth of the design size)—that surrounds the em-dash.

This example is our first explicit encounter with *fontinst* command syntax. These commands are explained fully in the documentation accompanying *fontinst* and are summarized in the appendix to this chapter (page 197). Incidentally, *fontinst* assumes there are 1000 units in the default font size of 10 pt. Thus, an instruction above like \movert{167} will add a space of 1.67 pt at the default font size. If you use the font at a different size, the surrounding space will be scaled accordingly.

7.9.2 Adjusting font size

Even "at" the same design size, there is an astonishing range in the perceived sizes of fonts. Here are samples of Centaur and Lucida Bright each at a 10-pt design size.

Monotype Centaur, versus Lucida Bright

These differences in size mean that the density and printed length of documents can change dramatically with a new face.

One wants to assume that the font designer designed the font so that it looks best at the natural default size of 10 pt. Nevertheless, there may be times when you need to alter this size. For instance, if you plan to create a virtual font using pieces of fonts in different font families, you may well wish to scale one set of characters to match the cap-height, say, of the other characters. Suppose we wanted to add the uppercase Greek letters to a virtual font; after all, the OT1 encoding provides space for them at the beginning of the font. These symbols occur in the Symbol font, resident in every PostScript printing device. The cap height of these Greek letters is 673 units (as we find by inspecting the .afm file; use an editor to open the .afm file, and search for the string CapHeight that occurs about 12 lines from the top of the file). In the same way, we determine that the capitals in an

Adobe Garamond regular font are 663 units tall. If we scale the Symbols by a factor of 98.5% (this scale factor is the result of dividing 663 by 673), then the symbols will match the Garamond caps, at least in height. (We have no guarantee that they will be visually compatible no matter how we scale it— after all, it belongs to a different font family.) Therefore, an \installfont command should look as follows.

```
\installfont{padr7t}{padr8a,psyr scaled 985,%
    [padr8x,]latin}{OT1}{OT1}{pad}{m}{n}{}
```

(The bracketed material is optional.) Proceed as usual. An entry needs to be made in psfonts.map for the Symbol font (psyr), but that is usually present already.

7.9.3 Oldstyle figures

In nontechnical contexts, it often makes more visual sense to use oldstyle figures throughout a document.

> The date 31 December 1500 cuts right across the most fertile period of the new art, halving the lives of some of its greatest practitioners such as Anton Koberger (1445–1513), Aldus Manutius (1450–1515), Anthoine Vérard (d. 1512), Johannes Froben (1460–1527), Henri Estienne (1460–1520), and Geofroy Tory (1480–1533)[Steinberg (1961)].

We can easily create a special Roman font in which the oldstyle digits occupy the positions of the usual digits, provided we have access to the expert font, which contains these quaint numerals. A short file OT19.etx, part of the *fontinst* distribution, governs this change; the suffix '9' is a convention for identifying fonts with oldstyle digits. To this end, place the command

```
\installfont{padr97t}{padr8a,padr8x,latin}%
    {OT19}{OT1}{pad}{m}{os}{}
```

in an installation file.

Plain TEX users select the font with a declaration like

```
\font\oldie=padr97t at 10pt
```

LATEX users can rely on built-in commands of NFSS. To select this font, say something like

```
\normalfont\fontshape{os}\selectfont
```

7.9.4 Better footnote numbers

Expert fonts contain a series of superior digits, altogether superior for type-setting footnote numbers. To create a special "footnote font," we need a

> **Oldstyle Figures; Better Footnote Numerals**
>
> To create fonts incorporating **oldstyle figures** create a virtual font as per the instructions on page 190.
>
> To create **better footnote numerals**, follow the instructions on page 190.

virtual font where the digits have been replaced by the superior figures from the expert font. First, we need a new encoding font `OT1fn.etx` modeled closely on `OT19.etx`. The following works.

```
\relax
    This is file OT1fn.etx, for use with fontinst.
\encoding
\setcommand\digit#1{#1superior}
\inputtx{OT1}% Then we call OT1.etx.
\endencoding
```

The `\installfont` command to create a footnote font resembles the following.

```
\installfont{padfn7t}{padr8a,padr8x,latin}{OT1fn}%
    {OT1}{pad}{m}{fn}{}
```

We are deviating a bit from the usual font-naming scheme, but when in a frenzy of font creation, it's difficult to know how to incorporate many of our new virtual fonts in a traditional naming scheme.

To use the new font in plain TEX, you must redefine the footnote macros to incorporate this new font `padfn`. Under NFSS, you'll need a redefinition like

```
\renewcommand{\@makefnmark}{\mbox{\normalfont\fontshape{fn}
    \selectfont\@thefnmark}}
```

but be careful—this only works in an environment where '@' acts like a letter (as in the interior of a `.sty` or `.cls` file, or between a pair of `\makeatletter` and `\makeatother` commands). Default footnote marks, like[12345] are not as successful as the "superior"[12345] marks.

7.9.5 Foreign languages

Many languages, such as French, German, Turkish, and so on, use the Latin alphabet together with accents. LATEX and TEX provides many ways to typeset accents but there is an important drawback: Words containing accents inhibit hyphenation by TEX when the accents are entered using the accent

Multilingual Typesetting: First Approximations

For limited typesetting of a foreign language, virtual fonts can ease keyboard entry.

1. Decide on the keyboard conventions that seem convenient, as in figure 7 on the next page.

2. Create a variant encoding file, as on this page, to set up ligature rules for TEX and to create slots in a font for accented and other special characters.

3. Use the new code beginning on page 194 as a model to install the new fonts using *fontinst*.

4. Handle the resulting .vpl and .fd files in the usual way.

commands \', \^, and so on. It's likely that a document with many accented words will display awkward line breaks as a result. Furthermore, TEX's normal keyboard conventions for accents pepper the document with numerous backslashes making the input file hard to read.

When a document is written in a language containing many accented words, virtual fonts can be of service. We can define an accented character as a single letter in a font so its presence will *not* prevent hyphenation. In this font, we can define new ligature patterns to select these characters for us, making it easier to both create and read the input file.

As an example, we can create a "mock" German font family. (German was chosen principally because there are relatively few accented characters to handle.) This font adheres to the keyboard conventions of figure 7 on the facing page.

Instructions for ligatures and inclusions of glyphs in a font are matters of encoding, so all changes are localized in a special encoding file (and, of course, a separate installation file). We edit a copy of OT1.etx called OT1de.etx; de=deutsch (German).

The new file requires three kinds of changes: (1) instructions for the umlaut ligatures; (2) an instruction for the double-s (ß) ligature; and (3) instructions to include the accented glyphs in the font.

Ligature instructions belong with the " character. The *fontinst* \ligature command controls TEX's awareness of ligatures, so we change

```
\setslot{quotedblright}
  \comment{An English double closing quote mark '\,''\,'.}
\endsetslot
```

(this is the fragment for which to search in OT1de.etx) to

```
\setslot{quotedblright}% new lines
  \comment{An English double closing quote mark '\,''\,'.}
  \ligature{LIG}{A}{Adieresis}
  \ligature{LIG}{O}{Odieresis}
  \ligature{LIG}{U}{Udieresis}
  \ligature{LIG}{a}{adieresis}
  \ligature{LIG}{o}{odieresis}
  \ligature{LIG}{u}{udieresis}
\endsetslot
```

and then TEX automatically replaces the designated character pairs when they occur by single German characters. Here, LIG declares to *fontinst* the kind of ligature involved (there are several varieties), the second argument (A or O, and so on) is the letter following the " that TEX scans for, and the final argument (Adieresis, etc.) is the character that TEX uses to replace the pair of characters that would otherwise appear. Encodings use *dieresis* for the usual umlaut and reserve "umlaut" for the Hungarian umlaut.

In the same way, we search OT1de.etx for

```
\setslot{\lc{S}{s}}
   \comment{The letter '{s}'.}
\endsetslot
```

and replace this code by

```
\setslot{\lc{S}{s}}% new lines
   \comment{The letter '{s}'.}
   \ligature{LIG}{s}{germandbls}
\endsetslot
```

Type...	To get...
"a	ä
"o	ö
"u	ü
"A	Ä
"O	Ö
"U	Ü
ss	ß

Figure 7: German input conventions.

The \ligature statement acts to replace two consecutive s's by ß when this font is the current font.

Finally, the font needs slots for ß, ä, and so on; these don't normally occur in an OT1-encoded font. But there's plenty of room—normally, only the initial 128 positions are filled in such a font, and TEX now has room for twice as many characters. To add these additional seven characters, replace

```
\setslot{dieresis}
   \comment{The umlaut or dieresis accent '\"a'.}
\endsetslot
```

(very near the end of the file) by

```
\setslot{dieresis}% new
   \comment{The umlaut or dieresis accent '\"a'.}
\endsetslot
\setslot{Adieresis}
\endsetslot
\setslot{Odieresis}
\endsetslot
\setslot{Udieresis}
\endsetslot
\setslot{adieresis}
\endsetslot
\setslot{odieresis}
\endsetslot
\setslot{udieresis}
\endsetslot
\setslot{germandbls}
\endsetslot
```

An installation file for these fonts resembles the simplest of *fontinst* installation files. The major change is a call to OT1de.etx over OT1.etx. In case we want to install an Adobe Garamond set of German fonts, assuming we had the expert fonts at hand, we can prepare a short installation file to do this:

```
\input fontinst.sty
%% This is file makede.tex
\installfonts
  \installfamily{OT1}{hansa}{}
  \installfont{der}
    {padr8a,padr8x,latin}{OT1de}{OT1}{hansa}{m}{n}{}
  \installfont{die}
    {padri8a,padri8x,latin}{OT1de}{OT1}{hansa}{m}{it}{}
  \installfont{das}
```

```
{pads8a,pads8x,latin}{OT1de}{OT1}{hansa}{m}{s}{}
\endinstallfonts
\bye
```

The fonts created here belong in the hansa family, include an expert font, and comprise three German fonts, a Roman, italic, and semibold.

For plain TeX, the three fonts are called der, die, and das, and after declarations like

```
\font\ger=der \font\gei=die \font\ges=das
```

we can select the fonts with \ger, \gei, and \ges. For NFSS and LaTeX, move OT1hansa.fd to a TeX-aware directory, and type

```
\renewcommand{\rmdefault}{hansa}
```

in the document preamble.

When these fonts are current, we need only type

```
Ein durchdringendes L"auten, der gellende Ruf: Das Theater
f"angt an! weckte mich aus dem sanften Schlaf, in den ich
versunken war; B"as{}se brummen
durcheinander---ein Paukenschlag---Trompetenst"osse---ein
klares A, von der Hoboe ausgehalten---Violinen stimmen
ein: ich reibe mir die Augen.
```

(from *Don Juan* by E. T. A. Hoffmann) to typeset

> Ein durchdringendes Läuten, der gellende Ruf: Das The-
> ater fängt an! weckte mich aus dem sanften Schlaf, in
> den ich versunken war; Bässe brummen durcheinander—
> ein Paukenschlag—Trompetenstöße—ein klares A, von
> der Hoboe ausgehalten—Violinen stimmen ein: ich reibe
> mir die Augen.

Note that the ß ligature can be broken by typing s{}s, s{s}, or something similar. (This display also indicates the importance of proper hyphenation for acceptable typesetting. LaTeX tried to set justified type using the patterns for American English and was unable to. The bad line breaks have been left as an object lesson.)

Lots more remains to be done to typeset documents entirely in German or any other language. Hyphenation patterns need to be set up, punctuation (especially quotation marks) needs adjustment, and other niceties need attention. Please see the languages subdirectory in any CTAN archive. The Babel packages for the current version of LaTeX (in ctan/macros/latex) created under the direction of Johannes Braams are also important resources for foreign-language typesetting. (The Babel keyboard conventions for German differ slightly from those offered above.) A fuller discussion of LaTeX in

Troubleshooting

This brief list contains many of the problems I encountered while preparing the virtual fonts for this book.

- Check and doublecheck that you followed all procedures faithfully and that no typos entered auxiliary files, .fd, or .map files.

- Some multitasking implementations of TEX should be terminated and restarted after new virtual fonts have been installed.

- The .fd files must be in a directory visible to LATEX.

- The .map file must be updated.

- In psfonts.map, there must be at least one space or tab separating each item on a line, including the download '<' character.

- Check the .afm file to make sure the glyph names assigned by the font designer bear some relation to the actual glyphs. (The next chapter discusses this problem with solutions.) That is, sometimes an unusual ligature or alternate form is assigned a glyph name based on its position in the font, rather than on its function.

- Check the values of font parameters in the .afm file to see that they are accurate.

- Make sure there are no out-of-date files on other parts of the input path.

- When rerunning *fontinst*, a new .fd file will overwrite an existing file descriptor. It is common that later runs of *fontinst* will concentrate on fewer files than earlier runs, so the earlier .fd file will have to be protected. You will also need to be careful to add the new font description information to the "protected" .fd file.

a multilingual environment appears in Goossens, Mittelbach, and Samarin (1994, chapter 9).

7.10   Appendix: summary of all *fontinst* commands

The following table only lists all the *fontinst* commands available. Each command is given as an example of its use; for explanations, see the forepart of this chapter or the *fontinst* documentation. These examples are listed alphabetically within category, and assume that all fonts are named strictly according to the Berry font-naming scheme.

Basic commands

`\input fontinst.sty \latinfamily{`*ptm*`}{}\bye`

Use these commands anywhere

`\ifiscommand{`*int*`}\then` *commands* `\fi`
`\ifisdim{`*dim*`}\then` *commands* `\fi`
`\ifisglyph{`*int*`}\then` *commands* `\fi`
`\ifisint{`*int*`}\then` *commands* `\fi`
`\ifisstr{`*int*`}\then` *commands* `\fi`
`\needsfontinstversion{`*version*`}`
`\resetcommand{`*command*`}{`*definition*`}`
`\resetdim{`*dim*`}{`*dimension*`}`
`\resetint{`*int*`}{`*integer expression*`}`
`\resetstr{`*str*`}{`*string*`}`
`\setcommand{`*command*`}{`*definition*`}`
`\setdim{`*dim*`}{`*dimension*`}`
`\setint{`*int*`}{`*integer expression*`}`
`\setstr{`*str*`}{`*string*`}`
`\unsetcommand{`*command*`}{`*definition*`}`
`\unsetdim{`*dim*`}{`*dimension*`}`
`\unsetint{`*int*`}{`*integer expression*`}`
`\unsetstr{`*str*`}{`*string*`}`

Creating integer expressions

`\add{`*integer expression*`}{`*integer expression*`}`
`\depth{`*glyph*`}`
`\div{`*integer expression*`}{`*integer expression*`}`
`\height{`*glyph*`}`
`\int{`*int*`}`
`\italic{`*glyph*`}`
`\kerning{`*left*`}{`*right*`}`
`\mul{`*integer expression*`}{`*integer expression*`}`
`\neg{`*integer expression*`}`
`\scale{`*integer expression*`}{`*integer expression*`}`
`\sub{`*integer expression*`}{`*integer expression*`}`
`\width{`*glyph*`}`

Use these in any *fontinst* file

\declareencoding{*string*}{*etx file*}
\declaresize{*size*}{*fd-size-range*}
\installfonts *Install commands* \endinstallfonts
\substitutenoisy{*from*}{*to*}
\substitutesilent{*from*}{*to*}
\transformfont{*font-name*}{*transformed font*}

Install commands

\installfamily{*encoding*}{*family*}{*fd-commands*}
\installfont{*font-name*}{*list of metric files*}{*encoding file*}%
  {*encoding*}{*family*}{*series*}{*shape*}{*size*}

Transformed fonts

\fromafm{*afm file*}
\frommtx{*mtx file*}
\frompl{*pl file*}
\reencodefont{*etx file*}{*transformed font*}
\scalefont{*integer expression*}{*transformed font*}
\slantfont{*integer expression*}{*transformed font*}
\xscalefont{*integer expression*}{*transformed font*}
\yscalefont{*integer expression*}{*transformed font*}

Encoding files

\relax
ignored material
\encoding
Encoding commands
\endencoding
ignored material

Encoding commands

\inputetx{*encoding file*}
\nextslot{*number*}
\setslot *Slot commands* \endsetslot

These encoding variables may be set in an encoding file

boundarychar   codingscheme   fontdimen(n)   \int{*glyph*}
letterspacing

Slot commands

\comment{*text*}
\ligature{*ligtype*}{*glyph*}{*glyph*}
\nextlarger{*glyph*}
\usedas{*Character type*}{*control sequence*}

\varchar *Varchar commands* \endvarchar

Character types

accent char mathaccent mathbin mathclose mathdelim mathopen
mathord mathpunct mathrel mathvariable

Varchar commands to create extensible characters

\varbot{*glyph*}
\varmid{*glyph*}
\varrep{*glyph*}
\vartop{*glyph*}

Metric files

\relax
ignored material
\metrics
Metric commands
\endmetrics
ignored material

Metric commands

\setglyph{*name*} *Glyph commands* \endsetglyph
\resetglyph{*name*} *Glyph commands* \endsetglyph
\unsetglyph{*name*}
\setrawglyph{*name*}{*font*}{*dimen*}{*integer*}
    {*integer*}{*integer*}{*integer*}{*integer*}
\setnotglyph{*name*}{*font*}{*dimen*}{*integer*}
    {*integer*}{*integer*}{*integer*}{*integer*}
\setkern{*glyph*}{*glyph*}{*integer expression*}
\setleftkerning{*glyph*}{*glyph*}{*integer expression*}
\setrightkerning{*glyph*}{*glyph*}{*integer expression*}
\inputmtx{*metric file*}

Metric variables may be set in metric files

ascender capheight descender designsize *glyph*-spacing
italicslant minimumkern monowidth rawscale underlinethickness
xheight

Glyph commands

\glyph{*glyph*}{*integer expression*}
\glyphpcc{*glyph*}{*integer expression*}{*integer expression*}
\glyphrule{*integer expression*}{*integer expression*}
\glyphspecial{*text*}
\glyphwarning{*text*}
\movert{*integer expression*}
\moveup{*integer expression*}

\push *Glyph commands* \pop
\resetdepth{*integer expression*}
\resetheight{*integer expression*}
\resetitalic{*integer expression*}
\resetwidth{*integer expression*}
\samesize{*glyph*}

· ·

VIRTUAL-FONT PROJECTS

The previous chapter defined and justified virtual-fonts. In this chapter, we'll roll up our sleeves and create several virtual fonts. The presentation will lead the reader through the philosophy behind *fontinst* virtual font tools.

8.1 Getting started

Begin by reviewing the previous chapter and installing *fontinst*. For every scalable, *outline font*, there must be an associated .afm file. The fonts as furnished by a retailer are not virtual fonts, but they become raw fonts in a virtual-font project.

For all of our *bitmap fonts*, we must have an associated .pl property list file. Many—but not all—of the Computer Modern .pl files come with the *fontinst* package. Should you need one of the files that doesn't accompany *fontinst* (or if you don't feel like cluttering up your disk with the files), you can generate these property files as you need them with the tftopl program that should be part of your TEX distribution. (You can issue a command like

```
tftopl /usr/local/lib/tex/fonts/tfm/cmfib8.tfm cmfib8.pl
```

at the terminal prompt—that is, tftopl needs to know where the .tfm files reside.)

Any .pl files and .afm files you use must be in a TEX input directory; that is, if any of these file names were part of an \input or \documentclass command, TEX would be able to read that file.

A *glyph* is a character that cannot be broken down into simpler components. 'A', '%', and ']' are examples of glyphs. An accented character like 'à' is often built out of two glyphs—an 'a' and an accent '`', although in some fonts, accented letters like à are designed as single, distinct, unbreakable glyphs.

Even *fontinst* has trouble making sense out of information in an .afm or .pl file. Who could have foreseen the need to make these files readable by

TEX? After reading one of these files, the first thing *fontinst* does is create an associated `.mtx` file with the metric information written in a way that is easier for *fontinst* to make sense of. After a *fontinst* run, your working directory will be littered with many new .mtx files, each named after some .afm or .pl file. These files are temporary and can be deleted at the conclusion of the virtual font process. Leave them for the interim, for if they exist, *fontinst* will read them in preference to their parent .afm file, and the virtual font process runs a little faster in their presence. (*Be careful* of issuing a command like del *.mtx or rm *.mtx until you make sure that permanent files like latin.mtx are in separate directories.)

8.1.1   Subsequent definitions in fontinst

In plain TEX, any definition quietly replaces an earlier definition of the same name. LATEX, on the other hand, flags as an error any attempt to redefine an existing macro command. The *fontinst* macros travel down yet a third road—the *first* definition of an object takes precedence; subsequent definitions of the same object are not errors, but are silently ignored. This way, if descriptions of a general case come at the end of the input process, we can easily specialize to our particular needs with only modest modification of the distribution files. We simply make sure that *fontinst* learns the details of our special case before it reads in the description of the general case.

Here's an example: suppose we want to create a SMALL CAPS font. The file latin.mtx is often the last metric file called by an \installfont command. This file of last resort contains the definitions of many Latin glyphs, more than any font could call for, and includes small caps.

- In case we *don't* have an expert font (the special font containing real small caps) at hand, instructions in latin.mtx explain how to fudge small caps from pint-sized uppercase letters.

- But if we *do* have the expert font, information about this font and its glyphs will precede the instructions in latin.mtx. Consequently, *fontinst* will ignore the definitions in latin.mtx, and the resulting small caps font will contain true small caps.

8.1.2   Names of Latin glyphs

For many of our projects, we'll need a file latin.gly that will be a base for systematically modifying all the Latin glyphs. We can edit a copy of latin.mtx into latin.gly in this way.

1. Look for all lines that contain either an occurrence of \unfakable or \setglyph. Change every line like

   ```
   \unfakable{Gamma}
   ```

or

```
\setglyph{dotlessj}
```

into lines like

```
\newglyph{Gamma}
\newglyph{dotlessj}
```

and *remove* all other lines in this file.

2. Include \newglyph{...} lines for any other special glyphs that you
   plan to have in your virtual font. Such special glyphs might be unusual
   ligatures (ct) or swash characters (M).

3. Add the lines

```
\relax
\metrics
```

   at the beginning of the file.

4. Add the line

```
\endmetrics
```

   at the very bottom of the file.

Hearty editors like Emacs or scripts in Perl, awk, or Icon make light work
of this task. Here is a Perl script to create the basic latin.gly file. (But you
still need to add special \newglyph commands to this file yourself.)

```
# This is file makegly.prl
open (LATIN,
  "/usr/local/lib/tex/inputs/latin.mtx");# <== adjust this
open (LATOUT, ">latin.gly");
print LATOUT "\\relax\n\n\\metrics\n\n"; # start file
while (<LATIN>) {
  next unless /^\\unfakable/ || /^\\setglyph/;# get line
  $_ =~ /\\[a-z]+\{([A-Za-z]+)\}/; # strip off junk
  print LATOUT "\\newglyph{$1}\n"; # build/write new line
}
print LATOUT "\n\\endmetrics\n";   # end the file
```

You may invoke this by typing

```
perl makegly.prl
```

assuming the Perl executable is part of your path. (Adjust the first open statement to reflect the location of latin.mtx on your system.)

8.2 Underline and strikeout fonts

LATEX and TEX provide several alternatives for underlining snippets of text, but they generally require switching to math mode or placing the text in a box. But what if you need to underline an entire paragraph? The underlining must not inhibit TEX from breaking lines properly and deciding on hyphenation, and so the foregoing strategies are no longer appropriate.

For fonts designed with METAFONT, it's straightforward to alter the font programs to automatically include an understroke as part of each character. But an underbar is such a simple typographic element that we can construct a virtual font to do the underlining for us. (Besides, font programs for non-META-fonts do not exist.)

In an underline font, each new character should be the old character under which we slip a horizontal rule segment exactly the width of the character. A construction like the following uses *fontinst* syntax to underline the argument of the \uline command.

```
\setcommand\uline#1{%      underlining
  \ifisglyph{#1}\then
    \resetglyph{#1}
      \push
        \moveup{-150}\glyphrule{\width{#1}}{40}
      \pop
      \glyph{#1}{1000}
    \endresetglyph
  \fi
}
```

Since \uline is a new command, \setcommand operates like \def or \newcommand. The \push-\pop pair makes sure that the intervening commands have no effect on the dimensions of the final glyph. Each unit in the arguments to the positioning commands refers to thousandths of the font size, so \moveup{-150} really means move down by 1.5 pt. The rule will be as wide as a character and 0.4 pt thick. After drawing the rule, TEX will insert the original character, and adopt its dimensions. The \ifisglyph command at the beginning ensures that the glyph in the argument already exists (there's no point underlining something that doesn't exist).

To use this command, you'll need to copy latin.gly to uline.mtx. Then, insert this definition of \uline at the beginning of the file, but after the \metrics statement. Following this command, but before the first \newglyph statement, add the instruction

```
\let\newglyph=\uline
```

to make \newglyph behave like \uline.

An installation file to create an underline Garamond font might resemble the following.

```
\input fontinst.sty
\installfonts
  \installfamily{OT1}{pad}{}
  \installfont{padru7t}{padr7t,uline}%
    {OT1}{OT1}{pad}{m}{un}{}
\endinstallfonts
\bye
```

There are a couple of noteworthy points in this construction:

1. We are allowed to use virtual fonts created in a previous exercise as raw fonts in a current project. The raw font for this font is the regular Garamond font—a virtual font—that has been previously created. Before we run this file through TEX, we need the property list file for the regular font (after all, there's no .afm file for a virtual font), so we type something like

```
tftopl
  /usr/local/lib/tex/fonts/tfm/padr7t.tfm
  padr7t.pl
```

(Unix syntax for a traditional system; type this all on a single line) or

```
tftopl
  /usr/local/lib/tex/fonts/tfm/adobe/agaramon/padr7t.tfm
  padr7t.pl
```

(for a TDS system).

2. Since the font family already exists, we must merge the new .fd file to the existing one.

3. We can dispense with a reference to latin.mtx in the installation file since any missing glyphs have already been handled at the time that the virtual font padr7t was born.

By the way, a similar procedure will underline a bit-mapped font like cmr10. After we've created a property file via

```
tftopl ⟨path⟩/cmr10.tfm cmr10.pl
```

Creating an Underline Font (or Overstrike Font)

- Create file `uline.mtx`.

- Create the property `.pl` files for each font that will be under-lined.

- Create the installation file as on page 205 (scalable fonts) or page 206 (Computer Modern). Run this file through TₑX.

- Create the new `.tfm` and `.vf` files for each new underline font using `pltotf` and `vptovf`. Move these files to the proper places on your hard disk.

- Merge the new `.fd` file with the existing `.fd` file for that family.

- You will most likely *not* need a new entry in `psfonts.map` be-cause each underline font resolves to raw fonts, each of which is already present in that file.

In case you need an overstrike (strikeout) font, you will also need a file `strike.mtx`, as described below.

then a short installation file like

```
\input fontinst.sty
\installfonts
   \installfamily{OT1}{cmr}{}
   \installfont{cmrun10}{cmr10,uline}%
     {OT1}{OT1}{cmr}{m}{un}{10}
\endinstallfonts
\bye
```

does the trick.

Follow the procedure in the box on this page to generate the virtual font. Those directions generated this font; you may care to adjust the thickness and position of the underline rule. Notice how line breaking and hyphen-ation proceed as usual.

8.2.1 Strikeout fonts

A ~~strikeout, or overstrike, font is the same as an underline font, but the rule appears above the baseline instead of below it.~~ A strikeout is just an underline that's lost its way. Clearly, we need only modify the definition of

\uline to place the bar above the baseline by some amount. Create a file called strike.mtx identical to uline.mtx except for a definition at the top of the file, which should read

```
\setcommand\strike#1{
  \ifisglyph{#1}\then
    \resetglyph{#1}
      \push
        \moveup{200}\glyphrule{\width{#1}}{40}
      \pop
      \glyph{#1}{1000}
    \endresetglyph
  \fi
}
\let\newglyph = \strike
```

The installation file should be augmented by a line like

```
\installfont{padrst7t}{padr7t,strike}{OT1}%
  {OT1}{pad}{m}{st}{}
```

for a scalable font, or

```
\installfont{cmrst10}{cmr10,strike}{OT1}%
  {OT1}{cmr}{m}{st}{10}
```

for a Computer Modern font. Otherwise, you should adhere to the procedure sketched on the preceding page.

Accessing new virtual fonts   In plain TeX, insert declarations like

```
\font\uline=padru7t   \font\strike=padrst7t
```

or perhaps

```
\font\uline=cmrun10   \font\strike=cmrst10
```

after which \uline or \strike select these fonts in the usual way.

Under LaTeX and the NFSS, you may select these fonts using the new shapes un (underline) and st (overstrike). That is, type something like

```
{\normalfont\fontshape{un}\selectfont ⟨Underlined text⟩}
```

or

```
{\normalfont\fontshape{st}\selectfont ⟨Overstruck text⟩}
```

to underline or overstrike the text.

8.2.2   One-hundred-percent underlining

<u>The underline font underlines words only. We have to work only a little harder to underline interword space as well.</u>

<u>   The technique we use exploits the equivalence between interword space and horizontal leaders. The normal, stretch, shrink components for a word space are given by</u> `\fontdimen` <u>parameters 2, 3, and 4 (a bunch of</u> `\font-dimen`<u>'s are always set each time we select a font).</u> (The typewriter words aren't underlined since I hadn't prepared a typewriter underline font.) The values of these parameters are available to us. Here's how we proceed in LATEX. First we capture the normal values of interword spacing. At the same time, we define a rule that will line up with the underline, and create leader glue that uses this rule.

```
\newskip\fontskip
{\normalfont\fontshape{un}\selectfont
 \global\fontskip=\fontdimen2\the\font%
 plus\fontdimen3\the\font minus\fontdimen4\the\font\relax}
\def\underrule{\hrule depth1.5pt height-1.1pt}
\def\underspace{\leaders\underrule\hskip\fontskip}
```

Next, we make sure that whenever a space or carriage return has *active status*, it invokes the underspace leader. Furthermore, this definition should hold only within the `underlining` environment, which is what the new 'weird-type' conditional allows us to test for. Outside of this environment, the active space and active carriage return the meaning we expect when `\obey-lines` and `\obeyspaces` are in force. (Any character that is *active* can be assigned a definition like any normal control sequence or control symbol, but it is only a single character in length.)

```
\newif\ifweirdtype \weirdtypefalse
{\obeyspaces\global\let\savespace= %
\gdef {\ifweirdtype\weirdspace\else\savespace\fi}}
{\catcode`\^^M=\active \global\let\savecr=^^M%
\gdef^^M{\ifweirdtype\weirdspace\else\savecr\fi}%
\gdef\Par^^M{\par}}
```

Incidentally, you must type these instructions *exactly* as shown. The `\Par` command is a paragraph separator within this environment. It *must* appear on its own line. (Here, `^^M` is how TEX refers to the end-of-line.) Finally, we define a LATEX environment to use this material.

```
\newenvironment{underlining}{\bgroup%
\let\weirdspace=\underspace%
\normalfont\fontshape{un}\selectfont%
\leavevmode\weirdtypetrue\catcode`\ =\active\relax%
```

```
\catcode'\^^M=\active\relax}{\egroup}
```

With these definitions and conventions in place, we typed

```
\begin{underlining}%
The creation of ...
   ...
...as well.
\Par
The technique...
   ...
...a font).%
\end{underlining}
```

to get the above display. Note well—it was necessary to end the final line of the text with the percent sign \%, otherwise we get one extra "underspace" before returning to normal text.

In plain TEX, we capture the value of the \fontdimens for \fontskip the same way. The definitions for \underrule and \underspace remain the same, as do the definitions for active spaces, carriage returns, and \Par. Formal environments don't exist in plain TEX, so we need to define two pseudo-environment commands. After

```
\def\underlining{\bgroup\let\weirdspace=\underspace%
\rmun\leavevmode\weirdtypetrue\catcode'\ =\active\relax%
\catcode'\^^M=\active\relax}
\def\endunderlining{\egroup}
```

where \rmun is the control sequence to select the underline font, we type

```
\underlining
The creation of ...
   ...
...font).%
\endunderlining
```

to completely underline a selection of text.

See page 255 for more adventures in underlining.

To completely overstrike text, we will follow the instructions above for complete underlining. It will be necessary to replace references to \underrule and \underspace by

```
\def\strikerule{\hrule height2.4pt depth -2pt}
\def\strikespace{\leaders\strikerule\hskip\fontskip}
```

but the definitions for active spaces and carriage returns remain the same.

Now, we can define environments for overstriking in the obvious way. For example, under LaTeX, after

```
\newenvironment{strikeout}{\bgroup%
\let\weirdspace=\strikespace%
\normalfont\fontshape{st}\selectfont%
\leavevmode\weirdtypetrue\catcode`\ =\active\relax%
\catcode`\^^M=\active\relax}{\egroup}
```

we can enclose text in a strikeout environment.

8.3   Poor man's bold fonts

The author of TeX has shown how to create "poor man's bold" characters by capturing a character and printing it several times with slight offsets from its original position [Knuth (1986a), p. 386]. The result is imperfect, but may be better than nothing. We can apply this to fonts, and boldly create fonts where no bold font existed before. The technique might be useful for creating bold math fonts or bold versions of fonts that don't otherwise exist.

Within the Computer Modern family, for example, there are typewriter fonts that lack bold variants. We can use the *The TeXbook* approach to create computer typewriter bold virtual fonts. (Since we have the METAFONT parameter files, we can also modify METAFONT parameters to produce bold variants, but we will not follow that approach here.)

We will now describe two slightly different procedures for generating "poor man's bold" fonts for bitmap and for scalable fonts. The complete details appear in the box on page 214.

In either case, we'll need a copy of latin.gly called pmb.mtx. Add the lines

```
\setcommand\pmb#1{%
  \ifisglyph{#1}\then
    \resetglyph{#1}
      \push\movert{-25}\glyph{#1}{1000}\pop
      \push\movert{ 25}\glyph{#1}{1000}\pop
      \push\moveup{ 43}\glyph{#1}{1000}\pop
      \samesize{#1}
    \endresetglyph
  \fi
}
\let\newglyph=\pmb
```

immediately following the line \metrics but before any \newglyph command. The \pmb command mimics the action of *The TeXbook*'s \pmb—it emboldens its argument (each individual character) by typesetting several copies of the character, each slightly offset from the others. The bold glyph is to have the same dimensions as the original glyph.

```
\input fontinst.sty
\installfonts
   \installfamily{OT1}{cmtt}{}
      \installfont{cmbtt10}{cmtt10,pmb}%
         {OT1tt}{OT1}{cmtt}{b}{n}{10}
      \installfont{cmbitt10}{cmitt10,pmb}%
         {OT1tt}{OT1}{cmtt}{b}{sl}{10}
      \installfont{cmbslt10}{cmsltt10,pmb}%
         {OT1tt}{OT1}{cmtt}{b}{it}{10}
      \installfont{cmbsct10}{cmtcsc10,pmb}%
         {OT1tt}{OT1}{cmtt}{b}{sc}{10}
\endinstallfonts
\bye
```

Figure 1: A `fontinst` file for a family of bold typewriter fonts.

Next, for each base font we seek to embolden, we will need property list files. Figure 1 lists an installation file for generating some bold additions to a Computer Modern typewriter family. For each of the raw fonts in this figure (namely `cmtt10`, `cmitt10`, `cmsltt10`, and `cmtcsc10`), we enter a series of commands like

```
tftopl ⟨path⟩/cmtt10.tfm cmtt10.pl
```

in our working directory. Once these files and `pmb.mtx` are present in an inputs directory, we'll follow the usual procedures to create the new virtual fonts. In plain TEX, a line like

```
\font\ttb = cmbtt10
```

makes `\ttb` select **bold typewriter type**. In LATEX, any command like

```
\fontfamily{cmtt}\fontseries{b}\selectfont
```

will select this same font.

The same procedure applies to outline fonts. We still need `pmb.mtx` and the `.pl` files. This time, the calls to `tftopl` look like

```
tftopl ⟨path⟩/bfar7t.tfm bfar7t.pl
```

where here, `bfa` is the font family (Bernhard Fashion, in this example) in the regular `r` weight in an OT1 (`7t`) encoding. We use previously installed virtual fonts as raw fonts. The installation file is like that of figure 2.

```
\input fontinst.sty
\installfonts
  \installfamily{OT1}{bfa}{}
  \installfont{bfab7t}{bfar7t,latin,pmb}{OT1}%
    {OT1}{bfa}{b}{n}{}
  \installfont{bfabc7t}{bfarc7t,latin,pmb}{OT1}%
    {OT1}{bfa}{b}{n}{}
  \installfont{bfabo7t}{bfaro7t,latin,pmb}{OT1}%
    {OT1}{bfa}{b}{n}{}
\endinstallfonts
\bye
```

Figure 2: A fontinst file for a family of bold fonts based on Bernhard Fashion.

Bernhard Fashion dates from the years preceding World War II. It adds a lovely Art Deco touch to typesetting:

This is Art Deco typesetting with TEX.

Although it's normally furnished in a single weight, the VFINST installation sets up mock small caps and oblique fonts. Using the procedures detailed above, we can then generate bold versions, and because the Bernhard strokes are all hairlines, it's possible to approximate several strengths of boldness. All this is illustrated in figure 3. There is a danger in increasing the offset in the \pmb command in a misguided effort to increase the degree of boldness. Here's what happens if you try that with Bernhard Fashion:

It's no longer poor man's bold; it's now another effect entirely.

8.4   f-words

In this book, an *f-word* is a word that *ends* in 'f'. Have you ever examined—closely examined—examples of tight typesetting? Magazines like *The New Yorker*, which use narrow columns in their layout, are good places to look. A problem often arises with f-words because the hook of the final f protrudes far to the right out of the intrinsic type box. With tight type, the hook appears to swallow the interword space, and it looks like the words run together. The reader should compare

self hatred, half Time, of X-rays, if Europe

which has been normally typeset, with the tightly set

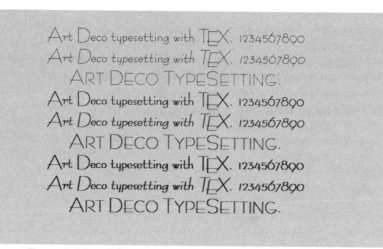

Figure 3: Virtual font magic with Bernhard Fashion types.

self hatred, half Time, of X-rays, if Europe

to see the difference. (This problem tends not to occur in Computer Modern fonts, as the outward protrusion of the f is restrained, at least in comparison with PostScript fonts.) Because two important little words ('if' and 'of') are f-words, this is an important problem.

We'd like to automatically add a small amount of extra space after any f-word. The recent versions of TEX have provision for designating an entry in a font table as a 'boundarychar'; not really a character, this construct denotes a word boundary. It can enter into kern and ligature combinations, so TEX can automatically select special glyphs for the beginnings and endings of words.

While this is certainly vital for Hebrew or Arabic TEX systems, it will be of some assistance even in this instance. Because the boundarychar behaves just like any other character, we can kern against it, and this solves our problem for us. We'll arrange things so anytime an f is adjacent and to the left of a boundarychar (that is, f is at the end of a word), TEX will add a kern, the effect of which will be to keep an f-word and its right neighbor well-spaced no matter how tight the typesetting. (This approach was suggested to the author by Alan Jeffrey.)

The box on page 216 summarizes the steps we need to take. We need to make changes to both the new metric file and the encoding file. Let's deal with the metric file first.

The metric changes are easy since we may encapsulate these revisions in a special file f.mtx that will follow latin.mtx in any \installfont command. Here are the contents of this short file.

```
\relax
```

"Poor Man's Bold" Fonts

This section described the general scheme for generating pseudo-bold typewriter fonts. This box presents the details.

- Create the file `pmb.mtx` as described above.

- Create a property list file for each base file with a command like

```
tftopl cmtt10.tfm cmtt10.pl
```

    (bitmap fonts) or

```
tftopl bfar7t.tfm bfar7t.pl
```

    (scalable fonts). Make sure to include the path prefix in front of each `.tfm` file so `tftopl` knows where to find the metric file.

- Create an installation file as on page 211 for bitmap fonts or as on page 212 for outline fonts, and run TEX on this file.

- Use `vptovf` on each `.vpl` file.

- Move the new `.vf` and `.tfm` files to the proper places on the hard disk.

- Merge the new `.fd` file with the pre-existing `.fd` file for the font family.

- Clean up the working directory: delete the `.mtx`, `.log`, `.pl`, `.vpl`, and other auxiliary files.

- An entry for the map file `psfonts.map` will almost certainly *not* be necessary. If the new fonts are built from outline fonts, then an entry for the base fonts already exists. If the new fonts are built from bitmap fonts, then map entries aren't needed.

```
This is file f.mtx, for specifying
the metric changes for an f-word font.
\metrics
  \setint{fcorr}{100}
    % approx 1/10 of the font size (1pt at 10pt)
  \setkern{f}{boundarychar}{\int{fcorr}}
  \setkern{ff}{boundarychar}{\int{fcorr}}
```

```
\endmetrics
```

This file begins by defining a correction factor fcorr, the amount of additional space to place to the right of an f-word. The command \setint is the *fontinst* way of defining a variable and setting its value. The amount here works well for Adobe Garamond, but some experimentation may be necessary for other fonts. Next, we let the kerning between a final f (which can either occur in isolation or as part of an ff ligature) be equal to this correction factor. In any installation file, we will call f.mtx after calling latin.mtx, for we want to make sure that glyphs f and ff have received some sort of definition (it's the purpose of latin.mtx to flesh out such definitions in case these glyphs aren't present in the font).

We record some brief changes to the encoding in a copy of OT1.etx called OT1f.etx. Simply change the final

```
\endencoding
```

instruction to

```
\setslot{boundarychar}
    \comment{The boundary character.}
\endsetslot
\endencoding
```

and save the file. This simple change allocates a slot to the font for the boundarychar that is not automatically present in the encoding. This alteration highlights the reason why we rely so heavily on OT1-encoded fonts in this narrative—there is plenty of space in the OT1 encoding for new characters. Cork-encoded fonts (designation T1) are full to the brim so there's no room for the boundarychar. It's possible to use these fonts, of course, but only after discarding some characters from the encoding to make room for new virtual characters. In an f-word font, we would want to discard one character and replace it by boundarychar.

The installation file for an Adobe Garamond f-font looks as follows.

```
\input fontinst.sty
\installfonts
  \installfamily{OT1}{pad}{}
  \installfont{padrf7t}{padr7t,latin,f}{OT1f}%
    {OT1}{pad}{m}{f}{}
\endinstallfonts
\bye
```

The presence throughout of the variant f should suggest the new functionality of the f-font. (This file assigns it a font shape called 'f'.)

Coping with f-words

An *f-word* is a word ending in f.

- Since previously created virtual fonts serve as raw fonts for each f-font, type a command like

  ```
  tftopl padr7t.tfm padr7t.pl
  ```

- We need to prepare an installation file as shown on the previous page. Run this file through plain TEX.

- Use `vptovf` to create the virtual font. Move the `.vf` and `.tfm` files where they belong.

- Merge the entries from the current `.fd` file into the pre-existing `.fd` file for this font family.

- New entries to `psfonts.map` will *not* be necessary as long as the pre-existing base fonts had been properly installed.

- In the usual way, clean up the working directory by deleting superfluous auxiliary files. (But make sure to preserve `f.mtx`.)

Typeset with our f-font, this nonsense paragraph,

Self hatred is a fearsome problem of emerging personalities. Half the problem with Eff Words or Eff Phrases is the shelf life (or is it Shelf Life?) of concern—we call this the half life of Eff problems.

shows that even in normal situations, the excess 'f'-space is not objectionable. In tight spots, such as

self hatred, half Time, of X-rays, if Europe

(compare this with the samples at the start of this section), our special final f glyph does preserve interword spacing.

In conclusion, it's instructive to consider an approach that fails. It's tempting to define a special glyph called 'finalf', which is indistinguishable from the usual lowercase f except that it is a little wider. The added width consists of extra space on the right of the type. We could set up a virtual font to automatically select this character whenever a final f is followed by white space (a ligature rule would check to see if an f is followed by the boundary character). That effectively adds a dollop of space after an f-word, but other interword spaces and the spacing surrounding the appearance of f elsewhere will be unaffected. However, if a line ends with an f-word, this extra space present may cause the right margin to appear slightly ragged to an especially sharp-eyed reader.

8.5   Composite fonts

The early history of italic fonts shows that they were originally a composite font composed of new italic forms for the lower case alphabet plus the standard upright Roman form for the upper case; see, for example, Aldus Manutius's 1501 edition of Virgil's *Æneid*. Although such a font is of limited use today, it provides a good example of a *composite font*, one created from large portions of existing fonts, that we can manufacture using the virtual font mechanism. (The MathInst utility described in chapter 10 creates new fonts for math typesetting that are themselves composite fonts.) Let's create a font that takes all lowercase letters, digits, punctuation, and other special characters from an italic font. Only the uppercase alphabet will come from an upright font.

The problem from *fontinst*'s point of view is that we read font information on an "all or none" basis; we can't pick and choose portions of a font without some care. A first attempt at installing the font by means of the (naïve) *fontinst* instruction

```
\installfont{padroi7t}{padri7t,padr7t,latin}%
  {OT1}{OT1}{pad}{m}{oi}{}
```

simply recreates an italic font under a new name. Here, we are using Adobe Garamond (pad) fonts as the raw fonts, and the 'oi' designation suggests "original italic" fonts; we are using the OT1 encoding. By the time TeX reads metric information for padr7t, the Roman raw font, all the slots have already been filled with glyphs from the italic font padri7t; recall that *fontinst* silently ignores later information (in this case, information concerning the upright font) in favor of prior information (here, the italic font).

We can selectively discard certain glyph information before ingesting the Roman font. A file ucoff.mtx, with the following structure, does the trick:

```
\relax
This is file ucoff.mtx for discarding upper case glyph
  information.
\metrics
  \unsetglyph{A}
  \unsetglyph{B}
  \unsetglyph{C}
    ...
    ...
```

```
    \unsetglyph{Z}
  \endmetrics
```

(Don't forget to replace the ellipses by \unsetglyph commands for the remainder of the alphabet.) Now when TEX reads metric information for the
Roman font, it ignores everything *except* the capital letters. The complete
installation file should resemble the following.

```
  \input fontinst.sty
    \transformfont{padri8r}%
      {\reencodefont{8r}{\fromafm{padri8a}}}
    \transformfont{padr8r}%
      {\reencodefont{8r}{\fromafm{padr8a}}}
  \installfonts
    \installfamily{OT1}{pad}{}
    \installfont{padroi7t}{padri7t,ucoff,padr7t,latin}%
      {OT1}{OT1}{pad}{m}{oi}{}
  \endinstallfonts
  \bye
```

If you have the appropriate expert fonts, you'll need to include the statement

```
    \transformfont{padri8x}{\reencodefont{8r}{\fromafm{padri8x}}}
```

with the other \transformfont's, and the \installfont command should
read

```
    \installfont{padroi7t}{padri7t, padri8x, %
      ucoff,padr7t,latin}\{OT1}{OT1}{pad}{m}{oi}{}
```

This is almost the virtual font used to typeset figure 4 on the facing page.
(Refer to page 238 to learn about 8r.)

Shortcomings of this composite font   Although only font fanatics are likely
to find the font described above unsatisfactory, it's important to at least understand its shortcomings. As constructed above, all kerning pairs involving
uppercase characters are wrong.

When we read in the information for the italic raw font, *fontinst* recorded both glyph and kern information for all characters. Unsetting the uppercase glyphs nullified the glyph information, but did nothing to the kern
information. Although the final glyph information is correct, the virtual
font uses kerning information for the uppercase letters that is appropriate
only for the original italic font. Unfortunately, there is no '\unsetkern'
command in *fontinst*.

What should the proper kerning information look like? Until a font
designer sits down and determines the actual values that pertain to upright

Arms, and the man I sing, who, forc'd by fate,
And haughty Juno's unrelenting hate,
Expell'd and exil'd, left the Trojan shore,
Long labors, both by land and sea, he bore,
And in the doubtful war, before he won
The Latian realm, and built the destin'd town;
His banish'd gods restor'd to rites divine,
And settled sure succession in his line,
From whence the race of Alban fathers come,
And the long glories of majestic Rome.

Figure 4: These lines are drawn from the beginning of the *Æneid*, translation by John Dryden.

capitals adjacent to lowercase glyphs, it's probably best to have these kern values be zero. Here's how we proceed.

First, we need to prevent italic kerning information from entering TEX's memory. When *fontinst* reads a metric .mtx file, this information is provided by a set of \setkern commands; a single command looks like

```
\setkern{A}{b}{-30}
```

which subtracts 30 units of space whenever 'Ab' is typeset. (Since there are 1000 units in the font size, 30 units represents three-tenths of a point at 10-pt.) We can cancel this effect by judiciously redefining \setkern. The short file kernoff.mtx does this for us.

```
\relax
  This is file kernoff.mtx, for cancelling kern information.
\metrics
  \let\savedsetkern=\setkern % save the original def'n.
  \resetcommand\setkern#1#2#3{}
\endmetrics
```

After ingesting the italic glyph information, we set the kern information for the vertical bar character. This glyph, called bar in the Adobe Standard Encoding, commonly has no kerning associated with it. We explicitly set the kerns to zero, intending to use these values later. This is the function of uckerns.mtx.

```
\relax
  This is file uckerns.mtx.
\metrics
```

```
    \let\setkern=\savedsetkern % restore original def'n.
    \setcommand\barkern#1{\setkern{bar}{#1}{0}%
      \setkern{#1}{bar}{0}}
    \barkern{A}
    \barkern{B}
    \barkern{C}
      ...
    \barkern{Y}
    \barkern{Z}
    \barkern{a}
      ...
    \barkern{z}
  \endmetrics
```

Now, to restore all kerning, we need the file `barkern.mtx`

```
    \relax
      This is file barkern.mtx
    \metrics
      \setcommand\setkerning#1#2#3{%
        \setleftkerning{#1}{#2}{#3}%
        \setrightkerning{#1}{#2}{#3}}
      \setcommand\nokernsfor#1{\setkerning{#1}{bar}{1000}}%
        % since bars are not kerned, this
        % should turn off kerning for glyph #1
      \nokernsfor A
      \nokernsfor B
        ...
      \nokernsfor Z
    \endmetrics
```

to explicitly assign the bar kerns for capital letters. Now, we reread the italic metrics to learn about the kern pairs for the nonuppercase letters, unset the uppercase glyphs (as above), and use the Roman capitals. We can continue to use the installation file described above, provided we use this new \installfont command:

```
    \installfont{padroi7t}{kernoff,padri8r,uckerns,barkern,%
      padri8r,ucoff,padr8r}{OT1}{OT1}{pad}{m}{oi}{}
```

It is *this* font used in figure 4 on the previous page.

8.6 New encodings, alternate fonts

An increasing number of fonts are now available together with special *alternate fonts*, fonts with wonderful alternative characters. Now that the work of translating most traditional fonts to digital format seems to have been

completed, more alternate fonts (and expert fonts) will appear. Among the
notable font families that already include alternate fonts are Adobe Garamond and Adobe Caslon; Centaur and Fournier from Monotype; Chiante
and Bernhard Modern from Bitstream; and Mantinia and the fine cutting of
Galliard from the Carter and Cone digital foundry. The reigning monarch
of alternate fonts is the Poetica font family from Adobe. [This last has been
considered in connection with TEX already; see Hoenig (1995).]

Although alternate fonts may never be suitable for common typesetting
tasks, the exercise of creating alternate virtual fonts for use by LATEX and
TEX is valuable because it ties together all threads from previous projects. In
this section, we will consider three projects—Adobe Garamond, Bitstream
Bernhard Modern, and the Mantinia font from Carter and Cone.

8.6.1 Adobe Garamond

Adobe Garamond has with it several alternate fonts, each containing special
old-fashioned glyphs that give character to a document (but a little such
character goes a long way—be frugal). There are two alternate fonts, which
match the roman and italic fonts. Our task is to create special roman and
italic virtual fonts that contain the usual and alternate characters, together
with special ligature rules that automatically typeset the special characters
in the proper circumstances. We can imagine that a new metric file will be
needed, but we will also need a new encoding with enough space to put the
new characters. As an additional challenge, we would like to use only a single new metric and encoding file for the new alternate roman and alternate
italic fonts.

The first task is a mini-installation of the alternate fonts. We install the
two alternate fonts under the names `padr81` and `padri81`, assuming we use
`pad` as the family designation.

A table like that of figure 5 on the following page combines all the alternate characters from both fonts into a single chart. Although the alternate
fonts don't have many glyph names in common, it is a good idea to create a
single set of files `padalt.mtx` and `padalt.etx` to avoid an unruly prolifera-
tion of auxiliary files (and to get some interesting practice with *fontinst*).

The new alternate fonts   How shall we select the wonderful characters of
figure 5 on the next page for typesetting? The `\char` mechanism is always
available, but too many `\char`'s can make an input file unreadable and anyway, who wants to depend on a font table to prepare an input file?

Some characters get selected in the obvious way. We'll expect the new ligatures ct, st, and so on to appear whenever ct or st are adjacent pairs in the
input. The italic swash caps will replace their plain Jane italic counterparts.
After all, if we need the plainer italic caps, we can always typeset them by
dropping down to the regular italic. In the same way, the alternate Q shall
replace the usual uppercase Q in the new alternate roman font.

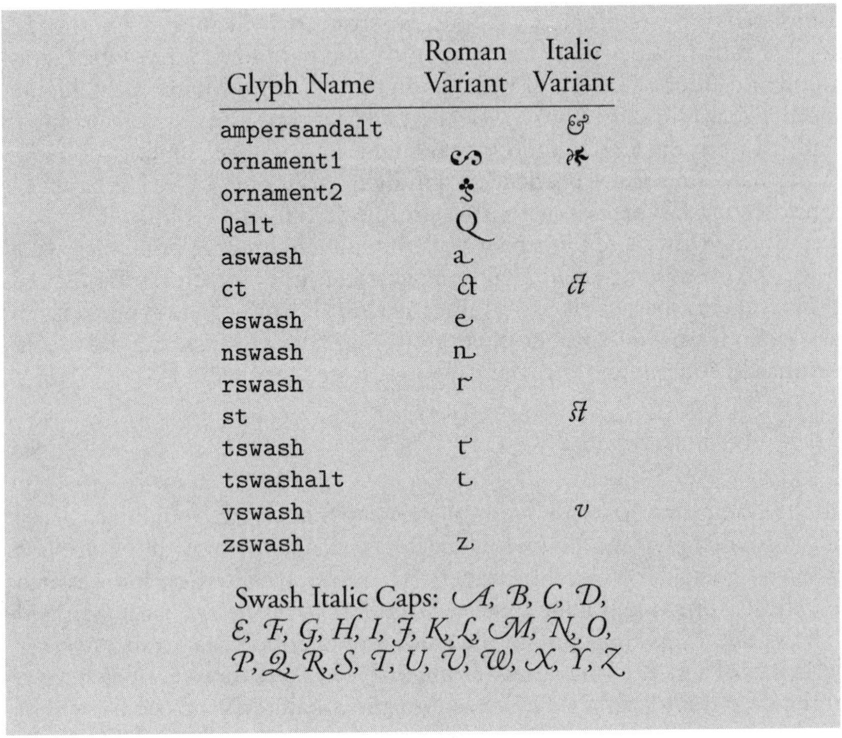

Glyph Name	Roman Variant	Italic Variant
ampersandalt		$\mathscr{E}$
ornament1	✍	✍
ornament2	♣	
Qalt	Q	
aswash	a	
ct	ct	ct
eswash	e	
nswash	n	
rswash	r	
st		st
tswash	t	
tswashalt	t	
vswash		v
zswash	z	

Swash Italic Caps: $\mathcal{A}$, $\mathcal{B}$, $\mathcal{C}$, $\mathcal{D}$,
$\mathcal{E}$, $\mathcal{F}$, $\mathcal{G}$, $\mathcal{H}$, $\mathcal{I}$, $\mathcal{J}$, $\mathcal{K}$, $\mathcal{L}$, $\mathcal{M}$, $\mathcal{N}$, $\mathcal{O}$,
$\mathcal{P}$, $\mathcal{Q}$, $\mathcal{R}$, $\mathcal{S}$, $\mathcal{T}$, $\mathcal{U}$, $\mathcal{V}$, $\mathcal{W}$, $\mathcal{X}$, $\mathcal{Y}$, $\mathcal{Z}$

Figure 5: Alternate characters.

The swash lowercase letters are more interesting. The roman glyphs, with their swash strokes extending to the right, are appropriate for word endings only, so we will rely on the boundarychar mechanism to select these characters automatically when they appear at word endings. In the same way, the italic v belongs only at the start of a word, and we'll rely on boundarychar yet again to select and typeset it automatically.

That leaves a small handful of characters for which these rules of "natural selection" won't suffice. We may appropriate another rule from the usual rules of input—some punctuation immediately followed by the single left quote enters into ligatures to typeset their Spanish counterparts (?' becomes ¿) and we can appropriate that convention for an alternate font. Let's agree to typeset the ornaments in these fonts via 1' and 2' to generate ✍ and ♣. And although cat typesets 'cat', we will agree to get cat by typing cat'.

Implementing these rules involves a metric file with the new kerning for the alternate characters, changes to an encoding file describing the new ligature rules, and an insignificant new installation file.

The font metric file   Metric information for the alternate characters arises from the .afm files themselves plus information about kerning that we'll place in a new metric file padalt.mtx.

We need to take certain precautions in `padalt.mtx` since this file will be used by both roman and italic variants. If we blithely specify kerning information on all alternate glyphs, vptovf will complain later that kerns have been supplied for nonexistent characters. Therefore, we proceed with some care. Here is the file.

```
\relax
  The file padalt.mtx, which contains kerning information
  for the alternate Adobe Garamond fonts.
\metrics
\setcommand\Setrightkerning#1#2#3{
  \ifisglyph{#1}\then\setrightkerning{#1}{#2}{#3}\fi}
\setcommand\Setleftkerning#1#2#3{
  \ifisglyph{#1}\then\setleftkerning{#1}{#2}{#3}\fi}
\setcommand\Setkern#1#2#3{
  \ifisglyph{#1}\then\setkern{#1}{#2}{#3}\fi}
\Setleftkerning{aswash}{a}{1000}
\Setleftkerning{ct}{c}{1000}
\Setrightkerning{ct}{t}{1000}
\Setleftkerning{eswash}{e}{1000}
\Setleftkerning{nswash}{n}{1000}
\Setleftkerning{rswash}{r}{1000}
\Setleftkerning{st}{s}{1000}
\Setrightkerning{st}{t}{1000}
\Setleftkerning{tswash}{t}{1000}
\Setleftkerning{tswashalt}{t}{1000}
\Setrightkerning{vswash}{v}{1000}
```

The `\Set...kerning` commands define alternatives to the standard ways of setting kerns. These alternatives, distinguished by the initial majuscule S, take effect only if the first glyph is defined. Finally, we use these commands to set the kerning. For example, the aswash appears only at word endings, so kerning appears only at the left, and the left kerning should mimic that of the standard a in that font. Similarly, since the ct behaves on the left like a c and on the right like a t, we kern to the left and right like those letters.

The encoding file   We'll need a copy of `OT1.etx` called `OT1padl.etx` to which we make the following alterations.

Search for the line near the top of the file that reads

```
\encoding
```

and replace it with the following lines.

```
\encoding
\ifisglyph{Aswash}\then
   \setcommand\uc#1#2{#1swash}
\else
```

```
   \setcommand\uc#1#2{#1}
\fi
\ifisglyph{ampersandalt}\then
   \setcommand\alternatechar#1{#1alt}
\else
   \setcommand\alternatechar#1{#1}
\fi
\setcommand\Ligature#1#2#3{
   \ifisglyph{#3}\then\ligature{#1}{#2}{#3}\fi}
\setcommand\atendofword#1{\Ligature{LIG}{boundarychar}{#1}}
\setcommand\atstartofword#1#2{\Ligature{LIG}{#1}{#2}}
```

The command \ifisglyph allows us to test that a certain glyph exists and take action accordingly. The usual uppercase glyphs will be selected unless a swash A exists, in which case it is these swash alternatives that will be selected. (Surely it's safe to assume that if Aswash exists, all the swash caps exist.) We make a similar test on the alternate ampersand.

In the same way, we defined a conditional ligature command, which only takes effect if the proposed replacement for an adjacent pair exists. With this syntax, the replacement of a terminal 'a' by its swash variant would be coded

```
\setslot{\lc{A}{a}}
   \atendofword{aswash}
\endslot
```

We need to create similar alterations—similar \atendofword commands— to the \setslot commands for 'a' (shown here), 'e', 'n', 'r', 't', and 'z', since these all have special final forms in the Garamond alternate fonts.

We need places for all the new glyphs in the alternate fonts. It is \setslot's role to make this room available. Therefore, we add commands like

```
\setslot{\alternatechar{ampersand}}\endsetslot
\setslot{ornament1}\endsetslot
\setslot{ornament2}\endsetslot
\setslot{Qalt}\endsetslot
\setslot{aswash}\endsetslot
\setslot{ct}\endsetslot
\setslot{eswash}\endsetslot
\setslot{nswash}\endsetslot
\setslot{rswash}\endsetslot
\setslot{st}\endsetslot
\setslot{tswash}\endsetslot
\setslot{tswashalt}\endsetslot
\setslot{vswash}\endsetslot
\setslot{zswash}\endsetslot
\setslot{boundarychar}
   \atstartofword{Q}{Qalt}
```

```
\atstartofword{v}{vswash}
\endsetslot
```

immediately preceding the final \endencoding near the end of the file. In these alternate fonts, the swash capitals sit in the slots otherwise occupied by normal uppercase letters.

All the \atstartofword commands must follow the

```
\setslot{boundarychar}
```

command. The first letter is replaced by the second. Thus, we get a variant v or Q at the beginning of a word (*variant* versus *variant*; Queen versus Queen) by virtue of the commands associated with the boundarychar slot.

We will also need to make provision for other special ligatures. In addition to making room for them via \setslot, we need to include ligature rules. We need two additions to two existing commands. Make the following modifications

```
\setslot{\lc{C}{c}}
   \Ligature{LIG}{t}{ct}
   \comment{The letter '{c}'.}
\endsetslot
 ...
 ...
\setslot{\lc{S}{s}}
   \Ligature{LIG}{t}{st}
   \comment{The letter '{s}'.}
\endsetslot
```

to the c and s slots. The \lc command selects a lowercase glyph.

8.6.2 Installation

Finally, we need a short *fontinst* file to pull these threads together. For the pad Garamond family, the following works.

```
\input fontinst.sty
\installfonts
\installfamily{OT1}{pad}{}
\installfont{padr7l}%     upright alt
   {padr7t,padr8l,latin,padalt}{OT1pad1}{OT1}{pad}{m}{ar}{}
\installfont{padri7l}%    italic alt
   {padri7t,padri8l,latin,padalt}{OT1pad1}{OT1}{pad}{m}{ai}{}
\endinstallfonts
\bye
```

These lines work, provided we have the property list files for padr7t and padri7t, that the alternate fonts have names padr7l and padri7l, and that

Creating Alternate Fonts for Adobe Garamond

- Begin by assembling a chart of all new alternate characters, and decide on the ligature rules by which the alternate font will operate.

- Create a file like `padalt.mtx` containing new kerning instructions and boundary character information.

- Create an encoding file like `OT1padl.etx` with new slot and ligature commands. Certain *fontinst* commands, like \uc, may also need revisions.

- Create the appropriate *fontinst* installation file, and proceed as usual to create the virtual fonts. That is,

  - create property list files for base fonts;

  - run the installation file through plain TEX;

  - use `vptovf` to create the virtual fonts, and place the resulting files where they belong;

  - combine the new `.fd` file with the pre-existing `.fd` file for this family; and

  - update `psfonts.map` to refer to the raw alternate fonts.

There is so much variation between alternate fonts that the information in this section should be regarded as suggestive and descriptive rather than rigid and prescriptive. Several additional alternate font projects appear below.

the shapes `ar` and `ai` select that alternate regular and alternate italic shapes under NFSS. We run this installation file through TEX, and proceed in the usual way.

8.6.3 *Bitstream Bernhard Modern*

The Bernhard Modern types, designed by Lucien Bernhard in 1937, include (in the Bitstream version) a large array of alternate characters, including many unusual forms and rare ligatures (such as the Dutch ij for a welcome change!) that we will have to make a careful selection of characters to use. We will need two italic variants—an alternate and a swash form. Here are samples showing Bernhard Modern typesetting using standard fonts prepared using VFINST.

These explorations of Alexander and Casanova left one enticing corner in the dark. That is, the nature—if not the personality—of their supreme adversary in the game, the unseen dealer of the hand they and society lost. At times, certainly, even under the thick whitewash Plutarch laid over the world's greatest exploit, I fancy we made out a wavering shadow, the traits of a presence that is neither Greek nor Persian, nor human at all; luring, spoiling, finally strangling with generosity the young demi-god. So, the track of his campaigning that he scribbled in impatience over the map of Asia, Europe, Africa, seems (unknown to him) to be in a planchette writing, the script of Destiny. This Destiny, Chance, Fate, Providence, lover and assassin of adventurers, each of whose names is an unproved theory and surmise, whatever its true identity, seems nearer because not so solemn, in the life of the Venetian rake. That midnight catastrophe in the Palace of Cardinal Acquaviva at Rome, that letter dropped by the canal-side by the old Senator, the rusty lock he found in the attics of the Piombi leave the curtain quaking, and a slight pricking of the scalp, even if we have not Casanova's own naïve mysticism.

These explorations of Alexander and Casanova left one enticing corner in the dark. That is, the nature—if not the personality—of their supreme adversary in the game, the unseen dealer of the hand they and society lost. At times, certainly, even under the thick whitewash Plutarch laid over the world's greatest exploit, I fancy we made out a wavering shadow, the traits of a presence that is neither Greek nor Persian, nor human at all; luring, spoiling, finally strangling with generosity the young demi-god. So, the track of his campaigning that he scribbled in impatience over the map of Asia, Europe, Africa, seems (unknown to him) to be in a planchette writing, the script of Destiny. This Destiny, Chance, Fate, Providence, lover and assassin of adventurers, each of whose names is an unproved theory and surmise, whatever its true identity, seems nearer because not so solemn, in the life of the Venetian rake. That midnight catastrophe in the Palace of Cardinal Acquaviva at Rome, that letter dropped by the canal-side by the old Senator, the rusty lock he found in the attics of the Piombi leave the curtain quaking, and a slight pricking of the scalp, even if we have not Casanova's own naïve mysticism.

The construction of the Bernhard alternate fonts is a task quite different in character from the construction of the Garamond alternate fonts. With Garamond, relatively few alternate forms needed incorporation in special fonts, and we agreed to typeset them by using new ligature rules. The Bernhard fonts have many more new letterforms, and many of these will simply replace standard glyphs in the font, although there are many new ligatures. An "alternate" raw font contains these variant glyphs, while it is the extension raw font that contains the collection of rare and unusual ligatures. Bitstream provides many of the alternate forms with diacritics, but in order to keep this text to manageable length, the new fonts we will create contain only unaccented letters.

It's worth reminding ourselves of the categories of characters in a font.

1. "Printable ASCII" characters need to be in the slots assigned to the ASCII character set. In this way, typing A results in whatever A-like glyph we place in that slot. (Note that "printable ASCII" is a relative term. European keyboards directly provide for accented letters so a

European's concept of "printable ASCII" encompasses an American's "printable ASCII.")

2. Ligatures need no special positioning in the font, since we will typeset them via sequences of standard characters that TEX converts to ligatures behind the scenes using the rules we will be building into a virtual font.

3. Another group of characters, like the Scandinavian ligatures æ and œ, are typeset via control sequences like \ae and \oe. If we ensure that these glyphs remain in the same places in a virtual font as they occupy in a TEX font, then the definitions of \ae and \oe will continue to be valid. Adhering as much as possible to one of the standard encodings, OT1 or T1, easily satisfies this requirement.

Although the extension fonts exist for regular and italic shapes, the alternate font exists only in an upright version. In partial compensation, though, there is an italic swash font.

Let's first discuss the *fontinst* encoding file OT1bb71.etx we'll need for the installation. To aid us, here is a table displaying standard letterforms with their alternate counterparts.

Standard   [& a g k r v w y ff ffi ffl G K Q V W]
Alternate ⤙ ℚ a g k r v w y ff ffi ffl G K Q V W ⤚

In the .afm file, the glyphs have names like aalt, ampersandalt, ffalt, and so on. The designation bb7 follows Karl Berry's font naming scheme.

OT1bb7.etx begins life as a copy of OT1.etx. Once again, we are using the original TEX encoding simply because this encoding has room for all of the new glyphs we'll need to add. We will also use a single encoding file for both regular and italic font shapes as a way of keeping the number of new files to a minimum.

Directly following the \needsfontinstversion{...} command, add the following lines to the new encoding file OT1bb7.etx.

```
\setcommand\Setslot#1{%
  \ifisglyph{#1alt}\then
    \edef\thisglyph{#1alt}
  \else
    \edef\thisglyph{#1}
  \fi
  \setslot{\thisglyph}}
\def\csetslot#1\endsetslot{% conditional setslot
  \ifisglyph{#1alt}\then
    \setslot{#1}\endsetslot
  \fi}
\setcommand\Ligature#1#2#3{%
  \ifisglyph{#3}\then\ligature{#1}{#2}{#3}\fi}
```

These commands allow us to define things conditionally. For example, with \Setslot in place, the instructions

```
\Setslot{K}
\endsetslot
```

defines a slot for the usual K glyph, unless Kalt exists, in which case the slot will contain the alternate K. But even if the alternate forms exist, we still need room in the font for the standard forms because we'll apply the kerning information from the standard glyphs to the alternates. (Oddly, the alternate .afm file contains no kerning information whatsoever.) That's where the conditional setslot command \csetslot is useful. When we type a line like

```
\csetslot{K}
\endsetslot
```

nothing happens unless Kalt exists, in which case we need another slot for the standard K. If there is no alternate K, then the K slot has been defined previously, and nothing further will be done by this \csetslot. Similarly, \Ligature is a conditional ligature command, which checks that the ligature glyph exists before it defines a ligature rule.

The alternate font contains alternate double-f ligatures. We handle them by inserting this code at the beginning of the encoding file.

```
\setcommand\ffig{ffi}\setcommand\fflg{ffl}
\setcommand\ffg{ff}
\ifisglyph{ffialt}\then\resetcommand\ffig{ffialt}\fi
\ifisglyph{fflalt}\then\resetcommand\fflg{fflalt}\fi
\ifisglyph{ffalt}\then\resetcommand\ffg{ffalt}\fi
```

These lines begin by embedding the names of the ligature glyphs in control words. (The final g in these names suggests "glyph.") In case the alternate forms exist, these control words are redefined accordingly.

The remaining revisions to this file involve making changes to implement these new commands and features. We will make several encoding changes with the .afm files of the alternate and extension fonts close at hand.

1. For each character with an alternate form, change the \setslot command to \Setslot. For example. \setslot{\uc{Q}{q}} would become

    ```
    \Setslot{\uc{Q}{q}}
    ```

    (Here, \uc selects an uppercase character.) For this font, there are alternate letterforms for the &, a, g, k, r, v, w, y, G, K, Q, V, W, the three double-f ligatures, and the two square brackets.

2. Revise the double-f ligature rules to use glyph names `ffg` and so on. For example, following `\Setslot{ff}`, the ligature rules should now read

```
\ligature{LIG}{\lc{I}{i}}{\ffig}
\ligature{LIG}{\lc{L}{l}}{\fflg}
```

and similarly for the ligature rule following f.

3. At the end of the file (preceding the final `\endencoding` command), add slots for all the unusual ligatures, ornaments, dingbats, and so forth. The file should contain lines like

```
\setslot{ch}\endsetslot
\setslot{ft}\endsetslot
    . . .
\setslot{AB}\endsetslot
\setslot{AF}\endsetslot
    . . .
\setslot{ornament1}\endsetslot
\setslot{ornament2}\endsetslot
    . . .
\setslot{ampersandalt1}
  \Ligature{LIG}{quoteleft}{ampersandalt2}
\endsetslot
\setslot{ampersandalt2}
  \Ligature{LIG}{quoteleft}{ampersandalt4}
\endsetslot
\setslot{ampersandalt4}\endsetslot
```

4. We need ligature rules for some unusual conventions. For example, there are four alternative ampersands, named ampersandalt, and ampersandalt1 through ampersandalt4, but omitting ampersandalt3 for some reason. The first alternative replaces the usual glyph we get by typing \& (⅋), and we further decide that *‘, *‘‘, and *‘‘‘ will typeset the remaining ampersands (℗, ℘, and ⅋). Several of these new rules already appear above in the \setslot commands.

We also need a way to access the ornaments that are part of the font. There are eleven of them, named ornament1 through ornament12, omitting ornament9. It is convenient to use the left quote adjacent to a digit to typeset these glyphs. That is, if we type

0‘ 1‘ 2‘ 3‘ 4‘ 5‘ 6‘ 7‘ 8‘ 9‘ a‘

we typeset

We get these by revising the digit slots to look like

```
\setslot{\digit{zero}}
  \Ligature{LIG}{quoteleft}{ornament1}
\endsetslot
```

(and we'll need a similar rule governing ornament12 in the slot for lowercase 'a').

5. We need ligature rules of the usual stamp to activate new ligatures. For example, we'll be able to typeset Æ or AW by typing AB or AW if we include rules

```
\Ligature{LIG}{B}{AB}
\Ligature{LIG}{W}{AW}
```

in the slot for \uc{A}{a}. We typeset IA or IA automatically from La or LA by means of

```
\Ligature{LIG}{A}{LA}
\Ligature{LIG}{aalt}{LAalt}
```

in the slot for \uc{L}{l}. (*Note well* that we use the alternate glyph name in the ligature rule if the alternate glyph exists in the encoding.) Prepare and place all other \Ligature commands with their proper \Setslot's.

6. For reasons to be discussed below, include the ligature rule

```
\Ligature{LIG}{H}{GH}
```

in the slot for G, and also include

```
\setslot{GH}
  \Ligature{LIG}{T}{GHT}
\endsetslot
\setslot{GHT}\endsetslot
```

in the encoding file.

7. Finally, the very last sequence of instructions in the encoding file (but they must precede \endencoding!) are conditional slot statements of the form

```
\csetslot{G}\endsetslot
\csetslot{K}\endsetslot
\csetslot{Q}\endsetslot
    ...
```

There must be one \csetslot command per \Setslot command.

We will support these encoding changes with metric changes described in a file bb71.mtx. The most important such changes are kerning information for the alternate glyphs in terms of standard characters, and these are made necessary only because the foundry has not included any such information in the .afm files.

For example, the ⒞ ligature should kern on the left like a 'c' but on the right like a 't'. In addition to the ⒞, the other rare and wonderful ligatures include Æ, Æ, Aⱳ, CO, Ꜳ, GⱵ, Ꜣ, KA, Ꜥ, Ꜵ, Ꞁ, Ꜽ, MD, MP, Mᶜ, Œ, Ꝏ, QU, Qu, TR, TT, TY, Ꞇh, Ti, ch, ck, fb, fh, fr, ft, ꜱp, tf, tt, and ty. Also, in the absence of kerning information regarding alternate forms like Ꝗ or ꝝ, we will use the kerns of the standard glyphs.

```
\relax
  This is bb71.mtx, for Bernhard Modern alternate fonts.
\metrics
\setcommand\setkerning#1#2#3{%
  \ifisglyph{#1}\then
    \setleftkerning{#1}{#2}{1000}%
    \setrightkerning{#1}{#3}{1000}%
  \fi}
\setkerning{ch}{c}{h}        \setkerning{ft}{f}{t}
\setkerning{ck}{c}{k}        \setkerning{fr}{f}{r}
\setkerning{Ti}{T}{i}        \setkerning{AB}{A}{B}
\setkerning{AF}{A}{F}        \setkerning{AW}{A}{W}
\setkerning{HE}{H}{E}        \setkerning{KA}{K}{A}
\setkerning{LA}{L}{A}        \setkerning{MD}{M}{D}
\setkerning{MP}{M}{P}        \setkerning{OC}{O}{C}
\setkerning{OO}{O}{O}        \setkerning{Th}{T}{h}
\setkerning{QU}{Q}{U}        \setkerning{Qu}{Q}{u}
\setkerning{TR}{T}{R}        \setkerning{ct}{c}{t}
\setkerning{fb}{f}{b}        \setkerning{fh}{f}{h}
\setkerning{tf}{t}{f}        \setkerning{tt}{t}{t}
\setkerning{ty}{t}{y}        \setkerning{Co}{C}{o}
\setkerning{sp}{s}{p}        \setkerning{st}{s}{t}
\setkerning{LE}{L}{L}        \setkerning{LL}{L}{L}
```

```
\setkerning{TT}{T}{T}        \setkerning{TY}{T}{Y}
\setkerning{Cr}{C}{r}        \setkerning{dutchij}{i}{j}
\setkerning{dutchIJ}{I}{J} \setkerning{GHT}{G}{T}
\setkerning{LAalt}{L}{L}
```

The new \setkerning command is syntactic sugar for setting kerning. For example,

```
\setkerning{st}{s}{t}
```

is the same as—but shorter than—the pair of *fontinst* statements

```
\setleftkerning{st}{s}{1000}
\setrightkerning{st}{t}{1000}
```

The remainder of the file is filled out by scanning the two .afm files for the alternative and extension fonts, and adding \setkerning command for each glyph that we want to include.

The odd GHT ligature requires special treatment. We want it to be a three-letter ligature—only the typed GHT should yield GHT. The strategy by which TEX typesets ffi when we type ffi is mirrored here. We create a new character called GH, which consists of a 'G' set next to an 'H', and only when this virtual glyph is followed by T should TEX select the GHT. The ligature rules don't belong here, but the construction of these glyphs is simple, and we add these instructions to bb71.mtx.

```
\setglyph{GH}
  \ifisglyph{Galt}\then
    \glyph{Galt}{1000}
    \movert{\kerning{Galt}{H}}
  \else
    \glyph{G}{1000}
    \movert{\kerning{G}{H}}
  \fi
  \glyph{H}{1000}
\endsetglyph
```

In a better world, the metric constructions we've outlined would be sufficient to create an alternate virtual font. Unfortunately, digital foundries are often sloppy in the metric information they provide with the font. (We will meet a particularly egregious example in our final project.) When I created virtual fonts using these constructions, I found that accents were poorly positioned (all accents were much too high) and the TEX logo printed incorrectly. (The 'E' did not drop down at all.) Some detective work revealed the problem—the entries at the beginning of the .afm file that should have recorded important thing like the x-height and descender height of the font had instead been zeroed out. That is, about 12 lines down from the beginning, I encountered lines like

```
CapHeight 0
XHeight 0
Ascender 0
Descender 0
```

The zeroes are incorrect. This information is easy to regenerate, and the following lines do just that. We replace the \endmetrics command in the file bb7l.mtx by the following

```
\resetint{capheight}{\height{B}}
\resetint{ascender}{\height{b}}
\resetint{descender}{\depth{p}}
\resetint{xheight}{\height{x}}
\endmetrics
```

to regenerate this data. (This fix will be correct, although unnecessary, even if a new release of the fonts fixes this problem.)

With these new metric and encoding files under our belt, it remains simply to stitch everything together with an appropriate installation file. Here's one way to do it.

```
\input fontinst.sty
\installfonts
  \installfamily{OT1}{bb7}{}
  \installfont{bb7rl7t}{bb7r8l,bb7r8e,bb7r7t,bb7l}%
    {OT1bb7l}{OT1}{bb7}{m}{ar}{}
  \installfont{bb7ril7t}{bb7ri8e,bb7ri7t,bb7l}%
    {OT1bb7l}{OT1}{bb7}{m}{ai}{}
  \installfont{bb7rsw7t}{bb7ri8w,bb7ri7t,bb7l}%
    {OT1bb7l}{OT1}{bb7}{m}{sw}{}
\endinstallfonts
\bye
```

Before running this file through TeX, we need to prepare property files for the roman and italic standard fonts. That is, issue commands like

```
        tftopl ⟨path⟩/bb7r7t.tfm bb7r7t.pl
        tftopl ⟨path⟩/bb7ri7t.tfm bb7ri7t.pl
```

(Unix syntax).

We assign font shapes of ar (alternate regular), ai (alternate italic), and sw (swash) to these fonts for use with NFSS. Within plain TeX documents, we need declarations like

```
  \font\beraltr=bb7rl7t
  \font\beraltri=bb7ril7t
  \font\bersw=bb7rsw7t
```

> ## Alternate Fonts: Bernhard Modern
>
> The following procedure applies strictly to the construction of Bernhard Modern alternate and swash fonts, but similar considerations apply to other font families containing fonts of rare ligatures and to alternate forms that replace standard letterforms. It applies in particular to other Bitstream families containing typographer sets of fonts.
>
> - Switch to a special work directory.
>
> - Use `tftopl` Prepare `.pl` files for the base fonts (in the text above, these base fonts were called `bb7r7t` and `bb7ri7t`).
>
> - Prepare files like `bb7l.mtx` and `OT1bb7l.etx`.
>
> - Prepare the *fontinst* installation file and run it through TEX.
>
> - Use `vptovf` to create the virtual font files that LATEX and TEX will use. Move these files to their proper places.
>
> - Use an editor to add the entries in the `.fd` file produced by these steps to the original `.fd` file for this font family in an inputs directory.
>
> - Save the installation file, the special metric files, and the new encoding file in case the fonts have to be re-installed, but delete all `.pl`, `.vpl`, and auxiliary files. Also delete files with names like `bb7*.mtx`.

to make `beraltr`, `beraltri`, and `bersw` control sequences to select these fonts.

With the installation complete, here's what the fonts look like. We need only type

```
\renewcommand{\rmdefault}{bb7}
```

in the preamble of a LATEX document file, after which statements like

```
\begin{center}
  {\fontshape{ar}\selectfont[ HERE CoMES PLENTY {\scshape of}
    FOOD FOR THOUGHT {\scshape For} ALL. ]\\
  \fontshape{ai}\selectfont] HERE CoMES PLENTY of
    FOOD FOR THOUGHT For ALL. ]\\
\end{center}
```

will generate

◄| HERE ©MES PLENTY of FOOD FOR THOUGHT For ALL. |►
◄| *HERE ©MES PLENTY of FOOD FOR THOUGHT For ALL.* |►

Upon typing something like

```
These explorations of Alexander and Casanova left one
enticing corner in the dark.  That is, the
nature---if not the personality---of their supreme
adversary in the game, the unseen dealer of the hand
they and society lost.  At times, certainly, even
under the thick whitewash Plutarch laid over the
world's greatest exploit, I fancy we made out a
wavering shadow, the traits of a presence that is
neither Greek nor Persian, nor human at all; luring,
spoiling, finally strangling with generosity the
young demi-god.  So, the track of his campaigning
that he scribbled in impatience over the map of Asia,
Europe, Africa, seems (unknown to him) to be in a
planchette writing, the script of Destiny.  This
Destiny, Chance, Fate, Providence, lover and assassin
of adventurers, each of whose names is an unproved
theory and surmise, whatever its true identity, seems
nearer because not so solemn, in the life of the
Venetian rake.  That midnight catastrophe in the
Palace of Cardinal Acquaviva at Rome, that letter
dropped by the canal-side by the old Senator, the
rusty lock he found in the attics of the Piombi leave
the curtain quaking, and a slight pricking of the
scalp, even if we have not Casanova's own na\"{\i}ve
mysticism.
```

(the text is drawn from Bolitho (1929, chapter 3)), we get either

These explorations of Alexander and Casanova left one enticing corner in the dark. That is, the nature—if not the personality—of their supreme adversary in the game, the unseen dealer of the hand they and society lost. At times, certainly, even under the thick whitewash Plutarch laid over the world's greatest exploit, I fancy we made out a wavering shadow, the traits of a presence that is neither Greek nor Persian, nor human at all; luring, spoiling, finally strangling with generosity the young demi-god. So, the track of his campaigning that he scribbled in impatience over the map of Asia, Europe, Africa, seems (unknown to him) to be in a planchette writing, the script of Destiny. This Destiny, Chance, Fate, Providence, lover and assassin of adventurers, each of whose names is an unproved theory and surmise, whatever its true identity, seems nearer because not so solemn, in the life of the Venetian rake. That midnight catastrophe in the Palace of Cardinal Acquaviva at Rome, that letter dropped by the canal-side by the old Senator, the rusty lock he found in the attics of the Piombi leave the curtain quaking, and a slight pricking of the scalp, even if we have not Casanova's own naïve mysticism.

(after `\fontshape{ar}\fontsize{9}{10.5}\selectfont`) or

These explorations of Alexander and Casanova left one enticing corner in the dark. That is, the nature—if not the personality—of their supreme adversary in the game, the unseen dealer of the hand they and society lost. At times, certainly, even under the thick whitewash Plutarch laid over the world's greatest exploit, I fancy we made out a wavering shadow, the traits of a presence that is neither Greek nor Persian, nor human at all; luring, spoiling, finally strangling with generosity the young demi-god. So, the track of his campaigning that he scribbled in impatience over the map of Asia, Europe, Africa, seems (unknown to him) to be in a planchette writing, the script of Destiny. This Destiny, Chance, Fate, Providence, lover and assassin of adventurers, each of whose names is an unproved theory and surmise, whatever its true identity, seems nearer because not so solemn, in the life of the Venetian rake. That midnight catastrophe in the Palace of Cardinal Acquaviva at Rome, that letter dropped by the canal-side by the old Senator, the rusty lock he found in the attics of the Piombi leave the curtain quaking, and a slight pricking of the scalp, even if we have not Casanova's own naïve mysticism.

after `\fontshape{ai}\fontsize{9}{10.5}\selectfont`,
Let's conclude with an example of the swash font:

These explorations of Alexander and Casanova left one enticing corner in the dark. That is, the nature—if not the personality—of their supreme adversary in the game, the unseen dealer of the hand they and society lost. At times, certainly, even under the thick whitewash Plutarch laid over the world's greatest exploit, I fancy we made out a wavering shadow, the traits of a presence that is neither Greek nor Persian, nor human at all; luring, spoiling, finally strangling with generosity the young demi-god. So, the track of his campaigning that he scribbled in impatience over the map of Asia, Europe, Africa, seems (unknown to him) to be in a planchette writing, the script of Destiny. This Destiny, Chance, Fate, Providence, lover and assassin of adventurers, each of whose names is an unproved theory and surmise, whatever its true identity, seems nearer because not so solemn, in the life of the Venetian rake. That midnight catastrophe in the Palace of Cardinal Acquaviva at Rome, that letter dropped by the canal-side by the old Senator, the rusty lock he found in the attics of the Piombi leave the curtain quaking, and a slight pricking of the scalp, even if we have not Casanova's own naïve mysticism.

which we get be selecting the `sw` font-shape. The LATEX logo you get by typing `La\TeX` in the alternate regular font shape

LATEX

may be the most typographically pure rendering of that logo ever.

	1 · ₁	2 fi ₂	3 fl ₃	4 / ₄	5 " ₅	6 Ł ₆	7 ł ₇
8 ، ₁₀	9 ° ₁₁		11 ˘ ₁₃	12 – ₁₄		14 Ž ₁₆	15 ž ₁₇
16 ˇ ₂₀	17 ˛ ₂₁						
						30 ˋ ₃₆	31 ' ₃₇
32 ₄₀	33 ! ₄₁	34 " ₄₂	35 # ₄₃	36 $ ₄₄	37 % ₄₅	38 & ₄₆	39 ' ₄₇
40 (₅₀	41) ₅₁	42 * ₅₂	43 + ₅₃	44 , ₅₄	45 - ₅₅	46 . ₅₆	47 / ₅₇
48 0 ₆₀	49 1 ₆₁	50 2 ₆₂	51 3 ₆₃	52 4 ₆₄	53 5 ₆₅	54 6 ₆₆	55 7 ₆₇
56 8 ₇₀	57 9 ₇₁	58 : ₇₂	59 ; ₇₃	60 < ₇₄	61 = ₇₅	62 > ₇₆	63 ? ₇₇
64 @ ₁₀₀	65 A ₁₀₁	66 B ₁₀₂	67 C ₁₀₃	68 D ₁₀₄	69 E ₁₀₅	70 F ₁₀₆	71 G ₁₀₇
72 H ₁₁₀	73 I ₁₁₁	74 J ₁₁₂	75 K ₁₁₃	76 L ₁₁₄	77 M ₁₁₅	78 N ₁₁₆	79 O ₁₁₇
80 P ₁₂₀	81 Q ₁₂₁	82 R ₁₂₂	83 S ₁₂₃	84 T ₁₂₄	85 U ₁₂₅	86 V ₁₂₆	87 W ₁₂₇
88 X ₁₃₀	89 Y ₁₃₁	90 Z ₁₃₂	91 [₁₃₃	92 \ ₁₃₄	93] ₁₃₅	94 ^ ₁₃₆	95 _ ₁₃₇
96 ` ₁₄₀	97 a ₁₄₁	98 b ₁₄₂	99 c ₁₄₃	100 d ₁₄₄	101 e ₁₄₅	102 f ₁₄₆	103 g ₁₄₇
104 h ₁₅₀	105 i ₁₅₁	106 j ₁₅₂	107 k ₁₅₃	108 l ₁₅₄	109 m ₁₅₅	110 n ₁₅₆	111 o ₁₅₇
112 p ₁₆₀	113 q ₁₆₁	114 r ₁₆₂	115 s ₁₆₃	116 t ₁₆₄	117 u ₁₆₅	118 v ₁₆₆	119 w ₁₆₇
120 x ₁₇₀	121 y ₁₇₁	122 z ₁₇₂	123 { ₁₇₃	124	₁₇₄	125 } ₁₇₅	126 ~ ₁₇₆	

Figure 6: A font table for a PostScript font (Adobe Garamond) in the 8r encoding.

8.6.4 New encodings, hidden characters

The bulk of a binary outline .pfb file (or its equivalent ASCII .pfa file) contains recipes for constructing the glyphs in the font. Each such recipe is a subroutine or macro for constructing one character, and each such routine has a name, the name of the matching glyph. Thus, a routine called K will draw a 'K', while the routine dagger draws a †, and so on.

We need to impose order on these routines and make a font out of them. This structure is imposed by an *encoding array*, which will inform an application of the names of the glyphs and the position number of that glyph in the font. Remember, there's room for 256 characters in any font, numbered 0–255. For most text fonts, we can see this encoding array defined by glancing at the header of the outline file. A statement like

```
/Encoding StandardEncoding def
```

near the beginning of the .afm file uses PostScript syntax to make this definition, and relies on the built-in definition of StandardEncoding to define

		130 , 202	131 f 203	132 „ 204	133 … 205	134 † 206	135 ‡ 207
136 ^ 210	137 ‰ 211	138 Š 212	139 ‹ 213	140 Œ 214			
			147 " 223	148 " 224	149 • 225	150 – 226	151 — 227
152 ~ 230	153 ™ 231	154 š 232	155 › 233	156 œ 234			159 Ÿ 237
	161 ¡ 241	162 ¢ 242	163 £ 243	164 ¤ 244	165 ¥ 245	166 ¦ 246	167 § 247
168 ¨ 250	169 © 251	170 ª 252	171 « 253	172 ¬ 254		174 ® 256	175 ‾ 257
176 ° 260	177 ± 261	178 ² 262	179 ³ 263	180 ´ 264	181 µ 265	182 ¶ 266	183 · 267
184 ¸ 270	185 ¹ 271	186 º 272	187 » 273	188 ¼ 274	189 ½ 275	190 ¾ 276	191 ¿ 277
192 À 300	193 Á 301	194 Â 302	195 Ã 303	196 Ä 304	197 Å 305	198 Æ 306	199 Ç 307
200 È 310	201 É 311	202 Ê 312	203 Ë 313	204 Ì 314	205 Í 315	206 Î 316	207 Ï 317
208 Ð 320	209 Ñ 321	210 Ò 322	211 Ó 323	212 Ô 324	213 Õ 325	214 Ö 326	215 × 327
216 Ø 330	217 Ù 331	218 Ú 332	219 Û 333	220 Ü 334	221 Ý 335	222 Þ 336	223 ß 337
224 à 340	225 á 341	226 â 342	227 ã 343	228 ä 344	229 å 345	230 æ 346	231 ç 347
232 è 350	233 é 351	234 ê 352	235 ë 353	236 ì 354	237 í 355	238 î 356	239 ï 357
240 ð 360	241 ñ 361	242 ò 362	243 ó 363	244 ô 364	245 õ 365	246 ö 366	247 ÷ 367

Figure 7: The upper half of a PostScript 8r-encoded font for Adobe Garamond text.

slots and names for the members of the encoding. Were we to expand the meaning of StandardEncoding, it would read

```
256 array
0 1 255 {1 index exch /.notdef put} for
dup 32 /space put
dup 33 /exclam put
dup 34 /quotedbl put
dup 35 /numbersign put
dup 36 /dollar put
dup 37 /percent put
   ...
dup 241 /ae put
dup 245 /dotlessi put
dup 249 /oslash put
dup 250 /oe put
dup 251 /germandbls put
readonly
```

(The first line creates an array with 256 positions, and the second line initializes each slot to the value `.notdef`. A series of instructions puts individual glyphs in the various slots.)

These considerations are suggestive. First of all, to include additional characters in a font, a font designer needs simply to include the relevant drawing routines in the outline file. Second, to make these characters accessible, we need only to include them in the encoding array.

A glance at the contents of many `.afm` files shows that often there are quite a number of *hidden glyphs* in a font—characters whose routines are present but whose names are not in the encoding array. It's easy to tell which ones are hidden—the character position is given as -1 rather than a number between 0 and 255. In an Adobe Garamond `.afm` file, the first such line is

```
C  -1 ; WX  623 ; N Aacute ; B -25 -3 643 841 ;
```

so we conclude that Aacute is a hidden character. Many of the hidden characters are diacritically adorned glyphs, but some are new, such as the Scandinavian thorn and edh, the brokenbar character, and a small collection of mathematical symbols (mu, plusminus, multiply symbol, and so on). The *fontinst* documentation refers to these hidden characters as "not" glyphs.

Recently, the TEX community has begun promulgating a new encoding system whereby many of these characters become accessible. This new encoding is the *TeXBase1Encoding*, which has been allocated the designation 8r for font naming purposes. The file `8r.enc` describes this encoding in PostScript terms, while `8r.etx` provides a *fontinst* description. (These files are now part of the *fontinst* distribution.) Figures 6 and 7 on pages 238 and 239 show the glyphs in this encoding.

Implementation of the new encoding is a two-stage process.

1. The metric `.tfm` files for a font need to follow and refer to the new encoding.

2. The outline font file itself needs to refer to and follow this new encoding.

Fortunately, both *fontinst* and *dvips* adhere to these principles and allow digital typographers to change font encodings easily.

The file `8r.etx` provides a prototype for the TeXBase1 encoding employing *fontinst* syntax. In the presence of this file, an installation file assumes the following schematic form.

```
\input fontinst.sty
% Times Roman re-encoding
\transformfont{ptmr8r}%
  {\reencodefont{8r}{\fromafm{ptmr8a}}}
⟨More re-encoding commands⟩
% Adobe Garamond re-encoding
\transformfont{padr8r}%
```

```
{\reencodefont{8r}{\fromafm{padr8a}}}
```
⟨*More re-encoding commands*⟩
⟨*Re-encoding commands for other fonts in other families*⟩
```
\installfonts
```
⟨*Installation commands using "8r" fonts as raw fonts*⟩
```
\endinstallfonts
\bye
```

That is, we need to transform a raw font according to the new encoding, and we use these re-encoded raw fonts as the constituents of subsequent

```
\installfont
```

commands. The result of running this installation file through TeX will be as usual, but there will be a series of new `.pl` files, one for each 8r-encoded raw file. Make sure to generate the corresponding `.tfm` file.

The *dvips* postprocessor needs additional information in `psfonts.map` to make sense of this new encoding. Revise an entry like

```
ptmr8r Times-Roman "TeXBase1Encoding ReEncodeFont" <8r.enc
```

for resident fonts or

```
padr8r AGaramond-Regular "TeXBase1Encoding ReEncodeFont"
  <8r.enc <padr8a.pfb
```

if *dvips* needs to download the font. (This last example is shown here in two lines on account of its length. You should take great care to include all the material for an entry on a *single* line and to get the upper- and lowercase spelling just right. The font file and the `.enc` file need to be in a place *dvips* knows about. Otherwise, you'll need to include the path prefix with the file name (for example, `/usr/local/tex/inputs/8r.enc` in Unix). The VFINST utilities automatically re-encode fonts that follow standard Adobe encoding, and the entries it creates in `psfonts.map` refer to the encoding described in `8r.enc`.

Following these changes, the virtual fonts created using the 8r-encoded raw fonts may be accessed in the usual manner.

Misleading metrics   Considerations of font re-encoding sometimes loom large for a font installer. It is sometimes true that glyphs will have been improperly named. For example, this table

	Bad Name	Good Name
ct	E	ct
ff	H	ffalt
sp	S	sp
st	V	st
tt	X	tt
st	w	stalt1
st	x	stalt2
th	y	th

shows some of the glyphs in one of the special Poetica fonts (from Adobe Systems, Inc.). The columns record the names in the .afm file, together with my suggestions for the names. It's not helpful to call a ct ligature by the name E, and particularly so for a *fontinst* enthusiast, since glyph names are the anchors by which *fontinst* creates virtual fonts. In my experience, .afm files that contain lines like

```
Comment Generated by Fontographer ...
```

or

```
Comment Generated by Metamorphosis ...
```

very near the top of the file are apt to contain inappropriate glyph names. Apparently, all but the most basic of metric information in an .afm file is ignored by virtually all non-TEX software. The name E is chosen for the ct, H for an alternate ff, and so on because these alternate glyphs occupy the slots normally reserved for the E, H, and so on.

Mantinia   But worse is yet to come. The Mantinia font distributed by Carter and Cone is a striking titling font compatible with Galliard Roman types. [See figure 8 on the facing page, with text drawn from Gibbon (1788, chapter 4).] Not only are glyphs names inappropriate but some of the (poorly named) glyphs are hidden from the casual user—they have been assigned slot positions of −1 and are not part of the standard Adobe encoding.

This matters for Mantinia, for this is an exceptionally handsome font. In addition to the standard

UPPERCASE ALPHABET

common to all titling fonts, it contains many rare ligatures

CT HE LA TT CI TT TY ME MB V

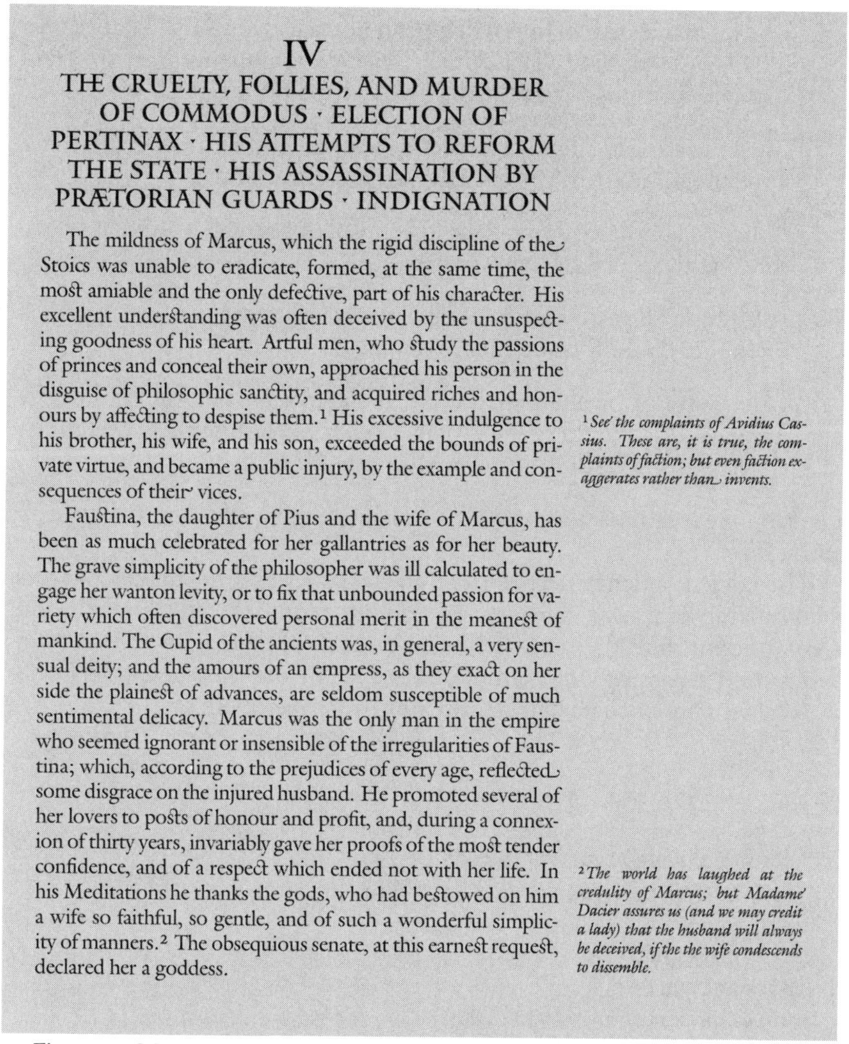

IV
THE CRUELTY, FOLLIES, AND MURDER OF COMMODUS · ELECTION OF PERTINAX · HIS ATTEMPTS TO REFORM THE STATE · HIS ASSASSINATION BY PRÆTORIAN GUARDS · INDIGNATION

The mildness of Marcus, which the rigid discipline of the Stoics was unable to eradicate, formed, at the same time, the most amiable and the only defective, part of his character. His excellent understanding was often deceived by the unsuspecting goodness of his heart. Artful men, who study the passions of princes and conceal their own, approached his person in the disguise of philosophic sanctity, and acquired riches and honours by affecting to despise them.[1] His excessive indulgence to his brother, his wife, and his son, exceeded the bounds of private virtue, and became a public injury, by the example and consequences of their vices.

> [1] See the complaints of Avidius Cassius. These are, it is true, the complaints of faction; but even faction exaggerates rather than invents.

Faustina, the daughter of Pius and the wife of Marcus, has been as much celebrated for her gallantries as for her beauty. The grave simplicity of the philosopher was ill calculated to engage her wanton levity, or to fix that unbounded passion for variety which often discovered personal merit in the meanest of mankind. The Cupid of the ancients was, in general, a very sensual deity; and the amours of an empress, as they exact on her side the plainest of advances, are seldom susceptible of much sentimental delicacy. Marcus was the only man in the empire who seemed ignorant or insensible of the irregularities of Faustina; which, according to the prejudices of every age, reflected some disgrace on the injured husband. He promoted several of her lovers to posts of honour and profit, and, during a connexion of thirty years, invariably gave her proofs of the most tender confidence, and of a respect which ended not with her life. In his Meditations he thanks the gods, who had bestowed on him a wife so faithful, so gentle, and of such a wonderful simplicity of manners.[2] The obsequious senate, at this earnest request, declared her a goddess.

> [2] The world has laughed at the credulity of Marcus; but Madame Dacier assures us (and we may credit a lady) that the husband will always be deceived, if the the wife condescends to dissemble.

Figure 8: Mantinia and Galliard fonts. The alternate Galliard fonts shown were constructed according to the principles of this chapter.

and some alternate forms and ornaments

· QUIET ✢ TREAT ✦ FOR ϙ YOU ·

to which we'd like easy access.

Let's explore one way to install the Mantinia font. Since the entire font package consists of a single raw font, it should be possible to construct a single virtual font containing everything, but it is not apparent how to use—*easily* use—such a font. For this reason, it's better to construct three distinct virtual fonts.

1. The regular (normal) font will typeset normal characters. That is, type
   QUIET RIOT to get QUIET RIOT. Lowercase input gives rise to certain
   superior forms of letters: QuIeT RiOT yields QᵁIᵉT RᵢOT.

2. An alternate font silently replaces normal glyphs with alternate forms.
   Type QUIET RIOT to get QUIET RIOT in this font.

3. A second alternate font replaces a handful of normal or alternate characters with special tall counterparts.

4. In all fonts, ligatures are selected automatically; we get
   TWENTY LAMBS from TWENTY LAMBS.

5. In fonts using the alternate R (R), then any time the R is followed by
   a vowel, TEX should select a smaller superior form of the vowel. That
   is, we get RᴬTTY RᴇRᵁNS from RATTY RERUNS.

(Later on we'll discuss a macro file to facilitate font selection in this new
family.)

The correspondence between the given names and the actual glyph is
established in manx.mtx. First, we printed out a font table for this font, and
in conjunction with the .afm file, we laboriously prepared this file. Certain
glyphs need renaming; for example, numbersign and mu typeset as TT and
Æ. The remaining characters already possess proper names.

```
\relax
   This is manx.mtx, to redefine glyphs in the Mantinia font.
\metrics
\setcommand\saveglyphas#1#2{%
   % eg. \saveglyphas{numbersign}{TT}
   \setglyph{#2}
     \glyph{#1}{1000}
   \endsetglyph
   \setleftkerning{#2}{#1}{1000}
   \setrightkerning{#2}{#1}{1000}}
\saveglyphas{numbersign}{TT}
\saveglyphas{percent}{dollarsuperior}
\saveglyphas{asterisk}{ornament1}
\saveglyphas{plus}{Qalt}
\saveglyphas{less}{TU}
\saveglyphas{equal}{qalt}
\saveglyphas{greater}{TW}
\saveglyphas{at}{Talt}
\saveglyphas{backslash}{ralt}
\saveglyphas{backslash}{ralt}
\saveglyphas{asciicircum}{CT}
\saveglyphas{bar}{Ralt}
\saveglyphas{asciitilde}{TH}
```

```
\saveglyphas{ellipsis}{UP}
\saveglyphas{dagger}{TE}
\saveglyphas{daggerdbl}{ampersandalt}
\saveglyphas{perthousand}{HE}
\saveglyphas{Scaron}{Esmall}
\saveglyphas{bullet}{ornament2}
\saveglyphas{endash}{rangedash}
\saveglyphas{emdash}{punctdash}
\saveglyphas{trademark}{MD}
\saveglyphas{scaron}{Hsmall}
\saveglyphas{Ydieresis}{Yalt}
\saveglyphas{currency}{Ttall}
\saveglyphas{brokenbar}{Ltall}
\saveglyphas{section}{ornament3}
\saveglyphas{copyright}{MP}
\saveglyphas{logicalnot}{LA}
\saveglyphas{registered}{TY}
\saveglyphas{plusminus}{CI}
\saveglyphas{twosuperior}{Itall}
\saveglyphas{threesuperior}{Zsmall}
\saveglyphas{mu}{ME}
\saveglyphas{paragraph}{ampersandsuperior}
\saveglyphas{periodcentered}{ornament4}
\saveglyphas{onesuperior}{Wsmall}
\saveglyphas{onequarter}{Usmall}
\saveglyphas{onehalf}{Tsmall}
\saveglyphas{threequarters}{Ysmall}
\saveglyphas{Eth}{Asmall}
\saveglyphas{multiply}{Ytall}
\saveglyphas{Yacute}{Ismall}
\saveglyphas{Thorn}{Rsmall}
\saveglyphas{germandbls}{MB}
\saveglyphas{eth}{Csmall}
\saveglyphas{divide}{VI}
\saveglyphas{yacute}{Osmall}
\saveglyphas{thorn}{Ssmall}
\saveglyphas{ydieresis}{yalt}
\endmetrics
```

Use \saveglyphas to rename a glyph. Be sure to choose a rename that is meaningful, and make sure this new name does not duplicate an existing glyph name!

One other metric file is needed, provided you agree with my proposal to do something special whenever the alternate R is followed by a vowel. A special file r.mtx contains *fontinst* instructions for forming special glyphs we'll call Ra, Re, and so on, to enter into special ligature rules.

```
\relax
  This if file r.mtx.
\metrics
\setglyph{Ra}
  \glyph{Ralt}{1000}
  \movert{\kerning{Ralt}{a}}
  \glyph{a}{1000}
\endsetglyph
\setglyph{Re}
  \glyph{Ralt}{1000}
  \movert{\kerning{Ralt}{e}}
  \glyph{e}{1000}
\endsetglyph
    ...
\endmetrics
```

The glyphs not shown here (Ri, Ro, and Ru) should be created in an analogous way.

We revise the encoding by revising an existing encoding. Since we'll need to include so many new glyphs corresponding to alternate forms, ornaments, the new 'R' glyphs, and so on, it is better to use the OT1 encoding as a base, since there is so much room in this encoding. Begin with a copy of OT1.etx called OT1man.etx.

The only changes for the first part of the file are \ligature statements added to various slots. I am fond of the left quote convention whereby 1', 2', and so on typesets the ornaments of a font. Mantinia contains four ornaments, and we get them by revising the slot for the digit "one" to look like

```
\setslot{\digit{one}}
  \ligature{LIG}{quoteleft}{ornament1}
  \comment{The number one '1'.}
\endsetslot
```

and so on for the remaining three ornamental glyphs. In the same way, add \ligature rules for each of the rare ligatures in Mantinia. To select Æ automatically any time A and E are adjacent, revise the A slot

```
\setslot{\uc{A}{a}}
  \ligature{LIG}{E}{AE}
  \comment{The letter '{A}'.}
\endsetslot
```

in the obvious way. (And do the same for all slots that contain the left character of a ligature pair.)

The font needs room for each additional glyph, so at the end of the file, the slots for the slashed l's can be removed (they don't exist in this font), and they should be replaced by instructions like

```
\setslot{TT}\endsetslot
\setslot{dollarsuperior}\endsetslot
\setslot{ornament1}\endsetslot
    . . .
```

where a new slot is needed for every '\saveglyphas' entry in manx.etx (this file renamed these glyphs). We will conclude with slots for the Ra, Re, ..., glyphs, although they won't be present in the normal font.

```
    . . .
\setslot{Ra}\endsetslot
\setslot{Re}\endsetslot
\setslot{Ri}\endsetslot
\setslot{Ro}\endsetslot
\setslot{Ru}\endsetslot
\endencoding
```

Next we need variations on this theme for the two additional fonts in the Mantinia family. Begin by copying OT1man.etx to OT1man1.etx. Only minor revisions are necessary for the alternate font.

It's easy to replace standard glyphs by their alternate forms—we need merely replace the slot name by the alternate name. For example, the slot in OT1man1.etx for T must now read

```
\setslot{ Talt }
    \ligature{LIG}{E}{TE}
    \ligature{LIG}{H}{TH}
    \ligature{LIG}{ Talt }{TT}
    \ligature{LIG}{U}{TU}
    \ligature{LIG}{W}{TW}
    \ligature{LIG}{Yalt}{TY}
    \comment{The letter '{T}'.}
\endsetslot
```

if Talt is the name of the alternate T. (The \ligature commands should already have been added.)

The ligature commands also need revision; they must now refer to the new, alternate forms instead of the original glyphs (after all, there is no plain 'T' glyph in this particular font anymore). There are eight alternate letter-forms: compare the alternate &, Q, R, T, Y, Q, R, and Y to the standard & Q, R, T, Y, Q, R, and Y. Ligature commands need to be altered to reflect the alternate forms in the slot for C (the CT ligature) and for Talt (governing the TT and TY ligatures; these changes are illustrated above).

In addition, we can activate the glyphs 'Ra', 'Re', and so on (which type-set as Ra̋, etc.) by adding the ligature commands

```
\ligature{LIG}{A}{Ra}
\ligature{LIG}{E}{Re}
\ligature{LIG}{I}{Ri}
\ligature{LIG}{O}{Ro}
\ligature{LIG}{U}{Ru}
```

to the slot for Ralt.

In light of these comments, the encoding changes for a "tall" font are trivial indeed. Begin by making a copy of OT1man1.etx called OT1mant.etx. There are four tall glyphs, which I named Itall, Ltall, Ttall, and Ytall. The slots for the standard I and L and for the alternate T and Y need to reflect the tall glyphs of this font. Thus, the slot for 'I' should look as follows:

```
\setslot{Itall}
   \comment{The letter '{I}'.}
\endsetslot
```

and likewise for L, T, and Y. Ligature commands need modification whenever they refer to these characters, so make changes to ligature commands in the lslashslash, C, R (actually Ralt), T (Ttall), and V glyphs. (Rest assured— all these machinations are far easier to carry out than they are to read about.)

A short installation file knits everything together. The *fontinst* package needs to know about the raw font, about renaming glyphs, and about the special 'R' glyphs we constructed for use with our special R-ligatures. The encoding information can be found in the OT1man...etx files we created. Let's agree to place all three fonts in the man family, the medium series m, and font shapes n (normal), al (alternate), and ht (tall; think "height"). The installation file

```
\input fontinst.sty
% This is file makeman.tex, an
% installation file for fontinst.
\transformfont{manr8r}{\reencodefont{8r}{\fromafm{manr8a}}}
\installfonts
\installfamily{OT1}{man}{}
  \installfont{manr7t}{manr8r,manx}%
    {OT1man}{OT1}{man}{m}{n}{}
  \installfont{manr7l}{manr8r,manx,r}%
    {OT1man1}{OT1}{man}{m}{al}{}
  \installfont{manr7h}{manr8r,manx,r}%
    {OT1mant}{OT1}{man}{m}{ht}{}
\endinstallfonts
\bye
```

does the trick. After running this file through TEX, run the `.vpl` and `.pl` files through `vptovf` and `pltotf`, move the font files where they belong, move the `.fd` file to an inputs directory, and the fonts are *almost* ready to use.

A special `Mantinia` environment for LATEX will make it easier to switch from font to font. Let's imagine that such an environment automatically switches into the alternate Mantinia font at a size of 16 pt. We redefine the square bracket and angle delimiters to do our font selection for us. If we surround text by [...] (here the ellipsis represents text for typesetting; see the following example), then typesetting will automatically use the tall alternative font. We can switch down to the normal Mantinia font by enclosing text in angle brackets <...>. One short LATEX style file to accomplish appears below.

```
% This is style file mantinia.sty.
\def\savetokens{% save original meanings, just in case.
  \let \[=[ \let\]=] \let\<=<  \let\>=>}
\def\mantall{\fontshape{ht}\selectfont}
\def\manalt{\fontshape{al}\selectfont}
\def\manreg{\fontshape{n}\selectfont}
\def\makedelimsactive{
  \catcode`\[=\active \catcode`\]=\active \catcode`\<=\active
  \catcode`\>=\active }
{\makedelimsactive
\gdef[{\bgroup\mantall}\gdef<{\bgroup\manreg}
  \global\let]=\egroup \global\let>=\egroup}
\newenvironment{Mantinia}{\bgroup\savetokens
  \fontfamily{man}\fontseries{m}\fontshape{al}
    \fontsize{16}{22}\selectfont
  \makedelimsactive
  }{\endgraf\egroup}
%% Now for some shortcuts for simple typesetting purposes.
\def\mann#1{{\fontfamily{man}\manreg #1}}  % 'n' shape
\def\manl#1{{\fontfamily{man}\manalt #1}}  % alt shape
\def\mant#1{{\fontfamily{man}\mantall #1}} % tall shape
\endinput
```

Plain TEX users can define a similar file to set up commands \Mantinia and \endMantinia that will behave like LATEX environment delimiters. Only the font-selection commands will need changing (commands like \fontfamily make no sense in plain).

With these conventions in place, we need only type

```
\documentclass{article}
\thispagestyle{empty}
\usepackage{mantinia}
\begin{document}
```

```
\begin{center}
  \begin{Mantinia}
    \noindent QUONIAM AD HUNC LOCUM PERvENTUM EST, NON
    A[Li]ENUM ESSE VIDETUR DE GALLIAE
    GERmANIAEQUE MORIBUS \& QUO DIFFERANT
    HAE NATIONES <INTER> SESE PROPONE<R>e.  IN
    GALLIA NON SOLUM IN OMNIBUS C\kernOptIVITA[T]IBUS
    A[T]QUE IN OMNIBUS PAGIS <PAR[T]IBUSQUE>, SED
    PAENE <ETIAM> IN SINGULIS DOMIBUS
    FACTIONES SUNT, <EARUMQUE> FACTIONUM
    PRINCIPES SUNT QUi SUMMAM AUCTORI[T]ATEM
    EORUM IUD[I]CIO HABERE EXIS[T]IMANTU<R>,
    QUORUM AD A<R>BI[T]RiUM IUDICIUMQUE SUMMA
    OMNIUM RERUM CONSI[Li]ORUMQUE REDEA<T>.
  \end{Mantinia}
\end{center}
\end{document}
```

to get the material in figure 9 on the next page.

The Poetica project [Hoenig (1995)] employs a different set of input convention to gain access to the many fonts and ligatures in the Poetica fonts. With the Poetica styles in CTAN, it is possible to typeset displays similar to figure 10 on page 252.

8.7 Two advanced projects

We conclude this chapter with two projects that exercise other virtual font capabilities.

8.7.1 *Motion picture credits*

Producers of film and television programs often engage in typographic acrobatics when displaying production credits. Although such displays may look awful, and be of limited use for conventional books and reports, such fonts are well within what virtual fonts can do. We consider one example. It illustrates other aspects of juggling characters in a virtual manner.

This display,

B̲RETT̲ M̲AVERICK

similar in style to the credits of some movies, is the product of typing

```
Brett Maverick
```

for some suitably defined (and suitably selected) virtual font. Here's what we propose for this font.

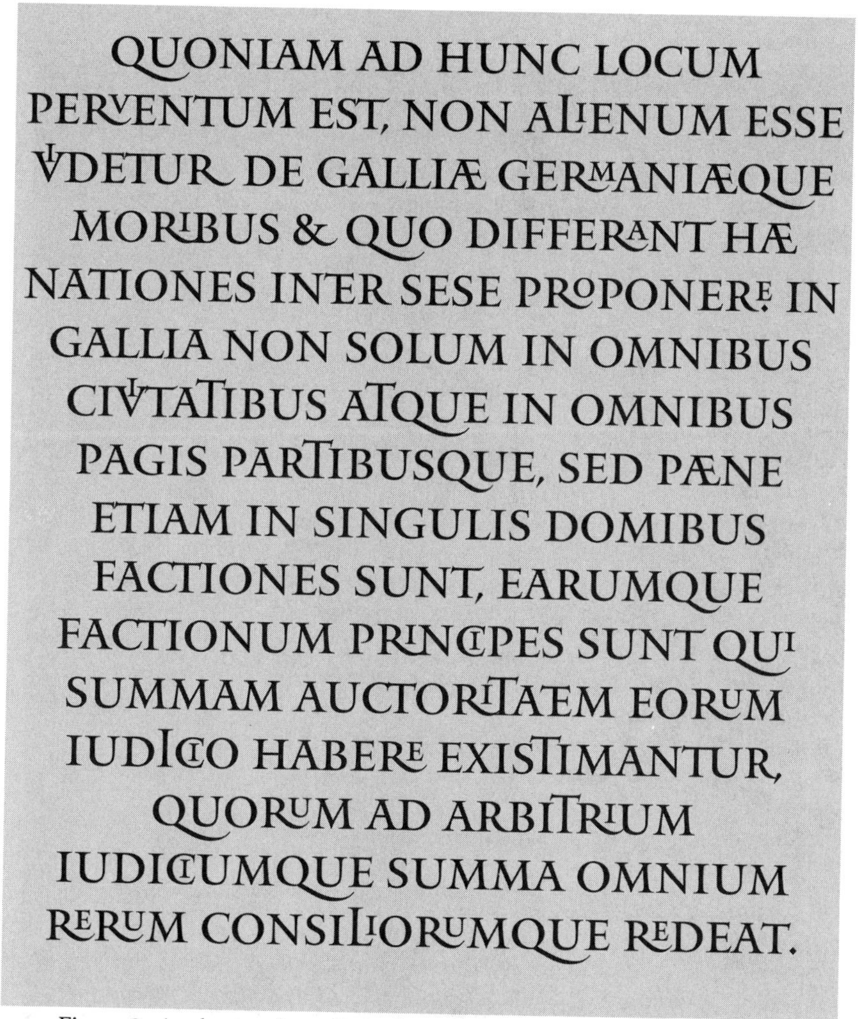

QUONIAM AD HUNC LOCUM
PERVENTUM EST, NON ALIENUM ESSE
VDETUR DE GALLIÆ GERMANIÆQUE
MORIBUS & QUO DIFFERANT HÆ
NATIONES INTER SESE PROPONERE IN
GALLIA NON SOLUM IN OMNIBUS
CIVTATIBUS ATQUE IN OMNIBUS
PAGIS PARTIBUSQUE, SED PÆNE
ETIAM IN SINGULIS DOMIBUS
FACTIONES SUNT, EARUMQUE
FACTIONUM PRINCIPES SUNT QUI
SUMMAM AUCTORITAEM EORUM
IUDICO HABERE EXISTIMANTUR,
QUORUM AD ARBITRIUM
IUDICUMQUE SUMMA OMNIUM
RERUM CONSILIORUMQUE REDEAT.

Figure 9: A selection from Caesar's *Gallic Wars* set with Mantinia fonts.

- The lowercase letters be uppercase glyphs scaled 70% and aligned at the tops of the letters (not the baselines).

- All letters have an overbar.

- The lowercase letters have an underbar at the baseline.

We'll use bold Galliard (family name bgl) as our base font, so rather than reconstruct it, we will reuse it. It is available to us if we create a property file from the font metric file; we type something like this:

```
tftopl ⟨path⟩/bglb7t.tfm bglb7t.pl
```

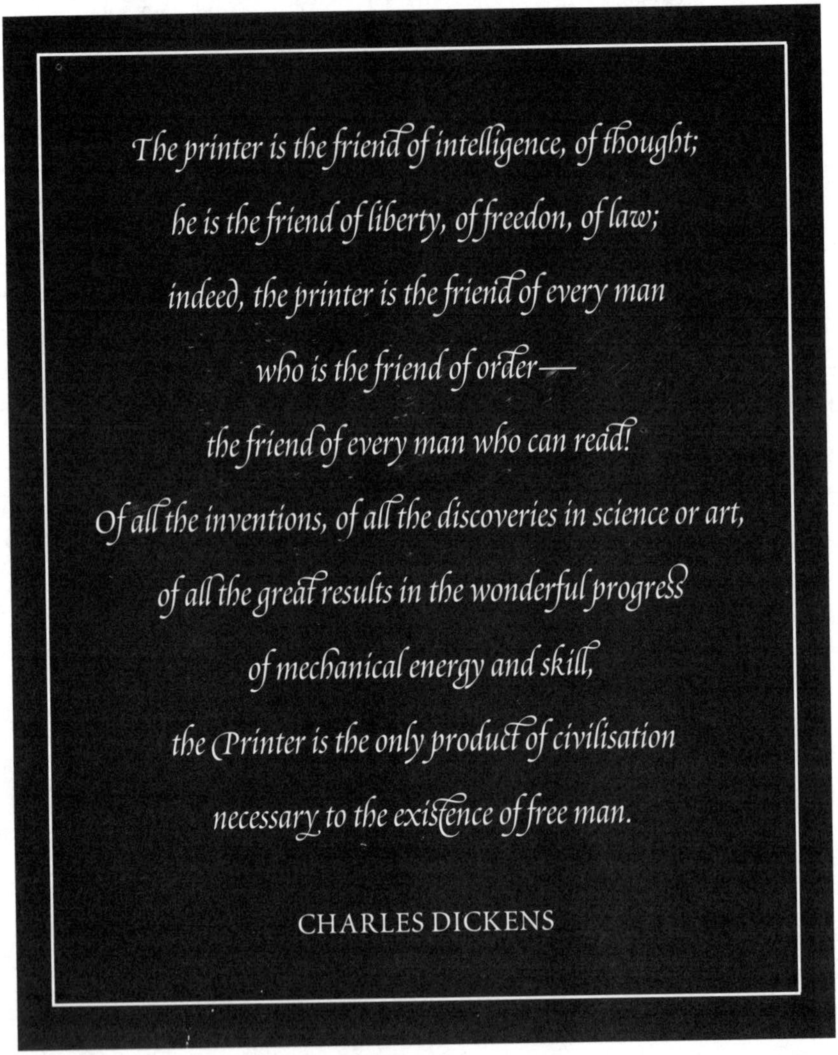

The printer is the friend of intelligence, of thought;

he is the friend of liberty, of freedon, of law;

indeed, the printer is the friend of every man

who is the friend of order—

the friend of every man who can read!

Of all the inventions, of all the discoveries in science or art,

of all the great results in the wonderful progress

of mechanical energy and skill,

the Printer is the only product of civilisation

necessary to the existence of free man.

CHARLES DICKENS

Figure 10: Virtual fonts helped set many special ligature characters in these Adobe Poetica fonts.

Alternate Fonts: Comparing and Contrasting

The three alternate font constructions of this chapter represent not only individual examples of fonts, but also show how to cope with different classes of difficulties. This chart summarizes the types of problems we encountered in these projects.

Font	*Description*
Adobe Garamond	Adding new ligatures to a font; implementing ligature rules to select these special glyphs automatically. New ligature selection mechanisms using the left quote character.
Bernhard Modern	Adding special new ligatures; seeing how to replace standard letterforms by alternate glyphs via a modification of a standard encoding. Dealing with a ligature formed from three characters. Coping with errors in .afm files: some font dimensions are incorrectly given.
Mantinia	Dealing with rare ligatures and two types of alternate characters; organizing several different alternate fonts; creating several different fonts to contain selections of alternate characters. Dealing with a new encoding and misleading glyph-naming; dealing with characters present in the font, but inaccessible (hidden characters). Creating a special macro file to make the selection of these special fonts as convenient as possible.

We need a command `\ucletter` to create new uppercase glyphs, with names like Abar, Bbar, and so on. In a similar way, `\lcletter` creates our peculiar lowercase letter from the uppercase. This, and other metric information, belongs in a file bars.mtx, which begins like this. (Refer to the *fontinst* documentation for the syntactical details of all the *fontinst* commands.)

```
\relax
  This is file bars.mtx, for a Hollywood-like virtual
  font.
\metrics
\setint{capheight}{\height{X}}
\setint{sccapheight}{\scale{\int{capheight}}{700}}
\setint{capdiff}{\scale{\int{capheight}}{300}}
\setint{obar}{\add{\int{capheight}}{\sub{\int{capdiff}}{60}}}
\setcommand\ucletter#1{
```

```
\setglyph{#1bar}
  \push
    \moveup{\int{obar}} % overhead bar
    \glyphrule{\width{#1}}{60}
  \pop
  \glyph{#1}{1000}
\endsetglyph
\setleftkerning{#1bar}{#1}{1000}
\setrightkerning{#1bar}{#1}{1000}}
\setcommand\lcletter#1{
  \resetint{scwidth}{\scale{\width{#1}}{700}}% width of
                                      % small caps glyph
  \setglyph{#1bbar}
    \push
      \moveup{\int{obar}} %  overhead bar
      \glyphrule{\int{scwidth}}{60}
    \pop
    \push
      \glyphrule{\int{scwidth}}{60}
    \pop% low bar
    \moveup{\int{capdiff}}
    \glyph{#1}{700}
  \endsetglyph
  \setleftkerning{#1bbar}{#1}{700}
  \setrightkerning{#1bbar}{#1}{700}}
\setcommand\makeletters#1{% some syntactic sugar
  \ucletter{#1}
  \lcletter{#1}}
    ...
    ...
```

Initial \setint commands define some useful quantities and show how to do arithmetic the *fontinst* way. A small-caps cap height (sccapheight) is scaled at 70% of the majuscule cap height. The capdiff variable is the difference between the two cap heights, and obar is the total height above the baseline for the overbar—it's the same distance above the letters as the base bar is below the raised small caps.

Now the uppercase letters are easy. For the bar-glyph, we draw the overbar first, then place the standard glyph, and finally appropriate the kerning. The \push and \pop are crucial to restore ourselves back to the position just before the \push. (Without them, the glyph would appear to the right of the overbar. If the purpose of \push and \pop is still unclear, simply remove them from bars.mtx before creating the virtual font. You'll soon appreciate what went wrong.)

Similar machinations appear within \lcletter. We create the glyph by first drawing the overbar, an underbar (enclosing each in \push and

\pop pairs to make sure that all bars begin at the left edge of the type), and then placing the small caps glyph so its top edge aligns with the cap height. As usual, we use the kerning information from the base font. Finally, \makeletters provides some keystroke shortcuts.

Now we continue by applying these constructions to each uppercase glyph. (We won't bother with other characters in the font.)

```
   ...
\makeletters{A}   \makeletters{B}
\makeletters{C}   \makeletters{D}
   ...
\makeletters{Y}   \makeletters{Z}
\endencoding
```

A short encoding file ensures that the encoding refers to these barred letters. Assuming OT1 encoding, create a file OT1bar.etx.

```
\relax
  This is file OT1bar.etx for Hollywood fonts.
\encoding
\setcommand\uc#1#2{#1bar}
\setcommand\lc#1#2{#1bbar}
\inputetx{OT1}
\endencoding
```

Since the letter slots in an encoding file are defined using the \lc and \uc commands, these definitions ensure that *fontinst* will pick up the barred letters for the font.

Finally, we need an installation file to create the font.

```
\input fontinst.sty
\installfonts
  \installfamily{OT1}{bgl}{}
  \installfont{bglbt7t}{bglb7t,bars}%
    {OT1bar}{OT1}{bgl}{b}{tv}{}
\endinstallfonts
\bye
```

For NFSS, the font will be a 'tv' shape in the bold series. We need only select the new font to typeset as shown above.

8.7.2 Better underlining

Earlier we described an underline font. But when underlining characters with descenders

Quit <u>playing goofy (jejune) games,
Jacques!</u>

it looks awkward that the underscore passes through the descenders. One quick fix—and an easy fix—is to recreate the virtual underline font, and this time move the underscore further down so it clears the descenders. A more interesting solution is to interrupt the underline whenever a descender gets in the way:

Quit playing goofy (jejune) games, Jacques!

How can we create such a virtual font without laboriously figuring out by hand where the descender appears?

One solution assumes we're using PostScript technology. First, we begin with a copy of `uline.mtx` called `uuline.mtx` in which we add a definition for better underlining.

```
\setcommand\uuline#1{
 \ifisglyph{#1}\then
  \resetglyph{#1}
    \push
      \moveup{-150}\glyphrule{\width{#1}}{40} % set u-line
    \pop
    \glyphspecial{ps: /SaveGray currentgray def 1 setgray}
    \push
      \movert{-40}\glyph{#1}{1000}
    \pop
    \push
      \movert{40}\glyph{#1}{1000}
    \pop
    \glyphspecial{ps: SaveGray setgray}
    \glyph{#1}{1000}
  \endresetglyph
 \fi}
```

This command draws the underline first, then prints several copies of the glyph, slightly to the left and right, in white ink, effectively erasing the part of the underline that would coincide with the letter's descending stroke. Finally, TEX prints the character in the current shade (usually black). The effect will be what we are after, and this example shows how to embed calls to PostScript within a virtual font.

Alas, if this definition is applied to every glyph in the font, the result is a monster font too large for TEX and friends to handle. A better approach is to apply the normal underline to all but those glyphs with descenders. For the Galliard font displayed above, this includes only parenleft, parenright, comma, semicolon, J, Q, g, j, p, q, and y (these are the standard glyph names). For these glyphs, we explicitly replace the \newglyph command by \uuline. Following the construction of uuline.mtx, follow the same procedure as above in the construction of normal underline fonts.

CHAPTER 9

· ·

MORE VIRTUAL FONTS

9.1 Letterspacing and tracking

When we *letterspace* text, we adjust the characters to sit a bit closer or farther apart from each neighbor by some fixed amount in addition to the normal kerns that apply between adjacent characters. Normally, we will subject only a word or short phrase to the Procrustean bed of *track kerning*—an equivalent term for letterspacing—and we do so for special purposes only, perhaps for a large display or in order to better fit type on particularly short lines (rarely). *The New Yorker* magazine, with a layout that centers about three narrow columns, is notorious for its frequent use of letterspacing to avoid large interword spaces. (An alternate approach often appears on the Op-Ed pages of *The New York Times*, which eschews letterspacing for its narrow columns. Odd layouts are apt to display immense interword spaces and occasional ragged right lines. Given the reality of short lines, it's not easy to decide which alternative is preferable.) Since tracking closes up the interword spacing when applied to several adjacent words, it sometimes looks as if several words have simply been run together. The author of TEX has rightly observed that it is easy to abuse tracking. Typesetters should be sparing in its use.

Close tracking—setting letters closer together—has only become feasible since the decline of hot metal technologies. In the old days, one was apt only to find examples of distance tracking—adding thin spaces between neighboring glyphs—since close tracking would have required craftsmen to laboriously file off bits of metal from each piece of type. It's possible to find books (especially German) of the last century in which letterspacing was used for e m p h a s i s rather than boldface or italic. (The German term for this typographic curiosity is *Sperrsatz*.)

Letterspacing Text

Two approaches exist.

1. Macros, such as provided by the `letterspace` package, provide tools for letterspacing. These macros can inhibit line breaks and break ligatures, but do make possible an infinite gradation of tracking.

2. It's possible to create virtual fonts in which the glyphs of the original font are automatically spaced closer or more distantly to each other. Although hyphenation, line breaking, and ligatures are not inhibited, this approach requires the creation of a new virtual font for each level of tracking.

Apply tracking sparingly!

9.1.1   A macro approach

Phil Taylor has created a set of macros for letterspacing. You can download the file `letterspace.sty` from the `macros/latex209/contrib/misc` area of any of the CTAN archives, but the style appears to work well with the current LaTeX. This file offers a `\letterspace` macro with a syntax like `\vbox` and `\hbox` of plain TeX.

9.1.2   A virtual-font approach

The *fontinst* package makes short work of creating special virtual fonts in which all letters are automatically letterspaced. With these fonts in place, letterspacing becomes an issue not of macros but of font selection.

With all the variations possible from a given base font, sometimes the hardest part of virtual font creation is the assignment of unique names to the new fonts. For letterspaced fonts, we'll append a 'k' plus a single additional letter to the name of each tracked font; the 'k' suggests trac*k k*erning. Let's assume four levels of tracking, so we'll need four new fonts, two with *positive* tracking (space is added between each pair of letters) and two with *negative* tracking letters (interletter spacing is removed, so neighbors appear closer together). We'll let 'a' and 'b' refer to the positive tracking and 'z' and 'y' to the negative. So if we create four tracked Adobe Garamond fonts, the names would be `padrka7t`, `padrkb7t`, `padrkz7t`, and `padrky7t` if we encode according to the OT1 convention; we recall that `pad` is the Berry name for Adobe Garamond.

For use with NFSS, we need to agree on a few further conventions. Let the font series remain the same (m for Roman text fonts), but let's name the font shapes after their tracking designations, that is ka, kb, kx, and ky.

We'll use an existing virtual font as the base font for this project. For this, we'll need the property file. In the Adobe Garamond font family (designation pad), we begin with a command like

```
tftopl ⟨path⟩/padr7t.tfm padr7t.pl
```

which we issue in the work directory.

The installation file   By great good fortune, an existing *fontinst* variable controls the letterspacing in a font. letterspacing is an encoding variable, and we give it a value in a *fontinst* encoding file. Although we normally need a single file OT1.etx, say, to install a text font, we'll need the additional files OT1ka.etx, and so on, to set letterspacing. The installation file maketrax.tex is straightforward to compose.

```
\input fontinst.sty
% This is the installation file maketrax.tex, to implement
% letterspaced (tracked) virtual fonts.
\installfonts
  \installfamily{OT1}{pad}{}
    \installfont{padka7t}{padr7t}{OT1ka}{OT1}{pad}{m}{ka}{}
    \installfont{padkb7t}{padr7t}{OT1kb}{OT1}{pad}{m}{kb}{}
    \installfont{padky7t}{padr7t}{OT1kz}{OT1}{pad}{m}{kz}{}
    \installfont{padkz7t}{padr7t}{OT1ky}{OT1}{pad}{m}{ky}{}
\endinstallfonts
\bye
```

Here, a previously created virtual font (padr7t) acts as a raw font in the definition of the new letterspaced virtual fonts.

New encoding files   We'll use track levels of ± 25 and ± 50. With 1000 integer units to the type size, $+50$ corresponds to letterspacing of 0.5 pt and -25 to -0.25 pt (that is, close tracking), if the type size is 10 pt. These values represent the values of the additional kerns added between all pairs of adjacent characters.

The new encoding files are short because we'll reuse virtually all of the standard OT1.etx. Here is OT1ka.etx.

```
\relax
% This is file OT1ka.etx
\encoding
\resetint{letterspacing}{25}
\inputtx{OT1}
\endencoding
```

and here is OT1ky.etx.

```
\relax
% This is file OT1ky.etx
\encoding
\resetint{letterspacing}{-50}
\inputetx{OT1}
\endencoding
```

You may feel it's proper to suppress ligatures in a tracked font—after all, ligatures preserve the look of normal, nonletterspaced text, which may be inappropriate in letterspaced setting. To do that, we realize that the normal \ligature command takes three arguments, and we can "dummy it out" by redefining it to do nothing. That is, you'll need to add the lines

```
\setcommand\gobblethree#1#2#3{}
\let\ligature=\gobblethree
```

immediately following the \encoding line of any of the OT1k...etx files.

Creating the tracked fonts   Once these files have been prepared, you follow the usual procedures for the actual installation.

1. First, create the .pl file for padr7t (or whatever), and then run plain TEX on the installation file.

2. At the end of the run, you will have several new files: some .vpl files and an .fd file for use by LATEX's NFSS. Run all the .vpl files through vptovf with commands like

```
vptovf gdrka.vpl gdrka.vf gdrka.tfm
```

and move .vf, and .tfm files to their proper directories.

3. Merge the entries in the .fd file with the pre-existing .fd file for this family.

Implementing tracking   The font names for the tracking fonts are messy. The best way to deal with them is by means of a macro interface. Suppose we associate four levels of tracking with our four letterspaced fonts. Then, after

```
\newcommand{\tr}[1]{\ifcase#1
  \or\fontshape{ka}\or\fontshape{kb}\or
  \fontshape{ky}\or\fontshape{kz}\fi
  \selectfont}
```

(assuming LATEX and NFSS syntax) we type

```
\begin{tabular}{rl}
  Normal&Letterspacing\\
  \tr{1}Wide&\tr{1}Letterspacing\\
  \tr{2}Wider&\tr{2}Letterspacing\\
  \tr{4}Tight&\tr{4}Letterspacing\\
  \tr{3}Tighter&\tr{3}Letterspacing
\end{tabular}
```

to get

Normal	Letterspacing
Wide	Letterspacing
Wider	Letterspacing
Tight	Letterspacing
Tighter	Letterspacing

Plain TEX users can define a similar \tr command. If we access the tracking fonts with declarations like

```
\font\ka=padka7t \font\kb=padkb7t
\font\ky=padky7t \font\kz=padkz7t
```

then we define

```
\def\tr#1{\ifcase#1
  \or\ka \or\kb \or\ky \or\kz \fi}
```

which we use in the same way.

Letterspaced fonts can also be useful in setting scalable fonts at small sizes; see subsection 9.4.4 on page 281. See the epigraph on page 2 for another example of letterspaced fonts.

9.2   Previewing PostScript: Hardware strategies

It's easy to preview bitmapped output. Monitors are raster devices just like laser printers, but a bit coarser. Previewers have learned how to display bit-mapped output on screen using special preview fonts or by sampling printer bitmaps in clever ways.

Special problems arise when working with outline fonts, for no bitmaps exist. Given both the ubiquity of PostScript software and the length of time it has been dominant, it's hard to explain why previewing PostScript output remains so onerous. Monitors remain bitmap devices, and it's hard coaxing them to display outline fonts.

Normally, the PostScript rasterizer (the program responsible for the ren-dition of outlines to the appropriate bitmap) resides in the printer and re-mains unavailable to the computer or monitor. Typically, previewer soft-ware is not able to directly render the outlines, and it may appear that we have to forego previewing when working with outline fonts. In fact, several alternatives exist. We can preview PostScript using hardware or software so-lutions.

Letterspacing: A Virtual-Font Approach

In a letterspaced font, each glyph is spaced a bit from its neighbors in a uniform way. Here's how to create a virtual letterspaced font.

1. Decide on the levels of letterspacing you may need, and create an installation file as on page 259.

2. Create several short encoding files OT1ka.etx and so on as per the suggestions of page 259.

3. Run TEX on the installation file.

4. Run vptovf on the resulting .vpl files. Place the resulting .tfm and .vf files in the proper directories. Place the .fd file in an input directory if you use NFSS.

5. You may care to add macros like the ones on page 260 to your document or style files. With them in place, it becomes easy to access the tracking fonts.

9.2.1   Display PostScript

Certain systems have always had access to *Display PostScript*; that is, the hardware or operating system contains a PostScript interpreter capable of rendering outlines on-screen. Those readers using a form of TEX on an Amiga system [Radical Eye Software (1990)] or any computer running the NextStep [NeXT Computer Corporation (1993)] operating system know how convenient this is. Running NextStep on a 486 box with video accelerator is fully as fast as a traditional pixel previewer and just as convenient. The image under Display PostScript tends to be sharper than with pixels, as the PostScript interpreter optimizes the image for the display better than most pixel previewers can.

Users of Display PostScript can view documents exactly whether they contain text, embedded Encapsulated PostScript (.epsf or .eps) or .tiff graphics, or both.

The NextStep operating system is a special windowing environment that sits on top of Unix, so anyone familiar with any flavor of Unix will have no trouble adapting to NextStep. NextStep windows are easy and intuitive to use, so anyone familiar with another windowing system will also feel right at home. Although NextStep does run on a 486 computer, this computer needs to be beefier than the standard off-the-shelf machine. Check with NeXT Computer Corporation before acquiring hardware!

Special mention should be made of the TEX that's bundled with Next-Step. *TEXView*, by Tom Rokicki, knits TEX (or LATEX) plus a previewer into one seamless application that feels as comfortable as a well-worn baseball glove. Previewing under *TEXView* takes advantage of the built-in Display PostScript capability of NextStep. For a further discussion of LATEX and TEX under NextStep, see Hoenig (1994). A hypertext version of *TEXView* is also available for downloading; see chapter 5. The manuscript for this book was prepared on a NextStep system.

Certain Unix xdvi previewers are also capable of direct PostScript display on X-windows systems. The Adobe Type Manager (ATM) on Macintosh and Windows systems also renders PostScript type and images on-screen, and does a particularly fine job.

The *Ghostscript* program provides another avenue for previewing Post-Script. Current versions of this public utility can render a font and send the bitmaps to an output stream. Utilities such as gs2pk and ps2pk take advantage of this capability.

9.3 Previewing PostScript: Software strategies

9.3.1 Pixel fonts from outline fonts

If we can replace the original outline fonts of a document by equivalent pixel fonts—bitmaps fonts that reproduce the look of the original and have identical metrics—then the document is previewable, if we simply request that TEX use the bitmap equivalents when compiling or previewing the document. Every outline font at every size must be given a pixel equivalent (unless your previewer makes clever font substitutions), so there is apt to be some work on your part in creating the suite of equivalent fonts. (Remember, even the "lite"-st of TEX installations requires 16 fonts.) Furthermore, any scalable object in your document that is neither a font nor a rule (included figures, etc.) will not have a pixel equivalent and so will not be previewable using this approach.

Bitmap equivalents to outline fonts   One firm [Kinch Computer Company (1987)] makes pixel files available that imitate the look of the 35 fonts normally resident in most PostScript laser printers. Each font in this collection consists of a pixel file and an associated font metric file.

Although this AP-TEX package contains a file collection of fonts at different sizes, be aware that the magnification and printer resolution is limited to the pixel files in the package. You can print on 300 dpi printers at a rich range of sizes between 5 and 24.9 pt. Certain headline fonts in this collection expand the range to 74.3 pt. The use of these fonts will allow us to preview a document that is entirely text, but it cannot enable us to preview a document containing a figure or graphic image of any kind (bitmap images present no problem).

Preparing pixel equivalents to outline fonts   Several utilities in the CTAN archives, in `fonts/utilities`, facilitate the creation of bitmap fonts from original outline fonts. Once valid `.pk` fonts have been created as the end result of this process, you can incorporate them into a LATEX or TEX document as you would any other font. They have the same—*exactly* the same— metrics as the original outline fonts.

The program `ps2pk` by Piet Tutelaers is the most straightforward of these tools. The pixel font is its end product. The program requires the original `.pfb` and `.afm` files for the font, the resolution of your printer, and the size of the font you need.

A second utility, `ps2mf` by Erik Jan Vens, requires an additional set of steps, for its output is a METAFONT program file, and this METAFONT file must then be rendered into bitmap form by METAFONT. This proce- dure gives you the opportunity of adjusting letterforms in a way unavailable to you using simple PostScript transformations. Follow the procedures of chapter 3 to install pixel fonts from the METAFONT programs. Only the source files for `ps2mf` appear to be in the archives, so it is probably up to you to perform the compilation.

Relatively recently, a new utility `gsf2pk` for Unix users, also on CTAN, has appeared. Its goal is to create bitmap equivalents for GhostScript fonts (see the next section), which are themselves a superset of standard Type 1 outline fonts. Therefore, `gsf2pk` should also be useful.

The use of these fonts will certainly allow us to preview a document that is entirely text, but it cannot let us preview a document containing a figure or graphic image unless the graphic has been provided in bitmap form. Also, successful use of these utilities requires a sure knowledge of precisely which fonts appear in the document. See subsection 9.3.3 on page 267 for a reso- lution of this issue.

9.3.2   *PostScript renderers*

Some third-party programs render PostScript into bitmap form, just like real PostScript interpreters. Whereas real interpreters rasterize within the printer, these programs do their work in the computer. Not only does this make it possible to view output on-screen, but we can also print this output to non-PostScript printers. Moreover, these renderers can display included PostScript graphics as well as type.

However, these programs may be expensive, are usually slow, and are often not user friendly. Some of this software does an inferior job of ren- dering even though this is their sole *raison d'être*. Smooth curves can come out as curve segments with noticeable joins. A few of these programs are *GoScript* [LaserGo, Inc. (1988)] and *Freedom of Press* [Custom Applica- tions Inc. (1988)]. A recent arrival is the *PSAlter* program [Quite Software (1996)], a very useful tool (for computers running Windows 3.1 and bet- ter) for creating PostScript programs and getting them right, but it also lets one preview a PostScript document via a particularly convenient interface.

Using Equivalent Bitmap Fonts

You should think of the bitmap fonts equivalent to scalable fonts as raw fonts. Your system may, for example, contain an outline font named like ptmr8a.afm (the metric file) and ptmr8a.pfb (the file containing the outline descriptions). According to the Berry font-naming scheme, these are the names for the Adobe Times Roman regular font resident in nearly every PostScript laser printer. To use this font with a bitmap previewer:

- we would need the pixel equivalent (something named like ptmr8a.pk or ptmr8a.300pk for 300 dpi resolution) and

- we need a TEX font metric file named ptmr8t.tfm. This .tfm file should have been distributed with the pixel file, if this is a commercial package, or should be part of the output of a utility like ps2pk or ps2mf. (If the .afm file is available, a utility like afm2tfm—part of *dvips*—can quickly generate the .tfm.)

With *PSAlter*, a PostScript artist can convert the document into other formats (Windows Bitmap, .tiff, or encapsulated PostScript).

The commercial Windows program dviwindo [Y&Y, Inc. (1996)] renders outline fonts when printing TEX documents.

CorelDRAW [Corel Corporation (1996)] is well known for graphic manipulation. It can also import a PostScript file for preview.

Acrobat   Adobe Acrobat is a multiplatform suite of several programs to make document images portable across platforms. The Acrobat *Distiller* renders a document in a new portable document format [Bientz and Cohn (1993)]; its files have extension .pdf. Acrobat *Reader*, a freely available utility, displays the portable document on a system monitor and will also print the document on a non-PostScript printer. Acrobat *Exchange* does everything *Reader* does but lets you add some hypertext structure to the portable document as well as some editorial comments. LATEX and TEX users can use Acrobat to preview documents—bitmap *or* PostScript—by running the document through the Distiller. As it creates the .pdf file, it displays it in a friendly way (lots of options exist for sizing, text searching, moving on a page, and moving throughout the document). Once you've built the .pdf file, anyone with Reader or Exchange can also view it.

Besides the cost of the Distiller program, the act of distilling the document takes time, sometimes lots of time. Long documents or lots of included graphics slow the process down. The program has been intelligently designed—Distiller displays the initial page as soon as it is ready, so you can begin previewing even as the distill process continues.

Ghostscript and Ghostview   GhostScript by Peter Deutsch exists in two versions. A relatively older version of the program is a part of the GNU suite of programs. GNU aims to create free versions of all major Unix programs, and GhostScript corresponds to the GNU version of PostScript. Normally, GNU programs run only on Unix architecture, but this is one of the components for which extraordinary demand appeared, and there are now versions of GhostScript for most platforms. GNU programs are distributed under the terms of the GNU General Public License, which allows free use, and free copying and redistribution under certain conditions (including, in some cases, commercial distribution).

A current version is distributed as Aladdin Ghostscript, under similar terms to the GNU version, but which prohibits commercial distribution. The GNU version lags the Aladdin version by about a year.

Both source and executables are available from many archives, including the support section of CTAN, and from many CD-ROMs and other sources of distribution. You can find Aladdin GhostScript at `ftp.cs.wisc.edu` in the directory `/ghost/aladdin` for `ftp` retrieval from its primary source.

GhostScript's *raison d'être* is to serve as renderer of PostScript output *within* the computer, rather than at the printer, as is the case with standard PostScript. This rendered, bitmap image can be displayed on the monitor, but since it is a bitmap image, it can even be sent to a non PostScript printer. GhostScript appears to be actively supported by its creator.

GhostScript's main disadvantage is its unfriendliness, although this is improving incrementally with each new release. Two software tools ease this unfriendliness. The shell GhostView, by Russell Lang, sits on top of GhostScript to make it easier to use this program in Windows/DOS, OS/2, or X11. A PostScript script by P. Pianowski and B. Jackowski called `ps-view.ps` make GhostScript more interactive. The `ps-view` and `ghostview` subdirectories of the CTAN support area contain this material.

GhostScript does its job well and robustly (but sometimes slowly), and it displays both fonts and graphics, but there are other advantages to this tool. It has been compiled for a wide variety of computers and has begun appearing as a component in other useful tasks. For example, it takes an important rôle in the `fontload` package of Basil Malyshev to accomplish *partial downloading* of fonts—only those characters used by a document get sent to the printer. Authors preparing files that must contain the font information for a service bureau will find their PostScript files of a far more manageable size with this package in place. (The `fontload` package can be found in the `fonts/utilities/fontload` area of CTAN.)

Once GhostScript is properly installed (a simple process; follow the directions in the `.doc` files that are part of the distribution), we first prepare a PostScript file from a `.dvi` file with a command like

```
dvips -o foo.ps foo.dvi
```

(The syntax will presumably vary with other postprocessors.) To view the document, type something like

```
gs foo.ps
```

at the operating system prompt. Press the "enter" key to go from one page to the next. Various switches control other aspects of the program. For example, to print foo.ps on a Hewlett Packard LaserJet printer, type something like

```
gs -sDEVICE=laserjet -dNOPAUSE -sOUTPUTFILE=LPT1 foo.ps
```

Recent versions of GhostScript (versions 3.51 and later) support the display of .pdf files and the conversion of .pdf to PostScript. As of this writing, version 4.x of GhostScript is unreleased, but it will both generate and preview .pdf output. At its release, it will provide an alternative to the Adobe Distiller component of *Acrobat*.

9.3.3   The virtual-font way

In his original announcement of virtual fonts, the author of TEX used as an example the generation of mock scalable fonts from Computer Modern pixel maps coupled to the metrics of an outline font. Such a mock font would make the document previewable—all line breaks, page breaks, and so on, are as in the actual document, and only the letterforms are different. With a suite of such fonts, previewing would be just as fast as when an author uses bitmap fonts, but perhaps not as visually satisfactory.

Owing to the general ubiquity of tools such as GhostScript, it may no longer be so important to generate such mock scalable fonts as we've described. Nevertheless, it is important to consider such a project if only for the additional practice with virtual fonts.

Which fonts?   If you choose to follow this approach, you may wish to impose some typographical discipline on yourself. Each outline font you use requires a mock, virtual companion, so you should limit the fonts you use and their sizes; typographically, this is a good idea anyway.

After you've been as "fontally" frugal as possible, you'll still need a list of all fonts used in the document. With the aid of the little-used utility dvitype, which should and must be part of your suite of TEX software, this information is easy to come by. Hardly anyone ever uses dvitype these days—it served as exemplar in the early days of TEX when people needed to be able to verify that a .dvi file had been properly created, or when developers needed a model to follow when writing a device driver. But one of the things recorded in its output file dvitype.out is a list of all fonts and their scalings. This information occurs at or near the beginning of this (potentially huge) file.

Suppose you've just produced the .dvi file foo.dvi. Then, after having made sure that dvitype lies on the computer's path, issue the command

```
dvitype foo.dvi
```

The program asks you to verify or modify a number of parameters, including the maximum number of pages to process. Since the resulting file dvitype.out can be truly huge—many megabytes in size, which can choke an almost-filled hard disk to death—you should make sure that you answer this with a maximum of one page (and even then, the output file can be uncomfortably large).

Near the beginning of dvitype.out is a series of lines beginning with Font.... You will want to collect these statements to a smaller file, for they provide the needed list of fonts for this document. For an early draft of one of the chapters of this book, this information looked like this.

```
Font 24: padr7t scaled 1200---loaded at size 786432 DVI units
Font 23: padri7t scaled 800---loaded at size 524288 DVI units
Font 22: cmbtt10---loaded at size 655360 DVI units
Font 21: padru7t---loaded at size 655360 DVI units
Font 20: cmtt10---loaded at size 655360 DVI units
Font 19: padr7t---loaded at size 655360 DVI units
Font 14: logo10---loaded at size 655360 DVI units
```

For each outline font in our document, we can create a virtual font that

- has the same metrics, but

- uses pixel files instead of outline files to generate the letterforms.

This technique will not work on included graphics.

> **Warning!! This virtual font method requires creating mock fonts that are inferior to fonts we print with, but which have their same names. When making these virtual fonts, take great care not to overwrite your good fonts with these mock fonts.**

Configuring the previewer   The virtual, mock fonts must have the same name as the real fonts. When you create them, carefully segregate them from the real ones. For example, if we store padr8a.pfb in directory /ps-fonts, (padr8a being Adobe Garamond regular), we will store the mock fonts padr8a.329pk, padr8a.300pk, and so on, *separately*. Most device drivers and previewers can be configured to look in special places for the fonts they use. The first thing you will want to do, then, is to check the relevant rules for your previewer software.

For example, some DOS authors use the emTeX implementation to compile and preview documents, and they might use *dvips* to print their

> **Previewing Outline Font Documents: Strategies**
>
> 1. Use Display PostScript, if possible.
>
> 2. Use AP-TEX fonts or create (`ps2pk`, `ps2mf`, `gsf2pk`) pixel fonts that approximate the original fonts. A pixel font is necessary for each scalable font at each size.
>
> 3. Use software—`ghostscript`, `dviwindo`, *CorelDRAW*, *Acrobat*, *Freedom of Press*—for rendering PostScript files into a bitmap equivalent.
>
> 4. Create virtual fonts that use the Computer Modern pixels with the metrics from the outline font. Such virtual fonts can be previewed in the usual way. (Although you need one such font for each outline font, the previewing is done at normal speed.)

documents. TEX and *dvips* will use the standard fonts, which belong in directories like `\emtex\fonts\tfm` and `\emtex\psfonts`. Special `.cnf` configuration files can be created that override default settings such as these. You would carefully craft such a file, and create a batch file or alias so that the invocation of the previewer automatically reads this configuration file. The previewer will then scoop up the mock fonts and their bitmapped images. (Most versions of TEX and their previewers work in similar ways.)

New virtual fonts   Here are the steps needed to create a virtual font with the properties we described above—same metrics but bitmap images. It's helpful to be explicit about our goals in creating a "mock Garamond" font.

   We arrange things so *fontinst* learns about `cmr10`. We carefully save all of this glyph information using different names and then free up the original glyph names for use in the mock font. Next we get the metric information for the real Garamond fonts. We reassemble all characters so that the `cmr10` metrics are ignored in favor of the Garamond metrics, while the Garamond glyphs are superseded by the CM glyphs. We expect a schematic of our `\installfont` to look something like

```
\installfont{padr7t}{⟨read CMR10 metrics⟩,
    ⟨selectively discard CM info⟩,⟨read Garamond metrics⟩,
    ⟨selectively use Garamond metrics plus CM glyphs⟩,latin}%
    {OT1}{OT1}{pad}{m}{n}{}
```

The *fontinst* package expects to find the `cmr10` metric information in a file

cmr10.pl (which you must create from cmr10.tfm using tftopl). It then
creates an equivalent file cmr10.mtx, which is easier for it to work with. This
.mtx file contains three types of commands:

1. \setint commands set parameters for the font;

2. \setkern commands set kern values; and

3. \setrawglyph commands set information about each glyph.

We'd like to ignore the \setint and \setkern commands, for all of this
should come from the scalable fonts. We need to save the glyph information and free up the glyph name. Three new files accomplish these goals.
A short file undim.mtx renders \setint and \setkern temporarily useless;
after saving their original meanings, these two commands are temporarily
redefined to simply swallow their arguments.

```
\relax
  This is file undim.mtx.
\metrics
  \global\let\savedsetint=\setint
  \global\let\savedsetkern=\setkern
  \resetcommand\setint#1#2{} \resetcommand\setkern#1#2#3{}
\endmetrics
```

After reading glyph information, each glyph is renamed to indicate its CM
origins; 'A' becomes 'ACM', 'a' becomes 'aCM', and so on. Then the original
glyphs are freed up for subsequent use by the Garamond fonts. This is done
by a lengthier file uncmr.mtx. (It was easy to edit a copy of OT1.etx into this
form.)

```
\relax
  This is file uncmr.mtx.
\metrics
  \setcommand\CMglyph#1{%
    \setglyph{#1CM}
      \glyph{#1}{1000}
    \endsetglyph
    \unsetglyph{#1}  }
  \CMglyph{Gamma}
  \CMglyph{Delta}
  \CMglyph{Theta}
    ...
    ...
  \CMglyph{rangedash}
  \CMglyph{punctdash}
  \CMglyph{hungarumlaut}
  \CMglyph{tilde}
```

```
\CMglyph{dieresis}
\endmetrics
```

Next, we'll need a file to restore the original meanings of \setkern and \setint in time to capture and use this information from the Garamond fonts. The short file redim.mtx accomplishes this goal.

```
\relax
  This is file redim.mtx.
\metrics
  \global\let\setint=\savedsetint
  \global\let\setkern=\savedsetkern
\endmetrics
```

After reading the Garamond metric files, we'll need to throw away the Garamond glyph information in favor of the Computer Modern glyphs. We can reuse uncmr.mtx for this purpose as long as we take care to redefine the command \CMglyph, which the file unpsfont.mtx does for us.

```
\relax
  This is file unpsfont.mtx.
\metrics
  \resetcommand\CMglyph#1{\ifisglyph{#1}\then
    \resetglyph{#1}
      \glyph{#1CM}{1000}\samesize{#1}
    \endresetglyph\fi}
  \inputmtx{uncmr}
\endmetrics
```

With these files in place, we can resolve the \installfont schematic on page 269.

```
\installfont{padr7t}{%
    undim,%      prepare to discard cmr metric info
    cmr10,%      read cmr font info
    uncmr,%      store cmr glyph info; free up these glyphs
    redim,%      prepare to gather outline font metrics
    padr8a,padr8x,%    gather outline font info
    unpsfont,%    discard outline glyphs; use cmr glyphs
  latin}{OT1}{OT1}{pad}{m}{n}{}
```

Your font-selection declarations no doubt select scalable fonts *at* a variety of sizes. How will the mock fonts be handled? The previewer will load the mock fonts at these various sizes, and that will require pixel files at the various new magnifications. For example, if you have typeset text in a scalable font at both 10- and 5-pt sizes, the mock fonts for a 300-dpi device will resolve into pixel files cmr10.300pk (10 pt) and cmr10.150pk (5 pt), and both those pixel fonts need to be present. (On traditional DOS systems, you will need files cmr10.pk in both directories \tex\fonts\dpi300 and tex\fonts\dpi150, or something similar.) You may well not have all of these fonts. It's a good idea to use a previewer that either runs METAFONT on the fly to generate any missing fonts or that generates a list of missing fonts for you to generate by hand. (After only a few documents, you'll likely have all the pixel files you need for your mock fonts.)

These instructions should give rise to an installation file similar to the *mock* code below. You should *take care to prepare this file in a distinct work directory*, one where there is no danger that any outputs from this process will contaminate the true .vf's that describe the scalable fonts.

```
\input fontinst.sty
%% Creating mock outline fonts.
\installfonts
  \installfamily{OT1}{pad}{}
    \installfont{padr7t}{undim,cmr10,uncmr,redim,
      padr8a,padr8x,unpsfont,latin}
      {OT1}{OT1}{pad}{m}{n}{}
    \installfont{padri7t}{undim,cmti10,uncmr,redim,
      padri8a,padri8x,unpsfont,latin}
      {OT1}{OT1}{pad}{m}{it}{}
    ⟨Other install commands.⟩
\endinstallfonts
\bye
```

This installation file reads expert font metric files; you will need to eliminate these clauses if expert fonts are not present.

After double-checking yet again that you are in a separate directory, run this installation file through TEX and through vptovf. As usual, the result will be a set of .vf files, a set of .tfm files, and an .fd file. You may safely delete the .tfm files and the .fd file; after all, they merely duplicate the metric information in your "good" .tfm files. The .vf files will provide to the previewer the details for how to construct the mock fonts. These files belong in a directory that your previewer has been instructed to look to for virtual font information.

Figure 1 on page 274 [drawn from Knuth (1979)] shows how a passage printed normally (using the Adobe Garamond fonts) appears using the new, mock, pixellated fonts.

9.4   Proper (optical) sizing of fonts

The author of TEX took great care during the design of the Computer Modern fonts to subtly redesign the proportions of each character at different sizes. The smaller the type, the more the eye needs help in resolving individual characters. The letterspacing—space between characters—must be increased, strokes must be thickened, contrast between thick and thin strokes

Previewing Scalable Fonts: A Virtual-Font Approach

It is possible to create mock virtual fonts possessing the same metrics as outline fonts but with bitmap images.

Warning: These mock fonts will have the same names as the real, outline fonts on your system. Take *great* care to keep the two sets of fonts separate.

1. Modify the previewer configuration file so the previewer will search a special directory for fonts, one that is invisible to your printer.

2. For each font whose bitmaps you plan to "steal," use `tftopl` to create the corresponding property list `.pl` file.

3. In aid of the eventual *fontinst* installation file, prepare files `undim.mtx` on page 270, the lengthy `uncmr.mtx` on page 270, `redim.mtx` on page 271, and `unpsfont.mtx` on page 271.

4. Use the installation file on the preceding page as a model for your own needs. Run this file through plain TEX.

5. After using `vptovf` on each `.vpl` property list file, delete the resulting `.tfm`'s. Move the `.vf`'s to a separate directory visible to the previewer but not to the printer.

reduced, and counters (islands of space entirely surrounded by ink, like the interior of the 'o' or the top of the 'e') need to be larger. An examination of the METAFONT parameter files for cmr10 and cmr5 verifies these trends, and a demonstration appears early on in *The TEXbook* (page 16).

Old-time metal typefounders took care that their font designs preserved these differences across sizes. Latter-day digital type designers are less careful—or perhaps the reigning software techniques will not permit designers to be so fussy. Nevertheless, a few options are available to the perfectionist who wants to branch out from Computer Modern.

There are signs that the digital-type business is now recognizing the importance of font changes across font sizes. Digital foundries have coined the term *optical scaling* and *optical size* to refer to these changes in proportion that occur with size.

ABCDEFGHIJKLMNOPQRSTUVWXYZ

Leonardo da Vinci made a sweeping statement in his notebooks: *Let no one who is not a mathematician read my works.* In fact, he said it twice, so he probably meant it.

Fortunately, a lot of people failed to heed his injunction. It turns out that non-mathematicians are quite capable of dealing with mathematical concepts, when the description isn't beclouded with too much jargon. So I would like to reverse Leonardo's dictum and say, *Let everyone who is not a mathematician read my works.* (Furthermore, mathematicians are invited too.)

ABCD EFG H IJKLMN O PQRSTU VW XYZ

Leonardo da Vinci made a sweeping statement in his notebooks: *Let no one who is not a mathematician read my works.* In fact, he said it twice, so he probably meant it.

Fortunately, a lot of people failed to heed his injunction. It turns out that non-mathematicians are quite capable of dealing with mathematical concepts, when the description isn't beclouded with too much jargon. So I would like to reverse Leonardo's dictum and say, *Let everyone who is not a mathematician read my works.* (Furthermore, mathematicians are invited too.)

Figure 1: These two paragraphs were set two ways. Conventional text faces were used on top, while the virtual preview fonts were used on bottom. Line breaks, hyphenation, and so on are the same in both cases. The italics were not in the original.

9.4.1 Optical scaling with bitmap fonts

The parameters necessary for generating Computer Modern fonts at a variety of sizes already exist, as do (for the most part) the fonts themselves. With the METAFONT parameter files, you can generate the fonts yourself with METAFONT; this is sometimes necessary if you acquire a printer with new attributes, or you wish to generate some fonts at nonstandard sizes.

Nonstandard sizes present a problem. Suppose you want to generate a true cmr14 font. Such a font doesn't exist, although cmr12 and cmr17 do (cmr17 is actually at 17.32 pt). It is *not* true that we can linearly interpolate (use simple proportions) all the numerical parameters of the two fonts to generate the values for our hypothetical cmr14.

It should be possible to create some more complicated relationships governing these values so that reasonable approximations to fonts like cmr14 are possible. John Sauter has done this work, and his apparatus for creating custom fonts appears in the CTAN archives in ctan/fonts/cm/sauter. (See chapter 3.)

Users of personal computer systems often wonder at the bewildering network of directories or folders necessary to contain all the CM fonts, but this is a consequence of the distinction between optically scaled and linearly (or geometrically) scaled fonts. A "12 pt" font can be either one truly designed for 12-pt size or a 10 pt magnified by 20%. The designation cmr12 is reserved for the true, optically scaled font, while another, separate number describes the magnified font. We now describe the meaning and derivation of this separate number.

Magnification is connected to the resolution of the printer. To see why, imagine what would happen if we tried printing with fonts developed for a 300 dpi (dots per inch) printer, but on a fancier printer capable of 600 dpi. Bitmap fonts, remember, provide instructions for blackening pixel patterns; that's why they are "maps." Each pixel on the fancy printer is half the width of the standard printer, so each character in fancy output is half its size in standard output. In the conventions of plain TEX, we have achieved magnification of 500 (that is, reduction by 50%). (This simplified discussion ignores certain other variables that may change with resolution and which may also vary from one type of printer to another. METAFONT can be instructed to take cognizance of these additional changes during font generation.)

If rrr is the resolution of a printer in (dpi units), mmm is the magnification of the font (where 1000 = magnification by 1) and nnn represents the special number for relating magnification and resolution, then

$$nnn = \frac{mmm \times rrr}{1000}$$

For a font magnified twice ($mmm = 2000$) on a fancy printer ($rrr = 600$), then $nnn = 1200$. For a standard printer ($rrr = 300$), $nnn = 600$. Fonts with the same number appear different on different printers. A font with $nnn = 450$ appears magnified by 50% on a 300 dpi printer but reduced by 25% on a 600 dpi printer.

On many operating systems, we can make the number nnn part of the font name. For example, two font files could have names cmr10.1200pk and cmr10.600pk, but file names with such lengthy last names are forbidden in DOS. A workable solution for this operating system is a branching network of subdirectories, with each subdirectory name incorporating nnn. In MS-DOS, both of these pixel files would have names cmr10.pk, but the file corresponding to cmr10.1200pk would be in something like

```
\tex\pixels\dpi1200
```

and the second would appear in

```
\tex\pixels\dpi600
```

(at least in a traditional TEX system).

Although the Computer Modern fonts are the most famous examples of properly scaled fonts, they are not the only such example. Damian Cugley has spent some time on his Malvern family of sans-serif fonts. Current versions of these fonts are at CTAN, in the `fonts/malvern` area.

Knuth's Concrete fonts are another example. They exemplify a different kind of font, even though the underlying programs are those of Computer Modern fonts. The METAFONT parameters have been tweaked to give the fonts slab-like serifs and less contrast between thick and thin strokes. These fonts have been used to typeset both the English and Russian versions of Graham, Knuth, and Patashnik (1989). All the METAFONT program files are in the `fonts/concrete` area of CTAN.

9.4.2 Optical scaling with "scalable" fonts

Although the very nature of linearly scalable fonts mitigates against optical scaling, there are modest grounds to hope that options for typesetting with optically scaled fonts may soon be increased.

Multiple Master fonts   Adobe Systems has developed and pioneered the Multiple Master font technology, which can create an instance of the master font at a particular type size. The master font might have been created to allow for one or more parameters to be properly varied across a wide range of sizes, and one such parameter is optical size. A Multiple Master is very like a set of METAFONT parameters from which vast families of fonts can be generated, and the master font suffers from a similar drawback of a META-FONT font—it's hard to create the master. Although a generous handful of faces have been tooled for Multiple Master technology, only one or two allow for variation of optical size.

Further, none of the familiar and beautiful Roman faces that one might want—Garamond, Baskerville, Caslon, Galliard, and so on—exist as Multiple Master master fonts. As of this writing, Minion is the only optically scaled roman master font, and it is not yet clear if this face will hold its own among the classic faces.

A Multiple Master font consists of two files—a familiar `.pfb` file (albeit somewhat larger than most such files) and a Multiple Master metric `.mmm` file, a binary file corresponding to an `.afm` file, but with lots more information. In principle, it should be straightforward to revise a program like *dvips* to scale such master fonts properly, and such capability may appear in the future.

Michel Goossens and Sebastian Rahtz were the first to show that it is possible to use Multiple Master fonts in TEX documents. The report of this work, Goossens, Rahtz, and Fairbairns (1995), is typeset in Multiple Master Minion types and illustrates the technology.

While this book was in production (July-August, 1997), a pair of useful tools for Multiple Master fonts appeared on CTAN, in the

```
fonts/utilities/mmtools
```

area. The first, mmafm, allows you to create an .afm file by interpolating in a Multiple Master design space (that is, you fix the MM parameters—thickness of stroke, size, degree of obliqueness, or whatever is appropriate for these particular fonts—and it creates the .afm file for a specific font with those properties). The second, called mminstance, performs a similar function for the font file and creates a .pfb file by the same process of interpolation. Both these tools, developed by Eddie Kohler, are Unix-specific and you will need a C++ compiler (but not its libraries) to prepare working executables for your computer. Of course, the resultant files can be passed to other font tools (afm2tfm, *fontinst*, VFINST, ps2pk, and so on) on Unix or other platforms.

9.4.3 Monotype Times New Roman

One family of properly scaled fonts lies quietly tucked in among the offerings of the Monotype catalog. Compatible with the Monotype Times New Roman fonts are Times Seven and Times Small Text fonts, that is, Times fonts optically scaled for 7-pt and 5-pt work. Comparison of the 5-pt type with the 10-pt yields

"Five point type" writ large adjacent to ten point Times,

and the comparison is more telling at five points:

The music-room in the Governor's House at Port Mahon, a tall, handsome, pillared octagon, was filled with the triumphant first movement of Locatelli's C major quartet. The players, Italians, pinned against the far wall by rows and rows of little round gilt chairs, were playing with passionate conviction as they mounted towards the penultimate crescendo, towards the tremendous pause and the deep, liberating final chord. And on the the little gilt chairs at least some of the audience were following the rise with an equal intensity: there were two in the third row, on the left-hand side; and they happened to be sitting next to one another.

The music-room in the Governor's House at Port Mahon, a tall, handsome, pillared octagon, was filled with the triumphant first movement of Locatelli's C major quartet. The players, Italians, pinned against the far wall by rows and rows of little round gilt chairs, were playing with passionate conviction as they mounted towards the penultimate crescendo, towards the tremendous pause and the deep, liberating final chord. And on the little gilt chairs at least some of the audience were following the rise with an equal intensity: there were two in the third row, on the left-hand side; and they happened to be sitting next to one another.

Figure 2 on the next page is a fairer demonstration—types designed for 5 pt and 7 pt are compared with the 10-pt font scaled to 6 pt and 7.4 pt. [The text is from O'Brian (1990).] We'll see later how to further improve the appearance of linearly scaled fonts.

Incidentally, all like-named fonts are *not* alike. Fonts with like names differ from one digital foundry to another in subtle but important ways—the number and accuracy of kern pairs, the shapes of the letterforms themselves, and so on. The Monotype Times is particularly distinguished.

The music-room in the Governor's House at Port Mahon, a tall, handsome, pillared octagon, was filled with the triumphant first movement of Locatelli's C major quartet. The players, Italians, pinned against the far wall by rows and rows of little round gilt chairs, were playing with passionate conviction as they mounted towards the penultimate crescendo, towards the tremendous pause and the deep, liberating final chord. And on the the little gilt chairs at least some of the audience were following the rise with an equal intensity: there were two in the third row, on the left-hand side; and they happened to be sitting next to one another.

The listener farther to the left was a man of between twenty and thirty whose big form overflowed his seat, leaving only a streak of gilt wood to be seen here and there. He was wearing his best uniform—the white-lapelled blue coat, white waistcoat, breeches and stockings of a lieutenant in the Royal Navy, with the silver medal of the Nile in his buttonhole—and the deep white cuff of his gold-buttoned sleeve beat the time, while his bright blue eyes, staring from what would have been a pink-and-white face if it had not been so deeply tanned, gazed fixedly at the bow of the first violin.

The music-room in the Governor's House at Port Mahon, a tall, handsome, pillared octagon, was filled with the triumphant first movement of Locatelli's C major quartet. The players, Italians, pinned against the far wall by rows and rows of little round gilt chairs, were playing with passionate conviction as they mounted towards the penultimate crescendo, towards the tremendous pause and the deep, liberating final chord. And on the the little gilt chairs at least some of the audience were following the rise with an equal intensity: there were two in the third row, on the left-hand side; and they happened to be sitting next to one another.

The listener farther to the left was a man of between twenty and thirty whose big form overflowed his seat, leaving only a streak of gilt wood to be seen here and there. He was wearing his best uniform—the white-lapelled blue coat, white waistcoat, breeches and stockings of a lieutenant in the Royal Navy, with the silver medal of the Nile in his buttonhole—and the deep white cuff of his gold-buttoned sleeve beat the time, while his bright blue eyes, staring from what would have been a pink-and-white face if it had not been so deeply tanned, gazed fixedly at the bow of the first violin.

The high note came, the pause, the resolution; and with the resolution the sailor's fist swept firmly down upon his knee. He leant back in his chair, extinguishing it entirely, sighed happily and turned towards his neighbour with a smile. The words 'Very finely played, sir, I believe' were formed in his gullet if not quite in his mouth when he caught the cold and indeed inimical look and heard the whisper, 'If you really must beat the measure, sir, let me entreat you to do so in time, and not half a beat ahead.'

Figure 2: The left text shows examples of Times Small Text (5 pt) and Times Seven fonts compared, on the right, to Times New Roman scaled six and 7.4 pt respectively.

Installing optical Times   We may wish to incorporate all these Times fonts into a single family with the mnt designation. The trouble is, the raw fonts themselves belong to three different families, named by their distributor as Times New Roman, Times New Roman Seven, and Times Small Text, all with font name designations mnt, mnt with a variant '7', and mtm.

Here's how I resolved this impasse. I named the raw fonts using their individual family names. But all subsequent virtual fonts using them will receive the family name mnt. The appendix to this chapter (starting on page 284) contains the addendum to my psfonts.map file, which also aids in the font renaming.

The installation process requires specific fonts for specific size ranges. For example, we'll want the New Times font for any size from 8 pt on up (scaled properly, of course), but from 6 pt up to (but not including) 8 pt, we'd prefer the corresponding member from the Times Seven family. Finally, for tiny type (less than 6 pt), we'll use the small text variants.

We can use the final argument of any \installfont command to specify the size or size range for a font. Since this information is only used by

```
<12>  exactly 12 pt
<->   all sizes
<-6>  sizes up to but not including 6 pt
<6-8> all sizes greater than or equal to 6 pt but strictly less than 8 pt
<8->  all sizes greater than or equal to 8 pt
```

Figure 3: *fontinst* size conventions and their meanings.

NFSS, we use NFSS conventions to set the sizes. When working with scalable fonts, we normally leave the final argument empty; *fontinst* thereby knows to scale the font.

NFSS syntax demands that angle brackets surround a size, which can be a single number for a single size, or a range of sizes; *fontinst* has adopted the same syntax. The list of examples in figure 3 illustrates the conventions we'll be using. We'll agree to use the usual Times Roman for sizes of 8 pt and larger, to use the 7-pt font for any sizes between 6 and 8 pt, and to use the small text fonts for sizes below 6 pt. With these conventions in hand, we can create the long (and mostly boring) installation file. One such appears in the appendix to this chapter.

There are a few points worthy of note. First, it is unfortunate that neither the small text nor the 'seven point' fonts contain expert fonts, and furthermore, there is no bold italic variant in the small text fonts. Had we been conscientious about creating italic small caps and unslanted italic fonts in both the medium and bold series, that would have led to virtual fonts with 9-character names (e.g., `mntric7t7`; it's the extra character for the type size that leads to problems)—anathema to the widely used DOS operating system and its derivatives. We can finesse the problem by creating those fonts using only the New Times fonts, and declaring these fonts linearly scalable across all font sizes.

Once the fonts have been renamed properly and moved to their ultimate destinations on the system, once `psfonts.map` has been updated according to the suggested lines in the appendix, and once the appendix's installation file has been run through TEX, it will be necessary in the usual way to create new `.tfm` and `.vf` files by exercising `pltotf` and `vptovf` on the `.pl` and `.vpl` files written by *fontinst*.

With plain TEX   The best way to use all these fonts is via the PDCFSEL font selection scheme for plain TEX by Damian Cugley. After getting hold of `pdcfsel.tex`, you'll need to include lines like

```
\input pdcfsel
```

```
\newfam\scfam  % small caps
```

```
\newfam\sifam   % italic small caps
\newfam\iufam   % unslanted italic
\newfam\bscfam  % bold small caps
\newfam\bslfam  % bold slanted
\newfam\bitfam  % bold italic
\newfam\bsifam  % bold italic small caps
\newfam\biufam  % bold unslanted italic
\def\tentemplate{%
  \@\f{rm}{mntr7t}\@\f{sc}{mntrc7t}\@\f{sl}{mntro7t}%
  \@\f{it}{mntri7t}\@\f{si}{mntric7t}\@\f{ui}{mntriu7t}%
  \@\f{bf}{mntb7t}\@\f{bsc}{mntbc7t}\@\f{bsl}{mntbo7t}%
  \@\f{bit}{mntbi7t}\@\f{bsi}{mntbic7t}\@\f{bui}{mntbiu7t}}
\def\seventemplate{%
  \@\f{rm}{mntr7t7}\@\f{sc}{mntrc7t7}\@\f{sl}{mntro7t7}%
  \@\f{it}{mntri7t7}\@\f{si}{mntric7t}\@\f{ui}{mntriu7t}%  <==
  \@\f{bf}{mntb7t7}\@\f{bsc}{mntbc7t7}\@\f{bsl}{mntbo7t7}%
  \@\f{bit}{mntbi7t7}\@\f{bsi}{mntbic7t}\@\f{bui}{mntbiu7t}}%  <==
\def\fivetemplate{%
  \@\f{rm}{mntr7t5}\@\f{sc}{mntrc7t5}\@\f{sl}{mntro7t5}%
  \@\f{it}{mntri7t5}\@\f{si}{mntric7t}\@\f{ui}{mntriu7t}%%  <==
  \@\f{bf}{mntb7t5}\@\f{bsc}{mntbc7t5}\@\f{bsl}{mntbo7t5}%
  \@\f{bit}{mntbi7t}\@\f{bsi}{mntbic7t}\@\f{bui}{mntbiu7t}}%  <==
\fontset{body}\tentemplate{10}{12pt}{}{}
\fontset{note}\seventemplate{7}{8pt}{}{}
\fontset{subnote}\fivetemplate{5}{6pt}{}{}
```

in a document or macro file; you may well decide not to include so many font shapes in each template. (The arrows at the left of some of these lines indicate lines that seem to require special care when typing.) Then, the act of switching to different fonts at different sizes, or in different contexts, is simply a matter of defining the proper fontset (here "body," "note," and "subnote" fontsets appear), and then selecting the proper fontset in the document. For example, after the above, we might type

```
\bodyfonts \bit Smaller
{\notefonts\bf and Smaller
\subnotefont\rm and Smaller Still.}
```

to get

Smaller **and Smaller** and Smaller Still.

With NFSS   To use these fonts, move the file OT1mnt.fd into an input directory. In a document, simply type

```
\renewcommand{\rmdefault}{mnt}
```

to use these fonts. Our .fd file insures that the proper fonts get selected at the proper sizes.

The music-room in the Governor's House at Port Mahon, a tall, handsome, pillared octagon, was filled with the triumphant first movement of Locatelli's C major quartet. The players, Italians, pinned against the far wall by rows and rows of little round gilt chairs, were playing with passionate conviction as they mounted towards the penultimate crescendo, towards the tremendous pause and the deep, liberating final chord. And on the the little gilt chairs at least some of the audience were following the rise with an equal intensity: there were two in the third row, on the left-hand side; and they happened to be sitting next to one another.

The listener farther to the left was a man of between twenty and thirty whose big form overflowed his seat, leaving only a streak of gilt wood to be seen here and there. He was wearing his best uniform—the white-lapelled blue coat, white waistcoat, breeches and stockings of a lieutenant in the Royal Navy, with the silver medal of the Nile in his buttonhole—and the deep white cuff of his gold-buttoned sleeve beat the time, while his bright blue eyes, staring from what would have been a pink-and-white face if it had not been so deeply tanned, gazed fixedly at the bow of the first violin.

The high note came, the pause, the resolution; and with the resolution the sailor's fist swept firmly down upon his knee. He leant back in his chair, extinguishing it entirely, sighed happily and turned towards his neighbour with a smile. The words 'Very finely played, sir, I believe' were formed in his gullet if not quite in his mouth when he caught the cold and indeed inimical look and heard the whisper, 'If you really must beat the measure, sir, let me entreat you to do so in time, and not half a beat ahead.'

Figure 4: The text on the left uses properly scaled fonts. On the right, the text is linearly scaled, but adjustments made in the letterspacing and in the nominal sizing make a better match to the left.

9.4.4 Approximations to optical scaling

Figure 2 on page 278 suggests that even with linear fonts, we can improve the appearance in two ways:

1. use a slightly larger size than the nominal size; and

2. increase the letterspacing at small sizes.

That is, suppose we need to do some typesetting at 5 pt. Instead of using a font at exactly half the 10-pt size, perhaps we might use it at a 5.5-pt size, and it will look even better if we add a little extra space between the letters. Figure 4 implements these ideas; compare it to figure 2 on page 278. In figure 4 the linear font appears at 5.5 pt and 7.3 pt, but letterspacing of 109 and 57 units are applied to the fonts. Properly scaled fonts are always best, but for fonts for which these are not available, these approximations may prove useful.

In preparation for the *fontinst* installation, we need encoding files called OT1v.etx and OT1vii.etx to set the letterspacing. Here is OT1v.etx.

```
\relax
  This is file OT1v.etx.
\encoding
\resetint{letterspacing}{109}
\inputetx{OT1}
\endencoding
```

And here is OT1vii.etx.

```
\relax
  This is file OT1vii.etx.
\encoding
\resetint{letterspacing}{57}
\inputetx{OT1}
\endencoding
```

The installation is straightforward. As we have begun doing in advanced projects, the raw fonts for this installation will be the already-created virtual fonts from earlier projects. Here is an installation file for Adobe Garamond using the original TEX encoding OT1.

```
\input fontinst.sty
\installfonts
  \installfamily{OT1}{pad}{}
  \installfont{padrn7t}{padr7t}{OT1}{OT1}{pad}{mn}{n}{<8->}
  \installfont{padrn7t7}{padr7t scaled 1043}{OT1vii}%
    {OT1}{pad}{mn}{n}{<6-8>}
  \installfont{padrn7t5}{padr7t scaled 1100}{OT1v}%
    {OT1}{pad}{mn}{n}{<-6>}
  ⟨Additional install commands as necessary⟩
\endinstallfonts
\bye
```

(Issue tftopl padr7t.tfm padr7t.pl before running this through TEX.) These fonts have been placed in a new font series, mn. When these fonts are appropriately created using the by-now usual procedure, a series of mock-nonlinear fonts are created, as shown in figure 5 on the facing page. In this figure, using the same text [O'Brian (1990)] we have encountered throughout this chapter, we see linearly scaled text on the right, and the nonlinear approximations on the left. Since we are using values for letterspacing derived for Times Roman, a particular user may well decide they need some fine-tuning.

The odd scale factors 1043 and 1100 in the \installfont commands have a simple explanation. If a font at 10.43 pt is scaled by 70%, it will have an actual type size of 7.3 pt (that is, $10.43 \times 0.7 \approx 7.3$); hence, the 1043.

The music-room in the Governor's House at Port Mahon, a tall, handsome, pillared octagon, was filled with
the triumphant first movement of Locatelli's C major
quartet. The players, Italians, pinned against the far
wall by rows and rows of little round gilt chairs, were
playing with passionate conviction as they mounted towards the penultimate crescendo, towards the tremendous pause and the deep, liberating final chord. And on
the little gilt chairs at least some of the audience were
following the rise with an equal intensity; there were
two in the third row, on the left-hand side; and they
happened to be sitting next to one another.

The listener farther to the left was a man of
between twenty and thirty whose big form
overflowed his seat, leaving only a streak of
gilt wood to be seen here and there. He
was wearing his best uniform—the white-
lapelled blue coat, white waistcoat, breeches
and stockings of a lieutenant in the Royal
Navy, with the silver medal of the Nile in
his buttonhole—and the deep white cuff of
his gold-buttoned sleeve beat the time, while
his bright blue eyes, staring from what would
have been a pink-and-white face if it had not
been so deeply tanned, gazed fixedly at the
bow of the first violin.

The music-room in the Governor's House at Port Mahon, a tall, handsome, pillared octagon, was filled with the triumphant first movement of
Locatelli's C major quartet. The players, Italians, pinned against the far
wall by rows and rows of little round gilt chairs, were playing with passionate conviction as they mounted towards the penultimate crescendo,
towards the tremendous pause and the deep, liberating final chord. And
on the little gilt chairs at least some of the audience were following the
rise with an equal intensity; there were two in the third row, on the left-
hand side; and they happened to be sitting next to one another.

The listener farther to the left was a man of between twenty and thirty whose big form overflowed
his seat, leaving only a streak of gilt wood to be
seen here and there. He was wearing his best uniform—the white-lapelled blue coat, white waistcoat, breeches and stockings of a lieutenant in the
Royal Navy, with the silver medal of the Nile in his
buttonhole—and the deep white cuff of his gold-
buttoned sleeve beat the time, while his bright blue
eyes, staring from what would have been a pink-
and-white face if it had not been so deeply tanned,
gazed fixedly at the bow of the first violin.

The high note came, the pause, the resolution; and with the resolution the
sailor's fist swept firmly down upon his knee. He leant back in his chair,
extinguishing it entirely, sighed happily and turned towards his neighbour
with a smile. The words 'Very finely played, sir, I believe' were formed in his
gullet if not quite in his mouth when he caught the cold and indeed inimical
look and heard the whisper, 'If you really must beat the measure, sir, let me
entreat you to do so in time, and not half a beat ahead.'

Figure 5: The paragraphs on the right display text at real font sizes of 5 pt and
7 pt; the bottom paragraph is 10 pt. Corresponding paragraphs on the left are
set in the mock-nonlinear fonts.

In the same way, an 11 pt font (scale factor 1100) scaled by 50% has a size
of 5.5 pt.

Purists may regard this deviation from linearity as unnatural. But after
all, the concept of font type size or design size is an inherently vague one.
Indeed, we have earlier seen how two fonts at the same type size may have
significantly different sizes. That being the case, perhaps it's wrong to automatically conclude that a context calling for a 7 pt font should be exactly
70% of the same font at 10 pt. The enhanced readability of the left part of
figure 5 makes a strong case for nonlinear font sizing.

9.4.5   Other optically scaled fonts

Hoeffler Type Foundry (1996) is a designer-type foundry, several of whose
font families explore the variation of a visual property across different fonts.

The Didot Roman fonts they offer display variation of optical size, and each weight and shape comes in 6, 11, 16, 24, and some larger display sizes. The company reports that their fonts contain all the f-ligatures.

International Typeface Corporation licenses several sizes of the Bodoni typeface that display optical scaling. ITC Bodoni comes in 6-, 12-, and 72-pt sizes, and these fonts are available from various vendors.

9.5 Appendix: Installing Times New Roman

Here follow the lines that need to be added to `psfonts.map`, provided the font files are properly renamed first. It may be necessary to preface file names in these lines with path prefixes (that is, you may have to say

```
... </usr/local/lib/tex/inputs/8r.enc ...
```

or whatever rather than simply ... `<8r.enc ...`). I used the family name mt7 for the 'Seven' fonts instead of the official Berry designation in order to avoid 9-character font names.

```
mntr8r   TimesNRMT   "TeXBase1Encoding ReEncodeFont" <8r.enc <mntr8a.pfb
mntro8r  TimesNRMT   ".286 SlantFont TeXBase1Encoding ReEncodeFont" <8r.enc
mntr8x   TimesNRExpertMT  <mntr8x.pfb
mntro8x  TimesNRExpertMT  ".286 SlantFont"
mntri8r  TimesNRMT-Italic   "TeXBase1Encoding ReEncodeFont" <8r.enc <mntri8a.pfb
mntriu8r TimesNRMT-Italic "-.286 SlantFont TeXBase1Encoding ReEncodeFont" <8r.enc
mntri8x  TimesNRExpertMT-Italic  <mntri8x.pfb
mntriu8x TimesNRExpertMT-Italic "-.286 SlantFont"
mntb8r   TimesNRMT-Bold  "TeXBase1Encoding ReEncodeFont" <8r.enc <mntb8a.pfb
mntbo8r  TimesNRMT-Bold ".286 SlantFont TeXBase1Encoding ReEncodeFont" <8r.enc
mntb8x   TimesNRExpertMT-Bold  <mntb8x.pfb
mntbo8x  TimesNRExpertMT-Bold ".286 SlantFont"
mntbi8r  TimesNRMT-BoldItalic  "TeXBase1Encoding ReEncodeFont" <8r.enc <mntbi8a.pfb
mntbiu8r TimesNRMT-BoldItalic "-.286 SlantFont TeXBase1Encoding ReEncodeFont" <8r.enc
mntbi8x  TimesNRExpertMT-BoldItalic  <mntbi8x.pfb
mntbiu8x TimesNRExpertMT-BoldItalic "-.286 SlantFont"
mt7r8r   TimesNRSevenMT  "TeXBase1Encoding ReEncodeFont" <8r.enc <mt7r8a.pfb
mt7ro8r  TimesNRSevenMT ".286 SlantFont TeXBase1Encoding ReEncodeFont" <8r.enc
mt7ri8r  TimesNRSevenMT-Italic  "TeXBase1Encoding ReEncodeFont" <8r.enc <mt7ri8a.pfb
mt7riu8r TimesNRSevenMT-Italic "-.286 SlantFont TeXBase1Encoding ReEncodeFont" <8r.enc
mt7b8r   TimesNRSevenMT-Bold  "TeXBase1Encoding ReEncodeFont" <8r.enc <mt7b8a.pfb
mt7bo8r  TimesNRSevenMT-Bold ".286 SlantFont TeXBase1Encoding ReEncodeFont" <8r.enc
mt7bi8r  TimesNRSevenMT-BoldItalic  "TeXBase1Encoding ReEncodeFont" <8r.enc <mt7bi8a.pfb
mt7biu8r TimesNRSevenMT-BoldItalic "-.286 SlantFont \
  TeXBase1Encoding ReEncodeFont" <8r.enc
mtmr8r   TimesSmallTextMT "TeXBase1Encoding ReEncodeFont" <8r.enc <mtmr8a.pfb
mtmro8r  TimesSmallTextMT ".305 SlantFont TeXBase1Encoding ReEncodeFont" <8r.enc
mtmri8r  TimesSmallTextMT-Italic  "TeXBase1Encoding ReEncodeFont" <8r.enc <mtmri8a.pfb
mtmriu8r TimesSmallTextMT-Italic "-.305 SlantFont TeXBase1Encoding ReEncodeFont" <8r.enc
mtmb8r   TimesSmallTextMT-Bold  "TeXBase1Encoding ReEncodeFont" <8r.enc <mtmb8a.pfb
mtmbo8r  TimesSmallTextMT-Bold ".305 SlantFont TeXBase1Encoding ReEncodeFont" <8r.enc
```

The line beginning

```
mt7biu8r TimesNRSevenMT-BoldItalic...
```

should be typed on a single long line; omit the \ continuation character. And here is a corresponding installation file.

```
\input fontinst.sty

\transformfont{mntr8r}{\reencodefont{8r}{\fromafm{mntr8a}}}
\transformfont{mntro8r}{\slantfont{286}{\frommtx{mntr8r}}}
\transformfont{mntro8x}{\slantfont{286}{\fromafm{mntr8x}}}
\transformfont{mntri8r}{\reencodefont{8r}{\fromafm{mntri8a}}}
\transformfont{mntriu8r}{\slantfont{-286}{\frommtx{mntri8r}}}
\transformfont{mntriu8x}{\slantfont{-286}{\fromafm{mntri8x}}}
\transformfont{mntb8r}{\reencodefont{8r}{\fromafm{mntb8a}}}
\transformfont{mntbo8r}{\slantfont{286}{\frommtx{mntb8r}}}
\transformfont{mntbo8x}{\slantfont{286}{\fromafm{mntb8x}}}
\transformfont{mntbi8r}{\reencodefont{8r}{\fromafm{mntbi8a}}}
\transformfont{mntbiu8r}{\slantfont{-286}{\frommtx{mntbi8r}}}
\transformfont{mntbiu8x}{\slantfont{-286}{\fromafm{mntbi8x}}}
\transformfont{mt7r8r}{\reencodefont{8r}{\fromafm{mt7r8a}}}
\transformfont{mt7ro8r}{\slantfont{286}{\frommtx{mt7r8r}}}
\transformfont{mt7ri8r}{\reencodefont{8r}{\fromafm{mt7ri8a}}}
\transformfont{mt7riu8r}{\slantfont{-286}{\frommtx{mt7ri8r}}}
\transformfont{mt7b8r}{\reencodefont{8r}{\fromafm{mt7b8a}}}
\transformfont{mt7bo8r}{\slantfont{286}{\frommtx{mt7b8r}}}
\transformfont{mt7bi8r}{\reencodefont{8r}{\fromafm{mt7bi8a}}}
\transformfont{mt7biu8r}{\slantfont{-286}{\frommtx{mt7bi8r}}}
\transformfont{mtmr8r}{\reencodefont{8r}{\fromafm{mtmr8a}}}
\transformfont{mtmro8r}{\slantfont{305}{\frommtx{mtmr8r}}}
\transformfont{mtmri8r}{\reencodefont{8r}{\fromafm{mtmri8a}}}
\transformfont{mtmriu8r}{\slantfont{-305}{\frommtx{mtmri8r}}}
\transformfont{mtmb8r}{\reencodefont{8r}{\fromafm{mtmb8a}}}
\transformfont{mtmbo8r}{\slantfont{305}{\frommtx{mtmb8r}}}


\installfonts
  \installfamily{OT1}{mnt}{}
  \installfont{mntr7t}{mntr8r,mntr8x,latin}{OT1}{OT1}{mnt}{m}{n}{<8->}
  \installfont{mntrc7t}{mntr8r,mntr8x,latin}{OT1c}{OT1}{mnt}{m}{sc}{<8->}
  \installfont{mntro7t}{mntro8r,mntro8x,latin}{OT1}{OT1}{mnt}{m}{sl}{<8->}
  \installfont{mntri7t}{mntri8r,mntri8x,latin}{OT1}{OT1}{mnt}{m}{it}{<8->}
  \installfont{mntric7t}{mntri8r,mntri8x,latin}{OT1c}{OT1}{mnt}{m}{si}{}
  \installfont{mntriu7t}{mntriu8r,mntriu8x,latin}{OT1}{OT1}{mnt}{m}{ui}{}
  \installfont{mntb7t}{mntb8r,mntb8x,latin}{OT1}{OT1}{mnt}{b}{n}{<8->}
  \installfont{mntbc7t}{mntb8r,mntb8x,latin}{OT1c}{OT1}{mnt}{b}{sc}{<8->}
  \installfont{mntbo7t}{mntbo8r,mntbo8x,latin}{OT1}{OT1}{mnt}{b}{sl}{<8->}
  \installfont{mntbi7t}{mntbi8r,mntbi8x,latin}{OT1}{OT1}{mnt}{b}{it}{<8->}
  \installfont{mntbic7t}{mntbi8r,mntbi8x,latin}{OT1c}{OT1}{mnt}{b}{si}{}
  \installfont{mntbiu7t}{mntbiu8r,mntbiu8x,latin}{OT1}{OT1}{mnt}{b}{ui}{}

  \installfont{mntr7t7}{mt7r8r,latin}{OT1}{OT1}{mnt}{m}{n}{<6-8>}
  \installfont{mntrc7t7}{mt7r8r,latin}{OT1c}{OT1}{mnt}{m}{sc}{<6-8>}
  \installfont{mntro7t7}{mt7ro8r,latin}{OT1}{OT1}{mnt}{m}{sl}{<6-8>}
  \installfont{mntri7t7}{mt7ri8r,latin}{OT1}{OT1}{mnt}{m}{it}{<6-8>}
  \installfont{mntb7t7}{mt7b8r,latin}{OT1}{OT1}{mnt}{b}{n}{<6-8>}
  \installfont{mntbc7t7}{mt7b8r,latin}{OT1c}{OT1}{mnt}{b}{sc}{<6-8>}
  \installfont{mntbo7t7}{mt7bo8r,latin}{OT1}{OT1}{mnt}{b}{sl}{<6-8>}
  \installfont{mntbi7t7}{mt7bi8r,latin}{OT1}{OT1}{mnt}{b}{it}{<6-8>}

  \installfont{mntr7t5}{mtmr8r,latin}{OT1}{OT1}{mnt}{m}{n}{<-6>}
  \installfont{mntrc7t5}{mtmr8r,latin}{OT1c}{OT1}{mnt}{m}{sc}{<-6>}
```

```
\installfont{mntro7t5}{mtmro8r,latin}{OT1}{OT1}{mnt}{m}{sl}{<-6>}
\installfont{mntri7t5}{mtmri8r,latin}{OT1}{OT1}{mnt}{m}{it}{<-6>}
\installfont{mntb7t5}{mtmb8r,latin}{OT1}{OT1}{mnt}{b}{n}{<-6>}
\installfont{mntbc7t5}{mtmb8r,latin}{OT1c}{OT1}{mnt}{b}{sc}{<-6>}
\installfont{mntbo7t5}{mtmbo8r,latin}{OT1}{OT1}{mnt}{b}{sl}{<-6>}
\endinstallfonts

\bye
```

CHAPTER 10

. . . .

NEW MATH FONTS

Typesetting math has always been a problem. Math fonts have to contain many odd and special-purpose characters, including extensible characters that come in pieces and out of which a typesetter must construct the right sizes to surround tall formulas. Decisions on the proper sizing of the fonts are always needed because the correct size depends on context. Finally, the spacing within math mode is completely different from nonmath spacing, and the metric files accompanying an aspiring math font have to reflect this spacing.

That's why there are only a few math font families other than the canonical Computer Modern for use by TEX. Several of these math fonts are commercial products, but fortunately are not very expensive (font prices are plummeting these days) and well worth the expense. In this chapter, we'll see how to use these few other fonts effectively.

Naïvely, a reader might wonder why we just can't replace the Computer Modern text fonts of a document by some other fonts for a brand-new look. This sample of math

If x and y are variables, then xy is too.

shows why. We have combined Computer Modern math with Times Roman text, but the variables are too light for the text letters, and in an extended document this incompatible contrast between text and math grates on the reader. You may find that some differences between math and text are acceptable—after all, math *is* different from prose—but the variations here are somehow too disparate.

This chapter contains the results of experiments—a "rogues' gallery"—showing how to use LATEX and TEX to generate technical documents using many handsome fonts. As has become our custom, we will be creating series of virtual fonts to do the typesetting for us. The first sample in subsection 10.8.1 on page 316 shows a passage set with traditional Computer Modern fonts. This selection from Weinberg (1972, p. 188) was chosen because it gives a good mix of text math plus display math, and it has a wide variety of characters drawn from all parts of the math fonts.

We will discuss several broad strategies for mathematical typesetting:

- switching to scalable versions of the Computer Modern fonts;

- replacing Computer Modern Roman with Monotype Modern;

- the use of commercial math fonts that can then be integrated with text fonts. Although vendors may supply macro and style files to perform this integration, we will explore virtual font approaches. The four special sets of raw math fonts include MathTime, Euler, Lucida New Math, and Mathematica fonts; and

- using variations of the usual Computer Modern bitmap math fonts whose parameters have been adjusted so they more closely match their accompanying text fonts.

In addition, readers may care to experiment with Alan Jeffrey's `mathptm`, a math font using the symbol font generally resident in every PostScript printer. The `mathptm` material is found with the current *fontinst* distribution on CTAN, but we will not discuss it further here.

10.1   Scalable Computer Modern fonts

One easy change to a TEX document is to switch from bitmapped Computer Modern fonts to their outline, scalable equivalents. The look of the documents won't change, but it may be easier to print on a PostScript phototypesetter.

The ability to print PostScript documents on any (PostScript) device is a great advantage. Normally, fine phototypeset LaTeX or TEX output requires hunting out a phototypesetter coupled to both the appropriate TEX printer driver and appropriate pixel fonts. The use of scalable fonts means any Post-Script phototypesetter can now perform this service.

There are two sources for outline equivalents to Computer Modern:

- A highly tuned commercial set has been developed and made available from Blue Sky Research, Inc. (1988). Recently, this company has donated these fonts to the public domain, and they may be downloaded from the

  ```
  fonts/cm/ps-type1/bluesky
  ```

  area of CTAN.

- A public domain version, the BaKoMa fonts (successor to the Paradissa fonts) by Basil Malyshev can be downloaded from any of the CTAN archives; visit the

  ```
  fonts/postscript/bakoma
  ```

Installing Scalable Computer Modern Fonts

- Place the .pfb files for these fonts in their proper place.

- Prepare additions to your dvi-to-PostScript .map file. Each outline font you plan to use should have a line like

cmtt10 CMTT10 <⟨*path*⟩/cmtt10.pfb

in the map file .psfonts.map (or its equivalent). Be *very* careful about the case of these entries, even in systems like MS-DOS which are allegedly case-insensitive. The Paradissa and BaKoMa fonts have internal font names like cmr10, cmmi10, and so on. The internal font names for the Blue Sky fonts are CMR10, CMMI10, and so on.

---

directory. In addition to members of the Computer Modern family proper, this collection includes additional fonts of interest, such as a Cyrillic font family and the Euler family of math fonts in outline form.

In either case, don't forget the matching .afm files. For the Blue Sky fonts, you may use the .afm files by Pierre MacKay found in the

fonts/cm/afm

area of CTAN. The first selection in subsection 10.8.1 on page 316 was produced via outline fonts.

10.2   Computer Modern math plus new text fonts

It may be typographically dangerous to willy-nilly change the text font of a document while retaining Computer Modern math, but it is possible to choose a font that does blend well with Computer Modern. Computer Modern fonts were designed using Monotype Modern No. 8A as a model. The digital font most resembling these fonts is Monotype's Modern font, available from Monotype Corporation (1997) and other digital font vendors. Weinberg (1972), the source of our "rogue's gallery" testbed, was set in this font.

You should install the fonts as per the procedures given in chapter 6 using VFINST or PSNFSS. LaTeX users should add the command

```
\renewcommand{\rmdefault}{mmo}
```

where mmo is the Berry name for the Modern font family. No changes need be made to the math font declarations, as we shall continue to use the Computer Modern math fonts.

The second sample on page 317 displays this combination of fonts working together.

10.3   New math raw fonts

In the next several sections, you will see how to replace Computer Modern math with other math fonts. Two tools for this are the MathInst utility and *MathKit*, collections of modules for creating the new virtual fonts automatically.

In an ideal world, math fonts would be 100% compatible with text fonts. For the math fonts available to TEX, this statement is true only when Computer Modern fonts are selected, when Times Roman is used with Math-Time or the Mathematica fonts, or when Lucida Bright is used with Lucida New Math. However, if reasonable compromises are permitted, a much wider selection of font matches is available.

To be sure, the text face will always be different from the mathematics, but that may be acceptable. A more serious problem arises from the relative proportions of the types. Even "at" the same design size, there are no size standards, so the effect of different fonts in a single document may be jarring unless some of the fonts are scaled. But what should be the standard for scaling? Three physical features of any font command our attention—the cap-height (distance above the baseline of a glyph like 'H'), the x-height (distance between the top of an 'x' and the baseline), and the descender depth (the distance that the lowest part of a letter like 'y' descends below the baseline). Figure 1 on the facing page shows these distances (plus a fourth, the ascender height, often close in value to the cap height). Ideally, we'd like to be able to scale a math font so that, after scaling, these three measurements for the math font match those for the text font. Practically, that's only possible for math fonts specifically designed for a particular text font. Normally, it will only be possible to match one of the dimensions of the scaled font to an original font, because the ratio between, say, x-height and cap-height also vary from font-to-font. The "before" and "after" scaling of figure 2 on the next page help make this clear.

The x-height is the dominant physical feature of a font, since so much of a document is lowercase. In our math fonts, we take pains to match the x-height of the math fonts with that of the text types. Moreover, it makes more sense to scale the math to the text, rather than vice versa, since there is almost always more text than math in a paper. Presumably, the 10-pt size for a text font is the optimal size for that font.

10.4   The MathInst utility

One way to install math fonts is via MathInst, written by the current author. MathInst creates an entire font environment for typesetting. At the

Figure 1: Type dimensions (Monotype Modern Bold is the example).

moment, MathInst knows about four math fonts, the MathTime, Lucida, Euler math, and *Mathematica* math fonts. MathInst consists of a Perl script, and several additional files needed by *fontinst*. The main purpose of these Perl scripts is to match a designated text family with a set of math fonts to create new math virtual fonts.

MathInst produces lots of output. First are the fonts themselves which combine the given math fonts with a family of text fonts. In case an author has provided the names of other fonts, such as

- a sans serif *family* of fonts;

- a typewriter font;

- a calligraphic font;

- a fraktur font;

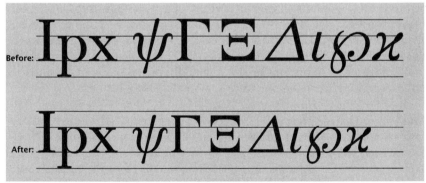

Figure 2: Monotype Bulmer juxtaposed to MathTime at a large size. The horizontals mark the levels of the cap-height, the x-height, the baseline, and the descender depth of Bulmer. Before scaling, the x-heights of the two fonts are off, although (by chance) the cap heights of the two are very close. After scaling, the x-heights match, but at the expense of the cap-height and descender depth.

- an uppercase bold Greek font; and

- a blackboard bold font,

MathInst will make them available as well (the uppercase Greek bold font will be used to create bold math fonts). In all cases, MathInst takes great care to size all fonts against the text fonts to make sure that all lowercase alphabets are visually compatible.

It's not enough to be provided fonts—they must be integrated into a set of macros for easy use by an author. For LATEX authors, MathInst provides a new package file that performs this integration and makes new commands available for the specialty fonts (Fraktur, blackboard bold, etc.) if these fonts are available.

Authors using plain TEX will find a new style performing this same integration. These authors will need to make sure Damian Cugley's PDCF-SEL font selection macros are available. (They can be downloaded from the `macros/plain/contrib/pdcmac` area of any of the CTAN archives; see chapter 6.)

Two test files are also provided—one for LATEX and one for plain—so authors can see examples of the new font selection commands at work. Finally, a log file records information about the virtual font process, including scale factors, to make it easy to rerun the process using override values of the scale factors if necessary.

MathInst itself is found on CTAN in the `fonts/utilities/mathinst` area.

10.4.1 Installing MathInst

Follow the detailed instructions in the file `mathinst.tex`, part of the package, to learn how to install this software. Consult the box on page 294 for a basic overview. You will also need the PDCFSEL font selection scheme for plain TEX mentioned above, and the text and math fonts themselves. You'll also need *fontinst*, version 1.5 or greater. Make sure that `pdcfsel.tex` and `fontinst.sty` are in one of the TEX input directories. Also, make sure the Perl executable appears on one of your system's path directories.

Customizing the installation   You'll also need to make adjustments to the `.par` parameter file that must accompany each type of math font. *MathInst will not run properly—and may not run at all—if these parameters are not set properly.* Changes need to made to some or all of the files `mt.par`, `lu.par`, `eu.par`, or `ma.par` depending on which math fonts you'll be using. Once these variables have been set, MathInst has been completely installed. Check the file `mathinst.tex` for complete details.

Installing raw math fonts   The *raw* math fonts consist of a series of outline font files plus the associated `.afm` files. It's easy to install these fonts. Here are the steps appropriate for traditional systems. The same steps apply to TDS systems, but it will be necessary to be more specific about the paths for the files. (For example, in a TDS system, the MathTime math fonts belong in places named like

⟨*texmf* ⟩/fonts/type1/texplora/mathtime/
⟨*texmf* ⟩/fonts/afm/texplora/mathtime/

and so on.)

1. Place the math font files with the other scalable fonts.

2. Place the .afm files with your other .afm files.

3. Make sure a proper entry exists for each math font in the .map file for your .dvi postprocessor.

Only the last point requires additional comment. For example, for the *dvips* psfonts.map file for a traditional TEX system, we need entries like

```
%% MathTime fonts...
mtsy    MTSY                    </psfonts/mtsy.pfa
mtex    MTEX                    </psfonts/mtex.pfa
rmtmi   RMTMI                   </psfonts/rmtmi.pfa

%% Lucida New Math fonts...
lbma LucidaNewMath-Arrows </psfonts/lbma.pfb
lbme LucidaNewMath-Extension </psfonts/lbme.pfb
lbms LucidaNewMath-Symbol </psfonts/lbms.pfb
lbmi LucidaNewMath-Italic </psfonts/lbmi.pfb
lbmo LucidaNewMath-AltItalic </psfonts/lbmo.pfb

%% Mathematica Math fonts...
Math1   Math1                   </psfonts/Math1.pfb
Math2   Math2                   </psfonts/Math2.pfb
Math3   Math3                   </psfonts/Math3.pfb
Math4   Math4                   </psfonts/Math4.pfb
Math5   Math5                   </psfonts/Math5.pfb
```

You'll have to adjust the path appropriately for a TDS system. Note that these fonts are proprietary; please respect the licenses under which these fonts are sold or distributed.

Euler math   Alone of the special math fonts, the Euler fonts are in the public domain. In the 1980s, the American Mathematical Society commissioned Hermann Zapf to draw a set of alphabets suitable for mathematical typesetting [Knuth and Zapf (1989), Siegel (1985)]. The Society has since graciously made these beautiful alphabets available for free. The first major

MathInst: Basic Installation

1. You will need: the MathInst modules, a version of *fontinst* with version 1.5 or greater, the PDCFSEL package, and a Perl executable for your computer. All but Perl are on CTAN; Perl is widely available from non-TEX archives and distributions of public-domain software.

2. Install the raw math fonts by placing them (outline font file, font metric file) on your disk in the proper place and updating the map file.

3. Install the text font family using the Berry font-naming scheme using VFINST (which does it automatically for you) or PSNFSS. The text fonts *must* be installed using the original OT1 TEX encoding.

4. Install any special purpose fonts (sans serif, blackboard bold, and so on) in the same way you installed the raw math fonts.

5. Create a mathinst directory with a work subdirectory.

use of these fonts was to typeset the book *Concrete Mathematics* [Graham, Knuth, and Patashnik (1989), Knuth (1989b)].

These fonts were implemented by METAFONT, and proper installation consists in placing the .tfm and .pk with their mates on your system. However, we will often be scaling these slightly to match various text fonts, and rather than regenerate many new bitmap fonts, it may be easier to use the scalable versions of these fonts, also available for free (courtesy of Basil Malyshev; they may be found in the fonts/postscript/bakoma section of CTAN—but there are certain licensing conditions). In this case, these fonts will also need entries in your .map file. These entries on a traditional TEX system should look something like

```
%% Euler fonts...
euex10    euex10    </psfonts/euex10.pfb
eufb10    eufb10    </psfonts/eufb10.pfb
eufb5     eufb5     </psfonts/eufb5.pfb
eufb7     eufb7     </psfonts/eufb7.pfb
eufm10    eufm10    </psfonts/eufm10.pfb
eufm5     eufm5     </psfonts/eufm5.pfb
eufm7     eufm7     </psfonts/eufm7.pfb
```

eurb10	eurb10	`</psfonts/eurb10.pfb`
eurb5	eurb5	`</psfonts/eurb5.pfb`
eurb7	eurb7	`</psfonts/eurb7.pfb`
eurm10	eurm10	`</psfonts/eurm10.pfb`
eurm5	eurm5	`</psfonts/eurm5.pfb`
eurm7	eurm7	`</psfonts/eurm7.pfb`
eusb10	eusb10	`</psfonts/eusb10.pfb`
eusb5	eusb5	`</psfonts/eusb5.pfb`
eusb7	eusb7	`</psfonts/eusb7.pfb`
eusm10	eusm10	`</psfonts/eusm10.pfb`
eusm5	eusm5	`</psfonts/eusm5.pfb`
eusm7	eusm7	`</psfonts/eusm7.pfb`

(The TDS path for these fonts will be something like `texmf/fonts/type1/ams/euler`.) Note that the Euler fonts come in a variety of weights and sizes; m and b represent medium and bold weights, and f, r, and s the fraktur, roman, and symbol fonts.

10.4.2 Installing the text fonts

The MathInst utilities expect the text font family (and the sans serif fonts too) to be installed using the Berry font-naming scheme. One way to do this is via the VFINST utility; see chapter 6. These text fonts *must* be installed using the original OT1 TEX encoding.

10.4.3 Running MathInst

Once the MathInst software has been properly installed, you execute a module by switching to a MathInst work directory like `mathinst/work` and issuing a command like

```
../mathinst mt mbv
```

The double dots '..' tell your computer to look for the MathInst script in the parent of the current working directory and to use the font families mt and mbv as arguments. This command installs a MathTime family of math fonts. If your computer doesn't seem to understand this command, issue the wordier incantation

```
perl ../mathinst mt mbv
```

instead. Then, follow the further instructions that appear on the computer screen.

MathInst: making the new fonts

- You'll need the three-character family designation for your text fonts.

- Switch to the work directory.

- Issue a command like

```
../mathinst mt mbv
```

  to create the new math fonts. Follow all further instructions.

- The new font family has a six-character designation, beginning with z, followed by the math font type (either mt, eu, lu, or ma as of this writing), and the three-character text family sequence.

- Compile and print or preview either of files `testmath.tex` (LaTeX) or `testmatp.tex` (plain) to test the new fonts.

- When the fonts are acceptable, complete the installation by placing the fonts and styles where they ultimately belong on your system. Do this via `../putfonts`.

10.5 New math virtual fonts with MathInst

MathInst uses the two-character designations

> mt MathTime
> lu Lucida New Math
> eu Euler
> ma Mathematica

to refer to the various math fonts. The new math font families use the *z naming convention*, whereby the font family name for the new math fonts uses the two-character math designations together with the text font family designation. Suppose we combine MathTime (mt) with Baskerville, whose family designation is mbv in the Berry scheme. The new fonts will be described in macro files `zmtmbv.tex` and `zmtmbv.sty` (for users of plain TeX or LaTeX). Baskerville plus Euler or Baskerville plus Lucida would form the z-names zeumbv and zlumbv. The z-name zmambv describes a marriage between Baskerville and the *Mathematica* math fonts.

The fonts themselves follow the Berry scheme, but you don't need to keep track of this, since the MathInst style files load the fonts for you automatically and establish their correspondence either with familiar nicknames (\it, \bf) or with the NFSS. But if you find yourself poking about your font directories, here's a quick key to the many new fonts you'll see.

Additional font variants m, e, l, or a indicate a math font, while variants m, y, or v following the encoding digit denote the math italic, symbol, or extension fonts. For Monotype Baskerville, the four math fonts at text size have names

- mbvrm7t, the math Roman font;

- mbvrm7m, the math italic font;

- mbvrm7y, the symbol font; and

- mbvrm7v, the extension font.

(The presence of the "7" in the font name reminds us we are using the original OT1 TEX encoding.) A math Roman font connecting Baskerville and Euler or Baskerville and Lucida would be called mbvre7t or mbvrl7t. A similar math Roman font for Baskerville plus Mathematica would be mbvra7t.

MathInst does its best to "fake out" new fonts at script and scriptscript sizes. Computer Modern fonts provide the rôle model—those fonts are subtly redesigned at different sizes. Smaller fonts sizes also display greater letterspacing (additional space between adjacent characters) at smaller sizes. We can't redesign a scalable font, but we can create virtual fonts which differ only in the letterspacing, for use in various contexts. MathInst creates installation files that take letterspacing into account. Therefore, you will see as many as three fonts for each of the above varieties listed above. In addition to mbvrm7t, the math Roman font for text sizes, you'll see mbvrm7t7 and mbvrm7t5, the same fonts fine-tuned for use in script and scriptscript contexts. (The suffixes "7" and "5" recall the sizes of seven and five points that Computer Modern typesetting uses for these designations.) There is only a single math extension font for any family.

10.5.1 Using the new fonts

Whether you use LATEX or plain TEX, you'll only need to remember the *z*-name for your new fonts. One purpose of the MathInst test files is to provide living examples showing just how the new fonts are invoked.

In a LATEX document, all the work is done by the package file whose first name is precisely the *z*-name for the math fonts. As with all package files, its extension is .sty. If you add a line like

```
\usepackage{zmtmbv}
```

MathInst: using the new fonts

To use the new fonts: add a command like

```
\usepackage{zmtmbv}
```

following the \documentclass command (LaTeX) or the command

```
\input zmtmbv
```

at or near the beginning of the document file (plain TeX). Here, zmtmbv is a font family (synergizing MathTime plus Baskerville). In general, the six-character font family identifier will be formed like

z+⟨*math identifier*⟩+⟨*text family identifier*⟩

At the moment, the ⟨*math identifier*⟩'s are mt, eu, lu, or ma.

following \documentclass{...} then all the usual LaTeX font-switching mechanisms will now apply to the zmtmbv fonts rather than to the default Computer Modern fonts.

No font-selection scheme for plain TeX is quite as all-encompassing as the LaTeX NFSS, but Damian Cugley's PDCFSEL comes gratifyingly close and does one or two things better than NFSS. Like the LaTeX package, the plain macro file has the font z-name as its first name, but the extension is .tex. To use these macros, simply place a statement like

```
\input zmtmbv
```

very near the beginning of your file. Thereafter, all the usual plain font commands like \it, \rm, \tt, $, $$, and so on, refer to the new math fonts. The PDCFSEL package itself provides more flexibility than plain users are used to, and it would be well worth any (plain) reader's time to gain familiarity with this package.

10.5.2   The MathTime fonts

Michael Spivak developed the MathTime math fonts to be used with the Times family of text fonts in a LaTeX or TeX document; Y&Y is the vendor. Many authors will find these fonts the most useful for math typesetting.

Their "Times Roman-y" look goes well with many other Roman fonts. Recently, the MathTime Plus family has become available. These new fonts make bold math, extra bold, upright Greek, and script faces available for math typesetting (but they have not as yet been incorporated into Math-Inst).

The package consists of three fonts—an extension font, a math italic font, and a symbol font. The extension font mtex is directly analogous to cmex10 (the same characters are in the same positions), but the remaining fonts have slightly different layouts from their Computer Modern counterparts. These differences are largely due to the elimination of the oldstyle digits and the calligraphic alphabet from the italic and symbol fonts. The slots opened up by these omissions have been filled with uppercase Greek letters and redesigned operator symbols. (The documentation that accompanies the fonts discusses the differences in greater detail.)

Users can also create MathTime math fonts in a second way—by following the instructions that accompany these fonts. This approach is not so heavily dependent on virtual fonts as is the MathInst way and relies on a well-written macro file accompanying this package.

10.5.3   The Euler fonts

Euler fonts consist of math literals (neither Roman nor italic, but a unique upright font which is a compromise between the two forms; see figure 3 on the next page, especially the eurm10 block), symbols (with a compatible uppercase calligraphic alphabet), Fraktur, and extension fonts. Because they predate virtual fonts, and because the font tables themselves follow slightly quirky layouts, they have not been as useful heretofore as they might have been. The extension font is quite sparse, but we can add virtual flesh using Computer Modern glyphs to fill in the blanks of the font table. Figure 3 on the following page displays a selection from the Euler suite in the medium weight (bold variants are also available).

10.5.4   Lucida New Math

The Lucida math fonts for TEX were designed by Charles Bigelow and Kris Holmes to follow normal LATEX and TEX typesetting conventions and yet be compatible with the extensive Lucida and Lucida Bright font families. An early version of these math fonts seems formerly to have been available through Adobe Systems and associated vendors. These fonts have disappeared from type catalogs, and new versions are available instead for purchase from Y&Y.

In this discussion, we will focus on a virtual-font approach for creating Lucida math fonts. The utilities that accompany the font package may follow other approaches.

This Lucida New Math family consists of five fonts. Because each contains the full complement of 256 characters, these fonts are crammed with

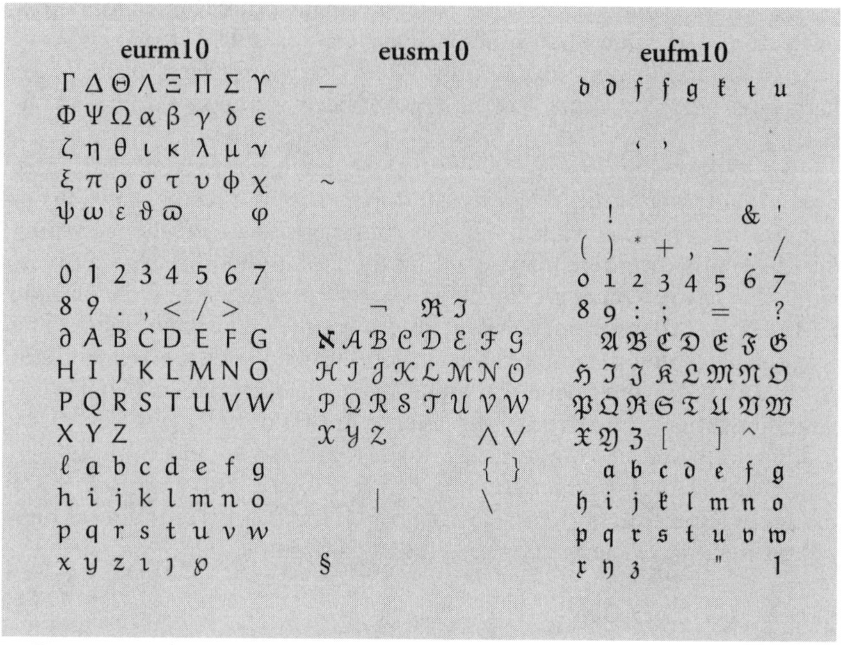

Figure 3: A selection of the Euler math fonts (roman, symbol, and Fraktur) in medium weight.

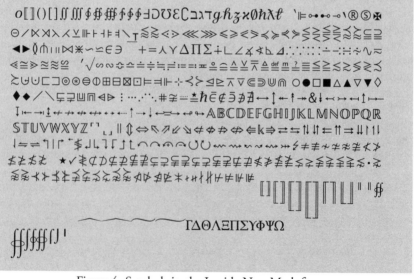

Figure 4: Symbols in the Lucida New Math fonts.

all kinds of additional glyphs. These additions include all the special symbols that occur in the additional symbol fonts commissioned and made available by the American Mathematical Society and include a Blackboard Bold font. Figure 4 on the preceding page displays these additional Lucida symbols. The three fonts useful for standard TEXnical typesetting are the symbol, math oblique, and math extension fonts. A math italic font doesn't follow the original math italic font quite as closely as the oblique font. Finally, a math arrow font contains many, many new symbols plus the Blackboard Bold alphabet.

Lucida math extension   Lucida math extension differs from other extension fonts in that it contains many new glyphs in its upper half. With this font properly in place, you can use a new extensible set of open brackets, additional wide accents, newly sized integral symbols, and a fully extensible integral. The font also contains the uppercase Greek alphabet, which we already use to construct the math Roman font. MathInst style files contain commands (where necessary) to use these new features.

The wide accent symbols are automatically in place; simply continue to use \widetilde and \widehat as before.

There are new kinds of square brackets that grow to enclose filler material. These brackets, invoked with commands \Lbrack and \Rbrack, are amenable to the usual "growth" mechanisms that govern \left, \right, \bigl, and so on.

The several new integral signs include new surface integrals, a new size for the regular and contour integrals, and pieces for a generally extensible integral. The new command \surfint and the existing integral commands \int and \oint work as expected. In addition, there are large variants, summoned into play by \lint, \loint, and \lsurfint. These control sequences ensure that the various integral signs change their size depending on a text or display context.

You might like to have TEX select the right size integral for you. For that reason, there are three variant integral commands, \varint, \varoint, and \varsint (for regular, contour, and surface integrals) that try to do that for you. Each of these takes as argument the contents of the integrand. Figure 5 on page 303 shows that this mechanism works poorly for the surface and contour integrals when the total height of the integrand is taller than the largest of the available integrals.

The \var.. integral commands have been designed so that normal TEX sub- and superscript conventions hold as usual. However, the \limits and \nolimits commands, which control the positioning of scripts, do not. You will have to use the new commands \setlimits and \setnolimits within the argument of the integral. (Here, \setnolimits is the default.) That is, if you type

```
\int\limits_0^1{\displaystyle{\sin x\over x}
    \above1pt\displaystyle{x\over\cos x}}\,dx
```

to get $\displaystyle\int_0^1 \frac{\dfrac{\sin x}{x}}{\dfrac{x}{\cos x}}\, dx$, you would type

```
\varint_0^1{\setlimits\displaystyle{{\sin x\over x}
  \above1pt\displaystyle{x\over\cos x}}\,dx}
```

when using the variable extensible integral.

MathInst automatically places the TEX-hackery necessary in the Lucida style files it writes. You could type

```
$$
  \overbrace{\vphantom{\lint}
    \hbox{$\int\lint\oint\loint\surfint\lsurfint$\ }}%
    ^{\hbox{text}}
  \overbrace{\int\lint\oint\loint\surfint\lsurfint}%
    ^{\hbox{display}}
$$
$$\varint_{-\infty}^{+\infty}{\setlimits\left\Lbrack
\vcenter{\halign{\strut\hfil$#$\hfil\cr
  \widehat 1\,\widehat{23}\,\widehat{456}\,
  \widehat{7890}\,\widehat{12345}
\cr
  \widetilde{67890}\,\widetilde{1234}\,\widetilde{567}\,
  \widetilde{89}\,\widetilde{0}
\cr
  \varoint{\short}\,\varoint{\med}\,\varoint{\tall}\,
  \varoint{\Tall}\,\varoint{\Talll}\,\varoint{\VTall}
\cr
  \varsint{\VTall}\,\varsint{\Talll}\,\varsint{\Tall}\,
  \varsint{\tall}\,\varsint{\med}\,
  \varsint_{\scriptscriptstyle\partial C}%
  {\setlimits\omega}
\cr
  \left\Lbrack x\right\Rbrack\
  \left\Lbrack\med\right\Rbrack\
  \left\Lbrack \tall \right\Rbrack\
  \left\Lbrack \Tall \right\Rbrack\
  \left\Lbrack \Talll\right\Rbrack\
  \left\Lbrack \ontop{42pt}\right\Rbrack
\cr
  \varint_0^9{\Talll}\ \varint_{-1}^{+1}{\Tall}\
  \varint{\tall}\
  \varint^{+\infty}_{-\infty}{\med}\ \varint{x}\cr
}}\right\Rbrack\,dx
}$$
```

to get figure 5 on the next page, which combines the Lucida math and Lucida Bright Roman fonts. Here, \short, \med, \tall and so on are simply temporary control sequences to generate arguments of various relative heights.

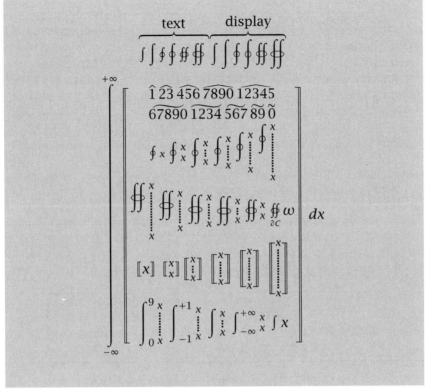

Figure 5: New Lucida math extension characters in action.

10.5.5 Mathematica math fonts

The Mathematica math fonts were in development as this book was written, but Wolfram Research graciously made their interim fonts available to me. The fonts in their eventual release may have different names, different characters, and a different ordering.

These fonts consist of five font series comprising all of the characters that TEX normally expects, a calligraphic and a Blackboard Bold alphabet, and many more additional characters. Each series consists of four variants, normal, bold, typewriter, and typewriter bold.

$\alpha\beta\chi\delta\epsilon\phi\gamma\eta\iota\varphi\kappa\lambda\mu\nu o\pi\theta\rho\sigma\tau\upsilon\varpi\omega\xi\psi\zeta\{|\}\aleph I R\wp\otimes\oplus\emptyset$

$\alpha\beta\chi\delta\epsilon\phi\gamma\eta\iota\varphi\kappa\lambda\mu\nu o\pi\theta\rho\sigma\tau\upsilon\varpi\omega\xi\psi\zeta\{|\}\aleph I R\wp\otimes\oplus\emptyset$

$\alpha\beta\chi\delta\epsilon\phi\gamma\eta\iota\varphi\kappa\lambda\mu\nu o\pi\theta\rho\sigma\tau\upsilon\varpi\omega\xi\psi\zeta\{|\}\aleph I R\wp\otimes\oplus\emptyset$

$\alpha\beta\chi\delta\epsilon\phi\gamma\eta\iota\varphi\kappa\lambda\mu\nu o\pi\theta\rho\sigma\tau\upsilon\varpi\omega\xi\psi\zeta\{|\}\aleph I R\wp\otimes\oplus\emptyset$

These are the glyphs in each series:

$!\forall\#\%\&\ni()*+,-./0123456789:;<=>?\cong A B X \Delta E \Phi \Gamma H$
$I \partial K \Lambda M N O \Pi \Theta P \Sigma T \Upsilon \varsigma \Xi \Omega \Psi Z [\therefore]\bot\_\,\alpha\beta\chi\delta\epsilon\phi\gamma\eta\iota\varphi\kappa\lambda\mu\nu o$

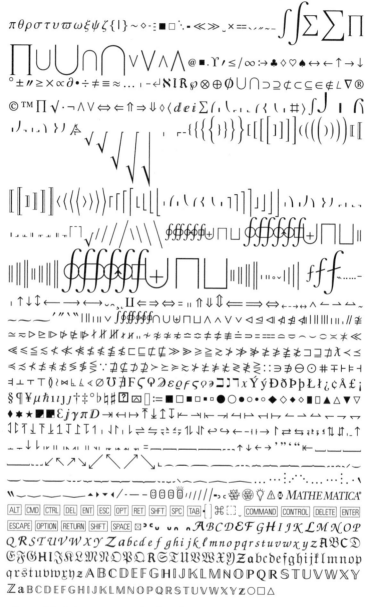

As far as TEX is concerned, the characters in these fonts are scrambled in a funny order, so we first create raw fonts, each of which appears more meaningfully ordered to TEX. You can do this with the script makemma.tex, part of MathInst. Running this script, and then creating virtual fonts in the usual way, creates three fonts mmami, mmasy, and mmaex (math italic, symbol, and extension), which are themselves suitable components for virtual font shenanigans. Although these three are in fact virtual fonts, we will treat them as raw fonts in the creation of additional virtual fonts.

10.6   Fine tuning the new math fonts

Each MathInst module contains a .par parameter file; any changes to the fonts involve straightforward revisions to these files.

10.6.1   Adding special-purpose fonts

Authors may want to add special fonts to their math style. Here's what MathInst allows you to add:

- a sans serif font *family*,

- a typewriter font,

- a blackboard bold font,

- a Fraktur font,

- a calligraphic font, and

- a bold Greek font (suitable for setting bold math).

You may add any, all, or none of these. If any of these fonts are present on your system, MathInst adds high-level font-switching commands to the style and macro files it creates that recognize the presence of these fonts.

Where do these fonts come from? Many of them are proprietary, but a large number of them reside in the public domain, albeit in unlikely or unsuspected places.

As far as typewriter type is concerned, I strongly recommend the freely available Computer Modern typewriter font cmtt10, which blends well with almost every other digital face. There are alternatives. The Pandora typewriter font pntt10 is also free from CTAN, and of course the printer-resident Courier font is widely available. There are several other variants of cmtt10 in the TEX suite that some users may prefer, and proprietary typewriter fonts include offerings in the Lucida Bright families and ITC American Typewriter. Other authors may use a monowidth sans serif font (such as Letter Gothic) or some other contrasting face entirely.

A wide choice exists for sans serif families. Common choices will be Computer Modern sans serif, and the Helvetica fonts resident in all Post-Script printers. I am personally partial to Gill Sans (from Monotype) and the Lucida Sans fonts (Bigelow & Holmes), but both of these are commercial fonts.

A calligraphic uppercase alphabet is necessary to make the \mathcal or \cal commands work properly. MathInst can add this alphabet (in a virtual way) to the math symbol font. Among the widely available candidates are alphabets from the Computer Modern symbol and Euler symbol fonts, and the printer-resident Zapf Chancery font. Several bitmap script fonts in the fonts area of CTAN (such as Calligra, the RSFS fonts, script fonts, and `twcal`) may be appropriate. Many commercial fonts are suitable, but authors should refrain from choosing too fancy a script.

There is less choice for a Blackboard Bold and Fraktur font. In CTAN, we find the `bbold` fonts (by Alan Jeffrey) and the `msbm` fonts developed and provided by the American Mathematical Society; both of these are in the `fonts` area of CTAN, the latter being in its `ams` subdirectory. Commercial sources include the Lucida New Math family (the "arrows" font contains the Blackboard Bold glyphs) and Adobe's Math Pi fonts (the sixth of these contains the Blackboard Bold). Choices on CTAN for fraktur include Euler fraktur `eufm` in `fonts/ams` (a scalable version is part of the BaKoMa collection, also on CTAN) and the `yfrak` fonts in `fonts/gothic/yfrak`. Commercial choices include the Math Pi package from Adobe (check out the second font in the series for Fraktur) and a font called Fraktur from Bitstream.

Mathematicians often want formulas in bold type. MathInst will create bold math fonts for you, but the sticking point might be bold variants of the uppercase Greek letters. Computer Modern, Euler, and Mathematica fonts contain bold Greek alphabets, but neither Lucida nor MathTime do. If a bold version of the Greek letters is available, MathInst would like to know about it. There seems to be nothing available that exactly matches the Lucida Greek types, but bold Greek Times fonts can be purchased (from Monotype and other font vendors).

If these fonts are available, they should be installed properly. For the sans serif *family*, that means installing them following the Berry font naming scheme, perhaps by using VFINST. For the other individual fonts, the installation is much simpler. Here is the pertinent procedure applicable to traditional systems:

- Place the `.tfm` file with other TEX font metric files, and

- Place the bitmap font file in the proper spot with the other bitmap files of that resolution.

- If the font is an outline font, use the `afm2tfm` utility to create a `.tfm` file from the `.afm` file, and then move the `.tfm` to its proper spot.

- Place the outline font file with your other outline fonts, and

- Update the `.map` to reflect the presence of this file on your system.

For example, in `psfonts.map`, you'll need a line like

```
pmp6  MathematicalPi-Six  </psfonts/pmp6.pfb
```

(traditional systems) or something like

```
pmp MathematicalPi-Six <⟨texmf⟩/fonts/type1/adobe/mathpi
```

on a TDS system to make the correspondence between file `pmp6` and the `MathematicalPi-Six` font.

To make these fonts visible to MathInst, you'll need to enter the names of the font files to the right of the equal signs in the statements making assignments to $tt_, $sansserif_, and so on. Don't forget to remove any comment characters from the beginning of the line! Thus, to use pmp6 as the source for Blackboard Bold, we need the line

```
$bbold_ = "pmp6";
```

in the parameter .par file. Note that font names in these statements need double quotes fore and aft. Note too that these changes need to be part of *all* the .par files (or at least all the ones you'll be using).

10.6.2 Controlling font scaling

Normally, MathInst calculates the scale factors for itself, under the assumption that the roman types will be at their natural size and that all other fonts are scaled so that all lowercase letters are at the same height. The scale factors that MathInst uses in any run are recorded in the MathInst log file.

An author is entitled to overrule these decisions. There is a series of variables with names like $...SF_ that control the scale factors. The scale factor represents the amount by the special font has to be enlarged or made smaller to guarantee a fit between its lowercase letterforms and the Roman letterforms (actually, the scale factor is 1000 times the magnitude of the magnification). If you type an actual value, MathInst uses this given value as the scale factor and will not calculate any other. If you make its value zero, MathInst uses its natural size—it refuses to scale the special font at all. If you do not set the scale factor variable, MathInst computes the amount of scaling and uses this value. So, to make a calligraphic font slightly larger than expected, enter the line

```
$calSF_ = 1330;
```

into the parameter file. To use the typewriter font at its natural size, enter

```
$ttSF_ = 0;
```

To use a fraktur font at the size MathInst deems appropriate, keep the variable $frakSF_ commented out.

10.6.3 Sizing fonts at small sizes

The subtle redesign of Computer Modern fonts at different sizes helps make characters at script and scriptscript sizes (that is, 7 pt and 5 pt) easier to read than linearly scaled fonts would be. Part of this redesign includes adding extra space (letterspacing or tracking) between adjacent characters at small sizes, and the smaller the size, the more such spacing. With few (if any) exceptions, it is impossible to redesign scalable fonts at different sizes—we can only scale them up and down in a linear fashion. Type printed at seven and five points is really hard to read.

We can't do anything involving font redesign, but we can mitigate the harshness at small sizes in two ways—we can adjust the letterspacing and we can use the type at a slightly larger nominal size. By default, Math-Inst uses fonts at 5.5 pt and 7.3 pt at script and scriptscript sizes; compare these to the Computer Modern values of 5 pt and 7 pt. But you can change values by adjusting the variables `$sssize_` and `$ssize_` in the `.par` file. Normally, though, they should not be touched. To adjust the letterspacing at these smaller sizes, you'll need to enter the distribution files with names like `OM...s.etx` and `OM...ss.etx` and vary the values for the *fontinst* `letterspacing` variable.

10.6.4   Other adjustments

MathInst produces test files `testmath.tex` for LaTeX and `testmatp.tex` for plain TeX. These files show how to implement the fonts you've just created and exercises these fonts in some reasonably complete manner. The files themselves are closely modeled after a similar test file originally designed by Alan Jeffrey for his installation of the `mathptm` fonts. (The original of this file appears on CTAN in the `fonts/utilities/fontinst` area.) It is a good idea to compile these tests and print one out each time you create a new math font family.

This document may reveal details that need attention. As an example, consider the first efforts at installing MathTime + Adobe Garamond, the text font for this book. The first printout reveals that the test construction `]f[` looks like

$$]f[$$

when it should look like `]f[`. Furthermore, `$\vec f$` comes out

$$\vec{f}$$

instead of $\vec{f}$.

Details such as these may be repaired by inspecting the two `...hax.mtx` and the `...skw.mtx` files that MathInst prepares. That is, given a text family like pad (say), the files `padrhax.mtx`, `padihax.mtx`, and `padiskw.mtx` provide places to alter the glyph dimensions for the Roman and italic fonts. Once these files exist, MathInst takes care not to overwrite them, as that would destroy an author's efforts at fine tuning.

The reader is also reminded of TeX's `\skew` command that helps adjust superaccents within documents in case fontwise tinkering is not done; see Knuth (1986a, p. 136).

10.7   New math fonts via Metafont

Think of the reasons that Computer Modern math fonts clash with other text fonts—they are somehow too skinny, the wrong height and depth, and their shapes may not harmonize well with text fonts. Being that they are meta-fonts, can we not alter the parameters to generate math fonts that more closely approximate text fonts we may be using? This strategy lies behind the *MathKit* scripts I have developed. *MathKit* aids in the creation of math fonts that may be compatible with a text font family. It consists of a Perl script and some auxiliary files to help an author—even one ignorant of virtual fonts or of METAFONT—to perform these tasks. This material can be found in the fonts/utilities/mathkit area of CTAN.

MathKit takes METAFONT parameters that are appropriate to an outline font family and uses these to create math fonts. The symbols and other special characters look pretty good—and are compatible with your outline fonts—but the italics and numerals look ghastly. Using TEX's virtual font mechanism, we create math fonts that combine the new special symbols with letters and numerals from the outline fonts. *MathKit* does some of this work for you, and provides scripts for the remaining steps (described in the accompanying documentation). It also provides style files for plain TEX and for the NFSS of LATEX for you to use these fonts in your documents.

The current version of *MathKit* comes with three sets of font templates. Since Palatino and Times-Roman are so common, I prepared templates for these fonts. For fun, I prepared a template for Monotype Baskerville. Times comes in regular and bold series, and Baskerville in regular and semibold; Palatino is regular only.

MathKit itself produces a number of scripts and batch files. Once these are properly executed, you get the following:

1. Virtual fonts for math and text typesetting. You will also get fonts for bold math if you have supplied a template containing bold parameters.

2. Style files for plain TEX and LATEX (NFSS) . These files support bold math if bold parameter templates were present.

10.7.1 Installation and execution

Follow the directions in the documentation file mathkit.tex for proper installation; this mostly involves making sure that various files are in their proper locations and ensuring that certain Perl variables are given proper values.

The main *MathKit* script requires three parameters. These are:

1. The name of the parameter template. 'tm' refers to Times-like parameters, 'pl' to Palatino-like, and 'bv' to Baskerville-like.

2. The name under which text fonts are installed. This is apt to be something like ptm or mnt for Adobe Times or Monotype Times New Roman, ppl for Palatino, and mbv for Monotype Baskerville (which is *quite* different from ITC New Baskerville).

3. The encoding your fonts follow. Only OT1 or ot1 (original TEX encoding) are allowed.

For example, I type

```
perl ../mathkit tm ptm OT1
```

in my work directory to create Times-like fonts following the original TEX encoding. (If your system supports the #! syntax for specifying the name of an interpreter, then put the proper path at the very top of mathkit, make sure the execute bit is set, and type the simpler injunction ../mathkit tm ptm OT1 from the work directory.)

I've had success matching bv (Baskerville-like) parameters to other Roman fonts. For example, I typed

```
../mathkit bv mjn OT1
```

to generate a nice-looking set of fonts combining Monotype Janson text with Bsakerville-like math fonts.

The following steps complete the font creation. Perform them all within the *MathKit* work directory.

1. Use the mkdirs script to create any missing directories.

2. Execute the file makegf.bat to have METAFONT create the pixel fonts for your fonts. This step will take some time.

3. You'll need to pack all the pixel files. Inside Unix, you can do this via a series of commands like

```
foreach X (*.600gf)
foreach? gftopk $X $X:r.600pk
foreach? end
```

Not all operating systems are so accommodating, so there is a file called makepk.bat that may be helpful in this regard. *Caution:* before executing this script, it may be necessary to edit it.

4. Execute the script makepl.bat to create some property list files needed by the next step.

5. Run the file makevp.tex through TEX. That is, execute the command tex makevp or something appropriate for your system. This step will take some time. Along with lots of superfluous files, this creates many "virtual property list" files with extension .vpl.

6. Create the actual virtual files by running every .vpl file through the program vptovf. You can do this easily in Unix with commands like

```
foreach X (*.vpl)
foreach? vptovf $X $X:r.vf $X:r.tfm
foreach? end
```

But there's an easier way—execute the file makevf.bat which *MathKit* creates for you.

7. Execute the file putfonts.bat to place the font and other files where they belong.

This sequence is summarized for you again on the computer screen when you execute *MathKit*.

After you place all the font files properly, this still leaves behind files with extensions .log, .mtx, .pl, .vpl, .bat, .600gf (or something similar) and perhaps one or two other miscellaneous files. You may safely delete all these.

10.7.2 Naming the new fonts

METAFONT will make many new fonts with names like the usual Computer Modern fonts, except the first two letters will be replaced by the abbreviation you specified in the *MathKit* command. Thus, when making Times-like fonts, you'll be making new fonts tmr10, tmbx10, and so on for other varieties and sizes. There will be some bold variants of these if you've provided a bold parameter template.

There will be lots of new virtual fonts for Math roman and italic (and perhaps in bold variants). These fonts have names beginning with the font family indicator (such as ptm or mbv), a weight indicator (r, s, or b for regular, semibold, or bold), a single letter referring to the bitmaps that have been incorporated (this will be the first of the two-letter abbreviation for the bitmap family), an encoding digit "7" (for OT1 encoding), a further encoding symbol (either t or m for text or math italic), and a character for the font size (no digit for 10 pt, a single digit for smaller sizes, and a "c," hexadecimal digit representing "12," for the 12-pt size). All font names are eight or fewer characters.

10.7.3 Using the new fonts

MathKit produces two style files, one for LATEX and one for plain TEX. Their file names are formed according the naming scheme

$$z\langle \textit{mock-family}\rangle\langle \textit{font-family}\rangle$$

Here, ⟨*mock-family*⟩ is the two-character designation for one of the font parameter templates (such as tm, pl, or bv); the word "mock" refers to the fact that these fonts imitate but don't equal the actual fonts in this family. ⟨*font-family*⟩ is the Berry family designation. Thus, if I create a Times-like set of fonts for use with font family ptm, I would find files ztmptm.sty (LATEX) and ztmptm.tex (plain). In the same way, the style files for mock-Palatino and mock-Baskerville fonts are named zplppl and zbvmbv (with the appropriate extensions).

At the top of a plain TeX file, include the statement

```
\input ztmmnt
```

(or whatever the style file name is). Then, standard font nicknames like \bf and \it and math toggles like $ and \(will thenceforward refer to these new fonts.

If bold fonts have been generated, a command \boldface typesets everything in its way in boldface—prose, mathematics, whatever. Bold math may be appropriate for bold captions, sections heads, and the like. Like any other font changing command, this command should be placed within grouping symbols.

In LaTeX documents, you simply need to include the style name as part of the list of packages that you use in the document. Thus, a typical document would have a statement like

```
\usepackage{ztmptm,epsf,pstricks,...}
```

at the outset.

If *MathKit* has created bold math fonts, a boldface environment will typeset everything in that environment as bold, including all mathematics.

Occasionally, you may need to fine tune a file or two by hand. As with MathInst, there are a series of ...x.mtx and ...w.mtx files to assist you in that fine tuning.

If your outline fonts have been installed using expert fonts, you may need to alter the \rmdefault command. It might be necessary, say, to type

```
\rmdefault{ptmx}
```

instead of \rmdefault{ptm}.

In files named like OT1⟨*whatever*⟩.fd it may be necessary to replace the bx series designation by b. Or it may be necessary to add entries at the bottom instructing NFSS to substitute fonts in the bx series with fonts in a b or sb (bold or semibold) series.

10.7.4 Preparing parameter files

It was surprisingly easy to prepare these parameter files. I prepared a test document in which individual characters are printed on a baseline at a size of 750 pt. It's (relatively) easy to measure the dimensions of such large characters, and METAFONT can be asked to divide by 75 to compute the proper dimension for 10-pt fonts. It was particularly easy for me to make these measurements, as I use Tom Rokicki's superior implementation of TeX for NextStep. This package contains on-screen calipers, which take all the work out of this chore.

If you plan to create your own parameter files for other font families, please use the supplied files as models (those files with extensions .mkr,

.mks, or .mkb). Make sure all measurements are given in terms of "pt#"; *MathKit* looks for this string. And please consider placing this information in CTAN.

10.8   Rogues' gallery

The displays beginning on page 316 show the results of mixing and matching various math families to many text fonts. VFINST installed all the text fonts, and MathInst or *MathKit* generated all the math + text fonts. Additional details on these (and other) types appear in Lawson (1990). The classic reference by Updike (1980) has recently appeared in an inexpensive Dover edition.

These displays should be regarded as experiments only. I showed these pages to several people, and all concluded that some of the experiments are successful and others are failures. However, no one agreed which were the successes and which were the failures!

Many of the fonts available for digital typesetting are as beautiful as any created anywhere, in any age. The text faces, by and large, fall into either of two categories—tried and true fonts, beauties that came into existence many years, often several centuries, ago; and modern aspirants to typographical immortality.

Let's briefly consider the venerable class of types that appear in our experiments. All digital Caslon fonts trace their ancestry to William Caslon's eighteenth-century Roman fonts. The family Adobe Caslon has a pleasing old-timey look and contains many alternate characters and ligatures.

Adobe has also put their stamp on Garamond, a name describing many fonts based on those of the sixteenth-century French punchcutter Claude Garamond. The contemporary designer Robert Slimbach worked hard to develop a Garamond that was as true to the original cutting as possible. However, the so-called Garamond italic fonts were actually designed originally by Robert Granjon, a rough contemporary of Garamond.

John Baskerville, a talented amateur typefounder and printer who flourished in the middle of the eighteenth century, designed many popular fonts. Type cast from his original matrices is still available today (from Schriftgiesserei Walter Fruttiger AG). The Monotype version of his text fonts are among the finest of the several versions available digitally, perhaps because it follows the hot-metal version the closest.

The "Bulmer" of the Bulmer font was the proprietor of the firm that secured the services of William Martin as punch cutter. His Bulmer fonts of 1790 anticipate the modern Bodoni faces, while retaining many attributes from old style faces. The Monotype digital version is closely based on a hot-metal version from the 1930s.

The Janson fonts shown below were revived by Monotype in 1937 and are based on fonts cut by the Hungarian Nicholas Kis in the late 1600s. It's hard to explain their misattribution to Anton Janson. (These fonts are totally different from the Jansen fonts that now appear in the Adobe catalog.)

Many twentieth-century type designs hark back to classic type forms of earlier centuries, such as the beautiful font Galliard. Matthew Carter designed Galliard in 1978, and based its look on that of French old-style types designed by Granjon but added liveliness and zest from the dance for which it is named. We use the cutting from the Carter and Cone foundry, which makes available many wonderful alternate characters and ligatures, a true small caps font, and a handsome titling font (called Mantinia).

Bruce Rogers designed Centaur (named for the title of the first book it appeared in) at the behest of the Metropolitan Museum of Art in New York City which needed a font for their exhibition labels. First used in 1915, it remains one of the most elegant faces of modern times.

The Gill Sans serifless type of 1928 designed by Eric Gill rapidly became the most popular sans serif type in Great Britain. Travelers will note its similarity to the fonts used in the London Underground system.

The Lucida Bright and Lucida Sans fonts are the text and sans serif fonts designed by Charles Bigelow and Kris Holmes to accompany the Lucida New Math fonts (or is is the other way round?) we've already encountered.

"Modern" styles of text fonts actually date from Thomas Jefferson and are distinguished from old-style faces in several ways, chief among them being the high contrast between thick and thin elements and the repeatability of component letter parts [Knuth (1986e)]. Perhaps it is this last that helped recommend the modern style to Knuth as a model for Computer Modern. The English Monotype Corporation produced a series of Modern fonts, named numerically Monotype Modern No. 1, 7, 13, 14, and so on. Its American cousin produced Modern No. 8a, which was the direct model for the Computer Modern fonts. (An edition of the novel *Typee* [Melville (1962)]—wonderfully named, under the circumstances—that I own is set entirely in Modern fonts 8 and 20, and shows how handsome these fonts are.) Among digital offerings, Monotype Modern appears a very bright relative of the numerical Modern fonts, but it was actually born as Linotype Modern and designed in 1969 by Walter Tracy.

Although designed in 1937 by Lucien Bernhard, Bernhard Modern remains popular to this day. It has a particularly small x-height, and although a modern font, is quite different from the Monotype Modern fonts. Finally, everyone knows about Times Roman and Palatino since these fonts are resident in every PostScript printer. Their ubiquity can blind a reader to their inherent beauty. In the tests that follow, we use the cutting of Times called Times New Roman from Monotype; Times Roman was first used to set the British newspaper of that name in October 1932 (but this face is no longer in use with that paper). Everyone recognizes Palatino—the face whose appearance in 1950 put Hermann Zapf on the typographic map. Zapf was one of the original advisors in typographical matters to Knuth, and we have already encountered him as the designer of the Euler math fonts.

10.8.1 Notes on the rogues' gallery

The first sample shown is a testbed piece of text typeset in traditional Computer Modern, and this is followed by a demonstration replacing Computer Modern by Monotype Modern. Then, all the MathTime, Euler, Lucida, and Mathematica specimens are grouped together, followed by demonstrations of *MathKit*.

Since every PostScript printer contains Times Roman and Palatino, I included samples showing how both these fonts work together with each of our four math font groups. You will also find examples of math using sans serif types for text fonts.

With few exceptions (noted in the labels), all specimens are shown at the natural 10-pt type size of the text font. Centaur was just too small and Lucida Bright and Lucida Sans just too big under this criterion, so changes were made. More often, the bold-faced title was reduced in size if it caused the title to spill over to a second line. In such cases, the specimen would then not fit on a single page unless this adjustment was made.

Computer Modern math + Computer Modern text

Unbound Orbits: Deflection of Light by the Sun

Consider a particle or photon approaching the sun from very great distances. At infinity the metric is Minkowskian, that is, $A(\infty) = B(\infty) = 1$, and we expect motion on a straight line at constant velocity V

$$b \simeq r \sin(\varphi - \varphi_\infty) \simeq r(\varphi - \varphi_\infty)$$
$$-V \simeq \tfrac{d}{dt}\left(r \cos(\varphi - \varphi_\infty)\right) \simeq \tfrac{dr}{dt}$$

where b is the "impact parameter" and φ_∞ is the incident directions. We see that they do satisfy the equations of motion at infinity, where $A = B = 1$, and that the constants of motion are

$$J = bV^2 \tag{1}$$
$$E = 1 - V^2. \tag{2}$$

(Of course a photon has $V = 1$, and as we have already seen, this gives $E = 0$.) It is often more convenient to express J in terms of the distance r_0 of closest approach to the sun, rather than the impact parameter b. At r_0, $dr/d\varphi$ vanishes, so our earlier equations give

$$J = r_0 \left(\frac{1}{B(r_0)} - 1 + V^2\right)^{1/2}$$

The orbit is then described by

$$\varphi(r) = \varphi_\infty + \int_r^\infty \left\{ \frac{A^{\frac{1}{2}}(r)\,dr}{r^2 \left(\frac{1}{r_0^2}\left[\frac{1}{B(r)-1+V^2}\right]\left[\frac{1}{B(r_0)-1+V^2}\right]^{-1} - \frac{1}{r^2}\right)^{\frac{1}{2}}} \right\}.$$

The total change in φ as r decreases from infinity to its minimum value r_0 and then increases again to infinity is just twice its change from ∞ to r_0, that is, $2|\varphi(r_0) - \varphi'_\infty|$. If the trajectory were a straight line, this would equal just π;

$$\Delta\varphi = 2|\varphi(r_0) - \varphi_\infty| - \pi.$$

If this is positive, then the angle φ changes by more than $180°$, that is, the trajectory is bent *toward* the sun; if $\Delta\varphi$ is negative then the trajectory is bent away from the sun.

Reprinted by permission of John Wiley & Sons, Inc. from Weinberg, *Gravitation and Cosmology* © 1972, John Wiley & Sons, Inc.

Computer Modern math + Monotype Modern

Unbound Orbits: Deflection of Light by the Sun

Consider a particle or photon approaching the sun from very great distances. At infinity the metric is Minkowskian, that is, $A(\infty) = B(\infty) = 1$, and we expect motion on a straight line at constant velocity V

$$b \simeq r \sin(\varphi - \varphi_\infty) \simeq r(\varphi - \varphi_\infty)$$
$$-V \simeq \frac{d}{dt}\left(r \cos(\varphi - \varphi_\infty)\right) \simeq \frac{dr}{dt}$$

where b is the "impact parameter" and φ_∞ is the incident directions. We see that they do satisfy the equations of motion at infinity, where $A = B = 1$, and that the constants of motion are

$$J \;=\; bV^2 \tag{1}$$
$$E \;=\; 1 - V^2. \tag{2}$$

(Of course a photon has $V = 1$, and as we have already seen, this gives $E = 0$.) It is often more convenient to express J in terms of the distance r_0 of closest approach to the sun, rather than the impact parameter b. At r_0, $dr/d\varphi$ vanishes, so our earlier equations give

$$J = r_0 \left(\frac{1}{B(r_0)} - 1 + V^2\right)^{1/2}$$

The orbit is then described by

$$\varphi(r) = \varphi_\infty + \int_r^\infty \left\{ \frac{A^{\frac{1}{2}}(r)\,dr}{r^2 \left(\frac{1}{r_0^2}\left[\frac{1}{B(r)-1+V^2}\right]\left[\frac{1}{B(r_0)-1+V^2}\right]^{-1} - \frac{1}{r^2}\right)^{\frac{1}{2}}} \right\}.$$

The total change in φ as r decreases from infinity to its minimum value r_0 and then increases again to infinity is just twice its change from ∞ to r_0, that is, $2|\varphi(r_0) - \varphi'_\infty|$. If the trajectory were a straight line, this would equal just π;

$$\Delta\varphi = 2|\varphi(r_0) - \varphi_\infty| - \pi.$$

If this is positive, then the angle φ changes by more than $180°$, that is, the trajectory is bent *toward* the sun; if $\Delta\varphi$ is negative then the trajectory is bent away from the sun.

Unbound Orbits: Deflection of Light by the Sun

Consider a particle or photon approaching the sun from very great distances. At infinity the metric is Minkowskian, that is, $A(\infty) = B(\infty) = 1$, and we expect motion on a straight line at constant velocity V

$$b \simeq r\sin(\varphi - \varphi_\infty) \simeq r(\varphi - \varphi_\infty)$$
$$-V \simeq \tfrac{d}{dt}\left(r\cos(\varphi - \varphi_\infty)\right) \simeq \tfrac{dr}{dt}$$

where b is the "impact parameter" and φ_∞ is the incident directions. We see that they do satisfy the equations of motion at infinity, where $A = B = 1$, and that the constants of motion are

$$J = bV^2 \tag{1}$$
$$E = 1 - V^2. \tag{2}$$

(Of course a photon has $V = 1$, and as we have already seen, this gives $E = 0$.) It is often more convenient to express J in terms of the distance r_0 of closest approach to the sun, rather than the impact parameter b. At r_0, $dr/d\varphi$ vanishes, so our earlier equations give

$$J = r_0 \left(\frac{1}{B(r_0)} - 1 + V^2\right)^{1/2}$$

The orbit is then described by

$$\varphi(r) = \varphi_\infty + \int_r^\infty \left\{ \frac{A^{\frac{1}{2}}(r)\,dr}{r^2 \left(\frac{1}{r_0^2}\left[\frac{1}{B(r)-1+V^2}\right]\left[\frac{1}{B(r_0)-1+V^2}\right]^{-1} - \frac{1}{r^2}\right)^{\frac{1}{2}}} \right\}.$$

The total change in φ as r decreases from infinity to its minimum value r_0 and then increases again to infinity is just twice its change from ∞ to r_0, that is, $2|\varphi(r_0) - \varphi'_\infty|$. If the trajectory were a straight line, this would equal just π;

$$\Delta\varphi = 2|\varphi(r_0) - \varphi_\infty| - \pi.$$

If this is positive, then the angle φ changes by more than 180°, that is, the trajectory is bent *toward* the sun; if $\Delta\varphi$ is negative then the trajectory is bent away from the sun.

MathTime + Palatino (Adobe)

Unbound Orbits: Deflection of Light by the Sun

Consider a particle or photon approaching the sun from very great distances. At infinity the metric is Minkowskian, that is, $A(\infty) = B(\infty) = 1$, and we expect motion on a straight line at constant velocity V

$$b \simeq r\sin(\varphi - \varphi_\infty) \simeq r(\varphi - \varphi_\infty)$$
$$-V \simeq \frac{d}{dt}(r\cos(\varphi - \varphi_\infty)) \simeq \frac{dr}{dt}$$

where b is the "impact parameter" and φ_∞ is the incident directions. We see that they do satisfy the equations of motion at infinity, where $A = B = 1$, and that the constants of motion are

$$J = bV^2 \tag{1}$$
$$E = 1 - V^2. \tag{2}$$

(Of course a photon has $V = 1$, and as we have already seen, this gives $E = 0$.) It is often more convenient to express J in terms of the distance r_0 of closest approach to the sun, rather than the impact parameter b. At r_0, $dr/d\varphi$ vanishes, so our earlier equations give

$$J = r_0\left(\frac{1}{B(r_0)} - 1 + V^2\right)^{1/2}$$

The orbit is then described by

$$\varphi(r) = \varphi_\infty + \int_r^\infty \left\{ \frac{A^{\frac{1}{2}}(r)\,dr}{r^2\left(\frac{1}{r_0^2}\left[\frac{1}{B(r)-1+V^2}\right]\left[\frac{1}{B(r_0)-1+V^2}\right]^{-1} - \frac{1}{r^2}\right)^{\frac{1}{2}}} \right\}.$$

The total change in φ as r decreases from infinity to its minimum value r_0 and then increases again to infinity is just twice its change from ∞ to r_0, that is, $2|\varphi(r_0) - \varphi'_\infty|$. If the trajectory were a straight line, this would equal just π;

$$\Delta\varphi = 2|\varphi(r_0) - \varphi_\infty| - \pi.$$

If this is positive, then the angle φ changes by more than 180°, that is, the trajectory is bent *toward* the sun; if $\Delta\varphi$ is negative then the trajectory is bent away from the sun.

MathTime + Baskerville (Monotype)

Unbound Orbits: Deflection of Light by the Sun

Consider a particle or photon approaching the sun from very great distances. At infinity the metric is Minkowskian, that is, $A(\infty) = B(\infty) = 1$, and we expect motion on a straight line at constant velocity V

$$b \simeq r\sin(\varphi - \varphi_\infty) \simeq r(\varphi - \varphi_\infty)$$
$$-V \simeq \frac{d}{dt}\left(r\cos(\varphi - \varphi_\infty)\right) \simeq \frac{dr}{dt}$$

where b is the "impact parameter" and φ_∞ is the incident directions. We see that they do satisfy the equations of motion at infinity, where $A = B = 1$, and that the constants of motion are

$$\mathcal{J} \;=\; bV^2 \tag{1}$$
$$E \;=\; 1 - V^2. \tag{2}$$

(Of course a photon has $V = 1$, and as we have already seen, this gives $E = 0$.) It is often more convenient to express $\mathcal{J}$ in terms of the distance r_0 of closest approach to the sun, rather than the impact parameter b. At r_0, $dr/d\varphi$ vanishes, so our earlier equations give

$$\mathcal{J} = r_0 \left(\frac{1}{B(r_0)} - 1 + V^2\right)^{1/2}$$

The orbit is then described by

$$\varphi(r) = \varphi_\infty + \int_r^\infty \left\{ \frac{A^{\frac{1}{2}}(r)\,dr}{r^2 \left(\frac{1}{r_0^2}\left[\frac{1}{B(r)-1+V^2}\right]\left[\frac{1}{B(r_0)-1+V^2}\right]^{-1} - \frac{1}{r^2}\right)^{\frac{1}{2}}} \right\}.$$

The total change in φ as r decreases from infinity to its minimum value r_0 and then increases again to infinity is just twice its change from ∞ to r_0, that is, $2|\varphi(r_0)-\varphi'_\infty|$. If the trajectory were a straight line, this would equal just π;

$$\Delta\varphi = 2|\varphi(r_0) - \varphi_\infty| - \pi.$$

If this is positive, then the angle φ changes by more than 180°, that is, the trajectory is bent *toward* the sun; if $\Delta\varphi$ is negative then the trajectory is bent away from the sun.

MathTime + Bernhard Modern (Bitstream)

Unbound Orbits: Deflection of Light by the Sun

Consider a particle or photon approaching the sun from very great distances. At infinity the metric is Minkowskian, that is, $A(\infty) = B(\infty) = 1$, and we expect motion on a straight line at constant velocity V

$$b \simeq r \sin(\varphi - \varphi_\infty) \simeq r(\varphi - \varphi_\infty)$$
$$-V \simeq \frac{d}{dt}(r\cos(\varphi - \varphi_\infty)) \simeq \frac{dr}{dt}$$

where b is the "impact parameter" and φ_∞ is the incident directions. We see that they do satisfy the equations of motion at infinity, where $A = B = 1$, and that the constants of motion are

$$J = bV^2 \tag{1}$$
$$E = 1 - V^2. \tag{2}$$

(Of course a photon has $V = 1$, and as we have already seen, this gives $E = 0$.) It is often more convenient to express J in terms of the distance r_0 of closest approach to the sun, rather than the impact parameter b. At r_0, $dr/d\varphi$ vanishes, so our earlier equations give

$$J = r_0 \left(\frac{1}{B(r_0)} - 1 + V^2 \right)^{1/2}$$

The orbit is then described by

$$\varphi(r) = \varphi_\infty + \int_r^\infty \left\{ \frac{A^{\frac{1}{2}}(r)\,dr}{r^2 \left(\frac{1}{r_0^2}\left[\frac{1}{B(r)-1+V^2}\right]\left[\frac{1}{B(r_0)-1+V^2}\right]^{-1} - \frac{1}{r^2} \right)^{\frac{1}{2}}} \right\}.$$

The total change in φ as r decreases from infinity to its minimum value r_0 and then increases again to infinity is just twice its change from ∞ to r_0, that is, $2|\varphi(r_0) - \varphi_\infty'|$. If the trajectory were a straight line, this would equal just π;

$$\Delta\varphi = 2|\varphi(r_0) - \varphi_\infty| - \pi.$$

If this is positive, then the angle φ changes by more than $180°$, that is, the trajectory is bent *toward* the sun; if $\Delta\varphi$ is negative then the trajectory is bent away from the sun.

MathTime + Bulmer (Monotype)

Unbound Orbits: Deflection of Light by the Sun

Consider a particle or photon approaching the sun from very great distances. At infinity the metric is Minkowskian, that is, $A(\infty) = B(\infty) = 1$, and we expect motion on a straight line at constant velocity V

$$b \simeq r \sin(\varphi - \varphi_\infty) \simeq r(\varphi - \varphi_\infty)$$
$$-V \simeq \tfrac{d}{dt}\left(r \cos(\varphi - \varphi_\infty)\right) \simeq \tfrac{dr}{dt}$$

where b is the "impact parameter" and φ_∞ is the incident directions. We see that they do satisfy the equations of motion at infinity, where $A = B = 1$, and that the constants of motion are

$$\mathcal{J} = bV^2 \tag{1}$$
$$E = 1 - V^2. \tag{2}$$

(Of course a photon has $V = 1$, and as we have already seen, this gives $E = 0$.) It is often more convenient to express $\mathcal{J}$ in terms of the distance r_0 of closest approach to the sun, rather than the impact parameter b. At r_0, $dr/d\varphi$ vanishes, so our earlier equations give

$$\mathcal{J} = r_0 \left(\frac{1}{B(r_0)} - 1 + V^2\right)^{1/2}$$

The orbit is then described by

$$\varphi(r) = \varphi_\infty + \int_r^\infty \left\{\frac{A^{\frac{1}{2}}(r)\,dr}{r^2\left(\frac{1}{r_0^2}\left[\frac{1}{B(r)-1+V^2}\right]\left[\frac{1}{B(r_0)-1+V^2}\right]^{-1} - \frac{1}{r^2}\right)^{\frac{1}{2}}}\right\}.$$

The total change in φ as r decreases from infinity to its minimum value r_0 and then increases again to infinity is just twice its change from ∞ to r_0, that is, $2|\varphi(r_0) - \varphi'_\infty|$. If the trajectory were a straight line, this would equal just π;

$$\Delta\varphi = 2|\varphi(r_0) - \varphi_\infty| - \pi.$$

If this is positive, then the angle φ changes by more than $180°$, that is, the trajectory is bent *toward* the sun; if $\Delta\varphi$ is negative then the trajectory is bent away from the sun.

Unbound Orbits: Deflection of Light by the Sun

Consider a particle or photon approaching the sun from very great distances. At infinity the metric is Minkowskian, that is, $A(\infty) = B(\infty) = 1$, and we expect motion on a straight line at constant velocity V

$$b \simeq r \sin(\varphi - \varphi_\infty) \simeq r(\varphi - \varphi_\infty)$$
$$-V \simeq \tfrac{d}{dt}(r\cos(\varphi - \varphi_\infty)) \simeq \tfrac{dr}{dt}$$

where b is the "impact parameter" and φ_∞ is the incident directions. We see that they do satisfy the equations of motion at infinity, where $A = B = 1$, and that the constants of motion are

$$J = bV^2 \tag{1}$$
$$E = 1 - V^2. \tag{2}$$

(Of course a photon has $V = 1$, and as we have already seen, this gives $E = 0$.) It is often more convenient to express J in terms of the distance r_0 of closest approach to the sun, rather than the impact parameter b. At r_0, $dr/d\varphi$ vanishes, so our earlier equations give

$$J = r_0 \left(\frac{1}{B(r_0)} - 1 + V^2 \right)^{1/2}$$

The orbit is then described by

$$\varphi(r) = \varphi_\infty + \int_r^\infty \left\{ \frac{A^{\frac{1}{2}}(r)\,dr}{r^2\left(\frac{1}{r_0^2}\left[\frac{1}{B(r)-1+V^2}\right]\left[\frac{1}{B(r_0)-1+V^2}\right]^{-1} - \frac{1}{r^2} \right)^{\frac{1}{2}}} \right\}.$$

The total change in φ as r decreases from infinity to its minimum value r_0 and then increases again to infinity is just twice its change from ∞ to r_0, that is, $2|\varphi(r_0) - \varphi_\infty'|$. If the trajectory were a straight line, this would equal just π;

$$\Delta\varphi = 2|\varphi(r_0) - \varphi_\infty| - \pi.$$

If this is positive, then the angle φ changes by more than 180°, that is, the trajectory is bent *toward* the sun; if $\Delta\varphi$ is negative then the trajectory is bent away from the sun.

Unbound Orbits: Deflection of Light by the Sun

Consider a particle or photon approaching the sun from very great distances. At infinity the metric is Minkowskian, that is, $A(\infty) = B(\infty) = 1$, and we expect motion on a straight line at constant velocity V

$$b \simeq r\sin(\varphi - \varphi_\infty) \simeq r(\varphi - \varphi_\infty)$$
$$-V \simeq \frac{d}{dt}\left(r\cos(\varphi - \varphi_\infty)\right) \simeq \frac{dr}{dt}$$

where b is the "impact parameter" and φ_∞ is the incident directions. We see that they do satisfy the equations of motion at infinity, where $A = B = 1$, and that the constants of motion are

$$J = bV^2 \tag{1}$$
$$E = 1 - V^2. \tag{2}$$

(Of course a photon has $V = 1$, and as we have already seen, this gives $E = 0$.) It is often more convenient to express J in terms of the distance r_0 of closest approach to the sun, rather than the impact parameter b. At r_0, $dr/d\varphi$ vanishes, so our earlier equations give

$$J = r_0 \left(\frac{1}{B(r_0)} - 1 + V^2\right)^{1/2}$$

The orbit is then described by

$$\varphi(r) = \varphi_\infty + \int_r^\infty \left\{ \frac{A^{\frac{1}{2}}(r)\,dr}{r^2\left(\frac{1}{r_0^2}\left[\frac{1}{B(r)-1+V^2}\right]\left[\frac{1}{B(r_0)-1+V^2}\right]^{-1} - \frac{1}{r^2}\right)^{\frac{1}{2}}} \right\}.$$

The total change in φ as r decreases from infinity to its minimum value r_0 and then increases again to infinity is just twice its change from ∞ to r_0, that is, $2|\varphi(r_0) - \varphi'_\infty|$. If the trajectory were a straight line, this would equal just π;

$$\Delta\varphi = 2|\varphi(r_0) - \varphi_\infty| - \pi.$$

If this is positive, then the angle φ changes by more than 180°, that is, the trajectory is bent *toward* the sun; if $\Delta\varphi$ is negative then the trajectory is bent away from the sun.

MathTime + Galliard (Carter & Cone)

Unbound Orbits: Deflection of Light by the Sun

Consider a particle or photon approaching the sun from very great distances. At infinity the metric is Minkowskian, that is, $A(\infty) = B(\infty) = 1$, and we expect motion on a straight line at constant velocity V

$$b \simeq r\sin(\varphi - \varphi_\infty) \simeq r(\varphi - \varphi_\infty)$$
$$-V \simeq \frac{d}{dt}(r\cos(\varphi - \varphi_\infty)) \simeq \frac{dr}{dt}$$

where b is the "impact parameter" and φ_∞ is the incident directions. We see that they do satisfy the equations of motion at infinity, where $A = B = 1$, and that the constants of motion are

$$J = bV^2 \tag{1}$$
$$E = 1 - V^2. \tag{2}$$

(Of course a photon has $V = 1$, and as we have already seen, this gives $E = 0$.) It is often more convenient to express J in terms of the distance r_0 of closest approach to the sun, rather than the impact parameter b. At r_0, $dr/d\varphi$ vanishes, so our earlier equations give

$$J = r_0 \left(\frac{1}{B(r_0)} - 1 + V^2\right)^{1/2}$$

The orbit is then described by

$$\varphi(r) = \varphi_\infty + \int_r^\infty \left\{ \frac{A^{\frac{1}{2}}(r)\,dr}{r^2 \left(\frac{1}{r_0^2}\left[\frac{1}{B(r)-1+V^2}\right]\left[\frac{1}{B(r_0)-1+V^2}\right]^{-1} - \frac{1}{r^2}\right)^{\frac{1}{2}}} \right\}.$$

The total change in φ as r decreases from infinity to its minimum value r_0 and then increases again to infinity is just twice its change from ∞ to r_0, that is, $2|\varphi(r_0) - \varphi_\infty'|$. If the trajectory were a straight line, this would equal just π;

$$\Delta\varphi = 2|\varphi(r_0) - \varphi_\infty| - \pi.$$

If this is positive, then the angle φ changes by more than 180°, that is, the trajectory is bent *toward* the sun; if $\Delta\varphi$ is negative then the trajectory is bent away from the sun.

> MathTime + Adobe Garamond

Unbound Orbits: Deflection of Light by the Sun

Consider a particle or photon approaching the sun from very great distances. At infinity the metric is Minkowskian, that is, $A(\infty) = B(\infty) = 1$, and we expect motion on a straight line at constant velocity V

$$b \simeq r\sin(\varphi - \varphi_\infty) \simeq r(\varphi - \varphi_\infty)$$
$$-V \simeq \frac{d}{dt}\left(r\cos(\varphi - \varphi_\infty)\right) \simeq \frac{dr}{dt}$$

where b is the "impact parameter" and φ_∞ is the incident directions. We see that they do satisfy the equations of motion at infinity, where $A = B = 1$, and that the constants of motion are

$$J = bV^2 \tag{1}$$
$$E = 1 - V^2. \tag{2}$$

(Of course a photon has $V = 1$, and as we have already seen, this gives $E = 0$.) It is often more convenient to express J in terms of the distance r_0 of closest approach to the sun, rather than the impact parameter b. At r_0, $dr/d\varphi$ vanishes, so our earlier equations give

$$J = r_0\left(\frac{1}{B(r_0)} - 1 + V^2\right)^{1/2}$$

The orbit is then described by

$$\varphi(r) = \varphi_\infty + \int_r^\infty \left\{ \frac{A^{\frac{1}{2}}(r)\,dr}{r^2\left(\frac{1}{r_0^2}\left[\frac{1}{B(r)-1+V^2}\right]\left[\frac{1}{B(r_0)-1+V^2}\right]^{-1} - \frac{1}{r^2}\right)^{\frac{1}{2}}} \right\}.$$

The total change in φ as r decreases from infinity to its minimum value r_0 and then increases again to infinity is just twice its change from ∞ to r_0, that is, $2|\varphi(r_0) - \varphi'_\infty|$. If the trajectory were a straight line, this would equal just π;

$$\Delta\varphi = 2|\varphi(r_0) - \varphi_\infty| - \pi.$$

If this is positive, then the angle φ changes by more than $180°$, that is, the trajectory is bent *toward* the sun; if $\Delta\varphi$ is negative then the trajectory is bent away from the sun.

MathTime + Janson (Monotype)

Unbound Orbits: Deflection of Light by the Sun

Consider a particle or photon approaching the sun from very great distances. At infinity the metric is Minkowskian, that is, $A(\infty) = B(\infty) = 1$, and we expect motion on a straight line at constant velocity V

$$b \simeq r \sin(\varphi - \varphi_\infty) \simeq r(\varphi - \varphi_\infty)$$
$$-V \simeq \frac{d}{dt}\left(r \cos(\varphi - \varphi_\infty)\right) \simeq \frac{dr}{dt}$$

where b is the "impact parameter" and φ_∞ is the incident directions. We see that they do satisfy the equations of motion at infinity, where $A = B = 1$, and that the constants of motion are

$$\mathcal{J} = bV^2 \tag{1}$$
$$E = 1 - V^2. \tag{2}$$

(Of course a photon has $V = 1$, and as we have already seen, this gives $E = 0$.) It is often more convenient to express $\mathcal{J}$ in terms of the distance r_0 of closest approach to the sun, rather than the impact parameter b. At r_0, $dr/d\varphi$ vanishes, so our earlier equations give

$$\mathcal{J} = r_0 \left(\frac{1}{B(r_0)} - 1 + V^2\right)^{1/2}$$

The orbit is then described by

$$\varphi(r) = \varphi_\infty + \int_r^\infty \left\{ \frac{A^{\frac{1}{2}}(r)\,dr}{r^2 \left(\frac{1}{r_0^2}\left[\frac{1}{B(r)-1+V^2}\right]\left[\frac{1}{B(r_0)-1+V^2}\right]^{-1} - \frac{1}{r^2}\right)^{\frac{1}{2}}} \right\}.$$

The total change in φ as r decreases from infinity to its minimum value r_0 and then increases again to infinity is just twice its change from ∞ to r_0, that is, $2|\varphi(r_0) - \varphi_\infty'|$. If the trajectory were a straight line, this would equal just π;

$$\Delta\varphi = 2|\varphi(r_0) - \varphi_\infty| - \pi.$$

If this is positive, then the angle φ changes by more than $180°$, that is, the trajectory is bent *toward* the sun; if $\Delta\varphi$ is negative then the trajectory is bent away from the sun.

> Euler + Times New Roman (Monotype)

Unbound Orbits: Deflection of Light by the Sun

Consider a particle or photon approaching the sun from very great distances. At infinity the metric is Minkowskian, that is, $A(\infty) = B(\infty) = 1$, and we expect motion on a straight line at constant velocity V

$$b \simeq r \sin(\varphi - \varphi_\infty) \simeq r(\varphi - \varphi_\infty)$$
$$-V \simeq \tfrac{d}{dt}(r\cos(\varphi - \varphi_\infty)) \simeq \tfrac{dr}{dt}$$

where b is the "impact parameter" and φ_∞ is the incident directions. We see that they do satisfy the equations of motion at infinity, where $A = B = 1$, and that the constants of motion are

$$J = bV^2 \tag{1}$$
$$E = 1 - V^2. \tag{2}$$

(Of course a photon has $V = 1$, and as we have already seen, this gives $E = 0$.) It is often more convenient to express J in terms of the distance r_0 of closest approach to the sun, rather than the impact parameter b. At r_0, $dr/d\varphi$ vanishes, so our earlier equations give

$$J = r_0 \left(\frac{1}{B(r_0)} - 1 + V^2 \right)^{1/2}$$

The orbit is then described by

$$\varphi(r) = \varphi_\infty + \int_r^\infty \left\{ \frac{A^{\frac{1}{2}}(r)\, dr}{r^2 \left(\frac{1}{r_0^2} \left[\frac{1}{B(r)-1+V^2} \right] \left[\frac{1}{B(r_0)-1+V^2} \right]^{-1} - \frac{1}{r^2} \right)^{\frac{1}{2}}} \right\}.$$

The total change in φ as r decreases from infinity to its minimum value r_0 and then increases again to infinity is just twice its change from ∞ to r_0, that is, $2|\varphi(r_0) - \varphi'_\infty|$. If the trajectory were a straight line, this would equal just π;

$$\Delta\varphi = 2|\varphi(r_0) - \varphi_\infty| - \pi.$$

If this is positive, then the angle φ changes by more than $180°$, that is, the trajectory is bent *toward* the sun; if $\Delta\varphi$ is negative then the trajectory is bent away from the sun.

Euler + Palatino (Adobe)

Unbound Orbits: Deflection of Light by the Sun

Consider a particle or photon approaching the sun from very great distances. At infinity the metric is Minkowskian, that is, $A(\infty) = B(\infty) = 1$, and we expect motion on a straight line at constant velocity V

$$b \simeq r\sin(\varphi - \varphi_\infty) \simeq r(\varphi - \varphi_\infty)$$
$$-V \simeq \frac{d}{dt}(r\cos(\varphi - \varphi_\infty)) \simeq \frac{dr}{dt}$$

where b is the "impact parameter" and φ_∞ is the incident directions. We see that they do satisfy the equations of motion at infinity, where $A = B = 1$, and that the constants of motion are

$$J = bV^2 \tag{1}$$
$$E = 1 - V^2. \tag{2}$$

(Of course a photon has $V = 1$, and as we have already seen, this gives $E = 0$.) It is often more convenient to express J in terms of the distance r_0 of closest approach to the sun, rather than the impact parameter b. At r_0, $dr/d\varphi$ vanishes, so our earlier equations give

$$J = r_0 \left(\frac{1}{B(r_0)} - 1 + V^2 \right)^{1/2}$$

The orbit is then described by

$$\varphi(r) = \varphi_\infty + \int_r^\infty \left\{ \frac{A^{\frac{1}{2}}(r)\,dr}{r^2 \left(\frac{1}{r_0^2} \left[\frac{1}{B(r)-1+V^2} \right] \left[\frac{1}{B(r_0)-1+V^2} \right]^{-1} - \frac{1}{r^2} \right)^{\frac{1}{2}}} \right\}.$$

The total change in φ as r decreases from infinity to its minimum value r_0 and then increases again to infinity is just twice its change from ∞ to r_0, that is, $2|\varphi(r_0) - \varphi'_\infty|$. If the trajectory were a straight line, this would equal just π;

$$\Delta\varphi = 2|\varphi(r_0) - \varphi_\infty| - \pi.$$

If this is positive, then the angle φ changes by more than $180°$, that is, the trajectory is bent *toward* the sun; if $\Delta\varphi$ is negative then the trajectory is bent away from the sun.

Euler + Galliard (Carter & Cone)

Unbound Orbits: Deflection of Light by the Sun

Consider a particle or photon approaching the sun from very great distances. At infinity the metric is Minkowskian, that is, $A(\infty) = B(\infty) = 1$, and we expect motion on a straight line at constant velocity V

$$b \simeq r\sin(\varphi - \varphi_\infty) \simeq r(\varphi - \varphi_\infty)$$
$$-V \simeq \tfrac{d}{dt}(r\cos(\varphi - \varphi_\infty)) \simeq \tfrac{dr}{dt}$$

where b is the "impact parameter" and φ_∞ is the incident directions. We see that they do satisfy the equations of motion at infinity, where $A = B = 1$, and that the constants of motion are

$$J = bV^2 \tag{1}$$
$$E = 1 - V^2. \tag{2}$$

(Of course a photon has $V = 1$, and as we have already seen, this gives $E = 0$.) It is often more convenient to express J in terms of the distance r_0 of closest approach to the sun, rather than the impact parameter b. At r_0, $dr/d\varphi$ vanishes, so our earlier equations give

$$J = r_0 \left(\frac{1}{B(r_0)} - 1 + V^2 \right)^{1/2}$$

The orbit is then described by

$$\varphi(r) = \varphi_\infty + \int_r^\infty \left\{ \frac{A^{\frac{1}{2}}(r)\,dr}{r^2 \left(\frac{1}{r_0^2} \left[\frac{1}{B(r)-1+V^2} \right] \left[\frac{1}{B(r_0)-1+V^2} \right]^{-1} - \frac{1}{r^2} \right)^{\frac{1}{2}}} \right\}.$$

The total change in φ as r decreases from infinity to its minimum value r_0 and then increases again to infinity is just twice its change from ∞ to r_0, that is, $2|\varphi(r_0) - \varphi'_\infty|$. If the trajectory were a straight line, this would equal just π;

$$\Delta\varphi = 2|\varphi(r_0) - \varphi_\infty| - \pi.$$

If this is positive, then the angle φ changes by more than 180°, that is, the trajectory is bent *toward* the sun; if $\Delta\varphi$ is negative then the trajectory is bent away from the sun.

Euler + Adobe Garamond

Unbound Orbits: Deflection of Light by the Sun

Consider a particle or photon approaching the sun from very great distances. At infinity the metric is Minkowskian, that is, $A(\infty) = B(\infty) = 1$, and we expect motion on a straight line at constant velocity V

$$b \simeq r\sin(\varphi - \varphi_\infty) \simeq r(\varphi - \varphi_\infty)$$
$$-V \simeq \tfrac{d}{dt}(r\cos(\varphi - \varphi_\infty)) \simeq \tfrac{dr}{dt}$$

where b is the "impact parameter" and φ_∞ is the incident directions. We see that they do satisfy the equations of motion at infinity, where $A = B = 1$, and that the constants of motion are

$$J = bV^2 \qquad (1)$$
$$E = 1 - V^2. \qquad (2)$$

(Of course a photon has $V = 1$, and as we have already seen, this gives $E = 0$.) It is often more convenient to express J in terms of the distance r_0 of closest approach to the sun, rather than the impact parameter b. At r_0, $dr/d\varphi$ vanishes, so our earlier equations give

$$J = r_0 \left(\frac{1}{B(r_0)} - 1 + V^2\right)^{1/2}$$

The orbit is then described by

$$\varphi(r) = \varphi_\infty + \int_r^\infty \left\{ \frac{A^{\frac{1}{2}}(r)\,dr}{r^2 \left(\frac{1}{r_0^2}\left[\frac{1}{B(r)-1+V^2}\right]\left[\frac{1}{B(r_0)-1+V^2}\right]^{-1} - \frac{1}{r^2}\right)^{\frac{1}{2}}} \right\}.$$

The total change in φ as r decreases from infinity to its minimum value r_0 and then increases again to infinity is just twice its change from ∞ to r_0, that is, $2|\varphi(r_0) - \varphi'_\infty|$. If the trajectory were a straight line, this would equal just π;

$$\Delta\varphi = 2|\varphi(r_0) - \varphi_\infty| - \pi.$$

If this is positive, then the angle φ changes by more than 180°, that is, the trajectory is bent *toward* the sun; if $\Delta\varphi$ is negative then the trajectory is bent away from the sun.

> Euler + Gill Sans (Monotype)

Unbound Orbits: Deflection of Light by the Sun

Consider a particle or photon approaching the sun from very great distances. At infinity the metric is Minkowskian, that is, $A(\infty) = B(\infty) = 1$, and we expect motion on a straight line at constant velocity V

$$b \simeq r \sin(\varphi - \varphi_\infty) \simeq r(\varphi - \varphi_\infty)$$
$$-V \simeq \frac{d}{dt}(r \cos(\varphi - \varphi_\infty)) \simeq \frac{dr}{dt}$$

where b is the "impact parameter" and φ_∞ is the incident directions. We see that they do satisfy the equations of motion at infinity, where $A = B = 1$, and that the constants of motion are

$$J = bV^2 \tag{1}$$
$$E = 1 - V^2. \tag{2}$$

(Of course a photon has $V = 1$, and as we have already seen, this gives $E = 0$.) It is often more convenient to express J in terms of the distance r_0 of closest approach to the sun, rather than the impact parameter b. At r_0, $dr/d\varphi$ vanishes, so our earlier equations give

$$J = r_0 \left(\frac{1}{B(r_0)} - 1 + V^2 \right)^{1/2}$$

The orbit is then described by

$$\varphi(r) = \varphi_\infty + \int_r^\infty \left\{ \frac{A^{\frac{1}{2}}(r)\, dr}{r^2 \left(\frac{1}{r_0^2} \left[\frac{1}{B(r)-1+V^2} \right] \left[\frac{1}{B(r_0)-1+V^2} \right]^{-1} - \frac{1}{r^2} \right)^{\frac{1}{2}}} \right\}.$$

The total change in φ as r decreases from infinity to its minimum value r_0 and then increases again to infinity is just twice its change from ∞ to r_0, that is, $2|\varphi(r_0) - \varphi'_\infty|$. If the trajectory were a straight line, this would equal just π;

$$\Delta\varphi = 2|\varphi(r_0) - \varphi_\infty| - \pi.$$

If this is positive, then the angle φ changes by more than $180°$, that is, the trajectory is bent *toward* the sun; if $\Delta\varphi$ is negative then the trajectory is bent away from the sun.

Lucida New Math + Times New Roman (Monotype)

Unbound Orbits: Deflection of Light by the Sun

Consider a particle or photon approaching the sun from very great distances. At infinity the metric is Minkowskian, that is, $A(\infty) = B(\infty) = 1$, and we expect motion on a straight line at constant velocity V

$$b \simeq r \sin(\varphi - \varphi_\infty) \simeq r(\varphi - \varphi_\infty)$$

$$-V \simeq \frac{d}{dt}\left(r \cos(\varphi - \varphi_\infty)\right) \simeq \frac{dr}{dt}$$

where b is the "impact parameter" and φ_∞ is the incident directions. We see that they do satisfy the equations of motion at infinity, where $A = B = 1$, and that the constants of motion are

$$J = bV^2 \tag{1}$$

$$E = 1 - V^2. \tag{2}$$

(Of course a photon has $V = 1$, and as we have already seen, this gives $E = 0$.) It is often more convenient to express J in terms of the distance r_0 of closest approach to the sun, rather than the impact parameter b. At r_0, $dr/d\varphi$ vanishes, so our earlier equations give

$$J = r_0 \left(\frac{1}{B(r_0)} - 1 + V^2\right)^{1/2}$$

The orbit is then described by

$$\varphi(r) = \varphi_\infty + \int_r^\infty \left\{\frac{A^{\frac{1}{2}}(r)\,dr}{r^2\left(\frac{1}{r_0^2}\left[\frac{1}{B(r)-1+V^2}\right]\left[\frac{1}{B(r_0)-1+V^2}\right]^{-1} - \frac{1}{r^2}\right)^{\frac{1}{2}}}\right\}.$$

The total change in φ as r decreases from infinity to its minimum value r_0 and then increases again to infinity is just twice its change from ∞ to r_0, that is, $2|\varphi(r_0) - \varphi'_\infty|$. If the trajectory were a straight line, this would equal just π;

$$\Delta\varphi = 2|\varphi(r_0) - \varphi_\infty| - \pi.$$

If this is positive, then the angle φ changes by more than 180°, that is, the trajectory is bent *toward* the sun; if $\Delta\varphi$ is negative then the trajectory is bent away from the sun.

Lucida New Math + Palatino (Adobe)

Unbound Orbits: Deflection of Light by the Sun

Consider a particle or photon approaching the sun from very great distances. At infinity the metric is Minkowskian, that is, $A(\infty) = B(\infty) = 1$, and we expect motion on a straight line at constant velocity V

$$b \simeq r\sin(\varphi - \varphi_\infty) \simeq r(\varphi - \varphi_\infty)$$
$$-V \simeq \frac{d}{dt}(r\cos(\varphi - \varphi_\infty)) \simeq \frac{dr}{dt}$$

where b is the "impact parameter" and φ_∞ is the incident directions. We see that they do satisfy the equations of motion at infinity, where $A = B = 1$, and that the constants of motion are

$$J = bV^2 \tag{1}$$
$$E = 1 - V^2. \tag{2}$$

(Of course a photon has $V = 1$, and as we have already seen, this gives $E = 0$.) It is often more convenient to express J in terms of the distance r_0 of closest approach to the sun, rather than the impact parameter b. At r_0, $dr/d\varphi$ vanishes, so our earlier equations give

$$J = r_0 \left(\frac{1}{B(r_0)} - 1 + V^2\right)^{1/2}$$

The orbit is then described by

$$\varphi(r) = \varphi_\infty + \int_r^\infty \left\{ \frac{A^{\frac{1}{2}}(r)\,dr}{r^2\left(\frac{1}{r_0^2}\left[\frac{1}{B(r)-1+V^2}\right]\left[\frac{1}{B(r_0)-1+V^2}\right]^{-1} - \frac{1}{r^2}\right)^{\frac{1}{2}}} \right\}.$$

The total change in φ as r decreases from infinity to its minimum value r_0 and then increases again to infinity is just twice its change from ∞ to r_0, that is, $2|\varphi(r_0) - \varphi'_\infty|$. If the trajectory were a straight line, this would equal just π;

$$\Delta\varphi = 2|\varphi(r_0) - \varphi_\infty| - \pi.$$

If this is positive, then the angle φ changes by more than $180°$, that is, the trajectory is bent *toward* the sun; if $\Delta\varphi$ is negative then the trajectory is bent away from the sun.

Lucida New Math + Adobe Caslon

Unbound Orbits: Deflection of Light by the Sun

Consider a particle or photon approaching the sun from very great distances. At infinity the metric is Minkowskian, that is, $A(\infty) = B(\infty) = 1$, and we expect motion on a straight line at constant velocity V

$$b \simeq r\sin(\varphi - \varphi_\infty) \simeq r(\varphi - \varphi_\infty)$$
$$-V \simeq \frac{d}{dt}(r\cos(\varphi - \varphi_\infty)) \simeq \frac{dr}{dt}$$

where b is the "impact parameter" and φ_∞ is the incident directions. We see that they do satisfy the equations of motion at infinity, where $A = B = 1$, and that the constants of motion are

$$J = bV^2 \tag{1}$$
$$E = 1 - V^2. \tag{2}$$

(Of course a photon has $V = 1$, and as we have already seen, this gives $E = 0$.) It is often more convenient to express J in terms of the distance r_0 of closest approach to the sun, rather than the impact parameter b. At r_0, $dr/d\varphi$ vanishes, so our earlier equations give

$$J = r_0 \left(\frac{1}{B(r_0)} - 1 + V^2 \right)^{1/2}$$

The orbit is then described by

$$\varphi(r) = \varphi_\infty + \int_r^\infty \left\{ \frac{A^{\frac{1}{2}}(r)\,dr}{r^2 \left(\frac{1}{r_0^2} \left[\frac{1}{B(r)-1+V^2} \right] \left[\frac{1}{B(r_0)-1+V^2} \right]^{-1} - \frac{1}{r^2} \right)^{\frac{1}{2}}} \right\}.$$

The total change in φ as r decreases from infinity to its minimum value r_0 and then increases again to infinity is just twice its change from ∞ to r_0, that is, $2|\varphi(r_0) - \varphi_\infty'|$. If the trajectory were a straight line, this would equal just π;

$$\Delta\varphi = 2|\varphi(r_0) - \varphi_\infty| - \pi.$$

If this is positive, then the angle φ changes by more than 180°, that is, the trajectory is bent *toward* the sun; if $\Delta\varphi$ is negative then the trajectory is bent away from the sun.

Lucida New Math + Lucida Bright (Bigelow & Holmes; 8/10)

Unbound Orbits: Deflection of Light by the Sun

Consider a particle or photon approaching the sun from very great distances. At infinity the metric is Minkowskian, that is, $A(\infty) = B(\infty) = 1$, and we expect motion on a straight line at constant velocity V

$$b \simeq r\sin(\varphi - \varphi_\infty) \simeq r(\varphi - \varphi_\infty)$$
$$-V \simeq \tfrac{d}{dt}(r\cos(\varphi - \varphi_\infty)) \simeq \tfrac{dr}{dt}$$

where b is the "impact parameter" and φ_∞ is the incident directions. We see that they do satisfy the equations of motion at infinity, where $A = B = 1$, and that the constants of motion are

$$J = bV^2 \tag{1}$$
$$E = 1 - V^2. \tag{2}$$

(Of course a photon has $V = 1$, and as we have already seen, this gives $E = 0$.) It is often more convenient to express J in terms of the distance r_0 of closest approach to the sun, rather than the impact parameter b. At r_0, $dr/d\varphi$ vanishes, so our earlier equations give

$$J = r_0 \left(\frac{1}{B(r_0)} - 1 + V^2 \right)^{1/2}$$

The orbit is then described by

$$\varphi(r) = \varphi_\infty + \int_r^\infty \left\{ \frac{A^{\frac{1}{2}}(r)\,dr}{r^2 \left(\frac{1}{r_0^2} \left[\frac{1}{B(r)-1+V^2} \right] \left[\frac{1}{B(r_0)-1+V^2} \right]^{-1} - \frac{1}{r^2} \right)^{\frac{1}{2}}} \right\}.$$

The total change in φ as r decreases from infinity to its minimum value r_0 and then increases again to infinity is just twice its change from ∞ to r_0, that is, $2|\varphi(r_0) - \varphi_\infty'|$. If the trajectory were a straight line, this would equal just π;

$$\Delta\varphi = 2|\varphi(r_0) - \varphi_\infty| - \pi.$$

If this is positive, then the angle φ changes by more than $180°$, that is, the trajectory is bent *toward* the sun; if $\Delta\varphi$ is negative then the trajectory is bent away from the sun.

Lucida New Math + Lucida Sans (Bigelow & Holmes; 8/10)

Unbound Orbits: Deflection of Light by the Sun

Consider a particle or photon approaching the sun from very great distances. At infinity the metric is Minkowskian, that is, $A(\infty) = B(\infty) = 1$, and we expect motion on a straight line at constant velocity V

$$b \simeq r\sin(\varphi - \varphi_\infty) \simeq r(\varphi - \varphi_\infty)$$
$$-V \simeq \frac{d}{dt}(r\cos(\varphi - \varphi_\infty)) \simeq \frac{dr}{dt}$$

where b is the "impact parameter" and φ_∞ is the incident directions. We see that they do satisfy the equations of motion at infinity, where $A = B = 1$, and that the constants of motion are

$$J = bV^2 \qquad (1)$$
$$E = 1 - V^2. \qquad (2)$$

(Of course a photon has $V = 1$, and as we have already seen, this gives $E = 0$.) It is often more convenient to express J in terms of the distance r_0 of closest approach to the sun, rather than the impact parameter b. At r_0, $dr/d\varphi$ vanishes, so our earlier equations give

$$J = r_0 \left(\frac{1}{B(r_0)} - 1 + V^2\right)^{1/2}$$

The orbit is then described by

$$\varphi(r) = \varphi_\infty + \int_r^\infty \left\{ \frac{A^{\frac{1}{2}}(r)\,dr}{r^2 \left(\frac{1}{r_0^2}\left[\frac{1}{B(r)-1+V^2}\right]\left[\frac{1}{B(r_0)-1+V^2}\right]^{-1} - \frac{1}{r^2}\right)^{\frac{1}{2}}} \right\}.$$

The total change in φ as r decreases from infinity to its minimum value r_0 and then increases again to infinity is just twice its change from ∞ to r_0, that is, $2|\varphi(r_0) - \varphi_\infty'|$. If the trajectory were a straight line, this would equal just π;

$$\Delta\varphi = 2|\varphi(r_0) - \varphi_\infty| - \pi.$$

If this is positive, then the angle φ changes by more than $180°$, that is, the trajectory is bent *toward* the sun; if $\Delta\varphi$ is negative then the trajectory is bent away from the sun.

Mathematica + Times New Roman (Monotype)

Unbound Orbits: Deflection of Light by the Sun

Consider a particle or photon approaching the sun from very great distances. At infinity the metric is Minkowskian, that is, $A(\infty) = B(\infty) = 1$, and we expect motion on a straight line at constant velocity V

$$b \cong r\sin(\varphi - \varphi_\infty) \cong r(\varphi - \varphi_\infty)$$
$$-V \cong \tfrac{d}{dt}(r\cos(\varphi - \varphi_\infty)) \cong \tfrac{dr}{dt}$$

where b is the "impact parameter" and φ_∞ is the incident directions. We see that they do satisfy the equations of motion at infinity, where $A = B = 1$, and that the constants of motion are

$$J = bV^2 \tag{1}$$
$$E = 1 - V^2. \tag{2}$$

(Of course a photon has $V = 1$, and as we have already seen, this gives $E = 0$.) It is often more convenient to express J in terms of the distance r_0 of closest approach to the sun, rather than the impact parameter b. At r_0, $dr/d\varphi$ vanishes, so our earlier equations give

$$J = r_0\left(\frac{1}{B(r_0)} - 1 + V^2\right)^{1/2}$$

The orbit is then described by

$$\varphi(r) = \varphi_\infty + \int_r^\infty \left\{ \frac{A^{\frac{1}{2}}(r)\,dr}{r^2\left(\frac{1}{r_0^2}\left[\frac{1}{B(r)-1+V^2}\right]\left[\frac{1}{B(r_0)-1+V^2}\right]^{-1} - \frac{1}{r^2}\right)^{\frac{1}{2}}} \right\}.$$

The total change in φ as r decreases from infinity to its minimum value r_0 and then increases again to infinity is just twice its change from ∞ to r_0, that is, $2|\varphi(r_0) - \varphi'_\infty|$. If the trajectory were a straight line, this would equal just π;

$$\Delta\varphi = 2|\varphi(r_0) - \varphi_\infty| - \pi.$$

If this is positive, then the angle φ changes by more than $180°$, that is, the trajectory is bent *toward* the sun; if $\Delta\varphi$ is negative then the trajectory is bent away from the sun.

Mathematica + Palatino (Adobe)

Unbound Orbits: Deflection of Light by the Sun

Consider a particle or photon approaching the sun from very great distances. At infinity the metric is Minkowskian, that is, $A(\infty) = B(\infty) = 1$, and we expect motion on a straight line at constant velocity V

$$b \cong r\sin(\varphi - \varphi_\infty) \cong r(\varphi - \varphi_\infty)$$
$$-V \cong \frac{d}{dt}(r\cos(\varphi - \varphi_\infty)) \cong \frac{dr}{dt}$$

where b is the "impact parameter" and φ_∞ is the incident directions. We see that they do satisfy the equations of motion at infinity, where $A = B = 1$, and that the constants of motion are

$$J = bV^2 \qquad (1)$$
$$E = 1 - V^2. \qquad (2)$$

(Of course a photon has $V = 1$, and as we have already seen, this gives $E = 0$.) It is often more convenient to express J in terms of the distance r_0 of closest approach to the sun, rather than the impact parameter b. At r_0, $dr/d\varphi$ vanishes, so our earlier equations give

$$J = r_0\left(\frac{1}{B(r_0)} - 1 + V^2\right)^{1/2}$$

The orbit is then described by

$$\varphi(r) = \varphi_\infty + \int_r^\infty \left\{\frac{A^{\frac{1}{2}}(r)\,dr}{r^2\left(\frac{1}{r_0^2}\left[\frac{1}{B(r)-1+V^2}\right]\left[\frac{1}{B(r_0)-1+V^2}\right]^{-1} - \frac{1}{r^2}\right)^{\frac{1}{2}}}\right\}.$$

The total change in φ as r decreases from infinity to its minimum value r_0 and then increases again to infinity is just twice its change from ∞ to r_0, that is, $2|\varphi(r_0) - \varphi_\infty|$. If the trajectory were a straight line, this would equal just π;

$$\Delta\varphi = 2|\varphi(r_0) - \varphi_\infty| - \pi.$$

If this is positive, then the angle φ changes by more than $180°$, that is, the trajectory is bent *toward* the sun; if $\Delta\varphi$ is negative then the trajectory is bent away from the sun.

Mathematica + Adobe Garamond

Unbound Orbits: Deflection of Light by the Sun

Consider a particle or photon approaching the sun from very great distances. At infinity the metric is Minkowskian, that is, $A(\infty) = B(\infty) = 1$, and we expect motion on a straight line at constant velocity V

$$b \cong r\sin(\varphi - \varphi_\infty) \cong r(\varphi - \varphi_\infty)$$
$$-V \cong \frac{d}{dt}\left(r\cos(\varphi - \varphi_\infty)\right) \cong \frac{dr}{dt}$$

where b is the "impact parameter" and φ_∞ is the incident directions. We see that they do satisfy the equations of motion at infinity, where $A = B = 1$, and that the constants of motion are

$$J = bV^2 \tag{1}$$
$$E = 1 - V^2. \tag{2}$$

(Of course a photon has $V = 1$, and as we have already seen, this gives $E = 0$.) It is often more convenient to express J in terms of the distance r_0 of closest approach to the sun, rather than the impact parameter b. At r_0, $dr/d\varphi$ vanishes, so our earlier equations give

$$J = r_0\left(\frac{1}{B(r_0)} - 1 + V^2\right)^{1/2}$$

The orbit is then described by

$$\varphi(r) = \varphi_\infty + \int_r^\infty \left\{ \frac{A^{\frac{1}{2}}(r)\,dr}{r^2\left(\frac{1}{r_0^2}\left[\frac{1}{B(r)-1+V^2}\right]\left[\frac{1}{B(r_0)-1+V^2}\right]^{-1} - \frac{1}{r^2}\right)^{\frac{1}{2}}} \right\}.$$

The total change in φ as r decreases from infinity to its minimum value r_0 and then increases again to infinity is just twice its change from ∞ to r_0, that is, $2|\varphi(r_0) - \varphi_\infty|$. If the trajectory were a straight line, this would equal just π;

$$\Delta\varphi = 2|\varphi(r_0) - \varphi_\infty| - \pi.$$

If this is positive, then the angle φ changes by more than 180°, that is, the trajectory is bent *toward* the sun; if $\Delta\varphi$ is negative then the trajectory is bent away from the sun.

Unbound Orbits: Deflection of Light by the Sun

Consider a particle or photon approaching the sun from very great distances. At infinity the metric is Minkowskian, that is, $A(\infty) = B(\infty) = 1$, and we expect motion on a straight line at constant velocity V

$$b \simeq r \sin(\phi - \phi_\infty) \simeq r(\phi - \phi_\infty)$$
$$-V \simeq \frac{d}{dt}(r\cos(\phi - \phi_\infty)) \simeq \frac{dr}{dt}$$

where b is the "impact parameter" and ϕ_∞ is the incident direction. We see that they do satisfy the equations of motion at infinity, where $A = B = 1$, and that the constants of motion are

$$J = bV^2 \tag{1}$$
$$E = 1 - V^2 \tag{2}$$

(Of course a photon has $V = 1$, and as we have already seen, this gives $E = 0$.) It is often more convenient to express J in terms of the distance r_0 of closest approach to the sun, rather than the impact parameter b. At r_0, $dr/d\phi$ vanishes, so our earlier equations give

$$J = r_0 \left(\frac{1}{B(r_0)} - 1 + V^2 \right)^{1/2}$$

The orbit is then described by

$$\phi(r) = \phi_\infty + \int_r^\infty \left\{ \frac{A^{\frac{1}{2}}(r)\,dr}{r^2 \left(\frac{1}{r_0^2} \left[\frac{1}{B(r)-1+V^2} \right] \left[\frac{1}{B(r)-1+V^2} \right]^{-1} - \frac{1}{r^2} \right)^{\frac{1}{2}}} \right\}.$$

The total change in ϕ as r decreases from infinity to its minimum value r_0 and then increases again to infinity is just twice its change from ∞ to r_0, that is, $2|\phi(r_0) - \phi'_\infty|$. If the trajectory were a straight line, this would equal just π;

$$\Delta\phi = 2|\phi(r_0) - \phi_\infty| - \pi.$$

If this is positive, then the angle ϕ changes by more than 180°, that is, the trajectory is bent *toward* the sun; if $\Delta\phi$ is negative then the trajectory is bent away from the sun.

Unbound Orbits: Deflection of Light by the Sun

Consider a particle or photon approaching the sun from very great distances. At infinity the metric is Minkowskian, that is, $A(\infty) = B(\infty) = 1$, and we expect motion on a straight line at constant velocity V

$$b \simeq r\sin(\phi - \phi_\infty) \simeq r(\phi - \phi_\infty)$$
$$-V \simeq \tfrac{d}{dt}(r\cos(\phi - \phi_\infty)) \simeq \tfrac{dr}{dt}$$

where b is the "impact parameter" and ϕ_∞ is the incident direction. We see that they do satisfy the equations of motion at infinity, where $A = B = 1$, and that the constants of motion are

$$J = bV^2 \tag{1}$$
$$E = 1 - V^2 \tag{2}$$

(Of course a photon has $V = 1$, and as we have already seen, this gives $E = 0$.) It is often more convenient to express J in terms of the distance r_0 of closest approach to the sun, rather than the impact parameter b. At r_0, $dr/d\phi$ vanishes, so our earlier equations give

$$J = r_0 \left(\frac{1}{B(r_0)} - 1 + V^2 \right)^{1/2}$$

The orbit is then described by

$$\phi(r) = \phi_\infty + \int_r^\infty \left\{ \frac{A^{\frac{1}{2}}(r)\,dr}{r^2 \left(\frac{1}{r_0^2} \left[\frac{1}{B(r)-1+V^2} \right] \left[\frac{1}{B(r)-1+V^2} \right]^{-1} - \frac{1}{r^2} \right)^{\frac{1}{2}}} \right\}.$$

The total change in ϕ as r decreases from infinity to its minimum value r_0 and then increases again to infinity is just twice its change from ∞ to r_0, that is, $2|\phi(r_0) - \phi'_\infty|$. If the trajectory were a straight line, this would equal just π;

$$\Delta\phi = 2|\phi(r_0) - \phi_\infty| - \pi.$$

If this is positive, then the angle ϕ changes by more than $180°$, that is, the trajectory is bent *toward* the sun; if $\Delta\phi$ is negative then the trajectory is bent away from the sun.

Unbound Orbits: Deflection of Light by the Sun

Consider a particle or photon approaching the sun from very great distances. At infinity the metric is Minkowskian, that is, $A(\infty) = B(\infty) = 1$, and we expect motion on a straight line at constant velocity V

$$b \simeq r\sin(\phi - \phi_\infty) \simeq r(\phi - \phi_\infty)$$
$$-V \simeq \tfrac{d}{dt}(r\cos(\phi - \phi_\infty)) \simeq \tfrac{dr}{dt}$$

where b is the "impact parameter" and ϕ_∞ is the incident direction. We see that they do satisfy the equations of motion at infinity, where $A = B = 1$, and that the constants of motion are

$$J \;=\; bV^2 \tag{1}$$
$$E \;=\; 1 - V^2 \tag{2}$$

(Of course a photon has $V = 1$, and as we have already seen, this gives $E = 0$.) It is often more convenient to express J in terms of the distance r_0 of closest approach to the sun, rather than the impact parameter b. At r_0, $dr/d\phi$ vanishes, so our earlier equations give

$$J = r_0 \left(\frac{1}{B(r_0)} - 1 + V^2 \right)^{1/2}$$

The orbit is then described by

$$\phi(r) = \phi_\infty + \int_r^\infty \left\{ \frac{A^{\frac{1}{2}}(r)\,dr}{r^2 \left(\frac{1}{r_0^2} \left[\frac{1}{B(r)-1+V^2} \right] \left[\frac{1}{B(r)-1+V^2} \right]^{-1} - \frac{1}{r^2} \right)^{\frac{1}{2}}} \right\}.$$

The total change in ϕ as r decreases from infinity to its minimum value r_0 and then increases again to infinity is just twice its change from ∞ to r_0, that is, $2|\phi(r_0) - \phi'_\infty|$. If the trajectory were a straight line, this would equal just π;

$$\Delta\phi = 2|\phi(r_0) - \phi_\infty| - \pi.$$

If this is positive, then the angle ϕ changes by more than 180°, that is, the trajectory is bent toward the sun; if $\Delta\phi$ is negative then the trajectory is bent away from the sun.

MathKit 'Baskerville' + Baskerville (Monotype)

Unbound Orbits: Deflection of Light by the Sun

Consider a particle or photon approaching the sun from very great distances. At infinity the metric is Minkowskian, that is, $A(\infty) = B(\infty) = 1$, and we expect motion on a straight line at constant velocity V

$$b \simeq r\sin(\phi - \phi_\infty) \simeq r(\phi - \phi_\infty)$$
$$-V \simeq \tfrac{d}{dt}(r\cos(\phi - \phi_\infty)) \simeq \tfrac{dr}{dt}$$

where b is the "impact parameter" and ϕ_∞ is the incident direction. We see that they do satisfy the equations of motion at infinity, where $A = B = 1$, and that the constants of motion are

$$\mathcal{J} \;\; = \;\; bV^2 \tag{1}$$
$$E \;\; = \;\; 1 - V^2 \tag{2}$$

(Of course a photon has $V = 1$, and as we have already seen, this gives $E = 0$.) It is often more convenient to express $\mathcal{J}$ in terms of the distance r_0 of closest approach to the sun, rather than the impact parameter b. At r_0, $dr/d\phi$ vanishes, so our earlier equations give

$$\mathcal{J} = r_0 \left(\frac{1}{B(r_0)} - 1 + V^2 \right)^{1/2}$$

The orbit is then described by

$$\phi(r) = \phi_\infty + \int_r^\infty \left\{ \frac{A^{\frac{1}{2}}(r)\,dr}{r^2 \left(\frac{1}{r_0^2} \left[\frac{1}{B(r)-1+V^2} \right] \left[\frac{1}{B(r)-1+V^2} \right]^{-1} - \frac{1}{r^2} \right)^{\frac{1}{2}}} \right\}.$$

The total change in ϕ as r decreases from infinity to its minimum value r_0 and then increases again to infinity is just twice its change from ∞ to r_0, that is, $2|\phi(r_0) - \phi'_\infty|$. If the trajectory were a straight line, this would equal just π;

$$\Delta\phi = 2|\phi(r_0) - \phi_\infty| - \pi.$$

If this is positive, then the angle ϕ changes by more than $180°$, that is, the trajectory is bent *toward* the sun; if $\Delta\phi$ is negative then the trajectory is bent away from the sun.

CHAPTER II

. . . .

GRAPHIC DISCUSSIONS

The urge to draw is a powerful one, as a glance at a New York City subway or at the walls of a public bathroom amply attests. It was clear early on that TEX gave precise control over the placement and formatting of text on a page, and it did not take long for authors to clamor for the ability to do the same with images. In the formative years of TEX, the situation regarding graphics was limited, but now there are so many ancillary utilities and sophisticated drivers that we can be optimistic at preparing and including graphic images that match the style and appearance of the paper.

Interest in the general subject "TEX + graphics" continues unabated. No matter how comprehensive an overview is, it is sure to be out of date almost immediately. Interested readers must consult proceedings of TEX meetings and journals of the various TEX user groups (*TUGboat, Cahiers Gutenberg, TEXnische Komödie, GUST*, and so on) to stay current with what's being done and should also plan to prowl through the graphics subdirectory on CTAN and other archives. The book by Sowa (1994), charmingly designed, is another important reference, but is currently only available in German. Walsh (1994) lists many graphic techniques applicable to LATEX and TEX (with brief descriptions), but there is a Unix bias to his discussion. Goossens, Rahtz, and Mittelbach (1997) is an important recent resource because of (or despite?) its predilection towards LATEX.

Our goal in this and the next few chapters is straightforward. We seek answers to two questions:

- How can we prepare graphic images both with and without the aid of TEX tools, and

- how do we include these images in a LATEX or TEX document?

As we'll see, several satisfactory answers to these questions exist. One caveat: we'll largely restrict ourself to techniques that work across all platforms and will tend to ignore platform-specific programs and utilities that, while great for MS-DOS users (say), are irrelevant to Macintosh or Unix folks.

11.1   General graphics

There are two ways to generate graphics:

- without TEX, or

- with TEX

where by "TEX" we mean TEX, LATEX, or any of its friends like METAFONT, MetaPost, or other packages and programs. Each approach has advantages and disadvantages.

11.1.1   *Without TEX*

Without using TEX, you will need to rely on some external program. Since many of these come with convenient interfaces and extensive capabilities, this sounds like an attractive alternative.

On the other hand, how do we place these externally produced graphics into a document? Many people know that the \special command has been provided as a hook for things like a non-TEX graphic file, but \special is not so much a hook as a handle, and it's up to the device driver or previewer to turn the handle and open the document for the graphic inclusion. The device driver may not be able to include the graphic file.

There may be other disadvantages to this approach. Externally produced graphics may not be previewable even if printable since most previewers usually work only with packed pixel fonts. These graphics will not be automatically revised with the document since they are outside the document. Often, TEX authors want their drawings to show precise, mathematical relationships, and such precision may be all but impossible for external programs.

External figures containing text pose a larger problem—the text in the figure may not match the typeface of the document! The printed article will look funny.

Finally, and most damning, documents with graphic inclusions may no longer be portable. Graphics are often dependent on a particular resolution. If the resolution of a draft printer doesn't match that of (say) a phototypesetter, it will be necessary to regenerate the graphic at the higher resolution, but this regeneration is something the device driver cannot do on its own, nor can we assume (as we can with the case of Computer Modern fonts) that the second printer automatically has access to the graphic at this higher resolution. The onus on preparing graphics in multiple resolutions—and keeping them from getting mixed up!—falls squarely on the shoulders of the document's author.

11.1.2   *With TEX*

TEXish graphics tend not to be as flashy as external graphics, but these approaches offer other inducements. Included text matches the document, the figures may be revised automatically as you make changes to the commands creating the figure, it may be less of a problem to print and preview the figure, and it may be easier to maintain document portability. It's often easy to express and display precise relationships with LaTeX or TeX drawing tools.

Here's one "easy" way to make drawings with LaTeX or TeX—we just create special fonts to piece together drawings and figures. Special macros can make the "piecing together" process somewhat less painful than otherwise. In this approach, the heart of the graphic process is just another font, one which can be tuned to the resolution of the printer like any other font. Even with macros, it can be tedious to artfully join arcs, line segments, and dingbats together except for simple diagrams. The LaTeX `picture` environment, and its descendants `epic` and `eepic` and some other packages like XY-Pic, follow this font-like approach (see chapter 12). The PiCTeX macro package (chapter 12) uses symbols from current fonts to draw elaborate images. A line segment at an angle will be drawn from dozens of little dots placed next to one another, so TeX works harder.

Many readers know that TeX has a graphic sibling METAFONT, the tool for creating all the Computer Modern fonts. After all, a font is nothing but a collection of graphics gathered together in a special way. MetaPost is a descendant of METAFONT that creates PostScript output. Both of these languages are perfect for creating graphics for TeX documents, as their output is specially designed to be used by LaTeX or TeX. While some people complain at the relative difficulty of METAFONT or MetaPost, others complain of their addictive nature! Using these languages, it's possible to integrate text—text that perfectly matches that of the document—within the figure and to create drawings whose components are precisely connected by precise relations.

11.1.3 Hybrid approaches

A wide range of hybrid techniques aim to combine the best parts of the pure strategies we discussed above with fewer of the disadvantages. Several people have created graphic front ends to make the TeX drawing tools easier and more familiar. For example, the PSTricks package produces PostScript output, but the PostScript language, which is unfamiliar to most LaTeX and TeX users, has been replaced by calls to TeX macros, which should be easier to master. In the same way, MFPiC produces METAFONT output, but uses TeX commands to do so, so authors will feel comfortable with the drawing process.

Several front ends use non-TeX interfaces to generate output which TeX can easily incorporate into a document. One such program is `gnuplot`, useful for effortlessly creating scientific plots. People using this program can arrange to generate LaTeX or TeX output (in any of several flavors—LaTeX, LaTeX+emTeX specials, Eepic, PSTricks, and TPic) or METAFONT output. Other programs such as *Mathematica, Maple,* or other mathematical assistants can generate TeX output and so serve as unwitting front ends to TeX as well.

Graphics With/Without TeX: Pros and Cons

Pros	*Cons*
Without TeX	
Greater professionalism.	May be hard to include in document.
	Document may no longer be preview-able.
	Embedded text may not match document.
	Document may not be portable.
	Precise, mathematical shapes may not be possible.
	Figure is not automatically revised with document.
With TeX	
Easily included in document.	Graphics might possess little panache.
Often previewable.	
Embedded text usually matches document.	
Precise shapes possible.	
Automatic revision is often possible.	
Document remains portable.	

11.1.4   Plan of attack

The list on the facing page lists all the graphic techniques we will be discussing in this volume. We'll finish this chapter by exploring some ways of importing graphic files into a TeX document. Subsequent chapters will present the remaining techniques.

11.2   Graphic inclusions

General Caveat. There is no single strategy that applies to all types of graphic formats and files. Be prepared to network freely, to experiment boldly, and to endure patiently.

There are dozens, if not hundreds, of distinct graphic formats; see, for example, Murray and van Ryper (1994), Kay and Levine (1994), and Rimmer (1993). A graphic inclusion comes in the form of files, and so possesses a complete file name like any other file. A common convention is

> ### Preparing and Including Graphics: Techniques
>
> 1. Use of external programs.
>
> 2. Siblings of TEX: METAFONT, MetaPost.
>
> 3. A fontal attack I: special fonts (`picture`, `epic`, and `eepic` environments in LATEX; XY-Pic) with attendant macros are used to create drawings.
>
> 4. A fontal attack II: using ordinary fonts in clever ways: PICTEX.
>
> 5. TEX front ends: PSTricks (TEX front end to PostScript), MFPIC (TEX front end to METAFONT).
>
> 6. Non-TEX front ends: `gnuplot`, *Mathematica*, etc. (which are not discussed in this volume).

to use the file extension to identify the graphic format. Thus, `data.epsf` (which might be `data.eps` on DOS systems) is an Encapsulated PostScript file, while `plot.tiff` (or `plot.tif` for DOS) is a tagged image format file. No one rigidly enforces this rule, so files that appear to follow one format may not. Furthermore, even if the extension properly identifies the graphics format, the artist may be using a nonstandard variation of the format. This is a substantial problem with `.tiff` files (tagged image format files).

> ### Placing Externally Prepared Graphics in a Document
>
> - Check to see if your device driver handles the graphic (for example, Encapsulated PostScript can usually be included with little problem using a dvi-to-PostScript postprocessor).
>
> - Use the `pbmplus` package to translate from one graphic format to another with which your device driver can cope.
>
> - Use `bm2font` to create a special `.pk` font out of the image file.

11.2.1   Encapsulated PostScript and eps

The easiest external files to include in a document seem to be *Encapsulated PostScript* files, but this will be of value only to those readers with ready access to PostScript printers, and the inclusion is done by means of TEX's \special command. For example, for Nelson Beebe's dvialw utility, one would include a statement like

```
\special{language "PS", include "⟨epsf-file⟩"}
```

Y&Y's program dviwindo supports both .eps and .tif files via syntax of the form

```
\special{insertimage: ⟨file⟩⟨width⟩⟨height⟩}
```

The account by Reckdahl (1996) is an excellent summary of the several ways of including Encapsulated PostScript in LATEX documents.

Perhaps the most robust treatment of Encapsulated PostScript is accomplished by using the epsf macros in conjunction with the *dvips* postprocessor. Plain TEX users say

```
\input epsf
```

near the top of the file, while LATEX users should say

```
\usepackage{epsf}
```

in the document's preamble. Of course, both files epsf.tex and epsf.sty, available from CTAN but which should have been part of the *dvips* distribution, should be in a TEX-aware directory on your system. To include an Encapsulated PostScript graphic in a document, say something like

```
\epsfbox{⟨complete-graphic-file-name⟩}
```

wherever the figure is to go. LATEX or TEX expects the *complete* file name of graphic including the extension. This command works in all flavors of TEX, but LATEXers may have to precede this command with \leavevmode or \noindent in certain environments. The LATEX commands to generate figure 1 on the next page look something like

```
\begin{center}
  \leavevmode \epsfxsize=2in \epsfbox{scribe.eps}
\end{center}
```

This image appears courtesy of *Yale Alumni Magazine*.

Since PostScript material—graphics or fonts—is scalable, it's possible to perform some simple transformations on the fly. For *dvips*, the two registers

Figure 1: Including an Encapsulated PostScript file.

\epsfxsize and \epsfysize control the width and height of the figure. Changes to these values should be made right before the call to \epsfbox. In LaTeX, I typed

```
\begin{center}
  \leavevmode
  \epsfxsize =1.6in \epsfbox{scribe.eps} \quad
  \epsfysize = 1.2in \epsfbox{scribe.eps} \quad
  \epsfxsize = 1.3in \epsfysize = .8in \epsfbox{scribe.eps}
\end{center}
```

to get figure 2 on page 353; notice that it is possible to alter the aspect ratio by setting values to both registers. (Otherwise, *dvips* scales the figure naturally.) Changes to the aspect ratio of a PostScript figure mostly look ghastly (the aspect ratio being the ratio of the width to height). Prudent artists and authors avoid changing the aspect ratio at all costs.

All dvi-PostScript postprocessors allow shenanigans like this; check the accompanying documentation to see how to (and check the *dvips* documentation for a few additional features associated with epsf).

Creating graphics files with dvips   The *dvips* program can create graphics files for use in other documents, even non-TeX documents (providing the environment is PostScript). If a document fits on a single page, then the -E switch tries to write an Encapsulated PostScript file with the name given as argument to the -o switch. Thus, if I've typeset 1page.tex successfully to create 1page.dvi then

```
dvips -E -o 1page.eps 1page
```

creates 1page.eps, which I can include elsewhere via \epsfbox. (It can also be included in non-TeX documents, provided that the external application

Using Encapsulated PostScript

With the `epsf` macros and *dvips*, say

```
\input epsf
   ...
\epsfbox{⟨epsf-file⟩}
```

in plain TEX.

In LATEX, say

```
\usepackage{epsf}
   ...
\leavevmode\epsfbox{⟨epsf-file⟩}
```

The `\leavevmode` may be unnecessary.

The file name ⟨*epsf-file*⟩ must be the complete file name, including extension.

- **Pros:**

    - Easy to use.
    - Properly renders all TEX output—bitmap or outline—on a PostScript device.

- **Cons:**

    - Limited to use in a PostScript environment.

knows how to include Encapsulated PostScript files.) Take careful note of this valuable approach:

- Making an Encapsulated PostScript file from a LATEX page means you can include the LATEX page in a plain TEX document.

- Making an Encapsulated PostScript file from a plain TEX page means you can include a bit of plain TEX in a LATEX document.

- Making an Encapsulated PostScript file from any bit of LATEX or TEX means you can include TEX output in any other document or application that accepts Encapsulated PostScript.

Figure 2: Scaled variations on an Encapsulated PostScript file.

dvips as a Graphics Generator

The program *dvips* (and perhaps other .dvi-to-PostScript postprocessors) can generate Encapsulated PostScript files for use in other LaTeX or TeX documents.

- Prepare the input file for the proposed .eps file. Its typeset form should *not* be longer than a single page.

- Run this file through LaTeX or TeX.

- Run the resulting .dvi file through *dvips* using the -E switch to Encapsulate the PostScript material and the -o switch to make sure the PostScript translation is stored in an output file; that is, use a command line of the form

```
dvips -o myfile.eps -E myfile
```

- Certain complicated pieces of TeX can be embedded in .epsf files for inclusion into the main part of a document. Thus, while the remainder of the report is still undergoing revision, the complicated material need not be repeatedly recompiled.

If the document makes use of bitmap fonts, then *dvips* is smart enough to include the bitmaps in the right way so that they can be included by another PostScript application, even non-TeX ones. However, if you include bitmap material in this way, your Encapsulated PostScript is now device-dependent, and you'll have to regenerate this file in case you plan on printing on printers with various resolutions.

From PostScript to Encapsulated PostScript   It may be possible to convert a regular PostScript file to an encapsulated form, provided the document is a *single page* in length and the PostScript instructions are reasonably well-behaved. Often, too, it happens that *dvips* makes an otherwise perfectly fine `.eps` file which, for some reason, lies about the rectangular dimensions of the figure. (This may be the case with graphics produced with PSTricks, a package described further in chapter 14.)

The beginning of a PostScript file should contain a series of lines beginning with percent signs. By convention, the first line (beginning with `%!`) identifies the PostScript version. The comments are terminated by a comment of the form

```
%%EndComments
```

and if a bounding box comment is supplied after the first line but before this line, that may be sufficient to "encapsulate" your file. The bounding box comment is of the form

```
%%BoundingBox: ⟨llx⟩ ⟨lly⟩ ⟨urx⟩ ⟨ury⟩
```

where the ⟨*llx*⟩, ⟨*lly*⟩, and so on, represent coordinates for the lower left corner and upper right corner of an imaginary rectangle—the *bounding box*—which surrounds the graphic image. Single spaces should separate the components of the coordinates. These coordinates must be in PostScript units, which are what *The TEXbook* calls *big points*.

The coordinates are measured from the lower left corner of the page. To "encapsulate" your graphic, print it out, and make a series of measurements. The distance from the left edge of the sheet to the leftmost mark of ink is ⟨*llx*⟩, while the distance from the bottom of the sheet to the bottom-most ink mark is ⟨*lly*⟩. The distance from the left edge to the rightmost blob of ink is ⟨*urx*⟩, while the distance from the sheet's bottom to the highest mark is ⟨*ury*⟩.

For example, a bounding-box comment

```
%%BoundingBox: 72 72 350 325
```

means that the lower left corner of the image's bounding box is one inch to the right and up from the lower left corner of the page (there are 72 PostScript units to the inch). The upper right corner of the image is 350 big points to the right of the lower left corner of the sheet and 325 units above it. In case your ruler is not calibrated in big points (PostScript units), measure according to the ruler, and multiply by the scaling factors of figure 3 on the next page.

This technique may not always work. Consult Reckdahl (1996) for other tips and techniques.

If you measure in ...	Multiply by ...
Inches	72
Centimeters	28.35
"Regular" points	0.9963
Picas	11.96

Figure 3: Scaling factors when measuring images.

11.2.2 Other graphic formats and pbmplus

It's easiest to stick—if possible—to graphic formats that your device drivers support. For example, the printer drivers that are part of the emTeX suite can accommodate Microsoft Paint .msp files, Paintbrush .pcx, and black and white bitmap .bmp files.

If the printer driver can't handle the graphic format, it may be possible to transform the graphics file into a format that can be handled, and this strategy relies on the *portable bitmap* formats developed by Jef Poskanzer. He realized that all graphic images form three natural groups—purely black and white images (like black-and-white comic strips), grayscale images (remember those boxes of old black-and-white photos in your grandparents' living room?), and full color images. He developed three generic formats for representing these image types. Portable bitmap files with extension .pbm render black and white images in the first group. Portable graymap .pgm files record gray images from the second group, and the *portable pixmap* .ppm format handles the third group. The extension .pnm—*portable anymap*—is used as a generic extension to represent any of the three formats.

With the .pnm formats in hand, it's straightforward to design utilities of the form xxxtopnm and pnmtoxxx to convert a graphic to and from the anymap format. The pbmplus collection of (over 100) utilities lets us do just that. The pbmplus package is freely and widely available. With luck, particularly nice interfaces to this package may exist, such as Lennart Lövstrand's *ImageViewer* for NextStep (downloadable from ftp.cs.orst.edu) and the shareware program *Graphic Workshop* for Windows (available from many servers and on the 4AllTeX CD-ROM). Figure 4 on the following page lists the formats supported by pbmplus.

Figure 5 on page 357 shows the results of manipulations by which a .tiff file becomes part of this manuscript. In Unix, the command

```
tifftopnm reader.tiff > reader.pbm
```

created a portable bitmap file from the original .tiff file, and

```
pnmtops reader.pbm > reader.eps
```

Ascii graphics	MTV or PRT ray tracer output
Abekas YUV bytes	NCSA ICR format
Andrew Toolkit raster object	.pcx
Atari Degas .pi1	portable bitmap
Atari Degas .pi3	portable graymap
Atari compressed Spectrum file	portable pixmap
Atari uncompressed Spectrum file	PostScript "image" data
Bennet Yee "face" file	PostScript
BitGraph graphics	Printronic printer graphics
CMU window manager bitmap	QRT ray tracer output
DEC sixel format	raw RGB bytes
doodle brush	raw grayscale bytes
Epson printer graphics	Sun icon
FITS	Sun rasterfile
GEM .img file	text
Gould scanner file	.tiff (or .tif) file
GraphOn graphics (compressed)	TrueVision Targa file
Group 3 fax file	Unix plot(5) file
HIPS	unknown
HP LaserJet format	Usenix FaceSaver(tm)
HP PaintJet	X10 bitmap
IFF ILBM	X10 window dump
Img-whatnot	X11 "puzzle" file
Lisp Machine bitmap	X11 bitmap
MGR bitmap	X11 pixmap
MacPaint	X11 window dump
Macintosh PICT	Xim file
Motif UIL icon file	Zinc bitmap

Figure 4: Graphic formats supported in the pbmplus package.

created the (encapsulated) PostScript files for use with \epsfbox. Having known that the image would be printed in black-and-white rather than color, I translated the original into a bitmap file rather than a greymap or pixmap.

The pbmplus package contains several useful utilities in addition to routines for converting to and from the various .pnm formats. Several dozen software tools allow us to resize, adjust the color, rotate an image, smooth an image, and create special effects (make the image look like an oil painting, shear the image, apply Conway's rules of the Game of Life to an image, and so on).

Figure 5: Encapsulated PostScript file from a `.tiff` file. This image appears courtesy of *Yale Alumni Magazine*.

11.2.3 The LaTeX graphics bundle

The LaTeX `graphics` bundle is a collection of styles allowing an author to include graphics files in a document. The styles are dependent on the version of TeX or the device driver in use, and so the only graphics that may be included are those that the driver can handle. Figure 6 on the next page lists the driver support available as of Spring 1996. Useful references to this material include both Carlisle (1996c) and Lamport (1994).

The `graphics` package consists of a half-dozen or so commands for performing graphic tricks. The `graphicx` package is similar, but extends the syntax available.

Two commands provide for the resizing and scaling of material. The `\scalebox` takes two arguments—the scale factor and the text to scale. A second, optional argument provides separately for a vertical scale factor. The `\resizebox` command takes three arguments, for LaTeX needs to know the width and height of the box, and the text for the distorted box. Authors can

Using pbmplus: Pros and Cons

- **Pros:**

  - Easy to use, particularly those implementations that have added a nice interface to the utilities.

- **Cons:**

  - May be hard to locate an implementation for your computer; you may have to compile the sources.

Look on page 355 for an example of its use.

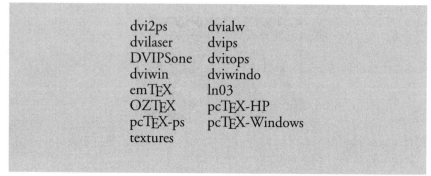

dvi2ps	dvialw
dvilaser	dvips
DVIPSone	dvitops
dviwin	dviwindo
emTEX	ln03
OZTEX	pcTEX-HP
pcTEX-ps	pcTEX-Windows
textures	

Figure 6: Driver support for the graphics package.

use a "!" in place of any of the two dimensions to maintain the aspect ratio after scaling.

The \rotatebox command rotates by a specified angle. The command \reflectbox is a special case of \rotatebox—it simply reflects the text about a vertical line.

Finally, \includegraphics imports a named graphics file, providing (of course) that it is a graphics type that your device driver understands. There is a star-form of this command that clips the image to a rectangle formed by coordinates to a lower left and upper right corner given in optional arguments.

The graphicx allows an author to do (essentially) the same things as the graphics package, but the command interface is more convenient. For example, one need only type

```
\includegraphics[scale=.5, angle=66]{foo.ps}
```

to rotate the graphic file at half-size by 66°. The equivalent command in graphics would require a series of nested calls, \includegraphics inside \scalebox inside \rotatebox.

If we type

```
\usepackage[dvips]{graphics}
\begin{document}
\scalebox{2.5}{Testing}\quad
Testing\quad
\scalebox{1}[3]{Testing}

\resizebox{2in}{\height}{Fat Cat}\
\resizebox{2in}{!}{Pudgie Budgie}

\rotatebox{22.5}{\resizebox{1.5in}{!}{Hail, C{\ae}sar!}}%
\hspace{-1in}
\TeX--\reflectbox{\TeX}
```

Figure 7: Output from graphics commands.

```
\vspace{-2in}\noindent
\includegraphics{path.3}\
\includegraphics*[-.1in,-.1in][.7in, 5in]{path.3}
\end{document}
```

we get figure 7. The LaTeX commands \height, \width, and \depth are always available to provide the dimensions of the typeset box. The graphic in path.3 was produced by MetaPost.

Color   Color is also a device-dependent option. There is a color package as part of the graphics bundle. After typing something like

```
\usepackage[dvips]{color}
```

in the preamble, several color commands add color to the document (alas, we cannot display the results here). The color of the page is controlled via

```
\pagecolor{⟨color⟩}
```

where the ⟨color⟩ is any one of the predefined colors black, white, red, green, blue, yellow, cyan, or magenta. The instructions

```
\colorbox{⟨color⟩}{⟨text⟩}
```

and

```
\fcolorbox{⟨border color⟩}{⟨color⟩}{⟨text⟩}
```

put text into boxes of color. The command \fcolorbox surrounds the box with a border of color.

Text itself can be typeset in colors, using the command \textcolor or the declaration \color. For further information on all these color commands, and on the ability to define your own colors using various color models, please refer to Lamport (1994) and to Carlisle (1996c).

Color is available to TeX authors in other contexts. The program *dvips* supports the use of color in specials, although it's probably better to use the standard LaTeX interface if you're a LaTeX author. The PSTricks package (see chapter 14) supports color using a slightly different set of commands. Note too the package pstcol that loads both PSTricks and the color package and repairs some incompatibilities between them. Finally, MetaPost (see chapter 13) allows an artist to embed colors directly within its output.

11.2.4 Including graphics with bm2font

Friedhelm Sowa's bm2font utility takes a different tack towards the inclusion of images. He realized that LaTeX and TeX already do have provisions for including very special kinds of graphic images—letterforms that have been organized into fonts. The TeX program does not check that indeed the letter "A" of a font really looks like an A, so another strategy might involve the designing of a special purpose font, each of whose characters looks like the graphic we are trying to include. TeX does expect its fonts to conform to certain standards, so our conversion utility must make sure that the graphic font looks to TeX like any other font.

This is what bm2font does. It receives for input the name of a graphics file together with various options and attempts to produce a special-purpose font, each of whose characters represents a portion of the graphic. Including the picture becomes a simple matter of selecting the special font and selecting the proper characters in this font. These tasks are made even simpler since bm2font produces a short .tex file that contains the definition of a macro to do this for us.

Figure 8: Graphics via bm2font. This is Dürer's 1519 etching, *Saint Anthony Reading*.

It may not be possible to have a single letter represent a single image, as that might make the letter look too large from the point of view of TEX (or of a previewer or device driver). For that reason, bm2font will slice the image into smaller tiles and assign each tile to a character. The bm2font software ensures that all these tiles are placed on the page with no white space "grout" between them. The graphic font it produces adheres to the packed pixel .pk format used by the Computer Modern collection of fonts; this just means that its fonts are usable by TEX. More to the point: An author can preview the graphic image in the document (otherwise a difficult task).

Fortunately, bm2font makes it particularly convenient to use the fonts it produces. Not only does its output consist of appropriate .pk and .tfm files, but also a short .tex file that contains the mach nery for setting up the fonts, piecing the "tiles" together, and typesetting with them. Recent versions of this program handle full color, and accept at least the following graphic types: .pcx, .gif, .bmp, .iff, .lbm, .tif and .tiff, .img, .cut, and .raw.

To generate figure 8 (available on CD-ROM for royalty-free duplication from Planet Art (1995)), I typed

```
bm2font duerer.tif
```

to make my pixel files—duerera.pk, duererb.pk, and so on (together with their .tfm files)—and duerer.tex. Actually this invocation assumes default values for the program; for production purposes, it was necessary to type

```
bm2font duerer.tif -h1200 -v1200 -b3 -m86
```

Here, the h and v options prepare font files with horizontal and vertical resolutions of 1200 dpi, a parameter to reduce halftone colors (the program itself suggested this value to me when I ran without it), and the m option to

---

bm2font: Pros and Cons

- **Pros:**

  - Easy to use;
  - Available for many computer platforms;
  - Document remains previewable; and
  - Applicable for a wide variety of graphic formats.

- **Cons:**

  - Graphic font files need regeneration for each printer type.

---

force the width of the picture to 86 mm. (A separate parameter controls the height in case you wanted to change the aspect ratio of the object.) Simply type bm2font to get a list of options and their meanings.

To include the picture, I move the font files to places where TEX and the drivers know about, and I typed

```
\input duerer
   . . .
\setduerer
```

in the document (for both plain TEX and LATEX). bm2font automatically creates the \setduerer command and writes its definition in duerer.tex. It's \setduerer's job to lay the graphic tiles properly.

Options to bm2font   Authors can specify a wide variety of options to control the behavior of bm2font. For example, it's wise to specify the length or height of the image (in millimeters only) with the m and n switches;

```
bm2font duerer.tif -m86
```

makes sure that the various fonts duerera.300pk, duererb.300pk and so forth, generate a picture whose width is 86 mm. To obtain picture fonts for a printer with horizontal and vertical resolution of 600 dpi, we might say something like

```
bm2font duerer.tif -m86 -h600 -v600
```

where we need to specify both the horizontal and vertical resolution of the

Using bm2font

- Issue the command

bm2font ⟨*graphic-file*⟩.⟨*ext*⟩ ⟨*options*⟩

where ⟨*ext*⟩ can be any of pcx, gif, bmp, iff, lbm, tif or tiff, img, cut, or raw. Check the bm2font documentation for the options that may be necessary.

- Move the .tfm and .pk files to appropriate places on your hard disk.

- Type

\input ⟨*graphic-file*⟩ \set⟨*graphic-file*⟩

to typeset the graphic.

device. (The simple command bm2font duerer.tif is actually equivalent to bm2font duerer.tif -h300 -v300.)

Many different switches control other aspects of the conversion process, including sizing and scaling and the way in which the original pixels are converted to .pk pixels. The bm2font manual, in English and German, does an excellent job of discussing these matters, and presents a good introduction to some essential topics in computer graphics at the same time.

bm2font *caveats* It's tempting to leave these bit-map font files in the current working directory (the area containing the current document, with which it would be natural to keep the special bitmap fonts we create), but many implementations of TEX will *not* look for fonts in this location.

- If LATEX or TEX complains about a missing font, you will need either to move the .tfm file with your other font metric files or place the current directory on the environment variable that tells TEX where to get its fonts. (In many implementations, this environment variable is called texfonts or something comparable.)

- If the image appears empty or as a big, black square, or if the previewer/driver complains in any other way, you will need to move the .pk file with the other pixel files for that size and that resolution.

For the emTEX implementation for DOS and OS/2, for example, these might be the directories `\emtex\tfm` and `\texfonts\pixel.lj\300dpi`. Your own implementation might adopt some other strategy.

The `bm2font` approach is *device-dependent*. Default `.pk` files produced by bm2font were at a resolution of 300 dpi, fine for my ancient laser printer, but new pixel files had to be developed for use by the phototypesetter, whose resolution was so much greater than this.

11.3 PSfrag

The PSfrag LATEX package is useful to authors who have prepared include-able PostScript graphics for their documents by means of non-TEX software tools. Such graphics often contain text which, though presentable enough, does not match the typographical standard of a TEX document. PSfrag (originally by Michael Grant and recently revamped and currently maintained by David Carlisle) lets an author modify this embedded text. This discussion should be read in conjunction with the PSfrag documentation; the entire package appears at any CTAN site. PSfrag has recently been thoroughly revised; it no longer needs special preprocessing, and authors who have previously made use of this package should obtain version 3 (or better) and recompile their documents.

Figure 9 on the facing page displays a perfectly respectable graphic that has been prepared by an external utility (in this case, the *MatLab* program). Nevertheless, a conscientious author would have just cause for complaint about the labels in the figure. They are all done in the standard Helvetica sans serif, which doesn't match the sans serif used in this book. As the labels show, the typesetting is naive, at least when compared to TEX's high standard. For example, the "minus" signs in labels of the vertical axis are just dashes that have been stuck in front. If you peek ahead to figure 10 on page 366, you'll see the difference PSfrag makes.

Two special commands lie at the heart of PSfrag. The `\tex` instruction contains the LATEX commands that PSfrag will later interpret, while `\ps-frag` specifies tags that we later ask PSfrag to replace with snippets of text for LATEX to typeset. We assume that we can easily embed ASCII strings in the figure. The simple document file to process figure 10 on page 366 might look as follows:

```
\documentclass[dvips]{article}
\usepackage{graphics,epsf,zmtpad,psfrag,...}
\begin{document}
\begin{figure}
  \begin{center}
    \psfragscanon \psfrag{p1}[l]{$\ \sin(t)$}
    \psfrag{p2}[][l]{$\bullet$} \psfrag{p3}{$\cos(t)$}
    ⟨axis-label replacement commands⟩
    \epsfbox{example.eps}
```

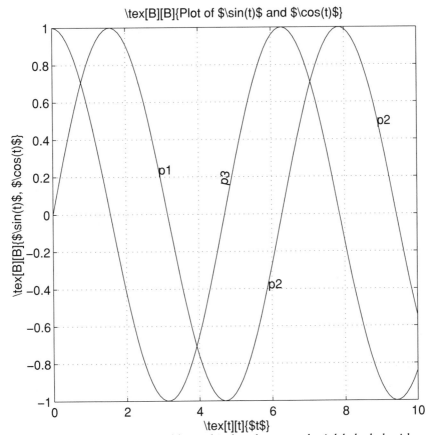

Figure 9: A perfectly respectable graphic, but the tags and axis labels clash with the rest of this book.

```
    \end{center}
    \end{figure}
    \end{document}
```

The contents of the graphics must be loaded before that of the psfrag package. The optional arguments in the \tex and \psfrag commands control the placement of the LATEX replacement with respect to the original PostScript text. Associated with each text fragment is a *bounding box*—the imaginary box that snugly encloses each bit of text. Normally, the left end of the baseline of the LATEX replacement coincides with the left end of the baseline of the PostScript tag, but other effects are possible.

How can we replace the axis labels with TEX equivalents? In this example (figure 9), it's easy enough to add a \psfrag for each label:

```
    \psfrag{-0.2}[r][r]{$-.2$}
```

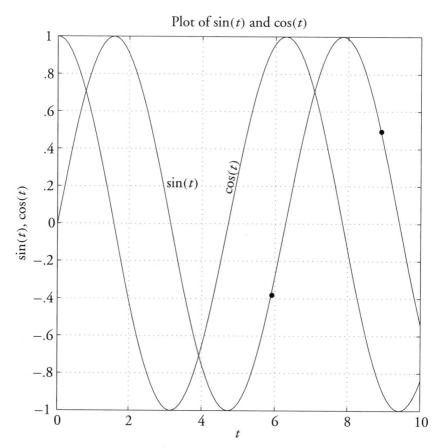

Figure 10: A well-nigh perfect graphic.

and so on. For labels vertically placed at the vertical axis, it makes sense to align the right end of the PostScript bounding box baseline with the right end of the LaTeX replacements.

But what if there were a huge number of such labels, so many that adding \psfrag commands for each such label would be a tedious labor? Observing the regularity of the labels, it would be reasonable to attempt to use TeX's \loop mechanism to issue a series of \psfrag commands. This reasonable approach fails, for PSfrag waits until the last moment before making the substitutions, so all replacements are made in terms of the final value of the loop counter, rather than in terms of all the intermediate values of this counter. But plain TeX code similar to the following works:

```
\newcount\n
\let\PSF=0
\newwrite\tmp \immediate\openout\tmp=\jobname.tmp
\loop \advance\n by 2
```

```
\ifnum\n<10
  \immediate\write\tmp{\PSF{0.\the\n}[r][r]{$.\the\n$}}%
  \immediate\write\tmp{\PSF{-0.\the\n}[r][r]{$-.\the\n$}}%
\repeat
\n=-2
\loop \advance\n by 2
\ifnum\n<12
 \immediate\write\tmp{\PSF{\the\n}{$\the\n$}}%
\repeat
\immediate\closeout\tmp
\psfrag{1}[r][r]{$1$}\psfrag{-1}[r][r]{$-1$}
\let\PSF=\psfrag \input \jobname.tmp
```

and here is a brief explanation. We can't generate intermediate \psfrag commands in the document, so let's instead generate them and write them to an external file. Then we read this file to make all typesetting commands known to LATEX.

The first few lines perform some necessary setup: a counter and an output stream are allocated, a temporary file is opened, and a control sequence is \let equal to an unexpandable token. When we create the temporary file, we will redefine this control sequence to be \psfrag. Next, a series of loops create strings for the axis labels (horizontal and vertical axes) and writes them to the temporary file. Finally, two commands take care of special axis labels, the control sequence \PSF is redefined, and the temporary file is read in.

. . . .

CHAPTER 12

GRAPHICS VIA
LaTeX and TeX

This chapter will serve as a travelog through the LaTeX picture environment and the PICTeX macro package. If authors need either of these systems, they should be able to tour these pages to get an idea if they will be appropriate. These two systems use LaTeX or TeX commands to generate graphic images.

12.1 Coordinate geometry

Anyone planning to use graphic techniques will need to know basic elements of coordinate geometry, the universal language that makes it possible to locate and place things on a flat surface.

Fancy terminology like "coordinate axes" disguises the simple intent of these conventions—to define a reference point from which it is possible to locate things. This fixing is done by drawing—or imagining—two perpendicular lines on a page. The *origin*—the point where the lines cross—is our reference point. It's common to call the horizontal axis the *x*-axis, while the vertical axis is the *y*-axis. Each axis is marked into equal sized units, and the size of the unit is usually up to whoever prepares the graph. A unit might be one printer's point in size, an inch, a kilometer, or anything else. People who draw graphs generally choose a convenient size. Of course, we imagine that both axes (plural of axis) extend to infinity, but we can only draw a portion of these infinite lines on a finite sheet, as shown in figure 1 on the facing page.

It's often helpful to imagine that additional horizontal and vertical lines are drawn in the axis, to form a grid like that of figure 2 on page 370. With these grid lines in place, the coordinate system immediately suggests the grid-like map of many large cities (Manhattan, Hoboken, etc.). This analogy, a bit of a cliché, is nevertheless useful, for just as we may fix our position in a city by describing a place by giving its east-west and north-south

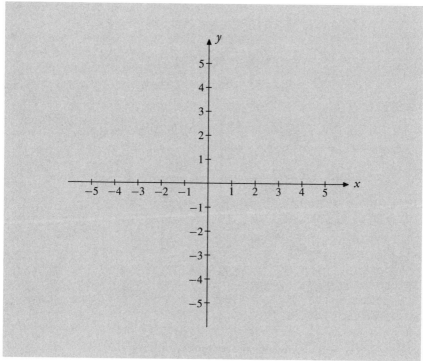

Figure 1: Coordinate axes.

positions, so too may we fix a point in the plane by giving its east or west positions (right or left of the origin) and north or south position (above or below the origin). By longstanding convention, positions left or below are negative. Positions are always given as a pair of numbers, with the horizontal position *always* appearing first. In books, we separate these numbers by commas and surround them with parentheses, like $(-1, 2)$.

The analogy with city streets is useful, but it goes only so far. Urban street grids involve positive whole numbers and are finite in extent. Mathematical coordinates may be positive or negative or zero, or whole number or fraction. Figure 3 on the following page shows some points with their coordinates.

Most TeX, LaTeX, METAFONT, ..., systems rely on this description for the position of graphic elements. The syntax may vary, but positions on the sheet are given by pairs of numbers, and the horizontal measure always precedes the vertical measure.

Some purely TeX solutions base themselves on the simple \point macro [Knuth (1986a), p. 389]. Using a simple variant, we type something like

```
\newdimen\unit \unit=10pt
\def\plotsymbol{\hbox{\tt\char`\*}}
```

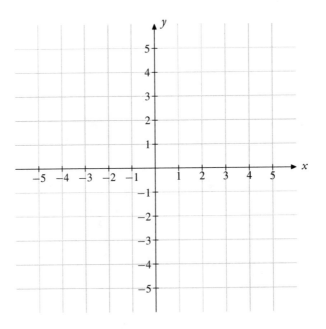

Figure 2: Coordinate axes define a grid.

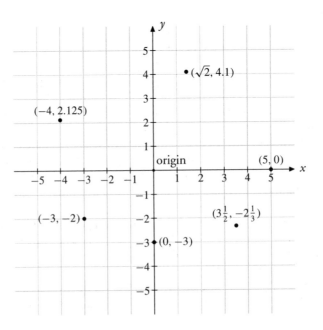

Figure 3: Plotting points.

```
\def\point#1 #2 {\rlap{\kern#1\unit
  \raise#2\unit\plotsymbol}}
$$
\hbox{%
  \point 5 -1 \point 5 1 \point 5 2 \point 6 3
  \point 7 4 \point 7 5 \point 6 6 \point 5 6 \point 4 6
  \point 3 5 \point 3 4 }
$$
```

to get

```
        * * *
      *       *
      *       *
                *
            *
            *

            *
```

(in \point 5 -1, 5 and -1 are the *x*- and *y*-coordinates). There's an under-lying unit, and if we make this distance a little smaller (\unit=2pt), and if we change the plotting symbol

```
\def\plotsymbol{\hbox{$\bullet$}}
```

we get the following.

Adding more dots would also improve the appearance. Clever enhance-ments to this \point macro form the basis of LATEX's picture environment and of several other graphic packages, including PICTEX. (That's why the picture environment and PICTEX system are naturals for treatment in a single chapter.)

12.2   The LATEX picture environment and extensions

Since there are relatively few drawing characters in the normal suite of TEX fonts, additional fonts have been provided so that the LATEX \put command (analogous to the raw \point command) can create angled lines and vec-tors, circles, and ovals in several sizes and inclinations. Lamport (1994) and Goossens, Mittelbach, and Samarin (1994) provide the definitive doc-umentation for this material.

All picture instructions belong inside the picture environment, whose argument is a point giving the width and height of the picture. Behind the scenes is a \unitlength register that determines the unit. Its default value is 1 pt, but this can be changed (as can any LATEX length) via \setlength. Since elements of a LATEX picture are formed out of characters from special fonts, a unit length of 1 pt is natural.

The basis of virtually all picture commands is the \put command for placing elements within a picture. Any \put needs to know where to place the object and what to place, so the syntax is

\put(⟨*x-coord*⟩,⟨*y-coord*⟩){⟨*stuff*⟩}

The ⟨*stuff*⟩ can be any valid picture drawing instructions—to typeset text, circles, ovals, lines, or arrows. For example, we get

from

```
\begin{picture}(20,70) % Pa
  \put(10,60){\circle{20}} % face
  \multiput(1.5,60)(6,0){4}{\makebox(0,0){$\bullet$}}% eyes, ears
  \put(10,55){\makebox(0,0){$\bullet$}} % nose
  \put(6.8,53){\line(1,0){6}} % mouth
  \put(10,50){\line(0,-1){20}}%
  \put(0,40){\line(1,0){20}}% trunk, arms
  \put(5,30){\line(1,0){10}}%
  \put(5,10){\line(1,0){10}}% belt, cuffs
  {\thicklines\put(2,8){\line(1,0){16}}} % shoes
  \put(5,30){\line(0,-1){20}}\put(15,30){\line(0,-1){20}} % pants
  \put(10,24){\line(0,-1){14}} % pants
  \put(10,0){\makebox(0,0){Pa}}
\end{picture}
```

This example shows how to place commands together. The \multiput command is shorthand for \put'ting several identical elements on a page. Let's look again at Pa, this time superimposed on a coordinate grid (each square is five units on a side).

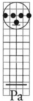

We can also add other curves and angled lines.

```
\begin{picture}(20,70) % Ma
  \put(10,60){\circle{20}} % face
  \put(7,60){\makebox(0,0){$\bullet$}}
  \put(13,60){\makebox(0,0){$\bullet$}}
  \put(10,55){\makebox(0,0){$\bullet$}} % eyes, nose
  \put(6.8,53){\line(1,0){6}} % mouth
  \put(-5,60){\oval(10,10)[br]}\put(25,60){\oval(10,10)[bl]}% hair
  \put(10,50){\line(0,-1){20}}%
  \put(0,40){\line(1,0){20}}% trunk, arms
  \put(5,30){\line(1,0){10}} % belt
  \put(5,30){\line(-1,-2){9}}\put(15,30){\line(1,-2){9}} % skirt
  \put(8,8){\line(-1,0){6}}\put(8,8){\line(0,1){3}} % left shoe
  \put(12,8){\line(1,0){6}}\put(12,8){\line(0,1){3}} % right shoe
  \put(10,0){\makebox(0,0){Ma}}
\end{picture}
```

Beginners may have trouble with \lines. You draw a line by \put'ting it somewhere, and then telling LATEX its inclination and length. The trouble is, while the means for specifying these bits of information are quite reasonable for mathematicians, more (or less?) ordinary authors may not be so comfortable with these conventions. LATEX needs a pair of numbers to decide on the slope of the line, and only a certain repertoire of inclined lines are possible. (A final argument is responsible for the segment's length.) Figure 4 on the next page lists the entire range of LATEX sloped lines, and small line segments themselves. In this figure, bullets mark the head of each line segment.

LATEX needs to know how long to draw the line, but you specify the length not by its actual "length," but by the length of the shadow cast on the horizontal axis by a distant overhead sun; see figure 5 on page 375. (This does *not* apply to horizontal or vertical lines—in these special cases, you use the exact length.) In figure 4 on the next page, all lines have a "length" of 20 units, and despite the many different real lengths, these segments obligingly line up in columns, since they all cast horizontal shadows of the same length. Thus, to get a line proceeding from the origin at a 45° angle /, we type

```
\begin{picture}(10,10)
\put(0,0){\line(1,1){10}}
\end{picture}
```

Similar conventions apply to arrows, or \vectors in the LATEX lexicon, except the range of allowable vectors is somewhat more restricted.

One command, \qbezier, helps draw arbitrary curves. The 'qbezier' stands for quadratic Bézier curve, a variant of the curves METAFONT and MetaPost draw. It takes three points as an argument, but only the first and

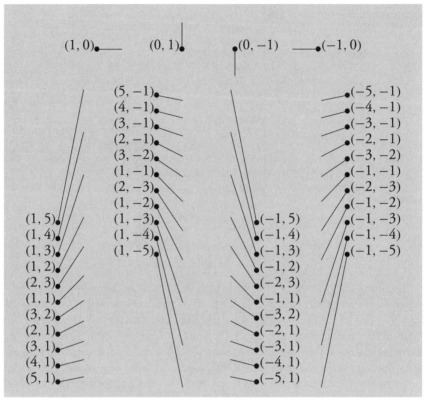

Figure 4: Drawing angled lines in the LATEX picture environment. The "co-ordinates" at each segment head are the LATEX designations for the segment's slope.

third of these actually lie on the curve. The drawing

is the product of

```
\begin{picture}
  ...
  \qbezier(0,0)(50,-90)(90,0)
```

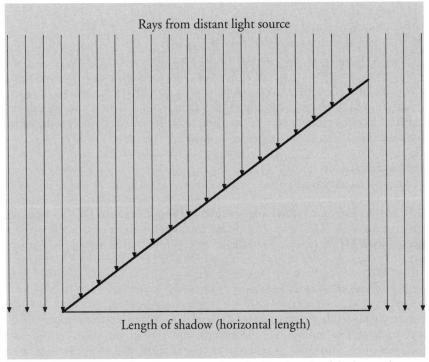

Figure 5: Horizontal length versus true length. The length of the heavy diagonal line is the "true length" of a line.

```
    ...
\end{picture}
```

is an illustration. The three points define a "snowcone" into which the scoop
of ice droops in such a way that the edges of the snow are tangent to the
cone at the cone's rim. It may also help to think of the curve as a flexible,
extensible magnetic wire pinned to the page at the first and third points and
attracted to a strong magnet held at the second point.

12.2.1   Plain pictures

Malcolm Clark (1992, p. 273) reminds us that the LATEX picture environment macros are so modular they can be ripped from `lplain.tex` or `la-
tex.tex` and inserted into a `plain` document with little difficulty. David
Carlisle has recently done this ripping, and the files and documentation that
support this are in the

```
macros/plain/graphics
```

area of CTAN.

There is another way to incorporate these pictures in a plain document. Although much of the functionality is provided for plain TEX users by the PICTEX package of macros (see page 377), part of this package consists of the file latexpicobjs.tex, which allows an author-artist to use LATEX picture objects in a plain TEX, PICTEX source file. Of course, you will need to adhere to PICTEX conventions. In particular, the PICTEX \put and \multiput commands have a completely different syntax. (Also, the \qbezier command is not mimicked, but the functionality of pictex reproduces it in other ways.) To do this, type the command

```
\input pictex
\input latexpicobjs
```

(The file latexpicobjs.tex may be just latexpic.tex on DOS systems.) Then, use the PICTEX \put command (or its relatives) to place the object formed with LATEX syntax. See Wichura (1987, p. 54) for further information.

12.2.2 Extensions to `picture`

Two freely available packages extend the LATEX picture environment. The epic package (by Sunil Podar) extends the functionality of the picture environment but continues to rely on the special fonts that picture uses. It's easier to specify lines and large groups of objects using the extended commands provided by epic.

Just as epic is an extension to picture, so is eepic (by Conrad Kwok) an extension to epic. Although it provides additional functionality, it is also a superset of epic, so all epic graphics may be processed by eepic. eepic relies on post-processing the document by a sympathetic dvi-processor, such as *dvips*, for many eepic commands are embedded in \special commands whose meaning may only be resolved, say, in a PostScript environment. In this way, lines of arbitrary orientation and length, circles of any size, ellipses, arcs, and fancier curve drawing all become possible.

Further details for these three environments appear in Lamport (1994) and Goossens, Mittelbach, and Samarin (1994), as well as in the software itself.

12.2.3 `picture`-*like packages*

The picture environment requires special fonts for its use. If you are willing to resort to auxiliary fonts for special effects, there are other packages to explore. In the cases below, the special fonts are available both in pixel form (ready-to-use) and METAFONT source for customization for a particular printer or previewer.

Michael Spivak's LAMS-TEX system was designed to be a complete environment for technical typesetting, comparable to LATEX. It's a powerful package and does things easily that LATEX cannot yet handle. A significant

---

Some Commands for the "picture" Environment

\put(⟨*x-coord*⟩,⟨*y-coord*⟩){⟨*stuff*⟩}
  puts *stuff* at the point whose coordinates are given by *x-coord*
  and *y-coord*.
\multiput(⟨*x-coord*⟩,⟨*y-coord*⟩)(⟨*x-inc*⟩, ⟨*y-inc*⟩){⟨*n*⟩}{⟨*stuff*⟩}
  typesets *n* copies of *stuff*; first copy is at (*x-coord, y-coord*), and
  successive copies are displaced from each other by the increment (*x-inc, y-inc*).
\line(⟨*x-coord*⟩,⟨*y-coord*⟩){⟨*x-len*⟩}
\vector(⟨*x-coord*⟩,⟨*y-coord*⟩){⟨*x-len*⟩}
  draws lines or arrows; see this text for further details.
\circle{⟨*diam*⟩}, \circle*{⟨*diam*⟩}
  draws circles or disks as close as possible to the diameter *diam*.
\oval{⟨*len*⟩,⟨*ht*⟩}
  draws a rectangle of dimension *len*×*ht* using appropriate
  rounded corners (optional arguments allow selection of halves
  or corners of the oval).
\qbezier(⟨*x1*⟩,⟨*y1*⟩)(⟨*x2*⟩,⟨*y2*⟩)(⟨*x3*⟩,⟨*y3*⟩)
  draws a quadratic Bézier curve; see this text for additional discussion.

---

portion of this system was devoted to macros for commutative diagrams and complicated matrices and other diagrams that consist only of arrows and arrow-like things. LAMS-TEX is available from CTAN. It is not known whether this part of LAMS-TEX can be "ripped out" and used with LATEX.

Kristoffer Rose's XY-Pic package is designed for similar purposes—the creation of graphics, with an emphasis on those requiring arrows of all sorts in their construction, such as commutative diagrams. Since these macros are generic, they can be part of LATEX or TEX documents. XY-Pic diagrams are matrix-like constructs within the confines of a "diagram" environment. The nodes of the drawing are like the elements of a matrix or array, and various commands allow the nodes to be connected in artful ways.

The DraTeX package of macros provides an extensive structured environment in which to create an astonishing selection of figures and graphs. Although the macros and styles are public, it will be necessary to consult Gurari (1993) to proceed.

12.3   PↃCTEX

The PↃCTEX package is one of the oldest of the "graphics extensions" to TEX, dating from 1986. The essential reference for this package is Wichura

(1987). The discussion here should be viewed as an introduction containing a variety of examples, all of which only supplement the documentation.

It achieves its aims by placing many small dots (usually taken from a 5-pt font) close together. The resulting shapes are good approximations to smooth curves or to lines with arbitrary orientations.

Since all of PICTEX's curves are collections of dots, it follows that PICTEX instructions make TEX work hard. It's easy to generate huge .dvi files in a PICture. It may be best to create small documents, each containing one PICture, and then to include each picture in the final document using techniques from chapter 11.

We'll see later how to draw PICtures in LATEX documents, but for now let's assume we are working with plain TEX. Near the beginning of a PICTEX document, include the statement

```
\input pictex
```

Each PICture must appear within a pair of instructions.

```
\beginpicture
  ⟨PICTEX instructions⟩
\endpicture
```

PICTEX commands often need to take cognizance of many optional arguments, as well as several required ones. Consequently, PICTEX commands have been designed to adhere to the following conventions.

- PICtures will be enclosed in pairs of \beginpicture and \endpicture commands.

- PICTEX commands contain lots of clauses, each of which must be separated from its neighbor by at least one space. So,

  ```
  \put {Hello, world.} [tr] <3pt,1mm> at 0 0 % Good :-)
  ```

  is correct, whereas

  ```
  \put{Hello, world.}[tr]<3pt,1mm>at0 0  % Bad :-(
  ```

  is not. The many kinds of delimiters in PICTEX reflect the different nature of optional arguments for commands.

- The most frequent cause of PICTEX errors is failure to pay close attention to delimiters <, >, [,]. (,), and /. Errors of omission generate screens full of obscure error messages.

- Many instructions control the placement of a TEX box. You will want to place this box "at" a point. But what part of the box goes at the point? The box reference point can be at the top, at the bottom, or at the baseline; it can be at the right or left; or it can be centered. In most commands, we will enclose the reference-point attributes in square brackets. An r or l orients the box to its right or left edge. A t, B, or b orients at its top, baseline, or bottom. The default orientation is centering.

- Coordinates and other lists delimited by angle brackets < and > are separated by commas.

- Undelimited coordinates and other P$_{I}$CT$_{E}$X items must be separated from one another by at least one space.

- The P$_{I}$CT$_{E}$X macros are themselves freely available; CTAN contains them. TUG (1979) sells the manual [Wichura (1987)].

The summary of basic P$_{I}$CT$_{E}$X commands on page 388 is necessarily skeletal. Most of the optional arguments are missing; you'll need to consult Wichura (1987) after all.

The remainder of this section consists of a small selection of P$_{I}$Ctures together with the P$_{I}$CT$_{E}$X code that generated them and perhaps a few brief comments.

Figure 6 on the next page reveals P$_{I}$CT$_{E}$X's secret—lots of little dots carefully placed next to one another simulate diagonal lines as well as curves of surprising sophistication. I measured the height of the period in a 5-pt font (by placing a 5-pt period in an \hbox and saving its height), which is the P$_{I}$CT$_{E}$X's usual plotting symbol, and made sure the right horizontal rule was that thickness. In that way the rule maintains visual compatibility with the rest of the figure.

The basic drawing unit of figure 7 on page 381 is an example of some of the most elementary P$_{I}$CT$_{E}$X commands. In addition, it shows how it is possible to incorporate P$_{I}$CT$_{E}$X graphics as part of macros (and other L^{A}T$_{E}$X and T$_{E}$X constructs) and so to build more complicated drawings using these components. Here, using the conventions of plain T$_{E}$X, the macro \corners draws a picture consisting of four corner pieces (arguments 1–4) surrounding a central device (argument 5). A new macro \arrows is a special case of this one, and the \arrows themselves can be part of a bigger \corners drawing.

Figure 7 on page 381 also demonstrates the ways that variations in the basic \put command effect placement in a picture. Each box placed in a figure can have one of 11 reference points; these appear in figure 8 on page 382.

12.3.1 Command syntax

It's worthwhile examining the syntax of \put in detail, since it nicely encapsulates all the syntax conventions of P$_{I}$CT$_{E}$X. At the most basic, \put needs

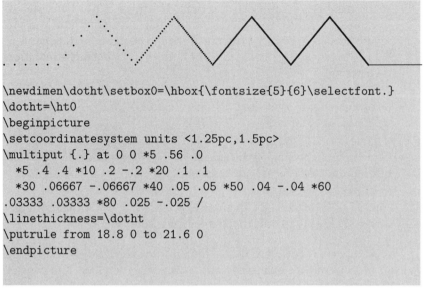

```
\newdimen\dotht\setbox0=\hbox{\fontsize{5}{6}\selectfont.}
\dotht=\ht0
\beginpicture
\setcoordinatesystem units <1.25pc,1.5pc>
\multiput {.} at 0 0 *5 .56 .0
  *5 .4 .4 *10 .2 -.2 *20 .1 .1
  *30 .06667 -.06667 *40 .05 .05 *50 .04 -.04 *60
.03333 .03333 *80 .025 -.025 /
\linethickness=\dotht
\putrule from 18.8 0 to 21.6 0
\endpicture
```

Figure 6: PICTEX zig-zags.

to know what to \put, and where to put it. Divested of all options, then, we always need to say at the least

\put {⟨*stuff*⟩} at ⟨*x*⟩ ⟨*y*⟩

so that, for example,

\put {$\bullet$} at 3 4

places a bullet at a point three units to the right of the origin and four units up; \setcoordinatesystem will have set the magnitude of the units.

But what part of the bullet? In the absence of instructions, PICTEX will place ⟨*stuff*⟩ (here, the bullet) and center this box at the point. This may not be what is wanted, so you may place up to two position holders in square brackets:

r	right
l	left
t	top
B	baseline
b	bottom

An author-artist may choose at most one from the top part of this table and at most one from the bottom. So

\put {$\bullet$} [lb] at 3 4

places the bottom left corner of the box at the point $(3, 4)$.

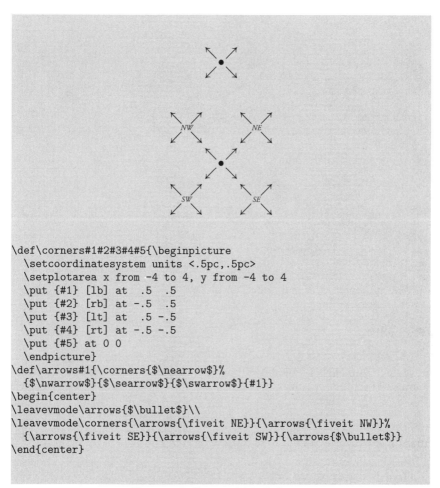

```
\def\corners#1#2#3#4#5{\beginpicture
  \setcoordinatesystem units <.5pc,.5pc>
  \setplotarea x from -4 to 4, y from -4 to 4
  \put {#1} [lb] at  .5  .5
  \put {#2} [rb] at -.5  .5
  \put {#3} [lt] at  .5 -.5
  \put {#4} [rt] at -.5 -.5
  \put {#5} at 0 0
  \endpicture}
\def\arrows#1{\corners{$\nearrow$}%
  {$\nwarrow$}{$\searrow$}{$\swarrow$}{#1}}
\begin{center}
\leavevmode\arrows{$\bullet$}\\
\leavevmode\corners{\arrows{\fiveit NE}}{\arrows{\fiveit NW}}%
  {\arrows{\fiveit SE}}{\arrows{\fiveit SW}}{\arrows{$\bullet$}}
\end{center}
```

Figure 7: PｌCtures within PｌCtures.

It's often convenient to be more specific about the amount by which you need to shift some ⟨*stuff*⟩, so PｌCTEX allows you to specify this information. If you type

```
\put {$\bullet$} <10pt,0pt> at 3 4
```

then PｌCTEX will locate the point $(3, 4)$ and place the center of the bullet 10 pt to the right of it, but at the same vertical level. You are allowed to use both the square bracket and the angle bracket options in a single \put statement, but the square bracket option must come first. Figure 8 on the next page thoroughly exercises the \put command.

Every picture here requires a \setcoordinatesystem command. Figure 9 on page 383 shows what happens when coordinate system units are changed. The left part of this display is completely accurate (at least, as ac-

```
\beginpicture
\setcoordinatesystem units <1pc,1pc>
\linethickness=.4pt
\putrectangle corners at 0 -1 and 8 4
\linethickness=.2pt \putrule from 0 0 to 8 0
\multiput {$\scriptscriptstyle\bullet$}
  at 0 0 0 4 8 4 8 0 8 -1 0 -1 /
\put {\tt lt} [rb] <-3pt,0pt> at 0 4
\put {\tt lB} [r]  <-3pt,0pt> at 0 0
\put {\tt lb} [rt] <-3pt,0pt> at 0 -1
\put {\tt rt} [lb] <3pt,0pt>  at 8 4
\put {\tt rB} [l]  <3pt,0pt>  at 8 0
\put {\tt rb} [lt] <3pt,0pt>  at 8 -1
\put {\tt t}  [b]  <0pt,3pt>  at 4 4
\put {\tt b}  [t]  <0pt,-3pt> at 4 -1
\put {\tt l}  [r]  <-3pt,0pt> at 0 1.5
\put {\tt r}  [l]  <3pt,0pt>  at 8 1.5
\put {$\bullet$} at 4 1.5 \setdashes
\putrule from 4 -1 to 4 4
\putrule from 0 1.5 to 8 1.5
\endpicture
```

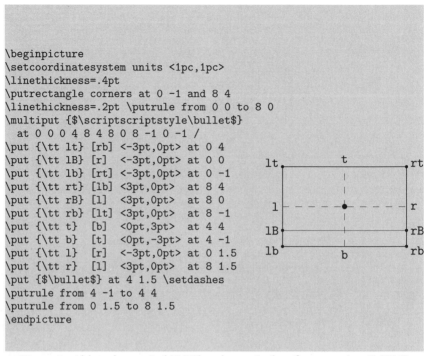

Figure 8: Although a typical TEX box has a single reference point, PICTEX knows 11 reference points.

curate as the printing device!) and allows you to compare TEX big points to 50ths of an inch.

PICTEX can do much fancier things. Figure 10 on page 384 shows off many of the ways graphs can be drawn. For fun, we also see what happens when PICTEX uses a file sin.d containing external data to prepare a plot. This file contains pairs of *x*- and *y*-values like this.

```
-5.0   3.4979
-4.8   2.5395
-4.6   1.6464
  ...
 4.6  -1.6464
 4.8  -2.5395
 5.0  -3.4979
```

It makes sense to use an external program to prepare data like this since LATEX or TEX would be poor at computing. (These data were prepared using the freely available Perl utility.)

PICTEX can draw a smoother graph, as figure 11 on page 385 shows. The dog's leg kink in the left portion of the curve is the algorithm's way of

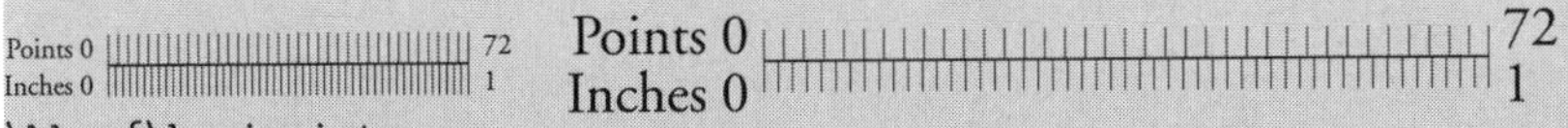

Points 0 |||||||||||||||||||||||||||||| 72   Points 0 |||||||||||||||||||||||||||||||||||||||||||||||| 72
Inches 0 ||||||||||||||||||||||||||||| 1   Inches 0 ||||||||||||||||||||||||||||||||||||||||||||||||| 1

```
\hbox{\beginpicture
\setcoordinatesystem units <1bp,1bp> % bp = big point
\linethickness=.4pt
\putrule from 0 0 to 72 0 % axis
\multiput
  {\vrule width.2pt height6pt depth 0pt} [b] at 0 0 *36 2 0 /
\put {\fiverm Points\ 0} [rb] <-3pt,1.5pt>  at 0  0
\put {\fiverm 72}        [lb] <3pt,1.5pt>    at 72 0
\multiput
  {\vrule width.2pt height6pt depth 0pt} [t] at 0 0 *50 1.44  0 /
\put {\fiverm Inches\ 0} [rt] <-3pt,-1.5pt> at 0 0
\put {\fiverm 1}         [lt] <3pt,-1.5pt>   at 72 0
\endpicture
\hskip.15in
\beginpicture
\setcoordinatesystem units <2bp,1bp>
\linethickness=.4pt
\putrule from 0 0 to 72 0 % axis
\multiput
  {\vrule width.2pt height6pt depth 0pt} [b] at 0 0 *36 2 0 /
\put {\fiverm Points\ 0} [rb] <-3pt,1.5pt>  at 0  0
\put {\fiverm 72}        [lb] <3pt,1.5pt>    at 72 0
\multiput
  {\vrule width.2pt height6pt depth 0pt}
  [t] at 0 0 *50 1.44 0 /
\put {\fiverm Inches\ 0} [rt] <-3pt,-1.5pt> at 0  0
\put {\fiverm 1}         [lt] <3pt,-1.5pt>   at 72 0
\endpicture}
```

Figure 9: Rulers, accurate and inaccurate.

alerting us that the data points are too far apart in that region. When we augment the data

0.2 5.0000   0.4 2.5   0.6 1.6667   0.8 1.25 ...

to

0.2 5   0.3 3.33333   0.4 2.5   0.5 2   0.6 1.6667 ...

(\setquadratic expects an even number of points), then the troublesome portion changes from

to

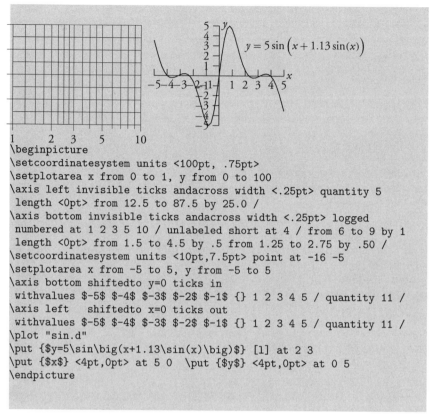

```
\beginpicture
\setcoordinatesystem units <100pt, .75pt>
\setplotarea x from 0 to 1, y from 0 to 100
\axis left invisible ticks andacross width <.25pt> quantity 5
 length <0pt> from 12.5 to 87.5 by 25.0 /
\axis bottom invisible ticks andacross width <.25pt> logged
 numbered at 1 2 3 5 10 / unlabeled short at 4 / from 6 to 9 by 1
 length <0pt> from 1.5 to 4.5 by .5 from 1.25 to 2.75 by .50 /
\setcoordinatesystem units <10pt,7.5pt> point at -16 -5
\setplotarea x from -5 to 5, y from -5 to 5
\axis bottom shiftedto y=0 ticks in
 withvalues $-5$ $-4$ $-3$ $-2$ $-1$ {} 1 2 3 4 5 / quantity 11 /
\axis left   shiftedto x=0 ticks out
 withvalues $-5$ $-4$ $-3$ $-2$ $-1$ {} 1 2 3 4 5 / quantity 11 /
\plot "sin.d"
\put {$y=5\sin\big(x+1.13\sin(x)\big)$} [1] at 2 3
\put {$x$} <4pt,0pt> at 5 0  \put {$y$} <4pt,0pt> at 0 5
\endpicture
```

Figure 10: Graphing a curve with PICTEX.

PICTEX can draw four types of plots. In addition to smooth and line-like curves controlled by \setquadratic and \setlinear, it can plot histograms and bar graphs via the \sethistograms and \setbars declarations. To a non-statistician, histograms are bar graphs whose bars are drawn with no intervening space between them. Figure 12 on page 386 shows one graph combining these four forms. A simple Perl program prepared the data for this display, the top half of which superimposes a bar graph and a quadratic graph. The bottom half of this graph is the mirror image of the top, drawn this time with a linear graph and a histogram.

Associated with bar graphs is the concept of breadth. Normally, a horizontal bar looks something like ⬜ and its vertical counterpart resembles ⬜. The length of the narrow side is the *breadth*, and we can adjust the appearance of the bar graph by tweaking the breadth keyword in the \setbars command. For example, we can draw a solid line by increasing the value of PICTEX's \linethickness parameter but making the breadth zero points in width. This does *not* make the line invisible; the short sides vanish, but the long sides are still drawn.

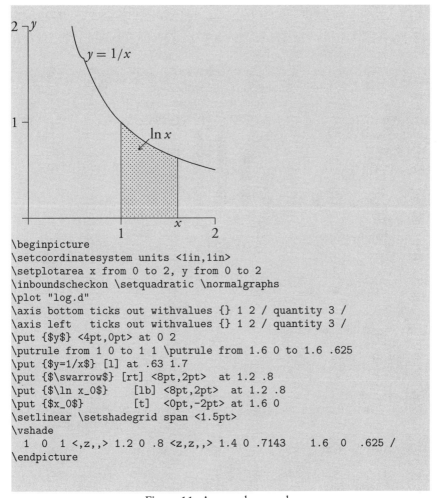

```
\beginpicture
\setcoordinatesystem units <1in,1in>
\setplotarea x from 0 to 2, y from 0 to 2
\inboundscheckon \setquadratic \normalgraphs
\plot "log.d"
\axis bottom ticks out withvalues {} 1 2 / quantity 3 /
\axis left   ticks out withvalues {} 1 2 / quantity 3 /
\put {$y$} <4pt,0pt> at 0 2
\putrule from 1 0 to 1 1 \putrule from 1.6 0 to 1.6 .625
\put {$y=1/x$} [l] at .63 1.7
\put {$\swarrow$} [rt] <8pt,2pt>  at 1.2 .8
\put {$\ln x_0$}    [lb] <8pt,2pt>  at 1.2 .8
\put {$x_0$}        [t]  <0pt,-2pt> at 1.6 0
\setlinear \setshadegrid span <1.5pt>
\vshade
  1  0  1 <,z,,> 1.2 0 .8 <z,z,,> 1.4 0 .7143   1.6  0  .625 /
\endpicture
```

Figure 11: A smoother graph.

Figure 13 on page 387 shows how to manipulate these quantities to draw sophisticated displays. We want a graph such that pairs of bars include a solid and an open bar and such that the boundary between them is located at the y-value. We draw the solid bars by increasing \linethickness and making the breadth equal to zero points. It must also be shifted upwards by half its width. To draw the open bar, we reset \linethickness to be .4pt or something similar, at the same time shifting it down by half the breadth.

12.3.2 PjCTEX plus LATEX

Only minor modification is needed to use PjCTEX within LATEX file. Since PjCTEX predates the current LATEX, the syntax follows the old style LATEX,

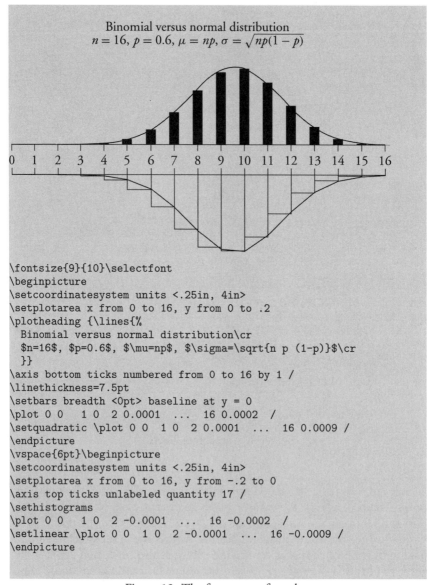

```
\fontsize{9}{10}\selectfont
\beginpicture
\setcoordinatesystem units <.25in, 4in>
\setplotarea x from 0 to 16, y from 0 to .2
\plotheading {\lines{%
 Binomial versus normal distribution\cr
 $n=16$, $p=0.6$, $\mu=np$, $\sigma=\sqrt{n p (1-p)}$\cr
 }}
\axis bottom ticks numbered from 0 to 16 by 1 /
\linethickness=7.5pt
\setbars breadth <0pt> baseline at y = 0
\plot 0 0   1 0   2 0.0001  ...  16 0.0002  /
\setquadratic \plot 0 0   1 0   2 0.0001  ...  16 0.0009 /
\endpicture
\vspace{6pt}\beginpicture
\setcoordinatesystem units <.25in, 4in>
\setplotarea x from 0 to 16, y from -.2 to 0
\axis top ticks unlabeled quantity 17 /
\sethistograms
\plot 0 0   1 0   2 -0.0001  ...  16 -0.0002  /
\setlinear \plot 0 0   1 0   2 -0.0001  ...  16 -0.0009 /
\endpicture
```

Figure 12: The four types of graphs.

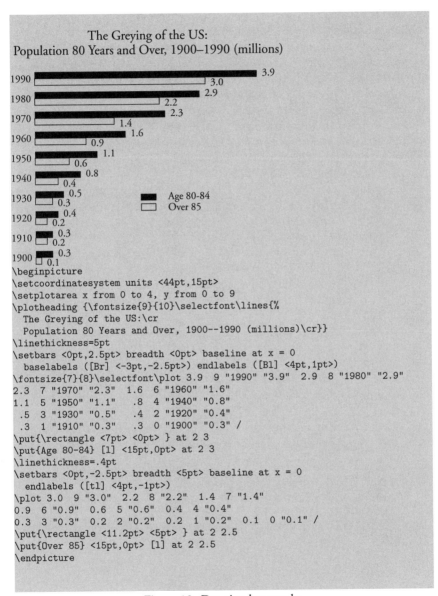

The Greying of the US:
Population 80 Years and Over, 1900–1990 (millions)

```
\beginpicture
\setcoordinatesystem units <44pt,15pt>
\setplotarea x from 0 to 4, y from 0 to 9
\plotheading {\fontsize{9}{10}\selectfont\lines{%
  The Greying of the US:\cr
  Population 80 Years and Over, 1900--1990 (millions)\cr}}
\linethickness=5pt
\setbars <0pt,2.5pt> breadth <0pt> baseline at x = 0
  baselabels ([Br] <-3pt,-2.5pt>) endlabels ([Bl] <4pt,1pt>)
\fontsize{7}{8}\selectfont\plot 3.9  9 "1990" "3.9"  2.9  8 "1980" "2.9"
2.3  7 "1970" "2.3"  1.6  6 "1960" "1.6"
1.1  5 "1950" "1.1"   .8  4 "1940" "0.8"
 .5  3 "1930" "0.5"   .4  2 "1920" "0.4"
 .3  1 "1910" "0.3"   .3  0 "1900" "0.3" /
\put{\rectangle <7pt> <0pt> } at 2 3
\put{Age 80-84} [l] <15pt,0pt> at 2 3
\linethickness=.4pt
\setbars <0pt,-2.5pt> breadth <5pt> baseline at x = 0
  endlabels ([tl] <4pt,-1pt>)
\plot 3.0  9 "3.0"  2.2  8 "2.2"  1.4  7 "1.4"
0.9  6 "0.9"  0.6  5 "0.6"  0.4  4 "0.4"
0.3  3 "0.3"  0.2  2 "0.2"  0.2  1 "0.2"  0.1  0 "0.1" /
\put{\rectangle <11.2pt> <5pt> } at 2 2.5
\put{Over 85} <15pt,0pt> [l] at 2 2.5
\endpicture
```

Figure 13: Drawing bar graphs.

PiCTEX: Some Basic Commands

```
\beginpicture
\endpicture
\setcoordinatesystem units <⟨x-unit⟩,⟨y-unit⟩>
\put {⟨stuff⟩} at ⟨x-coord⟩ ⟨y-coord⟩
\multiput {⟨stuff⟩} at
  ⟨x-coord⟩ ⟨y-coord⟩ *⟨n⟩ ⟨x-inc⟩ ⟨y-inc⟩ ... /
\stack{⟨item1⟩,⟨item2⟩,...}
\lines{⟨item1⟩\cr ⟨item2⟩\cr ...}
```
useful for creating vertical blocks of text for labels.
```
\setplotarea x from ⟨x-left⟩ to ⟨x-right⟩ ,
  y from ⟨y-bot⟩ to ⟨y-top⟩
\axis /
```
This command has *numerous* options; check the examples here and in Wichura (1987).
```
\plotheading{⟨heading⟩}
```
places a title over the graph.
```
\grid{⟨cols⟩}{⟨rows⟩}
```
creates a rectangular grid of the specified columns and rows.
```
\longticklength, \shortticklength, \linethickness, etc.
\putrule from ⟨x1⟩ ⟨y1⟩ to ⟨x2⟩ ⟨y2⟩
\putrectangle corners at ⟨x1⟩ ⟨y1⟩ and ⟨x2⟩ ⟨y2⟩
\sethistograms, \setbars breadth ⟨wd⟩ baseline at ⟨var=val⟩
```
Controls plotting of histograms and bar graphs.
```
\setlinear, \setquadratic
```
Controls the types of plots.
```
\plot ⟨x1⟩ ⟨y1⟩ ... /
```
Basic plotting command.

See the manual[Wichura (1987)] for many additional commands controlling arrows, shading, arcs, dot and dash patterns, rotations, and much more. All options for these new commands and those listed above are also explained here.

although it appears to work well with the current LATEX. PiCTEX requires access to a font called \fiverm from which it draws the period as the endlessly repeated element for creating curves. In the old days, \fiverm was predefined, but now you'll need a line like

```
\newfont{\fiverm}{padr at 5pt}
```

towards the beginning of the file. Some few things have to be redefined, so you'll need to type

```
\input prepictex \input pictex \input postpictex
```

in the document. Obviously, this string of commands will look different for systems like MS-DOS that don't allow long filenames. This plain TEX syntax is necessary since there are no LATEX-appropriate style or package files in the PICTEX package.

CHAPTER 13

· ·

USING METAFONT AND METAPOST

METAFONT and MetaPost—the META twins—are serious tools for creating images, but they are also great fun. One of the purposes of this chapter is to demonstrate how interesting these tools are.

Another purpose is instructional. There is a need for clear, well-written texts for these languages, but the length of this chapter precludes presenting a comprehensive tutorial here. Nevertheless, I hope that the approach I have adopted will prove beneficial. There is some discussion of the main concepts underlying a METAFONT or MetaPost program, and there are many examples—both code and output—illustrating this discussion. The problem lies with the underlying generality of these languages; there is simply no room here for a discussion of every topic. I hope that readers will tolerate this state of affairs, and I also hope that the visual output of the programs shown will let careful readers infer what is going on. The current chapter should accompany perusal of the main references for these tools, Knuth (1986c), Hobby (1992), and Hobby (1993).

With luck, the remarks in this chapter will be useful for getting started with these remarkable languages, but this chapter can in no way replace the standard references [Knuth (1986c), Hobby (1992)]. Since these two accounts tell essentially the same story from different points of view, they are both valuable regardless of which language is of concern. Also, the conscientious reader should have at least glanced above at chapter 3 concerning METAFONT. Throughout this discussion, we use "META" to refer jointly to METAFONT and MetaPost. It is possible to treat these two languages in a single discussion because they share so many similarities.

13.1 Basics

The highest and best drawing packages are those that allow for the creation of *structured graphics* files, analogous to the structured documents of LATEX.

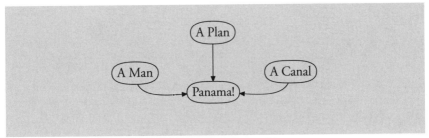

Figure 1: A sample graphic.

In a structured graphic, changes in single instructions propagate properly throughout the image.

Figure 1 is an image showing relationships between several short pieces of text. After seeing this, the artist may decide that "Panama!" should be a little larger and more emphatic, and the four balloons should be spread out a bit more, as in figure 2 on the next page. It's easy to specify a larger font, and it's easy to spread everything out a bit. If, after these changes, the graphic realigns itself properly, we can call it structured. In this case, the enclosing balloon sizes itself and the connecting arrows follow the repositioned balloons properly. This image appears well-structured. Only METAFONT and MetaPost offer fully structured graphics capabilities for LATEX or TEX graphics.

13.1.1 Basic truths

Both METAFONT and MetaPost require some computer sophistication on the part of the artist. Some familiarity with (and tolerance for) mathematical concepts is even better. Furthermore, aspiring META-artists should be prepared to spend some considerable amount of time acquiring the basics of these tools.

It's possible to delude oneself that LATEX or TEX are not programming languages, but this deception is impossible to maintain with METAFONT and MetaPost. Instructions for drawing characters or graphics are issued sequentially and bear a strong (but superficial) resemblance to the C and C++ languages. It is only by dealing with META as a programming language that it is possible to extract their great power. However, in case you care to use either of them as a (relatively) simple drawing engine, you may find it useful to learn about mfpic (chapter 15), which provides a TEX front end to METAFONT.

13.1.2 Variables

In order to create a picture, METAFONT or MetaPost needs certain quantities. Rather than refer to these things explicitly, these languages allow us to

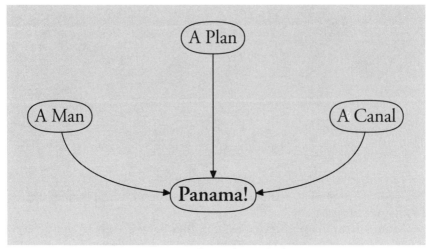

Figure 2: A sample graphic with changes.

refer to them symbolically, and these symbols take the form of names collectively called *variables*.

META variables are very similar to algebraic variables, although while algebraic variable names consist of a single letter, that is not true of META variables. Simple variable names consist of a mixture of upper- and lowercase letters, intermingled possibly with the underscore character. So z, AlPhA, upper_case, and Hannah could be names of variables. Since META is case sensitive, variables Sam, sam, and SAM represent three entirely different variables.

META artists often find it convenient to group related quantities together. This group of items will have the same variable name, and individual items will be distinguished one from the other by their *subscripts*.

For example, points are important in a META construction. It's convenient to let z refer collectively to a group of points and to distinguish points from each other using subscripts: z1, z2, z4, and so on. META subscripts need not be numeric; z.center presumably refers to a point in the center of something. As these examples show, numeric subscripts simply stand next to the variable, while the single period "." or a blank serves as the punctuation for subscripts. By this criterion, this list

```
a1
z2
a d
a.d
```

represents valid variable names as well, variables that might look like a_1, z_2, and a_d using traditional mathematical notation. (The whole story about variable names is more general than these comments indicate.)

> **MetaFont and MetaPost versus Other Methods**
>
> • **Pros:**
>
>   ○ Precise control over drawing.
>
>   ○ Graphic can be tailored to the raster printing device.
>
>   ○ Allows descriptive sets of statements.
>
> • **Cons:**
>
>   ○ Requires learning a new computer language.
>
>   ○ Not appropriate for free-hand drawings, sketches, or other nonmathematical graphics.
>
>   ○ May require mathematical aptitude or computer sophistication on the part of the artist.

What's a drawing made of? A final picture is built up of paths, each of which is constructed of points whose components are numbers. Therefore, no one should be surprised that the META interpreters provide for many different kinds of quantities. All variables, of whatever type, have names conforming to the conventions above. META knows what a variable's type is through a *type declaration*. After the line

```
numeric a[]; path p; picture pic;
```

variables like a5 or a.upper refer to numbers, while p and pic refer to a path and to a picture. The juxtaposed square brackets in the numeric statement lets the META interpreters know that all names to numeric variables with the first name a must be followed by a single subscript. Variables whose types have not been declared are legal, but META then assumes they refer to numeric quantities. In this example, a picture variable pic3 is illegal because this declaration has not permitted pic to have a subscript.

METAFONT provides for eight variable types, and MetaPost provides for these plus a color type. In this chapter we will mainly be concerned with numbers, paths, and pictures.

13.1.3 File organization

For both METAFONT and MetaPost, a program consists of a series of statements. Formatting of the program file is flexible. Statements are separated from each other using the semicolon, as they are in the C language. Only printable ASCII characters are permitted in a META source file.

METAFONT   If we direct METAFONT output to produce a font, it's easy to include in a LATEX or TEX document. To this end, all METAFONT drawing instructions should be enclosed by pairs of beginchar and endchar statements. That is, the program file resembles a set of sandwiches:

> beginchar(⟨*char-name*⟩,⟨*width*⟩#,⟨*height*⟩#,⟨*depth*⟩#) ;
> ⟨*drawing instructions*⟩
> endchar;

where the sandwich filling can be any valid sequence of commands. The ⟨*char-name*⟩ will be the character label of the place in the font that will contain the image. This should be "A", for example, if the image will be typeset in the document by typing A. The three dimensions following ⟨*char-name*⟩ should be sharped quantities giving the width, height, and depth (in reverse alphabetic order, for mnemonic reference) of the image. There can be no more than 256 of these sandwiches in any METAFONT file, since TEX fonts may not contain more characters than this.

MetaPost   MetaPost is designed for the production of figures, not fonts, so the end product of a MetaPost program is a figure rather than a character. A MetaPost program file also resembles a set of sandwiches, but the structure is

> beginfig(⟨*number*⟩) ;
> ⟨*drawing instructions*⟩
> endfig;

There is no point in specifying the dimensions of the figure—that computation is part of MetaPost's job, and bounding box information is part of the output file. Since it's not a character, there is no inherent depth below the baseline. The ⟨*number*⟩ argument to the beginfig command has no special relation to the figure itself, but it becomes the extension to the file containing the drawing instructions for that figure. That is, if a file foo.mp contains programs for figures 1 and 2, the output will be two PostScript files called foo.1 and foo.2. (In this chapter, there is no correspondence between the figure number of a MetaPost program and the figure number as it appears in the figure's display in the text.)

Both   The input file for either program must end either with a command bye or with end so the interpreter knows it's time to quit.

    In the examples of this chapter, the statements will *not* include the enclosing begin... and end... commands. You will need to provide the proper set, depending on the context—METAFONT or MetaPost.

13.1.4   Coordinate systems and points

Refer to chapter 11 for greater detail about coordinate systems.

Individual locations on a coordinate plane are *points*. Points are important because they can be connected in artful ways to form pictures (or elements of pictures).

Points, like other quantities, can be named. The META twins support the familiar *z convention*, whereby points are collectively named 'z' and are distinguished one from each other by a unique subscript. Furthermore, the individual *x*- and *y*-components can be retrieved by saying x or y followed by the proper subscript. That is, if we say

```
z12'=(2pt,-1pc);
```

in a META program file, then $z'_{12} = (2pt, -1pc)$ and we can use x12' or y12' whenever we want. They automatically have the values x12'=2pt and y12'=-1pc. Points are called "pairs" in META terminology, and though it is possible to say

```
pair dot;
dot=(2pt,1pc);
```

to name an arbitrary point, there is no *x*- or *y*-convention associated with pair names other than those called *z* (with an arbitrary collection of subscripts). To get at the individual components of dot, we need to use xpart and ypart.

```
pair newdot;
xpart newdot = 2 xpart dot;
ypart newdot = 3 ypart dot;
```

By the way, you should **not** say

```
pair z[]
```

in a META program. The *z*-convention is set up using a special macro, and META will complain about the conflicting usage.

13.2   Paths into pictures

We will see here how to create simple pictures out of paths, the connections between points. It's possible to use simple pictorial elements as components of more complicated drawings.

There's nothing inherently fascinating about dots, but there's art in connecting them gracefully. META can perform this connecting when told to draw a path between some points. There are two important path connectors: --, which draws straight line segments; and .., for curves. META goes

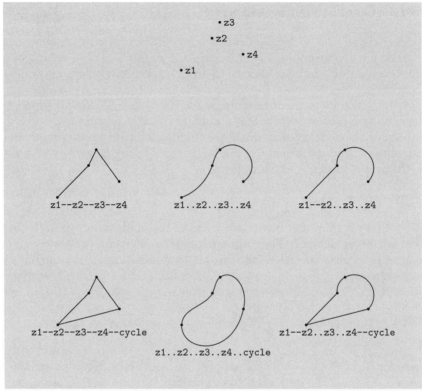

Figure 3: Different ways to connect the same points.

to great pains to choose the most pleasing curve possible when drawing a curve with the ".." path connector.

In addition to connecting adjacent points, the cycle keyword is available to form a closed path. Note that META pays attention to the path connector preceding the cycle command.

Figure 3 shows how these work, and how they can be mixed, for four particular points. Individual paths can be formed using mixtures of all the path connectors.

It's often convenient to assign a path name to a *path*—a collection of points and their connections—and to then stroke (draw) the path. The simplest way to control the stroking of a path is with the pickup command. The effect of

```
pickup pencircle scaled 1pt;
```

will be to draw everything after this (and until the next pickup command) with a circular pen whose diameter is 1 pt. This seems small, but is visually quite heavy; this rule | is 1 pt thick. By default, META draws with a circular

Basic Concepts of Metafont and of MetaPost

File structure. Main files consist of sequences of statements separated by semicolons. Such files must be terminated by the command bye or end. Usable output is sandwiched between command pairs beginchar and endchar (METAFONT) or between beginfig and endfig (MetaPost).

Objects. Objects must be named and are declared by type declarations such as numeric, path, and so on. Both META interpreters support the z-convention for points (pairs).

Path Connectors

--	connect points with a straight line
..	connect points with a smooth curve
cycle	construct a closed path
{...}	direction specifiers for pen
up, down, right, left	common directions

Basic Commands

pickup ...	select pen for drawing
draw ...	draw a path
fill ...	darken the interior of a cyclic path

pen that is 0.4 pt thick. (The penoptions keyword in MetaPost only makes it easier to set pen drawing choices.)

Paths, once named, can be transformed for simple effect. For example, I type

```
u=1pc; path petal;
z1=origin; z2=(0,3u);
z3=(3u,3u); z4=(3u,0);
petal=z1..{up}z2..z3..
  z4{left}..z1..cycle;
draw petal;
```

to get a petal-like structure, and I can draw a flower by saying

```
u=1pc; path petal;
z1=origin; z2=(0,3u);
z3=(3u,3u); z4=(3u,0);
```

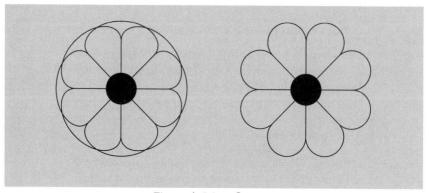

Figure 4: More flowers.

```
petal=z1..{up}z2..z3..z4{left}..z1..cycle;
for i=0 upto 3:
  draw petal rotated (90*i);
endfor
pickup pencircle scaled 2u;
drawdot origin;
```

which gives

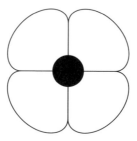

This fragment illustrates some useful features. The direction the pen nib should travel at a point is enclosed in curly brackets; this is the meaning of {up} and {left}; {right} and {down} are also available. Loop structures control repetitive actions, and if we rotate and draw a petal within the loop, we get our flower. Two basic META verbs are draw and fill.

Figure 4 shows variations on this basic flower shape. Readers should try to generate these figures themselves.

The discussion up until now constitutes a very basic introduction to the simplest uses of METAFONT and MetaPost. Our discussion will now explore several miscellaneous and more advanced META capabilities.

13.3 Calculating

Most computer languages have no concept of algebraic equality, so

$$x + y = 3$$

is gibberish to them. It's generally only possible to assign values to a variable, and in modern languages this *assignment operator* is denoted by `:=`. The META interpreters have this ability, too. After

```
numeric theta, sfactor; path p, q;
```

the instructions

```
theta:=theta+dtheta;
q:=p scaled sfactor rotated theta;
```

create a new value of `theta` from the sum of the existing value of `theta` and `dtheta`. In the same way, a new value for the path q comes from the path p after it has been scaled down and rotated. Readers who enjoy a challenge may care to see why the META code

> %   some initial computation.
> **boolean** *timetofillbox*;
> *sfactor* := .95; % scale factor
> **path** *p, q*; *u* := 8*pc*;
> *p* := (*u, u*) -- (−*u, u*) -- (−*u, −u*) -- (*u, −u*) -- cycle; %   a square
> *theta* := 0; *dtheta* := .005; %   tolerance
> **forever**: %   search for angle of rotation
>   *theta* := *theta* + *dtheta*;
>   *q* := *p* scaled *sfactor* rotated *theta*;
>   **exitif** ypart(**point** 0 **of** *q*) > *u*;
> **endfor**
>
> % computing the boxes.
> **beginfig**(5);
>   **fill** *p*; *timetofillbox* := **false**;
>   **for** *i* := 1 **upto** 51: %   successive boxes
>   *p* := *p* scaled *sfactor* rotated *theta*;
>   **if** *timetofillbox*:
>   **fill** *p*; *timetofillbox* := **false**;
>   **else**:
>   **unfill** *p*; *timetofillbox* := **true**;
>   **fi**
>   **endfor**
> **endfig**;

leads to figure 5 on the following page.

The code does illustrate some new features. Variables may be of type boolean, and there is a `forever` variant of the usual `for` loop; the command `exitif` can test a condition and exit from this loop sooner than forever.

The milestones on any path are the points that META connects in simple or artful ways. These points are numbered internally by META starting from zero, and an expression like

```
point 0 of q
```

Figure 5: Nifty nested boxes.

tells META to select the initial milestone point on path q—here, (u,u)—after the square has been scaled and rotated. Since we ask META to exit from the loop the first time the y-value of this point rises above the level of the original, this procedure has the effect of determining the amount $d\theta$ by which a slightly shrunken nested square needs to be rotated in order to kiss its enclosing box at its four corners.

As in LaTeX and TeX, the percent symbol introduces comments. Finally, we see our first examples of the META if statement.

The *mediation* operator lets us determine a point that is part of the way between two known points. That is, if we know z1 and z2, then

```
z3=.5[z1,z2];
```

creates z_3, which is one-half of the way between the line connecting z_1 with z_2. Any mediation value is acceptable, but if the number is greater than one or less than zero, then z_3 won't be between the given points.

The left part of figure 6 on the next page is the output of

```
u := 1 in;  partway := .5; %                              some parameters
z₀ = (.5u, −1pc); %                                       triangle vertices
z₁ = origin;  z₂ = (.5u, u);  z₃ = (u, .1u);
draw z₁ -- z₂ -- z₃ -- cycle;%                            outer triangle
z₄ = partway[z₁, z₂]; %                       observe the use of mediation
z₅ = partway[z₂, z₃];
z₆ = partway[z₃, z₁];
draw z₄ -- z₅ -- z₆ -- cycle;%                            inner triangle
```

which also shows the advantages of parametrization. We can scale the figure up or down by adjusting the value of u. We can alter the interior triangle by changing the value of partway, as this figure shows.

It's possible now to generalize in quite a different way the nested boxes of figure 5 on the facing page. We can set the vertices of an immediately nested box as points that are part of the way between two of the outer vertices. At the same time, we might as well parametrize the number of vertices, and we might as well do the same for the mediation value. Here is the generic code.

```
boolean timetofillbox;  timetofillbox := true;%            some parameters
n := ⟨number⟩;  partway := ⟨fraction⟩;
l := 1 in;  u := ⟨value⟩;  theta := 360/n;
z₁ = (0, u);%                                               initial point
for i := 2 upto n:
    z[i] = z₁ rotated ((i − 1) * theta);%         determine additional vertices
endfor
forever:
    path p;  p := z₁ for j := 2 upto n: -- z[j] endfor -- cycle;%  nested polygon
    if timetofillbox:
        fill p;  timetofillbox := false;
    else:
        unfill p;  timetofillbox := true;
    fi
    pair Z[];  for j = 2 upto n: Z[j] := partway[z[j − 1], z[j]];  endfor
    Z₁ := partway[z[n], z₁];
    for j := 1 upto n: x[j] := xpart Z[j];  y[j] := ypart Z[j];  endfor
    if not timetofillbox: l := abs(z₁);  fi exitif l < .2u;
endfor
```

(It's up to you to replace the angle-bracketed expressions by numeric quantities.) One new feature shown here is the use of abs to compute the distance of z_1 from the origin. If this distance gets too small, then the loop terminates. (Otherwise, the next ring is computed and drawn.) Another important feature appears in the definition of p in the line following the forever. We want p to be the polygon formed by connecting the vertices z_1 through z_n with straight lines. We could write something like

```
p:=z1--z2--z3--z4--z5--cycle;
```

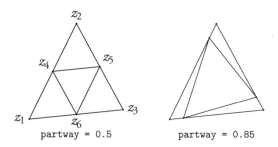

Figure 6: Examples of mediation.

if only we knew how many sides the polygon contained. We don't, so META allows us to build up the polygonal shape using a for loop. The bracket notation simply requests META to evaluate the contents of the brackets. That is, if j=3, then z[j] is the same as z3 (z_3), but different from z.j (z_j).

The output, for a variety of polygons and with partway assuming values of 0.5, 0.7, and 0.9, appears in figure 7 on the next page.

In addition to assignment :=, META also possesses the concept of equality as presented in an old-fashioned algebra class. Given equations like

```
X + 2Y = 10;
2X -  Y =  0;
```

the META interpreters solve for X and Y behind the scenes whether or not you need to explicitly know the results (here, X=2, Y=4). That is, rather than assign the value of one side of the relation to the other, META accepts the statement as expressing a relationship between the two sides. This relationship may change as METAFONT or MetaPost encounters additional information in subsequent statements, although META will complain if new information contradicts or repeats earlier information. (That's why this ability, coupled with the high degree of accuracy and the large repertoire of operations, makes META handy as a personal calculator. See chapter 3 for additional details.)

From a designer's point of view, it makes it easy to specify graphic elements by *describing* the elements and by eliminating the need for *prescribing* the elements. Here are some examples of this description process, made possible by META's ability to solve equations.

As part of some image, imagine we have drawn a rectangle of width and height a and b centered at the point z_c. We need to enclose it in an oval balloon, and we could do that easily by determining the corner points z.ul, z.ll, z.ur, and z.lr, where the subscripts suggest upper left corner, lower left corner, and so on. Here's one way to draw the box and its enclosing oval.

$z_{ur} - z_{ll} = (a, b); \quad z_{ul} - z_{lr} = (-a, b);$
$.5[z_{ll}, z_{ur}] = .5[z_{lr}, z_{ul}] = z_c;$
path *oval*; *oval* $= z_{ur} \mathinner{..} z_{lr} \mathinner{..} z_{ll} \mathinner{..} z_{ul} \mathinner{..}$ cycle;

Figure 7: Nested polygons.

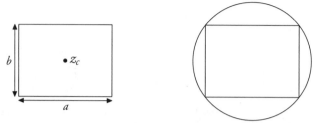

Figure 8: Surrounding a box with a closed curve.

path *box*; *box* = z_{ur} -- z_{lr} -- z_{ll} -- z_{ul} -- cycle;
draw *box*; **draw** *oval*;

The corner points are defined by their relationship to the rectangle. If drawn, the vector proceeding up from the lower left to the upper right would be (a, b), while the vector extending from the lower right to the upper left is $(-a, b)$. (If A and B are two points, then $A - B$ represents a line originating at the origin that points in the same direction as would a line drawn from B to A. Its length is the distance between A and B.) These vectors are fixed on the page by requiring their midpoints to coincide with the given point z_c. (MetaPost contains macros for doing this same thing more conveniently.)

A similar problem is presented by the following situation. If we have two points lying on each leg of an asymmetric V, as in the left of figure 9, where is the vertex z.bot? The slick META answer works because these programs have the power to solve linear equations automatically. The designation whatever stands for some unknown quantity, so a statement like

```
z.bot = whatever[z2,z1];
```

asserts that z.bot lies somewhere on the line passing through z1 and z2. If we combine that with a similar statement

```
z.bot = whatever[z3,z4]
```

we will have determined z_{bot} uniquely, for z_{bot} is the only point lying on both lines. META carries out the necessary calculations silently.

Suppose further we want to frame the V in such a way that the vertex lies on the lower horizontal strut, as in the right part of figure 9. We need

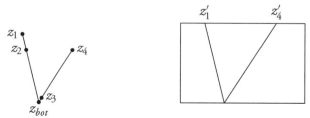

Figure 9: Drawing and framing a V-shaped path.

Figure 10: A geometrically regular figure.

to compute points z1' and z4', which lie both on the sides of the V and on the top horizontal. If we require that

```
z1'=whatever[z1,z2]=whatever[z.ul,z.ur];
z4'=whatever[z3,z4]=whatever[z.ul,z.ur];
```

then z1'--z.bot--z4' is the framed V. The framing box is easier:

```
z.ll=(0pc,y.bot); z.lr=(a,y.bot);
z.ul=(x.ll,y.bot+b); z.ur=(x.lr,y.bot+b);
draw z.ll--z.lr--z.ur--z.ul--cycle;
```

where *a* and *b* are the length and width of the box and will have been given values earlier on.

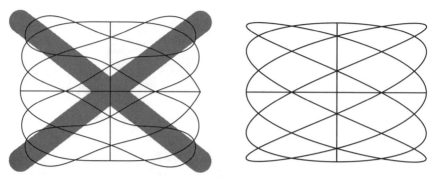

Figure 11: Graphing parametric equations.

13.4 Uses and applications

The META interpreters are especially good at rendering geometric patterns, as figure 10 on the previous page (and other figures in this chapter) show. For fun, the code to generate this graphic is

$u := 9pc$; $n = \langle first\ integer \rangle$; %   n=36 works well.
$sep = kappa * u$; $kappa = 1/60$; $nlevels := \langle second\ integer \rangle$;
path $p[]$; $p_1 = fullcircle$ scaled $2u$; $theta := 360/n$;
$side := 2u * sind(180/n)$; %   side of n-gon
$fudge := .06side$;
path $tile$;
$z_0 = (0,\ u)$; $z_1 = z_0 + (.5side + fudge,\ .5\ sqrt(3) * side)$; $z_2 = z_0$ rotated $-theta$;
$z_3 = (0,\ u - sep)$ rotated $-2theta$; $z_4 = (0,\ u - 2sep)$ rotated $-3theta$;
$u' = u - .5\ sqrt(3) * side$; $p_2 = halfcircle$ scaled $2u'$;
$z_{5'} = p_2$ intersectionpoint $(origin -- z_1)$; $y_{5'} := y_{5'} - 1.5sep - .2pt$;
$z_5 = z_{5'}$ rotated $-2theta$;
$lambda = (u - y_{5'})/u$;
$sfactor := (1 - lambda)/(1 + sqrt(3) * sind(180/n))$;
$z_6 = (0,\ u - 2sep)$ rotated $-2theta$; $z_7 = (0,\ u - sep)$ rotated $-theta$;
$tile = z_0 -- z_1 -- z_2 -- z_3 -- z_4 -- z_5 -- z_6 -- z_7 --$ cycle;
for $i = 0$ **step** 2 **until** n: **fill**$(tile$ rotated $-(i * theta))$; **endfor**%   ring
for $i = 1$ **step** 2 **until** n:
  draw $tile$ rotated $-(i * theta)$;
endfor
picture pic; $pic = currentpicture$;
for $i = 1$ **upto** $nlevels - 1$:
  $pic := pic$ scaled $sfactor$ rotated $-theta$;
  addto $currentpicture$ **also** pic;
endfor

Figure 10 on the preceding page uses `nlevels=10` and n=72. Complex effects are built from simple transformations of objects. [This and many other of the interesting geometric figures in this chapter were inspired by images in Grünbaum and Shephard (1987).]

13.4.1 Drawing engines

It's easy to regard METAFONT and MetaPost as "plotting machines" or even as drawing machines, as at left [courtesy of Jeremy Gibbons (1995)]. For the the case of plotting data, see section 13.6 on page 411 below for a discussion of the special abilities of MetaPost. In the case of mathematical expressions, either program makes an excellent drawing tool, but figure 11 on the facing page shows a common pitfall. In this figure, a graph of the parametric equations $x = a\cos 5\theta$ and $y = b\sin 3\theta$, we see the end result of

```
i := 0; %                                          initialize counter
for theta = 0 step ⟨ increment-value ⟩ until 360:
  X := cosd(5theta);  Y := sind(3theta);
  z[i] = (X * a, Y * b);  i := i + 1; %               compute points
endfor
draw z₀ for j = 0 upto i − 1: .. z[j] endfor; %          draw path
draw(−a, 0) -- (a, 0);  draw(0, −b) -- (0, b); %              axes
```

If an author is careless about the number of points, the sloppy graph shown on the left is the result. In this unacceptable version, the parameter varies in steps of $10°$, and this is not fine enough. In the acceptable drawing on the right, the step size is $1.5°$. (Any attempt to decrease the step size further leads to another problem. META reported on the console that its capacity was exceeded. This common problem often means that you are trying to do too many things in METAFONT, MetaPost, or in LATEX and TEX for that matter. A solution is to somehow do less of the offending activity. Here, increasing the step size back up to $1.5°$ meant that MetaPost has fewer data points to compute, and this resolved the problem.)

No computer artist can afford to turn META loose on equations without careful supervision. Figure 12 on the next page shows one difficulty. Graphs that should be drawn in two distinct pieces may appear, as on the left, in a single, continuous, and misleading curve. The right figure is a better depiction.

The proper representation of cusps presents another problem. Simple "connect-the-dots" drawing can transform what should be a corner point into a smooth region of the curve. Suppose we have three points forming the vertices of an isosceles triangle, and we need to connect them with curves in such a way as to form a Gothic arch. The instruction

```
draw z0..z1..z2;
```

won't work, as the left portion of figure 13 on the following page shows; both METAFONT and MetaPost connect the points smoothly. A better command would be either

```
draw z0..z1..z1..z2;
```

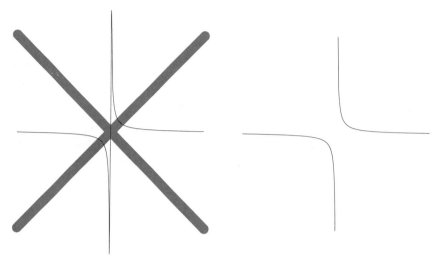

Figure 12: A graphing problem: dealing with discontinuities.

in which the pointed vertex is repeated, or

```
draw z0..z1 & z1..z2;
```

in which the arch becomes the joining together (via the concatenation operator &) of two distinct paths. The right portion of figure 13 displays the proper arch.

13.5   Simple transformations

META provides superior control over the stroke of an electronic nib. Here we'll consider only a few of the easy things that can be done to add variety to an image.

Changing the pen's nib is an easy way to add change. By default, we draw with a circular pen of diameter 0.4 pt, the diameter of a hairline rule

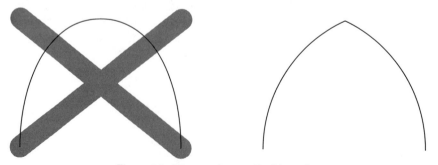

Figure 13: How to draw a Gothic arch.

Figure 14: Drawing with different nibs.

in LATEX or TEX. We use the `pickup` command to change the shape and/or size of the nib. If we type something like

```
path p; p=fullcircle scaled 2u; draw p;
pickup pencircle scaled 4pt; draw p shifted (4u,0);
pickup pencircle scaled 6pt yscaled .08pt;
draw p shifted (8u,0);
pickup pencircle scaled 6pt yscaled .08pt rotated 45;
draw p shifted (12u,0);
pickup pencircle scaled .4pt; draw p shifted (16u,0);
```

we get the circles of figure 14.

But the META twins allow additional transformations, and samples appear in figure 15 on the next page. If `tile` is the name for the outline shape of figure 10 on page 405, then we see the effect of META transformations in this figure. In each case, the shadow represents the transformed tile. The shadows in the first column were the effect of

```
path p[];
p1=tile shifted (.5u,.2u);
p2=tile scaled 1.5;
p3=tile xscaled 2;
p4=tile yscaled 3;
```

The statements

```
p5=tile slanted -2;
p6=tile rotated 35;
p7=tile zscaled (-1/3,1/6);
p8=tile rotatedaround ((u,u),30);
p9=tile reflectedabout (z0,z4);
```

created the shapes in the second column. (Here, u is some unit we need to define in the program. Also, z_0 and z_4 represent the left and right extreme vertices of `tile`.)

The great strength of META transformations is that they can be used as elements to form more complicated transforms. Both `reflectedabout` and `rotatedaround` are formed from simpler transforms. For example, rotatedaround is the "product" of a shift, followed by a rotation, followed by a final shift. [See Knuth (1986c, p. 266) for the interesting details.]

Figure 15: Transformed shapes.

The tile of figure 10 on page 405 and of figure 15 itself involves trans-formations. The META code given by the fragment

$u := 9pc$; $n = 36$;
$sep = kappa * u$; $kappa = 1/60$;
path $p[]$; $p_1 = fullcircle$ scaled $2u$; $theta := 360/n$;
$side := 2u * \text{sind}(180/n)$; %   side of an n-gon
$fudge := .06side$;
path $tile$;
$z_0 = (0, u)$; $z_1 = z_0 + (.5side + fudge, .5 \text{ sqrt}(3) * side)$;
$z_2 = z_0$ rotated $-theta$;
$z_3 = (0, u - sep)$ rotated $-2theta$; $z_4 = (0, u - 2sep)$ rotated $-3theta$;
$u' = u - .5 \text{ sqrt}(3) * side$; $p_2 = halfcircle$ scaled $2u'$;
$z_{5'} = p_2$ intersectionpoint $(origin -- z_1)$; $y_{5'} := y_{5'} - 1.5sep - .2pt$;
$z_5 = z_{5'}$ rotated $-2theta$;
$z_6 = (0, u - 2sep)$ rotated $-2theta$; $z_7 = (0, u - sep)$ rotated $-theta$;

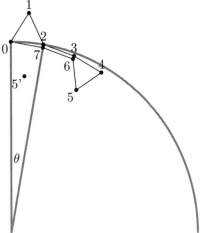

Figure 16: Anatomy of a tile. Points z_0 and z_2 lie on a circle of radius u. Points z_3 and z_7 lie on a quarter circle of radius u-sep. Finally, points z_4 and z_6 lie on a circle whose radius is u-2sep.

$$tile = z_0 \mathbin{--} z_1 \mathbin{--} z_2 \mathbin{--} z_3 \mathbin{--} z_4 \mathbin{--} z_5 \mathbin{--} z_6 \mathbin{--} z_7 \mathbin{--} \text{cycle};$$

produced the tile, where n is the number of sides in a circumscribed polygon, fudge is a small horizontal displacement of the upper triangle's vertex, and sep is the amount of separation between one dark tile and the one it underlaps to the right. Figure 16 helps make these notions clear. The tile itself is the component out of which figure 10 on page 405 has been formed.

13.6   Just MetaPost

John Hobby's MetaPost was designed as a graphics program rather than a font program, so no one should be surprised that the two programs differ in some of the capabilities they offer. MetaPost, for example, cannot create a font for use by LATEX or TEX. In this section, we will see examples of some of the things easy for MetaPost, but hard (or impossible) for METAFONT.

MetaPost knows more drawing options than METAFONT. It can draw arrows or dashed lines. MetaPost can also include text in its drawings.

MetaPost also supports additional file handling operations. Command readfrom returns the next line of a file as a string. Its opposite, write...to writes a line of text to a named file.

13.6.1   Getting MetaPost

Like most of the other programs in the TEX milieu, MetaPost is available in source and executable form from any CTAN archive. As of this writing, there are no commercial implementations available.

MetaPost versus MetaFont

- **Pros:**

  - Easy and natural integration of text with graphics.
  - Sophisticated graph package makes it easy to visualize data.
  - Language is similar to that of METAFONT.

- **Cons:**

  - Can't generate fonts—just graphics.
  - MetaPost requires a PostScript printer.
  - Language is similar to that of METAFONT.

13.6.2   Shades of gray and color

MetaPost allows shades of gray. If I type

```
draw p withcolor .4[white,black];
```

for some path p, I get a gray path. The mediation operator offers a convenient method for choosing a shade of gray or a color intermediate to two other hues. It's probably better to recode this as follows.

color *mygray*; *mygray* = .7[*white*, *black*];
draw p **withcolor** *mygray*;

Note the use of the `color` declaration.

MetaPost does understand simple color, as does PostScript. Pre-defined colors include `white`, `black`, `red`, `blue`, and `green`, but not `yellow`. New colors can be defined through the `color` keyword. For example, after

color *yellow*;
yellow = *red* + *green*;

it is now possible to draw `yellow` paths and pictures.

On displays with Display PostScript, the judicious use of color spices up the display, although few printers can yet exploit this capability. Those readers who do have access to color facilities might enjoy running the code

color *yellow*, *hue*[];

Including MetaPost Output

It may be necessary to use the *dvips* postprocessor. Make sure the epsf macros are included in the document. Then, to include a Meta-Post graphic, say

\epsfbox{⟨*graphic-name*⟩}

in the document, as for any encapsulated PostScript file.

```
yellow = red + green;
hue₁ = green;  hue₂ = blue;  hue₃ = red;
beginfig(1);
u = 1pc;
for j = 0 upto 10:
  for i = 0 upto 10:
    fill fullcircle scaled 2u shifted (i * .2 * u, u − j * .2 * u)
      withcolor(1 − j/10)[(1 − i/10)[hue₁, hue₂], hue₃];
  endfor
endfor
endfig;
end
```

through MetaPost and displaying the results. (Change the hues to alter the color effects.)

13.6.3   Typesetting a MetaPost graphic

MetaPost output is quite different from a METAFONT font, so the simple procedure for including MetaPost output in a document is different. It works reliably only for the *dvips* postprocessor. Consult the box on this page.

Plain TEX users will say '\input epsf' early in the document, and then MetaPost output file foo.1 is included via a command

\epsfbox{foo.1}

LATEX authors invoke the epsf macros by means of the statement

\usepackage{epsf}

after \documentclass and then will call the graphic by means of the same \epsfbox call. The epsf documentation details many ways to adjust the size, slant, orientation, and so on of the graphic.

13.6.4 Layers

One aspect of the PostScript model often makes it easier to construct figures, and that is this—any stroke, no matter how light, completely covers and obliterates anything underneath, no matter how dark. If a graphic can be resolved into layers, the MetaPost construction becomes much simpler.

At first glance, the MetaPost compass rose of figure 17 looks complicated. But it is the result of superposing five layers on each other, each of which is easy to construct. We see these individual layers in figure 18 on the next page. Most of the PostScript-generated graphics in this volume take advantage of this technique in some way.

13.6.5 Including text

Among the most important of MetaPost's shows of strength is its ability to include text within a graphic. MetaPost assumes that an artist includes text

Figure 17: A compass rose.

Figure 18: The components of the compass rose.

to label or tag some part of the figure, so the `label` (or `dotlabel`) command provides the mechanism for including text.

The basic form of a label command is

    label⟨.suffix⟩(⟨label-text⟩,⟨anchor-point⟩);

Labels are positioned with respect to a point, so it will be necessary to decide on an anchor point. Then, other questions need answering—should the label be centered on the anchor, or above it, or below it, or to the lower right of it, or ..., and so on. MetaPost uses the optional suffix to place the label with respect to the anchor. If no suffix is present, the label is centered on the anchor point. Otherwise, the suffix gives the placement. Thus

    label.bot("a",z0);

places a label below a point z_0, while

    label.urt(btex $\sqrt{x}$etex, u*(10, sqrt(10)));

affixes the tag $\sqrt{x}$ to the upper right of the point $u(10, \sqrt{10})$. The allowable suffix combinations are

    top   bot   rt   lft   urt   ulft   lrt   llft

for top, bottom, right, left, upper right, upper left, lower right, and lower left. If `dotlabel` is used, MetaPost sets a dot at the anchor point, but of course typesets the label text as well.

String text   A glance at the preceding two examples shows there are two different ways to specify the label text. The first way is to include the text as a string as the first argument to `label`. In MetaPost, strings are delimited by double quotes, which accounts for the double-quote syntax. MetaPost typesets this material simply—it uses the shape information from the `.tfm` file to position the characters next to each other.

In this "string" mode, MetaPost ignores all kerning and ligature information. That is, if we typed

    label("fifth", z0);

we would see "fifth" rather than "fifth" centered at z_0. (Look sharp to see the absence of the "fi" ligature.) When typesetting "string" labels, MetaPost uses the typeface given by the parameter `defaultfont`. To deviate from the default `cmr10` typesetting, insert a statement like

```
defaultfont := "cmti9";
```

(to select Computer Modern text italic) or perhaps

```
defaultfont := "ptmr8a";
```

if `ptmr8a` corresponds to the raw font for Times Roman. It may be necessary also to add a statement like

```
defaultscale := 0.8;
```

to adjust the size of the scalable font; this demonstrates the use of `default-scale` to control the size of label text. MetaPost runs TEX to typeset the labels, and TEX needs only metrics to do its work, so string values like `"cmti10"` or `"ptmr8a"` *must* refer to the names of `.tfm` files on your system.

Typeset text   The "string mode" method of text insertion is somewhat restrictive. A more satisfactory method of text inclusion is available. At any point in a MetaPost file, you can type

```
verbatimtex
⟨any valid TEX commands⟩
etex;
```

and text in a `label` command can contain blocks of the form

```
btex ⟨any TEX commands⟩ etex;
```

which rely on the setup in the preceding `verbatimtex` block. For example, people using plain TEX can type something like

```
verbatimtex \font\bf = pads7t at 8pt
  \font\rm = padr7t at 8pt\rm
etex;
beginfig(21);
u := 1pc;  path p[];
p0 = fullcircle scaled 2u shifted (u, 0);
p1 = fullcircle scaled 2u yscaled 2
   shifted (4u, 0);
p2 = (−2u, 2u)
  for i = −1.8 step .2 until 2: .. (i * u, .5i * i * u)
  endfor;
p2 := p2 shifted (8u, −u);
draw p0;  draw p1;  draw p2;
```

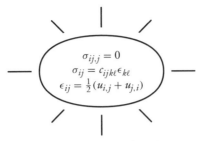

Figure 19: MetaPost plus LATEX.

label(btex{\ *bf Some Conic Sections*} **etex**, $(5u, 3u)$);
label *bot*(btex *Circle* **etex**, $(u, -2u)$);
label *bot*(btex *Ellipse* **etex**, $(4u, -2u)$);
label *bot*(btex *Parabola* **etex**, $(8u, -2u)$);
endfig;

to get

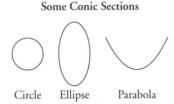

Here, pads7t and padr7t are the semibold and regular variants of Adobe Garamond. Note that the \rm is necessary to select the 8-pt regular as the default text font within the TEX "document" that MetaPost invokes.

Users of LATEX are not out in the cold, but some care is necessary. First, MetaPost's TEX environment variable must point to LATEX. I do this on my (Unix) system by saying

```
setenv TEX latex
```

Then, be careful in the MetaPost file to mention all the LATEX details necessary in a document. Carefully study this example, which generated figure 19.

```
verbatimtex
  \documentclass{article}\usepackage{zmtpad}
  \begin{document}
etex;
input boxes;
beginfig(17);
  u := 1pc;  path p[];  p₀ = (−6u, 0) -- (6u, 0);
  p₁ = (0, −4u) -- (0, 4u);
  p₂ = (0, −3.5u) -- (0, 3.5u);  p₂ := p₂ rotated −45;
  circleit mech(btex
    \ fontsize{8}{10}\selectfont
    $\begin{array}{c}
```

```
        \sigma_{ij, j} = 0\\
        \sigma_{ij} = c_{ijk\ell}\epsilon_{k\ell}\\
        \epsilon_{ij} = \frac{1}{2}(u_{i, j} + u_{j, i})
      \ end{array}$
  etex);
  mech_{dx} = mech_{dy};  mech_c = origin;
  pickup pencircle scaled 1pt;
  draw p_0;  draw p_1;  draw p_2;  draw p_2 rotated 90;
  pickup pencircle scaled u;  unfilldraw bpath_{mech};
  pickup pencircle scaled 1pt;  drawboxed(mech);
endfig;
verbatimtex
  \ end{document}
etex;
```

The LATEX preamble and \begin{document} statement should precede the first beginfig statement, and the \end{document} should follow the final endfig. The input statement brings in boxes.mp, which helps MetaPost circle and box things.

Text caveats   Don't be guilty of using the wrong parameters to control inserted text!

- The defaultfont and defaultscale commands only control text in "string" mode.

- Any commands in a verbatimtex/etex block control typesetting in subsequent btex/etex blocks.

Additional discussion of some advanced topics relating to the inclusion of text appears in several of the subsequent examples.

13.6.6 Drawing graphs

The package contained in the file graph.mp (part of the MetaPost package) defines a complete set of commands for creating graphs that are picture objects as far as MetaPost is concerned. Hobby (1993) describes these graphing macros and contains addenda to the main manual [Hobby (1992)]. In this section, we will see how to create a simple graph and how to successively enhance it. The best way for a casual user to prepare a graph is to peruse the manual [Hobby (1993)] and simply appropriate the code for the graph that best matches your own, with whatever minor revisions are necessary to personalize this code.

Any MetaPost input file should begin with

```
input graph;
```

to make the graph macros known to MetaPost. Typically, we create a graph
with a series of programs schematically similar to

```
beginfig(⟨number⟩);
  ⟨commands⟩
  draw begingraph(⟨width⟩,⟨height⟩);
    ⟨graph drawing commands⟩
  endgraph;
  ⟨more commands⟩
endfig;
```

In the simplest instance, the graph data are in a file like mydata.d, and a call
to the drawing command gdraw creates the curve. Many graph commands
resemble their nongraph counterparts to which a g has been prefixed.

I used an auxiliary program (in this case, Perl) to create a file sincos.d,
whose lines look like

```
0.00 0.000
0.05 0.999
   . . .
```

—that is, each line of the file contains two values separated by (at least) one
space. The first value is a horizontal value, and the second is the corresponding vertical value. One of the simplest ways to plot these data is via

```
beginfig(20);
  draw begingraph(4in, 2in);
  gdraw "sincos.d";
  endgraph;
endfig;
```

which generates figure 20 on the next page.

It's astonishing how few instructions were needed to get such a professional result. Nevertheless, additional instructions may be necessary to improve its appearance. For example, if we type

```
beginfig(21);
  draw begingraph(4in, 2in);
  setrange(0, −1, 6.28, 1);
  for x = 0, 1.57, 3.14, 4.71, 6.28:
    grid bot(format("%g", x), x) withcolor .6white;
  endfor
  for y = −1, −.5, 0, .5, 1:
    grid lft(format("%g", y), y) withcolor .6white;
  endfor
  gdraw "sincos.d";
  endgraph;
endfig;
```

we get figure 21 on the following page. Here, setrange focuses on the
proper range of values while the grid commands provide great control over

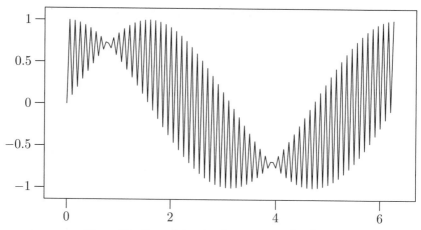

Figure 20: One of the simplest ways to plot data.

the axis labeling. The usual range of MetaPost color and drawing options continue to be available.

We strive for additional refinements in the final depiction, figure 22 on page 422. This augmented code

```
verbatimtex
  \documentclass{article}\usepackage{zmtpad}
  \begin{document}
  \fontsize{8}{10}\selectfont
etex;
init_numbers(btex $ − $ etex, btex $1$ etex, btex ${\times}10$ etex,
  btex ${}^{−}$ etex, btex ${}^2$ etex);
beginfig(22);
  numeric pi, hu, width, height;  pi = 3.14159265;
  width = 4in;  height = 2in;  2pi ∗ hu = width;
  draw begingraph(width, height);
```

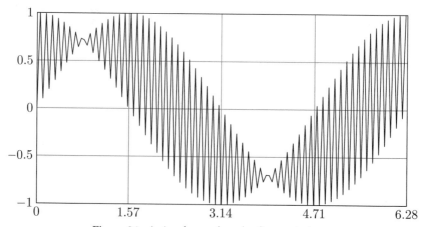

Figure 21: A simple graph—the first variation.

```
          setrange(0, −1, 2pi, 1);
          for x = pi/2, pi, 3pi/2:
            grid bot(format("", x), x) withcolor .6white;
          endfor
          for y = −1, −.5, 0, .5, 1:
            grid lft(format("%g", y), y) withcolor .6white;
          endfor
          gdraw "sincos.d";
          glabel top(btex{\bf Some Test Data} etex, OUT);
          glabel lft(btex The vertical coordinate $y$ etex
            rotated 90, OUT);
        endgraph;
        label bot(btex $\mathstrut0$ etex, (0, 0));
        label bot(btex $\mathstrut\pi/2$ etex, (hu ∗ pi/2, 0));
        label bot(btex $\mathstrut\pi$ etex, (hu ∗ pi, 0));
        label bot(btex $\mathstrut3\pi/2$ etex, (hu ∗ 3pi/2, 0));
        label bot(btex $\mathstrut2\pi$ etex, (hu ∗ 2pi, 0));
        label bot(btex The horizontal coordinate, $x$ etex, (hu ∗ pi, −1pc));
      endfig;
      verbatimtex \ end{document} etex;
```

is necessary for two major modifications: replacing some axis labels with exact (rather than numerical) values and typesetting with fonts other than the default Computer Modern. The typesetting in this example will actually be done by LaTeX, so before starting the MetaPost program, I issued

```
setenv TEX latex
```

Within the MetaPost source file, I began with a verbatimtex block to set up the proper prelude to a LaTeX document. The zmtad package simply selects MathTime math fonts with Adobe Garamond text fonts. The special label location OUT places a label relative to the entire graph.

Next, the init_numbers command serves as a MetaPost template for setting numerical labels on the axes. This is the default form of the statement, but reiterating it after LaTeX has been invoked will select and use the nondefault fonts that we've selected. Whenever you select a suite of nonstandard fonts for use in typesetting within a graphic, make sure you invoke this command after the verbatimtex block which switches type, but before the first beginfig command. The manual [Hobby (1993)] explains the significance of its five arguments, but most of the time you can use it exactly as presented in this example.

Within the begingraph block, we use the glabel command for several of the labels. One way to draw a grid with nonnumeric labels is to typeset them as shown in figure 22 on the following page. The special location OUT centers a label with respect to the entire graph.

It would be hard to typeset nonnumeric labels such as $\pi/2$. In this example, a horizontal scaling factor hu is defined by the statement

```
2pi*hu=width;
```

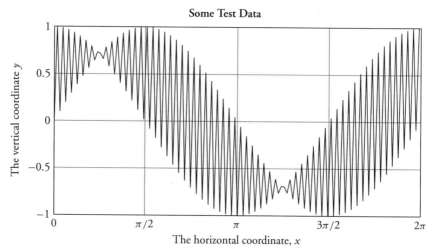

Figure 22: A simple graph—final variation.

so that the point (2pi*hu,0) corresponds to the point $(2\pi, 0)$ on the graph. Now it's possible to position typeset labels using the label command outside the begingraph block.

Finally, let's note that graph objects, for all their complexity, are merely picture objects to MetaPost, and are therefore subject to any of the special effects to which any other picture is subject. So if we type

```
beginfig(23);
  h = 3pc;  w = 27pc;  numeric sfactor;  sfactor = 1/3;
  fill(origin --- (w, 0) -- (w, h) -- (0, h) -- cycle) slanted sfactor
    withcolor .75[white, black];
  draw begingraph(w, h);
    setrange(0, −1, 6.28, 1);  autogrid(, );
    gdraw "sincos.d" withpen pencircle scaled 1.2pt
      withcolor white;
    endgraph slanted sfactor;
  endfig;
```

we get figure 23. Here, we have properly parametrized the height and width of the graph as parameters w and h. Normally, autogrid controls normal graph labeling; its invocation without arguments suppresses all labels.

Figure 23: A simple graph—an odd variation.

13.6.7 Text in graphics: Advanced topics

Because of the way TEX and MetaPost interact, it is not possible to use strings for typesetting as arguments in macros. Situations requiring this construct demand that we work around this limitation.

Consider, for example, the calendar page in figure 24 on the following page. Each of the daily blocks suggests the phase of the moon that would be visible that night. One would like to embed a loop like

```
for today =1 to 31: doday(today); endfor  % October
```

where the hypothetical doday macro is responsible for drawing a large dark square at the right place in the calendar page, chiseling out the moon's silhouette, and placing the white day number in each block's corner. We cannot do this for the reason mentioned above, and the alternative—placing numerous explicit label statements in the body of this figure, and in each figure for the remaining months of 1996—seems too painful to contemplate. One alternative and successful strategy exploits MetaPost's ability to write to external files.

If we say

string s; **numeric** pi; $pi = 3.14159265$;
$s = $ **str** pi & " = " & **str**$[pi]$ & ";";
write s **to** "myfile.tmp";
write *EOF* **to** "myfile.tmp";

then the string s has the value pi = 3.14159265; and this value—which is expressed in valid MetaPost syntax, by the way—becomes part of the file myfile.tmp. MetaPost opens this file if it needs to but otherwise appends this string to the file. Note, too, the two uses of the str command—str pi converts the name of the variable to a string, while str[pi] converts the value of this variable to a string. EOF is a predefined string which, when written to a file, has the effect of closing that file. Upon execution of these statements, the file myfile.tmp contains the following single line.

```
pi = 3.14159265;
```

These remarks form the kernel of our strategy for creating a lunar calendar. Before the loop controlling the blocks for each day, we write

string s;
$s = $ "verbatimtex \font\1=pads7t at 8pt \1 etex; picture P;"
write s **to** "myfile.tmp";

because all nondefault font declarations need to be redeclared when used in an auxiliary file such as myfile.tmp. Next, the doday macro shall create a pair of strings and write them to the auxiliary file.

$s := $ "P := thelabel(btex " & **str**$[today]$ & " etex, (";

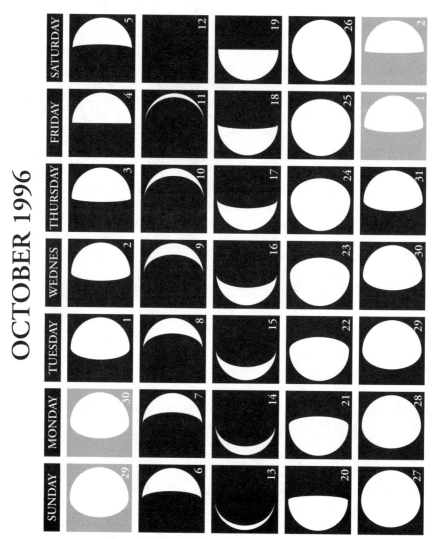

Figure 24: Month from a "lunar" calendar.

```
s := s & str[col] & ", " & str[row] & ")) ;";
write s to "myfile.tmp";
s := "draw P withcolor white;";
write s to "myfile.tmp";
```

As today cycles through all the days of the month, this places statements like

```
P := thelabel(btex 22 etex, (3,-4));
draw P withcolor white;
```

into the temporary file. (Here, we are using the `thelabel` variant of `label` to create a picture object that we can then typeset in white ink. It's up to the hypothetical doday macro to assign values to `row` and `col`.) At the conclusion of the loop, we

```
write EOF to "myfile.tmp";
input "myfile.tmp";
```

first to close the file and so prepare it for reuse, and then to read in the file's contents. We've taken care to create statements in the auxiliary file that are themselves valid MetaPost statements. If finer control is required when retrieving the contents of `myfile.tmp`, we can say

```
s := readfrom "myfile.tmp";
```

after which s is the string containing the next line of text from that file.

Figure 25 on page 428 plots the atomic weight (rounded to the nearest whole number) of the lighter elements versus the atomic number. We'd like to use graphing capabilities of MetaPost but the text on the vertical axis appears to be difficult if we restrict ourselves to those macros. Here is a version of the code that will generate this figure.

```
verbatimtex\font\lab=lsd at7pt \font\lar=lsr at7pt etex;
color TextColor, BackGroundColor;
                % Uncomment the next line for white text on a dark background:
%                       TextColor=white; BackGroundColor=.8[white, black];
          % Uncomment the next line for traditional black on white background:
TextColor := black; BackGroundColor := white;
input graph;
string t[]; numeric width, height, xmax, ymax;
width + 2pc = 27pc; height = 41pc;
xmax := 50; ymax := 120;        % max atomic number, max atomic weight
numeric vsf, hsf;                       % vertical and horizontal scale factors
ymax * vsf = height;
xmax * hsf = width;
beginfig(1);
  picture pic;
  t0 := "verbatimtex \font\lab=lsd at7pt ";
  t0 := t0 & "\font\lar=lsr at7pt etex; picture P;";
  write t0 to "chem.tmp"; write t0 to "chem1.tmp";
```

```
t₀ := "verbatimtex \input chemmacs etex;";
write t₀ to "chem.tmp";
draw begingraph(width, height);
    setrange(origin, xmax, ymax);                    % set bounds for graph
    autogrid(, );                                    % suppress labels
    gdata("elements.d", s,                           % deal with the data
        X := scantokens s₂; Y := scantokens s₃;
        gdraw(X, Y) -- (0, Y)
            withpen pencircle xscaled 2pt yscaled .2pt rotated 75
            withcolor TextColor;
        gdraw(X, Y) -- (X, 0)
            withpen pencircle xscaled 2pt yscaled .2pt rotated 75
            withcolor TextColor;
        t₀ := "P:=thelabel.lft(btex\\" & s₁ &
            " " & s₃ & ": etex, (0, " & s₃ & "vsf));";
        t₁ := " draw P withcolor TextColor;";
        write t₀ to "chem.tmp";
        write t₁ to "chem.tmp";
    );
endgraph;
for T = 1, 10, 20, 30, 40, 50:                       % generate horizontal labels
    t₀ := "P:=thelabel.bot(btex\lab " & str[T]&
        " etex, (" & str[T] & "hsf, 0));";
    t₁ := " draw P withcolor TextColor;";
    write t₀ to "chem.tmp";
    write t₁ to "chem.tmp";
endfor
write "endinput;" to "chem.tmp";
write EOF to "chem.tmp";                              % close the file
                              % Now to square the ends of the lines...
pickup penrazor scaled 1.5pt;  draw(−.75pt, −1.5pt) -- (−.75pt, ymax*vsf)
    withcolor TextColor;
pickup penrazor scaled 1.5pt rotated 90;
    draw(0, −.75pt) -- (xmax * hsf, −.75pt) withcolor TextColor;
              % Finally, we do the text typesetting (vertical labels).
input chem.001;
pic = currentpicture;
currentpicture := nullpicture;
fill bbox pic withcolor BackGroundColor;             % draw background
draw pic withcolor TextColor;                        % overlay TextColor paint
zₜ = ulcorner bbox currentpicture;                   % We will use these to get info
z_b = llcorner bbox currentpicture;                  % about the vertical extent of graph.
t₀ :=
"label.top(btex \lab Atomic weight versus atomic number ";
t₀ := t₀ & "for light elements etex, (" & str[.5xmax * hsf] & ", ";
t₀ := t₀ & str[yₜ + 3pt] & "));";
write t₀ to "chem1.tmp";
t₀ := "label.bot(btex \lar Atomic Number etex, ("&
    str[.5xmax * hsf] & ", ";
t₀ := t₀ if y_b − 3pt < 0: &"−" & str[−y_b + 3pt] else: str[y_b − 3pt] fi &"));";
write t₀ to "chem1.tmp";
write "endinput" to "chem1.tmp";
write EOF to "chem1.tmp";                             % close the file
input chem1.tmp;
```

endfig;

end

This example displays use of the bbox command, by which we can access the bounding box of a figure. Note too that various ..corner commands (ulcorner where ul is the upper left, llcorner for the lower left; urcorner and lrcorner also exist) give access to the corners of this box.

The file elements.d contains lines looking like this.

```
Al 13 27
Ar 18 40
As 33 75
    . . .
```

Each line of data contains the element's standard symbol, its atomic number, and the atomic weight. One of the verbatimtex blocks refers to the file chemmacs.tex, a short file containing the definition of the TeX macro we later use.

```
\def\\#1 #2:{\hbox{\lar\ #2\ \lab #1}}
```

Most of this MetaPost code for this figure is straightforward, especially with the manuals in hand. Be sure to consult the manual [Hobby (1993)] for the very interesting details behind the gdata command. Nevertheless, there are some interesting aspects to the construction.

Typesetting commands are written to two side files. The file chem.tmp contains information for the side labels, and the shorter chem1.tmp contains information for the labels at the top and bottom of the graph. Data within the begingraph block use natural coordinates for plotting—aluminum (Al) is at $(13, 27)$—and it's the responsibility of MetaPost to scale these numbers properly so all points fit properly on the graph. Since our typesetting occurs after the terminating endgraph command, it's up to us to create and keep track of the proper scale factors. That's the purpose of the statements

```
ymax*vsf=height; xmax*hsf=width;
```

where hsf and vsf suggest horizontal and vertical scale factors. The actual coordinates of aluminum, say, are $(13hsf, 27vsf)$, and it is now possible for us to precisely add material to the graph after the graph macros have finished their work. No auxiliary files may be reread by MetaPost unless they have been closed first; that's the purpose of a write EOF to ... statement.

Alert readers will note that in fact it is not chem.tmp that is input by MetaPost, but another file, chem.001. This second file is just a copy of chem.tmp with a few revisions made so some adjacent side labels won't vertically overlap.

13.7   Prettyprinting

Many of the code fragments throughout this chapter were prettyprinted using the mft tool, part of the original suite of software that accompanied TeX

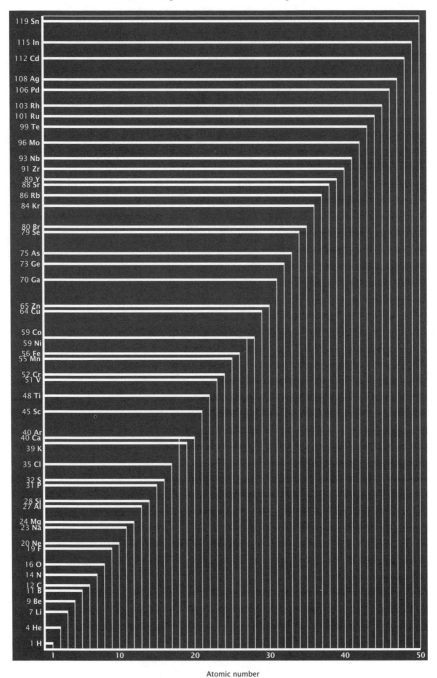

Figure 25: Atomic weights depend on atomic number.

and METAFONT. This program takes a METAFONT program, and, in the presence of a style file and possibly change files, creates a TEX listing for that file. The change file is necessary in case you wish to alter the formatting from that which mft thinks is proper. The program and its usage is described by Knuth, Rokicki, and Samuel (1989).

MetaPost is sufficiently similar to METAFONT that mft is useful. To prettyprint the file foo.mp, I first create a copy of it called foo.mf since mft expects an .mf file as input. Then, in the presence of the mp2.mft style file (by Ulrik Vieth; available from CTAN) I issue the command

```
mft foo -s mp2
```

to create the file foo.tex for typesetting.

13.8 Appendix: summary of MetaPost

The source for the following series of helpful tables summarizing the Meta-Post language was graciously provided by John Hobby. The special tables help make clear the differences between MetaPost and METAFONT. META-FONT and MetaPost are sufficiently similar that these tables should be useful to the METAFONT coder as well.

Keywords not prefixed by any symbols are MetaPost primitives; other symbols provide information about the package defining the command.

- A leading box ▪ means the command is part of the boxes.mp package. The statement input boxes must appear.

- A plain circle ○ means the command is part of the plain package.

- An infinity ∞ applies to the sarith.mp package for working with large numbers. You must type input sarith.

- The symbol +, to suggest a small set of coordinate axes, refers to features defined in graph.mp; type input graph to access these features.

These tables do not include certain administrative commands, loops and conditionals, and certain other constructs; consult Hobby (1992, pp. 73-78) for these.

Table 1: Internal variables with numeric values	
○ahangle	angle for arrowheads in degrees (default: 45)
○ahlength	size of arrowheads (default: 4bp)
○bboxmargin	extra space allowed by bbox (default 2bp)
charcode	the number of the next character to be output
▪circmargin	clearance around contents of a circular or oval box
day	the current day of the month
▪defaultdx	usual horizontal space around box contents (default 3bp)
▪defaultdy	usual vertical space around box contents (default 3bp)

ₒdefaultpen	numeric index used by pickup to select default pen
ₒdefaultscale	font scale factor for label strings (default 1)
+Gmarks	Minumum number of ticks per axis for auto and autogrid. Default 3
+Gminlog	Minimum largest/smallest ratio for logarithmic spacing with auto and autogrid. Default 3.0
ₒlabeloffset	offset distance for labels (default 3bp)
linecap	0 for butt, 1 for round, 2 for square
linejoin	0 for mitered, 1 for round, 2 for beveled
miterlimit	controls miter length as in PostScript
month	the current month (e.g, 3 ≡ March)
pausing	> 0 to display lines on the terminal before they are read
prologues	> 0 to output conforming PostScript using built-in fonts
showstopping	> 0 to stop after each show command
time	the number of minutes past midnight when this job started
tracingcapsules	> 0 to show capsules too
tracingchoices	> 0 to show the control points chosen for paths
tracingcommands	> 0 to show commands and operations as they are performed
tracingequations	> 0 to show each variable when it becomes known
tracinglostchars	> 0 to show characters that aren't infont
tracingmacros	> 0 to show macros before they are expanded
tracingonline	> 0 to show long diagnostics on the terminal
tracingoutput	> 0 to show digitized edges as they are output
tracingrestores	> 0 to show when a variable or internal is restored
tracingspecs	> 0 to show path subdivision when using a polygonal a pen
tracingstats	> 0 to show memory usage at end of job
tracingtitles	> 0 to show titles online when they appear
truecorners	> 0 to make llcorner etc. ignore setbounds
warningcheck	controls error message when variable value is large
year	the current year (e.g., 1998)

Table 2: Other predefined variables

Name	Type	Explanation
ₒbackground	color	Color for unfill and undraw (usually white)
ₒcurrentpen	pen	Last pen picked up (for use by the draw command)
ₒcurrentpicture	picture	Accumulate results of draw and fill commands
ₒcuttings	path	Subpath cut off by previous cutbefore or cutafter
ₒdefaultfont	string	Font used by label commands for typesetting strings
EOF	string	End-of-file indicator
ₒextra_beginfig	string	Commands for beginfig to scan
ₒextra_endfig	string	Commands for endfig to scan

Name	Type	Explanation
+Autoform	string	Format string used by autogrid
∘beveled	numeric	linejoin value for beveled joins [2]
∘black	color	Equivalent to (0,0,0)
∘blue	color	Equivalent to (0,0,1)
∘bp	numeric	One PostScript point in bp units [1]
∘butt	numeric	linecap value for butt end caps [0]
∘cc	numeric	One cicero in bp units [12.79213]
∘cm	numeric	One centimeter in bp units [28.34645]
∘dd	numeric	One didot point in bp units [1.06601]
∘ditto	string	The " character as a string of length 1
∘down	pair	Downward direction vector $(0, -1)$
∘epsilon	numeric	Smallest positive MetaPost number $[\frac{1}{65536}]$
∘evenly	picture	Dash pattern for equal length dashes
false	boolean	The boolean value *false*
+Fe_base	picture	What precedes the exponent when typesetting a power of ten
+Fe_plus	picture	Picture of the leading plus sign for positive exponents
∘fullcircle	path	Circle of diameter 1 centered on $(0, 0)$
+Gpaths	string	Coordinate types, either linear or log
∘green	color	Equivalent to (0,1,0)
∘halfcircle	path	Upper half of a circle of diameter 1
∘identity	transform	Identity transformation
∘in	numeric	One inch in bp units [72]
∘infinity	numeric	Large positive value [4095.99998]
∘left	pair	Leftward direction $(-1, 0)$
∘mitered	numeric	linejoin value for mitered joins [0]
∘mm	numeric	One millimeter in bp units [2.83464]
+Mten	numeric	The Mlog form for 10.0
nullpicture	picture	Empty picture
∘origin	pair	The pair $(0, 0)$
∘pc	numeric	One pica in bp units [11.95517]
pencircle	pen	Circular pen of diameter 1
∘pensquare	pen	square pen of height 1 and width 1
∘pt	numeric	One printer's point in bp units [0.99626]
∘quartercircle	path	First quadrant of a circle of diameter 1
∘red	color	Equivalent to (1,0,0)
∘right	pair	Rightward direction $(1, 0)$
∘rounded	numeric	linecap and linejoin value for round joins and end caps [1]
∘squared	numeric	linecap value for square end caps [2]
true	boolean	The boolean value true
∘unitsquare	path	Path (0,0)--(1,0)--(1,1)--(0,1)--cycle
∘up	pair	Upward direction $(0, 1)$

Table 3: Predefined constants

∘white	color		Equivalent to (1,1,1)
∘withdots	picture		Dash pattern that produces dotted lines

Table 4: Operators			

Name	Arguments and results			Explanation
	left	**right**	**result**	
&	string	string	string	Concatenation for paths *l*&*r* if *r*
	path	path	path	starts exactly where the *l* ends
*	numeric	color	color	Multiplication
		numeric	numeric	
		pair	pair	
*	color	numeric	color	Multiplication
	numeric		numeric	
	pair		pair	
**	numeric	numeric	numeric	Exponentiation
+	color	color	color	Addition
	numeric	numeric	numeric	
	pair	pair	pair	
++	numeric	numeric	numeric	Pythagorean addition $\sqrt{l^2 + r^2}$
+-+	numeric	numeric	numeric	Pythagorean subtraction $\sqrt{l^2 - r^2}$
-	color	color	color	Subtraction
	numeric	numeric	numeric	
	pair	pair	pair	
-	-	color	color	Negation
		numeric	numeric	
		pair	pair	
/	color	numeric	color	Division
	numeric		numeric	
	pair		pair	
< = >	string	string	boolean	Comparison operators
<= >=	numeric	numeric		
<>	pair	pair		
	color	color		
	transform	transform		
∘abs	-	numeric	numeric	Absolute value
		pair		
and	boolean	boolean	boolean	Logical and
angle	-	pair	numeric	2-argument arctangent (degrees)
arclength	-	path	numeric	Arc length of a path
arctime of	numeric	path	numeric	Time on a path where arclength from the start reaches a given value
ASCII	-	string	numeric	ASCII value of first character in string
∘bbox	-	picture	path	A rectangular path for the bounding box
		path		
		pen		
bluepart	-	color	numeric	Extracts the third component
boolean	-	any	boolean	Is the expression of type boolean?

bot	–	numeric	numeric	Bottom of current pen when centered
		pair	pair	at the given coordinate(s)
bounded	–	path	boolean	Is the path setbounded?
ₒceiling	–	numeric	numeric	Least integer greater than or equal to
ₒcenter	–	picture path pen	pair	Center of the bounding box
char	–	numeric	string	Character with a given ASCII code
clipped	–	picture	boolean	Picture begins with clipped path?
color	–	any	boolean	Is the expression of type color?
cosd	–	numeric	numeric	Cosine of angle in degrees
ₒcutafter	path	path	path	Left argument with part after the intersection dropped
ₒcutbefore	path	path	path	Left argument with part before the intersection dropped
cycle	–	path	boolean	Is path cyclic?
dashpart	–	path	boolean	Is path dashed?
decimal	–	numeric	string	The decimal representation
ₒdir	–	numeric	pair	$(\cos\theta, \sin\theta)$ given θ in degrees
ₒdirection of	numeric	path	pair	The direction of a path at a given "time"
ₒdirection- point of	pair	path	numeric	Point where a path has a given direction
direction- time of	pair	path	numeric	"Time" when a path has a given direction
ₒdiv	numeric	numeric	numeric	Integer division $\lfloor l/r \rfloor$
ₒdotprod	pair	pair	numeric	Vector dot product
filled	–	path	boolean	Is path filled?
floor	–	numeric	numeric	Greatest integer less than or equal to
fontpart	–	picture	boolean	What is the font of text component?
fontsize	–	string	numeric	The point size of a font
greenpart	–	color	numeric	Extract the second component
hex	–	string	numeric	Interpret as a hexadecimal number
infont	string	string	picture	Typeset string in given font
ₒintersec- tionpoint	path	path	pair	An intersection point
intersec- tiontimes	path	path	pair	Times (t_l, t_r) on paths l and r when the paths intersect
ₒinverse	–	transform	transform	Invert a transformation
known	–	any	boolean	Does arg have a known value?
length	–	path	numeric	Number of arcs in a path
length	–	picture	numeric	Number of components of picture
ₒlft	–	numeric	numeric	Left side of current pen when its
		pair	pair	center is at the given coordinate(s)

llcorner	–	picture path pen	pair	Lower-left corner of bounding box
lrcorner	–	picture path pen	pair	Lower-left corner of bounding box
makepath	–	pen	path	Cyclic path bounding pen shape
makepen	–	path	pen	A polygonal pen made from the convex hull of the path knots
mexp	–	numeric	numeric	The function $\exp(x/256)$
mlog	–	numeric	numeric	The function $256\ln(x)$
∘mod	–	numeric	numeric	The remainder function $l - r\lfloor l/r \rfloor$
normal-deviate	–	–	numeric	Choose a random number with mean 0 and standard deviation 1
not	–	boolean	boolean	Logical negation
numeric	–	any	boolean	Is the expression of type numeric?
oct	–	string	numeric	Interpret a string as an octal number
odd	–	numeric	boolean	Is the closest integer odd or even?
or	boolean	boolean	boolean	Logical inclusive or
pair	–	any	boolean	Is the expression of type pair?
path	–	any	boolean	Is the expression of type path?
pathpart	–	picture	path	Yields clipped or setbounds path
pen	–	any	boolean	Is the expression of type pen?
penoffset of	pair	pen	pair	Point on the pen furthest to the right of the given direction
penpart	–	picture	pen	Pen doing the drawing
picture	–	any	boolean	Is the expression of type picture?
point of	numeric	path	pair	Point on a path given a time value
postcontrol of	numeric	path	pair	First Bézier control point on path segment starting at the given time
precontrol of	numeric	path	pair	Last Bézier control point on path segment ending at the given time
readfrom	–	string	string	Returns next line from named file
redpart	–	color	numeric	Extract the first component
reverse	–	path	path	"Time"-reversed path with beginning swapped with ending
rotated	picture path pair pen transform	numeric	picture path pair pen transform	Rotate counterclockwise a given number of degrees
∘round	–	numeric pair	numeric pair	Round argument to the nearest integer
∘rt	–	numeric pair	numeric pair	Right side of current pen when centered at given coordinate(s)
∞Sabs	–	string	string	Absolute value of large number
∞Sadd	number	number	string	Adds large numbers

scaled	picture path pair pen transform	numeric	picture path pair pen transform	Scale all coordinates by the given amount
∞Scvnum	–	string	number	Converts string to number
∞Sdiv	string	string	string	Computes quotient of large numbers
shifted	picture path pair pen transform	pair	picture path pair pen transform	Add the given shift amount to each pair of coordinates
sind	–	numeric	numeric	Sine of an angle in degrees
slanted	picture path pair pen transform	numeric	picture path pair pen transform	Apply the slanting transformation that maps (x, y) into $(x + sy, y)$, where s is the numeric argument
∞Sleq	string	string	boolean	Returns Boolean result of $x \leq y$
∞Smul	string	string	string	Product of large numbers
∞Sneq	string	string	string	Returns Boolean result of $x \neq y$
sqrt	–	numeric	numeric	Square root
∞Ssub	string	string	string	Returns the numeric string for $x-y$
str	–	suffix	string	String representation for a suffix
string	–	any	boolean	Is the expression of type string?
stroked	–	picture	boolean	Is first component a stroked line?
subpath of	pair	path	path	Portion of a path for given range of time values
substring of	pair	string	string	Substring within given indices
textpart	–	picture	picture	Returns the text part of current picture component
textual	–	picture	boolean	Is current picture component text?
ₒtop	–	numeric pair	numeric pair	Top of current pen when centered at the given coordinate(s)
transform	–	any	boolean	Is the argument of type transform?
transformed	picture path pair pen transform	transform	picture path pair pen transform	Apply the given transform to all coordinates
ulcorner	–	picture path pen	pair	Upper-left corner of bounding box
uniform-deviate	–	numeric	numeric	Random number between zero and the value of the argument
ₒunitvector	–	pair	pair	Rescale a vector so its length is 1
unknown	–	any	boolean	Is the value unknown?

`urcorner`	–	picture path pen	pair	Upper-left corner of bounding box
ₒ`whatever`	–	–	numeric	Creates new anonymous unknown
`write to`	string	string	–	Writes string to named file
`xpart`	–	pair transform	number	x or t_x component
`xscaled`	picture path pair pen transform	numeric	picture path pair pen transform	Scale all x coordinates by the given amount
`xxpart`	–	transform	number	t_{xx} entry in transformation matrix
`xypart`	–	transform	number	t_{xy} entry in transformation matrix
`ypart`	–	pair transform	number	y or t_y component
`yscaled`	picture path pair pen transform	numeric	picture path pair pen transform	Scale all y coordinates by the given amount
`yxpart`	–	transform	number	t_{yx} entry in transformation matrix
`yypart`	–	transform	number	t_{yy} entry in transformation matrix
`zscaled`	picture path pair pen transform	pair	picture path pair pen transform	Rotate and scale all coordinates so that $(1, 0)$ is mapped into the given pair; i.e., do complex multiplication.

Table 5: Commands

`addto`	Low-level command for drawing and filling
`clip`	Applies a clipping path to a picture
ₒ`cutdraw`	Draw with butt end caps
ₒ`draw`	Draw a line or a picture
ₒ`drawarrow`	Draw a line with an arrowhead at the end
ₒ`drawdblarrow`	Draw a line with arrowheads at both ends
ₒ`fill`	Fill inside a cyclic path
ₒ`filldraw`	Draw a cyclic path and fill inside it
`interim`	Make a local change to an internal variable
`let`	Assign one symbolic token the meaning of another
ₒ`loggingall`	Turn on all tracing (log file only)
`newinternal`	Declare new internal variables
ₒ`pickup`	Specify new pen for line drawing
`save`	Make variables local
`setbounds`	Make a picture lie about its bounding box
`shipout`	Low-level command to output a figure
`show`	print out expressions symbolically
`showdependencies`	print out all unsolved equations

showtoken	print an explanation of what a token is
showvariable	print variables symbolically
special	print a string directly in the PostScript output file
∘tracingall	Turn on all tracing
∘tracingnone	Turn off all tracing
∘undraw	Erase a line or a picture
∘unfill	Erase inside a cyclic path
∘unfilldraw	Erase a cyclic path and its inside

Table 6: Function-like macros

Name	Arguments	Result	Explanation
+augment	variable, points	–	Append to a given path
+auto	x or y	–	Generate default x or y coordinates for tick marks
+autogrid	axis label commands	–	Draws axis labels
+begingraph	numbers	–	Begins new graph
•boxit	suffix, picture	–	Define a box containing the picture
•boxit	suffix, string	–	Define a box containing text
•boxit	suffix, ⟨empty⟩	–	Define an empty box
•boxjoin	equations	–	Give equations to connect boxes
•bpath	suffix	path	A box's bounding circle or rectangle
∘buildcycle	list of paths	path	Build a cyclic path
•circleit	suffix, picture	–	Put picture in a circular box
•circleit	suffix, picture	–	Put a string in a circular box
•circleit	suffix, ⟨empty⟩	–	Define an empty circular box
∘dashpattern	on/off distances	picture	Create a pattern for dashed lines
∘decr	numeric variable	numeric	Decrement and return new value
∘dotlabel	suffix, picture, pair	–	Mark point & draw picture nearby
∘dotlabel	suffix, string, pair	–	Mark point and place text nearby
∘dotlabels	suffix, point numbers	–	Mark z points with their numbers
•drawboxed	list of suffixes	–	Draw the named boxes and their contents
•drawboxes	list of suffixes	–	Draw the named boxes
∘drawoptions	drawing options	–	Set options for draw commands
•drawunboxed	list of suffixes	–	Draw contents of named boxes
+endgraph	–	picture	Ends a graph
•fixpos	list of suffixes	–	Solve for the size and position of the named boxes
•fixsize	list of suffixes	–	Solve for size of named boxes
+format	string, text	picture	Typeset the string as a picture
+frame	suffix, options	–	Frame all or part of a graph
+gdata	string, variable, commands		Read a file, execute commands on each input line
+gdotlabel	suffix, pic or string, location		Dots and labels a graph position

+gdraw	path or string	–	Draws a graph
+gdrawarrow	path or string	–	Draws a graph with arrows
+gdrawblarrow	path or string	–	Draws a graph with double arrows
+gfill	path or string	–	Fills a graph
+glabel	suffix, pic or string, location		Labels a graph position
+grid	suffix, format, point	–	Draw labeled grid line on graph
image	draw commands	picture	Finds result of given commands
+init_numbers	pictures	–	Provides templates for future formats
∘incr	numeric variable	numeric	Increment and return new value
+itick	suffix, format, point	–	Like grid, but draws inward tick mark
∘label	suffix, picture, pair	–	Draw picture near given point
∘label	suffix, string, pair	–	Place text near given point
∘labels	suffix, point numbers	–	Draw z point numbers; no dots
∘max	list of numerics	numeric	Find the maximum
∘max	list of strings	string	Find lexicographically last string
∘min	list of numerics	numeric	Find the minimum
∘min	list of strings	string	Find lexicographically first string
+Mreadpath	string	–	Converts a path into Mlog form
+otick	suffix, format, point	–	Like grid, & draws outward tick mark
•pic	suffix	picture	Box contents shifted into position
+setcoords	flags	–	Sets up a graph coordinate system, ±linear or ±log
+setrange	coordinates	–	Sets upper and lower limits for current coordinate system
∘thelabel	suffix, picture, pair	picture	Picture shifted as if to label a point
∘thelabel	suffix, string, pair	picture	Text positioned as if to label a point
∘z	suffix	pair	The pair $x\langle\text{suffix}\rangle, y\langle\text{suffix}\rangle$

Table 7: MetaPost primitives for making .tfm files

commands	charlist, extensible, fontdimen, headerbyte, kern, ligtable
ligtable operators	::, =:, =:|, =:|>, |=:, |=:>, |=:|, |=:|>, |=:|>>, ||:
internal variables	boundarychar, chardp, charext, charht, charic, charwd, designsize, fontmaking
other operators	charexists

Table 8: Macros, internal variables defined only in mfplain package

Defined in the mfplain package

beginchar	font_identifier
blacker	font_normal_shrink

capsule_def	font_normal_space
change_width	font_normal_stretch
define_blacker_pixels	font_quad
define_corrected_pixels	font_size
define_good_x_pixels	font_slant
define_good_y_pixels	font_x_height
define_horizontal_corrected_pixels	italcorr
define_pixels	labelfont
define_whole_blacker_pixels	makebox
define_whole_pixels	makegrid
define_whole_vertical_blacker_pixels	maketicks
define_whole_vertical_pixels	mode_def
endchar	mode_setup
extra_beginchar	o_correction
extra_endchar	proofrule
extra_setup	proofrulethickness
font_coding_scheme	rulepen
font_extra_space	smode

Defined as no-ops in the mfplain package

cullit	proofoffset
currenttransform	screenchars
gfcorners	screenrule
grayfont	screenstrokes
hround	showit
imagerules	slantfont
lowres_fix	titlefont
nodisplays	unitpixel
notransforms	vround
openit	

Table 9: Macros and internal variables defined in MetaPost only

MetaPost primitives not found in Metafont

bluepart	infont	redpart
btex	linecap	setbounds
clip	linejoin	tracinglostchars
color	llcorner	truecorners
dashed	lrcorner	ulcorner
etex	miterlimit	urcorner
fontsize	mpxbreak	verbatimtex
greenpart	prologues	withcolor

Variables and macros defined only in plain MetaPost

ahangle	cutbefore	extra_beginfig

ahlength	cuttings	extra_endfig
background	dashpattern	green
bbox	defaultfont	label
bboxmargin	defaultpen	labeloffset
beginfig	defaultscale	mitered
beveled	dotlabel	red
black	dotlabels	rounded
blue	drawarrow	squared
buildcycle	drawdblarrow	thelabel
butt	drawoptions	white
center	endfig	
cutafter	evenly	

Table 10: Internal variables defined in Metafont only

autorounding	fillin	proofing	tracingpens	xoffset
chardx	granularity	smoothing	turningcheck	yoffset
chardy	hppp	tracingedges	vppp	

CHAPTER 14

. . . .

PSTRICKS

Postprocessors like *dvips* translate each .dvi command into a PostScript equivalent. Might it not be possible to anticipate that activity and embed PostScript commands directly into a TeX document? After all, the \special command is a mechanism that exists precisely for purposes like this. The advantage of placing direct PostScript commands into a source file is that a clever macro package can use the LaTeX and TeX input language— familiar to so many LaTeX and TeX users—to generate useful graphic constructs in the PostScript language, which is familiar to relatively few users.

This seems to be the philosophy behind the PSTricks package of Timothy van Zandt, which is nothing less than an implementation of most of the PostScript language in terms of LaTeX and TeX syntax. This chapter presents a description of principles behind the use of this package and a demonstration of some of the astonishing things that can be done with it. Information for PSTricks may be found in the various documentation files that accompany the package, which is itself freely available from CTAN (in graphics/pstricks). However, if you are serious about PSTricks, you should make strenuous efforts to obtain the monograph by Denis Girou (1994), which contains numerous virtuoso displays with code of PSTricks constructs in a multihued display. With this reference in hand, it's easy to page through until you find an image close to what you need, at which point you can adapt the instructions that created it. You may also want to consult van Zandt and Girou (1994), which contains a useful discussion of the ways in which the PSTricks macros were created.

PSTricks works its magic by writing special commands to the .dvi file for the dvi postprocessor. You'll need to check the file pstricks.con, which details the adjustments necessary to match PSTricks to your program. The most extensive support is given for Tom Rokicki's *dvips*. This driver supports color, but you'll see only shades of gray in these pages.

14.1   Essentials

PSTricks works with plain TEX, LATEX, and almost every other large-scale macro package. No one should be surprised that a document file should contain the command

    \input pstricks

(plain TEX users) or

    \usepackage{pstricks}

(LATEX) near the beginning of the file. Some of the more exotic of the PSTricks are described in separate macros, so additional \input... statements or additional \usepackage arguments may be necessary.

14.2   Getting started

We will learn a lot by examining one of the more essential, yet most simple, of the PSTricks instructions. The command \pscircle draws a circle. I get

if I type $$\pscircle{.5}$$. PSTricks has obligingly drawn a circle whose radius is .5 cm.

   If you think about this command, there are clearly things you may wish to alter: the width of the outline, the radius, the interior (can it be filled?), its position. A careful reader may also find the proximity between the bottom of displays like this and the next line of text irksome.

14.2.1   Graphic parameters

PSTricks lets us alter graphic parameters easily enough, and well-chosen defaults control these parameters in case we neglect to specify them. For example, the default line width is .8 pt and the default unit is 1 cm; that's why PSTricks knew that .5 meant 0.5 cm. Dozens of parameters control the looks of PSTricks's output.

   Whenever you need to adjust a parameter for an extended portion of a document, use the \psset command, which accepts as argument a string of parameters and their values separated by commas. For example, after

    \psset{linewidth=.4pt, unit=1pc}

the same command \pscircle{.5} generates

instead. With the default unit 1 pc, the .5 refers now to 0.5 pc. Any number of parameters and values may appear in any \psset command. Several such commands may appear in a document—wherever and whenever it becomes necessary to set or reset a PSTricks parameter. The examples that follow will usually reference new graphic parameters without extensive (or any) explanation (the documentation is the resource for additional explanation). The purpose of a parameter is usually made self-evident by its name.

It may be necessary to temporarily adjust a parameter. TEX's grouping mechanism can be used in the usual way, but PSTricks makes it easier. Most commands accept *optional arguments*, delimited in proper LATEX fashion by square brackets (but this works also for plain TEX). Thus, we get

either by using optional parameters and typing

```
\pscircle{.5}
\pscircle[linewidth=2pt]{.75}
\pscircle{1}
```

or surrounding a new \psset value within a group like this:

```
\pscircle{.5}
{%
 \psset{linewidth=2pt}\pscircle{.75}
}%
\pscircle{1}
```

Some figure drawing commands have a variant form. The *star form* of a command often draws the figure and fills it in, and so we get

from

```
\pscircle*[fillstyle=solid, linecolor=gray]{10pt}
```

The parameter linecolor generally controls the color of a filled object.

In addition to true optional arguments and star variants, there is another class of options that belong to many commands. This will be a list of one or more coordinate pairs. For \pscircle, this option consists of a single pair, which determines the location of the circle's center. If we omit this pair,

PSTricks assumes that the center of the circle sits at the origin of the local coordinate system. So we get

whether we type

```
\pscircle*[linecolor=black]{1}
\pscircle*[linecolor=darkgray](.5,0){1}
\pscircle*[linecolor=gray](1,0){1}
\pscircle*[linecolor=lightgray](1.5,0){1}
\pscircle*[linecolor=white](2,0){1}
\pscircle[linewidth=.4pt](2,0){1}
```

(where we explicitly provide the centers of the disks) or

```
\pscircle*[linecolor=black]{1}\hskip.5cm
\pscircle*[linecolor=darkgray]{1}\hskip.5cm
\pscircle*[linecolor=gray]{1}\hskip.5cm
\pscircle*[linecolor=lightgray]{1}\hskip.5cm
\pscircle*[linecolor=white]{1}%
\pscircle[linewidth=.4pt]{1}
```

(where we use \hskip to move forward and establish a new local coordinate system for each disk; \hskip is the plain TEX equivalent of \hspace). This example illustrates another important lesson of PostScript graphics: an object that overwrites another obliterates the overlapped portion completely, even if the second object is lighter than the first; see also chapter 13, section 136.4.

14.2.2   The unit *parameter*

Regardless of the value of unit, you may always set a length to whatever value you want by including the dimension. So, for example,

```
\pscircle[unit=1cm]{10pt}
```

draws a circle of radius 10 pt even though each unit is normally 1 cm. But this is a bad a habit; you'll find it better to adjust values of unit as need be and record all lengths as generic values. That way, any time a PSTrick has to be scaled up or down, it's easy to do so via a simple change to the value of unit.

For example, if you type

```
\psset{unit=3pt}
\pspolygon[linewidth=.4pt]%
   (0,1)(0,2)(1,3)(2,3)(3,2)(3,1)(2,0)(1,0)
```

you get ○ . It may happen that such a drawing is too small, say by half. Rather than adjust all the coordinates by 100%, it's easy enough to adjust the default coordinate—that is, if we say

```
\psset{unit=6pt}
```

then ⬡ now comes out right.

14.2.3 *Other files*

The entire PSTricks system is quite large, and it might be quite a waste of TEX's memory to load in the entire set of macros each time the macros were called. Therefore, it has been built in a modular manner, with a collection of main macros forming the file pstricks.tex. Certain specialized "tricks" require additional macro files. This will be pointed out below when necessary, and is made quite clear in the article by Girou (1994) and in the documentation files that are part of the PSTricks package.

14.3   About PSTricks coordinate systems

Most drawing commands generate items that look to TEX and LATEX as if they have a width, height, and depth of 0 pt. So, if you type something like

```
...something like \pspolygon[unit=5pt, linewidth=.4pt](0,1)%
   (0,2)(1,3)(2,3)(3,2)(3,1)(2,0)(1,0)this.
```

in your file, you get something like this. Because the "trick" has no dimensions, neither TEX nor LATEX leave room for it. The reason for a displayed PSTrick 'bumping' its feet into the next line of text (as on page 442) becomes apparent—since TEX thinks it has no height, it has not left enough room to properly space it.

Furthermore, you must be careful about spaces. Typing

```
{\psset{linecolor=gray}\psellipse*(0,0)(1.5,1)}%
\psellipse*[linecolor=white](0,0)(1.3,.8)
```

> **PSTricks: Pros and Cons**
>
> • **Pros:**
>
>   ○ TEX macros for graphics are easy to learn and use.
>
> • **Cons:**
>
>   ○ As with all PostScript software, these macros require special PostScript hardware.

generates

but if you remove the %, you get instead

which may not be what you wanted. The second ellipse drawing command uses its own coordinate system displaced from the first by the width of a space. Like sets of high-tech Lego blocks, PSTricks artists construct complex figures out of simple shapes.

In the forgoing displays of octagons, I made sure that LATEX left enough room by placing the PSTrick in a box of the proper width. An invisible rule (that is, its width is zero) of the proper height adds vertical substance. This approach smacks of inelegance, and for that reason, PSTricks makes the pspicture environment available to LATEX users; plain TEXers use the commands \pspicture and \endpspicture instead. It's up to the artist to specify the width and total height of the drawing, as in

```
\psset{unit=1pc}
\pspicture(-1.5,-.5)(1.5,.5)
\psellipse*[linecolor=darkgray](1.5,.5)
\psellipse*[linecolor=lightgray](1.1,.45)
\endpspicture
```

to draw ⬛. LaTeX users would have typed

```
\psset{unit=1pc}
\begin{pspicture}(-1.5,-.5)(1.5,.5)
⟨drawing commands⟩
\end{pspicture}
```

for this or any picture. These declarations should be part of the document. The coordinate pairs following \pspicture or \begin{pspicture} provide the position of the lower left and upper right corners of the imaginary bounding box that surrounds the graphic construction.

14.4   Elementary examples

In the case of learning a graphics package, pictures really are worth thousands of words. In this section, we show several examples of simple PSTricks pictures and the commands to create them. Note well that I make no effort to explain all conventions and commands, and the extensive documentation that accompanies PSTricks should always be at hand.

14.4.1   Errors

Everyone makes mistakes. The easy errors are logical rather than syntactical—the PSTricks commands work, but you get something other than you expected. The solution is simply to revise the commands and run the file again through PSTricks and TeX or LaTeX. A common source of error arises from the presence of extra spaces in the PSTricks commands. From time to time, these extra spaces will make everything appear a little off. The habit of including comment characters % at the end of each line removes one common source of extra spaces. (Remember, TeX converts a line end to a space.)

The messy errors arise from a problem of syntax—you have mistyped a command or omitted some parameter or syntactical necessity. When you run this file through LaTeX or TeX, you generate error messages that are mystical, opaque, and vaguely frightening. Experience soon teaches you that the best thing is to ignore the messages, but simply to check the offending statement very carefully. Keep your well-thumbed copy of the PSTricks documentation close by.

14.4.2 A PSTricks gallery

First, here are some simple circles.

```
\psset{unit=1pc}
\pscircle[linewidth=.4pt](.5,.5){.5}
\pscircle[linewidth=.8pt](1.5,.5){.5}
\pscircle[linewidth=1.2pt](2.5,.5){.5}
```

There are many ways to superpose axes or grids on a picture, and we'll show several such ways during the course of the examples.

```
\psset{unit=1pc}
\pscircle[linewidth=.4pt](.5,.5){.5}
\pscircle[linewidth=.8pt](1.5,.5){.5}
\pscircle[linewidth=1.2pt](2.5,.5){.5}
\psgrid[gridlabels=7pt, gridcolor=gray, gridwidth=.4pt,
    subgriddiv=0](3,1)
```

The grid extends from the origin to the third columns and first row, which is the significance of $(3,1)$.

We can also draw lines given a sequence of points, as the following LATEX code demonstrates.

```
\usepackage{pst-plot}
\psline[linewidth=.4pt, labels=none,
    showpoints=true]{*->}%
    (0,0)(1,2)(5,0)(3,-1)(-1,4.5)(2.5,2)(5,5)
\psline[linestyle=dotted, linecolor=darkgray]%
    (2,3)(-1,3)(2,-1)(4,5)
\psaxes[linewidth=.4pt, labels=none,
    linecolor=gray](0,0)(-1,-1)(5,5)
```

The file pst-plot.sty that \usepackage refers to contains an extensive array of graphing and plotting commands for PSTricks users. Lists of coordinates mean different things to different commands. For \psline, they specify the dots to be connected by straight-line segments. For \psaxes, the first point [here, (0,0)] is the place where the axes cross, and the remaining two points provide the locations for the lower left and upper right corners of the graph.

It's a good idea to present some elementary examples of drawing. These are coded using the conventions of plain TEX. Note that because all graphic objects have no dimension, we include an invisible vertical rule (\vrule width 0pt ...) to provide vertical dimensions, and we explicitly use horizontal glue commands to ensure proper horizontal dimensions.

```
$$
\psset{unit=1.5pc,linewidth=.4pt}
\hbox{\vrule width0pt height3pc
  \psline(0,0)(3,2)\hskip5pc
  \psline[linestyle=dashed](3,2)\hskip5pc
  \psline[doubleline=true,doublesep=1pt]{|->}(3,2)\hskip5pc
  \psline[linestyle=dotted,linewidth=1pt]{|->}(3,2)(0,0)%
    \hskip4.5pc}
$$
```

```
$$
\psset{unit=1.5pc,linewidth=.4pt}
\hbox{\vrule width0pt height2pc
  \psline{->}(3,2)(0,1)(2,0)\hskip5pc
  \psline[linewidth=1pt,linearc=.3,cornersize=relative]{|-*}%
  (3,2)(0,1)(2,0)\hskip5pc
  \psline[linearc=.3,cornersize=absolute]{<<-}%
    (3,2)(0,1)(2,0)\hskip4.5pc}
$$
```

These commands demonstrate a new kind of optional argument delimited by curly brackets that are appropriate for a line drawing command like \psline. Lines may be more than lines—particularly when initiated and terminated by finials like dots, bars, and arrowheads. PSTricks provide a wide variety of lineal decoration to be specified in a suggestive manner. For example, the option {<-|} causes the line to begin with an arrow and to end with a short perpendicular line segment.

```
$$
\psset{unit=1.5pc,linewidth=.4pt}
\hbox{\vrule width0pt height3pc
  \pswedge[linewidth=2pt,linecolor=gray](0,0){3}{0}{60}%
  \hskip5pc
  \psarc[linestyle=dashed,linewidth=1pt]{<->}(1.5,1)%
    {1.5}{220}{0}%
    \hskip5pc
  \psarc*[showpoints=true](1.5,1){1.5}{220}{0}\hskip5pc
  \psdiamond[fillstyle=solid,fillcolor=lightgray]%
    (1.5,1)(1.5,1)
  \psframe*[linecolor=darkgray](1,.5)(2,1.5)\hskip4.5pc}
$$
```

(Your document will need to read in pst-beta.tex to use \psdiamond.)

```
$$
\psset{unit=1.5pc,linewidth=.4pt}
\hbox{\vrule width0pt height3pc
  \psellipse[fillstyle=vlines,hatchangle=0,
    linestyle=dashed](1.5,1)(1.5,1)\hskip5pc
  \psellipse[fillstyle=hlines*,hatchangle=0](1.5,1)(1.5,1)%
    \hskip5pc
  \psellipse[fillstyle=crosshatch](1.5,1)(1.5,1)\hskip4.5pc}
$$
```

14.4.3 Curves

Several commands control the creation of curves. The command \pscurve and its relatives draw a smooth curve connecting a sequence containing an arbitrary number of points. In contrast, \psbezier uses exactly four points to construct the scaffolding from which a Bézier curve is erected, and the resulting curve actually touches only the first and fourth point.

The next example displays the difference between curves—one Bézier and one not—specified by the same quartet of points.

```
\pscurve(-1,-1)(2,5)(3,1)(5,4)
\psbezier[linecolor=darkgray]%
  (-1,-1)(2,5)(3,1)(5,4)
\psgrid[gridwidth=.4pt,subgriddiv=2,
  subgridwidth=.2pt, gridcolor=lightgray,
  gridlabels=0](0,0)(-1,-1)(5,5)%
```

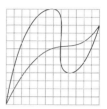

When drawing curves, the showpoints parameter is useful for showing the location of the keypoints. The following display redraws these curves, and also lays the grid down before the curves. Note well the difference in the final display.

```
\psgrid[gridwidth=.4pt,subgriddiv=2,
  subgridwidth=.2pt, gridcolor=lightgray,
  gridlabels=0](0,0)(-1,-1)(5,5)%
\pscurve[showpoints=true]
  (-1,-1)(2,5)(3,1)(5,4)
\psbezier[linecolor=darkgray,
  showpoints=true]%
  (-1,-1)(2,5)(3,1)(5,4)%
```

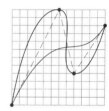

14.4.4 Drawing engine

The curve-drawing commands are the commands most useful to digital artists who need to represent complicated objects in a document. For those who contemplate using PSTricks as a drawing engine, it's important to become familiar with a related command, \pscustom, which can group related graphic components together connecting consecutive commands with line segments if need be. After

```
\newcommand\mycurve{\pscurve(-1,-1)(2,5)(3,1)(5,4)}
\newcommand\mybezier{\psbezier(-1,-1)(2,5)(3,1)(5,4)}
```

the commands

```
\psset{unit=1.75pc}\pscustom{\mybezier\psline(5,-1)}
\pscustom[linewidth=2pt]{\mycurve\psline(5,5.2)(-1,5.2)}
```

generate

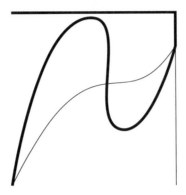

But PSTricks treats these constructs as fillable regions, and if we alter the above code to

```
\pscustom[fillstyle=solid,fillcolor=darkgray]%
  {\mybezier\psline(5,-1)}
\pscustom[linewidth=2pt,fillstyle=solid,fillcolor=lightgray]%
  {\mycurve\psline(5,5.2)(-1,5.2)}
```

we get

instead. Bunches of \pscurve commands (together with the gradient fill style discussed on page 466) contributed to the figure on the facing page. The code for this figure appears in the appendix to this chapter on page 482.

14.4.5 Clipping

PSTricks provides commands by which material can be clipped to a path. Although there is temptation to use this capability for frivolous purposes (see figure 2 on page 456), serious mathematicians and technicians will welcome it.

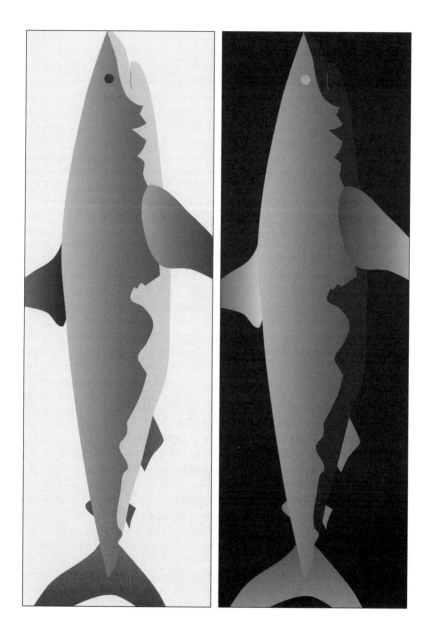

Figure 1: Jaws, two.

And indeed—here's a frivolous example of some "type-egg-raphy." The ovine

is a product of these instructions.

```
\fontsize{7}{8}\selectfont
\setbox0=\hbox{Typography}\dimen0=\wd0
\dimen2=10\dimen0 % now \dimen2 > \textwidth
\newcommand{\typoa}{\hbox to\textwidth{%
  \cleaders\hbox{Typography}\hskip\dimen2 \hss}}
\newcommand{\typob}{\hbox to\textwidth{\hskip.5\dimen0%
  \cleaders\hbox{Typography}\hskip\dimen2 \hss }}
\newcommand{\hleads}{\vbox{%
  \typoa\noindent\hskip-\dimen0\typob}}
\psclip{\psellipse[unit=.3in,linestyle=none]
  (.5\textwidth,1.5in)(.5\textwidth,4.5)}%
\vbox to3in{%
  \leaders\hleads\vfill}
\endpsclip
```

The clipping was done via the \psclip command, whose syntax is

```
\psclip{⟨any graphic construct⟩}%
  ⟨text, graphics, or anything else⟩
\endpsclip
```

Clipping like this is at the heart of figure 2 on the next page, in which we slavishly draw the profile and clip text to it. Previously, though, we had printed the full text in gray ink and backed up vertically in such a way that the clipped portion exactly overlays the gray text, to give the effect we're after. Selections from the LaTeX code that generated this figure appear below.

```
\fontfamily{pac9}\fontsize{12}{15}\selectfont
\setbox0=\hbox{()}\dimen0=\ht0 \dimen2=\dp0
\advance\dimen0 by1.5pt \advance\dimen2 by1.5pt
\edef\strut{\vrule width0pt height\dimen0 depth\dimen2 }
\setbox0=\vbox{\parindent 1em \noindent
\strut Four score and seven years ago our
   fathers brought forth ...
      ...shall not perish from the earth.\strut
}
\vbox{\null\gray\copy0\relax
\null\vspace{-23\baselineskip}\vspace{-11.6pt}}%
\noindent
  \psclip{\pscurve[unit=8.4pt]%
   (0,-1)(12,-1)%
     (12,-1)(12,0)(12,2)(7,6)        % segment 1 (shirtfront)
     (7,6)(6.9,6.7)(6,7)             % segment 2 (necktie)
     (6,7)(5,8)(4.2,9)(5,10.2)(6,9.7)% neck up to beard
     (6,9.7)(9,11)(10.5,13.6)(9,15.6)% beard
     (9,15.6)(9.5,16)(9.1,17)        % lower lip
     (9.1,17)(9.5,17)(9.8,18)(9.5,19)%
       (9.6,19.5)(10.6,19.8)(11.8,20)% upper lip
     (11.8,20)(12,21)(11,23)(9.6,25)%  & nose
     (9.6,25)(9.6,25.8)(10.5,27)      % eye socket
     (10.5,27)(10.3,27.8)(9.3,30)(8.5,31.5)% forehead
     (8.5,31.5)(9.4,32.8)(10.6,34.8)%
       (10.2,36.8)(9.3,38.2)(7.5,38.7)%        hair
     (7.5,38.7)(6.5,41)(6.5,41)(0,41)%
     }%
  \black\copy0
\endpsclip}
\begin{center}
\fontsize{10}{12}\selectfont\gray November 19, 1863
\end{center}
```

In a less frivolous vein, these tactics are useful to mathematicians seeking to shade areas between curves, a common task. For \psclip is smart enough

Four score and seven years ago our fathers brought forth on this continent, a new nation, conceived in Liberty, and dedicated to the proposition that all men are created equal.

Now we are engaged in a great civil war, testing whether that nation, or any nation so conceived and so dedicated, can long endure. We are met on a great battle-field of that war. We have come to dedicate a portion of that field, as a final resting place for those who here gave their lives that that nation might live. It is altogether fitting and proper that we should do this.

But, in a larger sense, we can not dedicate—we can not consecrate—we can not hallow—this ground. The brave men, living and dead, who struggled here, have consecrated it, far above our poor power to add or detract. The world will little note, nor long remember what we say here, but it can never forget what they did here. It is for us the living, rather, to be dedicated here to the unfinished work which they who fought here have thus far so nobly advanced. It is rather for us to be here dedicated to the great task remaining before us—that from these honored dead we take increased devotion to that cause for which they gave the last full measure of devotion—that we here highly resolve that these dead shall not have died in vain—that this nation, under God, shall have a new birth of freedom—and that government of the people, by the people, for the people, shall not perish from the earth.

November 19, 1863

Figure 2: A Lincoln portrait.

to recognize as a "region" the area between two curves. Since

```
\pscustom[unit=5pt]{\mybezier\psline(5,5.1)(-1,5.1)}%
```

and

```
\pscustom[unit=5pt]{\mycurve\psline(5,-1)}%
```

generate

we can clip to the region formed by superimposing the curves. That is,

```
\psclip{%
   \pscustom[linestyle=none]{\mycurve\psline(5,-1)}%
   \pscustom[linestyle=none]{\mybezier\psline(5,5.1)(-1,5.1)}}
   \psframe*[linecolor=lightgray](-1,-1)(5.1,5.1)%
\endpsclip
```

produces

Here, the gray rectangle formed by \psframe* is clipped to the region of
overlap. We need to redraw the curves to show them too. That is, one way

to get

is via

```
\psclip{%
  \pscustom[linestyle=none]{\mycurve\psline(5,-1)}%
  \pscustom[linestyle=none]{\mybezier\psline(5,5.1)(-1,5.1)}}
  \psframe*[linecolor=lightgray](-1,-1)(5.1,5.1)%
\endpsclip%
\pscustom{\mybezier}
\pscustom{\mycurve}
```

Of course, there are actually two regions "between" these two curves, and it's a more interesting challenge to color both of these. Make sure you see why

```
\pspicture(5.1,5.1)
\psgrid[subgridwidth=.4pt,gridwidth=1pt,%
  gridcolor=lightgray,subgridcolor=lightgray,%
  subgriddiv=3,gridlabels=0](0,0)(-1,-1)(5,5)
\rlap{%  good stuff
\psclip{%
  \pscustom[linestyle=none]{\mybezier\psline(5,-1)}%
  \pscustom[linestyle=none]{\mycurve\psline(-1,5)}}%
  \psframe*[linecolor=gray](-1,-1)(5,5)%
\endpsclip}%
\psclip{%
  \pscustom[linestyle=none]{\mybezier\psline(5,5.1)(-1,5.1)}%
  \pscustom[linestyle=none]{\mycurve\psline(5,-1)}}%
  \psframe*[linecolor=darkgray](-1,-1)(5,5)%
\endpsclip
\mycurve \mybezier
\endpspicture
```

yields the following:

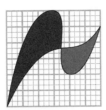

14.4.6   Cusps

It's easy to use \pscurve (or its siblings) to produce a smooth curve. But what of a curve containing a *cusp* (a sharp point or corner)? You may break the curve drawing in two and use two \pscurve's on the portions before and after the cusp, but if you double the cusp point, PSTricks draws the cusp properly. In the following display, I specified the two curves in the same way except for doubling the cusp point in the black graph.

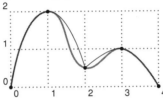

```
$$\psset{unit=1cm}
\pspicture(0,0)(4,2)
  \psgrid[griddots=10, gridlabels=7pt, gridcolor=darkgray,
    subgriddiv=0](4,2)
  \pscurve[linecolor=gray,linewidth=1.2pt]%
    (0,0)(1,2)(2,.5)(3,1)(4,0)
  \pscurve[linewidth=.4pt, showpoints=true]%
    (0,0)(1,2)(2,.5)(2,.5)(3,1)(4,0)
\endpspicture
$$
```

PSTricks does plots as well. Pie charts can be built up from wedges. From the code

```
\psset{unit=2cm}\degrees[100]
\pspicture(-1,-1)(1,1)
  \pswedge[fillstyle=solid,fillcolor=lightgray]{1}{0}{18}
  \pswedge[fillstyle=solid,fillcolor=gray]{1}{18}{33}
  \pswedge[fillstyle=solid,
    fillcolor=darkgray]{1}{33}{53}
  \pswedge[fillstyle=solid,
```

```
    fillcolor=lightgray]{1}{53}{78}
\pswedge[fillstyle=solid,
    fillcolor=gray]{1}{78}{90}
\pswedge[fillstyle=solid,
    fillcolor=darkgray]{1}{90}{100}
\uput{1.1}[9](0,0){\box\fries}
\uput{1.1}[25](0,0){Munchies}
\uput{1.1}[43](0,0){Red meat}
\uput{1.1}[65](0,0){Pizza}
\uput{1.1}[84](0,0){Soda}
\uput{1.1}[95](0,0){Other}\SpecialCoor
\rput(.7;9){\psframebox*{18\%}}
\rput(.7;25){\psframebox*{15\%}}
\rput(.7;43){\psframebox*{20\%}}
\rput(.7;65){\psframebox*{25\%}}
\rput(.7;84){\psframebox*{12\%}}
\rput(.7;95){\psframebox*{10\%}}
\endpspicture
```

we get

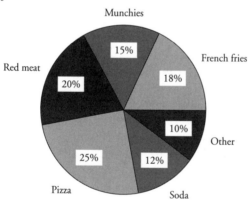

The arguments to \pswedge control the radius of the circle from which the wedge is sliced and the angular positions of the lower and upper radii of the wedge. Commands \uput and \rput are two of the many ways to put PSTricks constructs or text in a picture. The wedges are easy to lay out by virtue of the \degrees command, which allows an author to divide the circle into any arbitrary number of degrees. In this case, one hundred "degrees" means there is a simple correspondance between angles and percentages. Finally, \box\fries is a box to hold the label for french fries.

The \SpecialCoor provides another timesaving device. After this command is issued, PSTricks accepts *polar coordinate* specifications for a point. The polar coordinates $(r; \theta)$ of a point mean that the point lies r units from the origin on an imaginary line attached at the origin and rotated to an angle θ counterclockwise above the horizon, as at left. The semicolon here is an artifact of PSTricks syntax. (Mathematicians normally use a comma to separate the two quantities.) The side diagram is the outcome of this PSTricks code:

```
\psset{unit=3pc,framesep=0pt}
\pspicture[1](1.2,1.2)
  \psarc[arcsep=1pt]{->}(0,0){.7}{0}{72}
  \SpecialCoor \psline[linewidth=1pt]{-*}(1;0)(0;0)(1;72)
  \rput(.85;36){\psframebox*{$\theta$}}
  \rput[br](.4;76){\psframebox*{$r$}}
  \rput[bl](1.05;70){\psframebox*{$(r\,,;\theta)$}}
\endpspicture
```

PSTricks can accept data from other programs and use this information to prepare graphs. As an example, we plot the function

$$y = \cos(x + 3\cos(x)).$$

The program *Mathematica* prepared the data. I generated 41 pairs of points via the *Mathematica* command

```
Table[ {x, N[Cos[x/8 + 3Cos[x/8]]]}, {x,0,40}]
```

which generates values in the interval $0 \le x \le 5$. In a PSTricks document, we type

```
\pspicture(0,-2)(40,4)
\psset{xunit=6pt,yunit=3pc}
\savedata{\mydata}[
{{0, -0.989992}, {1, -0.9992}, {2, -0.999885},
  ...
 {38, 0.149851}, {39, 0.60383}, {40, 0.908047}}
]
```

which makes this data available through the shorthand reference "\mydata." The ellipses indicate the many data values not shown here. Next, we plot this material.

```
\dataplot[plotstyle=curve]{\mydata}
```

```
\psaxes[dx=8]{->}(0,0)(0,-1.5)(45,1.5)
\rput(45,0){\quad$x$}\rput(0,1.5){\qquad$y$}
\endpspicture
```

to get

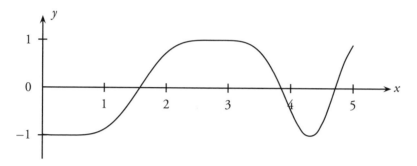

We have to work a bit harder to graph

$$y = \cos(x + |\sqrt{\cos(x)}|)$$

for $0 \le x \le 5$, because of the two cusps in this interval. To get the graph

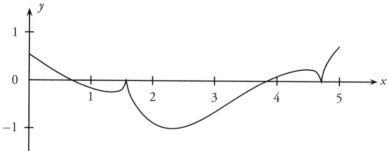

we have to include each of the two cusp points *twice* to make sure PSTricks doesn't go through the points in a smooth curve. (Mathematical aside: The two points all have y-values of zero, and x-values of $\pi/2$ and $3\pi/2$. We're using a horizontal coordinate system that stretches each x-value by a factor of 8, so we add two pairs of double points $\{12.56, 0\}, \{12.56, 0\}$ and $\{37.70, 0\}, \{37.70, 0\}$ to the list of points making up \mydata.) For this trick, the list of points generated for us by *Mathematica* must be augmented as follows.

```
\savedata{\mydata}[
  {{0, 0.540302}, ...
```

```
  ...
{12, -0.193932},  {12.56,0}, {12.56,0}, {13, -0.283041},
  ...
{37, 0.206542},  {37.70,0},{37.70,0}, {38, 0.229461},
  ... }]
\dataplot...
```

I added the second point in each box by hand. Once \mydata has been set up properly, the commands for this graph are the same as for the preceding cosine graph.

14.5 More advanced examples

Many of these examples are drawn from Girou (1994); I am grateful to Jacques André and Denis Girou, editor and author, for their permission to use this material. Those taken from this source are marked with DG, and have suffered but small modifications. (Text has been translated from French to English, and the brilliant hues of the original have been reduced to shades of gray.)

For fun, PSTricks can draw boxes. Which are possible and which not? Compare this to the demonstration by Knuth (1986c, p. 113).

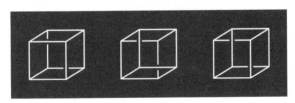

```
\pspicture(0,0)(7.5,2.3)
  \rput[lb](0,0){\psset{linewidth=1pt,
    linecolor=white, bordercolor=darkgray}
    \psframe*[linecolor=darkgray](-.5,-.5)(2,1.8)%
    \psline{c-c}(.5,.3)(0,0)\psline{c-c}(.5,.3)(1.5,.3)
    \psline{c-c}(.5,.3)(.5,1.3)%
    {\psset{border=1.5pt}%
      \psline{c-c}(1,1)(1,0)\psline{c-c}(1,1)(0,1)
        \psline{c-c}(1,1)(1.5,1.3)%
    }\psline{c-c}(1,1)(1,0)\psline{c-c}(1,1)(0,1)
        \psline{c-c}(1,1)(1.5,1.3)%
    \psline{c-c}(1,0)(0,0)\psline{c-c}(1,0)(1.5,.3)%
    \psline{c-c}(0,1)(0,0)\psline{c-c}(0,1)(.5,1.3)
```

```
    \psline{c-c}(1.5,1.3)(1.5,.3)\psline{c-c}(1.5,1.3)(.5,1.3)
}
\rput[lb](2.5,0){\psset{linewidth=1pt,
    linecolor=white, bordercolor=darkgray}
    \psframe*[linecolor=darkgray](-.5,-.5)(2,1.8)%
    \psline{c-c}(1,1)(1,0)\psline{c-c}(1,1)(0,1)
     \psline{c-c}(1,1)(1.5,1.3)%
    {\psset{border=1.5pt}\psline{c-c}(.5,.3)(0,0)
     \psline{c-c}(.5,.3)(1.5,.3)\psline{c-c}(.5,.3)(.5,1.3)%
    }\psline{c-c}(.5,.3)(0,0)\psline{c-c}(.5,.3)(1.5,.3)
     \psline{c-c}(.5,.3)(.5,1.3)%
    \psline{c-c}(1,0)(0,0)\psline{c-c}(1,0)(1.5,.3)%
    \psline{c-c}(0,1)(0,0)\psline{c-c}(0,1)(.5,1.3)
     \psline{c-c}(1.5,1.3)(1.5,.3)\psline{c-c}(1.5,1.3)(.5,1.3)
}
\rput[lb](5,0){\psset{linewidth=1pt,
    linecolor=white, bordercolor=darkgray}
    \psframe*[linecolor=darkgray](-.5,-.5)(2,1.8)%
    \psline{c-c}(1,1)(0,1)\psline{c-c}(1,1)(1.5,1.3)
    \psline{c-c}(.5,.3)(1.5,.3)\psline{c-c}(.5,.3)(0,0)%
    {\psset{border=1.5pt}\psline{c-c}(.5,.8)(.5,1.3)
     \psline{c-c}(1,.5)(1,0)%
    }\psline{c-c}(.5,.3)(.5,1.3)\psline{c-c}(1,1)(1,0)%
    \psline{c-c}(1,0)(0,0)\psline{c-c}(1,0)(1.5,.3)%
    \psline{c-c}(0,1)(0,0)\psline{c-c}(0,1)(.5,1.3)
    \psline{c-c}(1.5,1.3)(1.5,.3)
     \psline{c-c}(1.5,1.3)(.5,1.3)
}
\endpspicture
```

PSTricks is good about enclosing text in a variety of framed boxes.

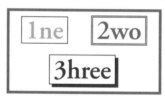

```
\fontsize{18}{20}\bfseries\selectfont
\psframebox[linecolor=gray, linewidth=2pt]{\begin{tabular}{c}
\psframebox{\lightgray 1ne}\hspace{18pt}
  \psdblframebox{\gray 2wo}\\[6pt]
```

```
\psshadowbox{\darkgray 3hree}\end{tabular}}
```

Framed boxes may also be circular, oval, diamond-shaped, or triangular.

```
\input pst-beta \input pst-3d
\pstribox[fillstyle=solid, fillcolor=gray, trimode=R]
  {\Large\bf\white Yale}\quad
\pscirclebox[linecolor=gray,linewidth=3pt]
  {\psshadow{\Large\bf H}}
```

Some workers, including me, have shown how to use METAFONT to generate rotated characters to typeset characters on curved paths. This task is now almost trivial with PSTricks (DG); it requires the file textpath.tex or textpath.sty.

```
\usepackage{textpath}
\begin{pspicture}(0,0)(6,2.5)
\psset{linecolor=lightgray,linewidth=2pt}
\pstextpath{\pscurve(0,0)(2,2)(4,0)(6,2)}
{Text/math ($(x+y)^2=x^2+2xy+y^2$)
 fits obligingly atop. }
\end{pspicture}
```

And another example (DG) ...

```
\usepackage{textpath}
\psset{linecolor=gray}\newcommand{\myR}{1.3}
\begin{pspicture}(0,0)(3,3)
\pstextpath[c]{\psarcn(\myR,\myR)%
 {\myR}{180}{0}}{\Large
   Chance favors the}
\pstextpath[c]{\psarc(\myR,\myR)%
 {\myR}{180}{0}}{\Large prepared mind.}
\end{pspicture}
```

It's hard to imagine a use for the following (DG) in a scientific paper, but it's nice to know it can be done if necessary.

TYPOGRAPHY

```
\font\reallybig=lssb7t at 1.5cm \font\teensy=padr at 6pt
\newcount\scratch \scratch=120
\setbox0=\vbox{\hsize=2cm \parindent=0pt
 \baselineskip=6.5pt \teensy \loop ff ffi ffl fi fl
 \advance\scratch by-1 \ifnum\scratch>0 \repeat}
\input charpath
\noindent
   \pscharclip[linecolor=darkgray,fillstyle=solid,%
   fillcolor=lightgray]{\rput[tl](0,0){\reallybig TYPOGRAPHY}}
\rput[t]{90}(-1,-1){\box0}
\endpscharclip
```

One additional file controls the creation of a special *gradient* style to fill regions. The model for the gradient is a brush that begins painting a region from the top down, starting with a color given by the gradbegin parameter. The color changes toward that specified by gradend as the brush moves. At some point in the brush's journey, specified by the numerical value of grad-midpoint, the brush will have reached the gradend color and will change color back to gradbegin, which it reaches at the opposite end of the region. The direction in which the brush moves is controlled by a final parameter, that of gradangle. (We've seen previously in figure 1 on page 453 how gradients help bring life to an otherwise simple sketch.)

```
\input gradient
\psset{linewidth=0pt, fillstyle=gradient, gradbegin=white,
 gradend=gray, gradmidpoint=.5}
\pspicture(0,0)(8,2)
```

```
\psframe(0,0)(2,2)
\psframe[gradmidpoint=.99](3,0)(5,2)
\psframe[gradangle=45](6,0)(8,2) \endpspicture
```

The table of figure 3 on the next page shows how gradients can add spice to a chart. The plain TEX code for this figure appears in the appendix to this chapter on page 485. The typography was modeled after that of *Publish* magazine.

Three dimensions PSTricks does 3-D graphics. We present the code from a slick example (DG) in its plain TEX form. Readers should type it in and observe the result.

```
\input pst-beta \input pst-3d \input gradient
\psset{dimen=middle, viewpoint=-1 -1 1}
\pspicture(0,-1)(4,6)
\ThreeDput[normal=0 -1 0]{\psframe[fillstyle=solid,
  fillcolor=gray](3,3)
 \rput(1.5,1.5){\it See no evil.}}
\ThreeDput[normal=-1 0 0](0,3,0){\psframe[fillstyle=solid,
  fillcolor=lightgray](3,3)\rput(1.5,1.5){Hear no evil.}}
\ThreeDput[normal=0 0 1](0,0,3){\psframe[fillstyle=gradient,
  gradmidpoint=.95,
  gradbegin=darkgray, gradend=white](3,3)\rput(1.5,1.5){%
  \psframebox[fillstyle=solid, fillcolor=white]%
   {Trick no evil!}}}
\endpspicture
```

The effect of three dimensions can also be hacked by creative use of simpler commands (DG), such as:

```
\psset{unit=1.5pc, linestyle=none, fillstyle=solid}
\pspicture(0,0)(10,12)
\newcommand{\cube}{
  \pspolygon[fillcolor=gray](0,0)(0,1.2)(1,1)(1,-0.4)
  \pspolygon[fillcolor=darkgray](1,-0.4)(1,1)(2,1.2)(2,0)
  \pspolygon[fillcolor=lightgray](0,1.2)(1,1.4)(2,1.2)(1,1)}
\rput(5,4)%(-6.5,-1.4)
  {\multirput(-1.4,-0.5){4}
    {\multirput(0,1.6){4}
      {\multirput(1.4,-0.6){4}{\cube}}}}
\endpspicture
```

World Temperature Extremes

Region	Place	Date	Deg (F)	Deg (C)
Highs				
World (Africa)	El Azizia, Libya	Sep 13, 1922	136	58
North America (US)	Death Valley, CA	Jul 10, 1918	134	57
Asia	Tirat Tsvi, Israel	Jun 21, 1942	129	54
Australia	Cloncurry, Queensland	Jan 16, 1889	128	53
Europe	Seville, Spain	Aug 4, 1881	122	50
South America	Rivadavia, Argentina	Dec 11, 1905	120	49
Canada	Midale & Yellow Grass, Sask.	Jul 5, 1937	113	45
Persian Gulf (sea surface)		Aug 5, 1924	96	36
South Pole		Dec 27, 1978	7.5	−14
Antarctica	Vanda Station	Jan 5, 1974	59	15
Lows				
World (Antarctica)	Vostok	Jul 21, 1983	−129	−89
Asia	Verkhoyansk/Oimekon	Feb 6, 1933	−90	−68
Greenland	Northice	Jan 9, 1954	−87	−66
N. America (exc Greenland)	Snag, Yukon, Canada	Feb 3, 1947	−81	−63
Alaska	Prospect Creek, Endicott Mts,	Jan 23, 1971	−80	−62
US (exc Alaska)	Pogers Pass, MT	Jan 20, 1954	−70	−57
Europe	Ust'Shchugor, USSR		−67	−55
South America	Sarmiento, Argentina	Jan 1, 1907	−27	−33
Africa	Ifrane, Morocco	Feb 11, 1935	−11	−24
Australia	Charlotte Pass, NSW	Jul 22, 1947	−8	−22
United States	Prospect Creek, AK	Jan 23, 1971	−80	−62

Figure 3: Gradients in tables.

to give:

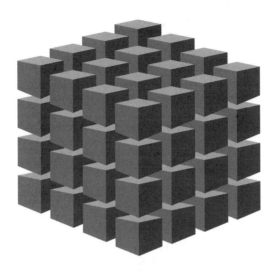

With other macros PSTricks macros are carefully crafted to work in conjunction with major macro packages. For example, after typing

```
\newenvironment{fancyfig}[1]{
  \psset{linewidth=0.4pt, unit=1pc}\edef\mytitle{#1}%
  \setbox0=\vbox\bgroup\advance\hsize -6.8pt
      \leftskip=1pc \rightskip=\leftskip}
  {\egroup\begin{figure}\dimen0=\ht0\advance\dimen0\dp0
      \advance\dimen0 5.5pc
  \pspicture(0,0)(\hsize,\dimen0)%
  \rput[lb](0,0){\psframebox[fillstyle=gradient,
      gradbegin=black,gradend=white,
  gradmidpoint=.98]{\vbox{\vspace{1.5pc}
  \begin{center}\white\large\bf\mytitle\end{center}
  \vspace{12pt}\box0\vspace{.5pc}}}}\endpspicture
    \vspace{1pc}\end{figure}
  }
```

in a LATEX document or macro file (plus the \usepackage commands to read the PSTricks files you will need), it is necessary only to type

```
\begin{fancyfig}{A Hymn}\vspace{1.5pc}
```

```
\begin{verse}
  Rise, traveller, the sky is light.\\
  Why do you sleep ... ?
  ...
  ... your hands in vain?
  \end{verse}
\end{fancyfig}
```

to get the text block appearing on page 472. The excerpt is a translation, by Vikram Seth (1994), of a hymn in the hymnbook of Mahatma Gandhi's ashram.

14.6 Text connections

Because of the underlying model TEX uses when typesetting, it is rarely possible to know the exact position of some text on a page until the page has been typeset, by which time that information is too late to be of use. One great strength of PSTricks is the ability to internally extract that information to make it possible to physically connect (with a wide variety of lines and shapes) one piece of text with another, even though we as the document's author have no way of knowing the position of either piece. In PSTricks parlance, these are *nodes*, and many commands control internode connections. Node connections allow authors to use actual connections on a page to connect ideas. The only real restriction on nodes and connectors is that they appear on the same page, and authors must keep this stricture in mind as TEX reflows paragraphs and text during the revision process.

The node macros, the "trickiest tricks in PSTricks," reside in separate files `pst-node.tex` and `pst-beta.tex` (and their `.sty` counterparts); the beta file contains useful extensions to PSTricks's node capabilities. (And don't forget the accompanying files `pst-doc1.ps` and `pst-doc2.ps`, which explain the beta features of PSTricks.) The macros must be read via a command like

```
\input pst-node \input pst-beta
```

for plain TEX or

```
\usepackage{pst-node,pst-beta}
```

for LATEX after the main PSTricks macros have been assimilated. Using nodes involves assigning names to privileged positions on a page, deciding how to display these nodes (plain, encircled, framed in a box, etc.), deciding on the connections between the nodes, and printing any labels for these connections. A wide and varied syntax is available for these tasks, and the examples we present here only skim the subject.

We create a node by giving it a name and placing something there. Its location is fixed at typeset time by TeX. In this example, we typed

```
...we type\rnode{alpha}{d}
   ...
\noindent\hskip12pt\rnode{omega}{t}o create two no...
\ncangles[angleA=180, angleB=-90]{*->}{omega}{alpha}
```

to create two nodes with names "omega" and "alpha." These nodes contain the characters "." and "t" which will also be typeset by the node mechanism. An \rnode is only one of several kinds of nodes. There are a few restrictions on nodes, the most important being that any nodes that will be connected must lie on the same page and have node names that must contain only letters and numbers and must commence with a letter.

Once nodes have been defined, we may may connect them with any number of different connecting strokes—lines, curves, loops—controlled by a generous handful of new options. The connection above is a product of

`\ncangles[angleA=180, angleB=-90]{*->}{omega}{alpha}`

(Here, "A" and "B" refer to the first and second nodes in the connection, whatever the node names that you actually assign.) The nc that begins most connection commands recalls the phrase "node connection." The optional argument in the curly brackets indicates the termination of the node connection (here, we've chosen dot and arrow.) The final mandatory arguments name the nodes for PSTricks to connect.

The next example shows off the arsenal of permissible node types.

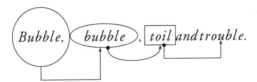

```
$$ \circlenode{circle}{Bubble,} \ovalnode{oval}{bubble},
   \rput[1B](0,0){\rnode{box}{\psframebox{toil}}}%
\hphantom{\hskip6pt toil} and \rnode{null}{trouble}.
\ncbar[angle=-90, offsetB=3pt]{->}{circle}{oval}
\nccurve[angleA=-90,angleB=270,offsetA=3pt, offsetA=3pt]%
   {*->}{oval}{box}
\ncbar[angleA=-90, offsetA=3pt]{*->}{box}{null} $$
```

A Hymn

Rise, traveller, the sky is light.
Why do you sleep? It is not night.
The sleeping lose, and sleep in vain.
The waking rise, and rise to gain.

Open your eyelids, you who nod.
O heedless one, pay heed to God.
Is this the way to show your love?
You sleep below, he wakes above.

What you have done, that you must bear.
Where is the joy in sin then, where?
When on your head your sins lie deep,
Why do you clutch your head and weep?

Tomorrow's task, enact today.
Today's at once, do not delay.
When birds have robbed the standing grain
What use to wring your hands in vain?

Although there is no "\boxnode" command, we simulate it easily by combining \rnode with \psframebox. However, because the dimensions of any \rnode are all zero points in magnitude, we use \hphantom to set the proper spacing.

The next demonstration shows off the several ways that labels can be applied to node connections and also shows the difference between the normal label placement and its star form.

```
\psset{unit=.05\textwidth, linewidth=.4pt}
\hbox{\vrule width0pt height.333\textwidth
```

```
  \pspolygon(0,0)(3,3)(3,0)
  \pcline[offset=12pt]{|-|}(0,0)(3,3)
  \lput*{:U}{Hypotenuse}
%%
  \pspolygon(3,0)(6,3)(6,0)
  \pcline(3,0)(6,3)\lput{:U}{Hypotenuse}
%%
  \pspolygon(6,0)(9,3)(9,0)\pcline(6,0)(9,3)
  \lput*{:D}{Hypotenuse}
%%
  \pspolygon(9,0)(12,3)(12,0)\pcline(9,0)(12,3)
  \lput*{0}{Hypotenuse}
  \hskip12cm
}
```

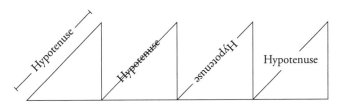

PSTricks has a special matrix environment. The following simple matrix

```
\begin{psmatrix}%
    [mnode=circle,colsep=1]
    & A \\
B & E & C \\
    & D &
\end{psmatrix}
```

(plain TEX users may type \psmatrix and \endpsmatrix) is clear, but in the background the psmatrix environment defines nodes whose names are given by the coordinate pairs of the entries; row always precedes column. Thus, *A* in the figure defines a node identified by {1, 2} because it lies on the first row and second column of the matrix, while B defines a node called $\{2, 1\}$, and so on. It's easy now to use standard node connections. (The mnode parameter sets every node to be of type "circle.") For example,

```
\ncarc[arcangle=-40]{3,2}{1,2}_[npos=.3]{d}^[npos=.7]^{e}
```

connects the D and A with an arc that starts 40° above the horizontal. There are two labels at roughly 0.3 and 0.7 along the connecting arc (default position is halfway) and we use the shortcuts ^ and _ to specify above and below the connection. A fully fleshed commutative diagram might look as follows.

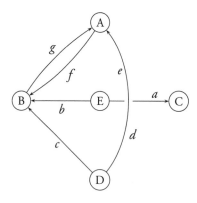

```
\begin{psmatrix}[mnode=circle,colsep=1]
& A \\
  B & E & C \\
& D &
\end{psmatrix}
\psset{shortput=nab,arrows=->,labelsep=2pt}
\everypsbox{\small\it}
\ncline{2,2}{2,3}^[npos=.75]{a}\ncline{2,2}{2,1}^{b}
\ncline{3,2}{2,1}^{c}
\ncarc[arcangle=-40,border=3pt]%
   {3,2}{1,2}_[npos=.3]{d}^[npos=.7]{e}
\ncarc[arcangle=12]{1,2}{2,1}^{f}
\ncarc[arcangle=12]{2,1}{1,2}^{g}
```

(This demonstration has been drawn from the PSTricks documentation.)
    These node connections are perfect for creating commutative diagrams like the following.

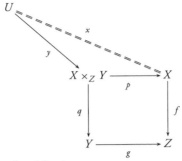

```
$$\fontsize{8}{9}\selectfont
\begin{psmatrix}
  U \\
    & X\times_Z Y & X \\
    & Y            & Z \\
  \psset{arrows=->, nodesep=2pt}\everypsbox{\scriptstyle}
  \ncline{1,1}{2,2}_{y}
  \ncline[doubleline=true,linestyle=dashed]
    {-}{1,1}{2,3}^{x}\ncline{2,2}{3,2}<{q}
  \ncline{2,2}{2,3}_{p}\ncline{2,3}{3,3}>{f}
  \ncline{3,2}{3,3}_{g}
\end{psmatrix}$$
```

This example is also from the documentation and shows two other abbreviations in use—the use of angle brackets to position labels to the left and right of connecting arcs.

Nodes and connections are sometimes helpful in completely different contexts. For example, it's possible to use this package to draw diagonal lines in column headings; that is, something like this.

Column 1	Column B	Last Column	
1	2	3	
3.999	5	The End.	

This construction demands cooperation between PSTricks and the rotating package by Sebastian Rahtz and Leonor Barroca, and we deviate a bit from standard LaTeX coding practices. I've created simple commands to measure the longest column heading, to rotate material, to typeset a rule, and to generate modes and mode connections. Within the table itself, rules are set explicitly in their own column—I have forborne using the usual "|"

convention to set vertical rules, and this is because vertical rules are not wanted in the top row. Within the tabular environment, @{} suppresses some intercolumn space at the left and right. Here are the LATEX instructions.

```
\usepackage{rotating}
  ...
\newdimen\lablength
\newcommand{\longesthead}[1]{\setbox0=\hbox{#1}%
  \global\lablength=\wd0}
\newcommand{\R}[1]{\begin{rotate}{-45}\ #1\end{rotate}}
\renewcommand\|{\vrule width.4pt }
$$
\renewcommand{\/}{\vrule width0pt height.71\lablength
  \pnode(0,0){A}\pnode(1,1){B}\ncline{A}{B}}
  \longesthead{Last Column}
  \psset{unit=.71\lablength,linewidth=.4pt}
  \begin{tabular}{@{}clcrccc@{}}
    \/&\R{Column 1}&\/&\R{Column B}&\/&\R{Last Column}&\/\\
      \noalign{\vskip-3.2pt\hrule}
    \|&1&\|&2&\|&3&\|\\ \hline
    \|&3.999&\|&5&\|&The End.&\|\\ \hline
  \end{tabular}
$$
```

If the longest column head has length \lablength and we print it at $45°$, then its vertical extent is roughly 71% of that amount ($.71 \approx \sqrt{2}/2$). If we set the PSTricks unit to equal .71\lablength, then coordinates $(0, 0)$ and $(1, 1)$ will mark the start and end of a label printed at an angle. The redefined \/ command creates nodes at these positions and connects them via \ncline. Note that the node names of A and B are reused by each call to \/.

14.7   Repetition

Repetition of actions is an important ability for graphic constructions, as one figure might be made up of the same component repeated according to some simple pattern. Plain TEX and LATEX provide the \loop and \whiledo constructions for this purpose, but they are often not good enough. For this reason, there is a separate \multido component to PSTricks, and although developed for use in PSTricks constructions, it is a separate module that can be appropriated for any purpose. The official source for this information is the document `multido.doc`; the `multido` package, although intended for generic TEX, is on any CTAN archive in the area `macros/latex/contrib`.

Since the macros are contained in a separate file, you'll need to say something like `\input multido` or `\usepackage{multido}` unless a previous module, such as `pst-plot`, has already caused TEX to read it in.

Here is the basic form of the `\multido` command.

`\multido{⟨variable and increment⟩} {⟨number of times⟩}{⟨stuff⟩}`

Thus, the command

`\multido{}{8}{\TeX\ }`

generates

TEX TEX TEX TEX TEX TEX TEX TEX

The first argument, not needed in this example, allows us to specify a variable with an initial value and increment, much as in other programming languages, although the syntax is more unusual. For one thing, the choice of variable name is limited. The variable name must *begin* with any of the four letters d, n, i, or r, or the uppercase equivalents. Like the Fortran of several decades ago, these leading letters serve to type the variables. Leading "d," "n," "i," and "r" identify the counting variable as a dimension register, integers or numbers with the same number of decimal places, integers only, or real numbers. (But see the documentation for important qualifications.) So if we type

`\multido{\ichar=65+1}{26}{\char\ichar}\endgraf`
`  \multido{\ichar=90+-1}{26}{\char\ichar}`

we get

ABCDEFGHIJKLMNOPQRSTUVWXYZ
ZYXWVUTSRQPONMLKJIHGFEDCBA

In each case, the loop counter is `\ichar` and each iteration is performed 26 times. In the first instance, the initial value is 65 (since A has ASCII code 65) and the counter increments by $+1$ each time. In the second example, we begin with the ASCII value of Z, and decrement by 1 (that is, the increment value is -1). Notice how we specified a negative value of the increment.

In this next example (DG), we see the use of `\hskip` (comparable to LATEX's `\hspace`) to translate to a new, simple coordinate system.

```
\psset{unit=.6cm}% this command sets \psunit=.6cm
\multido{\i=0+1}{6}{%
\psframe[linecolor=gray](0,0)(1,1)%
\rput{0}(.5,.5){$x_{\i}$}\psline{->}(0.5,-0.2)(1.5,-1)%
  \hskip\psunit}
```

This next example is an improvement on the "smear tactics" of page 444. If we type

```
\newgray{mygray}{0}\psset{unit=1cm, linecolor=mygray}
\multido{\n=0.0+.05}{20}{%
 \newgray{mygray}{\n}
 \pscircle*(\n,0){.5}}
```

we get

Here, \multido continually updates the definition of mygray at each iteration. With many tiny increments, we get this smear. We can improve these tactics by exploiting some of the other PSTricks tools for placing spheres or other shapes.

```
$$\pspicture(0,0)(5,3)
\newgray{mygray}{1.0}\psset{unit=10pt}
\SpecialCoor \degrees[100]
\pscircle[linewidth=.2pt,linecolor=black](4;51){.8}
\multido{\i=50+-1,\r=1.0+-.02}{51}{
  \pscircle*[linecolor=mygray](4;\i){.8}
  \newgray{mygray}{\r}\smallskip}
\endpspicture$$
```

We use the \degrees command to get an angular system that contains $100°$ instead of the canonical $360°$. The command \SpecialCoor allows polar coordinates; in (4;\i), a circle is placed four units from the origin at \i degrees above the horizontal axis. The value of grey is continuously changed, using anothor \multido for that purpose.

Here's one way to typeset calendars with LATEX + PSTricks.

	Sunday	Monday	Tuesday	Wednesday	Thursday	Friday	Saturday
							1997
	26	27	28	29	30	31 Halloween	1
	2	3	4 Election Day	5	6	7	8
NOVEMBER	9	10	11	12	13	14	15
	16	17	18	19	20	21	22
	23	24	25	26	27 Thanksgiving	28	29
	30	1	2	3	4	5	6
DECEMBER	7	8	9	10	11	12	13
	14	15	16	17	18	19	20
	21	22 1st Day Winter	23	24	25 Christmas	26	27
	28	29	30	31	1 New Year's Day 1998	2	3

The typography is after that of PerAnnum, Inc.

```
\psset{xunit=4pc,yunit=1.5pc}
\newcounter{row}\newcounter{col}% row and column counters
\newcommand{\calstrut}{\vrule width0pt height8pt}
\newcommand{\adjustdays}{\addtocounter{col}{1}%
  \ifnum\value{col}=7
    \setcounter{col}{0}\addtocounter{row}{-1}%
  \fi}
\begin{pspicture}(0,0)(7,11)
\rput[rb](7,11.1){\bf 1997}\psline[linewidth=1pt,linecolor=gray]%
  (0,11)(7,11)
\multido{\i=0+1}{7}{\rput[lb](\i,10.2){\footnotesize\ifcase\i
  Sunday\or Monday\or Tuesday\or Wednesday\or
  Thursday\or Friday\or Saturday\fi}}%
\pspolygon[linestyle=none,
  fillstyle=solid,fillcolor=lightgray](0,9)(6,9)(6,10)(0,10)
\pspolygon[linestyle=none,fillstyle=solid,fillcolor=lightgray]%
  (0,4)(1,4)(1,5)(7,5)(7,1)(4,1)(4,0)(0,0)
\multido{\i=0+1}{11}{\psline[linewidth=.4pt](0,\i)(7,\i)}
\rput{90}(-6pt,2.5){\sans DECEMBER}\rput{90}(-6pt,6.5)%
  {\sans NOVEMBER}
% the last few days of October
\setcounter{row}{10}\setcounter{col}{0}
\multido{\i=26+1}{6}{\rput[tl](\value{col},\value{row}){\tiny\i
  \calstrut}\adjustdays}%
% days of November
\multido{\i=1+1}{30}{\rput[tl](\value{col},\value{row}){\tiny\i
```

```
  \calstrut}\adjustdays}%
% now for December!
\multido{\i=1+1}{31}{\rput[tl](\value{col},\value{row}){\tiny\i
  \calstrut}\adjustdays}%
% the New Year!
\multido{\i=1+1}{3}{\rput[tl](\value{col},\value{row}){\tiny\i
  \calstrut}\adjustdays}%
% Now for holiday labels
\rput[tl](5.15,10){\tiny Halloween\calstrut}
\rput[tl](2.15,9){\tiny Election Day\calstrut}
\rput[tl](4.15,6){\tiny Thanksgiving\calstrut}
\rput[tl](4.15,2){\tiny Christmas\calstrut}
\rput[tl](1.15,2){\tiny 1st Day Winter\calstrut}
\rput[tl](4.15,1){\tiny New Year's Day \calstrut}
\rput[tl](4.15,.6){\tiny 1998\calstrut}
\end{pspicture}
```

This final example, inspired by DG, uses the \psdot command found in pst-beta. The plain TeX code follows.

```
\def\clockface{\multido{\i=1+1}{60}{\psline(.9;\i)(1;\i)}%
 \multido{\i=5+5}{12}{\psline[linewidth=.8pt](.87;\i)(1;\i)}%
}
\newcount\num \num=1
\newcount\angle \angle=-5
\psset{unit=1in,linewidth=.4pt}
\pspicture(-1,-1)(1,1)
  % The crown...
  \psline[linewidth=6pt](-.2,1.18)(.2,1.18)
  \psdot[dotsize=6pt](-.2,1.18)\psdot[dotsize=6pt](.2,1.18)
  % The case and dial...
  \pscircle[linewidth=.8pt]{1.09}
  \pscircle[linewidth=1.2pt]{1.13}
  \pscircle[linestyle=none,fillstyle=solid,%
    fillcolor=lightgray]{1.05}
  \pscircle{1.05}\degrees[60]\SpecialCoor
  \clockface
  \rput(0,-.65){\psset{unit=.2in}\clockface}  % little dial
  \psline[linewidth=1.6pt]{->}(0,0)(.6;-3.7)     % hour hand
  \psline[linewidth=1.2pt]{*->}(0,0)(.8;-27)   % minute hand
  \psline[linewidth=.8pt](0,-.8)(0,-.6)
  \psdot[dotsize=4pt](0,-.65)
  % The numbers on the dial...
  \multido{\i=10+-5}{5}{\rput{\the\angle}(.8;\i){\the\num}
    \global\advance\num by 1 \global\advance\angle by -5 }
  \num=7 \angle=-35
  \multido{\i=-20+-5}{6}{\rput{\the\angle}(.8;\i){\the\num}
    \global\advance\num by 1 \global\advance\angle by -5 }
\endpspicture
```

14.8   Other tricks

There are several other topics that are part of PSTricks but not part of this discussion. Readers interested in typesetting trees, transforming graphics in various ways, in slides, and in adding color to tables and table entries should consult the documentation. Please also visit the Web site http://www.tug.org/applications/PSTricks for additional examples—some of them smashing—by Denis Girou and others.

14.9   Late-breaking news

It was reported, in early 1997, that an interim release of PSTricks has appeared (PSTricks97) which merges all "beta" material with the main package. (It was not possible to redo this chapter in light of this news.) This is the material which now resides at

```
graphics/pstricks
```

in CTAN.

To subscribe to a new PSTricks-related mailing list, send a message saying

```
subscribe
```

to pstricks-request@mail.tug.org.

PSTricks Basic Facts and Tips

Plain TEX: Place the statement \input pstricks near the top of a document file. Depending on which facilities used, you may also need to \input other files—pst-plot, pst-node, pst-coil, pst-3d, and pst-beta.

LATEX: A \usepackage command with the argument pstricks must appear after the \documentclass statement. The \usepackage command may need other arguments—pst-plot, pst-node, pst-coil, pst-3d, and pst-beta—depending on which facilities of PSTricks you use.

Common Procedures: Keep your copy of the documentation available. Often, mistakes are due to a failure to adhere strictly to the PSTricks syntax. Use small test files to create an individual trick and only transfer its contents to your document when you're sure it works. It's a good idea to surround a PSTricks construction in a group so that parameters inadvertently altered with \psset will not alter subsequent pictures.

It greatly speeds up your work to have access to a PostScript previewer on hand, such as either the Display PostScript facility of the NextStep operating system or the ghostscript utility that runs on most operating systems and is freely available. (There are also a multitude of commercial products for this purpose.)

14.10   Appendix 1: Some PSTricks projects

14.10.1   Shark

The following code "drew" the figure on page 453.

```
%% Because PostScript does not paint adjacent areas well (boundary
%% problems), we paint areas, and and then superimpose the next area
%% on top of them.  Here's the order of superposition:
%%   * Large dorsal fin;
%%   * small dorsal fin;
%%   * tail;
%%   * small ventral fin;
%%   * med ventral fin;
%%   * entire body painted belly color;
```

```
%%    * mouth line;
%%    * dorsal part of body;
%%    * large axial fin;
%%    * eye.
\documentclass{article}

\usepackage{pstricks}
\usepackage{pst2eps}
\usepackage{epsf}

\input gradient

\begin{document}
\thispagestyle{empty}

\psset{unit=.06in,linestyle=none}
\def\largedorsalfin{\pscurve
  (6.6,63)(6.2,62)(4.9,60.2)(1.5,58)(0,57)
  \pscurve[liftpen=1](0,52)(4,51)(6.9,48.6)(7.2,49)(7.5,50)
  \psline(8,50.5)}
\def\smalldorsalfin{\psline(14,20)(12.6,19)\pscurve
  (12.6,19)(11.2,17.4)(13,15.5)\psline(14,15)}
\def\tail{\pscurve
  (13.8,11,8)(12.8,9.7)(4.8,3.8)(2,0)
  \pscurve[liftpen=1](9,0)(12.7,1.5)(15,2)(16.8,1.9)(20.4,0)
  \pscurve[liftpen=1](25.6,0)(24,2.8)(17,11)}
\def\smallventralfin{\psline
  (18.4,15)(19.1,13.5)\pscurve(19.3,14.8)(20.2,17.1)
  \psline(19,17.9)}
\def\medventralfin{\psline(21,24.7)(21.7,23.5)\pscurve
  (23,26.2)(25,28.8)(25,29)(24.6,30.1)(23.1,33.2)}
\def\body{\pscurve
  (14.5,100)(10.6,88)(6.6,63)(7.5,50)(8.3,42)(12,19)%
  (15.3,4.9)% defining the back
  \pscurve(16.8,7.7)(17,11)(17.8, 12.7)(18.4,15)(19,17.9)%
  (21,24.7)(23.1,33.2)%
  (25.5,40.5)(26,51)(26,59)(24,78)(23,85.5)(22,90)(21,93)(20,94.5)%
  (19.1,94.8)%belly
  \pscurve(18.8,94.6)(18.7,92.5)%lower lip
  \pscurve(17.7,97)(15.4,100)}
\def\mouth{\psline
  (18.8,93)(18.7,91)(19,89.8)}
\def\dorsal{\pscurve
  (14.5,100)(10.6,88)(6.6,63)(7.5,50)(8.3,42)(12,19)%
  (15.3,4.9)% back
  \pscurve(16.8,7.7)(17,11)(17.8, 12.7)% small bit on belly
  (17,14)(17.5,20.5)(18,23.2)(18.7,24)(17.2,28)(18.5,30)(18.5,32)%
  19.2,33)(18.5,35)
  \pscurve(21,37)(22,40.5)
  \pscurve(21,42)(20.4,43.3)(22,46)(23,49.3)(21.3,52)(19,53.5)%
  (19.7,55.6)
  \pscurve(20,55.3)(20.9,56.2)(21.6,55.8)
  \psline(24.2,57.6)
  \pscurve(24,59.6)(21.9,73)(21.1,75)(21.2,77.3)(20,78.2)
  \pscurve(21,79.5)(21.6,81)
```

```
  \psline(19,83)
  \pscurve(20.4,83.3)(21.6,84)
  \psline(20.4,85.6)\psline(21,87)\pscurve(20,87.2)%
  (18,88.8)(16.2,95.3)}
\def\axialfin{\pscurve
  (33.6,57)(30,58.6)(28.8,58.8)(25,59)(24,59.6)(21.8,63.4)(21.9,73)%
  (22.6,73.3)(30,67.8)(33.6,64.3)}
\def\eye{\pscircle(14.9,91.7){0.9}}
\def\positivecolors{%
  \newgray{bellycol}{.85}
  \newgray{fincol}{.4}
  \newgray{dorsalcol}{.5}
  \newgray{tailcol}{.3}
  \newgray{darkdarkgray}{0}
  \newgray{lightgray}{.75}
  \newgray{darkgray}{.25}
  \newgray{framecol}{.95}
}
\def\negativecolors{%
  \newgray{bellycol}{.15}
  \newgray{fincol}{.6}
  \newgray{dorsalcol}{.5}
  \newgray{tailcol}{.7}
  \newgray{darkdarkgray}{1}
  \newgray{lightgray}{.25}
  \newgray{darkgray}{.75}
  \newgray{framecol}{.05}
}
\def\shark#1{%
  \PSTtoEPS[bbllx=0,bblly=0,bburx=35,bbury=100]{#1}{%
    \psframe*[linecolor=framecol]
      (0,0)(33.6,100)
    \pscustom[fillstyle=gradient,
      gradbegin=fincol, gradend=darkdarkgray,
      gradmidpoint=.99,gradangle=90]{
      \largedorsalfin}
    \pscustom[fillstyle=solid,fillcolor=fincol]{
      \smalldorsalfin}
    \pscustom[fillstyle=gradient, gradend=tailcol,
      gradbegin=dorsalcol, gradmidpoint=.99]{
      \tail}
    \pscustom[fillstyle=solid, fillcolor=fincol, linestyle=none]{
      \smallventralfin}
    \pscustom[fillstyle=gradient, gradend=dorsalcol, gradbegin=fincol,
      gradangle=90, gradmidpoint=.99, linestyle=none]{
      \medventralfin}
    \pscustom[fillstyle=solid, fillcolor=bellycol, linestyle=none]{
      \body}
    \pscustom[linestyle=solid, linecolor=gray, linewidth=.4pt]{
      \mouth}
    \pscustom[fillstyle=gradient, gradangle=90, gradmidpoint=.99,
      gradbegin=tailcol, gradend=lightgray]{
      \dorsal}
    \pscustom[linestyle=none, fillstyle=gradient, gradbegin=darkgray,
      gradend=lightgray, gradmidpoint=.01, gradangle=90]{
```

```
      \axialfin}
    \pscustom[linestyle=none,fillstyle=solid,fillcolor=darkgray]{
      \eye}
    \pscustom[linestyle=solid,linewidth=.4pt]{psline %% frame
      (0,0)\psline(0,100)\psline(33.6,100)%
      \psline(33.6,0)\psline(0,0)}
  }
}

%% Uncomment this line to obtain a self-contained .eps file:
%\psset{headers=all,headerfile={pst-dots.pro,gradient.pro}}

%% Uncomment this line to force a new .eps file:
%\psset{makeeps=all} %% Parameter values are new/none/all/all*

\positivecolors % the default
\shark{shark-p.eps}
\negativecolors
\shark{shark-n.eps}

\begin{flushright}
  \leavevmode\epsffile{shark-p.eps}\epsffile{shark-n.eps}
\end{flushright}

\end{document}
```

An initial version of these sharks compiled properly in TEX, displayed perfectly under NEXTSTEP's Display PostScript capabilities, but nevertheless caused *dvips* to abort. Each \pscustom command creates a command whose potentially lengthy argument is the PostScript code generated by \pscustom. In at least one case, this argument was far too long for *dvips* to handle. (One can also resolve this problem by recompiling *dvips* after increasing the value of the C variable maxstring, defined in either of the files dvips.h or structures.h.) As a result, it was necessary to use the \PSTtoEPS command to create encapsulated PostScript which can be re-read thereafter, and thereby sidestepping the original problem. (I am grateful to Tim van Zandt for pointing out this approach to me.)

14.10.2 Gradient table

Most of these statements are straightforward. The admittedly tricky detabling part of \endgradtable is drawn directly from similar code in *The TEXbook* [Knuth (1986a), p. 392].

```
\font\rm=... \font\bf=... % Make sure you define fonts for
\font\Bf=... \font\mymath=... % \rm, \bf, \Bf, and \mymath

%% PSTricks STUFF
\input pstricks \input gradient
\newgray{lg1}{.9} \newgray{dg1}{.3}
```

```
\newgray{lg2}{.9} \newgray{dg2}{.3}

\psset{unit=1pc, linestyle=none, fillstyle=gradient, gradangle=90,
  gradend=dg1, gradbegin=lg1, gradmidpoint=.99}
\def\g{\psset{gradbegin=lg1, gradend=dg1}\global\let\makegray=\G}
\def\G{\psset{gradbegin=lg2, gradend=dg2}\global\let\makegray=\g}
\let\makegray=\g

\newdimen\theight \newdimen\tdepth \newdimen\twidth \newdimen\colwd
\def\parsedims{\expandafter\doparse\\}
\def\doparse#1!#2?{\dimen0=#1 \xdef\\{#2?}}

\newif\ifmore \moretrue
\def\finished{\morefalse}

\newdimen\lu \lu=18pt % line unit
\def\strut{\vrule width0pt height.75\lu depth.25\lu}
\def\-{{\mymath\char0\relax}}% cheap trick for minus sign
\def\Hrule{\hrule height.8pt }
\newdimen\shortheight % height of table without top row

\def\gradtable#1{\edef\ttitle{#1}\setbox0=\vbox\bgroup}
\def\endgradtable{\egroup \twidth=\wd0 % box0 holds alignment
  \setbox0=\vbox{\unvbox0 \setbox0=\lastbox % box0 contains last row
    \nointerlineskip \copy0 % put it back
    \global\setbox1=\hbox{}\xdef\\{?}%
    \setbox4=\hbox{\unhbox0 % open up bottom row
      \loop \skip0=\lastskip \unskip % remove tabskip glue
        \setbox2=\lastbox %
        \ifhbox2 \xdef\\{\the\wd2!\the\skip0!\\}%
          \setbox2=\hbox{\kern\wd2}\repeat\xdef\\{\the\skip0!\\}}}%
  \theight=\ht0 \tdepth=\dp0 % height and depth of table
  \shortheight=\theight \advance\shortheight by-\lu
  \parsedims \colwd=.5\dimen0 % ''prime the pump''; get leading tabskip value
  \hbox to\twidth{\hskip\tabskip
    \Bf\strut\ttitle\ \leaders\Hrule\hfill\hskip\tabskip}\vskip2pt
  \noindent\hskip\colwd
  \loop \parsedims \advance\colwd by\dimen0 % get a column's width
    \parsedims \advance\colwd by.5\dimen0 % get next tabskip value
    \makegray
    \psframe(0,\the\theight)(\the\colwd,-\the\tdepth)%
    \psframe[gradangle=-90](0,\the\shortheight)(\the\colwd,\the\theight)%
    \hskip\colwd \colwd=.5\dimen0
    \if?\\\finished \fi \ifmore \repeat
  \hskip.5\dimen0\llap{\box0}%
}


\newskip\mytabskip \mytabskip=9pt
\gradtable{World Temperature Extremes}
\tabskip=\mytabskip
\halign{\strut#\hfil\tabskip=\mytabskip &#\hfil&&\hfil#\cr
\bf Region&\bf Place&\omit\bf Date\hfil&\bf Deg (F)&\bf Deg (C)\cr
  \noalign{\white{\Hrule}}
\cr\bf Highs&&&&\cr \noalign{\white{\hrule}}
World (Africa)& El Azizia, Libya & Sep 13, 1922&136&58\cr
```

```
  \noalign{\white{\Hrule}}
North America (US)& Death Valley, CA & Jul 10, 1918&134&57\cr
  \noalign{\white{\Hrule}}
  ...
Antarctica& Vanda Station& Jan 5, 1974&59&15\cr
  \noalign{\white{\Hrule}}
\cr
\bf Lows&&&&\cr  \noalign{\white{\Hrule}}
  ...
United States& Prospect Creek, AK& Jan 23, 1971&\-80&\-62\cr}
\endgradtable

\bye
```

14.11   Appendix 2: PSTricks commands and parameters

This appendix summarizes all the commands and keywords currently discussed in PSTricks documentation, so this list includes all mainstream commands and all "beta test" commands, but not 3-D commands. Certain highly specialized commands, of use mainly to driver writers and gurus, may or may not be included in this list.

Most of these have *not* been discussed in this chapter, and you will have to consult the PSTricks documentation for explanation. Fortunately, most commands suggest their function by their name. Especially check to see which arguments are optional and which are required. It's a good idea to print and flip through all of the documentation.

We list all commands and keywords alphabetically, grouped according to the file containing their definitions. Commands and parameters that end with an asterisk also have an unstarred form.

For parameters, the key that follows each keyword attempts to suggest its argument type, and where there is no such suggestion, that means that it takes a dimension. Keyword keys are found at the end of the command reference list. Every so often, parameters apply to only a single command, and in that case the parameters are listed in the following line.

General commands: \input pstricks *or* \usepackage{*pstricks*}

```
\altcolormode
\black
\blue
\clipbox[dimension]{instructions}
\cput*[parameters]{angle}(x, y){instructions}
    linearc framearc(N) cornersize(R) dimen(L) framesep boxsep(B)
\cyan
\darkgray
\degrees[number]
\everypsbox{commands}
```

```
\gray
\green
\lightgray
\magenta
```
\multips*{*angle*}(*x_0, y_0*)(*x_1, y_1*){*whole number*}{*graphics instructions*}
\multirput*[*reference point*]{*rotation*}(*x_0, y_0*)(*x_1, y_1*){*whole number*}{*instructions*}
\newcmykcolor{*color*}{*num1 num2 num3 num4*}
\newgray{*color*}{*number*}
\newhsbcolor{*color*}{*num1 num2 num3*}
\newpsobject{*name*}{*object*}{*parameter list*}
\newpsstyle{*name*}{*parameter list*}
\newrgbcolor{*color*}{*num1 num2 num3*}
```
\NormalCoor
\overlaybox...\endoverlaybox
```
\parabola*[*parameters*]{*arrows*}(*x_0, y_0*)(*x_1, y_1*)
\psaddtolength{*command*}{*dimension*}
\psarc*[*parameters*]{*arrows*}(*x, y*){*radius*}{*angle A*}{*angle B*}
```
    arcsep
```
\psarcn*[*parameters*]{*arrows*}(*x, y*){*radius*}{*angle A*}{*angle B*}
\psbezier[*parameters*]{*arrows*}(*x_0, y_0*)(*x_1, y_1*)(*x_2, y_2*)(*x_3, y_3*)
\psccurve*[*parameters*]{*arrows*}(*x_0, y_0*)...(*x_n, y_n*)
\pscircle[*parameters*](*x_0, y_0*){*radius*}
```
    dimen (L)
\pscircle[*parameters*](*$x_0, y_0$*){*radius*}
    dimen (L)
\pscirclebox*[*parameters*]{*instructions*}
    linearc framearc (N) cornersize (R) dimen (L) framesep boxsep (B)
\pscustom*[*parameters*]{*commands*}
    liftpen (2)
\psdblframebox*[*parameters*]{*instructions*}
    linearc framearc (N) cornersize (R) dimen (L) framesep boxsep (B)
\psdots*[*parameters*](*$x_0, y_0$*)(*$x_1, y_1$*)...(*$x_n, y_n$*)
    dotstyle (S) dotscale (*) dotangle (A)
\psecurve*[*parameters*]{*arrows*}(*$x_0, y_0$*)...(*$x_n, y_n$*)
\psellipse*[*parameters*](*$x_0, y_0$*)(*$x_1, y_1$*)
    dimen (L)
\psframe*[*parameters*](*$x_0, y_0$*)(*$x_1, y_1$*)
    linearc framearc (N) cornersize (R) dimen (L)
\psframebox*[*parameters*]{*instructions*}
    linearc framearc (N) cornersize (R) dimen (L) framesep boxsep (B)
\psgrid(*$x_0, y_0$*)(*$x_1, y_1$*)(*$x_2, y_2$*)
    gridwidth gridcolor (C) griddots (N) gridlabels gridlabelcolor (C)
    subgriddiv (I) subgridwidth subgridcolor (C) subgriddots (N)
\pslabelsep
\pslbrace
\psline[*parameters*]{*arrows*}(*$x_0, y_0$*)(*$x_1, y_1$*)...(*$x_n, y_n$*)
    linearc framearc (N) cornersize (R)
\pslinecolor
\pslinewidth
```

```
\pslongbox{name}{command}
\psmathboxfalse
\psmathboxtrue
\psovalbox*[parameters]{instructions}
    linearc framearc (N) cornersize (R) dimen (L) framesep boxsep (B)
\psoverlay{string}
\pspicture[baseline] (x₀, y₀) (x₁, y₁) ... \endpspicture
\pspolygon*[parameters] (x₀, y₀) (x₁, y₁) ... (xₙ, yₙ)
    linearc framearc (N) cornersize (R)
\psrbrace
\pssetlength{command}{dimension}
\psset{parameter assignment list}
\psshadowbox*[parameters]{instructions}
    linearc framearc (N) cornersize (R) dimen (L) framesep boxsep (B)
\PSTricksoff
\pstverb{explicit PostScript code}
\psverbboxfalse
\psverbboxtrue
\pswedge*[parameters] (x₀, y₀) {radius}{angle1}{angle2}
    dimen (L)
\putoverlaybox{string}
\qdisk (coordinates) {radius}
\qline (x₀, y₀) (x₁, y₁)
\radians
\red
\rotatedown{instructions}
\rotateleft{instructions}
\rotateright{instructions}
\rput*[reference point]{rotation}(x, y){instructions}
\scaleboxto (x, y){instructions}
\scalebox{num1 num2}{instructions}
\SpecialCoor
\uput*{labelsep}[reference angle]{rotation}(x, y){instructions}
\white
\yellow
```

LATEX environments
overlaybox pspicture Rotatedown Rotateleft Rotateright

General: keywords and parameters
border bordercolor (C) curvature dash (*) dotsep doublecolor (C) doubleline (B) doublesep fillcolor (C) fillcolor (C) fillstyle (S) fillstyle (S) hatchangle (A) hatchcolor (C) hatchsep hatchwidth labelsep linecolor (C) linestyle (S) linetype (I) linewidth origin (Co) runit shadow (B) shadowangle (A) shadowcolor (C) shadowsize showpoints (B) swapaxes (B) unit xunit yunit

Arrows: keywords and parameters
arrowinset (N) arrowlength (N) arrows (Ar) arrowscale (*) arrowsize (*) bracketlength (N) dotsize (*) rbracketlength (N) tbarsize (*)

Plotting package: \input pst-plot *or* **\usepackage{***pst-plot***}**

\dataplot*[*parameters*]{*commands*}
\dataplot[*parameters*]{*commands*}
\listplot*[*parameters*]{*list*}
\listplot[*parameters*]{*list*}
\multido
\parametricplot[*parameters*]{*start*}{*stop*}{*function*}
\plotfile*[*parameters*]{*file*}
\plotfile[*parameters*]{*file*}
\psaxes[*parameters*]{*arrows*}$(x_0, y_0)(x_1, y_1)(x_2, y_2)$
\psaxes[*parameters*]{*arrows*}$(x_0, y_0)(x_1, y_1)(x_2, y_2)$
\psplot[*parameters*]{*start*}{*stop*}{*function*}
\psxlabel
\psylabel
\readdata{*command*}{*file*}
\savedata{*command*}[*data*]

Plotting package keywords

axesstyle (Ax) labels (X) plotpoints (I) plotstyle (S) showorigin (B)
ticks (X) ticksize tickstyle (T)

Commands for use within \pscustom only

\arrows{*arrows*}
\closedshadow[*parameters*]
\closepath
\code{*code*}
\coor$(x_0, y_0)(x_1, y_1) \ldots (x_n, y_n)$
\curveto$(x_0, y_0)(x_1, y_1)(x_2, y_2)$
\dim{*dimension*}
\file{*file*}
\fill[*parameters*]
\grestore
\gsave
\lineto(*coordinates*)
\movepath(*corrdinates*)
\moveto(*coordinates*)
\mrestore
\msave
\newpath
\openshadow[*parameters*]
\rcoor$(x_0, y_0)(x_1, y_1) \ldots (x_n, y_n)$
\rcurveto$(x_0, y_0)(x_1, y_1)(x_2, y_2)$
\rlineto(*coordinates*)
\rotate{*angle*}
\scale{*num1 num2*}
\setcolor{*color*}
\stroke[*parameters*]
\swapaxes
\translate(*corrdinates*)

Nodes and node connections: \input pst-node *or* \usepackage{*pst-node*}

\Aput*[*label separation*]{*instructions*}
\aput*[*label separation*]{*rotation*}(*position*){*instructions*}
\Bput*[*label separation*]{*instructions*}
\bput*[*label separation*]{*rotation*}(*position*){*instructions*}
\circlenode*[*parameters*]{*name*}{*instructions*}
\cnode*[*parameters*](*x, y*){*radius*}{*name*}
\cnodeput*[*parameters*]{*angle*}(*x, y*){*instructions*}
\lput*[*refpoint*]{*rotation*}(*position*){*instructions*}
\mput*[*refpoint point*]{*instructions*}
\ncangle*[*parameters*]{*arrows*}{*node A*}{*node B*}
\ncangles*[*parameters*]{*arrows*}{*node A*}{*node B*}
\ncarc*[*parameters*]{*arrows*}{*node A*}{*node B*}
    ncurv (N) arcangle (A)
\ncbar*[*parameters*]{*arrows*}{*node A*}{*node B*}
\nccircle*[*parameters*]{*arrows*}{*node*}{*radius*}
\nccurve*[*parameters*]{*arrows*}{*node A*}{*node B*}
    ncurv (N)
\ncdiag*[*parameters*]{*arrows*}{*node A*}{*node B*}
\ncdiagg*[*parameters*]{*arrows*}{*node A*}{*node B*}
\ncLine*[*parameters*]{*arrows*}{*node A*}{*node B*}
\ncline*[*parameters*]{*arrows*}{*node A*}{*node B*}
\ncloop*[*parameters*]{*arrows*}{*node A*}{*node B*}
    loopsize
\ovalnode*[*parameters*]{*name*}{*instructions*}
\pcangle*[*parameters*]{*arrows*}(x_0, y_0)(x_1, y_1)
\pcarc*[*parameters*]{*arrows*}(x_0, y_0)(x_1, y_1)
\pcbar*[*parameters*]{*arrows*}(x_0, y_0)(x_1, y_1)
\pccurve*[*parameters*]{*arrows*}(x_0, y_0)(x_1, y_1)
    ncurv (N)
\pcline*[*parameters*]{*arrows*}(x_0, y_0)(x_1, y_1)
\pcloop*[*parameters*]{*arrows*}(x_0, y_0)(x_1, y_1)
    loopsize
\pdciag*[*parameters*]{*arrows*}(x_0, y_0)(x_1, y_1)
\pnode(*x, y*){*name*}
\Rnode(*x, y*){*name*}{*instructions*}
\rnode[*reference point*]{*name*}{*instructions*}
\RnodeRef

Node connection parameters

---

angle (A) arm nodesep offset

Coils/zigzags: \input pst-node \input pst-coil *or* \usepackage{*pst-node,pst-coil*}

\nccoil*[*parameters*]{*arrows*}{*node A*}{*node B*}
\nczigzag*[*parameters*]{*arrows*}{*node A*}{*node B*}
\pccoil*[*parameters*]{*arrows*}(x_0, y_0)(x_1, y_1)
\pczigzag*[*parameters*]{*arrows*}(x_0, y_0)(x_1, y_1)
\psCoil*[*parameters*]{*angle 1*}{*angle 2*}
\pscoil*[*parameters*]{*arrows*}(x_0, y_0)(x_1, y_1)
\pszigzag*[*parameters*]{*arrows*}(x_0, y_0)(x_1, y_1)

Coil and zigzag parameters

`coilarm coilaspect`(A) `coilheight`(N) `coilinc`(A) `coilwidth`

Gradient fill style parameters: \input gradient *or* \usepackage{*gradient*}

`gradangle`(A) `gradbegin`(C) `gradend`(C) `gradlines`(I) `gradmidpoint`(N)

Typesetting text along a path: \input textpath *or* \usepackage{*textpath*}

\pstextpath [*position*] (*x, y*) {*graphics object*}{*text*}

Stroking and filling character paths:\input charpath *or* \usepackage{*charpath*}

\pscharclip*[*parameters*]{*text*}...\endpscharclip
\pscharpath*[*parameters*]{*text*}

Exporting encapsulated PostScript files: \input pst2eps *or* \usepackage{*pst2eps*}

\PSTtoEPS[*parameters*]{*file*}{*graphic objects*}
\TeXtoEPS...\endTeXtoEPS

Parameters for exporting encapsulated PostScript

`bbllx bblly bburx bbury headerfile`(F) `headers`(H)

New commands or options: \input pst-beta *or* \usepackage{*pst-beta*}

\psdiabox*[*parameters*]{*instructions*}
\psdiamond*[*parameters*] (*x*₀, *y*₀) (*x*₁, *y*₁)
   `gangle`(A)
\psdot*[*parameters*] (x_0, y_0)
\pstriangle*[*parameters*] (x_0, y_0) (x_1, y_1)
   `gangle`(A)
\pstribox*[*parameters*] {*instructions*}
   `trimode`(Tr)

New node and tree commands:\input pst-nodes \input pst-beta

~*[*parameters*]{*instructions*}
\dianode*[*parameters*]{*name*}{*instructions*}
\dotnode*[*parameters*]{*name*}{*instructions*}
\fnode*[*parameters*] (x_0, y_0){*name*}
\MakeShortNab{*character 1*}{*character 2*}
\MakeShortTablr{*character 1*}{*character 2*}{*character 3*}{*character 4*}
\MakeShortTab{*character 1*}{*character 2*}
\MakeShortTnput{*a character*}
\naput*[*parameters*]{*instructions*}
   `ref`(*)
\nbput*[*parameters*]{*instructions*}
   `ref`(*)
\ncarcbox*[*parameters*]{*node A*}{*node B*}
   `boxsize`
\ncbox*[*parameters*]{*node A*}{*node B*}
   `boxsize`
\ncput*[*parameters*]{*instructions*}
   `ref`(*)
\psedge
\pspred
\psrowhook...

\psspan{*whole number*}
\pssucc
\psTree{*root node*}
\pstree{*root node*}{*trees, subtrees, nodes, and terminal nodes*}...\endpstree
\skiplevel*[*parameters*]{*nodes or subtrees*}
\skiplevels*[*parameters*]{*whole number*}...\endskiplevels
\taput*[*parameters*]{*instructions*}
\tbput*[*parameters*]{*instructions*}
\TC*[*parameters*]
\Tc*[*parameters*]{*dimension*}
\Tcircle*[*parameters*]{*instructions*}
\Tdia*[*parameters*]{*instructions*}
\Tdot*[*parameters*]
\Tf*[*parameters*]
\Tfan*[*parameters*]
\tlput*[*parameters*]{*instructions*}
\Tn
\Toval*[*parameters*]{*instructions*}
\Tp*[*parameters*]
\TR*[*parameters*]{*instructions*}
\Tr*[*parameters*]{*instructions*}
\trinode*[*parameters*]{*name*}{*instructions*}
\trput*[*parameters*]{*instructions*}
\tspace
\Ttri*[*parameters*]{*instructions*}
\tvput*[*parameters*]{*instructions*}

Options for the new beta commands

bbd bbh bbl bbr colsep edge (Com) emnode (S) fansize href (N) levelsep
mcol (Pos) mnode (S) mnodesize name (Na) nodealign (B) nrot (A) radius rowsep
shortput (Sh) showbbox (B) tndepth tnheight tnpos (*l/r/a/b*) tnsep tnyref (N)
tpos (N) treefit (Lo) treeflip (B) treemode (Tre) treenodesize treesep vref
xbbd xbbh xbbl xbbr

Parameter types

No specification means any valid dimension. * = nonstandard notation; check the documentation. **2** = 0/1/2. **Ar** (arrow types) = -, <, >, <<, >>, |, |*, [,], (,), o, *, oo, **, c, cc, or C. **Ax** (axes) = axes/frame/none. **A** (angle) = angle in degrees. **B** (boolean) = true/false. **Com** = none/any valid PSTricks command. **Co** = coordinates. **C** (color) = red, green, blue, cyan, magenta, yellow, black, darkgray, gray, lightgray, white. **F** = file name. **H** (headers) = none/all/user. **I** (integer) = whole number. **Lo** (tree looseness) = tight/loose. **L** = outer/inner/middle. **Na** = a meaningful name. **N** = number. **Pos** (horizontal positioning) = l/r/c. **R** = relative/absolute. **Sh** (shortput form) = none/nab/tablr/tab. **S** (style) = many sets of valid styles exist; check documentation. **Tre** (tree mode) = R/L/U/D. **Tr** (triangle mode) = */U/D/R/L. **T** = full/top/bottom. **X** = all/x/y/none.

. . . .

CHAPTER 15

MFPIC PICTURES

I have a fondness for both METAFONT and MetaPost, and I hope therefore the reader has been duly impressed with the material in chapter 13. But no matter how impressive the results of that chapter, not everyone is in a position to spend the time necessary to master the METAFONT or MetaPost languages. Furthermore, not everyone will have a need for all the power these tools provide. For that reason, the appearance of the `mfpic` package is welcome. The `mfpic` macros provide a TEX interface for METAFONT. An author includes drawing commands with a TEX-like syntax into the document. Processing the document file in the usual manner generates an additional auxiliary file, which is a METAFONT input `.mf` file. Thereafter, a mechanical set of procedures translates the METAFONT file into a font, each character of which is one of the graphics. A final run of the document file through LATEX or TEX embeds the figures into the manuscript.

To be sure, using this package requires learning the drawing commands in the `mfpic` package. This is easier than learning METAFONT, since only a portion of the METAFONT capabilities have been provided for in these macros. (This is not a pejorative statement—the `mfpic` macros are remarkable in themselves.) Even within the confines of the package, there are certain limitations. Aspiring artists cannot, for example, create arbitrarily large pictures. METAFONT itself and various device drivers will not process drawings that are too large or too complicated.

Tom Leathrum began developing `mfpic` in 1992. Recent developments and bug fixes have been handled by Geoffrey Tobin.

It should be a straightforward task to generate an "mppic" package from `mfpic` that works with MetaPost but this task remains to be done.

15.1 Getting started

15.1.1 How mfpic works

An artist embeds `mfpic` drawing commands in the document file. Each time the file is run through LATEX or TEX, these commands generate a special

The mfpic Package: Pros and Cons

- **Pros:**

  - Although this package requires learning a new series of commands, they are easy to learn.

  - The drawing commands are part of the document, so any changes to the input file propagate automatically to the figures.

  - Provides a LATEX or TEX front end to METAFONT.

  - Output is METAFONT output, and can be tailored to any output device.

- **Cons:**

  - This package doesn't harness all the power of METAFONT.

auxiliary file containing pure METAFONT drawing commands. After the first successful run of the document through TEX, the auxiliary .mf file can be run through METAFONT and gftopk to generate a font whose characters are the graphics. Each time thereafter that we run the original document through TEX, TEX will typeset the character from this font in the document. The box on page 506 spells out the details.

15.1.2 Some syntax rules

Although it makes sense to regard the mfpic output file as an auxiliary file, akin to the .aux, .toc, .lof, .bbl, ... files that LATEX produces, this file differs in that the author specifies the file name explicitly. (Normally, other auxiliary files use the same file name, the \jobname, as the document file.) Before the first set of mfpic commands, type something like

```
\opengraphsfile{⟨name⟩}
```

In the file for this chapter, \opengraphsfile{mymfpic} appears early on. After the last set of mfpic commands, type something like

```
\closegraphsfile
```

One document can refer to several graph files, but before an alternative file can be opened with \opengraphsfile, the prior one must be closed with

```
\documentclass{article}

\input mfpic

\begin{document}

\opengraphsfile{⟨font name⟩}

\begin{mfpic}⟨scale factors and boundary values⟩
⟨various drawing commands⟩
\end{mfpic}
    · · ·
\begin{mfpic}⟨scale factors and boundary values⟩
⟨various drawing commands⟩
\end{mfpic}
    · · ·

\closegraphsfile

\end{document}
```

Figure 1: A general LaTeX document containing mfpic commands.

\closegraphsfile. The form of these commands is the same in plain TeX or LaTeX.

In plain TeX, we will place all drawing commands between pairs of commands

    \mfpic

and

    \endmfpic

commands. In LaTeX, we use

    \begin{mfpic}

and

    \end{mfpic}

statements instead.

These commands take a number of arguments, all of which pertain to the extent of the coordinate system which mfpic sets up for that graphic.

That is, we must say

   \mfpic[⟨*xscale*⟩] [⟨*yscale*⟩]{⟨*xmin*⟩}{⟨*xmax*⟩}{⟨*ymin*⟩}{⟨*ymax*⟩}

in plain TEX, or

   \begin{mfpic}
      [⟨*xscale*⟩] [⟨*yscale*⟩]{⟨*xmin*⟩}{⟨*xmax*⟩}{⟨*ymin*⟩}{⟨*ymax*⟩}

for LATEX.

Although the two scale parameters appear to be optional, in fact at least one must be present. These parameters establish the length of a unit in the local coordinate system, as a multiple of an internal unit. If only one of these parameters is present, they are presumed to be equal. The remaining parameters establish the smallest and largest values for the horizontal and vertical coordinate values.

For example,

   \mfpic[1] [1]{0}{35}{0}{50}

sets up a coordinate system in which the horizontal and vertical units are identical to mfpic's internal unit. Both the x- and y- coordinates begin at zero, and while the largest value of x should be 35, the largest value of y will be 50. In LATEX, this statement would be typed as

   \begin{mfpic}[1] [1]{0}{35}{0}{50}

Special effects are possible by varying the scale factors and boundary parameters. For example, I get ⏡ by typing

```
... For example, I get \begin{mfpic}[1] [1]{0}{10}{0}{10}
\cyclic{(2,10),(5,9),(8,10),
   (10,8),(9,5),(10,2),
   (8,0),(5,1),(2,0),
   (0,2), (1,5),(0,8)}
\end{mfpic}
by typing ...
```

but I get ⏠ by typing

   \begin{mfpic}[2] [2]{0}{10}{0}{10}

as the initial statement for this figure. Furthermore, if I butt several of the original characters together, I get

```
\input mfpic

\opengraphsfile{⟨font name⟩}
  . . .
  ⟨text⟩
  . . .
\mfpic⟨scale factors and boundary values⟩
⟨various drawing commands⟩
\endmfpic
  . . .
\mfpic⟨scale factors and boundary values⟩
⟨various drawing commands⟩
\endmfpic
  . . .

\closegraphsfile

\bye
```

Figure 2: A general plain TEX document with mfpic commands.

but if I perform the same experiment, this time changing the initial statement to

```
\begin{mfpic}[1][1]{1}{9}{1}{9}
```

I get

The characters overlap each other because I have changed the beginning and
ending positions of the character's bounding box.

Within the mfpic environment, one simply inserts a sequence of mfpic
commands. The full repertoire is described in the file mfpicdoc.tex, a component of the mfpic package.

Several commands control basic shapes and curves. We get a primitive
bomb by typing something like

```
\begin{mfpic}[1][1]{0}{35}{0}{56}
  \circle{(20,20),20}
  \rect{(18,38), (22,50)}
  \curve{(20,50),(21,54),(25,56)}
\end{mfpic}
```

which gives

As we'll see, there are several other commands to control basic geometric shapes.

The mfpic package can be of use in the creation of graphs. For example, I type

```
\begin{mfpic}[24][40]{0}{6.28}{-1}{1}
  \axes
  \xmarks{0,1.57,3.14,4.61,6.28} \ymarks{-1,-.5,0,.5,1}
  \connect
  \curve{(0.00, 0.000),(0.10, 0.995),...}
  \endconnect
\end{mfpic}
```

to get

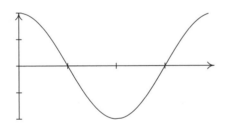

The actual curve data was the output of a short Perl program.

Two commands, \label and \caption, allow the placement of text (via TEX) in the picture. For example,

```
$$\fontsize{8}{10}\selectfont
\begin{mfpic}[24][40]{0}{6.28}{-1}{1}
  \axes
  \xmarks{0,1.57,3.14,4.71} \ymarks{-1,-.5,0,.5,1}
  \label[cr](-.1,1){$+1$} \label[cr](-.1,-1){$-1$}
  \label[cr](-.1,0){$0$} \label[cl](-.75,.5){$y$}
  \label[tc](3.14,-.1){$\mathstrut\pi$}
  \label[tc](6.28,-.1){$\mathstrut2\pi$}
  \label[cl](6.35,0){$x$}
  \caption[1.2,1]{{\bf The Cosine Curve}}
  \connect\curve{(0.10, 0.995),(0.30, 0.955),...}\endconnect
\end{mfpic}
```

produce

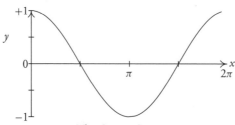

The Cosine Curve

The comma-separated numbers in the optional argument to \caption refer to scale factors to regulate the width of the caption text; the documentation explains their use. The \label command has two mandatory arguments for specifying the location (anchor point) and text of each label. The two-sequence characters in the optional argument regulate the placement of the label with respect to the anchor. The first character—t, c, or b—determines the vertical placement (top, center, bottom), while the second letter—l, c, or b—controls horizontal placement (left, center, or right).

15.1.3 Prefix macros

A few prefix commands provide convenient ways to get special effects. We type

```
\begin{mfpic}[1][1]{0}{35}{0}{56}
   \fill\circle{(20,20),20}
   \fill\rect{(18,38), (22,50)}
   \curve{(20,50),(21,54),(25,56)}
\end{mfpic}
```

to get

Other prefixes include \white, \shade, \hatch, \arrow, \dotted, and \rotate. These commands, applied to

```
\cyclic{(0,6), (5,10), (10,4), (15,12),
   (18,4), (14, 8), (11,3), (4,2)}
```

generated the following sequence:

(The first figure redraws the original shape with a thicker pen with larger dots to highlight the location of the defining points. In the second example, a filled rectangle was drawn so the whitened region would be distinct. The \rotate command requires as arguments the coordinates of a point to rotate about and a value for the rotation. The \hatch command could not be illustrated; it exceeded METAFONT's capacity at production-quality resolutions.) Some of the effects can be combined. I obtained

by means of the statement

```
\dotted\draw\rotate{(10,6),45}
\cyclic{(0,6), (5,10), (10,6), (15,12),
(18,4), (14, 6), (11,3), (4,2)}
```

within the mfpic environment.

15.1.4 Transforming shapes

The mfpic macros know many ways to transform shapes. In order to use transforms, it's necessary to enclose the statements describing the transformation within the coords environment—otherwise, mfpic uses the transformation for all subsequent drawing, even for all subsequent mfpictures. For example, I got

by typing

```
\begin{mfpic}[1][1]{0}{35}{0}{56}
  \begin{coords}
    \rotates{45}
    \fill\circle{(20,20),20}
    \fill\rect{(18,38), (22,50)}
    \curve{(20,50),(21,54),(25,56)}
  \end{coords}
\end{mfpic}
```

in LᴬTEX, or by typing

```
\mfpic[1][1]{0}{35}{0}{56}
  \coords
    \rotates{45}
    \fill\circle{(20,20),20}
    \fill\rect{(18,38), (22,50)}
    \curve{(20,50),(21,54),(25,56)}
  \endcoords
\endmfpic
```

in plain TEX. (LᴬTEX accepts the plain TEX form perfectly well.)

Quite a variety of transforms are available. To get them, simply replace the boxed statements above by any of the commands of figure 3 on the next page. The \shift transform is not shown here because the command simply moves a picture to a new location but otherwise leaves it untouched.

Contrary to the documentation, the transform \xyswaps must be entered as

```
\xyswaps{}
```

This transformation reflects an object about the 45° diagonal line connecting the upper right corner to the lower left.

Transforms can be combined. I obtained

via the compound transform statement

```
\xscales{1.3} \rotates{45}
```

The order in which we apply the transformation counts. The "reverse" transform statement

```
\rotates{45} \xscales{1.3}
```

generates

Transforms are applied from right to left.

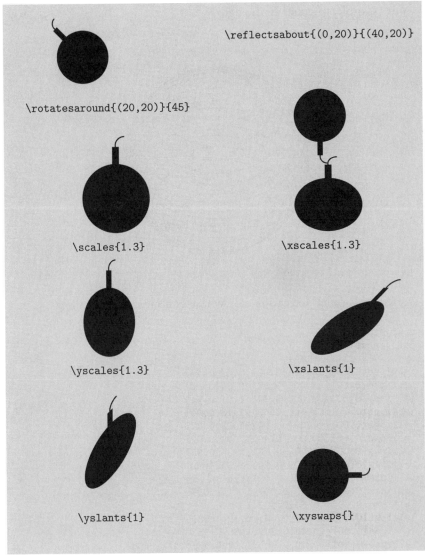

Figure 3: A plethora of transforms.

The appendix to this chapter presents a reference to all MFPIC commands as of summer 1994.

15.2   The mfpic process

The box 2 on page 506 summarizes the complete series of steps necessary to include an mfpic set of graphics in a document. Since the output of a mfpic run is a METAFONT program file, this procedure is essentially equivalent to creating a new file for use by LaTeX or TeX.

For example, to generate the figure

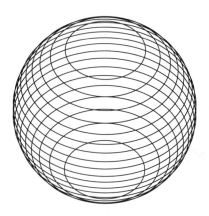

I created a file called `ellipses.tex` whose contents were as follows.

```
\input mfpic
\opengraphsfile{ell}
\mfpic[50]{-1}{1}{-1}{1}
  \ellipse[0.00]{(0.00,-0.90),0.62,0.44}
  \ellipse[0.00]{(0.00,-0.80),0.85,0.60}
  \ellipse[0.00]{(0.00,-0.70),1.01,0.71}
  \ellipse[0.00]{(0.00,-0.60),1.13,0.80}
  \ellipse[0.00]{(0.00,-0.50),1.22,0.87}
  \ellipse[0.00]{(0.00,-0.40),1.30,0.92}
  \ellipse[0.00]{(0.00,-0.30),1.35,0.95}
  \ellipse[0.00]{(0.00,-0.20),1.39,0.98}
  \ellipse[0.00]{(0.00,-0.10),1.41,0.99}
  \ellipse[0.00]{(0.00,0.00),1.41,1.00}
  \ellipse[0.00]{(0.00,0.10),1.41,0.99}
  \ellipse[0.00]{(0.00,0.20),1.39,0.98}
  \ellipse[0.00]{(0.00,0.30),1.35,0.95}
  \ellipse[0.00]{(0.00,0.40),1.30,0.92}
  \ellipse[0.00]{(0.00,0.50),1.22,0.87}
  \ellipse[0.00]{(0.00,0.60),1.13,0.80}
  \ellipse[0.00]{(0.00,0.70),1.01,0.71}
  \ellipse[0.00]{(0.00,0.80),0.85,0.60}
  \ellipse[0.00]{(0.00,0.90),0.62,0.44}
\endmfpic
\closegraphsfile
\bye
```

(The various \ellipse statements were generated for me in a painless way by a quick Perl program.) I ran this file through TEX a first time:

```
tex ellipses
```

which silently produced a new auxiliary file `ell.mf`. On my Unix system, the command

```
mf '\mode=imagen; input ell'
```

is sufficient to process `ell.mf`; syntax and mode might be different on your system. It is now necessary to convert the generic font format to packed pixels with a command like

```
gftopk ell.600gf ell.600pk
```

Now I run TEX on the document one final time: `tex ellipses` includes all proper fonts, and `ellipses.dvi` is ready for previewing.

15.2.1 *Other front ends to Metafont*

The graphics area of CTAN contains three other front-end tools to META-FONT. By chance, these three occur next to each other in lexicographical sequence. The packages `fig2mf` and `fig2mfpic` make it possible to convert `fig` output to METAFONT or MFPIC files; `fig` is a mostly-Unix tool for creating graphics files in a device-independent way (like TEX). The `gnuplot` program is a powerful curve-plotting utility that can deliver its output in any of a number of ways, one of which is as METAFONT code.

The mfpic Production Cycle

- Create the document file, incorporating `mfpic` instructions and conventions. Follow the templates of figure 1 on page 496 and figure 2 on page 498.

- Run the document file through LATEX or TEX.

- The output of the TEX process includes a METAFONT program file. Run METAFONT on this file with a command like

  ```
  mf 'mode=imagen; input myfont'
  ```

  where `myfont.mf` has been created by the `mfpic` `\opengraphs-file` command.

- Create the packed pixel font with a command like

  ```
  gftopk myfont.300gf myfont.300pk
  ```

  Leave the packed pixel file and the `.tfm` file in the current work directory, if your implementation of TEX permits this. This is advantageous as it makes it easy to delete the special `mfpic` fonts when you are finished with them.

- Run the document through LATEX or TEX once again to incorporate the completed font in the document. (No further changes to the document are called for, unless you are still in the process of revising the text.)

15.3 Appendix: mfpic reference

Setting up the environment

`\mfpic` [*xscale*] [*yscale*] {x_{min}}{x_{max}}{y_{min}}{y_{max}}...`\endmfpic`
    Determines the environment for a particular picture.

`\opengraphsfile`{*font name*}...`\closegraphsfile`
    Opens the font file.

LATEX environments

`mfpic connect coords`

Points, lines, and rectangles

\lines{$(x_0, y_0),(x_1, y_1),\dots$ }
  Connects the dots with lines segments.

\point{$(x_0, y_0),(x_1, y_1),\dots$ }
  Draws points at the given locations.

\rect{$(x_0, y_0),(x_1, y_1)$}
  Draws the rectangle with the lower left and upper right corners as given.

Axes and axis marks

\axes
  Draws two perpendicular coordinate axes.

\xmarks{$x_1,x_2,\dots$ }
  Places ticks at the given locations.

\ymarks{$y_1,y_2,\dots$ }
  Places ticks at the given locations.

Circles and ellipses, circular arcs, odd figures, and general curves

\arc[c]{$(x_0, y_0), (x_1, y_1), angle$}
  Draws an arc of a circle centered at the initial point starting from the other point which subtends the angle.

\arc[p]{$(x_0, y_0),angle\ 1, angle\ 2, radius$}
  Draws an arc centered at the point starting from the first and proceeding to the second angles.

\arc[s]{$(x_0, y_0),(x_1, y_1), angle$}
  Draws a circular arc from the initial to terminal points subtending the given angle.

\arc[t]{$(x_0, y_0), (x_1, y_1), (x_2, y_2)$}
  Draws a circular arc through the three given points.

\circle{$(x_0, y_0),radius$}
  Draws a circle centered at the given point with the given radius.

\curve{$(x_0, y_0), (x_1, y_1),\dots$ }
  Draws a Bézier curve through the sequence of points.

\cyclic{$(x_0, y_0), (x_1, y_1),\dots$ }
  Draws a closed Bézier curve through the sequence of points.

\ellipse[$theta$]{$(x_0, y_0), semi\text{-}major, semi\text{-}minor$}
  Draws an ellipse centered at the given point with the given major and minor axes.

\turtle{$(x_0, y_0), (\theta_0, r_0), (\theta_1, r_1),\dots$ }
  Draws a figure originating at initial point consisting of a sequence of connected straight line segments. A segment begins at the origin or terminus of the preceding segment for a distance given by r_i traveling in a direction θ_i from the horizontal axis.

\wedge{$(x_0, y_0), angle\ 1, angle\ 2, radius$}
  Draws a wedge-shaped region of the circle centered at the given point with the radius. The wedge is that "slice of the pie" lying between the two angles.

Polar coordinate macros

\plrcurve{$(\theta_0, r_0), (\theta_1, r_1),\dots$ }

\plrcyclic{(θ_0, r_0), (θ_1, r_1),... }
\plrlines{(θ_0, r_0), (θ_1, r_1),... }
\plrpoint{(θ_0, r_0), (θ_1, r_1),... }

Prefix macros

\arrow [*head length*] [*rotation*] [*backset*]
\bclosed
   Closes a figure with a Bézier curve.

\cbclosed
   Closes a figure with a cubic Bézier spline.

\closed
   Closes a figure with a line segment between the end points.

\connect...\endconnect
   Draws line segments between the terminus of one open figure and the start of
   another figure.

\dotted [*dash length, dashspace*]
\draw
\fill
\hatch [*hatch space*]
\reverse
\rotate{(x_0, y_0), *angle*}
   Rotates a figure about the point by the angle.

\sclosed
   Closes a figure with a smooth curve.

\shade [*shade space*]
\white

Transforming figures

\applyT{*transformation*}
   General transformation tool; rarely used explicitly.

\boosts{*amount*}
   Applies a special relativity boost by the given amount.

\coords...\endcoords
   Environment which must enclose transformation commands.

\reflectsabout{*point 1*}{*point 2*}
   Reflects about the line connecting the two points.

\rotatesaround{*point*}{*angle*}
\rotates{*angle*}
\scales{*factor*}
\shifts{*point*}
   Shifts a figure in a direction and by the magnitude of the vector from the
   origin to the given point.

\xscales{*factor*}
\xslants{*factor*}
\xyswaps{ }
   Reflects the figure about the line $y = x$.

\yscales{*factor*}
\yslants{*factor*}
\zscales{*point*}
   Scales by the magnitude of the point (*its distance from the origin*)and rotates the
   figure by the angle of the point.

`\zslants{`*factor*`}`

Functions

When drawing functions, the *curve type* may be either s, smooth, or p, polygonal line segments. The *expression* must by a valid METAFONT expression. The subscript tells what name of the independent variable *must* be.

`\btwnfnc[`*curve type*`]{`x_{min}, x_{max}, *step size*`}{`*first expression$_x$, second expression$_x$* `}`
    Draws the region between two functions.

`\function[`*curve type*`]{`x_{min}, x_{max}, *step size*`}{`*expression$_x$* `}`
    Draws a function.

`\parafcn[`*curve type*`]{`t_{min}, t_{max}, *step size*`}{`*first expression$_t$, second expression$_t$* `}`
    Draws a pair of parametric equations.

`\plrfcn[`*curve type*`]{`t_{min}, t_{max}, *step size*`}{`*expression$_t$* `}`
    Draws a polar plot of *r* as a funtion of *t* for θ.

`\plrregion[`*curve type*`]{`t_{min}, t_{max}, *step size*`}{`*expression$_t$* `}`
    Plots a polar region.

Labels and captions

`\caption[`*maximum width factor, graph width factor*`]{`*caption text*`}`
    Places a caption under a graph, and uses the factors as guides for line breaking.

`\label[`*placement parameter*`]` (x_0, y_0) `{`*label text*`}`
    Places a label. The [*placement parameter*]is a two-character sequence for proper positioning. The first character must be one of t, c, or b for top, center, or bottom, and the second is one of l, c, or r for left, center, or right.

Parameters

`\axisheadlin`
    Length of arrow on graph axes.

`\darkershade`
    Controls shading.

`\dashlen`
    Lengths of dashes.

`\dashlineset`
    Sets dashes to dashes.

`\dashspace`
    Widths of spaces in dashed material.

`\dotlineset`
    Sets dashes to dots.

`\hashlen`
    Length of axis tick marks.

`\hatchspace`
    Spacing between lines when hatching.

`\headlen`
    Length of an arrowhead.

`\headshape{`*ratio of arrow width to length*`}{`*tension of Bézier curves*`}{`*filled or not*`}`
    Affords precise control over arrowhead shapes.

`\lightershade`
    Controls shading.

\mfpicunit
>   Scaling unit; default is one point.

\pen{*pensize*}
\pointfilled
>   Should the pints be filled or left as circles?

\pointsize
>   Controls size of plotted points.

\shadespace
>   Establishes spacing between dots when shading.

For experts only!

\mfcmd{*instructions*}
>   The {*instructions*} should be proper Metafont code.

\mfobj{*path variable*}
>   Use an object previously \store'd.

\store{*path variable*}
>   Stores the following figure under the variable name.

APPENDIX I

. . . .

BASIC TEX COMMANDS

The goal of this appendix is to identify a minimal subset of commands with which functional reports, letters, and other documents can be fashioned. "Basic TEX" makes it easy and quick to start with TEX, builds self-esteem in budding TEXnical typesetters, and generates an interest in typesetting things of greater and greater difficulty. Moreover, this appendix is useful even for aspiring LATEX authors. The LATEX package uses many of the same conventions, and much of what applies to plain TEX (the subject of this appendix) applies to LATEX as well.

More experienced authors may well turn their noses up at the methods presented here, and you may review these pages in a few weeks with the same feeling. I offer no apology, for the purpose of this material is simply to enable a new user of TEX get started as fast as possible. In fact, it would be a surprise if the methods that served you well in your first day with TEX remained serviceable in the light of further knowledge and experience.

Let's recall the production cycle associated with TEX. We first produce the *document file*, which is the text on which your TEX formatting commands have been sprinkled. In addition to using commands properly, there are a few other conventions that govern the preparation of this file.

In the second stage, we run this document through the TEX program. TEX examines it for blatant errors (misuse of command syntax mostly) and reports any errors to you. It is up to you to correct these errors and rerun the document through TEX. Once there are no remaining errors, TEX produces the output `.dvi` file, which you use in the next and final step.

Along with TEX, you need a few other basic programs. The two important for the final phase are the *device driver* for your printer and *screen previewer* for your monitor. The `.dvi` file contains type-placement information for each character in your document, and the device driver translates this information into language understood by your printer. Therefore, it is the device driver that is responsible for painting the type on the page. The screen previewer does the same with respect to the computer monitor. Remember, TEX is not a wysiwyg system, and the screen previewer helps you

511

get an idea of what the document looks like before you print it. At best, your document file will approximately represent the final typeset appearance. However, there are many places in a document file where the document file will bear no visible relation to the printed page. In this appendix, we concern ourselves solely with the first stage—preparing the document file. Please also see the first nine or so chapters in *The TEXbook*.

A1.1   Basic keyboard conventions

The basic building blocks of any document are the characters of text and its paragraphs. Any group of letters, numerals, punctuation, and some special characters can be typeset by simply including those characters in your source file. For example, to typeset

> In 1492, Columbus sailed the ocean blue.

simply type

```
In 1492, Columbus sailed the ocean blue.
```

in the document file.

Typesetters signal the beginning of a paragraph in typeset text by means of a small indentation in the first line. TEX ignores any indentations in your document file, so we need some other signal to begin a paragraph. A reasonable convention, one that typists find easy to get used to, is to leave a blank line between successive paragraphs of text in the document file. For example, to get

> Although she herself was ill enough to justify being in bed had she been a person weakminded enough to give up, Rose Sayer could see that her brother, the Reverend Samuel Sayer, was far more ill. He was very, very weak indeed, and when he knelt to offer up the evening prayer the movement was more like an involuntary collapse than a purposed gesture, and the hands which he raised trembled violently.
>
> Rose could see, in the moment before she devoutly closed her eyes, how thin and transparent those hands were, and how the bones of the wrists could be seen with almost the definition of a skeleton's.
>
> The damp heat of the African forest seemed to be intensified with the coming of the night, which closed in upon them while they prayed.

type

```
Although she herself was ill enough to justify being
in bed had she been a person weakminded enough to give
up, Rose Sayer could see that her brother, the
Reverend Samuel Sayer, was far more ill.  He was very,
very weak indeed, and when he knelt to offer up the
```

```
evening prayer the movement was more like an
involuntary collapse than a purposed gesture, and the
hands which he raised trembled violently.

Rose could see, in the moment before she devoutly
closed her eyes, how thin and transparent those hands
were, and how the bones of the wrists could be seen
with almost the definition of a skeleton's.

The damp heat of the African forest seemed to be
intensified with the coming of the night, which closed
in upon them while they prayed.
```

in your file. (The text is from C. S. Forester's *The African Queen*.) Notice that we got the special ligatures 'ff' and 'fi' by merely typing `definition` or `intensified` or `offer`; TEX was smart enough to take care of them by itself.

You get quotation marks " and " by typing `` ` ` `` and `' '`. There are three dashes

- – —

which you get by typing

```
-    --    ---
```

(Another "dash" is the mathematical minus sign; see below.) You might typeset another selection from *The African Queen*

> "Where's everybody, Miss?" he asked as he came
> up to her.
> "They've all gone," said Rose.
> "Where's the Reverend—your brother?"
> "He's in there—. He's dead," said Rose.

by typing

```
``Where's everybody, Miss?'' he asked as he came up to her.

``They've all gone,'' said Rose.

``Where's the Reverend---your brother?''

``He's in there---. He's dead,'' said Rose.
```

(The odd use of hyphens is per the original.) By the way, TEX takes care of hyphenation for you, in case a word at the end of the line needs to be broken across the line. You do *not* need to break a word yourself or worry about adding the hyphen.

Some TEX Jargon

The following few terms tend to become part of a TEXer's vocabulary.

- **The document file** is the file containing the text and TEX commands for your document.

- **Source file** is another name for *document file.*

- **Compiling a document** is the process of running the document file through the TEX program.

- **Macros** are customized TEX typesetting commands that experienced TEX'ers create out of simpler commands. A *macro package* aims to make using TEX simpler for some particular purpose.

- **LATEX** is a common macro package.

- **The** `.dvi` **file** is the output of successful document compilation.

- **The** `.log` **file** is the file, produced automatically and unsuppressibly, that contains a record of everything that appears on the screen as a result of running the document file through TEX, plus some additional diagnostic information.

- **Previewing** is the process whereby you display the TEX'ed document on the computer screen.

- **Rendering the document** is the same as printing it.

- **The device driver** is the program that can render the `.dvi` file on your printer.

- **Font files** contain information for actually painting the characters of your fonts on the printed page. Bitmap font descriptions appear in **pixel files**, while **outline** or **scalable fonts** require special printer technology.

- **The resolution** of your printer measures the degree of sharpness with which the document can be printed. It has become customary to express this measure in terms of *dpi*—dots per inch. (For example, most laser printers have resolutions of 600 dpi.)

A1.2   Default parameters, parameters, simple commands

When they begin composing a document, most people give some thought to specifying various page-layout parameters—how wide the text will be, how large the margins will be, the size of the paragraph indentation, and

Some Document File Conventions

- To get most printable characters, simply type them in the source file.

- Signal the start of new paragraph by inserting a blank line in the document file.

- Remember the special conventions for quotes and dashes. The word "quotes" is entered as ``quotes''.

- See below in case you need to include a special character in the document.

so on. TEX provides easy ways for adjusting these parameters (and many others), but in case you forget to adjust them to your satisfaction, TEX will have chosen various *default values* of these parameters.

You adjust these values and specify format conventions by entering commands in your document file. Most of the time, it's easy to pick out a TEX command. A TEX command consists of one or more letters (or perhaps a single numeral or special character) preceded by the backslash character '\'. Most TEX command names suggest their function; the command \TeX, for example, is the command to typeset the logo "TEX."

The backslash has a special meaning for TEX, so it's reasonable to expect that you have to do something special if you need the \ character in your document. In fact, there are a handful of other characters whose presence signals something special to TEX. We'll shortly see what they are and how to arrange to typeset them.

A1.2.1 Spaces

TEX is liberal in its interpretation of the spaces you enter in a source file. One space is the same as several spaces, and a single carriage return is equivalent to a space (but a double carriage return begins a new paragraph). Thus, the command

```
\hskip 1in
```

which inserts one inch of horizontal spacing in your typeset text, could be entered as \hskip1in, \hskip␣1␣in, \hskip␣␣␣␣␣␣1␣␣␣␣␣␣in, or even as

```
\hskip
    1   in
```

(here, the character ␣ represents a space character). You should exploit this flexibility to make the input file as easy to read as possible.

A related problem pertains to adding space after a command. While it *is* true that \TeX␣is, \TeX␣␣␣is, and even

```
\TeX
    is
```

are all equivalent, they all typeset the phrase "TₑXis", probably not the desired result. Here, the spacing you enter serves merely to terminate the command. At that point, TₑX gobbles it up and there is nothing left to add an actual space. One way to deal with this is via the control space command \␣. Thus,

```
\TeX\␣is
```

properly generates "TₑX is". An empty group {} can also terminate a command;

```
\tex{} is
```

also prints properly.

In general, TₑX ignores spaces after macro or command names. The conventions in this section apply equally to plain TₑX and LATₑX.

A1.3   Simple page layout

It's easy to adjust the most important aspects of page layout. First, a word on measurements.

Certain commands have to be followed by a dimension. TₑX can only know how wide a page of text will be, for example, if you tell it the text width. Such a dimension will consist of some number *always* followed by a unit abbreviation. That is, 1in means one inch to TₑX, 0.5cm means a half-centimeter, but 0 is not the same as 0mm (zero millimeters). In addition to these standard measures, TₑX knows about printer's *points* (pt) and *picas* (pc). There are 72.27 pt in an inch, and 12 pt make 1 pc. Despite the tininess of a point, the eye is sensitive to point-like dimensions, at least on the printed page. A long rule that is one point wide looks heavy:

Typically, a fine rule will be 0.4 pt or 0.5 pt wide or thick. See how the thin rule looks more genteel?

One additional caveat before we resume our discussion. TₑX's commands are *case-sensitive*. A capital letter (A, B, C, etc.) is uppercase; the minuscule or small letters (a, b, c, and so on) are lowercase. It makes a difference to TₑX whether you spell a command with upper- or lowercase characters. The commands "\hsize", "\Hsize", and "\HSIZE" are three completely different, unrelated commands. All the commands we will discuss use only lowercase letters in their spelling.

The TEX commands \hsize and \vsize control the *horizontal size* of the text and the *vertical size* (the text width and text length). Place them as near as possible to the beginning of the document. You might say, for example,

```
\hsize=30pc \vsize=9in
```

to make pages whose text forms blocks that are 30 pc by 9 in (30 picas are about five inches).

A printer speaks of the *baseline skip* as the distance between baselines of two consecutive lines in a normal paragraph. The baseline is the line on which the type appears to sit.

Type sits on a baseline.

Often, the baseline skip for text type is 12 pt, and this is TEX's default value. One way to adjust it is by typing a command like

```
\baselineskip=24pt
```

at the beginning of the document. Notice that the command

```
\baselineskip
```

is typed as a single word (and that it's spelled in lowercase). We rarely need to change the baseline separation, but you can achieve a poor person's double spacing with this command. (After all, if normal single spacing is a 12 pt baseline, then double spacing is twice that.)

A simple command that is unexpectedly useful is \noindent which suppresses the indentation of a paragraph. Place the command at the beginning of the paragraph. For example, we began this paragraph with

```
\noindent A simple command . . .
```

(preceded by a command to get some extra vertical space). The \noindent command comes in handy to suppress indentation in the initial paragraph following a section head. As we'll see, it's useful too in typesetting the salutation of a letter.

A1.4   Controlling lines of text

People frequently need to put text on various parts of a line, and at least three commands help in those tasks. The first is

```
\leftline{. . .}
```

which causes TEX to place your text (denoted here by the three dots) flush with the left edge of text. The text must be surrounded by the left and right curly braces { and }. It's a good idea to precede and follow \leftline with a blank line. Remember, blank lines signal the completion of paragraphs to TEX, so there will be no possibility that the \leftline becomes part of a paragraph when preceded and followed by a blank line.

Thus, if you type

```
\leftline{Left of Center}
```

(preceded and followed by blank lines) you get

Left of Center

Directly analogous are \rightline and \centerline, which do what you expect, and which have the same curly-brace syntax involving as \leftline. Quick examples follow. If we type

```
\rightline{Radical Right}

\centerline{Politically Powerless}
```

we get

Radical Right

Politically Powerless

A1.5   Spacing

A crowded document is difficult to read, so TEX provides several mechanisms for controlling the appearance of white space.

A1.5.1   Vertical spacing

Three useful commands for vertical space are \smallskip, \medskip, and \bigskip, which provide small, medium, and big skips (that is, 3 pt, 6 pt, and 12 pt). In general, you can also say

```
\vskip . . .
```

replacing the dots by any valid TEX measurement. For example,

```
\vskip 12pt
```

is almost the same as \bigskip.

You can issue these commands between paragraphs or between any of the

```
. . .line{. . .}
```

commands. If you issue them within a paragraph, TEX terminates that paragraph at that point, skips the space, and prepares to begin a new paragraph.

Figure 1: This gives some idea of the amounts of space provided by common vertical skip commands.

We often use these commands to adjust the vertical white space surrounding the title and author of a report, say. If you type

```
\centerline{How I Spent My Summer Vacation}
\medskip
\centerline{by B. C. Dull}
\bigskip
\noindent This past summer was memorable for me. . .
```

you get

> How I Spent My Summer Vacation
>
> by B. C. Dull
>
> This past summer was memorable for me. . .

The . . .skip commands can even take negative values. One way to get
Alpha   Omega
is to type

```
\leftline{Alpha}\vskip-12pt\rightline{Omega}
```

This works because the baseline separation is 12 pt.

Note well one TEXnical quirk that often confuses beginning TEXers. If a vertical skip command appears at a point corresponding to the beginning of a new page, TEX simply discards that skip command. There's good reason for this behavior, and there are several ways of getting space at the top of a page if you really need it, but these discussions are out of place here.

A1.5.2 *Horizontal spacing*

One way to *force* some interword spacing is with the command \␣—that is, the backslash followed by a space. (The ␣ is a convention for making the space visible to readers. Of course, you wouldn't enter this symbol at the keyboard; for one thing, it doesn't exist on the keyboard.) Every so often, it will appear to you that TEX has forgotten to put in a space when it should have. This is actually due to some more advanced feature of TEX, but rather than worry about it at this stage, simply use the *control space* command \␣.

A finer control over horizontal spacing is provided by \hskip. If, in a paragraph or ...line command, you say something like

    \hskip 1pc

or

    \hskip .5\hsize

then TEX will skip 1 pc horizontal space or half the text width on that line. One common example of \hskip, which also demonstrates the way it's possible to combine TEX commands, is given by

    \leftline{\hskip.5\hsize December 31, 1999}

which typesets as

December 31, 1999

and shows one way to put text left-aligned with the central axis of the page. This might be appropriate for a letter.

(Do you see how it works? \leftline puts some text at the left edge of the page. The text is a dollop of space followed by the date. We tell TEX that the width of the space should be half the text width, so this puts the left edge of the date where we want it.)

A1.6 Selecting new fonts

There are three important commands for selecting different type styles. You type \it to select *italic* type, \bf for **bold** type, and \tt for a `typewriter`-like display.

The syntax for changing fonts *requires* that the font command, together with the text, be surrounded by curly braces. To get

This is a bold initiative we embark on today.

type

    This is a {\bf bold initiative} we embark on today.

We can get a

more delicate style

of emphasis by typing

    . . . can get a {\it more delicate style\/} of emphasis . . .

`Computer programmers` and certain others like the effect from typing

`{\tt Computer programmers} and certain others . . .`

In the *italic* example, notice the presence of the *italic correction* command \/, which adds a tad more space (if necessary) due to the way the last letter in an italic phrase may appear to lean too close to the beginning of the next word. To get a feel for the importance of \/, compare

I met her   versus   I met her

which was typed as

`I {\it met\/} her     I {\it met} her`

Don't forget the closing brace } in the font-changing commands! If you do, you'll never get back to the normal Roman typesetting.

By the way, the curly braces that must surround a font change may double as the curly braces in the syntax for some other command. Thus, to center some authorial byline in italic type, like this

Etaoin Shrdlu

simply type

`\centerline{\it Etaoin Shrdlu}`

which is another useful demonstration of the way TEX commands can be used together.

(Sharp-eyed readers will notice that the results of typesetting TEX commands don't match the typeface used throughout this volume. That's because, in the absence of instructions to the contrary, TEX uses the Computer Modern font family. TEX works well with other faces as well, and other chapters in this book address—in great detail—the issues involved in using other fonts. In particular, see chapter 6.)

Simple document structure

With two or three more commands, you're ready to begin composing simple reports on your own. You can use \centerline and the . . .skip commands to place titles and bylines at the beginning of a document. You probably also need a way to indicate new sections, to start a new page, and to tell TEX that the document is complete.

It's a good idea to separate a lengthy document into component sections. One way to do that in TEX is via the \beginsection command. We used this command to begin this section, rather than the usual sectioning command we use elsewhere in this volume, just as an example (and that's why the section header looks a little different). The syntax for this command demands that the section title follow the command \beginsection and that there be a blank line following this title. *Don't forget this blank line!* This command has been constructed specially to treat everything following the command up to the next new paragraph indicator (that is, the blank line) as the section title. Without the blank line, TEX will assume that the entire text of the following paragraph is part of the section title, surely not what you had in mind. Here's how the end of the previous section and the beginning of this section appear in the text file for this article.

```
  . . . see chapter~6.).

\beginsection{Simple document structure}

With two or three more commands, . . .
```

Pay close attention to the blank lines in the example.

Normally, TEX makes its own decisions about where to finish one page and begin another, but you may care to force TEX's hand in special cases. You can force a new page with the command sequence

```
\vfill\eject
```

\eject will work by itself, but TEX will try to even out the spacing between the paragraphs on the page before the break. The effect of \vfill is to "push up from the bottom," so that all the paragraphs have the spacing they should, and all the extra spacing is concentrated at the bottom.

It's worth a quick illustration of this effect. Study figure 2 on the facing page carefully.

Finally, the last command in your document should be \bye, the signal that you are ready to sign off. TEX knows then it has reached the end of the document.

A1.7   Mathematics

Even though TEX excels at mathematics, there's little we can say about it in this brief survey. As you might expect, some special knowledge will be needed to properly typeset all the different kinds of math there are. All the comments in this section apply both to LATEX and plain TEX.

But certain things are simple. TEX typesets math in two modes—either within the text of a paragraph, such as $s = \int_0^t g\tau \, d\tau = \frac{1}{2}gt^2$, or displayed in the middle of a paragraph, like this.

$$s = \int_0^t g\tau \, d\tau = \frac{1}{2}gt^2$$

As you see, subtle details of spacing and sizing are different in the two contexts.

```
Imagine that this is a page
with a series of short
paragraphs on it.  Shortly, we
will try to force the end of
this page and begin a new
page.

Let's see how the different
ways we force the page break
affect the appearance of this
page.

A short paragraph.

Another short paragraph.

A final paragraph, and here we
force the page break.

\vfill\eject
```

Imagine that this is a page with a series of short paragraphs on it. Shortly, we will try to force the end of this page and begin a new page.

Let's see how the different ways we force the page break affect the appearance of this page.

A short paragraph.

Another short paragraph.

A final paragraph, and here we force the page break.

```
Imagine that this is a page
with a series of short
paragraphs on it.  Shortly, we
will try to force the end of
this page and begin a new
page.

Let's see how the different
ways we force the page break
affect the appearance of this
page.

A short paragraph.

Another short paragraph.

A final paragraph, and here we
force the page break.

\eject
```

Imagine that this is a page with a series of short paragraphs on it. Shortly, we will try to force the end of this page and begin a new page.

Let's see how the different ways we force the page break affect the appearance of this page.

A short paragraph.

Another short paragraph.

A final paragraph, and here we force the page break.

Figure 2: The minipages on the left show the source for the minipages typeset on the right. On the top, we use a \vfill with the \eject, and the page appears as we probably want it to. On bottom, we omit the \vfill and TeX responds by stretching the space between paragraphs so that there is no extra white space at the bottom. This effect is probably not what we wanted.

You should first convince yourself that math modes are necessary. In straight text, the equation $3x + 4y = 7$ comes out as "3x+4y=7", not very impressive. If you typeset in italics, you get *3x+4y=7*, not much better. The best is $3x + 4y = 7$.

To typeset text math, surround the math material in single dollar signs. To get $3x + 4y = 7$, I typed

```
$ 3x+4y=7 $
```

Surround the math material in double dollar signs $$ to get display mode. To typeset

$$3x + 4y = 7$$

I typed

```
    .  .  .   To typeset
$$
      3x+4y=7
$$
I typed . . .
```

By the way, you can get a minus sign by typing a single dash. The minus sign is yet a different kind of dash. We get $4 - 3 = 1$ by typing $4-3=1$, different from 4-3=1 typed without the math dollar sign toggles.

Within a math mode, TEX ignores virtually every space you type in. Spacing within formulas and displays is a serious matter, so serious that TEX dare not relinquish any control over spacing to an author (unless special spacing commands are present to override or enhance TEX's natural inclinations). Thus, input like $Ax+By=C$ or

```
$  A  x      +      B  y      =      C  $
```

or even

```
$
A
x
+
B
y
=
C
$
```

are all equivalent, and typeset $Ax + By = C$.

There isn't much more sophisticated math you can typeset at this point, but you may enjoy flipping through the math chapters or glancing at the chart of special math characters in *The TEXbook* [Knuth (1986a), chapters 16–19; Appendix F]. If you see an example that is close to some math you need, copy the example and try to adapt it for your purposes.

The commands we discussed in this brief appendix appear summarized in the table of figure 3 on the next page.

A1.8   Special characters

You've seen that certain special characters, like \, {, }, and $, have special meanings for TEX. Thus, you have to do something special if you need those characters in your text. There are a few more such characters, the &, ~, #, %, _, and ^, which require special action. Figure 4 on page 527 summarizes these characters and the actions you need to get them in your document.

The characters at the bottom of the table can only be gotten in a math mode. Whereas you can type \& to get & or \^{} to get ^, you have to type $\backslash$ to get \ or $\}$ to get }, but that's no real problem—you just have to remember to type the math signs $.

A1.9   White lies—where to now?

In the interest of keeping this appendix brief and to the point, many simplifying statements have been placed before you. They aren't wrong exactly, they just aren't the whole truth. You don't really know (yet) the true significance of the curly braces, or some of the subtleties involved with entering spaces in the document file. Not to worry—these things will become clear. The object was to get you up and running with TEX as quickly as possible.

If you become even a semiserious user of TEX, you should have a copy of *The TEXbook* at your computer. Written by Donald Knuth (1986a), the author of TEX, it contains everything there is to know about the TEX language.

One aspect of TEX that we have until now kept hidden is its ability to accept new commands that you create from pre-existing commands. These new commands, called *macros*, are similar to procedures and subroutines in Pascal or Fortran. The language of TEX is itself so rich that macros can be vastly more useful than their component commands. As a matter of fact, it's possible to virtually redefine the syntax of TEX using ingenious macros. Several people have created vast *macro packages* that do something close to that and may make TEX more convenient for you to use at the same time. The most important such package is LATEX.

A1.10   Examples: Simple letters and reports

With the commands of this appendix securely under your belt, you should be able to type simple letters and reports. Refer to figure 5 on page 528 to see how a simple letter might look, and how to generate that letter. Then,

Page Layout Parameters		
Command	Example	Comments
\hsize	\hsize=36pc	*Controls width of text.*
\vsize	\vsize=9in	*Controls maximum amount of vertical space taken by text.*
\baselineskip	\baselineskip=24pt	*Determines distance between any two successive baselines.*
\noindent	\noindent New par...	*Suppresses indentation of a paragraph.*
Vertical Spacing Commands		
\vskip	\vskip 15cm	*Ends a paragraph and skips an arbitrary amount of vertical space, either up or down.*
\bigskip	\bigskip	*Ends a paragraph and skips down 12 points.*
\medskip	\medskip	*Ends a paragraph and skips down 6 points.*
\smallskip	\smallskip	*Ends a paragraph and skips down 3 points.*
Horizontal Space Commands		
\␣	\␣	*Put a hard space between words.*
\hskip	\hskip 1.5pc	*Skip arbitrary amounts of horizontal space.*
Font Changing Commands		
\it	{\it emphasis\/}	*Italic font.*
\/	{\it emphasis\/}	*Italic correction.*
\bf	{\bf more} emphasis	**Bold** *font.*
\tt	{\tt typewriter} type	`Typewriter` *font.*
Line and Section Commands		
\centerline	\centerline{A Title }	*Centers text.*
\rightline	\rightline{Pg. 1009}	*Places text at right of line.*
\leftline	\leftline{B. C. Dull}	*Places text at left of line.*
\beginsection	\beginsection New Section	*Starts a new section. Don't forget to leave a blank line after the section name!*
\vfill\eject	\vfill\eject	*Start a new page.*
\bye	\bye	*End your document. This is the only command that* must *be present in any TEX document.*
Very Simple Math		
$...$	$8u-5v=3$	*This typesets* $8u - 5v = 3$ *in* text *mode.*
$$...$$	$$8u-5v=3$$	*This typesets* $8u - 5v = 3$ *in* display *mode.*

Figure 3: This summarizes the basic set of TEX commands presented in this appendix.

To get...	Type ...
#	\#
$	\$
%	\%
^	\^
&	\&
~	~
_	_
\	$...\backslash...$
{	$...\{...$
}	$...\}...$

Figure 4: Here's how to typeset TEX's special characters. Observe that the three characters in the bottom portion of the table must occur in math mode. Although these characters are all special, we don't discuss all of them in this appendix.

in figure 6 on page 529 the beginning of a simple report appears, along with its TEX coding instructions.

The following code, which generates the letter of figure 5 on the next page, is perhaps the most naïve way in TEX to print a letter. For a better method, please see Appendix E in *The TEXbook* (that example is more advanced—and more convenient to use—than the example below).

```
\centerline{\bf Ross Dean, M.\thinspace D.}
\centerline{\bf 512 Twelfth Street}
\centerline{\bf Baltimore, MD}
\vskip3pc

\leftline{\hskip .5\hsize December 12, 1999}
\vskip4pc

\noindent
Dear Mr. Adler,

Thanks for bringing the matter of the missing
medication to my attention.  I assure you my
staff has the situation completely under
control.  Please be prompt to our next
appointment.

My best regards to your wife and children.
\bigskip

\leftline{\hskip.5\hsize Sincerely,}
\vskip4pc
```

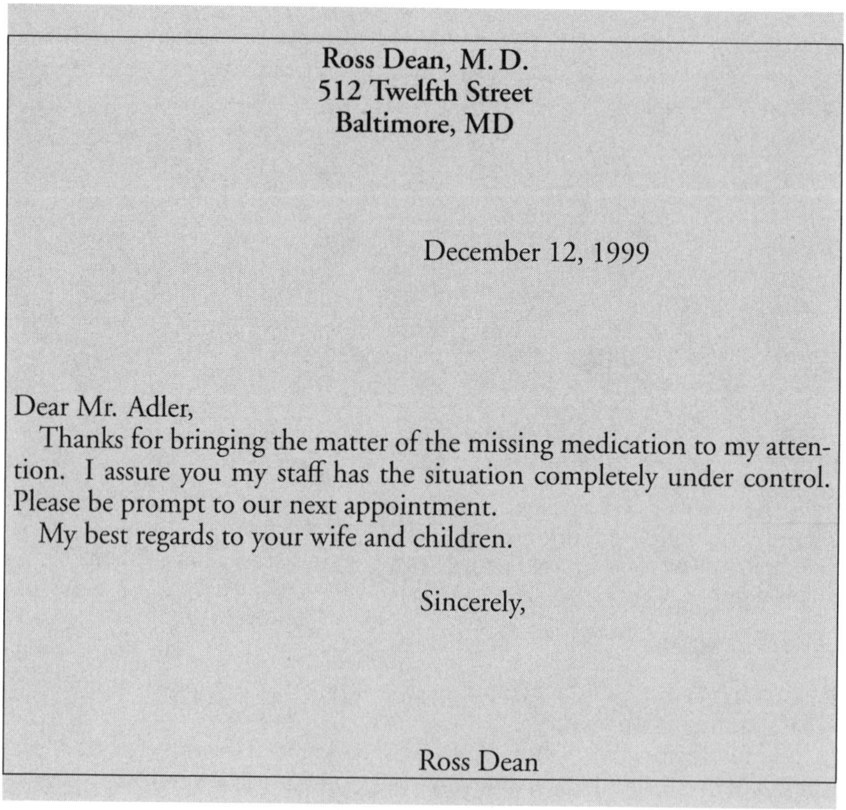

> **Ross Dean, M. D.**
> **512 Twelfth Street**
> **Baltimore, MD**
>
>
> December 12, 1999
>
>
> Dear Mr. Adler,
>   Thanks for bringing the matter of the missing medication to my atten-
> tion. I assure you my staff has the situation completely under control.
> Please be prompt to our next appointment.
>   My best regards to your wife and children.
>
> Sincerely,
>
>
> Ross Dean

Figure 5: A simple letter.

```
\leftline{\hskip.5\hsize Ross Dean}
\bye
```

The following set of input, which gives rise to figure 6 on the facing page,
is probably more acceptable to the experienced TEX user, who might only
wonder why special \title and \author commands were not created.

```
\centerline{\bf Necking in Bars}
\medskip
\centerline{\it by B. C. Dull}
\bigskip

\beginsection Introduction

Necking in bars under tension is closely
associated with the study of the buckling
of structural elements under compression.
Both phenomena refer to modes of failure
of a component beyond a certain critical
level of applied stress.
```

Necking in Bars

by B. C. Dull

Introduction

Necking in bars under tension is closely associated with the study of the buckling of structural elements under compression. Both phenomena refer to modes of failure of a component beyond a certain critical level of applied stress.

A change of sign of the stress is all that distinguishes necking from buckling, at least as far as the description of the problem is concerned.

Earlier Work

Important early work in this field was supervised by B. Budiansky at Harvard University...

Figure 6: A simple report.

```
A change of sign of the stress is all that
distinguishes necking from buckling, at
least as far as the description of the
problem is concerned.

\beginsection Earlier Work

Important early work in this field was
supervised by B. Budiansky at Harvard
University . . .

\bye
```

APPENDIX 2

· ·

MORE ABOUT LATEX

An author who needs education in LaTeX might want to begin by reading the previous appendix, especially the bits detailing the input conventions. This appendix contains additional useful information.

A2.1 Two flavors of LaTeX

There are two flavors of LaTeX. The first is the older, now-unsupported LaTeX209, and the second is the new, current LaTeX2_ε. The "209" part of the old LaTeX refers to its version number (2.09) in effect at the time the decision was made to release and support LaTeX2_ε. LaTeX2_ε itself represents a compromise between the older LaTeX and a revamped LaTeX still in the works (as of this writing). It was felt that it was more efficient to issue the interim LaTeX2_ε in place of continual patched and bug-fixes to the older package. LaTeX2_ε should be easier to customize, and of course it features the New Font Selection Scheme, which itself is reason enough to use this package. A dedicated band of workers will fix genuine bugs in LaTeX2_ε, but you are on your own with the original LaTeX.

As far as an author is concerned, there aren't many major syntax changes between the two versions of LaTeX. The advantage of LaTeX2_ε lies in its increased modularity, its incorporation of the New Font Selection Scheme (NFSS), and (most important) its being the only LaTeX officially supported.

Perhaps the most important syntax change occurs smack at the beginning of any source file. In the older LaTeX, document structures and additional groups of macros were all prescribed by distinct styles (whose files had extensions .sty) called into play by the beginning \documentstyle command. LaTeX2_ε recognizes the distinction between classes of documents that have different structures and macro packages that can be used by documents of whatever structure.

> ### More Jargon
>
> - **Class files** determine the structure of a LaTeX2$_\varepsilon$ document.
>
> - **Package files** represent collections of macros acting as tools to extend LaTeX functionality.
>
> - **Style files** represent external macro files used by the older LaTeX209 standard. Style files combine the functionality of package and class files in LaTeX2$_\varepsilon$.
>
> - **Options** are optional arguments that influence the behavior of some command. Not every command has optional arguments.
>
> - **Star forms** are available for some LaTeX commands, and represent a similar but distinct command behavior.
>
> - **Floats** are portions of text that may appear in different, apparently unpredictable portions of the document as the text is revised. The floating behavior arises from the need to keep the material in the float together at all costs, so TeX can only place it on pages for which there is room. (The material in this shaded box is treated by LaTeX as floating material, for example.)
>
> - **Markup** is the general term for instructions added to a document to influence and control its typeset appearance.
>
> - **NFSS** or New Font Selection Scheme refers to the font-selection scheme built-in to LaTeX2$_\varepsilon$. PSNFSS refers to the collection of packages that incorporate PostScript text fonts into the NFSS.
>
> - **Babel** and its options allows typesetting in many non-English, western-European languages.
>
> - **BibTeX**, an external program, processes bibliographic data into a form that can be incorporated into a plain TeX or LaTeX document.
>
> - *MakeIndex* is an external program to sort index data produced by an initial run of LaTeX on a document. The output of *MakeIndex* is a file that can then be typeset by LaTeX on a subsequent pass.

A2.1.1 "209"

It is easy to tell which LaTeX a document requires by glancing at the very first command of the document;

```
\documentstyle{...}
```

declares its allegiance to the older LATEX209 standard. There are still many sites working with this brand of LATEX, and a vast collection of style files and supporting software remains in existence. On any CTAN archive, this material can be found in the area macros/latex209.

A2.1.2   *Enhanced LATEX*

Document classes are now specified by the initial

```
\documentclass
```

command, so software can detect the requirement of LATEX2ε by examining this command. LATEX2ε has a compatibility mode by which it can process 209 documents as well as pure LATEX2ε documents.

The most important classes are the article, report, book, and perhaps letter classes. The CTAN archives contain many more class files than this but they tend to be variations of these classes. All LATEX2ε material appears in the area macros/latex in the CTAN archives.

Package files contain sets of macros usable by macros of whatever class. They do not have any effect on the general structure of the typeset document. LATEX2ε expects package files to have the extension .sty.

For example, a document might start life as a report intended for French audiences. The preamble for it might look something like

```
\documentclass[twoside]{article}
\usepackage[french]{babel}
```

where the usual square bracket convention for options holds. Later on, when the document becomes a book, a document of a different class, only the class needs changing. The babel package with its French option in force remains applicable to the new class.

A2.2   Getting classes and packages

Files with recognizable file name extensions of ".cls" and ".sty" declare their nature. Users of LATEX2ε will notice new extensions—namely .dtx and .ins—and will wonder how these files fit in to the LATEX2ε scheme of things.

Authors of LATEX2ε tools are encouraged to prepare their material in a form that incorporates documentation and LATEX commands together. Files with the extension .dtx conform to this convention. Further processing in the presence of the file docstrip.tex will create the requisite package or class file. This procedure is explained in greater detail in Goossens, Mittelbach, and Samarin (1994, chapter 14). A few essential details are discussed below.

The `.ins` file helps generate—install—the required file. For example, if I retrieve files `foo.dtx` and `foo.ins` from CTAN, then the command

```
tex foo.ins
```

will generate either `foo.cls` or `foo.sty` and perhaps a documentation file (plus the ever present `.log` file). An author can tailor some other existing `.ins` file to the present case. Typically, it suffices to create a file, say `foo.ins`, whose contents are something like

```
\def\batchfile{ foo .ins}
\input docstrip.tex
\generateFile{ foo .drv}{t}{\from{ foo.dtx }{driver}}
\generateFile{ foo .sty}{t}{\from{ foo.dtx }{package}}
```

The `.drv` driver file is helpful in creating the documentation. Simply type

```
tex foo .drv
```

to generate this information.

In the absence of the `.ins` file, you can simply run TEX on `docstrip`. You will need to respond to several questions:

- What is the extension of the input file? *Answer*: dtx.

- What is the extension of the output file? If you plan to generate the package file itself, respond with sty. If you want the driver file to generate a user manual, type drv.

- What options will you exercise? Type package or driver.

- What packages are you interested in currently? Type the package file-name, minus its extension.

When processing is complete, you'll need to indicate whether you have additional packages or options you want to exercise. Type y or n as appropriate.

In the absence of `docstrip.tex`, it is enough to rename the `.dtx` file to be a `.sty` or `.cls` file (you have to know which; the first few lines of the `.dtx` file should make it clear). Because the `.dtx` file contains all the lines of the derivative macro file, while the lines of documentation are commented out by at least one comment character, this strategy will work. Of course, the resulting macro file is much swollen with comments and will take some time for TEX to read, but this should do until you obtain `docstrip.tex`.

A2.3 Page layout

Although adjusting details of page layout is generally a simple matter in plain TEX, it can be a challenge in LATEX. First of all, there are many more such parameters in LATEX than in TEX. Second, the ones that correspond to plain TEX parameters have different names.

The diagram in figure 1 on the facing page (using the layout package of Kent McPherson) helps make clear what the page layout parameters are. One uses the \setlength and \addtolength commands in the preamble or in a package to alter their values. For example, one version of the author's package file for this manuscript contained commands like

```
\setlength{\textwidth}{27pc}
\addtolength{\textheight}{-24pt}
\setlength{\headsep}{1.5pc}
```

With commands like these in place, it was possible to adapt the generic article or book classes to meet the publisher's layout requirements.

A2.4 Some environments

A LATEX environment is delimited by a pair of \begin-\end commands whose argument is the name of the environment. Within that environment, all text is typeset according to conventions pertaining to that environment.

Perhaps the most important environment is the document environment in which all typesetting must be done.

For example, three environments, flushleft, center, and flushright, set type as "raggedright," "raggedcenter," and "raggedleft." The command \\ acts as line separator. For example, we get

Pippa's Song
ROBERT BROWNING

The year's at the spring,
And day's at the morn;
Morning's at seven;

The hill-side's dew-pearl'd;
The lark's on the wing;
The snail's on the thorn;

God's in His heaven—
All's right with the world!

by typing

```
\begin{center}
   \it Pippa's Song\\
   \sc Robert Browning\\[1pc]
\end{center}
\begin{flushleft}
   The year's at the spring,\\
   And day's at the morn;\\
```

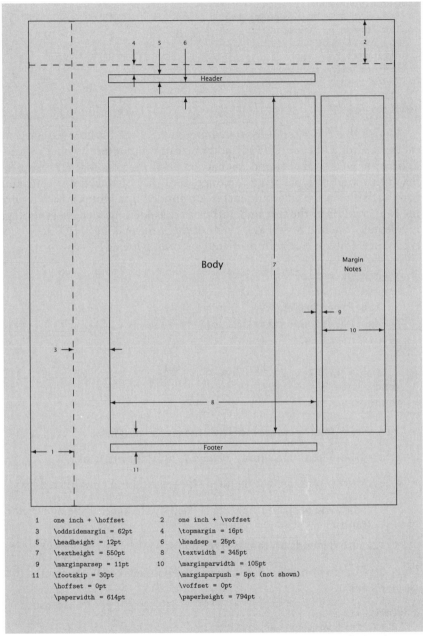

The following labels and values appear within the figure:

1   one inch + \hoffset   2   one inch + \voffset
3   \oddsidemargin = 62pt   4   \topmargin = 16pt
5   \headheight = 12pt   6   \headsep = 25pt
7   \textheight = 550pt   8   \textwidth = 345pt
9   \marginparsep = 11pt   10   \marginparwidth = 105pt
11   \footskip = 30pt   \marginparpush = 5pt (not shown)
     \hoffset = 0pt   \voffset = 0pt
     \paperwidth = 614pt   \paperheight = 794pt

Figure 1: Page-layout parameters in LaTeX with some of their default values.

```
   Morning's at seven;
\end{flushleft}
\begin{flushright}
   The hill-side's dew-pearl'd;\\
   The lark's on the wing;\\
   The snail's on the thorn;\\
\end{flushright}
\begin{center}
   God's in His heaven---\\
   All's right with the world!
\end{center}
```

Notice that \\ takes an optional argument to add a little extra verti-cal space after a line, so \\[1pc] add one extra pica after the poet's name. (There are verse, quote, and quotation environments that are also use-ful in this kind of typesetting.) Notice, too, that each environment (and here, each line in the environment) is surrounded by a group, which is why the font changes in the title and author to this poem needed no grouping. Incidentally, there is a verbatim environment for making LaTeX act like a typewriter. I obtained the immediately preceding listing by typing

```
\begin{verbatim}
\begin{center}
   \it Pippa's Song\\
   \sc Robert Browning\\[1pc]
\end{center}

   ...

   All's right with the world!
\end{center}
\end{verbatim}
```

Two environments control the two most common lists:

- lists whose items are simply *itemized* (as is this one), and

- lists whose items are enumerated. Observe that in enumerated lists,

  1. the style of the numbering is fixed by the class of the document, and

  2. also depends on the level of the list.

These two list environments are itemize and enumerate. We generated this list by means of

```
\begin{itemize}
   \item lists whose items are simply {\em itemized\/}
   (as is this one), and
   \item lists whose items are {\em enumerated}.  Observe that in
   enumerated lists,
   \begin{enumerate}
      \item the style of the numbering is fixed by the class of the
```

```
       document, and
       \item also depends on the level of the list.
    \end{enumerate}
\end{itemize}
```

which shows that environments may be nested within each other.

A2.4.1 Letters

It's best to prepare letters in LATEX using the letter class, but as an exercise the reader may care to produce the letter shown in appendix 1 using only the environments discussed above. Before undertaking this challenge, note that \hspace is the LATEX way to add horizontal white space; \hspace{1cm} skips one centimeter horizontally. There is a corresponding \vspace command for vertical skips.

Here is one way to generate that letter using LATEX.

```
{\bf
 \begin{center}
    Ross Dean, M.\thinspace D.\\
       ...
    Baltimore, MD\\[3pc]
 \end{center}
}
\begin{flushleft}
    \hspace{.5\textwidth}December 12, 1999\\[4pc]
\end{flushleft}
\noindent Dear Mr.\ Adler,

Thanks ...
 ... children.

\begin{flushleft}
    \hspace{.5\textwidth}Sincerely,\\[4pc]
    \hspace{.5\textwidth}Ross Dean
\end{flushleft}
```

A2.5 Document structure

Some environments and commands especially make clear and enforce the structure of a document. An abstract environment sets an abstract, and the command \maketitle typesets the title and accompanying authors, affiliations, and so on, provided commands like \title, \author and so on have previously been invoked.

Several commands—\chapter, \section, \subsection, and the like—control the segments of the document. Each such command takes as argument the title for the segment. Normally, each such segment is numbered (the style being controlled by the class of the document), but star forms of each suppress numbering.

Necking in Bars

B. C. Dull

August 23, 1997

Abstract

Necking in bars under tension is closely associated with the study of the buckling of structural elements under compression. Both phenomena refer to modes of failure of a component beyond a certain critical level of applied stress.

Introduction

A change of sign of the stress is all that distinguishes necking from buckling, at least as far as the description of the problem is concerned.

1 Earlier Work

Important early work in this field was supervised by B. Budiansky at Harvard University ...

Figure 2: A simple LATEX report.

We saw a sample of a simple report in appendix 1. Using LATEX, a slightly different version of this report appears in figure 2. The LATEX instructions behind it are as follows.

```
\documentclass{article}

\title{Necking in Bars}
\author{B. C. Dull}
\begin{document}

\maketitle

\begin{abstract}
    Necking in bars under tension is closely associated
    with the study of the buckling of structural
    elements under compression.  Both phenomena refer to
    modes of failure of a component beyond a certain
    critical level of applied stress.
```

```
\end{abstract}

\section*{Introduction}\thispagestyle{empty}
A change of sign of the stress is all that
distinguishes necking from buckling, at least as far as
the description of the problem is concerned.

\section{Earlier work}
Important early work in this field was supervised by
B. Budiansky at Harvard University...
\end{document}
```

Floating material in a document tends either to be a big table or figure, for which there might not be room on a typeset page at the point in the document where its presence makes most sense. This material belongs inside either the figure or table environment. For example, figure 2 on the facing page was generated by instructions very similar to the following.

```
\begin{figure}
   \begin{center}
      \noindent\epsffile{lreport.eps}
   \end{center}
\caption{A simple \LaTex\ report.}
\end{figure}
```

(The epsf package has previously been loaded. The file lreport.eps has been prepared separately, and placed in the document via \epsffile by centering it and adding a caption. Notice how \epsffile needs to be preceded by \noindent in this context. The command \epsffile is a synonym for \epsfbox.) Note the use of \caption to add a caption. The table environment works in a similar fashion to insert tables prepared with the tabular environment, a discussion of which is outside the scope of this appendix.

A2.6   Additional tools

Beginning users of LATEX should be made aware of additional tools to extend LATEX's usefulness. These packages are all at any CTAN archive and may be retrieved from the macros/latex/packages/tools area. Brief descriptions of some of the more relevant packages follow, but Carlisle (1996c) discusses all of these packages in greater detail. Beginners will need to come up to speed with the canonical LATEX before experimenting with these.

A2.6.1   Some new tools

Here are some of the new tools.

- With the extended `array` environment, an author has much greater control over a table's columns. In particular, it is now possible to precede and follow all items of a column with LATEX commands.

- The package `fileerr` provides greater control in the event you inadvertently ask TEX to read a nonexistent file.

- The `longtable` environment enables tables to be split across pages.

- The new `multicol` environment makes it possible to typeset up to ten columns on a page and to switch back and forth from different numbers of columns. Columns are balanced at the end.

- With the `theorem` package, an author can define new theorem-like environments.

- Readers find it useful when an author has taken the trouble to refer to a figure as "figure 5 on the facing page" or "table 7 on the following page". Commands in the `varioref` package make this possible.

- The `verbatim` package provides a flexible and far more robust version of the existing `verbatim` environment.

- With the `xr` (think "*ex*ternal *re*ference") package, one can refer to labels defined in other document files.

A2.6.2 Installation and use

All the `tools` packages come distributed as `.dtx` docstrip files, so use the procedures we describe beginning on page 532. To enable any of these packages in a document, include the package name in the `\usepackage` command as usual.

APPENDIX 3

· ·

PRODUCING THIS BOOK

And I mean it!
AYN RAND

TEX and TEX-friendly software tools were used to prepare *everything* in this book. This appendix provides some commentary on how this was done.

A3.1 General details

The text fonts for this book have been drawn from the Adobe Garamond font family. Quite apart from the beauty of these types, this family was chosen because it contains several members that are not normally present in a family, such as alternate fonts, as well as the complete suite of fonts that TEX can work with. Sans serif fonts were drawn from the Lucida Sans family. The typewriter fonts used in verbatim modes is cmtt10, in my opinion, the nicest of all typewriter fonts.

LATEX was used to prepare the input files. Of course, some tinkering went into some of the style files. The preamble to each input file began with declarations similar to these:

```
\documentclass[twoside]{article}
\usepackage{mybook,myfonts,path,colordvi,epsf,%
  xchicago,myxbib,varioref}
```

where the files mybook.sty and myfonts.sty contain local variations to the article class. In a book like this, frequent mention is made to directory paths, and path.sty contains a \path macro (by Philip Taylor) useful for splitting long path names sensibly so as to avoid large numbers of overfull boxes.

This book was a PostScript project throughout, and *dvips* was used to translate the ordinary .dvi into .ps form. The files epsf.sty and colordvi.sty were useful in this regard. The former allowed us to easily integrate encapsulated PostScript files (.eps or .epsf). With the macros of colordvi.sty in place, it is possible to give color commands for coloring the document. Although this is a one-color volume, this material was necessary for getting the shaded boxes (gray *is* a color) that appear throughout the text.

Two styles pertain to the bibliography. Charles Wells created xbib.sty for bibliographies with back references. An annotation at each bibliography item lets the reader know where the item was cited. I added a few trivial modifications to this file; it then became myxbib.sty. This style describes how to make changes to the TEX and BibTEX files you will use. I elected to follow the conventions of the *Chicago Manual of Style*; files xchicago.bst and xchicago.sty have been trivially modified to work with xbib. The xbib style generates an additional auxiliary file, with extension .xbi. Since the file xbix.sty is not generally available, I include it verbatim at the conclusion of this appendix.

With the varioref package (available from CTAN) in place, intelligent references become possible. That is, references like "figure 1 on the facing/preceding/following/current page" take advantage of the proximity between a \label and its \ref or \pageref.

The front end paper, the TEX ruler, is by Victor Eijkhout. The file ruler.tex that produces it is in CTAN. After retrieving this file, print it on heavy acetate for best use.

The design on page 2 was a collaborative effort between *fontinst*, Meta-Post, and PSTricks. The coordinates for the ellipse were generated by Meta-Post, which spat them out in a separate file. (PSTricks draws very nice ellipses but those paths begin at the wrong place, so we couldn't use them.) *fontinst* generated a new font with lots of space between each character. The short installation file

```
\input fontinst.sty
\setint{letterspacing}{450}
\installfonts
  \installfamily{OT1}{lss}{}
  \installfont{lsrz}{lssr,latin}{OT1}{OT1}{lss}{m}{z}{}
  \installfont{lsdz}{lssd,latin}{OT1}{OT1}{lss}{m}{z}{}
\endinstallfonts
\bye
```

takes care of that for us. (The font family lss refers to Lucida Sans.) At a 10-pt size, each pair of characters has an additional 9 pt of space in between. Finally, the textpath package within PSTricks typeset the text around the ellipse. The TEX commands to do this look like this:

```
\pstextpath{
  \rput(3in,-4.3in){\input path.pst }}%
{WE ARE INDEBTED ... }
```

where the file path.pst contains the coordinate pairs defining the ellipse's shape.

A3.2 Specifics

A reviewer had strongly urged that authors of works cited appear in the index. No generally available BibTeX style makes that possible, so a workaround was necessary. Entries in the .bib file for this book contained an index annotation, like this.

```
@BOOK{joy,
  author    = "Michael D. Spivak",
  title     = "The Joy of \TeX ",
  address   = "Providence, RI ",
  publisher = "The American Mathematical Society ",
  year      = 1986
}
%\index{Spivak, Michael}
```

The commented \index entry is not visible to BibTeX, but we can write a short program to scan the .bib file and extract the index entries for each bibliographic key. This program then reads each input file and adds an invisible index entry for each citation that appears. I found it convenient to use Perl to write this program.

(Nelson Beebe kindly made me aware that a set of utilities for doing this would become publicly available, but unfortunately not soon enough to be useful in the current work. Interested readers should keep an eagle eye out for announcements of this utility.)

Many of the chapters in this book are so complex—typographically, that is—that it was not possible to compile the entire volume in one pass. Each chapter was done separately, which created some challenges for assembling the end matter (bibliography and index) properly. For each chapter, the .aux, .idx, .xbi, and .bbl files were retained and concatenated. From these, it was straightforward to generate the master bibliography and index for the entire book.

This sanitized account omits all the last minute fine-tuning that invariably accompanies the production of any book. It often seemed that the last one percent of the work took 99% of the time!

A3.3 Addendum: The file **xbib.sty**

Here follows the file xbib.sty.

```
% Copyright 1992, 1993, 1994 by Charles Frederick Wells.  This file
% may be freely redistributed as long as it is unchanged and
% contains this copyright notice.  Please report errors or send
% suggestions for changes to cfw2@po.cwru.edu or to Charles Wells,
% Department of Mathematics, Case Western Reserve University,
% University Circle, Cleveland, OH 44106-7058, USA.
%   This file should be saved as "xbib.tex".  It causes a list of
% the pages on which a bibliographic entry is cited to be printed
% after the entry.  The document must be TeX'd twice to make
```

```
% this work.
%    To use this file, you have to do two things:  (1) Type "\input
% xbib" in the preamble of your LaTeX document.  (2) Enclose each
% bibliographical entry in braces.  Thus, instead of
%
% \bibitem{LG} Leonard Gillman, {\bf Writing Mathematics
% Well}.  Mathematical Association of America, 1987.
%
% you should write
%
% \bibitem{LG}{Leonard Gillman, {\bf Writing Mathematics
% Well}.  Mathematical Association of America, 1987.}
%
% Note that if you later decide not to use \xbib, these extra
% braces will cause no harm.
%
% A message is printed at the beginning of the
% bibliography explaining the list of pages after the entries.
% This message is contained in the
% command \xbibmessage (near the end of this file) and can be
% changed.  If you want it to disappear, put
%        \def\xbibmessage{\relax}
% in the preamble AFTER the command \input xbib.
%
% THIS FILE MUST BE USED WITH LATEX VERSION 2.09 OR LATER.   IT
% WILL NOT WORK WITH EARLIER VERSIONS.
%
% If you want to use xbib with BibTeX you must change the .bst
% file you use.  Most .bst files contain the following two
% functions:
%
% FUNCTION {output.bibitem}
% { newline$
%    "\bibitem[" write$
%    label write$
%    "]{" write$
%    cite$ write$
%    "}" write$
%    newline$
%    ""
%  'output.state before.all :=
% }
%
% FUNCTION {fin.entry}
% { add.period$
%    write$
%    newline$
% }
%
% They should be changed to:
%
% FUNCTION {output.bibitem}
% { newline$
%    "\bibitem[" write$
%    label write$
```

```
%    "]{" write$
%    cite$ write$
%     "}{" write$
%    newline$
%     ""
%    'output.state before.all :=
% }
%
% FUNCTION {fin.entry}
% { add.period$ write$
%     "}" write$
%    newline$
% }
%
% I recommend that you rename the resulting file by prepending an X
% to its name.  Thus ALPHA.BST would become XALPHA.BST.  As far as
% I know, if you use such modified files no difference will result
% in the output if you don't use xbib.
%
% WARNING
% This file redefines  the LaTeX commands \@lbibitem, \@bibitem
% and \@citex, which are used in the definition of \bibitem and
% \citex.  Therefore, it may not work if you use a style file that
% redefines these terms (the article and book styles are OK).
%
% By redefining \xbibpointer, you can cause the cross reference
% list to refer to sections (define it to be \thesection) or other
% subheadings.
%
% Warning:  This file has not been extensively tested.
\typeout{xbib.tex 30 July 1994}

\makeatletter

% The following command causes the page numbers to be listed in
% parentheses, separated by commas, with no period.
\def\showcites#1{\@ifundefined{xb@#1}{\relax}
{(Cited on \@nameuse{xb@#1}.)}}

% The following two commands cause the reference list to be
% printed at the end of the bibliographic entry after a 1 em
% space.
\def\@lbibitem[#1]#2#3{\item[\@biblabel{#1}]\if@filesw
      { \def\protect##1{\string ##1\space}\immediate
\write\@auxout{\string\bibcite{#2}{#1}}}\fi\ignorespaces%
{#3}\hskip 1em  \showcites{#2}}

\def\@bibitem#1#2{\item\if@filesw \immediate\write\@auxout
%%    {\string\bibcite{#1}{\the\c@enumi}}\fi\ignorespaces%
    {\string\bibcite{#1}{\the\value{\@listctr}}}\fi\ignorespaces%
{#2}\hskip 1em \showcites{#1}}

\def\addcite#1#2{
\@ifundefined{xb@#1}{
\global\@namedef{xb@#1}{#2}\global\@namedef{xbb@#1}{#2}
```

```
}
{
\xdef\@tempc{#2}
\xdef\@tempb{\csname xbb@#1\endcsname}
\ifx\@tempb\@tempc%
%% changed 7-27-94 from \ifnum to allow
%% other forms of page number
\else
\global\@namedef{xbb@#1}{#2}
\xdef\@gtempa{\@nameuse{xb@#1}, #2}
\expandafter\xdef\csname xb@#1\endcsname{\@gtempa}
\fi
}
}
\def\xbibpointer{\thepage}

\@input{\jobname.xbi}
\if@filesw \newwrite\@xbibfile
\immediate\openout\@xbibfile=\jobname.xbi \fi

\def\@citex[#1]#2{%
  \if@filesw\immediate\write\@auxout{\string\citation{#2}}\fi
  \let\@citea\@empty
  \@cite{\@for\@citeb:=#2\do
    {\@citea\def\@citea{,\penalty\@m\ }%
     \def\@tempa##1##2\@nil{%
      \edef\@citeb{\if##1\space##2\else##1##2\fi}}%
     \expandafter\@tempa\@citeb\@nil
     \@ifundefined{b@\@citeb}{{\reset@font\bf ?}\@warning
       {Citation `\@citeb' on page \thepage \space undefined}}%
      \if@filesw{\let\thepage\relax
        \def\protect{\noexpand\noexpand\noexpand}%
        \xdef\@gtempa{\write\@xbibfile{%
        \string\addcite{\@citeb}{\xbibpointer}}}}\@gtempa\fi
{\csname b@\@citeb\endcsname}}}{#1}}


\def\thebibliography#1{\section*{%References
 \@mkboth
 {Bibliography}{Bibliography}}
\xbibmessage\list
 {[\arabic{enumi}]}{\settowidth\labelwidth{[#1]}%
 \leftmargin\labelwidth
 \advance\leftmargin\labelsep
 \usecounter{enumi}}
 \def\newblock{\relax}
 \clubpenalty4000\widowpenalty4000
 \sfcode`\.=1000\relax}

\def\xbibmessage{At the end of each entry, the pages on which
 that entry is cited are listed in parentheses.}
\makeatother
\endinput
```

SOURCES
AND RESOURCES

Abrahams, P., K. Berry, and K. A. Hargreaves (1990). *TEX for the Impatient*. Reading, MA: Addison-Wesley.

Barnett, M. P. and K. R. Perry (1994, September). Symbolic Computation for Electronic Publishing. *TUGboat 15*(3), 285–292. (Cited on page 129.)

Beebe, N. (1993a, October). Bibliography prettyprinting and syntax checking. *TUGboat 14*(3), 222. (Cited on page 109.)

Beebe, N. (1993b, December). Bibliography prettyprinting and syntax checking. *TUGboat 14*(4), 395–419. (Cited on page 109.)

Bientz, T. and R. Cohn (1993). *Portable Document Reference Manual*. Reading, MA: Addison-Wesley. (Cited on pages 125 and 265.)

Billawala, N. (1989). *Metamarks: Preliminary Studies for a Pandora's Box of Shapes*. Stanford, CA 94305: Stanford University. This is report STAN-CS-89-1256, Computer Science Department, Stanford University. (Cited on page 93.)

Blue Sky Research, Inc. (1988). *Textures*. 534 SW Third Avenue, Portland, OR 97204, USA; 1-800-622-8398.: Blue Sky Research. BSR furnishes the popular implementation Textures—TEX on the Macintosh. (Cited on page 288.)

Bolitho, W. (1929). *Twelve Against the Gods*. New York: Simon and Schuster. (Cited on page 236.)

Borde, A. (1992). *TEX by Example*. New York: Academic Press.

Borde, A. (1994). *Mathematical TEX by Example*. New York: Academic Press.

Buerger, D. (1990). *LATEX for Engineers and Scientists*. New York: McGraw-Hill.

Carlisle, D. (1996a, February). A LATEX Tour, part 1. *Baskerville 6*(1), 8–12. This excellent and ongoing series of articles is, as of this writing, up to part 3.

Carlisle, D. (1996b, March). A LATEX Tour, part 1: The basic distribution. *TUGboat 17*(1), 67–73. (Cited on page 101.)

Carlisle, D. (1996c, April). A LATEX Tour, part 2: the Tools and Graphics distributions. *Baskerville 6*(2), 2–5. (Cited on pages 357, 360, and 539.)

Clark, M. (1992). *A Plain TEX Primer*. Oxford, UK: Oxford University Press. An engagingly written guide to plain TEX, which is refreshingly complete. (Cited on page 375.)

Corel Corporation (1996). *Corel DRAW!* 1600 Carling Avenue, Ottawa, Ontario, Canada K1Z 8R7; (613) 728-8200: Corel Corp. (Cited on page 265.)

Custom Applications Inc. (1988). *Freedom of Press*. 5 Middlesex Technology Center, 900 Middlesex Turnpike, Billerica, MA 01821; (508) 667-8585: Custom Applications. (Cited on page 264.)

Dol, W. and E. Frambach (1995). *4AllTEX*. The Netherlands: NTG. This eminently worthwhile package should be obtainable from your local user

547

group. It is certainly available through TUG (TEX Users Group) and NTG (Nederlandstalige TEX Gebruikersgroep, the Dutch language oriented TEX User Group). (Cited on page 55.)

Doob, M. (1990). Gentle introduction to TEX. This electronic file is available from many sources. It has also been published in traditional form by Springer-Verlag under the title "TEX from Square 1". (Cited on page 38.)

Doob, M. and C. Platt (1993, October). Virtual fonts in a production environment. *TUGboat 14*(3), 275–281. (Cited on page 168.)

Doyle, M. (1995, June). The Los Alamos e-print archives: HyperTEX in action. *TUGboat 16*(2), 154–159. (Cited on page 127.)

Eijkhout, V. (1992). *TEX by Topic: A TEXnician's Reference*. Reading, MA: Addison-Wesley. Although not for beginners, this is an invaluable aid to advanced users. (Cited on page 38.)

Flynn, P. (1995, June). HTML & TEX: Making them sweat. *TUGboat 16*(2), 146–150. (Cited on pages 123 and 124.)

Gibbon, E. (1776-1788). History of the decline and fall of the roman empire. The standard edition, edited by J. B. Bury, has been reprinted many times. (Cited on page 242.)

Gibbons, J. (1995, September). Dotted and dashed lines in METAFONT. *TUGboat 16*(3), 259–264. (Cited on page 407.)

Gibbs, W. W. (1996, November). Profile: T. V. Raman: Envisioning speech. *Scientific American 275*(3), 52–54. (Cited on page 98.)

Girou, D. (1994, February). Présentation de PSTricks. *Cahiers Gutenberg* (16), 21–70. *Cahiers Gutenberg* is the official publication of the TEX user group of France. This number was devoted mainly to discussion of PSTricks and Seminar, Timothy van Zandt's package for slides. Although all text is in French, the many demonstrations with accompanying PSTricks code makes this a valuable source for anyone planning to seriously learn and use this package. (Cited on pages 441, 445, and 463.)

Goldfarb, C. F. (1990). *The SGML Handbook*. Oxford, UK: Oxford University Press. (Cited on page 100.)

Goossens, M., F. Mittelbach, and A. Samarin (1994). *The LATEX Companion*. Reading, MA: Addison-Wesley. An invaluable reference to the many style files, packages, and document classes for LATEX, but also to the enhancements and advanced features of LATEX. (Cited on pages 38, 101, 105, 108, 109, 110, 150, 157, 168, 196, 371, 376, and 532.)

Goossens, M., S. Rahtz, and R. Fairbairns (1995, September). Multiple master Minion. *TUGboat 16*(3), 253–258. (Cited on page 277.)

Goossens, M., S. Rahtz, and F. Mittelbach (1997). *The LATEX Graphics Companion: Illustrating Documents with TEX and PostScript*. Reading, MA: Addison-Wesley. (Cited on page 345.)

Goossens, M. and J. Saarela (1995, June). From LATEX to HTML and back. *TUGboat 16*(2), 174–214. (Cited on page 124.)

Graham, R. L., D. E. Knuth, and O. Patashnik (1989). *Concrete Mathematics*. Reading, MA: Addison-Wesley. (Cited on pages 276 and 294.)

Granger, G. (1994, June). Hints and Tips. *TUGboat 15*(2), 135. This is a summary of a lengthier report that originally appeared in *Baskerville* 4(1), February, 1994. (Cited on page 105.)

Grünbaum, B. and G. C. Shephard (1987). *Tilings and Patterns*. New York: W. H. Freeman. (Cited on page 406.)

Gurari, E. M. (1993). *TEX & LATEX: Drawing and Literate Programming*. New York: McGraw Hill. (Cited on page 377.)

Haralambous, Y. (1991a). TEX and those other languages. *TUGboat 12*(4), 539–548. (Cited on page 96.)

Haralambous, Y. (1991b). Typesetting old German: Fraktur, Schwabacher, Gotisch and initials. *TUGboat 12*(1), 129–139. (Cited on pages 76 and 96.)

Haralambous, Y. (1996, June). ΩTimes and ΩHelvetica fonts under development: Step one. *TUGboat 17*(2), 126–146. (Cited on page 16.)

Haralambous, Y. and S. Rahtz (1995, June). LATEX, hypertext and PDF, or the entry of TEX into the world of hypertext. *TUGboat 16*(2), 162–173. (Cited on page 126.)

Hayes, B. (1995, November–December). Pleasures of Plication. *American Scientist 83*(6), 504–509. (Cited on page ix.)

Hobby, J. (1992). A User's Manual for MetaPost. Technical Report 162, AT&T Bell Laboratories, Murray Hill, NJ. This is obtainable by sending mail send 162 from research/cstr to netlib@research.att.com. (Cited on pages 90, 96, 390, 418, and 429.)

Hobby, J. (1993). Drawing graphs with MetaPost. Technical Report 164, AT&T Bell Laboratories, Murray Hill, NJ. This is obtainable by sending mail send 164 from research/cstr to netlib@research.att.com. (Cited on pages 90, 96, 390, 418, 421, and 427.)

Hoeffler Type Foundry (1996). Hoeffler Type Foundry. This designer type foundry furnishes several handsome font families that display variation of a visual attribute across fonts in the family. (Cited on page 283.)

Hoenig, A. (1989, December). Fractal Images with TEX. *TUGboat 10*(4), 491–498. (Cited on page 28.)

Hoenig, A. (1990, September). A constructed Duerer alphabet. *TUGboat 11*(3), 435–439. (Cited on page 93.)

Hoenig, A. (1994, June). NextTEX: TEX plus the NextStep Operating System. *TUGboat 15*(2), 107–109. (Cited on pages 15 and 263.)

Hoenig, A. (1995, September). The Poetica Family: Fancy Fonts with TEX and LATEX. *TUGboat 16*(3), 244–252. (Cited on pages 221 and 250.)

International Typeface Corporation (1995). International Typeface Corporation. They can be reached at 866 Second Avenue, New York, NY 10017; telephone (212) 371-0699; email intltypco@aol.com.

Jeffrey, A. (1993, October). A PostScript font installation package written in TEX. *TUGboat 14*(3), 285–292.

Jeffrey, A. (1994). PostScript font support in LATEX2ε. *TUGboat 15*(3), 263–268.

Jeffrey, A. (1995). The fontinst package. Make sure you always have an up-to-date version, available from any CTAN site. (Cited on page 168.)

Kay, D. C. and J. R. Levine (1994). *Graphics File Formats*. Blue Ridge Summit, PA: Windcrest/McGraw-Hill. (Cited on page 348.)

Kinch Computer Company (1987). *AP-TEX*. 6994 Pebble Beach Court, Lake Worth, FL 33467; (561) 966-8400: Kinch Computer Company. These pixel files approximate the "Adobe 35"—the 35 fonts resident in most laser printers—at various sizes. (Cited on page 263.)

Knuth, D. E. (1979). *TEX and METAFONT: New Directions in Typesetting*. Providence, RI: Digital Press & American Mathematical Society (jointly). This book reprints a series of early publications on early version of TEX.

The current TeX is quite different, and historically minded readers will enjoy comparing and contrasting. Unfortunately, this volume has been out of print for some time.   (Cited on pages 9, 35, and 272.)

Knuth, D. E. (1983, September). WEB User Manual: The WEB System of Structured Documentation. Technical Report STAN-CS-83-980, Stanford University, Stanford, CA.   (Cited on page 36.)

Knuth, D. E. (1986a). *Computers and Typesetting, volume A (The TeXbook)*. Reading, MA: Addison-Wesley. One of life's main reference works, it should be beside any author's computer.   (Cited on pages vii, 38, 80, 146, 210, 308, 369, 485, and 525.)

Knuth, D. E. (1986b). *Computers and Typesetting, volume B (TeX: The Program)*. Reading, MA: Addison-Wesley.   (Cited on pages 35 and 38.)

Knuth, D. E. (1986c). *Computers and Typesetting, volume C (The META-FONTbook)*. Reading, MA: Addison-Wesley.   (Cited on pages 38, 64, 73, 74, 79, 82, 96, 390, 409, and 463.)

Knuth, D. E. (1986d). *Computers and Typesetting, volume D (METAFONT: The Program)*. Reading, MA: Addison-Wesley.   (Cited on pages 36, 38, and 96.)

Knuth, D. E. (1986e). *Computers and Typesetting, volume E (Computer Modern Typefaces)*. Reading, MA: Addison-Wesley.   (Cited on pages 38, 79, 83, 96, and 314.)

Knuth, D. E. (1986f). Remarks to celebrate the publication of *Computers & Typesetting. TUGboat* 7(2), 95–98.   (Cited on pages 8, 9, and 36.)

Knuth, D. E. (1987, December). Fonts for digital halftones. *TUGboat* 8(2), 135–160.   (Cited on page 27.)

Knuth, D. E. (1988, August). A punk meta-font. *TUGboat* 9(2), 152–168.   (Cited on page 93.)

Knuth, D. E. (1989a, November). The new versions of TeX and METAFONT. *TUGboat* 10(3), 325–328. Although virtual fonts are not mentioned in here at all, this discussion of TeX3 clarifies some virtual font issues.   (Cited on page 168.)

Knuth, D. E. (1989b, April). Typesetting *Concrete Mathematics. TUGboat* 10(1), 31–36.   (Cited on page 294.)

Knuth, D. E. (1990, April). Virtual Fonts: More Fun for Grand Wizards. *TUGboat* 11(1), 13–24. This contains the definitive statement on virtual fonts.   (Cited on pages 36 and 168.)

Knuth, D. E. (1991). *3:16 Bible Texts Illuminated*. Madison, WI: A-R Editions, Inc.   (Cited on page 9.)

Knuth, D. E. (1992). *Literate Programming*. Leland Stanford Junior University, Stanford, CA: Center for the Study of Language and Information.   (Cited on page 36.)

Knuth, D. E. (1993). *The Stanford Graphbase: A Platform for Combinatorial Computing*. Reading, MA and New York: Addison-Wesley and ACM.   (Cited on page 28.)

Knuth, D. E. and D. R. Fuchs (1986, April). TeXware. Technical Report STAN-CS-86-1097, Stanford University, Stanford, CA.   (Cited on page 36.)

Knuth, D. E., T. G. Rokicki, and A. L. Samuel (1989, April). METAFONTware. Technical Report STAN-CS-89-1255., Stanford University, Stanford, CA.   (Cited on pages 36 and 429.)

Knuth, D. E. and H. Zapf (1989, April). AMS Euler—a new typeface for mathematics. *Scholarly Publishing 20*(3), 131–157. An informal discussion by the authors of the processes and rationale that went into the design of these fonts. (Cited on page 293.)

Kopka, H. (1994). *LATEX—Eine Einführung.* Bonn: Addison-Wesley. This is a well-known series (three volumes) written in German. Only a partial English translation has appeared.

Krieger, J. and N. Schwarz (1990). *Introduction to TEX.* Amsterdam: Addison-Wesley Europe.

Krol, E. (1994). *The Whole Internet: User's Guide & Catalog, 2nd ed.* Sebastopol, CA: O'Reilly & Associates, Inc. (Cited on page 42.)

Lamport, L. (1994). *LATEX: A Document Preparation System* (second ed.). Reading, MA: Addison-Wesley. (Cited on pages vii, 38, 109, 110, 357, 360, 371, and 376.)

LaserGo, Inc. (1988). *GoScript.* 9235 Trade Place, Suite A, San Diego, CA 92126; (619) 530-2400: LaserGo. (Cited on page 264.)

Lawson, A. (1990). *Anatomy of a Typeface.* Boston, MA: David R. Godine, Publisher, Inc. Details and vignettes surrounding many of the popular and beautiful types currently in use are presented in this well-designed volume. (Cited on page 313.)

Lesenko, S. (1996, September). The DVIPDF Program. *TUGboat 17*(3), 252–254. (Cited on page 125.)

Martin, S. (1997, June 9). Times Roman Font Announces Shortage of Periods. *The New Yorker,* 110. The lighter side—definitely—of computer typesetting via the pen of Steve Martin.

Melville, H. (1962). *Typee.* New York: West Virginia Pulp and Paper Company. This special edition, designed by Bradbury Thompson, is set entirely in Monotype Modern fonts. (Cited on page 314.)

Monotype Corporation (1997). *Monotype Digital Typography.* 985 Busse Road, Elk Grove Village, IL 60007-2400: Monotype Corp. The toll-free telephone number within the United States is (800) MONOTYPE. (Cited on page 289.)

Murray, J. D. and W. van Ryper (1994). *Encyclopedia of Graphics File Formats.* Sebastopol, CA: O'Reilly & Associates, Inc. (Cited on page 348.)

NeXT Computer Corporation (1993). *TEXView.* 900 Chesapeake Drive, Redwood City, CA 94063; 1-800-848-next: NeXT Computer Corp. This excellent implementation of TEX is due to Tom Rokicki, and surpasses in convenience and number of bells and whistles any other implementation of TEX I have seen. Next Computer is now a part of Apple Computer; the NextStep operating system is now called OpenStep. (Cited on page 262.)

O'Brian, P. (1990). *Master and Commander.* New York: W. W. Norton. (Cited on pages 277 and 282.)

Plaice, J. (1994, September). Progress in the Ω project. *TUGboat 15*(3), 320–325. (Cited on page 16.)

Plaice, J. and Y. Haralambous (1996, June). The latest developments in Ω. *TUGboat 17*(2), 181–183. An excellent self-critique of the current version of Ω, this note also details the changes and enhancements due as part of the upcoming release of this software. (Cited on page 16.)

Planet Art (1995). *Planet Art Classic Graphics CD-ROMs.* 505 South Beverly Drive, Suite 242, Beverly Hills, CA 90212: Planet Art. This series of CD-ROMs contains many smashing images, all royalty-free. Their telephone number is (800) 200-3405. (Cited on page 361.)

Prime Time Freeware (1994). *Prime Time TEXcetera.* 370 Altair Way, Suite 150, Sunnyvale, CA 94086; (408) 433-9662; ptf@cfcl.com: Prime Time Freeware. (Cited on page 52.)

Quite Software (1996). *PSAlter.* 105 Ridley Road, London, E7 0LX, UK; 0181 257 1044: Quite Software. *PSAlter* is a convenient Post-Script previewer for Windows systems. Their amusing Web page is at http://ds.dial.pipex.com/quite/index.htm. (Cited on page 264.)

Radical Eye Software (1990). *Amiga-TEX.* P. O. Box 2081, Stanford, CA 94309: Radical Eye Software. This implementation is due to Tom Rokicki, the author of dvips. (Cited on page 262.)

Raman, T. V. (1995, September). An audio view of (LA)TEX documents. *TUGboat 16*(3), 310–314. (Cited on page 98.)

Reckdahl, K. (1996, March). Using EPS graphics in LATEX2$_\varepsilon$ documents. *TUGboat 17*(1), 43–53. This article (and a companion piece not yet published while this current volume was in progress) appears closely based upon an electronic document by the same author that is available in the CTAN archives. (Cited on pages 350 and 354.)

Rimmer, S. (1993). *Bit-Mapped Graphics.* Blue Ridge Summit, PA: Windcrest/McGraw-Hill. (Cited on page 348.)

Rokicki, T. (1992). The dvips package (software). dvips is indispensable for TEX users in a PostScript environment and includes afm2tfm, a tool for constructing simple virtual fonts. This software has been compiled for virtually every hardware platform, and source code is available for those who prefer to "roll their own." This public domain package is available at CTAN sites. Get it.

Salomon, D. (1995). *The Advanced TEXbook.* New York: Springer-Verlag. (Cited on page 38.)

Schwarzkopf, O. (1995, June). The Hyperlatex Story. *TUGboat 16*(2), 159–162. (Cited on page 124.)

Seth, V. (1994). *A Suitable Boy.* New York: HarperCollins. (Cited on page 470.)

Sewell, W. (1989). *Weaving a Program: Literate Programming in WEB.* New York: Van Nostrand Reinhold. (Cited on page 36.)

Siegel, D. R. (1985). *The Euler project at Stanford.* Stanford, CA: Department of Computer Science, Stanford University. This handsomely produced report discusses many of the technical details behind this project. (Cited on page 293.)

Smith, C. (1993). Notebooks into Books via LATEX. *Mathematica Journal 3*(3), 69–73. (Cited on page 129.)

Sojka, P., H. T. Thanh, and J. Zlatuška (1996, September). The joy of TEX2PDF—Acrobatics with an alternative to DVI format. *TUGboat 17*(3), 244–251. (Cited on page 125.)

Sowa, F. (1994). *TEX/LATEX und Graphik: Ein Überblick über die Verfahren.* Berlin: Springer-Verlag. Not only a welcome survey of the graphic methods available to a conscientious user of TEX or LATEX (with many well chosen and well-done figures), but this is a fine example of book making using TEX. (Cited on page 345.)

Spivak, M. D. (1987). *The PC-TEX Manual*. Mill Valley, CA: Personal TEX, Inc. (Cited on page 38.)

Spivak, M. D. (1989). *AMS-TEX: The Synthesis*. 3701 W. Alabama, Ste. 450-273, Houston, TX 77027: The TEXplorators Corp. (Cited on pages 38 and 114.)

Spivak, M. D. (1990). *The Joy of TEX* (second ed.). Providence, RI: The American Mathematical Society. (Cited on page 38.)

Steinberg, S. H. (1961). *Five Hundred Years of Printing* (second revised ed.). Harmondsworth, England: Penguin Books. (Cited on page 190.)

Taylor, P. (1994, September). ε-TEX & $\mathcal{N_TS}$: A progress report. *TUGboat 15*(3), 353–358. (Cited on page 16.)

Tenner, E. (1996). *Why Things Bite Back: Technology and the Revenge of Unintended Consequences*. New York: Alfred A. Knopf. (Cited on page 7.)

TEX Live (1997, May). *TEX Live 2 CDROM*. UKTUG, GUTenberg, and TUG. The compilers have stated their intention to issue revisions every six months or so. The contents contain implementations of TEX and friends for a wide variety of Unix platforms which are executable right from the disk. Non-Unix users may be attracted by the wealth of macro, font, and supplementary material included on the disk. All users will be attracted by its price, roughly twenty dollars or its equivalent. It's available through the offices of the TEX Users Group, GUTenberg, or the UK TEX Users Group. The original version first appeared in May, 1996. (Cited on page 56.)

Thiele, C. (1996, March). TUG'95 Questions and Answers with Professor Donald E. Knuth. *TUGboat 17*(1), 7–22. (Cited on page 9.)

Tobin, G. (1994). *METAFONT for beginners*. This file is available in the `documentation` section of the CTAN archives. (Cited on page 96.)

TUG (1979). TEX Users Group. P. O. Box 1239, Three Rivers, CA 93271-1239, (209) 561-0112; `TUG@mail.tug.org`. The original user organization (founded 1979) and source for many resources. (Cited on pages 40 and 379.)

Turner, R. C., T. A. Douglas, and A. J. Turner (1996). *README.1ST: SGML for Writers and Editors*. New Jersey: Prentice-Hall. (Cited on page 100.)

Updike, D. B. (1980). *Printing Types: Their History, Forms, and Use*. New York: Dover. This two-volume work is the classic on the subject. It is an unabridged republication of the second (1937) edition originally published by Harvard University Press, Cambridge, MA. (Cited on page 313.)

van Zandt, T. and D. Girou (1994, September). Inside PSTricks. *TUGboat 15*(3), 239–247. (Cited on page 441.)

von Bechtolsheim, S. (1994). *TEX in Practice*. New York: Springer-Verlag. This four-volume series suffers from poor proofreading and copyediting, but is such a trove of techniques and tricks that readers may forgive the publisher. (Cited on page 38.)

Vulis, M. (1993). *Modern TEX and Its Applications*. Boca Raton, FL: CRC. An explication of the TEX language and the extensions pertaining to VectorTEX. A contributed chapter by the current author discusses typesetting on curved baselines.

Walnut Creek (1995). *TEX CDROM*. 1547 Palos Verdes Mall, Suite 260, Walnut Creek, CA 94596; (510) 674-0783; `info@cdrom.com`: Walnut Creek CDROM. (Cited on page 52.)

Walsh, N. (1994). *Making TEX Work*. Sebastopol, CA: O'Reilly & Associates, Inc. A wide-ranging collection of facts and figures about LATEX and TEX and how to retrieve various resources from the Internet. (Cited on pages 96 and 345.)

Ward, S. A. and J. Robert H. Halstead (1990). *Computation Structures*. Cambridge and New York: M.I.T. Press and McGraw-Hill.

Weinberg, S. (1972). *Gravitation and Cosmology: Principles and Applications of the General Theory of Relativity*. New York: Wiley. (Cited on pages 287 and 289.)

Wichura, M. J. (1987). *The PICTEX Manual*. San Francisco, CA: TEX Users Group. This is number 6 in the "TEXniques" series. (Cited on pages 376, 377, 379, and 388.)

Wolfram, S. (1996). *The Mathematica Book*. 100 Trade Center Drive, Champaign, IL 61820: Wolfram Media, Inc. This volume describes in great detail the operation of the *Mathematica* system for mathematics. The program itself is provided by Wolfram Research Corp., at the above address. (Cited on page 128.)

Wujastyk, D. (1988a, December). Further faces. *TUGboat 9*(3), 246–251. (Cited on page 96.)

Wujastyk, D. (1988b, August). The many faces of TEX: a survey of digital metafonts. *TUGboat 9*(2), 131–152. (Cited on page 96.)

Y&Y, Inc. (1996). *Y&Y TEX Package*. Tuttle's Livery, 45 Walden Street, Concord, MA 01742; (508) 371-3286: Y&Y. In addition to this package, a dynamic implementation of TEX for the personal computer, they furnish other TEX packages: the DVIWindo previewer, DVIPSONE driver for PostScript, Adobe Type Manager, Acrobat Reader, and PostScriptType 1 fonts for use with the TEX package. (Cited on page 265.)

Zapf, H. (1970). *Manuale Typographicum*. Cambridge, MA: The M.I.T. Press.

INDEX

Italicized page numbers indicate locations where the entry is shown in an example, but where no explicit mention is made. Commands have the package to which they pertain indicated in parentheses.

␣, 516, 519
! in indexing, 107
#, 525
(octothorpe), 99
$ (math toggle), 524
$$, 121, *524*
&, 120, 525
& (META), 408, *423*, *427*
&cm (METAFONT), *83*
*, 21
* command, 103
** (TEX), 20, 21
** (METAFONT), 61
\, (TEX), *302*
-- (META), *64*, *77*, *79*, 395, *399*, *404*, *405*, *407*, *411*, *422*
.. (parent directory), 295
.. (META), 77, *77*, *79*, 395, 396, *404*
. (META), 392
.notdef, 172
\/ (TEX), 521
:= (META), 399, *399*, *401*, *407*, *425*, *427*
:D (PSTricks), *473*
:U (PSTricks), *473*
; (META), 66, 68, 394
<-> (LATEX), 158
= (METAFONT), 69
?' (¿), 222
@ in indexing, 107
@, 107
\@ (PDCFSEL), 147, 148
@ signs in command names, 111
\@ (LATEX), *476*
[...] (NFSS), 160
[...] (META), *401*, *413*
\[(LATEX), *165*
\␣ (control space; TEX), 516, 519
% (comment character), 209, 525
\\ (LATEX), 103, 120, 534
^, 525
^ (PSTricks), 474
^^M (carriage return), 208
_, 525
_ (PSTricks), 474
{}, 516
~, 525

2602, 72, 82
3-D graphics, 467
.300pk files, 139
.400pk files, 139
4AllTEX, 55, 355
4dos program, 56
.600gf files, 311
8A, 289
8r, 240
8r.enc file, 240, 241, 284
8r.etx file, 240
9 convention, 190

\above (TEX), *302*
Abrahams, Paul, 547
abs (META), 401, *401*
absolute (PSTricks), *449*
abstract environment, 537, 539
accents, 191, 192
accessing private commands, 111
acd program, 56
Acorn, 14
Acrobat, 123, 124, 127, 265, 267
active character, 120, 208
active command form, 152
active status, 208
\active (TEX), *120*, *209*, *210*
\add (*fontinst*), *254*
addiction to METAFONT, 35
addto (META), *406*
\addtocounter (LATEX), *480*
\addtolength (LATEX), 534
adjusting characters, 188
Adobe Caslon, 221, 313
Adobe Garamond, 133, 142, 145, 147, 217, 221, 282, 313
Adobe Illustrator, 88
Adobe Multiple Master, 80
Adobe Standard Encoding, 219
Adobe Systems, Inc., 132, 242
Adobe Times Roman, 142
Adobe Type Manager, 263
\advance (TEX), *115*, *367*, *455*, *466*, *469*, *480*, *487*
\ae (TEX), 228, *359*
Æneid (Virgil), 217, 219

.afm files, 131, 137, 140, 174, 179, 184–186, 189, 196, 201, 202, 205, 222, 228, 229, 232, 233, 238, 240, 242, 244, 253, 264, 265, 276, 277, 289, 292, 293, 306
   problems with, 233
afm2tfm program, 174–176, 178, 265, 277, 306
The African Queen (Forester), 513
Aladdin Ghostscript, 266
alias file, 136
also (META), *406*
alternate fonts, 220
alternate ligatures, 221
alternate virtual fonts, 226
\alternatechar (*fontinst*), *225*
alternative ampersands, 230
American Legion, 42
American Mathematical Society, 33, 40, 44, 293, 301, 306
Amiga, 14, 47, 262
AmigaTEX, 262
AMS-LATEX, 33
amsmath package, 34
$\mathcal{A}_\mathcal{M}\mathcal{S}$TEX, 13, 19, 33, 34, 38, 114
André, Jacques, 463
angleA (PSTricks), *471, 472*
angleB (PSTricks), *471, 472*
anonymous font freak, 94, 95
Apple Macintosh, 13, 14
AP-TEX, 263
arcangle (PSTricks), *474*
Archie, 45
Archie sites, 46
archives, 43
   software, 43, 45, 47
arcsep (PSTricks), *461*
array environment, 418
array package, 540
\arrow (MFPIC), 500
\arrows, 381
\arrows (PICTEX), 379
arrows (PSTricks), *474, 475*
Art Deco, 212
Art of Computer Programming (Knuth), 8
article class, 532, 541
article.cls file, 104, 112
ascender (*fontinst*), 234
ascender height, 290
ASCII, 227
ASCII code, 111
aspect ratio, 351
assignment operator, 399
asterisk convention, 103

Atari, 14, 47
\atendofword (*fontinst*), *224*
ATM, 263
\atstartofword (*fontinst*), *224*, 225, *225*
Auc TEX, 15
author's children, 392
\author (LATEX), 104, 537, *539*
autogrid (MetaPost), 422, *422, 427*
.aux files, 110, 495, 543
awk program, 88, 120
\axis (PICTEX), *384–386, 388*
Ayres for the Violin (Matteis), 30

Babel, 195, 531
babel package, 532
backmatter, 5
backslash, 29
backslash in METAFONT, 66
bad filenames, 61
BaKoMa fonts, 25, 288, 306
bar, 219
bar graphs, 384
\barkern (*fontinst*), *220*
barkern.mtx file, 220
Barnett, Michael, 129
Barroca, Leonor, 475
bars.mtx file, 253, 254
.bas files, 91
.base files, 91
base file, 60, 74
   creation of, 61
baseline skip, 517
\baselineskip (TEX), *455, 466*
basic TEX, 511–529
Baskerville, 297, 309, 320, 344
Baskerville (journal), 40, 123
Baskerville, John, 313
.bat files, 311
bb71.mtx file, 232–235
bbding font, 94
.bbl files, 495, 543
bbold, 306
bbold10 font, 95
$bbold_, 307
bbox (MetaPost), 427, *427*
Beebe, Nelson, x, 44, 109, 123, 350, 543
Beeton, Barbara, x
\begin (LATEX), 102, 103, *209*
beginchar (METAFONT), *64*, 77, *77*, 82, 394, 397
beginfig (MetaPost), *394, 397, 399, 413, 417*, 418, *419*, 421, *421, 422, 427*

begingraph (MetaPost), *419, 420*, 421, *421*, 422, *422*, 427, *427*

\beginpicture (PₖCTEX), 378, *380–383, 387, 388*

\beginsection (TEX), 521, *529*

Bernhard Fashion, 211, 212

Bernhard Modern, 221, 235, 314, 321

Bernhard, Lucien, 226, 314

Berry font-naming, 140

Berry, Karl, 74, 114, 132, 181, 228, 547

Bézier curves, 75

\bf (TEX), *121*, 130, 152, *417, 421, 487*, 520, *528, 529*

\bfdefault (LATEX), *164*

\bfseries (LATEX), *153*, 154, *154, 155*

\bgroup (TEX), *209, 210, 469, 487*

.bib files, 109, 543

bibclean program, 109

bible for TEX users, 38

bibliographic utilities, 109

bibliographies, 109

\bibliography (LATEX), 109

\bibliographystyle (LATEX), 109

BIBTEX, 6, 44, 56, 109, 110, 114, 115, 123, 542, 543

Bientz, Tim, 125, 265

big point, 89, *see* bp, 382, 383

big TEX, 17

Bigelow, Charles, 299, 314

\bigl (TEX), 301

\bigskip (TEX), 518, *528, 529*

Billawala, Neenie, 93

bilo (*Mathematica* + TEX), 129

bitmap fonts, 21, 201
    pros and cons, 23

bitmap fonts from outline fonts, 263, 264

bitmaps in a .ps file, 87

Bitstream, 133, 185

black (PSTricks), *444, 467, 469*

black (MetaPost), 412, *412, 422*

\black (PSTricks), *455*

Blackboard Bold, 95, 301, 306

blacker (METAFONT), *74*

.blg files, 110

Blue Sky Research, Inc., 15, 25, 288

blue (MetaPost), 412

bm2font program, 349, 360–362, 364

.bmp files, 355, 361

Bodoni, 284

bold version, 164

boldface, 210–212

book class, 532

book production, 541–546

boolean (META), 399, *399, 401*

\boosts (MFPₖC), *502*, 503

Borde, Arvind, 547

border (PSTricks), *464, 474*

bordercolor (PSTricks), *464*

bottomfraction (LATEX counter), 105

\bottomfraction (LATEX), *105*

boundary character, 212–217, 225

boundarychar, 213, 215, 222

boundarychar (*fontinst*), 224, 225

bounding box, 354, 365, 394

bounding box comment, 354

Bourbaki, Nicolas, 14

\box (TEX), *112, 487*

boxes, 18

boxes.mp file, 418, 429

bp (big point; PostScript unit), 383

Braams, Johannes, 195

bracket convention (NFSS), 158, 160

breadth, 384

\break (TEX), *100*

brokenbar, 240

Browning, Robert, 534

.bst files, 109

btex (MetaPost), *416–418, 425*

Budiansky, Bernard, 538

Buerger, David, 547

\bullet (TEX), *371–373, 380–382*

Bulmer, 291, 313, 322

bye (META), 62, *64, 77, 79*, 394, 397

\bye (TEX), *181, 211, 212, 215*, 522, *528, 529*

C language, 36, 68, 277

\c (TEX), *175*

Cahiers Gutenberg, 123, 345

\cal (TEX), 305

calculations via META, 74

\caldefault (LATEX), *164*

Calligra, 95, 305

calligraphic font, 95, 305

$calSF_, 307

Caml Language, 124, 125

canon for TEX, 38

cap-height, 290

capacity exceeded (METAFONT or MetaPost), 407

capheight (*fontinst*), 234

\caption (LATEX), 103, 106, 109, 111, *111*, 539

\caption (MFPₖC), 499

careless graphing, 407

Carlisle, David, 101, 357, 360, 364, 375, 539, 547

Carter and Cone, 221, 242, 314

Carter, Matthew, 314

case sensitivity, 516
Caslon, *see* Adobe Caslon, 313, 323, 335
\catcode (TEX), 120, *120, 208–210*
category code, 111
category codes, 111
CD-ROMs, 52–57
Centaur, 189, 221, 314, 324
center environment, 90, 102, 103, 350, 351, 365, 381, 455, 469, 534
\centerline (TEX), *518,* 521, *521, 528, 529*
change file, 429
\chapter (LATEX), 103, 537
\char (TEX), *174,* 221, *371, 477, 487*
character code, 111
character spacing, 188
charpath.tex file, 466
Chen, Pehong, 106
Chiante, 221
Chicago Manual of Style, 542
chmod (Unix), 144
circle (PSTricks), *473, 474*
\circle (LATEX), *372, 373, 377*
\circle (MFPIC), *500, 502*
\circle* (LATEX), *377*
circleit (MetaPost), *418*
\circlenode (PSTricks), *472*
circular pens, 408
Clark, Malcolm, 375
class file, 104, 531
\cleaders (TEX), *454*
clipping, 452
closed paths, 396
\closegraphsfile (MFPIC), *495,* 496
\closeout (TEX), *367*
.cls files, 104, 191, 533
cm, 516
cm.bas file, 61
cm.base file, 61, 81
cm.mf file, 61
cmb10 font, 66, 151, 169
cmbase base file, 60
cmbase.base file, 60
cmex10 font, 299
\CMglyph (*fontinst*), 271, *271*
cmitt10 font, 211
cmr10 font, 22, 80, 81, 83, 138, 160, 174, 181, 205, 269, 273, 416
cmr10.390 file, 83
cmr10.390gf file, 83
cmr10.mf file, 81
cmr10.pl file, 270
cmr10.tfm file, 83
cmr5 font, 80, 273
cmsltt10 font, 211

cmtcsc10 font, 211
cmtt10 font, 211, 305, 541
.cnf files, 269
code page, 151, 172
Cohn, Richard, 125, 265
color, 359–360, 542
color package, 359, 360
\color (LATEX), 360
color (MetaPost), 393, 412, *412, 413*
\colorbox (LATEX), *360*
colordvi.sty file, 541, 542
colsep (PSTricks), *473, 474*
column headings
    diagonal, 475
comma-separated variable format, 120
command option, 531
command.com file, 56
commands
    star form (LATEX), 531
\comment (*fontinst*), *215,* 246
commercial TEX implementations, 55
commutative diagrams, 114, 377, 474
comp.text.tex, 51
compatibility mode, 532
compiling a document, 10, 514
complicated documents parts as .epsf, 353
composite fonts, 8, 217
Comprehensive TEX Archive Network, *see* CTAN
computer graphics, 363
computer hardware, 12
Computer Modern fonts, 13, 22, 25, 34, 79–86, 276, 314
    custom variants of, 83, 84
    new magnifications, 83, 84
    outline fonts, 288
    scalable versions, 288
Computer Modern math, 316–317
Computer Modern Roman, 22
Computer Modern Roman Slanted, 143
Computer Modern sans serif, 305
Computer Modern symbol, 305
Computer Modern variants, 82
Computers and Typesetting, 34, 36, 38, 73
concatenation operator, 408
Concrete fonts, 276
control points, 75
control space, 519
controlling floats, 105
Conway, John, 356
coordinate geometry, 368
coordinate notation, 71
coordinate system, 71
coords environment, 501

\coords (MFPiC), *502*
Copland, Aaron, 456
\copy (TEX), *455, 487*
CorelDRAW, 88, 265
Cork encoding, 134, 162
Cork-encoded font, *see* T1
\corners, 381
\corners (PiCTEX), 379
cornersize (PSTricks), *449*
\cos (TEX), *302, 365*
cosd (META), *407*
cosine curve, 500
counter, 273
Courier, 305
\cr (TEX), 120, *121, 302, 386, 487*
creating a base file, 61
creating new commands, 31
crosshatch (PSTricks), *450*
\csetslot (*fontinst*), *229*
CTAN, 12, 14, 15, 25, 28, 43, 45, 46, 49,
    52, 53, 56, 75, 86, 89, 90, 93, 94, 96,
    97, 101, 109, 114, 118, 119, 126,
    140, 142, 143, 146, 177, 195, 250,
    258, 264, 266, 275–277, 288, 289,
    292, 294, 305, 306, 308, 309, 313,
    345, 350, 364, 375, 377, 379, 411,
    429, 441, 477, 481, 505, 532, 533,
    539, 542
    mirrors of, 46
    top level, 44
CTAN interfaces on the Web, 54
Cugley, Damian, 96, 146, 276, 279, 292,
    298
currentpicture (META), *406, 427*
curve (PSTricks), *462*
curve drawing (PSTricks), 450–452
\curve (MFPiC), *500, 502*
curved segments, 395
cusps, 459, 462
Custom Applications, Inc., 264
.cut files, 361
CWEB system, 36
cycle (META), *77, 79,* 396, *397, 398,*
    401, 404, 405, 411, 422
\cyclic (MFPiC), *497, 501*
Cyrillic fonts, 289

Dante, 43
darkgray (PSTricks), *444, 447, 448,*
    451, 452, 458–460, 464, 466, 467,
    469, 485
das font, 195
dashed (PSTricks), *449, 450, 475*
dashes, 513
data file in MetaPost, 419

\dataplot (PSTricks), *462, 463*
\date (LATEX), 104
\dblfloatpagefraction (LATEX), *105*
\dbltopfraction (LATEX), *105*
dbltopnumber (LATEX counter), 105
DEC programs, 47
declaration form, 152
\DeclareFontFamily (LATEX), 157, *158,*
    161, 162, *165*
\DeclareFontShape (LATEX), *84, 85,*
    157, 158, *158,* 159, *160,* 161, 162,
    165
\DeclareMathSizes (LATEX), 161, *161,*
    162
\DeclareMathVersion (LATEX), 161,
    165
\DeclareSymbolFont (LATEX), 161, 162,
    163, 164, *164*
Decline and Fall of the Roman Empire
    (Gibbon), 243
\def (TEX), 111, *112, 120, 122,* 204,
    480, 485, 487
default parameters, 513
default resolution, 82
defaultfont (MetaPost), *416, 416,* 418
defaultscale (MetaPost), *416, 416,*
    418
\define (LAMS-TEX), 114
define_pixels (METAFONT), *64, 79*
\degrees (PSTricks), *460, 460,* 478,
    478, 480
delimited parameters, 120
\depth (*fontinst*), *234*
\depth (LATEX), 359
der font, 195
descender (*fontinst*), 234
description, 402
descriptive computer languages, 73
Design Science, 118
design size, 80, 283
design_size (METAFONT), *86*
detex program, 12
Deutsch, Peter, 266
device driver, 11, 13, 21, 511, 514
device independence, 11
device-independence, 11
diagonal column headings, 475
Didot Roman, 284
die font, 195
dieresis, 193
\digit (*fontinst*), *191, 246*
Digital Equipment, 56
dimen (PSTricks), *467*
\dimen (TEX), *455, 469, 487*
dingbats, 34, 94

Direct TEX, 128
discarding vertical glue, 519
discarding white space, 103
discontinuities in graphing, 408
Display PostScript, 15, 262
\displaystyle (TEX), *302*
Distiller, 265, 267
docstrip package, 146, 540
docstrip.tex file, 532, 533
document environment, 102, 359, 365,
　　418, 421, 534, 539
document compilation, 10, 514
document file, 511, 514
\documentclass (LaTeX), *102*, 104, *104*,
　　201, *298*, *365*, 413, *418*, *421*, 482,
　　485, *539*, *541*
\documentstyle (LaTeX), 104, 530
dog's leg, 382
Dol, Wietse, 55, 56
Don Juan (Hoffmann), 195
Doob, Michael, 38, 168
DOS, 266, 275, 279, 364
　　caveat for METAFONT users, 68
　　software, 47
dotlabel (MetaPost), 415
dotsize (PSTricks), *480*
dotted (PSTricks), *448, 449*
\dotted (MFPIC), 500
double spacing, 517
double-f ligatures, 183
doubleline (PSTricks), *449, 475*
doublesep (PSTricks), *449*
Douglas, Timothy, 100
down (META), *77, 79, 398*
download, 136
downloading fonts, 136
Doyle, Mark, 127
\dp (TEX), *455, 469, 487*
DraTeX package, 377
draw (META), *64, 397*, 398, *398, 401,
　　404, 405, 407, 409, 412, 417–422,
　　425, 427*
\draw (MFPIC), *501*
drawboxed (MetaPost), *418*
drawdot (META), *398*
drawing \lines, 373
driver files, 81, 533
dropped capitals, 32
.drv files, 533
Dryden, John, 219
.dtx files, 146, 532, 533, 540
Dürer font, 92, 93
Dürer, Albrecht, 93, 361
\dump (TEX), *20*
Dutch ligature, 226

.dvi files, 11, 12, 14, 21, 23–27, 37, 60,
　　64, 87, 90, 127, 168, 172, 173,
　　266–268, 293, 353, 378, 441, 511,
　　514, 541
dvi language, 11
dvialw program, 350
dvihps program, 126–128
dvipdf tool, 125
dvips program, 12, 14, 24, 26, 27, 56,
　　87–90, 119, 125–128, 132, 136, 140,
　　142, 173–175, 177, 188, 240, 241,
　　265, 268, 269, 276, 293, 350–354,
　　360, 376, 413, 441, 485, 541
　　making encapsulated PostScript, 351
dvips-generated graphics, 353
dvips.h file, 485
dvitype program, 37, 267, 268
dvitype.out file, 267, 268
dviwindo program, 265, 350
dx (PSTricks), *462*

ecr font family, 181
ecr10 font, 181
\edef (TEX), *229, 455, 469, 487*
edh, 240
Eepic, 347
eepic environment, 347, 376
Egler, Andreas, 28
\egroup (TEX), *209, 210, 469, 487*
Eijkhout, Inge, endpaper
Eijkhout, Victor, endpaper, 38, 542
\eject (TEX), *100, 522, 523*
elements.d file, 427
\ell (TEX), *418*
\ellipse (MFPIC), *505*
else (META), *401*
\else (TEX), *112*
em-dash, 189
\em (LaTeX), 101, 103, *153*
Emacs, 13, 15, 29, 115, 203
e-math archive, 44
\emph (LaTeX), *153*
emTEX, 14, 268, 355, 364
.enc files, 241
encapsulated PostScript, 88, 265, 350
encapsulator, 107
encoding, 133, 150, 151
encoding array, 238
encoding files, 179
encoding variants, 134
encoding vector, 172
\encoding (*fontinst*), *191, 224, 260, 282*
\encodingdefault (LaTeX), *164*
\end (LaTeX), 102
end (META), 62, 394, 397

endchar (META), *64, 77*
endchar (METAFONT), *79, 82,* 394, 397
\endcoords (MFPIC), *502*
enddef (META), *74*
\endencoding (*fontinst*), *191,* 230, *282*
endfig (MetaPost), *394,* 397, *399, 413, 417,* 418, *418–422,* 427
endfor (META), *398, 399, 401, 406, 407, 413, 417, 420, 421, 427*
\endgradtable (PSTricks), 485
\endgraf (TeX), *477*
endgraph (MetaPost), *419–422,* 427, *427*
\endinstallfonts (*fontinst*), 178, *195,* 205, 206, *211, 212, 215, 218, 259, 286*
\endmetrics (*fontinst*), 203, *218–220, 234, 245, 246, 270, 271*
\endmfpic (MFPIC), *496, 502, 505*
\endpicture (PICTEX), 378, *381–388*
\endpscharclip (PSTricks), *466*
\endpsclip (PSTricks), *454, 455, 458*
\endpsmatrix (PSTricks), 473
\endpspicture (PSTricks), *446, 447, 458–461, 467, 469, 480, 485*
\endresetglyph (*fontinst*), 204, *207, 210, 256, 271*
\endsetglyph (*fontinst*), *233, 246, 254, 271*
\endsetslot (*fontinst*), *194, 215, 246*
\endslot (*fontinst*), *225*
\endunderlining (TeX), *209*
entasis, 77
enumerate environment, 102, 536
environment, 102
environment variable, 17, 60, 363, 417
EOF (MetaPost), 423, *423, 425, 427*
epic environment, 347, 376
epic package, 376
epigraph, 261
eplain package, 114, 115
.eps files, 89, 262, 350, 353, 354, 541
.epsf files, 262, 353, 541
epsf package, 91, 350–352, 413, 539
epsf.sty file, 104, 350, 541
epsf.tex file, 350
\epsfbox, 413
\epsfbox (TeX), *90,* 91, *350,* 351, *351,* 356, *365,* 413, 539
\epsffile (TeX), 91, 539
\epsfxsize (TeX), 351, *351*
\epsfysize (TeX), 351, *351*
\epsilon (TeX), *418*
equality, 402

error messages in METAFONT, 62
escape character, 29
Esser, Thomas, 57
etex (MetaPost), *416–418, 421, 425, 427*
.etx files, 177, 179
eu.par file, 292
eufm font, 306
Euler fonts, 293, 299
Euler fraktur, 306
Euler math, 291, 327–332
Euler math fonts, 289
Euler math fonts, 34, 314
Euler symbol fonts, 305
evaluating subscripts, 402
everypsbox (PSTricks), *475*
\everypsbox (PSTricks), *474*
examples of kerning, 5
Excel, 120
Exchange, 265
executable file, 16
exitif (META), 399, *399, 401*
\expandafter (TeX), *487*
expert font installation, 183
expert fonts, 133, 140, 145, 169, 174, 185, 218
extended plain macros, 114
extensible math symbols, 133, 301

f-words, 212–217
f.mtx file, 213, 215, 216
\f (PDCFSEL), 147, 148
Fairbairns, Robin, 277
family, 150
fancyfig environment, 470
FAQ, 51, 53
\fcolorbox (LaTeX), 360, *360*
fcorr, 215
.fd files, 142, 152, 158, 161, 163, 164, 175–178, 183, 192, 196, 205, 206, 214, 216, 226, 235, 249, 260, 262, 272, 280
ff, 183
\ffg (*fontinst*), *229*
ffi, 183
\ffig (*fontinst*), *229*
ffl, 183
\fflg (*fontinst*), *229*
\fi (TeX), *112*
fig package, 506
fig2mf package, 505
fig2mfpic package, 505
figure environment, 105, 106, 365, 469, 539
fileerr package, 540

files (META), 393
fill (META), *77*, 398, *399, 401, 413,
    422, 427*
\fill (MFPC), *500, 502*
fillcolor (PSTricks), *452, 460, 465,
    467, 469, 480, 485*
filldraw (META), *64, 79*
fillin (METAFONT), *74*
fillstyle (PSTricks), *443, 450, 452,
    460, 465–467, 469, 480, 485, 487*
finding files via Archie, 45
finding files via ftp, 45
\fiverm (LaTeX), 388, *389*
\fivetemplate (PDCFSEL), *280*
flames, 48
float placement, 105
\floatpagefraction (LaTeX), *105*
floats, 6, 105, 531
flushleft environment, 90, 534
flushright environment, 534
Flynn, Peter, 123, 124
.fmt files, 91
\font, 207
font attributes, 150
font descriptor file, 164, 177
font family, 132, 151
font family abbreviations, 132
font installation, 130, 136–145
    bitmap fonts, 139
    outline fonts, 139, 140
    outlinefonts, 143
font magnification, 21
font metric files, 18
font names, 80
font naming, 131–135
font nicknames, 130
font resolution
    automatic selection of, 87
font scale factors, 307
font scaling, 307
font selection, 130
font series, 151
font shapes, 133, 151
font sizes, 21, 189
font sizing, 151
font table, 170
    Computer Modern font, 169
    PostScript 8r fonts, 238, 239
    PostScript fonts, 170, 171
font variants, 133, 134
font weights, 133
font-descriptor file, 158
font-encoding vector, 172
\font (TeX), *68, 85, 175, 190, 195,* 208,
    211, *234, 261, 417, 425, 466, 487*

font_coding_scheme (METAFONT), *81*
font_size (METAFONT), 85
\fontdimen (*fontinst*), 208, 209
\fontdimen (TeX), *208*
\fontendcoding (LaTeX), *156*
\fontfamily (LaTeX), *156, 157, 211,*
    455
fontinst, 52, 141, 143, 150, 158, 163,
    174–196, 197, 201, 202, 204, 215,
    217–219, 221, 225, 226, 228, 233,
    235, 240, 242, 245, 248, 253–255,
    258, 259, 269, 273, 277, 279, 282,
    288, 291, 292, 294, 308, 542
    encoding files, 180
    metric files, 179
    simple font installation, 180
    summary of commands, 197–200
fontinst.sty file, 177, 181, 292
fontinst.tex file, 177
fontload package, 266
fontmaking (METAFONT), *74*
Fontographer, 88, 96, 242
fonts, 13
    expert, 174
    free, 140
    installation of, 130
    optical scaling of, 85
    outline, 23
    selection of, 130
    virtual, 166–200
\fontseries (LaTeX), 156, *156, 157,*
    211, 280
fontset, 146
\fontset (PDCFSEL), 148
\fontshape (LaTeX), 156, *156, 157,*
    190, 191, 209, 210, 235, 260
\fontsize (LaTeX), *85,* 156, 157, *157,*
    237, 380, 386, 387, 418, 421, 454,
    455, 465, 475
\fontskip, 208
footnote font, 190
footnote numbers, 190, 191
footnotes, 6
\footnotesize (LaTeX), *153, 155, 480*
for (META), *398,* 399, *399, 401,* 402,
    406, 407, 413, 417, 420, 421, 427
foreign hyphenation, 19
foreign language typesetting, 191, 192
foreign typesetting, 8
Forester, C. S., 513
forever (META), 399, *399,* 401, *401*
format file, 16, 19, 20, 60, 101
format (MetaPost), *420, 421*
formatting and revisions, 32
Fortran, 28, 36

foundry abbreviations, 132
Fournier, 221
\frac (LATEX), *165*
fractal images, 27
$frakSF_, 307
Fraktur, 306
Fraktur font, 95, 306
fraktur font, 95
Frambach, Erik, 55, 56
framesep (PSTricks), *461*
framing boxes, 464
free scalable fonts, 140
Freedom of Press, 264
frequently asked questions, 51
friends of TEX, 34
\fromafm (*fontinst*), *187, 218, 241, 248,
    286*
\frommtx (*fontinst*), *286*
front end graphics packages, 347
front ends to METAFONT, 505
ftp, 34
ftp archives, 43, 45, 47
ftp commands, 48
ftp sites, 45, 47
ftp.cs.umb.edu archive, 132
ftp.math.utah.edu archive, 109
Fuchs, David, 36
fullcircle (META), *64, 406, 409, 411,
    413, 417*

Galliard, 221, 251, 314, 325, 330
Game of Life, 356
Gandhi, Mahatma, 470
Garamond, 145, 157, *see* Adobe
    Garamond, 308, 313, 326, 331, 340,
    417, 541
Garamond, Claude, 313
gdata (MetaPost), 427, *427*
\gdef (TEX), *208*
gdraw (MetaPost), 419, *419–422*
generate (META), 81
generic font file, 58, 67, 505
Gentle Introduction to TEX, 38
German double s, 193
German language typesetting, 192
germandbls, 193
getting TEX, 13
getting MetaPost, 411
Gettysburg Address (Lincoln), 456
.gf files, 37, 58, 83
gftodvi program, 36, 37, 60, 64
gftopk program, 36, 37, 60, 67, 83, 86,
    495, 505
gftype program, 37
GhostScript, 125, 263, 264, 266, 267

GhostView, 125, 128, 266
Gibbon, Edward, 243
Gibbons, Jeremy, 407
Gibbs, W. Wayt, 98
.gif files, 361
Gill Sans, 305, 314, 332
Gill, Eric, 314
Ginsparg, Paul, 127
Girou, Denis, 441, 445, 463, 481
glabel (MetaPost), 421, *421*
\global (TEX), *208, 480, 487*
glyph, 58, 201
\glyph (*fontinst*), 204, *207, 210, 233,
    245, 246, 256, 271*
\glyphrule (*fontinst*), 204, *207, 254,
    256*
\glyphspecial (*fontinst*), *256*
GNU project, 124, 125
GNU archive site, 116
GNU General Public License, 266
GNU project, 266
gnuplot program, 347, 506
\gobblethree (*fontinst*), *260*
Goldfarb, Charles, 100
Goossens, Michel, 38, 101, 105,
    108–110, 124, 150, 157, 168, 196,
    277, 345, 371, 376, 532
GoScript, 264
gradangle (PSTricks), *466, 467, 485,
    487*
gradbegin (PSTricks), *466, 467, 469,
    485, 487*
gradend (PSTricks), *466, 467, 469, 485,
    487*
gradient, 466
gradient (PSTricks), *467, 469, 485,
    487*
gradient fill style, 452, 466
gradient.tex file, 467
gradmidpoint (PSTricks), *466, 467,
    469, 485*
Graham, Ronald, 276, 294
grampa.mf file, 62
Granger, Geeti, 105
Granjon, Robert, 313
Grant, Michael, 364
graph package, 419
graph.mp file, 418, 429
graph (MetaPost), *427*
graphic inclusions, 345–367
graphic layers, 414, 444
Graphic Workshop, 355
graphics package, 357, 358, 365
graphics files from *dvips*, 351
graphics from *dvips*, 353

graphics from fonts, 347
graphics within TEX, 34
graphicx package, 357, 358
graphs, 382, 499
  carelessness with, 407
  in MetaPost, 418–429
  kink in, 382
Gravitation and Cosmology (Weinberg), x
gray (PSTricks), *443, 444, 446, 448, 458–460, 465–467, 478, 480*
gray fonts, 64
gray levels in virtual fonts, 256
gray.mf file, 64
\gray (PSTricks), *455*
Greek boldface, 306
Greek Times, 306
green (MetaPost), 412
grey (PSTricks), *478*
grid (MetaPost), 420, *420, 421*
\grid (PICTEX), *388*
gridcolor (PSTricks), *448, 451, 458, 459*
griddots (PSTricks), *459*
gridlabels (PSTricks), *448, 451, 458, 459*
gridwidth (PSTricks), *448, 451, 458*
group, 516
Grünbaum, Branko, 406
gs2pk program, 263
gsf2pk program, 264, 269
Gurari, Eitan, 377
GUST, 45
GUST, 345
GUTenberg, 56
gzip program, 27

halfcircle (META), *406, 411*
halftone fonts, 27
\halign (TEX), *121, 302, 487*
Halstead, Robert Jr., 2
Haralambous, Yannis, 16, 76, 92, 93, 95, 96, 126
Hargreaves, Kathryn, 547
Harrison, Michael, 106
\hatch (MFPIC), *500*
hatchangle (PSTricks), *450*
Hayes's Principle, ix
Hayes, Brian, ix
\hbox (TEX), *112, 258, 302, 371, 379, 380, 383, 449, 450, 454, 455, 473, 487*
header files, 26
\height (*fontinst*), *234, 254*
\height (LATEX), 359, *359*
help, 48

Helvetica, 305
Hewlett-Packard, 56
Hewlett-Packard laser printers, 12
\hfil (TEX), *112, 121, 302, 487*
\hfill (TEX), *100, 454, 487*
hidden glyphs, 240
\hidewidth (TEX), *121*
high-energy physics, 127
high-quality output, 87
histograms, 384
hlines (PSTricks), *450*
Hobby, John, x, 34, 75, 89, 90, 96, 390, 411, 418, 421, 427, 429
Hoeffler Type Foundry, 283
Hoenig, Alan, 15, 28, 93, 140, 221, 250, 263, 290, 309
Hoenig, Jozefa, x
Hoffleit, Gregor, 15
Hoffmann, E. T. A., 195
Holmes, Kris, 299, 314
home improvement, 76
horizontal shadows, 373
horizontal spacing, 519
Horn, Berthold, 127
\hphantom (TEX), *472, 472*
\hrule (TEX), *209, 487*
\hsize (TEX), *112, 466, 469*, 517, *520*
\hskip (TEX), *209, 444, 449, 450, 454, 472*, 477, *478, 487*, 520, *520*
\hspace (LATEX), *359, 444, 477*, 537
\hss (TEX), *454*
\ht (TEX), *455, 469, 487*
HTML, 123
huge TEX, 17
\Huge (LATEX), *153*
\huge (LATEX), *153*
Hungarian umlaut, 193
hyper.dtx macros, 126
hyperbasics.tex macros, 126
Hyperlatex, 124, 125
hyperlatex.tex macros, 126
hyperref.dtx macros, 126
hyperref package, 126
hypertext, 122–127
hypertext archives, 127
hypertext links, 52
hypertext markup language, 123
hypertext transfer protocol, 52
HyperTEXview, 128
hypertools, 128
hyphen, 513
hyphen.tex file, 20
hyphenation, 4, 19, 513

IBM-type computers, 14

Ides of March, 8
.idx files, 108, 543
if (META), 400, *401*
\ifcase (TEX), *260, 261, 480*
\ifdim (TEX), *112*
.iff files, 361
\ifhbox (TEX), *487*
\ifisglyph (*fontinst*), 204, *207, 210, 223, 224, 229, 233, 256, 271*
\ifnum (TEX), *367, 466, 480*
ij, 226
illuminated initials, 92
ImageViewer, 355
.img files, 361
\immediate (TEX), *367*
in (abb.), 516
\inboundscheckon (PICTEX), *385*
\includegraphics* (LATEX), *359*
\includegraphics (LATEX), 358, *359*
including graphics, 345–367
.ind files, 108
index preparation, 6
\index (LATEX), 106, *106*, 107, *107*, 108, *108*
indexing authors in a bibliography, 543
indexing conventions, 107
indexing process, 108
.inf files, 131
Information Please almanac, 120
\infty (TEX), *165, 302*
inimf program, 60
init_numbers (MetaPost), 421, *421*
initex program, 19, 20, 101
initial letters, special treatment, 32
initialization procedure for TEX, 19
inking the page, 21
input files, 18
input (META), 81, *83, 86*, 418, *418, 419, 425, 427, 427*
\input (TEX), *178*, 201, *211, 212, 215, 218, 298, 350, 367, 465, 467, 485, 487, 542*
\inputetx (*fontinst*), *191, 260, 282*
\inputmtx (*fontinst*), *271*
.ins files, 532, 533
INSTALL file, 16
installation of fonts, 167
\installfamily (*fontinst*), 178, *178, 188*, 205, 206, *211, 212, 215, 218, 259, 286, 542*
\installfont (*fontinst*), 178, 179, 181, 183, 188, *188*, 190, *190, 191, 195*, 202, *207, 211, 212*, 213, *215, 217, 218, 220, 241, 259*, 269, 271, 278, 282, *286, 542*

\installfonts (*fontinst*), 178, 188, *195*, 205, 206, *211, 212, 215, 218, 259, 286, 542*
installing TEX, 16
InstantTEX, 15
\int (*fontinst*), *215, 254*
\int (TEX), *165*, 301, *302*
integral symbols, 301
interactive mode, 21
intermediate caps, 96
International Typeface Corporation, 284, 549
Internet, 34, 42–52
Internet lists, 48–50
intersectionpoint (META), *406, 411*
Iron Curtain, 40
\it (TEX), 98, 101, 130, *298, 474*, 520, *521*
italic correction, 521
ItalicAngle, 187
ITC American Typewriter, 305
ITC Bodoni, 284
itemize environment, 102, 536
iterated groups (loops), 476
\itshape (LATEX), *153–155*

Jackowski, Bogusław, 45, 88, 266
Jackson, Don, x
Jansen, 313
Janson, 313, 327
Janson, Anton, 313
Japanese heraldic crests, 63, 96
jargon, 514
 LATEX, 531
Jefferson, Thomas, 314
Jeffrey, Alan, x, 63, 95, 96, 139, 141, 143, 168, 176, 213, 288, 306, 308, 549
\jobname (TEX), *367, 495*
John Jay College, x
joining curves, 408
joining the TEX community, 40

k convention, 258
K-Talk Communications, Inc., 118
Kay, David, 348
kermit program, 27
kern, 4
\kern (TEX), *371, 487*
kerning in virtual fonts, 223
kerning information, 82
kernoff.mtx file, 219
keyboard conventions, 512–513
Kinch Computer Company, 263
kink in a graph, 382

Kis, Nicholas, 313
Knuth, Donald E., x, 8, 9, 15, 18, 27,
      28, 34–36, 38, 44, 58, 60, 64, 72–74,
      79, 82, 83, 85, 93, 96, 100, 114, 166,
      168, 210, 257, 267, 272, 276, 293,
      294, 314, 390, 409, 429, 463, 525
   home page of, 9
Kohler, Eddie, 277
Kopka, Helmut, 551
Krieger, Jost, 551
Krol, Ed, 42
Kwok, Conrad, 376

l2x program, 124, 125
label suffixes (MetaPost), 415
label text, 415
   advanced topics, 423
   LaTeX, 417
   string mode, 415, 418
   text mode, 416, 418
\label (LaTeX), 115, 126, 542
label (MetaPost), 415, *415*, 416, *417,*
      421, 422, 423, 425, *427*
\label (MFPiC), 499, 500
labels (PSTricks), *448*
labels in figures (MetaPost), 415
labelsep (PSTricks), *474*
labrea archive, 44
lampblack, 66
Lamport, Leslie, vii, 33, 38, 101,
      108–110, 357, 360, 371, 376
LAMS-TeX, 33, 38, 114, 115, 376, 377
Lang, Russell, 266
lanlmac.tex macros, 126, 127
\lap (TeX), *458*
large initial letters, 32
large integral symbols, 301
\LARGE (LaTeX), *153*
\Large (LaTeX), *153,* 155, *466*
\large (LaTeX), 130, *153,* 154, *154,*
      155, 469
laser printers, 12
LaserGo, Inc., 264
\lastbox (TeX), *487*
LaTeX, 11, 33, 101–113
   additional tools, 539
   equivalence to LaTeX2e, 101
   graphics in, 357
   modifying commands, 109–113
LaTeXcontrasted with TeX, 3
LaTeX conventions, 102
LaTeX text in plain TeX files, 352
latex.fmt file, 101
latex.ltx file, 111–113
latex.tex file, 375

LaTeX209, 104, 530, 531
LaTeX2$_\varepsilon$, 101
LaTeX2HTML, 124
LaTeX2HTML converter, 124, 125
LaTeX3, 33, 101
latexpic.tex file, 376
latexpicobjs.tex file, 376
latin.gly file, 202–204, 210
latin.mtx file, 180, 183, 186, 202, 204,
      205, 213, 215
\latinfamily (*fontinst*), *181,* 184
Lawson, Alexander, 313
layout package, 534
.lbm files, 361
\Lbrack (TeX), 301, *302*
\lc (*fontinst*), *224,* 255
\lcletter (*fontinst*), 253, *254*
leaders, 454
\leaders (TeX), *209, 487*
Leathrum, Tom, 494
\leavevmode (TeX), 90, 350, *351,* 352,
      381
left quote convention, 222, 230, 246
left (META), *397, 398*
\left (TeX), *165,* 301, *302*
\leftline (TeX), *517, 520, 528*
\leftskip (TeX), *469*
Leroy, Xavier, 124, 125
Lesenko, Sergey, 125
\let (TeX), *120, 208–210, 220,* 367,
      367, 487
letter class, 532
Letter Gothic, 305
letters, 537
letterspace, 257, 272
letterspace.sty file, 258
\letterspace (TeX), 258
letterspacing, 257–261, 297
letterspacing, 282
letterspacing (*fontinst*), 259, *260, 282,*
      542
Levine, John, 348
Levy, Silvio, 36
life cycle of TeX, 10
liftpen (PSTricks), *485*
LIG (*fontinst*), 193, 224
\Ligature (*fontinst*), *224, 225,* 229
\ligature (*fontinst*), 192, 194, *224,*
      246, 260, *260*
ligatures, 4
lightgray (PSTricks), *444, 447, 451,*
      452, 457, 458, 465–467, 469, 480,
      485
lightning Textures, 15
ligtable (METAFONT), 82

\limits (TEX), 301, *302*
Lincoln, Abraham, 456
Linde, Dmitri, 15
\line angles, 373
line breaking, 100
line terminators, 461, 464, 472, 480
line terminators (PSTricks), 449, 450
\line (LATEX), *372*, 373, *373*, *377*
linearc (PSTricks), *449*
linecolor (PSTricks), *443, 444,
    446–448, 451, 457–459, 464–466,
    478, 480*
\lines (PICTEX), *386–388*
linestyle (PSTricks), *448–450, 454,
    457, 458, 469, 475, 480, 485, 487*
\linethickness (PICTEX), *380, 382,
    383*, 384, 385, *386–388*
linewidth (PSTricks), *442, 443, 445,
    448–450, 452, 459, 461, 464, 465,
    467, 469, 473, 478, 480*
Linotronic, 25
\lint, 302
\lint (TEX), 301, *302*
Linux, 56
Lisp, 15, 124, 125
\listoffigures (LATEX), 106
\listoftables (LATEX), 106
lists, 536
lists and newsgroups, 47–51
Listserv lists, 48
\llap (TEX), *487*
llcorner (MetaPost), 427, *427*
local.mf file, 65, 73, 74
.lof files, 495
.log files, 64, 83, 88–90, 177, 214, 311,
    533
logical document structure, 98–116
logical structure, 99
\loint (TEX), 301, *302*
London Underground, 314
\long (TEX), *112*
longtable package, 540
\longticklength (PICTEX), *388*
\loop (TEX), 366, *367, 466*, 476, *487*
loops, 476
loops (META), 398
Los Alamos e-print archives, 127
Lövstrand, Lennart, 355
lplain.tex file, 19, 375
\lput (PSTricks), *473*
lrcorner (MetaPost), 427
ls-lr file, 45
lslashslash, 248
\lsurfint (TEX), 301, *302*
lu.par file, 292

Lucida, 291
Lucida Bright, 189, 299, 302, 314, 336
Lucida Bright sans serif, 157
Lucida math extension, 301
Lucida math fonts, 299
Lucida New Math, 306, 314
Lucida New Math family, 299
Lucida New Math math, 332–337
Lucida Sans, 305, 314, 337, 541, 542

m convention, 135
\M (PDCFSEL), 148
\m (PDCFSEL), 148
ma.par file, 292
Macintosh, 15, 47, 263
MacKay, Pierre, 289
macro packages, 13, 18, 33, 525
macros, 31, 514, 525
mag (META), 83, *83, 84*
magnification, 21, 22, 83
\magnification (TEX), *84*
\makeatletter (LATEX), 111, 113, *113*,
    191
\makeatother (LATEX), 111, *113*, 191
\makebox (LATEX), *372, 373*
makegf.bat file, 310
makeidx package, 108
MakeIndex program, 6, 56, 106, 108,
    114, 115
makeindex package, 108
\makeindex (LATEX), *104*, 108
\makeletters (*fontinst*), *254*
makemma.tex file, 304
makepad.tex file, 184
makepk.bat file, 310
makepl.bat file, 310
\maketitle (LATEX), 104, 537, *539*
maketrax.tex file, 259
makevf.bat file, 311
makevp.tex file, 310
Malvern, 93, 96, 276
Malyshev, Basil, 25, 266, 288, 294
Mantinia, 221, 242–250, 314
Mantinia environment, 249
Mantinia style file, 249
Manutius, Aldus, 217
manx.etx file, 247
manx.mtx file, 244
.map files, 196, 289, 293, 294, 306
map file, 136
Maple, 347
markup, 531
Martin, Steve, 551
Martin, William, 313

Master and Commander (O'Brian), x, 277, 282
math bold fonts, 306
math font naming conventions, 135, 297
math fonts, 160–165, 287–344
    installing raw, 292
math fonts via METAFONT, 308–313
math modes, 522
Math Pi, 306
math typesetting, 287–344
math version, 164
\mathbf (LaTeX), *153, 154, 164*
\mathcal (LaTeX), *153, 154, 164*, 305
\mathdefault (LaTeX), *164*
Mathematica, 128–129, 347, 461, 462
Mathematica math fonts, 291, 337–344
mathematics, 522
\mathextension (LaTeX), *164*
MathInst, 150, 217, 290–292, 294–297, 299, 301, 302, 304–308, 312, 313
mathinst.tex file, 292
\mathit (LaTeX), *153, 154, 164*
MathKit, 150, 290, 308–313, 315, 341–344
    demonstration of, 340–344
mathkit file, 310
mathkit.tex file, 309
\mathnormal (LaTeX), *153, 154*
mathptm package, 288, 308
\mathrm (LaTeX), *153, 154, 164*
\mathsf (LaTeX), *153, 154, 164*
\mathtemplate (PDCFSEL), 149
MathTime math fonts, 135, 147, 162, 165, 291, 293, 295, 298, 317–327
MathTime Plus math fonts, 299
\mathtt (LaTeX), *153, 154, 164*
\mathversion (LaTeX), 164, 165, *165*
MatLab package, 364
matrix environment, 473
Matteis, Nicola, 30
Mattes, Eberhard, 14
Maverick, Brett, 250
\mbox (LaTeX), *191*
mbvrm7t5 font, 297
mbvrm7t7 font, 297
McPherson, Kent, 534
\mdseries (LaTeX), *153, 155*
measurement in TeX, 516
mediation, 400
\medskip (TeX), 518, *529*
Melville, Herman, 314
mem file, 91
META, 390
meta design, 76, 78–80
METAFONT, viii–x, 14–16, 26, 27,

34–38, 40, 49, 56, 58–97, 136, 138, 139, 204, 210, 264, 272–276, 294, 309–312, 346, 347, 349, 369, 373, 376, 390–413, 429, 465, 494, 495, 504–506, 509
    calculator, 74
    conversion to PostScript, 75
    creating base files for, 61
    creating the base, 61
    front ends to, 505
    installation of, 59
    interface to PostScript, 88
    magnification in, 83
    printable fonts from, 69
    undocumented feature of, 62
    unpopularity, 75
    variable types, 69
The METAFONTbook, 38
METAFONT conventions, 68
METAFONT vs. MetaPost, 439–440
Metamorphosis, 242
MetaPost, viii, ix, 14, 16, 34–36, 59, 62, 69, 75, 76, 82, 89–92, 96, 141, 346, 347, 349, 359, 360, 373, 390–440, 494, 542
    commands, 436
    commands of, 429–440
    function-like macros, 437
    internal variables, 429, 430
    operators of, 432
    predefined constants, 431
    undocumented feature of, 62
MetaPost data files, 419
MetaPost vs. METAFONT, 439–440
metric files, 179
\metrics (*fontinst*), 203, 204, *219, 220, 233, 270, 271*
Metropolitan Museum of Art, 314
.mf files, 64, 429, 494, 495
mf program, 60
MFPiC, ix, 347, 349, 504, 506
mfpic environment, 496, 501
mfpic package, 391, 494–510
\mfpic (MFPiC), *496, 502, 505*
mfpicdoc.tex file, 498
mfplain.mem file, 91
mfplain.mp file, 91
mft program, 36, 37, 60, 429
MfToEps, 88, 89
Microsoft Paint, 355
Microsoft Word, 117
middle (PSTricks), *467*
Minion, 276, 277
minus sign, 524
Mitchell, Ross, 28

Mittelbach, Frank, 38, 101, 105,
    108–110, 150, 157, 168, 196, 371,
    376, 532
.mkb files, 313
.mkr files, 312
.mks files, 313
mm, 516
mmaex font, 304
mmafm program, 277
mmami font, 304
mmasy font, 304
mminstance program, 277
.mmm files, 276
mnode (PSTricks), *473, 474*
mode, 65, 138
mode (METAFONT), *83*
mode_def (METAFONT), *74*
mode_setup (METAFONT), *64, 77, 79,
    81*
Modern, 289, 314, 316
modes, 73
modes.mf file, 74
modifying LaTeX comands, 109–113
Modula-2, 36
Monotype, 314
Monotype Baskerville, 309
Monotype Corporation, 132, 289, 314
Monotype Modern, 289, 314, 316
\movert (*fontinst*), *233, 256*
\moveup (*fontinst*), *204, 207, 254, 256*
movie credits, 250
Mozart, Wolfgang, 122
mp2.mft file, 429
MS-DOS, 135
msbm, 306
.msp files, 355
mt.par file, 292
mtex font, 299
.mtx files, 177, 179, 202, 214, 219, 270,
    311
mu, 240
\mu (TeX), *386*
multicol package, 540
multido package, 477
multido.doc file, 477
\multido (PSTricks), 476, 477, *477,
    478, 478, 480*
Multiple Master, 22, 80, 276, 277
multiply symbol, 240
\multiput (LaTeX), *372, 372, 377*
\multiput (PiCTeX), 376, *380, 382,
    383, 388*
\multirput (PSTricks), *469*
Murray, James, 348
MusixTeX package, 28

nab (PSTricks), *474*
naming fonts, 80
naming math fonts, 135, 297
\ncangles (PSTricks), *471*
\ncarc (PSTricks), *474*
\ncbar (PSTricks), *472*
\ncline (PSTricks), *474, 475*, 476
\nearrow (TeX), *381*
Nederlandstalige TeX Gebruikersgroep,
    56
\NeedsTeXFormat (LaTeX), *164*
Ness, David, x
New Font Selection Scheme, *see* NFSS
new paragraphs, 512
new typesetting system, 16
New York Times, 257
New Yorker magazine, 212, 257
\newcommand (LaTeX), *68, 104, 108,
    164, 204, 260, 452, 454, 469, 480*
\newcount (TeX), *367, 466, 480*
\newcounter (LaTeX), *480*
newdash.mtx file, 188
\newdimen (TeX), *487*
\newdimen (TeX), *380*
\newenvironment (LaTeX), *209, 210,
    469*
\newfam (TeX), *280*
\newfont (LaTeX), *68, 389*
\newglyph (*fontinst*), *203, 204, 207*, 210
\newgray (PSTricks), *478, 485, 487*
\newif (TeX), *208*, 487
\newpage (LaTeX), *100*
\newpost (LAMS-TeX), 114
news.answers, 51
newsgroups, 51
\newskip (TeX), *121, 208*, 487
\newwrite (TeX), *367*
NeXT, 56
NextStep, 15, 47, 262
NextStep ftp archive, 144
NFSS, 103, 114, 115, 140, 150–165,
    176, 207, 279, 297, 298, 530, 531
    high-level commands, 152–155
    low-level commands, 157–165
    low-level math commands, 161
    mid-level commands, 156–157
    sizing fonts in, 158
nicknames, 130
\noalign (TeX), *121, 487*
nodes, 470
nodesep (PSTricks), *475*
\noindent (TeX), *29, 90, 350, 359, 455,
    466, 485, 487*, 517, *528*, 539
\nointerlineskip (TeX), *487*

\nokernsfor (*fontinst*), *220*
\nolimits (TEX), 301
non-English typesetting, 8
nondocument files, 29
none (PSTricks), *454, 457, 458, 469, 480, 485, 487*
normal (PSTricks), *467*
normal version, 164
\normalfont (LATEX), *155*, 157, *157, 190, 191, 208–210*
\normalgraphs (PJCTEX), *385*
\normalsize (LATEX), *153, 155*
"not" glyphs, 240
npos (PSTricks), *474*
NTS, 16
\null (TEX), *455*
nullpicture (META), *427*
numeric (META), 393, *393*, 397, *399, 421–423, 427*
\nwarrow (TEX), *381*

o_correction (METAFONT), *74*
\obeylines (TEX), 208
\obeyspaces (TEX), 208, *208*
oblique fonts, 186
O'Brian, Patrick, x, 277, 282
octothorpe, 99
\oe (TEX), 228
\Offset (LAMS-TEX), 114
offset (PSTricks), *473*
offsetA (PSTricks), *472*
offsetB (PSTricks), *472*
\oint (TEX), 301, *302*
oldstyle figures, 190, 191
Omega, 16
\omega (TEX), *302*
\omit (TEX), *121*
OML, 151, 162
OMS, 151, 162
OMX, 151, 162
online help, 53
\ontop (TEX), *302*
open brackets, 301
\opengraphsfile (MFPJC), 495, *495, 505*, 506
\openout (TEX), *367*
OpenStep, 15
optical illusions, 77
optical scaling, 22, 80, 85, 135, 273
optical size, 273
option, 531
optional arguments, 103, 443
\or (TEX), *480*
ordered pair, 71
ordered pair notation, 71

origin, 71, 368
origin (META), *77, 79, 397, 398, 401, 406, 411, 418, 422, 427*
original TEX encoding, 162
original italic font, 217
original math extension encoding, 162
original math letter encoding, 162
original math symbol encoding, 162
ornaments in fonts, 230
OS/2, 14, 47, 266, 364
OT1, 151, 162, 217
OT1.etx file, 180, 192, 194, 215, 223, 228, 246, 259, 270
OT19.etx file, 180, 190, 191
OT1bar.etx file, 255
OT1bb7.etx file, 228
OT1bb7l.etx file, 228, 235
OT1c.etx file, 180, 186
OT1de.etx file, 192–194
OT1f.etx file, 215
OT1fn.etx file, 191
OT1ka.etx file, 259
OT1ky.etx file, 260
OT1man.etx file, 246, 247
OT1manl.etx file, 247, 248
OT1mant.etx file, 248
OT1mnt.fd file, 280
OT1padl.etx file, 223, 226
OT1v.etx file, 282
OT1vii.etx file, 282
OUT (MetaPost), 421, *421*
outline fonts, 23, 25, 201
  expert font installation, 183
  installation of, 183, 184
  pros and cons, 26
output
  high-quality, 87
\oval (LATEX), *373, 377*
\ovalnode (PSTricks), *472*
\over (TEX), *302*
\overbrace (TEX), *302*
overstriking, 206–207

package file, 531
package files, 104
packed pixels, 67, 505
pad.map file, 142
padalt.etx file, 221
padalt.mtx file, 221–223, 226
padihax.mtx file, 308
padiskw.mtx file, 308
padr7t font, 205, 217, 259
padr8l font, 221
padrhax.mtx file, 308
padri7t font, 217

padri8l font, 221
page breaking, 100
page-layout parameters, 514
\pagecolor (LATEX), *360*
\pageref (LATEX), 115, 126, 542
Paintbrush, 355
pair (META), *395, 401*
Palatino, 309, 314, 319, 329, 334, *339*,
    343
palindrome, 391, 392
Pandora, 91, 93
.par files, 292, 305, 307, 308
\Par, 209
\par (TEX), 112
\Par (*fontinst*), *208*
Paradissa fonts, 288
parameter files, 81
parameters, 80
parameters (PSTricks), 442
\parindent (TEX), *455, 466*
\part (LATEX), 103, 105
Parthenon, 78
partial downloading, 266
\partial (TEX), *302*
party, 36
Pascal, 8, 11, 35
Patashnik, Oren, 109, 276, 294
path, 396
path.pst file, 542
path.sty file, 541
path (META), *393*, 397, *397–399, 401,*
    404, 406, 409, 411, 417, 418
\path (TEX), 541
.pbm files, 355
pbmplus package, 349, 355, 356
    formats supported by, 356
pc, 516
PC-DOS, 14, 131
pcdown program, 136
\pcline (PSTricks), *473*
pcsend program, 136
.pcx files, 355, 361
pdccode.tex file, 146
PDCFSEL, 146–150, 279, 292, 294,
    298
pdcfsel.dtx file, 146
pdcfsel.tex file, 146, 279, 292
.pdf files, 124–126, 265, 267
pdf files
    conversion of TEX to, 126
pen nib, 408
pencircle (META), *64, 79, 396, 398,*
    409, 418, 422, 427
penoptions (META), 397
penrazor (META), *427*

pens, 408
PerAnnum, Inc., 479
Perl, 120, 123–125, 143–145, 203, 291,
    292, 294, 309, 382, 384, 419, 499,
    505, 543
Perry, Kevin, 129
.pfa files, 131, 136, 140, 174, 238
.pfb files, 131, 136, 137, 140, 142, 174,
    238, 264, 276, 277, 289
Pfeffer, Mitch, x
.pfm files, 131
.pgm files, 355
phototypesetters, 25, 87
Pianowski, P., 266
picas, 516
pickup (META), *64, 79,* 396, *396, 398,*
    409, *409, 418, 427*
PICTEX, 347, 349, 368, 371, 376–382,
    384, 388, 389
pictex package, 376
picture environment, 347, 368,
    371–376
picture extensions, 376–377
picture (META), *393, 406, 425, 427*
pictures (LATEX) in plain documents,
    375
pie charts, 459
Pippa's Song (Browning), 534
pixel, 70
pixel files, 13, 21
pixels_per_inch (METAFONT), *74*
.pk files, 37, 68, 139, 182, 264, 294,
    349, 361, 363, 364
.pk format, 67
pkunzip program, 54
pkzip program, 27
.pl files, 37, 177, 179, 181, 184, 201,
    202, 206, 211, 214, 235, 241, 249,
    260, 273, 279, 311
Plaice, John, 16
plain package, 114, 115
plain TEX, 33
plain base (METAFONT), 60
plain package (MetaPost), 429
plain TEX, 442–444, 446, 449, 467,
    470, 473, 480
plain TEX, viii, 19, 24, 33, 68, 80, 120,
    121, 146, 150, 175, 177, 195, 207,
    209, 211, 258, 260, 292, 296, 298,
    308, 311, 312, 352, 366, 378, 379,
    389, 416, 496, 502, 511, 516, 522
plain TEX font selection, 146–150
plain TEX text in a LATEX document, 352
plain.bas file, 61
plain.base file, 60, 61

plain.bst file, 110
plain.fmt file, 19, 20
plain.mem file, 91
plain.mf file, 61
plain.mp file, 91
plain.tex file, 18, 19, 33
\plain (TEX), *20*
Planet Art, 361
Platt, Craig, 168
pleasing curves, 75
\plot (PICTEX), *384–388*
\plotheading (PICTEX), *386–388*
plotstyle (PSTricks), *462*
\plotsymbol, 371
\plotsymbol (TEX), *371*
pltotf program, 14, 36, 37, 174, 177,
      184, 206, 249, 279
plusminus, 240
\pmb (*fontinst*), 210, 212
\pmb (TEX), *210*
pmb.mtx file, 210, 211, 214
pmx program, 28
.pnm files, 355, 356
pntt10 font, 305
Podar, Sunil, 376
Poetica, 221, 242, 250
point on a plane, 395
point (META), *399*
\point (TEX), 369, *371*
points, 516
polar coordinates, 461
Polish TEX archive, 45
pool file, 60
pooltype program, 37
poor man's bold, 210–212
\pop (*fontinst*), 204, *207, 210*, 254, *254,*
      256
portable anymap, 355
portable bitmap, 355
portable document format, 124
portable graymap, 355
portable pixmap, 355
Poskanzer, Jef, 355
PostScript, 23, 75, 87–91
      METAFONT interface to, 88
      bitmaps in, 87
      Level 2, 23
      METAFONT into, 87
PostScript code in virtual fonts, 256
PostScript page description language, 12
PostScript points, 89
PostScript programming environments,
      264
PostScript units, 354

PostScript files to bitmap equivalents,
      264
.ppm files, 355
preamble, 102, 104
preparing a TEX source file, 29
prescription, 402
prescriptive computer languages, 72
prettyprinting METR code, 429
previewer, 21
Prime Time TEXcetera, 52
Prime Time Freeware, 52
primitive commands, 18
printable ASCII, 227
printer resolution, 514
printers, 12
\printindex (LATEX), 108
private command names, 111
producing this book, 541–546
production cycle of TEX, 9
prog, 46
program files, 29, 82
pronouncing TEX, 3
proof mode, 66
proof (METAFONT), 66
proofing, 66–67
proofing (METAFONT), *74*
protecting symbols in Unix, 21
\ProvidesPackage (LATEX), *164*
.ps files, 24–27, 125, 126, 541
ps-view.ps file, 266
ps2mf program, 264, 265, 269
ps2pk program, 263–265, 269, 277
PSAlter program, 264
\psarc (PSTricks), *450, 461, 466*
\psarcn (PSTricks), *466*
\psaxes (PSTricks), 448, *448, 462*
\psbezier (PSTricks), 450, *451, 452*
\pscharclip (PSTricks), *466*
\pscircle (PSTricks), 442, *442*, 443,
      443, 444, 448, 478, 480
\pscirclebox (PSTricks), *465*
\psclip (PSTricks), 454, *454*, 455, *455,*
      458
\pscurve (PSTricks), 450, *451, 452,*
      455, 459, 459, 465, 485
\pscustom (PSTricks), 451, *452, 457,*
      458, 485, 485
\psdblframebox (PSTricks), *465*
\psdiamond (PSTricks), *450*
\psdot (PSTricks), 480, *480*
\psellipse (PSTricks), *446, 447, 450,*
      454
psfnss2e.tex file, 140
.psfonts.map files, 289
psfonts.map file, 136, 140, 142, 173,

177, 182, 184, 188, 190, 196, 206, 214, 216, 226, 241, 278, 279, 284, 293, 306
PSfrag, 364–367
  axis label replacements, 365
\psfrag (PSfrag), 364, 365, *365*, 366, 367, *367*
\psfragscanon (PSfrag), *365*
\psframe* (PSTricks), 457
\psframe (PSTricks), *450, 457, 458, 464, 467, 478, 485, 487*
\psframebox (PSTricks), *460, 461, 465, 469, 472, 472*
\psgrid (PSTricks), *448, 451, 459*
\psline (PSTricks), 448, *448, 449, 452, 457, 458, 461, 464, 478, 480, 485*
psmatrix environment, 473–475
\psmatrix (PSTricks), 473
PSNFSS, 140, 142, 531
pspicture environment, 446, 447, 465, 466, 480
\pspicture (PSTricks), 446, 447, *447, 458–461, 464, 467, 469, 478, 480*
\pspolygon (PSTricks), *445, 469, 473, 480*
\psset (PSTricks), 442, *442, 443, 445, 447–450, 460, 461, 464–467, 469, 473–475, 478, 480, 482, 485, 487*
\psshadow (PSTricks), *465*
\psshadowbox (PSTricks), *465*
pst-3d.tex file, 465, 467
pst-beta file, 480
pst-beta.tex file, 450, 465, 467, 470
pst-doc1.ps file, 470
pst-doc2.ps file, 470
pst-node.tex file, 470
pst-plot package, 477
pst-plot.sty file, 448
pst2eps.sty file, 485
pstcol package, 360
\pstextpath (PSTricks), *542*
\pstextpath (PSTricks), *465, 466*
\pstribox (PSTricks), *465*
PSTricks, ix, 347, 349, 354, 360, 441–493, 542
  PSTricks97, 481
  command summary, 487–493
  creating PostScript files from, 485
  drawing engine, 481
  mailing list, 481
  other techniques, 481
  shark, 482
pstricks.con file, 441
pstricks.tex file, 445
\PSTtoEPS (PSTricks), 485, *485*

\psunit (PSTricks), *478*
\pswedge (PSTricks), *450*, 460, *460*
pt, 516
public domain, 33, 38
public domain TEX implementations, 14
Publish, 467
punct.mf file, 82
Punk, 91, 93
puns, bad, 454
\push (*fontinst*), 204, *207, 210*, 254, *254, 256*
\put (LATEX), 371, 372, *372*, 373, *373, 377*
\put (PICTEX), 376, *378*, 379, *380*, 381, *381–385, 387, 388*
putfonts.bat file, 311
\putrectangle (PICTEX), *382, 388*
\putrule (PICTEX), *380, 382, 383, 385, 388*

\qbezier (LATEX), 373, *375*, 376, *377*
\quad (TEX), *351, 359, 462*
quadratic Bézier, 373
Quite Software, 264
quotation environment, 102, 536
quotation marks, 513
quote environment, 536
quote mechanism, 114
quote site index, 45

r.mtx file, 245
Radical Eye Software, 262
Rahtz, Sebastian, 52, 56, 126, 140, 277, 345, 475
\raise (TEX), *371*
Raman, T. V., 98
Rand, Ayn, 541
.raw files, 361
raw fonts, 169, 416
\Rbrack (TEX), 301, *302*
Reader, 265
readfrom (MetaPost), 411, *425*
README file, 16
Reckdahl, Keith, 350, 354
\rect (MFPIC), *500, 502*
\rectangle (PICTEX), *387*
red (MetaPost), 412
redim.mtx file, 271, 273
ReEncodeFont, 284
\reencodefont (*fontinst*), *218, 241, 248, 286*
reencoding fonts, 241
\ref (LATEX), 115, 126, 542
\reflectbox (LATEX), 358, *359*
reflectedabout (META), 409, *409*

\refstepcounter (LaTeX), *111*
rehash (Unix), 144
relative (PSTricks), *449*
\relax (META), 74
\relax (*fontinst*), 203, *218–220, 282*
\relax (TeX), *191, 208–210, 455, 487*
rendering a document, 514
\renewcommand (LaTeX), *105, 110, 158,
    163, 164, 191, 195, 235, 280, 290*
.rep files, 126
\repeat (TeX), *367, 466, 487*
repeating a curve point, 408
report class, 532
reserved characters, 31
\resetcommand (*fontinst*), *219, 229, 270,
    271*
\resetglyph (*fontinst*), *207, 210, 256,
    271*
\resetint (*fontinst*), *234, 254, 260, 282*
resident fonts, 173
\resizebox (LaTeX), 357, *359*
resolution, 514
revenge effects, 7
revisions and formatting, 32
rich text format, 117–118
right (META), *398*
\right (TeX), *165*, 301, *302*
\rightline (TeX), *518*
\rightskip (TeX), *469*
Rimmer, Steve, 348
\rlap (TeX), *371*
\rm (TeX), *298*, 417, *417, 487*
\rmdefault (LaTeX), 158, *158, 163,
    164, 235, 280, 290*
\rmfamily (LaTeX), *153*, 154
\rmun (*fontinst*), 209
\rnode (PSTricks), *471, 472, 472*
Rogers, Bruce, 314
Rokicki, Tomas, x, 12, 14, 24, 36, 87,
    263, 312, 429, 552
romanu.mf file, 82
Rose, Kristoffer, 377
\rotate (MFPIC), 500, 501, *501*
\rotatebox (LaTeX), 358, *359*
rotated (META), *398, 399, 401, 406,
    409, 411, 418, 421, 427*
rotatedaround (META), 409, *409*
\rotates (MFPIC), *502, 504*
rotating package, 475
\rput (PSTricks), *542*
\rput (PSTricks), 460, *460–462, 464,
    466, 467, 469, 472, 478, 480, 485*
RSFS fonts, 305
.rtf files, 117
rtf2LaTeX, 119

rtf2TeX, 119
ruler.tex file, 542
running TeX, 19

Saarela, Janne, 124
SAIL, 8
Saint Anthony Reading (Dürer), 361
Salomon, David, 38
Samarin, Alexander, 38, 101, 105,
    108–110, 150, 157, 168, 196, 371,
    376, 532
\samesize (*fontinst*), *210, 271*
Samuel, Arthur, 36, 429
sans serif, 77, 305
$sansserif_, 307
sarith.mp file, 429
Sauter fonts, 86
Sauter, John, 86, 275
\savedata (PSTricks), *461, 463*
\saveglyphas (*fontinst*), *245*
\sbox (LaTeX), *112*
\sc (LaTeX), *121, 467*
scalable Computer Modern, 288
scalable fonts, 24
scalable typography, 24, 40
scale factor, 307
\scale (*fontinst*), *254*
\scalebox (LaTeX), 357, 358, *359*
scaled (TeX), 84
scaled (META), *64, 79, 396, 398, 399,
    406, 409, 411, 413, 417, 418, 422,
    427*
\scales (MFPIC), *504*
scaling factor, 160
Scandinavian ligatures, 228
scantokens (META), *427*
Schöpf, Rainer, 101, 150
scholarly detritus, 5
Schriftgiesserei Walter Fruttiger, 313
Schwarz, Norbert, 551
Schwarzkopf, Otfried, 124
screen previewer, 11–13, 511
script, 297
script fonts, 305
scriptscript, 297
\scriptscriptstyle (TeX), *302, 382*
\scriptsize (LaTeX), *153*
\scriptstyle (LaTeX), *475*
\scshape (LaTeX), *153, 155, 235*
\searrow (TeX), *381*
\section* (LaTeX), *539*
\section (LaTeX), 103–105, 131, 537,
    539
\selectfont (LaTeX), *85*, 156, *156*, 157,
    157, 190, 191, 209–211, 235, 260,

380, 386, 387, 418, 421, 454, 455, 465, 475
selecting font resolution, 87
semicolon, 68, 394
Seminar, 13
series, 150, 151
serif, 76
service bureaus, 25, 87
  preparing files for, 27
\setbars (PⅠCTEX), 384, *386–388*
\setbox (TEX), *380, 454, 455, 466, 469,* 487
\setcommand (*fontinst*), *191, 204, 207, 210, 220, 223, 224, 229, 233, 245, 246, 256, 260, 271*
\setcoordinatesystem (PⅠCTEX), 380, *380,* 381, *381–388*
\setcounter (LATEX), *105, 480*
\setdashes (PⅠCTEX), *382*
setenv, 421
\setglyph (*fontinst*), 203, *233, 245, 246, 254, 271*
Seth, Vikram, x, 470
\sethistograms (PⅠCTEX), 384, *386, 388*
\setint (*fontinst*), 215, *215, 254, 254, 270, 270, 271, 542*
\setkern (*fontinst*), *215,* 219, *219, 220, 270, 270, 271*
\setkerning (*fontinst*), 220, 233, *233*
\Setleftkerning (*fontinst*), *223*
\setleftkerning (*fontinst*), *220, 223, 233, 254*
\setlength (LATEX), 371, 534
\setlimits (TEX), 301, *302*
\setlinear (PⅠCTEX), 384, *385, 386, 388*
\SetMathAlphabet (LATEX), *164*
\setnolimits (TEX), 301
\setplotarea (PⅠCTEX), *381, 384–388*
\setquadratic (PⅠCTEX), 383, 384, *385, 386, 388*
setrange (MetaPost), 420, *420, 422, 427*
\setrawglyph (*fontinst*), 270
\Setrightkerning (*fontinst*), *223*
\setrightkerning (*fontinst*), *220, 223, 233, 254*
\setshadegrid (PⅠCTEX), *385*
\Setslot (*fontinst*), *229*
\setslot (*fontinst*), *194, 215,* 224, 225, *225,* 229, *246*
\SetSymbolFont (LATEX), 161, 164, 165, *165*
\seventemplate (PDCFSEL), *280*

Sewell, Wayne, 36
\sfdefault (LATEX), *164*
\sffamily (LATEX), *153, 155*
SGML, 100
sgml.bib file, 123
\shade (MFPⅠC), 500, *501*
shape, 150, 151
shape of a font, 133
shapes
  transformations of, 501
shark, 482
sharp convention (METAFONT), 70–71
Shephard, G. C., 406
\shift (MFPⅠC), 502
shifted (META), *64, 409, 413, 417*
shortput (PSTricks), *474*
\shortticklength (PⅠCTEX), *388*
show (META), *73*
showidx package, 108
showpoints (PSTricks), *448, 451, 459*
Siegel, David, 293
\sigma (TEX), *386, 418*
signoff, 51
Silicon Graphics, 56
Simons, Don, 28
Simtel archive, 47, 144
sin.d file, 382
\sin (TEX), *302, 365*
sincos.d file, 419
sind (META), *406, 407, 411*
single asterisk prompt, 62
size conventions in *fontinst,* 278
size conventions in NFSS, 279
size of TEX, METAFONT source
  modules, 35
size of text block, 516
size of type, 80
sizes of fonts, 21, 189, 283
sizing fonts, 158, 279
sizing math fonts, 135
\skew (TEX), 308
\skip (TEX), *487*
skipping vertical space, 31
slanted fonts, 186
slanted (META), *409, 422*
SlantFont, 284
\slantfont (*fontinst*), *187, 286*
Slimbach, Robert, 313
SliTEX, 13
\slshape (LATEX), *153*
small caps, 184, 185
\small (LATEX), *153, 155, 474*
\smallskip (TEX), *121,* 518
Smith, Cameron, 129
smoke mode, 65, 66

software archives, 43, 45, 47
software, sources for, 13
Sojka, Petr, 125
solid (PSTricks), *443*, *452*, *460*,
    465–467, *469*, *480*, *485*
source file, 9, 29, 514
sources for TEX software, 13
Sowa, Friedhelm, 345, 360
spaces, 515
spaces after a command, 516
spacing conventions, 189
Spanish ligatures, 222
special characters, 31, 525
special relativity, 503
\special (TEX), 346, 350, 376, 441,
    485
\SpecialCoor (PSTricks), 461, *461*,
    478, *478*, *480*
spell check programs, 12
Sperrsatz, 257
Spivak, Michael, x, 33, 38, 114, 298,
    376, 543
spliteps.tex file, 89
spreadsheets, 119–122
    too wide, 121
sqrt (META), *406*, *411*
\sqrt (TEX), *386*
square brackets, 393
$ssize_, 308
$sssize_, 308
\stack (PₓCTEX), *388*
StandardEncoding (PostScript), 238
Standardized General Markup Language,
    100
Stanford Artificial Intelligence Language,
    8
star convention, 103
star form, 443
star form of a command, 531
statement separator, 66, 68
Steinberg, S. H., 190
step (META), *406, 407*
str (META), 423, *423, 427*
straight line segments, 395
strike out fonts, 206–207
strike.mtx file, 206, 207
\strike (*fontinst*), *207*
strikeout environment, 210
\strikerule (TEX), *209*
\strikespace (TEX), *209*
string pool, 18
string subtleties in MetaPost, 423
string (META), *423, 425, 427*
structured documentation, 35
structured graphics, 390

structures.h file, 485
\strut (TEX), *302, 455*
.sty files, 104, 152, 191, 297, 470, 530,
    532, 533
style file, 31, 531
\sub (*fontinst*), *254*
subgridcolor (PSTricks), *458*
subgriddiv (PSTricks), *448*, *451*, *458*,
    459
subgridwidth (PSTricks), *451*, *458*
subscribe, 51
subscripts, 72, 392
\subsection (LATEX), 537
\subsection (TEX), 101
A Suitable Boy (Seth), x, 470
Sun Microsystems computers, 47, 56
superaccents, 308
suppressing paragraph indentation, 31
\surfint (TEX), 301, *302*
\swarrow (TEX), *381*
swash characters, 221, 224
symbol fonts, 301
\symbol (LATEX), *107, 174*

T1, 151, 162, 181, 215
T1c.etx file, 186
tabbing character, 120
table environment, 105, 539
\tableofcontents (LATEX), 105
tabskip glue, 122
\tabskip (TEX), *121, 122, 487*
tabular environment, 102, 103, 106,
    121, 261, 465, 476, 539
\tag (LAMS-TEX), 114
tagged image format files, 349
tangent, 187
TANGLE program, 36
Taupin, Daniel, 28, 119
Taylor, Philip, 16, 258, 541
TDS, 137, 172, 293, 295, 306
Tenner, Edward, 7
\tentemplate (PDCFSEL), *280*
testltx.tex file, 143
testmath.tex file, 308
testmatp.tex file, 308
testpln.tex file, 143
teTEX, 57
TEX
    bibliographies of, 44
    canon, 38
    execution of, 19
    graphics within, 34
    history of, 8–9
    implementations of, 14–15
    initialization of, 19

installation of, 16
magnification in, 83
other files of, 17
output in word processing, 119
overview of, 3–7
production cycle of, 9
recent changes in, 8
sources for, 13
traditional systems, 137
undocumented feature of, 62
why is it hard?, 6
why use it?, 3
.tex files, 20, 298, 360, 361
TEX cdrom, 52
TEX Directory Structure, 56, 57, *see* TDS
TEX files
conversion into pdf format, 126
TEX journals on the Web, 54
TEX Live CDROM, 56, 57, 137, 140
TEX packages and programs on the Web, 54
TEX Ruler (Eijkhout), endpaper
TEX systems, 11
TEX text in other applications, 352
TEX Users Group, 40, 56, 379
tex.poo file, 18
tex.pool file, 18
tex2pdf program, 125
tex2rtf, 119, 124, 125
TEX3.0, 8
\tex (PSfrag), 364, 365
\TeX (TEX), 515
TeXBase1Encoding, 240
font table, 238, 239
TeXBase1Encoding, 284
The TEXbook, 22, 38, 80, 85, 89, 110, 111, 130, 146, 171, 210, 273, 354, 485, 512, 525, 527
texfonts, 363
TeXForm (*Mathematica*), 128
texi2html, 124, 125
texihtml package, 124, 125
texinfo, 124, 125
texinfo package, 115, 116
texinfo.tex file, 115
texmf (TDS), 137
TEXnische Komödie, 345
text (node) connections (PSTricks), 470–476
text editor, 11, 29
text math, 524
\textbf (LATEX), *153*, 154, *155*
\textcolor (LATEX), 360
\textfraction (LATEX), *105*

\textit (LATEX), *153, 155*
\textmd (LATEX), *153, 155*
\textnormal (LATEX), *153, 155*, 157
textpath package, 542
textpath.sty file, 465
textpath.tex file, 465, 466
\textrm (LATEX), *153*, 154
\textsc (LATEX), *153, 155*
\textsf (LATEX), *153, 155*
\textsl (LATEX), *153*
\texttt (LATEX), *107, 108*, 152, *152, 153*, 154
\textup (LATEX), *153*
Textures, 15
\textwidth (LATEX), *454, 473*
TEXView, 14, 128, 144, 262, 263, 312
TEXware, 36
τεχ, 3, 9
.tfm files, 17, 18, 37, 62, 64, 68, 83, 137, 139, 140, 142, 172–174, 176, 177, 179, 182, 184, 201, 206, 214, 216, 240, 241, 260, 262, 265, 272, 273, 279, 294, 306, 361, 363, 415, 416, 506
tftopl program, 14, 36, 37, 174, 177, 179, 201, 211, 234, 235, 270, 273
Thanh, Han The, 125
\the (TEX), *115, 367, 480, 487*
thelabel (MetaPost), 425, *425, 427*
theorem package, 540
\thicklines (LATEX), *372*
Thiele, Christina, 9
\thinspace (LATEX), *121*
\thispagestyle (LATEX), *485, 539*
thorn, 240
Thorup, Kresten Krab, 15
three-dimensional graphics, 467
\ThreeDput (PSTricks), *467*
.tif files, 350, 361
.tiff files, 262, 265, 349, 355, 361
Times family, 298
Times New Roman, 277, 278, 314, 318, 328, 333, 338, 341, 342
Times New Roman Seven, 278
Times Roman, 148, 181, 309, 314
Times Seven, 277
Times Small Text, 277, 278
times.sty file, 142
\times (TEX), *114, 421, 475*
\tiny (LATEX), *153, 480*
\title (LATEX), 104, *104*, 537, *539*
Tobin, Geoffrey, 96, 494
.toc files, 105, 495
tools for working with hypertext, 128
\topfraction (LATEX), *105*

topnumber (LaTeX counter), 105
totalnumber (LaTeX counter), 105
TPic, 347
\tr (*fontinst*), 261
\tr (TeX), *260, 261*
tracingtitles (METAFONT), *74*
track kerning, 257, *see* letterspacing
tracking, *see* letterspacing
Tracy, Walter, 314
traditional systems, 137
transformations, 409
\transformfont (*fontinst*), *187*, 188,
    218, 241, 248, 286
transforming shapes, 501
trimode (PSTricks), *465*
Trinkle, Daniel, 12
Trip TeX, 9
troubleshooting, 178
true (PSTricks), *459, 475*
True Type font, 12
\tt (TeX), *108*, 152, *152, 298, 371*, 520
$tt_, 307
\ttb (TeX), *211*
\ttfamily (LaTeX), 152, *152, 153*, 154
$ttSF_, 307
TUG, 40, 379
TUG home page, 52
TUGboat, 40, 123, 345
tuglib archive, 44
Turner, Audrey, 100
Turner, Ronald, 100
Tutelaers, Piet, 264
twcal, 306
twoside, 104
type declaration, 393
type geometry, 290
type size, 22, 283
Typee (Melville), 314
typesetting, 3
typesetting in foreign languages, 8
typesetting mathematics (LaTeX), 154
typewriter fonts, 305

\uc (*fontinst*), *229*, 255
\uc (TeX), 226
uckerns.mtx file, 219
\ucletter (*fontinst*), 253, *254*
ucoff.mtx file, 217
UK TeX Users Group (UKTUG), *see*
    UKTUG
UK TUG, 14, 40
UKTUG, 56
ulcorner (MetaPost), 427, *427*
uline.mtx file, 204, 207, 256
\uline (*fontinst*), 204, *204*, 207

umlaut, 193
uncmr.mtx file, 270, 271, 273
uncompressing files, 54
underlining, 204–206, 209
    better, 255
    one-hundred-percent, 207
underlining environment, 208, 209
\underlining (TeX), *209*
\underrule (TeX), *208*, 209
\underspace (TeX), *208*, 209
undim.mtx file, 270, 273
unfakable glyph, 180
\unfakable (*fontinst*), 202
unfill (META), *399, 401*
unfilldraw (META), *418*
unformatted file, 29
\unhbox (TeX), *487*
uniform record locator, 52
unique TeX implementations, 14–15
unit (PSTricks), *442, 444, 445,
    447–450, 454, 455, 457, 460, 461,
    469, 473, 478, 480, 485, 487*
\unitlength (LaTeX), 371
Unix, 15, 47, 277
Unix quoting, 66
Unix TeX, 56
unix.bib file, 123
unpopularity of METAFONT, 75
unpsfont.mtx file, 271, 273
\unsetglyph (*fontinst*), 218, *218, 271*
\unskip (TeX), *487*
unslanted italic fonts, 186
unsubscribe, 51
until (META), *406, 407, 417*
\unvbox (TeX), *487*
unzip program, 54
up (META), *77, 79, 397, 398*
Updike, Daniel, 313
\upshape (LaTeX), *153, 155*
upto (META), *398, 399, 401, 407, 413*
\uput (PSTricks), 460, *460*
urcorner (MetaPost), 427
URL, 52
\usefont (LaTeX), 156, *156, 157*
\usepackage (LaTeX), *90*, 104, *104*, 108,
    113, 126, *298, 350, 359, 360, 365,
    418, 421, 448, 465, 466,* 469, 482,
    485, 540, *541*
user groups, 39
Utopia, 25
uuline.mtx file, 256

v convention, 135
\value (LaTeX), *480*
van Zandt, Timothy, 441, 485

vanRyper, William, 348
variables, 392
variant of a font, 133
\varint (TEX), 301, *302*
varioref package, 540, 542
\varoint (TEX), 301, *302*
\varsint (TEX), 301, *302*
Vasil'ev, Konstantin, 12
\vbox (TEX), *121,* 258, *454, 455, 466, 469, 487*
\vcenter (TEX), *302*
\vec (TEX), *308*
\vector (LATEX), 373, *377*
Vens, Erik Jan, 264
\verb* (LATEX), 102
\verb (LATEX), 102
verbatim environment, 536
verbatim package, 540
verbatimtex (MetaPost), *416–418,* 421, *421, 425, 427*
verse environment, 470, 536
version, 164
    creating a new math, 164
vertical bar in indexing, 107
vertical space, 518
vertical spacing, 518
.vf files, 37, 140, 142, 172, 176, 177, 182, 184, 206, 214, 216, 260, 262, 272, 273, 279
\vfill (TEX), *100, 454,* 522, *523*
VFINST, 138, 140, 143–145, 173, 183, 184, 187, 188, 212, 226, 241, 277, 289, 294, 295, 306, 313
vfinst.tex file, 144
vftovp program, 14, 36, 37, 174, 177
Vieth, Ulrik, 429
viewpoint (PSTricks), *467*
Virgil, 217
virmf program, 60
virtual fonts, 8, 36, 130, 166–200
    adjusting character metrics, 188
    alternate fonts, 220
    approximations to optical scaling, 272
    bold fonts, 210
    encodings, 220
    f-words, 212
    font scaling, 189
    footnote numbers, 190, 191
    foreign languages, 191, 192
    gray levels in, 256
    letterspacing, 258
    math fonts, 287–344
    movie credits, 250
    oblique (slanted) fonts, 186
    oldstyle figures, 191

    oldstyle numbers, 190
    overstrike, 209
    PostScript commands in, 256
    preview fonts, 267
    sizing fonts in installation, 279
    small caps, 185
    strikeout, 206
    summary of *fontinst* commands, 197–200
    tools for, 174
    tracking, 258
    troubleshooting, 196
    underlining, 204, 208, 255
    unslanted italic fonts, 186
visual structure, 99
vlines (PSTricks), *450*
von Bechtolsheim, Stephan, 38
\vphantom (TEX), *302*
.vpl files, 177, 178, 182, 184, 192, 214, 235, 249, 260, 262, 273, 279, 310, 311
vptovf program, 14, 36, 37, 174, 177, 184, 206, 214, 216, 223, 226, 235, 249, 260, 262, 272, 273, 279
\vrule (TEX), *449, 450, 455, 473, 480, 487*
\vshade (PICTEX), *385*
\vsize (TEX), 517
\vskip (TEX), *112, 487, 528*
\vspace* (LATEX), 103
\vspace (LATEX), *31,* 103, *359, 386, 455, 469,* 537
VTEX, 16
Vulis, Michael, 16, 553

w2latex, 119
W3, 51
Walnut Creek CD-ROM, 52
Walsh, Norman, 96, 345
Ward, Stephen, 2
\wd (TEX), *112, 487*
WEAVE program, 36
WEB system, 8, 11, 34–36, 38, 44, 49, 53, 58
.web files, 36
Web sites, 53–55
web2c program, 11, 15, 90
weight of a font, 133
Weinberg, Steven, x
Wells, Charles, 542
whatever (META), 404, *405*
\whiledo (LATEX), 476
white (PSTricks), *444, 446, 464, 467, 469*
white space, 518

white (MetaPost), 412, *412*, *420–422*, *425*, *427*
\white (MFPıC), 500
\white (PSTricks), *487*
Whitehouse, Kendall, 126
Wichura, Michael, 376, 378, 379, 388
wide accents, 301
\widehat (TEX), 301, *302*
\widetilde (TEX), 301, *302*
\width (*fontinst*), *207*, *256*
\width (LATEX), 359
Windows, 47, 263, 266
Windows 3.1, 264
Windows Bitmap, 265
WINW2L, 119
withcolor (MetaPost), *412*, *413*, *420–422*, *425*, *427*
withpen (META), *422*, *427*
Wolfram Research, 303
Wolfram, Stephen, 128
Word (word processor), 117
word processing, 10
word processors, 29, 117–119
    including TEX output, 119
WordPerfect, 117
World Wide Web, 9, 51, 123
write (MetaPost), *411*, *423*, *425*, *427*
\write (TEX), *367*
Wujastyk, Dominik, 96
WWW, 51
WYSIWYG, 10, 12, 32, 33

X Windows, 47
x-height, 290
X11, 266
.xbi files, 542, 543
xbib.sty file, 542, 543
xbix.sty file, 542
xchicago.bst file, 542
xchicago.sty file, 542
\xdef (TEX), *487*
xdvi program, 56, 263
\xfontset (PDCFSEL), 149
xhdvi previewer, 128
xheight (*fontinst*), 234

xpart (META), 395, *395*, *401*
xr package, 540
xscaled (META), *409*, *427*
xunit (PSTricks), *461*, *480*
X-Windows, 128
XY-Pic, 347
XY-Pic, 377
\xyswaps (MFPıC), 502

y convention, 135
yahoo, 52
Yale Alumni Magazine, 350, 357
Y &Y TEX, 265
yellow (MetaPost), 412
yfrak font, 306
ypart (META), 395, *395*, *401*
yscaled (META), *409*, *417*, *427*
yunit (PSTricks), *461*, *480*

z convention, 72, 135, 296, 395
Zapf Chancery, 305
Zapf, Hermann, 293, 314, 554
.zip files, 53–55
zip program, 27
Jiří Zlatuška, 125
Zobrist, William, x
zscaled (META), *409*
\zscales (MFPıC), *502*
\zslants (MFPıC), *502*
ztmptm.sty file, 311
ztmptm.tex file, 311